BAPTISTS
AROUND THE
WORLD

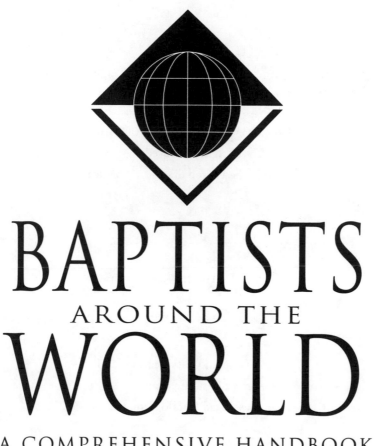

BAPTISTS
AROUND THE
WORLD

A COMPREHENSIVE HANDBOOK

ALBERT W. WARDIN, EDITOR

BROADMAN
&HOLMAN
PUBLISHERS

Nashville, Tennessee

© 1995

by BROADMAN & HOLMAN PUBLISHERS

All rights reserved

Printed in the United States of America

4210-76

0-8054-1076-7

Dewey Decimal Classification: 286

Subject Heading: Baptists

Library of Congress Card Catalog Number: 94-36271

Library of Congress Cataloging-in-Publication Data

Baptists around the world: a comprehensive handbook / Albert W. Wardin, Jr., editor

    p.   cm.

Includes bibliographical references

    ISBN 0-8054-1076-7 : $34.99

    1. Baptists—History. 2. Baptists—Missions. 3. Baptists—Statistics.

I. Wardin, Albert, W.

BX6231.B37   1995

286' ,09—dc20   94-36271

                      CIP

For my wife, Lucile,

for her patience and loving care

CONTENTS

CONTRIBUTORS

Addleton, Hubert F. . . . . .Karachi, Pakistan

Ajayi, Simon A. . . . . .Ila-Orangun, Osun State, Nigeria

Balders, Günter . . . . .Glinde, Germany

Bebbington, David W. . . . . .Stirling, Scotland, UK

Bradley, Linda . . . . .Mazini, Swaziland

Briggs, John H. Y. . . . . .Staffordshire, England, UK

Cadette, V. Anthony .Port-of-Spain, Trinidad

Canclini, Arnoldo .Buenos Aires, Argentina

Coops, Lorraine .Kingston, Ontario, Canada

Davidson, William F. . . . . .Columbia, South Carolina, USA

Downs, Frederick S. . . . . .Bangalore, India

Eidberg, Peder A. . . . . .Stabekk, Norway

Goodwin, Dan .Kingston, Ontario, Canada

Grijalva, Joshua . . . . .San Antonio, Texas, USA

Hill, Ronald C. . . . . .Lampang, Thailand

Hudson-Reed, Sydney . . . . .Pinelands, South Africa

Hylleberg, Bent . . . . .Tølløse, Denmark

Jenkins, Orville Boyd . . . . .Nairobi, Kenya

Latch, Ollie . . . . .Drasco, Arkansas, USA

Lorenzen, Thorwald . . . . .Obberrieden, Switzerland

Lozano, Alcides . . . . .La Chorrera, Panama

MacLeod, Angus H. . . . . .Auckland, New Zealand

McElrath, William N. .Bandung, Indonesia

Macek, Petr and Harriet . . . . .Prague, Czech Republic

Manley, Kenneth R. . . . . .Parkville, Victoria, Australia

Marseille, Sem . . . . .Port-au-Prince, Haiti

Neumann, Mike . . . . .Portland, Oregon, USA

Olson, Virgil A. . . . . .St. Paul, Minnesota, USA

Osei-Wusu, Kojo . . . . .Kumasi, Ghana

Patterson, Frank W. . . . . .San Angelo, Texas, USA

Patterson, W. Morgan . . . . .Novato, California, USA

Pierard, Richard V. . . . . .Terre Haute, India

Priestley, David T. . . . . .Edmonton, Alberta, Canada

Ramos, Marcos A. . . . . .Miami, Florida, USA

Rawlyk, George . . . . .Kingston, Ontario, Canada

Ridenour, Crea . . . . .Knoxville, Tennessee, USA

Russell, Horace O. . . . . .Wynnewood, Pennsylvania, USA

Sanford, Don A. . . . . .Janesville, Wisconsin, USA

Scaramuccia, Franco . . . . .Rome, Italy

Shelley, Bruce L. . . . . .Denver, Colorado, USA

Stamps, Stanley D. . . . . .El Progreso, Honduras

Stanley, Brian . . . . .Bristol, England, UK

Thobois, Michel . . . . .Paris, France

Towery, Britt E., Jr. . . . . .Waco, Texas, USA

Vehkaoja, Mai-Britt . . . . .Vaasa, Finland

Wardin, Albert W., Jr. . . . . .Nashville, Tennessee, USA

Whitson, Betty Ann . . . . .Iringa, Tanzania

Wiazowski, Konstanty . . . . .Warsaw, Poland

Younger, George D. . . . . .South Orange, New Jersey, USA

ABBREVIATIONS FOR MISSIONS

A. ABBREVIATIONS FOR BAPTIST AND BAPTIST-RELATED MISSIONS

Baptist missions include mission agencies sponsored by Baptist denominational bodies as well as agencies with independent boards. Some missions in the latter group consider themselves nondenominational but are included here if they were founded by Baptists, relate to the Baptist tradition, and help to nurture Baptist work abroad.

A code with capital letters only represents a mission from the United States of America. A code which includes a lowercase letter represents a mission from outside the United States with the initial letters representing the country itself.

ABA	American Baptist Association Missionary Committee, 1924
ABFMS	American Baptist Foreign Mission Society (now ABC)
ABMU	American Baptist Missionary Union (now ABC)
ABC	American Baptist Churches in the USA, Board of International Ministries, 1814
ABWE	Association of Baptists for World Evangelism, 1927
ArEBC	Evangelical Baptist Convention, Argentina, 1908
AuBMS	Australian Baptist Missionary Society, 1913
BBFI	Baptist Bible Fellowship International, 1950
BFM	Baptist Faith Missions, 1923
BGC	Baptist General Conference, Board of World Missions, 1944
BGEA	Billy Graham Evangelistic Association, 1950

SwO	Örebro Mission Society, Sweden, 1892
TIBM	Trinity International Baptist Mission, 1975
UkAET	Albanian Evangelical Trust, UK, 1986
UkBMS	Baptist Missionary Society, UK, 1792
UkGBM	Grace Baptist Mission, UK, 1861 (Strict Baptist)
UkHIM	Heartland International Ministries, UK
UkLA/LR	Light to Albania/Light to Romania, UK
UkRAD	Radstock Ministries, UK
UMBS	Ukrainian Missionary and Bible Society, 1945
WBF	World Baptist Fellowship Mission Agency, 1928

B. ABBREVIATIONS FOR NONDENOMINATIONAL MISSIONS

These nondenominational missions are included because of their contribution to Baptist work, particularly in the former USSR, southern Africa, and the Caribbean.

GerLIO	Licht im Osten/Light in the East, Germany, 1920
RM	Russian Ministries, 1991
SEND	Send International, 1947
SGA	Slavic Gospel Association, 1934
SoGM (AEF)	South Africa General Mission/Africa Evangelical Fellowship, 1906
UFMI	UFM International, 1931
UMN	United Mission to Nepal
WT	WordTeam USA, 1928

OTHER ABBREVIATIONS

ABHMS	American Baptist Home Mission Society
APBS	American Baptist Publication Society
BFBS	British and Foreign Bible Society
BWA	Baptist World Alliance
FMB	Foreign Mission Board
ICCC	International Council of Christian Churches
n/a	not available
TEE	Theological Education by Extension
USA	United States of America
USSR	Union of Soviet Socialist Republics
WABHMS	Woman's American Baptist Home Mission Society

MAPS AND CHART

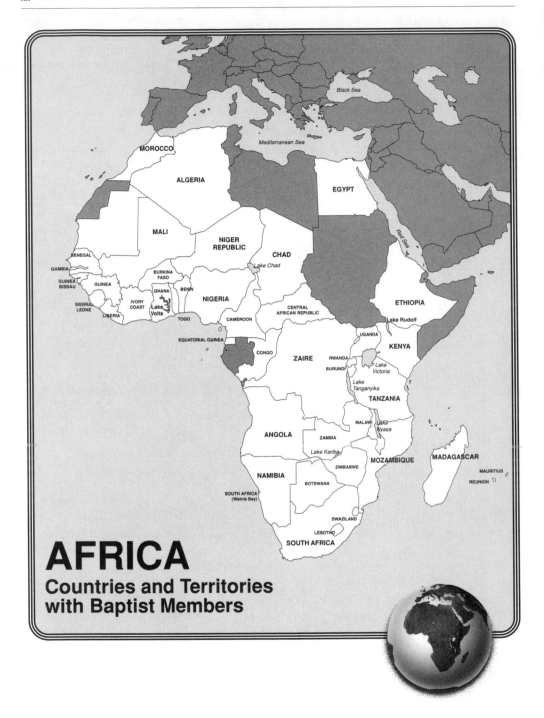

AFRICA
Countries and Territories
with Baptist Members

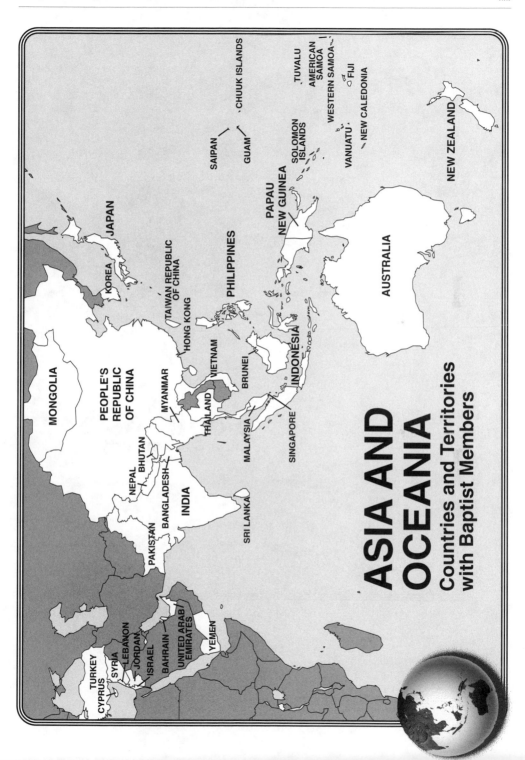

ASIA AND OCEANIA
Countries and Territories
with Baptist Members

South Asia
India Subcontinent

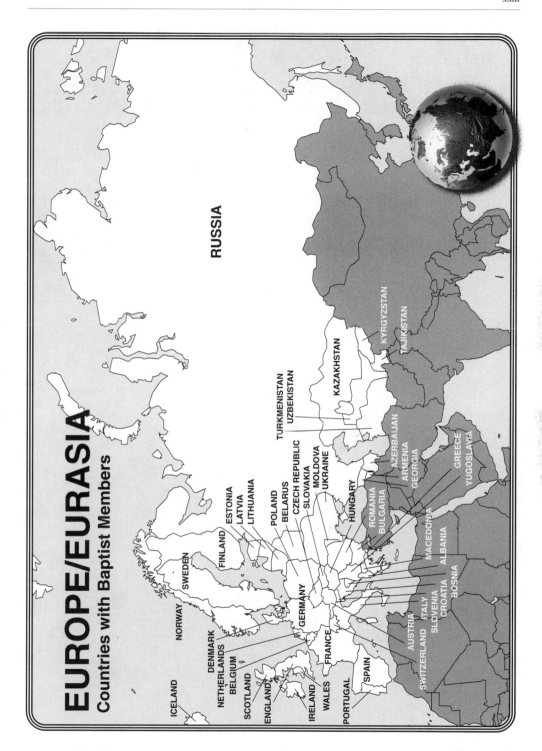

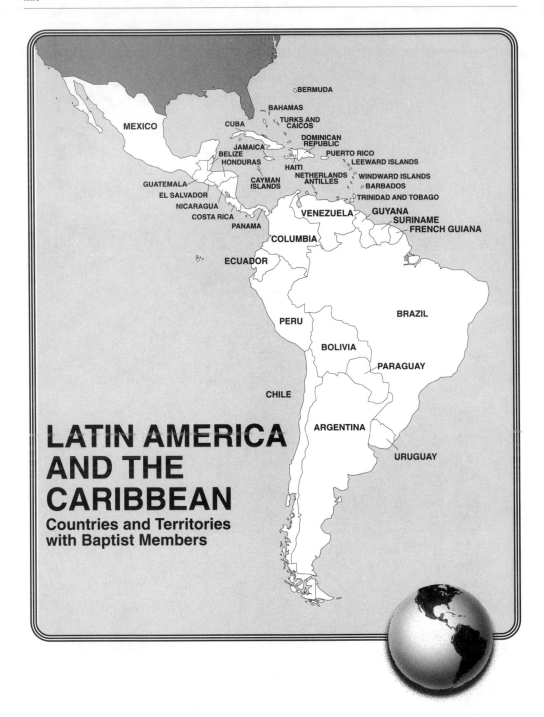

LATIN AMERICA AND THE CARIBBEAN
Countries and Territories with Baptist Members

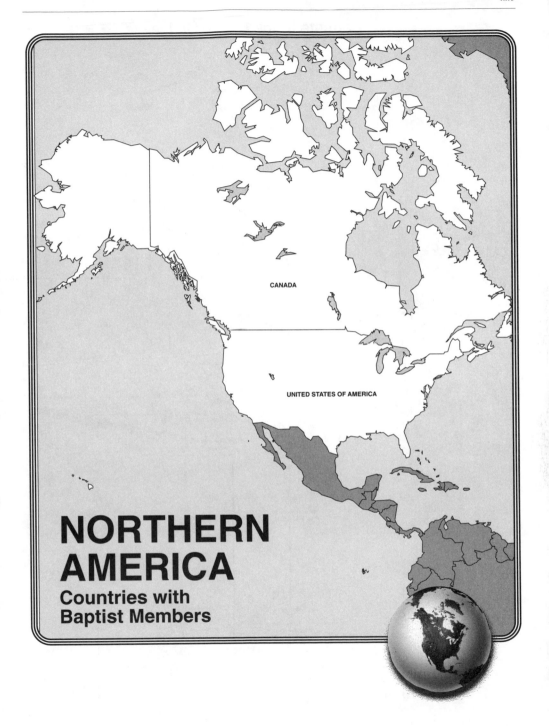

CANADA

UNITED STATES OF AMERICA

NORTHERN AMERICA
Countries with
Baptist Members

Baptists in the United States

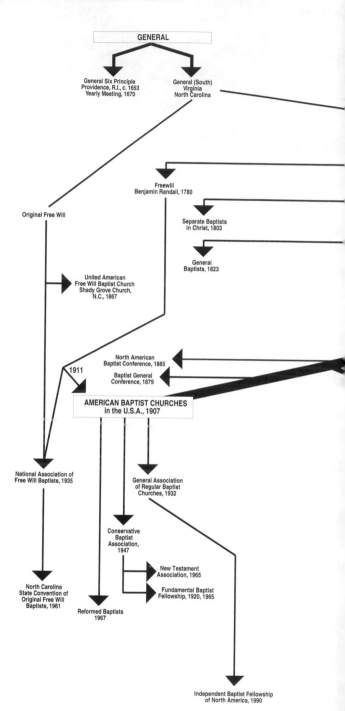

Baptists in the United States

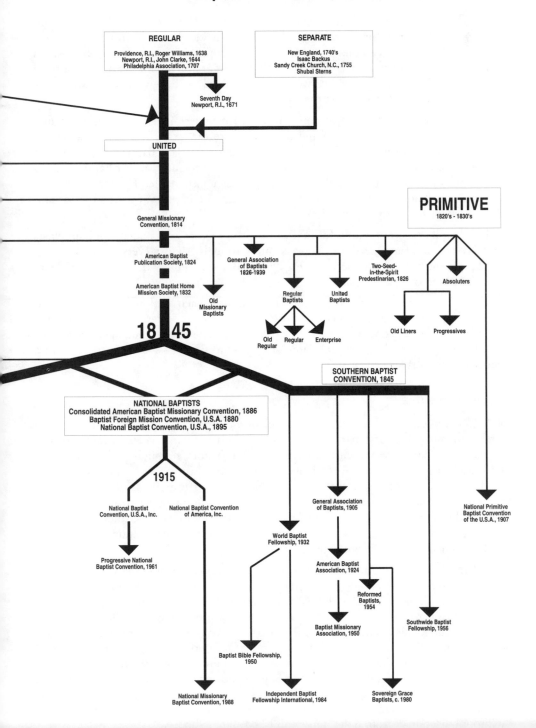

FOREWORD

Baptists Around the World: A Comprehensive Handbook is a significant contribution to understanding Baptist worldwide. Many histories of national conventions/unions have been written, emphasizing the story of Baptists in one particular country or area. This is the first attempt at a *handbook*, that is, a form of encyclopedia, a quick reference work to give a bird's eye view of Baptists in every conceivable geographical area of the world.

Albert W. Wardin, Jr. is to be complimented for undertaking this painstaking and monumental work. Perseverance and dedication are the stellar qualities of a Baptist historian that Wardin has exhibited. In addition to the 180 Baptists bodies in the Baptist World Alliance, there are numerous independent and separatist Baptist groups whose history and facts are unknown and almost unattainable. The fact that these groups are included in this book make it an even more important handbook for students of Baptist history and mission.

This handbook will be a useful tool for Baptist pastors and students, missiologists and lay-people everywhere. Its scope is international. Almost every country in the world is mentioned where there is some type of Baptist ministry if not in an article, at least in a footnote.

The book is divided into five geographical sections. Each section deals with Baptist work in a particular geographical area. This makes for easy reference when searching for a particular country. A brief historical account of Baptist beginnings in that area or country is given. Also, helpful dates of Baptist missionary society entrance into a particular country are given.

An Important Work

1. *The importance of studying Baptist history:* With the rapid growth of the world Christian movement and particularly that of the Baptists, it is important for new Christians to be aware of their history. Not only is history a reminder of heroes of the faith and their great sacrifice for kingdom work, but history serves as a lesson and guide. It has often been said that those that fail to learn from history will suffer from the same mistakes. History gives pointers along our pilgrimage as to where we have been and where we must go. It is important that Baptist seminarians, students and missionaries be aware of our past so that they might lead future generations with spiritual discernment and intelligent choices.

2. *Baptist identity*: With the rapid growth of the church around the world and particularly overseas, new Baptist Christians often have only a vague idea of what it means to be a Baptist. This handbook will help new Baptists gain an identity and learn what it means to belong to a particular group of world Christians called Baptists. It will help individuals define not only their doctrinal positions but their place in the larger community of the church. Contrary to prophets of doom who speak of the death of denominationalism, the fact is most evangelical denominations are growing and have a secure future. This is also true of the Baptist movement worldwide. In the Baptist World Alliance we are astounded at the many new Baptist conventions that are continually applying for membership, most of them from indigenous missionary work without any contact from older and established Baptist bodies.

3. *A mission resource*: The unevangelized world is often called today World A, or

the 10/40 window. This refers to peoples groups in that part of the world that has never heard the gospel and is geographically located within the 10/40 latitude and longitude on the world map. This handbook will be a useful tool for Baptist missiologists, and students of missions as all of us seek to evangelize the world in our generation. On the one hand this survey is an encouraging sign of the mighty movement of God's Spirit in many of the hard to reach places. For example, only recently Baptists in Nepal have organized themselves into a convention. For many years this area was closed to the gospel. We rejoice at the Christian work now taking place there. A study of this handbook will be cause for concern when one realizes the vast areas of the world without a Baptist or Christian witness.

4. *Statistics:* It was not easy for Noah to count all the animals as they entered the ark. Moses found it difficult to number the people of Israel. In the same way, it is an extremely difficult task to gather statistics on Christian world missions around the world. David B. Barrett unequivocally stated that there is a communion of at least one hundred million Baptists around the world. This includes children, family, and sympathizers. The Baptist World Alliance recognizes only baptized believers in its membership statistics. The BWA lists include almost forty million baptized believers in 180 Baptist conventions and unions worldwide.

In this handbook, Albert Wardin, concerned about dual alignment in a number of conventions, is more cautious and lists thirty-four million baptized believers in BWA member bodies. Membership in Baptist bodies and other Christian world organizations is always difficult to account for. For example, in Australia, Baptist churches clear their rolls every year of those who are members but have not attended. Whereas the Baptist Union of Australia lists 65,000 Baptist members, the Australians government census indicates almost 250,000 individuals who claim to be Baptist. In Eastern Europe a Baptist congregation may have 200 members, but on any Sunday there may be 500 in attendance. On the other hand, North American churches may have 1,000 members but only 500 in attendance on Sunday. In the larger Christian world when one considers that state churches of Europe, membership statistics become even more complicated. Whereas many countries would claim to have 99% Christians in their state churches, only 1% of the population many attend church services.

The Baptist World Alliance.

The Baptist World Alliance is "a home for every Baptist." In every corner of the world there are humble men and women, old and young, who follow the New Testament teachings concerning the church being a gathered body of believers who personally confess Jesus Christ as Lord and Savior and publicly confess that faith by immersion, in the name of the Father, Son and Holy Spirit. They gather together for prayer and worship and for the celebration of the Lord's Supper. They go to their homes, work, school and play with a burning desire that every believer must spread this light of Christ to others who have ever heard. They go, often with little education, but filled with the Spirit and passion of the early apostles, to tell the lost world that in Jesus Christ there is hope. These gathered Christians called Baptists have a unique history of suffering, for they arose in Europe in the 17th century during a period of religious intolerance and state churches which did not believe in the freedom of religion nor of soul competency. Baptists read the Scripture in the light of this freedom and thus became the early defenders of religious freedom around the world, but especially in the new world of North America. There they grew into the largest Protestant church in the USA and influenced greatly early decisions of religious freedom. On the continent the monarchies were less hospitable to freedom, but nevertheless Baptists grew. Even while imprisoned they preached the gospel and won many to Christ. In this century communism failed to eradicate the church. Many lost their lives witnessing to the power of the resurrection. Today a living church continues to bloom.

Since William Carey arrived in Calcutta, India in 1793 Baptists have spread around the world. In the Two-thirds world this same sense of urgency and zeal for evangelism has enabled Baptists to grow into one of the most widespread churches in the world. African, Asian, and Latin American Baptists outnumber their European brothers and sisters.

More than 90% of these Baptists have voluntarily joined together to form the Baptist World Alliance. Although formed in 1905, it is still a young organization with continual growth. To the 180 member bodies more are added every year. In 1995 there are twenty-five Baptist groups seeking membership in this worldwide fellowship of Baptists. The Baptist World Alliance (BWA) has a fourfold role among Baptists: The BWA unites Baptists worldwide, leads in evangelism, responds to people in need, and defends human rights. Whether defending the right of Baptist believers in Bulgaria to construct a church building, or protesting the imprisonment of believers in Middle Eastern prisons for religious reasons, or holding a conference on the unevangelized world, the BWA represents the worldwide Baptist concern in all areas of life.

Each quinquennium, that is, every five years, there is a Baptist World Congress where Baptists from around the world gather together in one city to celebrate our unity, network with one another, encourage the faithful, and deepen our spiritual life. The first congress was in London in 1905 and this year in Buenos Aires, Argentina. Since Baptist believe in a democratic congregational life, lay-people take an active part in the life of the BWA. Men, women, and youth play significant roles in encouraging lay witnessing and social concern. Commissions studying Christian ethics, human rights, Baptist history, worship and church leadership bring to bear the great intellectual and spiritual gifts of men and women from around the world to encourage and strengthen the church in its mission.

Baptist leaders from around the world benefit from the annual meetings of the general council. At these annual councils, committees and commissions meet. Networking outside of the meetings is probably the most significant aspect of these gatherings. To a certain extent the impetus and spiritual odyssey of this book was formed at meetings of the Baptist World Alliance attended by Albert Wardin. It therefore gives me great joy to commend this book to Baptists everywhere. We would encourage Baptist pastors and laity, professors and students to rediscover their history and thereby deepen their faith and commitment to Jesus Christ as Lord and Savior. May it be said of this generation of Baptists what Johannes Gerhard Oncken said of his German brothers and sisters, "Every Baptist, a missionary" (Jeder Baptist, ein Missionar)! Indeed read *Baptists Around the World* as a prayer calendar, a reminder to pray for the worldwide community of our brothers and sisters in Christ as we work and pray for that day when every knee shall bow and "every tongue confess that Jesus Christ is Lord!" (Phil. 2:11)

Denton Lotz

General Secretary

Baptist World Alliance

PREFACE

For many years there has been the need for a reference work on all Baptist groups around the world. The publication of such a volume is urgent since the Baptist world family is present today in most countries and its constituency is becoming increasingly interracial and international. There have been several Baptist histories—volumes by David Benedict (1848), Robert G. Torbet (1950), and H. Leon McBeth (1987)—which included historical material on Baptists in various parts of the world. Because of the prominence of Baptists in the British Isles and the United States of America, the focus of these works has been Anglo-American with the result that Baptists in the Two-Thirds World were treated only as mission extensions, if not ignored entirely.

Since the Second World War a multitude of nations have gained independence and demand proper treatment and recognition. Although within Baptist ranks many countries are still mission territory and are dependent on outside assistance, a large number of Baptist bodies outside the Anglo-American sphere stand on their own feet and are leaders in growth. Whatever the status of a Baptist group, each deserves consideration on its own terms. Although this volume does not overcome all inequities and often emphasizes the missionaries and their work rather than the believers themselves, it nevertheless attempts to remedy some of the deficiencies of past histories.

This volume has been a cooperative endeavor. After the presentation by the editor for the need of a Baptist handbook, the Heritage Commission of the Baptist World Alliance in Montreal, Canada, in July 1991 approved in principle the concept of such a work. One-fourth of the text was written by different individuals around the world in the attempt to make the work as international as possible. The remaining three-fourths of the book was written by the editor, who used a wide range of materials. Unsigned articles are his work.

The Heritage Commission also approved an editorial board, which, besides the editor, included John H. Y. Briggs, professor of history at the University of Keele, Keele, United Kingdom, and editor of *The Baptist Quarterly*; Horace O. Russell, professor of church history at Eastern Baptist Theological Seminary, Philadelphia, Pennsylvania; and Lynn E. May, Jr., executive director of the Historical Commission of the Southern Baptist Convention, Nashville, Tennessee. The editor greatly appreciated John Briggs' conscientious editing of the European section as well as the contributions and support of the other members of the board. The editor also acknowledges with gratitude the editorial assistance of Charles DeWeese of the Historical Commission; the contributions of Richard V. Pierard of Indiana State University in writing and translation; and the efforts of other individuals, including Polly Van Lear, Roy Chamlee, and Alfredo Colman, for their suggestions in correcting and improving the text.

The work has attempted to include a Baptist body if it carries the name "Baptist," has a historical relationship to other Baptist bodies, and maintains basic Baptist beliefs. For theological reasons, this work does not include the Christian Baptist Church of God (a holiness body); Brethren bodies; nor Pentecostal bodies, such as the Evangelical Baptist Church, Holiness Baptists, or the Pentecostal Free Will Baptist Church (even though all of them may carry the Baptist name). On the other hand, the volume includes the Örebro Mission of Sweden, although it favors Pentecostalism, since it is Baptist in heritage and considers itself a Baptist body. The volume also incorporates daughter bodies of the Örebro Society abroad which bear the Baptist name. Moreover, it includes the National Baptist Convention of Brazil and the National Baptist Convention of Zimbabwe, both Pentecostal bodies, since the Baptist World Alliance has accepted them as members.

The editor has used the earlier and more proper term "close communion," rather than "closed communion" for the practice of a local church in allowing only individuals of like faith and order or the members of the church to partake of the Lord's Supper.

The book contains several special features. Each country carries a date when Baptists first entered the country or were established in the country. The determination of such a date is, however, not always easy. For some countries the appropriate date is the coming of the first missionary, while for others it is the first baptism or the establishment of the first church.

After each regional subdivision, a listing is given of the missions currently related to Baptist work in the various countries. If available, the year when a mission first entered a country or designated it as a mission field follows the mission's name. Missions with dates are listed in chronological order. A special section of the book lists the code or abbreviation for each mission, the year of its establishment (if available), and its home country. Another feature of the book is the bibliographies for each country, some of which include foreign titles.

A further feature is the statistical data. Although memberships were unavailable or had to be estimated for many bodies, the volume nevertheless contains the most comprehensive statistical analysis of Baptists worldwide. Each country includes statistics, if available, of various Baptist bodies in that country. Two appendixes also include pertinent statistical data with one of them providing a distribution of Baptists in the USA by region and state.

The editor is a lifelong Baptist. Two of his grandparents came from Baptist families who migrated to the USA from East Prussia in Germany and Ukraine. His great-great-great uncle was the founder of the Baptist work in Poland and the first German Baptist minister in the Russian Empire. He has been a member of three different Baptist bodies in the United States, absorbing their distinct emphases. His wife is a cousin of Lottie Moon, one of the great missionary heroines of China.

The editor assumes full responsibility for the contents of the volume. Opinions of the various contributors, however, are their own and do not necessarily reflect the views of either the editor or publisher. The editor realizes the volume is a pioneer work and, if there are future editions, he would hope to improve its contents and provide additional data. Above all, the editor has attempted to be fair and balanced, reflecting both Baptist strengths and weaknesses, victories as well as defeats.

The editor hopes the volume will be useful in introducing Baptists to each other and the public at large. Baptists themselves could use the work in developing fellowship, in encouraging intercession for each other, and in the promotion and study of missions. It seeks to be a work of encouragement. In helping Baptists to see their past and current status, it should enable them to meet the challenges of the future more effectively not only for themselves but for God's glory.

Albert W. Wardin, Jr.

Baptist Identity

*T*hroughout their history Baptists have held to a number of basic principles which clearly set them aside from other major Christian bodies, while at the same time holding to Christian doctrines which place them within the mainstream of the Christian faith. Although some Baptists trace their history by means of an apostolic succession of churches or a spiritual succession through sects which dissented from the Roman Catholic Church, Baptist churches with the Baptist name and a self-defining identity clearly emerged in both England and the American colonies within the first half of the seventeenth century.

Unlike most other major Protestant bodies, Baptists have had no founder, such as a Martin Luther for the Lutherans, a John Calvin and an Ulrich Zwingli for the Reformed, or a John Wesley for the Methodists. In fact, John Smyth, whom many consider to be the first English Baptist, and Roger Williams, whom many regard as the founder of Baptists in America, both left the Baptist faith soon after their baptism as believers. Smyth led his congregation to accept Mennonite doctrine, and Williams became a Seeker, rejecting all existing denominations. In addition, Smyth baptized himself, a highly irregular practice, and neither Smyth nor Williams was immersed, today a universal Baptist practice, but were baptized by affusion if not sprinkling.

Over the years Baptist historians have debated the relative influences of Puritan Separatism and Anabaptism in the development of the Baptist movement. There is no attempt to resolve the debate here except to note that Thomas Helwys, who broke with Smyth and established the first General Baptist church on English soil, was Arminian in theology and had been under both Puritan and Anabaptist/Mennonite influences and rejected certain features of both systems. The later Particular or Calvinistic Baptists, clearly Puritan in doctrine, accepted believer's baptism by immersion after study of Scripture and were drawn to the example of the Collegiants, a group in the Netherlands which practiced it.

Although Baptists have been influenced by the theological currents of their day, they have insisted that they are "people of the Book," claiming Scripture as the sole norm of faith and practice. Besides this cardinal principle of the Protestant Reformation, they also have upheld a second principle of the Protestant Reformation—the priesthood of the believer, or soul competency. Whatever one may believe concerning their origins, the Baptist advocacy of these principles clearly place them within the Protestant tradition. On the other hand, from the beginning they separated themselves from most Protestants of their day by rejecting the magisterial Reformation. Protestant reformers, by and large, advocated territorial churches, supported and protected by the state, which incorporated an entire population under its discipline and brought the newborn into membership through infant baptism. With the earlier Anabaptists and Mennonites, Baptists countered by insisting that the local church is composed only of baptized believers and membership must be voluntary, thereby rejecting parish churches and infant baptism, as well as a union of church and state and religious coercion.

Such principles thereby place Baptists in what has been denominated as "the Believers' Church," a type of church in which Baptists were historical forerunners.

The principles which have made Baptists a distinct body do not, however, make them unique since many denominational bodies share these same principles today. In addition, these principles do not encompass all that Baptists believe since they hold with other Christians the cardinal doctrines of the Christian faith, such as acceptance of the Trinity, or with other Protestants the doctrine of justification by faith. Nevertheless, Baptists may make special claim to their principles since they were one of the first denominational bodies to support many of them. Baptists were also the first to link them in a distinct configuration and were generally more consistent and radical in applying them than other groups. Although all Baptist groups continue to hold to these principles, ironically today their interpretation and application are causing serious divisions among Baptists themselves. Even with these tensions within the Baptist fellowship, probably no other major denominational family has been able to be as united and stable in its doctrinal beliefs than Baptists, even among bodies with official creeds.

Baptists have rejected creeds as usurping the final authority of Scripture and as violating the soul competency of the believer. However, they have been a confessional people, adopting confessions for local churches, associations, conventions, and other denominational bodies. These confessions have sought to explain Baptist beliefs to others, to give doctrinal guidance, to provide a basis of unity, and to test heresy. Baptists have never adopted a universal confession for all Baptists, have generally allowed a degree of latitude in interpretation as not to coerce the conscience, have opposed placing any confession above the Bible as final authority, and feel free at any time to change their confessions. Since the fundamentalist controversies earlier in the twentieth century, Baptists have, however, been seriously divided over the role of the Bible. Many Conservatives claim it is completely inspired and inerrant and stress its supernatural character, while others, who hold to it as a spiritual standard, note the human factor in its composition. They do not consider it inerrant outside its religious content and would tend to stress the Lordship of Christ rather than Scripture as the fundamental principle.

Baptists have always held to a regenerate church membership and have generally stressed the need for a personal religious experience. The maintenance of a regenerate body of believers, however, is facing threats from several quarters. In many Baptist circles church discipline and the use of a church covenant which insured a regenerate membership are practically gone, and the erosion of a strong coupling of repentance with faith has opened the way for an "easy believism." In addition, the average age of persons baptized continues to get younger; in a number of cases child baptism is replacing believer's baptism. In their study of Scripture, Baptists came to believe that immersion was the correct biblical mode of baptism, which represented symbolically the rising of the believer from the watery grave to walk a new life with Christ. All Baptists continue to practice baptism by immersion, but a limited number of Baptist churches practice open membership and accept into membership, individuals who have been sprinkled either as infants or adults.

Soul competency, or the priesthood of the believer, has been a cherished doctrine for Baptists as well as its corollary, congregational church government. With other Protestants, Baptists maintain that a believer is his/her own priest who is competent to go directly to God through Christ. The church, composed of believers, is therefore competent to control its own affairs and also has the right to approach God directly without the jurisdiction of a synod, conference, convention, or any other ecclesiastical body over it. The formation of Baptist denominational organizations beyond the local association came not from an ecclesiology which required such structures but from the desire to support missions, Christian education, and benevolent enterprises more efficiently.

Soul competency, however, has become a fierce area of contention among Baptists. This is reflected in what Paul M. Harrison has noted as the tension between "the freedom of man" and "the freedom of God." Some Baptists stress the "freedom of man," that is, freedom to believe as conscience dictates. Other Baptists insist that belief must be determined by God's freedom as defined in Scripture. For the latter group, Christian freedom means the freedom to follow Scripture without interference from any state or ecclesiastical authority.

Baptists historically have been in the forefront of the struggle for religious liberty for all people and creeds. Its corollary, the separation of church and state, naturally follows whereby the state does not control the church, and the church does not seek to control government. Despised as a sect in their early days, Baptists often led the way for other free churches in gaining religious liberty in various parts of the world. Baptists today continue to struggle for freedom in undemocratic societies or in former Communist areas where traditional territorial churches wish to regain control. A great debate has occurred among Baptists in America, however, as to the role of religion in the public arena. Some Baptists interpret separation of church and state by principles enunciated by Thomas Jefferson, erecting a wall between the two wherein religious expression or activity may not be mandated or supported by the state. Other Baptists, while upholding religious freedom for all and rejecting state support for any one church or all churches, believe that religion should not be separated from the state. They uphold religious expression and activity in both public life and the public school.

With their congregational government, their spirit of independence, and differences among them, it is not surprising that there are so many different Baptist groups. In the USA, including ethnic bodies, there are at least fifty-three distinct bodies, which can be divided into a number of subcategories, each with its own ideological emphasis. Despite the many divisions, most Baptists would still consider themselves part of one Baptist denomination, accepting in one form or another the historic Baptist principles; they generally accept each other's members and, by and large, hold to a common core of belief. Primitivist, Landmark, and possibly Free Will Baptists would consider themselves ouside the major stream of Baptist life, but in comparison to the total Baptist population their number is small.

Even with their commonalities, Baptists are nevertheless deeply divided into three major parties—mainline ecumenical, conservative evangelical, and separatist fundamental—a division found not only in America but within the Baptist family around the world. Major divisions today are not between Calvinists and Arminians or between Missionary and Anti-Missionary Baptists— serious divisions in the past—but primarily over the interpretation of the Baptist principles themselves, social issues, and relations with other Christians.

The mainline ecumenical bodies, such as the Baptist Union of Great Britain and the American Baptist Churches/USA, tolerate a wide spectrum of belief ranging from conservative to liberal, permit open membership, exhibit a major concern for peace and human rights, tend to be rather liberal on social issues, and strongly support the ecumenical movement.

The second party—conservative evangelicals—contains the main bulk of Baptists.

dard histories of Baptists are Robert G. Torbet, *A History of the Baptists* (Valley Forge: Judson Press, 1950; 1963, rev. ed.; 1975, 3d ed.), and H. Leon McBeth, *The Baptist Heritage: Four Centuries of Baptist Witness* (Nashville: Broadman Press, 1987). Three works which contain valuable material on Baptist principles and identity are H. Wheeler Robinson, *The Life and Faith of the Baptists* (London: Kingsgate Press, 1927; 1946, rev. ed.); Paul M. Harrison, *Authority and Power in the Free Church Tradition: A Social Case Study of the American Baptist Convention* (Princeton: Princeton University Press, 1959); and William Henry Brackney, *The Baptists* (Westport, Conn.: Greenwood Press, 1988). The standard work on Baptist confessions is William L. Lumpkin, *Baptist Confessions of Faith* (Valley Forge: Judson Press, 1959; 1969, rev. ed.). For the relations of Baptists with other Christians, see William R. Estep, *Baptists and Christian Unity* (Nashville: Broadman Press, 1966); James Leo Garrett, ed., *Baptist Relations with Other Christians* (Valley Forge: Judson Press, 1974), and William Jerry Boney and Glenn A. Igleheart, eds., *Baptists and Ecumenism*, in *Journal of Ecumenical Studies*, 17 (spring 1980).

BAPTIST EXPANSION AND MISSIONS

*T*he Baptist denomination of today began in the seventeenth century as a small struggling sect on the fringe of the much larger Protestant world. Most Protestants were in the Lutheran, Reformed, Anglican, Presbyterian, and Congregational churches—all territorial churches established and supported by the state. Baptists established themselves first in England, Ireland, and the American colonies.

By 1750, after General Baptists had existed almost a century and a half and Regular or Particular Baptists for more than a century, Baptists were still a very minor body. In England the General Baptists, infected by Socinianism, and the Particular Baptists, affected by hyper-Calvinism, lost their spiritual vitality, and the Seventh Day Baptists were practically extinct. With secular indifference and rationalism infecting much of the population, Baptist prospects in the mid eighteenth century appeared bleak. In the American colonies at this time, Baptists numbered only a bit more than five thousand in around one hundred churches. In some areas American Baptists had faced or were facing restrictions, if not persecution. They did not have the advantage of the Anglicans and Presbyterians or the German and Dutch churches of the Middle Colonies of gaining large numbers of adherents from the territorial churches of Europe. Times, however, were soon to change.

In the British Isles, the Wesleyan or Evangelical Revival of the eighteenth century brought rejuvenation and growth to the Particular Baptists and produced a new evangelical body, the New Connexion of General Baptists. In America the First Great Awakening, occurring before the Revolutionary War, not only brought with its revivalism growth to the Regular Baptists but also produced an intensely evangelistic body, the Separate Baptists. After the Revolutionary War a Second Great Awakening helped to generate further expansion with Baptists becoming one of the major denominations in the United States, noted for its missionary zeal. In Virginia in 1768 a prosecuting attorney charged three Separate Baptist preachers as disturbers of the peace who "cannot meet a man upon the road, but they must ram a text of scripture down his throat." A Congregationalist minister of New England, Noah Worcester, who was critical of Baptist growth, in 1794 condemned them for their emotional appeals and irresponsible use of Scripture.

The Baptist witness spread with ministers itinerating to areas outside their own community. In America, the farmer-preacher, primarily in the South and western frontiers and providing most of his own support, moved with the migrating population and would often follow a circuit among a number of churches. Associations, which initially provided mutual encouragement and helped to set doctrinal and ministerial standards, also began to send out missionaries. At the end of the eighteenth century, the mission society for both home and foreign missions began to appear. It was generally a single-purpose regional, state, or national organization with membership based on financial support. It brought together like-minded individuals and by-passed the local church. Baptists in America later formed state conventions, which consolidated mission efforts on the state level, and later national conventions.

Even with growth and quickened evangelistic zeal, Baptists in 1790 were still an Anglo-American body, confined largely to Great Britain and the USA with only a handful of adherents abroad—primarily in Canada and Jamaica. The formation of the Baptist Missionary Society (1792) in England and the Baptist General Missionary Convention of the Baptist Denomination in the United States for Foreign Missions (1814), also known as the Triennial Convention, began to expand Baptist work abroad. In what Kenneth Scott Latourette, the noted Baptist historian of missions, called the "Great Century" (1815-1914), Baptists in Great Britain and the USA and elsewhere added an increasing number of foreign mission agencies. In addition, Johann Oncken, the great German Baptist leader who declared "every Baptist a missionary," began an indigenous European Baptist movement which extended across northern Europe into the Balkans and the Russian Empire.

In 1852 there were about 1,167,000 Baptists. By 1904, the year of the organization of the Baptist World Alliance, Baptists had become a world body with 6,188,000 in about forty-five countries and territories. Ninety years later in 1994 Baptists had grown to thirty-seven million in about 180 countries and territories. The distribution has changed remarkably:

	1852	*1904*	*1994*
British Isles	192,500	395,000	220,000
USA and Canada	922,000	5,450,000	28,385,000
West Indies	35,000	42,300	400,000
Continental Europe	4,200	124,000	680,000
Asia/Oceania	12,300	161,000	2,965,000
Africa	1,200	10,200	3,090,000
Middle and South America	_____	5,500	1,585,000
	1,167,200	6,188,000	37,325,000

In 1852 4½ percent of the Baptist population resided outside the British Isles and Northern America. In 1904 the percentage had grown to only 5½ percent. Today it exceeds 23 percent and, with present rates of growth, should soon reach 25 percent. About 30 percent of the Baptist population are members of the Black race, while 7½ percent are Asiatic and 4½ percent are of Latin origin. Baptists are becoming increasingly multiracial and multinational. Only 58 percent are of northern or eastern European stock.

The Baptist advance in the twentieth century has been remarkable. As Latourette would describe it, it has been an "advance through storm." With two devastating World Wars and Baptists living under totalitarian regimes, which would limit if not eliminate the Christian faith, Baptists have become one of the major Protestant bodies in the world. They rival if not surpass in active members Anglicans, Lutherans, Presbyterians, and Reformed and are established in more countries. Pentecostals appear to be the only significant free church body which is surpassing Baptists in rates of growth in various parts of the world, particularly in Scandinavia, southern Europe, and

Latin America. Pentecostalists and Seventh-Day Adventists are the only two Protestant bodies which can equal if not exceed Baptists in number of countries entered.

Significant Baptist growth and geographical spread has occurred since World War II. This is partly because of the surge of conservative evangelical strength in North America in this period. The largest Baptist mission agency, the Foreign Mission Board of the Southern Baptist Convention, which today has more than four thousand missionaries, embarked on an aggressive program which either expanded Baptist work or placed it in countries where it had not existed previously. Since the middle of the century, conservative evangelical or fundamentalist Baptist mission agencies in the USA, independent of the Baptist World Alliance, have grown in number and size and today have more than 3,800 career missionaries abroad who are located in most countries of the non-Moslem world. These missionaries must raise their own support by visiting the churches in their constituency. At the same time, the number of missionaries supported by ecumenical mainline bodies has declined. Baptists in the Two-Thirds World, generally considered mission territory, are also now sending their own missionaries to other lands. Many Baptists also serve in nondenominational evangelical missions and parachurch agencies. Baptist missions have also been adept in shifting mission forces from territories with closing doors to open ones, such as missionaries in French-speaking Africa moving to France and Belgium and missionaries in China settling after World War II in the Pacific area.

The career missionary continues to play a vital role, but the short-term volunteer has become increasingly important. In 1993 more than ten thousand volunteers served with the Foreign Mission Board of the Southern Baptist Convention. Through raising money for special projects and sending volunteers, churches themselves are becoming more involved personally in foreign missions. Evangelism remains the primary focus of most agencies. In their attempt to find opportunities to present the gospel as well as becoming more sensitive to the social needs of native populations, many Baptist missions, however, also provide an amazing range of social services from medical and educational services to hunger relief.

The church growth movement as well as the fundamentalist and traditional Baptist orientation of many Baptist boards has put a great emphasis on church planting and the desire for measurable results. With the collapse of Communism in Europe, Baptists have greatly increased their involvement in eastern Europe through both denominational and independent agencies. There is also a greater concern in reaching the previously unreached people groups in what missiologists call World A—a territory stretching across North Africa and much of southern and eastern Asia where millions have never heard the gospel. Professionals now seek to enter closed societies, not as career missionaries but as individuals with skills and services to share, who thereby gain opportunities for Christian witness. Theological Education by Extension (TEE), which decentralizes theological education and brings it to church leaders, is today an important adjunct to the residential seminary. Although problems of paternalism and strained relations between the Western missionary and native leaders at times persist, nevertheless there is a greater stress on partnership and recognition of the need to contextualize the gospel.

The Baptist mission scene has become practically an ecclesiatical free-for-all. With greater mobility and resources and opposition to the ecumenical movement, most Baptist mission agencies are not parties to any comity agreements. Today no Baptist mission agency can even stake out a country for itself or even a field, expecting other

Baptists to stay out. There may be some mutual consideration and even some cooperation with other Baptists or even non-Baptists, but each mission develops its own program and works out its own relationships. Some Baptist agencies attempt to work with a Baptist union or convention already present in a country, but others, particularly fundamentalist agencies, work independently, even in European countries with a long-established Baptist presence.

BIBLIOGRAPHY: The editor gained Baptist statistics for 1852, after excluding non-Baptist bodies, from J. Lansing Burrows, ed., *American Baptist Register, for 1852* (Philadelphia: American Baptist Publication Society, 1853), 495, and for 1904 from Baptist World Alliance, *Congress*, 1905, 343–44. He gained the 1994 statistics from sources noted elsewhere in this volume.

Material on Baptist growth in the United States may be found in the well-written volume by Edwin Scott Gaustad, *Historical Atlas of Religion in America* (New York and Evanston: Harper & Row, 1962). The study by Robert G. Gardner, *Baptists of Early America: A Statistical History, 1639–1790* (Atlanta: Georgia Baptist Historical Society, 1983) includes a valuable compilation of early Baptist statistics. Albert W. Wardin, Jr., *Baptist Atlas* (Nashville: Broadman, 1980), provides helpful statistical data on Baptists in the USA and abroad. A perceptive article on the problems in gathering Baptist statistics is by Carl W. Tiller, "How Useful Are Our Recent Statistical Data?" *Foundations*, 21 (Jan./Mar. 1978): 16–21.

Two perceptive articles on mission work as related to Baptists is Denton Lotz, "Baptist Identity in Mission and Evangelism," *Foundations*, 21, no. 1 (Jan./Mar. 1978): 32–49, and Justice C. Anderson, "Changing Patterns of World Mission Work," *Baptist History and Heritage*, 27, no. 3 (July 1992): 14–24. For a recent work on conservative evangelicals and missions, see Joel A. Carpenter and Wilbert R. Shenk, eds., *Earthen Vessels: American Evangelicals and Foreign Missions* (Grand Rapids: William B. Eerdmans, 1990).

It is surprising how few books have been written on Baptist missions as a whole. Two older volumes are G. Winfred Hervey, *The Story of Baptist Missions in Foreign Lands*, rev. ed. (St. Louis: Chaney R. Barnes Publishing Co., 1892), and Henry C. Vedder, *A Short History of Baptist Missions* (Philadelphia: Judson Press, 1927). The volume by A. L. Vail, *The Morning Hour of American Baptist Missions* (Philadelphia: American Baptist Publication Society, 1907), is an excellent study of the development of the mission spirit among Baptists in the USA, while the work by Frank W. Padelford, *The Commonwealths and the Kingdom* (Philadelphia: Griffith and Rowland Press, 1913), provides valuable material on state missions and state conventions in the Northern and Western states of the USA. A number of histories have appeared detailing the work of individual Baptist missions. Two very notable works are Robert G. Torbet, *Venture of Faith* (Philadelphia: Judson Press, 1955), for the foreign mission enterprise of the American Baptist Churches/USA, and Brian Stanley, *The History of the Baptist Missionary Society* (Edinburg: T&T Clark, 1992). The most beautifully edited and illustrated Baptist mission volume to date is the Conservative Baptist history by Hans W. Finzel, ed., *Partners Together: 50 Years of Global Impact—The CBFMS Story, 1943–1993* (Wheaton, Ill: CBFMS, 1993). The respected Baptist historian, William R. Estep, has recently completed, *Whole Gospel—Whole World: The Foreign Mission Board of the Southern Baptist Convention, 1845–1995* (Nashville: Broadman Holman, 1994), primarily an administrative history.

Several very fine books have appeared in recent years with material on Black Baptists and missions, one of which is Sandy D. Martin, *Black Baptists and African Missions* (Macon, Ga.: Mercer University Press, 1989). A valuable article on Blacks in missions from an African-American perspective is, Gayraud S. Wilmore, "Black Americans in Mission: Setting the Record Straight," *International Bulletin of Missionary Research*, 10, no. 3 (July 1986): 98–102. One great need is for studies on the work of the fundamentalist Baptist missions formed since the Second World War. Two excellent directories which include data on Baptist missions are, *Mission Handbook*, 1993–95 (Monrovia, Calif.: MARC, 1993), and *East + West Christian Organizations* (Evanston: Berry Publishing Services, 1993).

I. Africa

Africa is a vast continent with great diversity in lands and people, stretching from the Mediterranean Sea across the Sahara Desert and Sudan to the southern tip of South Africa. Until the nineteenth century most of Africa south of the Sahara was isolated from the world. Today Africa is seeking its place in the modern world. The old and the new live side by side. Modern technology coexists with ancient tribal life.

Africa and adjacent islands have more than fifty political entities. With few exceptions, all of these states had been colonial territories and gained their independence only in recent decades. With its attempt to modernize and at the same time shed its colonial past, Africa has also had to face a number of serious problems—tribal rivalries, civil war, political oppression, and economic dislocation and decline. But in spite of the difficulties, Africa is attempting to face the challenges of a new age.

Although the European colonial powers exploited Africa for its natural resources and manpower, at the same time they introduced political, economic, and social concepts and institutions. Missionaries brought the Christian faith together with Western education, literacy, medicine, and various practical arts. Today Africa is one of the most fruitful fields for the spread of the gospel. In spite of strong competition from Islam, which dominates North Africa and the Sudan and has pockets of strength in parts of West and East Africa, Christianity is becoming the dominant faith south of the Sudan region. For an African to forsake his or her tribal religion and accept either Christianity or Islam means far more than simply exchanging one religion for another; it signifies passage into world civilization.

Baptists were among the pioneers in bringing the gospel to Africa. Before World War I, the most notable work of Baptist missionaries was in Liberia, Nigeria, Cameroon, the Congo (Zaire) in Western Africa, and in Malawi and South Africa in Southern Africa. From the USA came the American Baptist Missionary Union, the Foreign Mission Board (FMB) of the Southern Baptist Convention, and FMB of the National Baptist Convention. From Europe came the Baptist Missionary Society of Great Britain and the Mission Society of German Baptists. In addition, a Baptist work took root among European settlers in South Africa. Since World War II there has been an acceleration of Baptist mission activity. Today there are Baptists in forty-two of the fifty-three countries or dependencies on the African continent and in the Indian Ocean. A number of these countries are experiencing an explosion of growth, often with the fastest rates of increase of Baptists anywhere in the world. In 1927 there were about

BURUNDI *(1928)*

	Members	Churches
Union of Baptist Churches in Burundi (1960)	32,000	(87)

*B*urundi is a small, densely populated territory located in highlands between the Congo and Nile Rivers. Belgium gained the territory from Germany after World War I, separating it from German East Africa (Tanzania). Burundi received independence in 1962. The population is composed of Hutu (85 percent) and Tutsi (14 percent), a nomadic people who until recently have dominated the Hutu for generations. Another one percent of the people are Pygmies. Baptist work has been primarily among the Hutu.

The Belgium government forbade German missionaries to return to their fields. The Neukirchener Mission Society turned over its five mission stations to the Danish Baptist Foreign Missionary Society, which at that time was seeking a field. The Neukirchener Society had been the only Protestant mission agency in Burundi, serving there from 1911 to 1916.

The first missionaries of the Baptist mission, Mr. and Mrs. N. P. Andersen, arrived in 1928, settling at Ibanga, where services and school work were begun. One of the successful extensions of the work was to Musema, where thirty-four young people were baptized on New Year's Day 1931. The formation of a Baptist congregation there on January 4 also signaled the establishment of the first Protestant church in the country. The mission opened schools, a most important evangelistic tool, as well as a clinic and maternity home. One of the missionaries established a printing shop, which printed reading books and a hymnbook.

Since Danish Baptists felt they could not occupy the entire field, in the 1930s they offered a division of the territory to other societies. The Danish Baptists in America were approached but could not enter. The Danish Baptists then transferred portions of the field to the Friends Africa Gospel Mission and to American Free Methodists and encouraged the Church Missionary Society (Anglican) to enter. In assisting these missions to start, Danish Baptists provided transportation and laborers to saw lumber for building. In 1935 the Protestant missions in Burundi and Rwanda formed a Protestant Council, which provided for comity, cooperative endeavor, and a united front with the government.

A revival movement broke in 1939, bringing spiritual renewal to church members and evangelistic outreach to others. In 1938 the number of members was 528, but in 1948 there were 1,448 members as well as 123 schools. In 1944 and 1945 the mission constructed the Emanuel Broholm Memorial Hospital at Musem with seventy beds. In spite of being cut off from financial support from Denmark because of World War II, the missionaries were able to continue work with financial assistance from Danish Baptists in America and other sources. The reduction of funds forced the Burundian churches to become self-supporting, a practice that continued after the war.

After the war, Baptists in Denmark again took up the work, and American Danish Baptists continued financial assistance. Attempts have been made to provide theological training. Although in 1956 a seminary was established at Rubura, today there is only a temporary pastors' school which was begun in 1990. In 1957 Baptists numbered only 2,900 but since then have grown over tenfold. During the unsuccessful rebellion by Hutus in 1972 and 1973, many Baptists lost their lives. Baptists formed in 1960 the Union of Baptist Churches in Ruanda-Urundi, which today is confined to Burundi. In 1988 Southern Baptists entered to work with the Danish Baptist mission and the Union of Baptist Churches.

BIBLIOGRAPHY: For the first three decades of the Danish Baptist mission in Burundi, see, Svend Aage Hagström, *A History of the Danish Baptist Mission in Ruanda-Urundi, 1928–1957* (B.D. treatise, Baptist Theological Seminary, Rüschlikon, 1958). The work by Donald Hohensee, *Church Growth in Burundi* (South Pasadena: William Carey Library, 1977), provides some material on Baptists.

ETHIOPIA (1950)

	Members	Churches
1. Baptist Evangelical Association of Ethiopia (1961)	8,009	(51)
2. Baptist Bible Fellowship International	1,300	n/a
3. Ethiopian Evangelical New Covenant Baptist Church (1990)	626	(20)
	9,935	(71)

*T*he ancient land of Ethiopia, located in the Horn of Africa, has a long Christian history, extending back to the fourth century. About half the population is Orthodox, a little more than 30 percent Moslem with the remainder either animist, Roman Catholic, or Protestant. Although Protestants are a bit less than 4 percent of the population, they represent a vital segment of Christian life in the country. The largest Protestant bodies are the Word of Life Evangelical Church, a product of the work of the Sudan Interior Mission, and the Ethiopian Evangelical Church Mekane Yesus (Lutheran). The Baptist presence is small but supported by three strongly active Baptist missions.

After the fall of the Ethiopian monarchy in 1974, a Communist regime ruled the nation until it collapsed in 1991. During this period, the nation suffered war and famine, while the Christian churches underwent persecution and even suppression. With the coming of renewed freedom, a new day of opportunity has dawned for Christian work.

Upon the suggestion of James Luckman, a former missionary of the Sudan Interior Mission, to open work in Ethiopia, the Baptist General Conference (BGC) sent him and Sten Lindberg in 1949 to explore the field. After gaining approval from the government, which desired medical and educational work, a station was opened in 1950 in the Ambo district, about eighty miles west of Addis Ababa. In 1954 the mission formed another station in the Bacoggi district, and a third station opened in the Gendeberet district around 1959. A number of institutions were established—a hospital at Hagere Hiywet in the Ambo district, a clinic at Bacoggi, and a hospital, leprosarium, and school in the Gendeberet district. In 1954 the mission opened an evangelistic center in Addis Ababa, where, in 1958, it also began a publication ministry. In cooperation with the Eastern Mennonite mission, it has operated Globe Publishing House. Even though much of its efforts were in institutional work, the mission did not neglect evangelism, but progress was slow. By 1960 three churches had been established; membership in 1966 was only 144. In 1961 Ethiopian Baptists formed the Baptist Evangelical Association.

The Communist regime brought nationalization of mission properties, reduction in missionary personnel, and persecution of Christians, including imprisonment. Under the new conditions, the Ethiopian churches adopted a greater program of self-reliance, and, in spite of restriction and oppression, membership grew. Fortunately, the mission was able to continue its ministry by providing relief and conducting rural clinics. It was forced, however, to work with discretion with the Baptist Evangelical Association. With the new freedom, the BGC today has fourteen missionaries on the field serving in church training, community development, and medical services.

The first missionaries of the Baptist Bible Fellowship International (BBFI) arrived in 1961. From that date until their forced withdrawal in 1977, twenty-three missionaries had served on the field. The BBFI established work in Addis Ababa and in the Welo district. By the mid-1970s, the membership had reached 1,300. In spite of the closure of the churches during the Communist period, secret meetings were held in the homes. The BBFI mission continued to maintain relations by visits of missionaries from Kenya who provided encouragement and training. During the Great Famine of 1984 and 1985, BBFI missionaries were able to return to Ethiopia, but, to avoid problems with the authorities, they used discretion in their relations with the believers.

After the collapse of the Communist regime, several churches regained their buildings, but most of them had to continue to petition the government for their property or for permission to acquire land to build a new structure. Today the BBFI has two missionary couples in the field, with one couple directing a Bible school in Addis Ababa. The work is growing in membership and congregations, but unfortunately recent statistics are not available.

In 1967 Southern Baptists entered Ethiopia and established a program of community development in the Menz-Gishe district, a strongly Orthodox area 150 miles north of Addis Ababa. Missionaries provided medical services, vocational training, and agricultural help. They conducted Bible studies in their homes, and the first converts were won in the 1970s. From 1977 to 1978, the missionaries had to leave but then were able to return. The relief efforts during the Great Famine of the mid-1980s gave the first true impetus to the work. In 1990 a collective body, the Ethiopian Evangelical New Covenant Baptist Church, was formed, which today has eleven churches. The Southern Baptist mission also has a congregation in Addis Ababa.

BIBLIOGRAPHY: Valuable material on the work of the BGC in Ethiopia may be found in David Guston and Martin Erikson, eds., *Fifteen Fruitful Years* (Chicago: Harvest Publications, 1961), and Donald E. Anderson, ed., *The 1970s in the Ministry of the Baptist General Conference* (Arlington Heights, Ill.: Baptist General Conference, 1981), 81–85. The article by Jim Singleton "Recently Persecuted, Christianity on the Rise in Ethiopia," *Baptist Bible Tribune*, Feb. 1993, 20–21, provides information on the work of the BBFI. For beginnings of the Southern Baptist mission, see Baker J. Cauthen and others, *Advance* (Nashville: Broadman Press, 1970), 175–76. For current Southern Baptist work, see *Your Guide to Foreign Missions*, 1992–1993, 29–30.

KENYA (1956)

	Members	Churches
1. Baptist Convention of Kenya (1971)	150,000	(2,000)
2. Nairobi Baptist Church (1958)	500	(1)
3. Grace Independent Baptist Fellowship (1964)	450	(5)
4. Fellowship of Independent Baptist Churches of East Africa (1964)	850	(17)
5. Conservative Baptist Fellowship (1972)	131	(4)
6. Reformed Baptists (1979)	120	(5)
7. African Christian Church and Schools (1949)	11,000	(43)
8. Other Independent Baptist congregations	n/a	(200)
	163,051	(2,275)

*B*efore the entry of Baptists into Kenya, many Baptists served as missionaries under the African Inland Mission, which established the African Inland Church, a body closely related to Baptists in belief and practice. Formal Baptist entry came in 1956 when Southern Baptists transferred three families from its field in Nigeria to East Africa.

Southern Baptists began in Mombassa, Kenya's major coastal city, and Nairobi, the capital. A third region of early work was Nyeri, near Mount Kenya, where churches quickly multiplied. In 1957 Davis and Mary Saunders started services in Nairobi which led to the formation in 1958 of the English-language Nairobi Baptist Church with twenty charter members. Davis Saunders also established the Nairobi Baptist Center, a business school and community center in Shauri Moyo, now under its own board. The Shauri Moyo Church, which initiated other congregations in Nairobi, met in the center until it obtained its own facilities in 1976.

In 1961 Kenyan Baptists formed the Nairobi Baptist Association, which has been very active in evangelism and social ministries. Local associations have continued to multiply—by the middle of 1993 there were fifty-seven, with others waiting acceptance. In 1971 the Baptist Convention of Kenya was established to serve as a national body. The convention and the Baptist mission of Kenya cooperate in a number of ministries. Today there are 130 Southern Baptist missionaries on the field.

Under the convention and the mission, Boards of Governors operate high schools at Mombassa and Nyeri. The Baptist Theological College, a non-residency school, has a very successful in-service training program, providing six two-week periods of instruction during the year, which can be completed in four and a half years. A very successful correspondence program is Bible Way which, in the early 1990s, had enrolled over 140,000 in addition to almost 20,000 in the Kenya prisons. The mission operates the Brackenhurst Baptist Assembly at Limuru, the site for conferences and a language school.

In 1993 the mission formed Kenya Baptist Media (KBM), replacing previous communications and publishing agencies with a new priority on church-oriented ministries, while continuing mass media work. Churches and missionaries with other Baptist groups use KBM literature and church supplies. KBM also produces newsletters for the Kenya Convention and Nairobi Baptist Association. Baptists in Kenya have developed Christian Studies, a program of Bible study training for local churches, as well as men's, women's, and youth work. Many local churches operate nursery schools. The mission has encouraged the use of indigenous music and worship styles, and a strong music program has been developed.

As part of its evangelistic and social ministry, the mission maintains Methare Medical Clinic in Nairobi, medical clinics in Nyanza, a relief ministry among refugees from Somalia, and water development projects. The mission is depending on local churches to begin new churches, while the missionaries, in addition to their work in religious and theological education, are attempting to reach those who have never heard the gospel. Only recently a most successful evangelistic effort among the nomadic Maasai is resulting in large numbers of converts and new churches. There has also been some outreach among the Pokot and Borons. As a result of the 1990 Kenya Coastal Crusade in the area of Mombassa, there were over fifty thousand professions of faith and the organization of eighty-four congregations. One of the leading Baptist churches in Kenya is Parklands, an English-language congregation in Nairobi. With a membership of eight hundred, including Asiatic Indians, it draws two thousand people in two services and is building a large sanctuary on choice property. The Kenya Baptist Convention is growing at a rate of 23 to 25 percent a year and is the most ethnically diverse church body in the country.

For several years Kenyan Baptists developed a successful partnership with the Kentucky Baptist Convention. It is currently working with the South Carolina Baptist Convention (SCBC) and the South Carolina Baptist Educational and Missionary Convention, the largest African-American Baptist body in the state, a most unusual three-way partnership. Because of political differences, the Kenya Convention withdrew from the National Christian Council of Kenya, but the Nairobi Association remains a member.

Most Baptists in Kenya are related to the Kenya Baptist Convention, but other Baptist groups and missions also exist. Although the Nairobi Association withdrew fellowship from it for its practice of open membership, the Nairobi Baptist Church has continued as an independent congregation, despite its acceptance of only immersed believers as members. Even though its membership is only five hundred, it has one of the largest Baptist congregations in the country, with three thousand worshipers on a Sunday attending four services with numbers sitting or standing outside and an additional three thousand children in Sunday School. It supports mission congregations, street preaching, and fifteen home Bible study fellowships. Many people in high government positions attend as well as many foreigners, including personnel from the embassies.

Forced to leave Uganda in 1972 and 1973, Conservative Baptist missionaries began work in the coastal area—a difficult field—which included Moslem, Hindu, and Christians with syncretized beliefs. Their work has included the formation of a predominantly Asiatic Indian church and a witness among the Digo and Duruma—both are tribal people influenced by Islam.

There are six independent Baptist missions in Kenya whose pastors participate in a fellowship meeting every other year. It is estimated that there are more than 200 congregations related to these missions. The oldest one is the Grace Independent Baptist Mission, begun in 1963 by Ed Weaver from Pennsylvania. Its headquarters is on Thika Road, north of Nairobi, where it has recently reopened a small Bible school. From this work has emerged Grace Independent Baptist Fellowship of Independent Baptist Churches with five churches, including Thika Road Baptist Church, as well as a Fellowship of Independent Baptist churches of seventeen churches among the Kamba and Kikuyu. The Baptist Bible Fellowship International (BBFI), which began in 1974 with the arrival of Jerry and Sherry Daniels, has churches in the Nairobi, Western, and Central areas of Kenya.

The American Baptist Association began its work in 1983 with a congregation started in 1978 by Chuck Shurley, a layman from the USA. Westwood Missionary Baptist Church of Winter Haven, Florida, sponsors three missionary families who serve in Nairobi, Kakamega (Western Kenya), and more recently at Naivasha in the Rift Valley. In 1985 Lynn Raburn established the Landmark Baptist Bible Institute in Nairobi.

The Independent Faith Baptist Churches are a result of the work of the Independent Faith Mission (Baptist) from Greensboro, North Carolina, which works in Samburu, north of Mount Kenya, and on the coast, where a Bible school has been established. The Association of Baptists for World Evangelism began a work in Karatina, which then affiliated with the Independent Faith Baptists. This mission reestablished work in Nairobi in 1991. In this same year the North American Baptist Missionary Association from Georgia started work in Nairobi under the auspices of BBFI.

Other mission efforts include the Reformed Baptists, led by Keith Underhill, who started the Trinity Baptist Church of Nairobi in 1979, and the Progressive Baptist Convention, which provides support for the Nyakonga Girls' Secondary School. Beginning in 1970 the Canadian Baptist Overseas Mission Board became associated with the African Christian Church and Schools and later with the African Brotherhood Church, both independent African bodies, to help them develop their work. In 1973 Don and Faye Smith, Conservative Baptists, moved their school, Daystar, from Zimbabwe to Nairobi. Today it is a leading evangelical educational institution. In 1976 Mickey Parrish and his wife, Southern Baptists from Florida, began an independent ministry, known today as the Christian Light Foundation. It supports five ministers in Kenya, and its program of evangelism includes an extensive prison ministry.

Orville Boyd Jenkins and Albert W. Wardin, Jr.

BIBLIOGRAPHY: For Southern Baptist work, see Davis Lee Saunders, *A History of Baptists in East and Central Africa* (Th.D. dissertation, Southern Baptist Theological Seminary, 1973), 170ff., 285–94. For a history of the first twenty years of the Kenya Baptist Mission, see Laura Lee Stewart, *Through God Who Strengthens* (Nairobi: Baptist Publications House, 1976), which is primarily a compilation of the minutes of the mission. For the Kenya Coastal Crusade, see *Commission*, Dec. 1990, 6–27, and for Baptist work among the Maasai and Borons, see *Commission*, Sep. 1993, 6–35, and Jan./Feb. 1994, 4–33. A description of Conservative Baptist work may be found in Hans W. Finzel, ed., *Partners Together* (Wheaton, Ill.: CBMFS, 1993), 30–33. The article by James O. Combs, "Kenya, a Nation Blessed with the Gospel," *Baptist Bible Tribune*, July 24, 1991, 12–13, includes reports from missionaries of the Baptist Bible Fellowship International.

RWANDA (1938)

	Members	Churches
1. Union des Églises baptistes du Rwanda (1962)	33,625	(36)
2. Association des Églises Baptistes du Rwanda (1967)	28,000	(76)
	61,625	(112)

B ecause of its snow-capped mountains and valleys, Rwanda has been called the Switzerland of Africa. Similar to Burundi, its neighbor to the south, it is densely populated with the Hutu (90 percent), the majority of the people who were dominated for generations by the Tutsi (9 percent). After Belgian control, the country gained its independence in 1962. Because of a struggle for power between Hutu and Tutsi, the country has suffered through warfare and political instability. The latest political disruption occurred in 1994 when thousands of Tutsi were massacred and thousands of Hutu fled the country.

The two Baptist groups who are in Rwanda today—the Union of Baptist Churches and the Association of Baptist Churches—are the result of their spilling over the border from neighboring countries. Both of them have been equally successful in growth. In 1939 Danish and African missionaries from Burundi entered territory in southern Rwanda, which the Church Missionary Society released to the Danish Baptist Mission. It was an area which had been affected by the East-African Revival. The first resident Danish missionaries were Jørgen and Nina Larsen, settling in 1961 at Runyombyi. The work of the mission spread to the east and west. Baptists in Rwanda formed their first two churches in 1962 at Nyantanga and Runyombyi, and in the same year formed a Union of Baptist Churches of Rwanda.

In 1977 Danish Baptist Mission invited the Southern Baptist FMB to assist in the work. It sent Earl Martin, who led in establishing a Baptist work in Kigali, the capital, and who also worked with rural churches. Theological Education by Extension (TEE), in which 150 are enrolled; a Bible Way correspondence program; and a health clinic and veterinary service at Mukoma all contribute in furthering Baptist work.

The first Conservative Baptist (CB) missionaries to enter Rwanda were Dr. and Mrs. Paul Hurlburt, Sr. Hurlburt left Uganda in 1965 to continue his work in translation but also engaged in personal witness. In 1967 because of conflict in Zaire, Paul and Nellie Okken, CB missionaries, were forced into Rwanda along with other refugees. Through their evangelistic effort, churches developed in the northwest corner of Rwanda. As early as 1967, the government recognized the Association of Baptist Churches of Rwanda, the body which represented Conservative Baptist work.

With immigrants, including some Baptists, moving to Bugesera in the south central part of the country for land granted by the government, an evangelistic effort was undertaken there in 1977. It resulted in an excellent response and the immediate formation of eight new churches. Conservative Baptist work has continued to spread—today it is in every prefecture. One goal is to plant small clusters of churches in neighboring areas. To be recognized as a church, a congregation must first form two daughter congregations.

The Association has established schools enrolling more than fourteen thousand on the primary level and up to another one thousand in secondary and vocational training. A literacy program seeks to help people read the Bible. TEE and Bible schools provide training for leaders. However, due to internal problems relating to discipline and church authority, the Conservative Baptist mission, has now terminated its official relationship with the Association.

Because of the intensification of civil conflict in 1994 which took many lives and caused countless others to flee, Baptist life has been seriously disrupted. A number of Baptist pastors were killed in the southern part, but others were able to evade the carnage, including the general secretary of the Baptist Union who escaped across the border.

BIBLIOGRAPHY: For Conservative Baptist work, see Hans W. Finzel, ed., *Partners Together* (Wheaton, Ill.: CBFMS, 1993), 40–43. For current work of Southern Baptists, see *Your Guide to Foreign Missions*, 1992–1993, 33–34.

TANZANIA (1956)

	Members	Churches
1. Baptist Convention of Tanzania (1971)	120,000	(1,381)
2. Baptist Bible Fellowship International (1988)	n/a	n/a
3. African Baptist Assembly	n/a	n/a
	120,000	(1,381)

*T*he seed for beginning Baptist work in Tanzania was planted when the Foreign Mission Board of the SBC sent I. N. Patterson and W. L. Jester of the Nigerian Baptist Mission to survey East Africa in 1954. An encouraging reception was recorded with the recommendation that Baptists begin work in Tanzania and Kenya. On July 2, 1956, three missionaries from Nigeria who were assigned to the new work arrived in the capital of Dar es Salaam. Shortly afterwards, the Wimpy Harpers arrived in Dar to open a community center, the Jack Walkers began making plans for a hospital in Mbeya, and requests went out for field evangelists. Southern Baptist work in Tanzania became a reality.

The Baptist Mission of East Africa coordinated personnel, finances, and mission activities. Missionaries served in evangelism, medicine, education, and agriculture. Other personnel were in special ministries shared by Tanzania, Kenya, and Uganda: publications (1961), seminary (1962), communications (1967), and Bible Way correspondence (1973). In 1977 a separate Baptist mission for Tanzania was formed.

In 1958 the first ten converts were baptized in a stream in Mbeya. The first two churches, the Majengo Baptist Church in Mbeya and the Magomeni Baptist Church in Dar es Salaam, were organized on Easter, March 29, 1959. Dar es Salaam Community Center opened in January 1959 with classes in adult education and literacy. Today

Tanzanian Baptists direct the Center, which has a training program from kindergarten and sewing to computer sciences and an adult night school. The hospital in Mbeya was dedicated in August 1959, but in 1978 it became a government institution. The mission at present supports medical clinics at Mbeya and Kikoma.

Because of the growing number of churches with inexperienced leadership, there was a critical need for training. Soon a Bible school was initiated for the southern region. Informal training continued at local levels, but with the need for formal pastoral training, the International Baptist Theological Seminary of Eastern Africa was established at Arusha in January 1962 with fifteen students. The residential program now has one hundred leaders and their families in theological studies and religious education. In 1988 the seminary with the Convention of Tanzania established a Department of Decentralized Theological Education (DTE). There are 180 DTE centers with 1,600 enrolled, twenty Bible schools equipping 340 church leaders, and four seminary branches with 130 pastors in both certificate and advanced studies. Swahili materials are being developed to meet the needs of each level.

The heartbeat of Baptist growth and development has been reaching individuals through evangelism, teaching, preaching, and witnessing in the villages and towns. Reading rooms, revivals, market preaching, medical clinics, and agricultural evangelism all provided opportunity to share the gospel. Personnel were stationed throughout the country where baptisms were numerous and preaching points rapidly became churches. Baptists became known as "the people of the Book," as many walked miles to hear about Jesus and get a Bible. During the 1960s the response was rapid: Kigoma in the west had six preaching points with 150 conversions the first year, and Joseph Abdullah became the first Muslim convert; Rungwe reported fifty-six churches and preaching points with baptisms passing 1,000.

Growth did not come without opposition. Baptists in Ujiji, a western Muslim stronghold, had many struggles with demonstrations trying to stop the work. Today the Ujiji church is one of the strongest in Tanzania with a Bible school and a seminary branch housed on the grounds. In 1964 when Baptists baptized their first seventeen converts in the southeastern Masasi area and opened a bookstore, it was not the Muslims (who were openly supportive because of the changed lives of the Christians) who objected but the long-term Roman Catholics and Anglicans. Even though they had the Baptist leader arrested, he was able to lead the three men on prison duty to Christ.

During the 1970s there was a unique beginning in the Bukoba area, when a large group of Greek Orthodox churches elected to become Baptists. With intensive teaching and preaching, this area has now grown into a center of Baptist work. Membership exploded in the 1980s with an average of more than 15,000 baptisms each year. With the aid of volunteers coming for revivals and teaching, the 1990s should continue the pattern of starting churches at a rate of more than 150 a year. Not all areas have exhibited rapid growth. Work along the coast has been slow and continues to be difficult. Urban areas have not responded as planned. There is yet the vast central area where there is little Baptist witness.

The first annual assembly was held in 1963 in Dodoma in conjunction with a crusade led by two Nigerian pastors. On June 21, 1971, a Baptist convention was organized. Priority was given to enlisting churches to support new work through evangelism. That same year the Easter offering for missions was begun with an offering of $400 to support the first home missionary. By 1993 offerings were supporting four home missionaries. The Stewardship and Evangelism Department, organized in 1974, continues this mission emphasis.

Since the first association was organized in 1960 in Rungwe/Mbeya, thirty-four associations have registered with the convention. To involve more local churches in the nationwide program, in 1992 the convention divided its constituency into five regions which meet annually, with a nationwide meeting every three years. Baptist Women of Tanzania was organized in 1972, and a Women's Work Department was established in 1989. Each area has trained women to assist in teaching and ministry. Some 1,600 women work in community missions, teach in children's organizations, and participate in nationwide seasons of prayers. Offerings are taken annually for mission projects.

Bible study has been a vital part in developing the work, and church training programs were started with Sunday School for children and adults. The Department of Religious Education, initiated in 1989, is promoting the use of "Bible Storying." Although there is a youth organization, most youth activities are local. The government has recognized Kipoke Baptist High School in Rungwe for academic excellence. Baptists plan a second high school in 1994.

Various ministries continue to aid the growth of the church. The year 1989 marked the beginning of Community Health Evangelism in the south; at Bukoba, an extensive AIDS ministry will assist thousands of orphans; in the north, taking veterinarian skills to the Maasai has opened the door for the gospel. From the first ten converts in 1959, Baptists in the Tanzanian convention now number over 120,000.

Unlike most African nations, Tanzania has had until recently only one Baptist mission. In 1988 Baptist Bible Fellowship International added Tanzania to its list of mission fields. There are a few churches of the African Baptist Assembly, an extension of the work of the Providence Industrial Mission (National Baptist, USA, Inc.) in Malawi.

Betty Ann Whitson

BIBLIOGRAPHY: For Southern Baptists beginnings in Tanzania, see Davis Lee Saunders, *A History of Baptists in East and Central Africa* (Th.D. dissertation, Southern Baptist Theological Seminary, 1973), 170–218, 284–85.

UGANDA (1961)

	Members	Churches
1. Baptist Union of Uganda (1974)	17,419	(360)
2. Baptist Fellowship of Uganda (1983)	n/a	(45)
	17,419	(405)

*T*he Conservative Baptist Foreign Mission Society (today CBI) was the first Baptist mission to enter Uganda. Because of political unrest in neighboring Zaire which forced the evacuation of missionaries, Dr. and Mrs. Paul Hurlburt, Sr., settled in Kampala in 1961. Hurlburt began holding services in his home but soon rented a hall. On July 18, 1965, the Kampala Baptist Church was organized—an international church with two congregations, one English-speaking and the other Swahili-speaking. Conservative Baptist missionaries began to teach in the schools, hold Bible studies in youth hostels, prepare and translate Christian literature into Luganda and Swahili, and plant churches. CB missionaries primarily centered their efforts in Kampala in urban evangelism but did extend work into the Masaka area among the Banyarwanda who had fled Rwanda because of tribal war. In 1969 twenty churches with nine hundred members formed a regional association.

When Southern Baptists entered East Africa in the mid-1950s, they considered including Uganda as one of their fields. Because of the opposition of the Church of Uganda (Anglican), the dominant Protestant body, they delayed entry until 1962. In April 1962 Charles Evans, assisted by Joram Muhando, a lay pastor, began services in a village bordering Kenya called Suam, six months before Ugandan independence. In December Mr. and Mrs. Hal Boone, the first resident Southern Baptist missionaries, moved to eastern Uganda. In 1963 Webster Carroll and his wife settled in Jinja, while Jimmy Hooten and his wife went to Mbale. By 1971 there were nine missionaries, including wives.

Unlike the Conservative Baptist missionaries, Southern Baptists spread to various areas, finding their greatest response in rural areas where Anglican or Roman Catholics had comparatively little mission work. In 1963 the Nile Baptist Church in Jinja was organized, the first in the country. In 1967 the Baptist Mission of Uganda was formed, separating from the Baptist Mission of East Africa. By 1972 there were 8,337 members with 144 congregations and 55 preaching points. In the 1960s Ugandan Baptists began to form associations, and in 1972 they established the Uganda Baptist Convention. To provide training for leaders, Bible schools with limited periods of instruction were conducted in various areas.

In January 1971 Idi Amin, a Moslem, seized power and began to force Christian missionaries out of the country. By the end of 1973 all Conservative Baptist missionaries had left, and the Southern Baptist mission force was reduced until only Webster Carroll and Jim Rice and their wives were permitted to remain.

In August 1973 forty churches related to the CB mission formed the Uganda Association of Baptist Churches. In the following year, the government forced the Uganda Association and the Baptist Convention to merge into a united body, the Baptist Union. Although there were reservations on both sides, the two bodies had to join or be banned. In 1977 Amin closed all Baptist churches, an order which remained in effect until he was overthrown in 1979. In this period a number of churches went underground, some joined the Anglicans, or disbanded. A few churches in remote areas, however, were able to continue services.

The Conservative Baptists, who continued to maintain relations with Ugandan Baptists, returned in 1982 and today have ten missionaries assigned to the country, while Southern Baptists have twenty-four. The two missions cooperate with each other and the Baptist Union. As in Kenya and Tanzania, Baptists are growing rapidly. One of the most productive endeavors has been among the Eteso people in the Teso and Kumi districts, where work was started in 1968.

In 1991 the Uganda Baptist Seminary graduated its first class. Six associational Bible schools provide additional training. The Bible Way correspondence course, which continued its ministry during the years of Idi Amin, now for the first time has a book in Luganda. Southern and Conservative Baptist missionaries are also working through seminars and literature to counter the AIDS epidemic, and money has been appropriated to assist in establishing an orphanage, primarily for children left without parents because of AIDS.

A break occurred in Baptist ranks in 1982 when the veteran missionaries, Webster Carroll and his wife, left the Southern Baptist mission to serve with Global Outreach, an agency which had been founded by Owen Cooper, a leading Southern Baptist layman. Carroll felt the Southern Baptist program was not meeting sufficiently the spiritual and physical needs of Uganda, which was emerging from the devastation of Amin's rule. A number of churches in the area of Jinja, where Carroll worked, pulled away from the Baptist Union and became part of the Baptist Fellowship of Uganda. There has been some attempt at reconciliation between the Fellowship and Union, and a joint service of worship was held in 1993 in Bugiri between the two groups. At present Global Outreach has nine missionaries in the country.

Another Baptist-related agency is the Christian Light Foundation which supports four ministers who engage in evangelism in schools, prisons, and churches. It is also engaged in an extensive program of literature distribution.

BIBLIOGRAPHY: For Conservative Baptist work in Uganda, see *Founded on the Word: Focused on the World* (Wheaton, Ill.: CBFMS, 1978), 245–58, and Hans W. Finzel, ed., *Partners Together* (Wheaton: CBFMS, 1993), 48–51. For a careful treatment of the beginnings of Southern Baptist work in Uganda, see Davis Lee Saunders, *A History of Baptists in Central and East Africa* (Th.D. dissertation, Southern Baptist Theological Seminary, 1973), 218–37. See, "Growth of Baptist Missions," in Gailyn Van Rheenen, *Church Planting in Uganda* (South Pasadena: William Carey Library, 1976), 88–96, for a comparative study of the Conservative and Southern Baptist missions in Uganda. For the work of Mr. and Mrs. Webster Carroll, see Global Outreach, Sep. 1983. The series of articles by Robert O'Brien in *Commission*, Feb./March, 1983, 7–32, provide a wealth of information.

BAPTIST AND BAPTIST-RELATED MISSIONS

1. BURUNDI DenBU (1928), SBC (1988)

2. ETHIOPIA BGC (1950), BBFI (1961), SBC (1967)

3. KENYA   SBC (1956), GIBM (1963), CBI (1972), IFM (1973), BBFI (1974), CLF (1976), RBMS (1979), ABA (1983), ABWE (1983) NABMA (1991), LC, PNBC

4. RWANDA DenBU (1938), CBI (1965), SBC (1977)

6. TANZANIA SBC (1956), BBFI (1988)

7. UGANDA CBI (1961), SBC (1962), GO (1982), CLF (1984), BBFI (1986)

B. EQUATORIAL AFRICA

*W*ith over one million adherents, Equatorial Africa has been one of the most productive fields for Baptists. Baptists were often the pioneers in bringing the gospel to the coastal area and the interior. Although their primary mission was evangelism, they helped to introduce modern medicine and education and provided numerous other services. Baptists are in each of these countries, except Gabon, and are united with an evangelical body in Congo.

Credit for heroic pioneer work must be given to British, German, Swedish and American Baptists who worked through the Baptist Missionary Society, the American Baptist Missionary Union, the Mission Society of the German Baptists, Baptist Mid-Missions, and the Örebro Society of Sweden. Other societies from Europe and America later joined, entering areas which needed extensive development also. Today Africans control the church bodies which have been formed, but the mission societies still play a supportive role.

	Members	*Churches*
1. Cameroon	182,486	1,001
2. Central African Republic	152,900	572
3. Chad	20,000	150
4. Congo	2,197	61
5. Equatorial Guinea	154	9
6. Zaire	<u>765,585</u>	<u>2,051</u>
	1,123,322	3,844

CAMEROON (1845)

1. Cameroon Baptist Convention (1954)	64,986	(686)
2. Union des Églises Baptistes du Cameroun (1952)	60,000	(180)
3. Église Baptiste Camerounaise		
(Native Baptist Church) (1945)	55,000	(135)
4. Confédération Baptiste du Cameroun (1964)	<u>2,500</u>	<u>n/a</u>
	182,486	(1,001)

*T*he history of Baptists in Cameroon is one of the most complex of any Baptist community. For one thing, a number of nationalities planted and furthered the Baptist cause—Jamaicans, British, Germans, Americans, and French. In addition, the colonial powers of Europe brought political division. The coastal region experienced British influence, which was followed by German occupation in 1884. This occupation was succeeded during the First World War by a division between the British who took West Cameroon, and the French who took the rest. In 1960 French Cameroon gained independence, and in the following year the southern area of West Cameroon, whose lingua franca was English, joined the new state.

Jamaicans, encouraged by British missionaries in Jamaica, urged the Baptist Missionary Society, (BMS) in London to establish a mission in West Africa. With the belief that such an enterprise, by bringing Christianity and Western civilization to Africa, would help to stop the slave trade and transform African society, the BMS was able to recruit four couples besides forty-two Jamaicans who would serve as teachers or settlers in a Christian community. In 1843 the BMS sent two mission parties to Fernando Po, an island off the coast of Cameroon, which the British were using as a naval base to counter the slave trade and which also served as a haven for liberated slaves. In 1845 one of the Jamaicans, Joseph Merrick, settled on the mainland at Bimbia (West Cameroon), learned the language of the Isubu people, and began translating the Scripture in their language. In the same year, Alfred Saker (1814–1880), one of the British missionaries, began to minister at Cameroons Town (now Duala in East Cameroon) on the Cameroon estuary. In spite of barbarous conditions, Saker persevered and in 1849 baptized his first convert and formed Bethel Church, the first Baptist church in Cameroon. In addition to the newly baptized convert, it was composed of Mr. and Mrs. Saker, Thomas Horton Johnson, who was Saker's first convert on Fernando Po and who served as pastor, and Mrs. Johnson.

With growing dissatisfaction, the majority of the Jamaicans returned home in 1848, and Merrick died an untimely death in 1849. One Jamaican, Joseph Jackson Fuller, however, became a full missionary of the BMS in 1850 and faithfully served until 1888. In 1858 the Spaniards expelled the Baptist mission from Fernando Po, which led Saker to found Victoria (now Limbe), a Christian settlement in West Cameroon over which he served as governor. Despite his opponents' attacks on his character, overbearing manner, and his emphasis on the civilizing aspects of the mission, the BMS sustained him until he retired from the field in 1876, worn out from service.

With the German occupation of Cameroon in 1884, the BMS was forced out. It sold its assets to the Basel Mission, a pietistic mission in Switzerland and Germany, rather than pay a subsidy to the Baptists in Germany to take over its work. At the time, there were 203 members with 368 children in Baptist schools. Although it was agreed that the Basel Mission would respect Baptist faith and practice, the Baptists began to resent the discipline of the Basel mission, and defections from it began—first in Douala in 1888, and in Victoria in 1889. Baptists in the Cameroons called upon Baptists in Germany for help, who in 1891 sent their first missionary, August Steffens, a German Baptist from the USA. Other missionaries followed, many from the USA, but the death toll was high. The German Baptists placed the work under a more formal structure by organizing in 1898 the Mission Society of the German Baptists. A spirit of independency among native Baptists again appeared with another division in Duala in 1897, dividing Baptists who worked with the mission and those who were independent. In 1914 the German mission had 6 stations, 4,000 members, and 1,600 pupils, while the independents, or Native Baptist Church, had 5 major congregations and around 2,500 members.

World War I brought another upheaval to the Baptist community. The occupation of Cameroon by the British, French, and Belgians in 1914 and 1915, terminated the work of all Baptist missionaries except for Carl Bender and his wife, who were American citizens. With West Cameroon becoming a British mandate and East Cameroon a French one, the Baptist work was separated into two segments. With the departure of the Benders in 1919, the British field had no resident missionary until the German Baptist society was allowed to return in 1927. In the meantime, however, Baptists expanded into the grasslands from the church in Victoria, whose pastor trained men who came to the coast for work as evangelists and who himself trekked twice into the interior.

German Baptists from America continued to serve as well in West Camroon but, beginning in 1935, went to the field under their own organization. Because of World War II, all Baptist missionaries from Germany were interned in 1940, which left the entire field of West Cameroon in the hands of the Americans, members of a body which now calls itself the North American Baptist Conference. This conference greatly expanded the institutional work and established two hospitals, a leprosy settlement, two Baptist teacher training colleges, a secondary school for girls, and two secondary schools for boys with the assistance of the Basel Mission for one of the two. In addition, the mission maintained an extensive network of primary schools and operated numerous medical and leprosy clinics. The institutional expansion, however, brought concern from some that it was hurting the personal and spiritual nature of the work.

In 1954 a Cameroon Baptist Convention was organized, and in the same year the Baptist Bible Training Center was established in Ndu for theological instruction. Today about 80 percent of the churches of the convention are in West Cameroon. About forty tribal languages are spoken in the churches, but the convention has adopted Pidgin English as the official common language. In the larger urban churches, proper English or French may be used.

The Baptist work in French Cameroon, which was the greater part of the German Baptist mission before the First World War, followed a different course. The French refused reentry to the German missionaries, and the Paris Evangelical Missionary Society assumed responsibility for the Baptist work and the Basel Mission. On their arrival in 1917, the French missionaries discovered among the Christians the widespread practice of polygamy and misappropriation of funds. In finding the Baptists divided between adherents of the German mission and the independents, the French insisted on the formation of a United Baptist Church. In the meantime Lotin Samē (1882–1946), a native pastor who had been ordained by Bender and had been elected a Baptist leader in 1915, resented French control and the imposition of a constitution which gave the French a dominant voice. Under French influence in 1922, the United Baptist Church expelled Samē, depriving him of all pastoral rights. Although there were attempts at reconciliation, especially in 1931, the break with Samē and his followers was never fully healed.

In September 1945 the Native Baptist Church organized as the Église Baptiste Camerounaise (EBC), electing Samē as president, one year before his death. In 1949 the French colonial regime recognized its statutes. Today EBC has adherents in both East and West Cameroon. From 1977 to 1986 David A. Rooks from the National Baptist Convention of America served as a missionary with this body. In 1952 the

Baptist churches that continued to cooperate with the Paris Society, called the Union des Églises Baptistes du Cameroun (UEBC), became an independent body and five years later gained full autonomy from the Society.

The three major Baptist bodies in Cameroon are about equal in size. Through the efforts of the UEBC, a Federation of Baptist Churches of Cameroon has been organized. All three bodies are members of the Baptist World Alliance (BWA). In 1964 the UEBC experienced a small schism with the formation of the Confédération Baptiste du Cameroun. In 1954 the European Baptist Mission, supported by the German Baptist Union and small European Baptist bodies, began to serve in northern Cameroon, close to Maroua, where no other mission worked. This mission also works in southern Cameroon and is in partnership with UEBC. In 1979 the Baptist General Conference entered the field to work with the Cameroon Baptist Convention.

BIBLIOGRAPHY: Material on the British phase of the Baptist mission may be found in Solomon Nfor Gwei, *History of the British Baptist Mission in Cameroon, with Beginnings in Fernando Po, 1841–1886* (B.D. treatise, Baptist Theological Seminary, Rüschlikon, 1966), and Brian Stanley, *The History of the Baptist Missionary Society 1792–1992* (Edinburgh: T&T Clark, 1992), 106–17. An excellent study of the British period and the subsequent history of Baptist work by German Baptists and the North American Baptist Conference in West Cameroon is Lloyd E. Kwast, *The Discipling of West Cameroon: A Study of Baptist Growth* (Grand Rapids: William B. Eerdmans, 1971). German Baptist material on the German phase of Baptist work may be found in Edward Scheve, *Die Mission der deutschen Baptisten in Kamerun (West-Afrika) von 1884 bis 1901* (Berlin: Verlag der Missions-Gesellschaft der deutschen Baptisten, 1901), and Alfred Sheve, "Die Mission der deutschen Baptisten in Kamerun," *Allgemeine Missions-Zeitschrift*, 44 (1917): 277–84, 323–44. For accounts of missionaries of the Paris Evangelical Missionary Society, see E. Allégret, *La Mission du Cameroun* (Paris: Evangelical Missionary Society, 1924), and Maurice Farelly, *Parmi les Églises Baptistes du Champ de Mission du Cameroun* (Denain [Nord]: "Témoin de la Vérité," 1936). Raymond Leslie Buell, *The Native Problem in Africa*, (New York: Macmillan, 1928), 2:302–5, provides valuable information on the Native Baptist Church in the period immediately after the First World War. For a history of Baptist work in Cameroon, including the development of the Native Baptist Church from an African viewpoint, see the paper by a vice-president of the UEBC, Pierre Mahend Betind, "Bilan de 145 ans de Baptisme au Cameroun de 1841–1986 inclus," typed mss., 1986. Carl F. H. Henry wrote a biography of Carl Bender, his father-in-law, entitled, *Bender in the Cameroons* (Cleveland: Roger Williams Press, c. 1941).

CENTRAL AFRICAN REPUBLIC (1920)

	Members	Churches
1. Églises Baptistes de la RCA (1920)	60,000	(375)
2. Églises Baptistes de l'Ouest (EBO) (1963)	50,000	(56)
3. Union Fraternelle des Églises Baptistes (1977)	42,900	(141)
4. Association des Églises Baptistes Centrafricaines	n/a	n/a
	152,900	(572)

*I*n 1960 the Central African Republic gained its independence. In the 1920s, while still part of French Equatorial Africa, two Baptist missions entered the territory—Baptist Mid-Missions (BM-M), as it was later called, and the Örebro Society. The first missionaries truly were pioneers, living in the most primitive conditions and facing the hostility of tribal peoples and medicine men who were gripped in animistic superstition. In spite of the early hardships, the Baptist denomination is today the largest Protestant community in the country.

After service as a missionary in the Belgian Congo with the Africa Inland Mission, William C. Haas formed an independent Baptist mission in Elyria, Ohio, today called Baptist Mid-Missions (BM-M). BM-M enabled him to begin mission work in French Equatorial Africa. In 1921 the first mission party, including Haas and five other missionaries, entered the territory, establishing the first stations at Sibut, Crampel, and Bangassou.

Although Haas died in 1924 and was buried at Bangassou, the mission continued to grow and expanded into more remote areas. By the 1960s it had one hundred churches, a hospital at Ippy, six dispensaries, a printing press, two regional Bible schools, seminary (1961), and bookstores. The mission translated and printed the New Testament in the Sango language and also completed the Old Testament with the assistance of the Grace Brethren Mission.

In 1963 the Association of Baptist Churches was formed with 191 churches. In spite of moral problems within the leadership of the Association, which led to its dissolution in the 1970s, the mission increasingly turned over more responsibilities to the Africans themselves. In the 1970s the missionaries introduced TEE, (Theological Education by Extension). In spite of serious economic problems and widespread crime, BM-M continues to maintain a strong program of evangelism and church planting. With over fifty missionaries, the Central African Republic continues to be the mission's largest as well as one of its most productive fields.

BM-M has experienced two schisms. One resulted in the formation in 1977 of the Fraternal Union of Baptist Churches with headquarters at Bangui, the capital. It claims a membership of fifty thousand, and is the only Baptist body in the country which belongs to the BWA. The European Baptist Mission works in partnership with it. Another division has been the Association of Central African Baptist Churches.

In 1923 the Örebro Society from Sweden established its first station at Bania. There was rapid expansion with eight stations by 1954. The mission established schools for children, two Bible schools, a seminary at Carnot (1953), a printing shop, and provided health care. On January 1, 1963, the Union of Baptist Churches of Western CRA with fifteen churches and ten thousand members came into being, later changing its name to the Baptist Churches of Western RCA (EBO). The new organization took over the mission work and properties of the mission, calling and assigning missionaries to various phases of the work. As more and more trained pastors became available, churches were divided. With the addition of new churches in towns and villages, EBO now has fifty-six churches and almost fifty thousand members. In 1984 national pastors began what today is a flourishing work among the Pygmies. A year later work was also started among Fulanis, with the first three baptized in 1992. With support from the mission, a school of home economics (1965) and a hospital (1972) have been established.

BIBLIOGRAPHY: The work of BM-M may be found in Polly Strong, *Burning Wicks* (Cleveland: Baptist Mid-Missions, 1984), and *Field Surveys* (Cleveland: Baptist Mid-Missions, c. 1977), 1–9. For the work of the Örebro Society, see Linné Eriksson, *I mänsklighetens tjänst* (Örebro: Libris, 1972), 93–95.

CHAD (1925)

	Members	Churches
Association of Baptist Churches (1963)	20,000	(150)

*C*had, once part of French Equatorial Africa, became an independent state in 1960. In the south the country is a wooded grassland, but the larger northern area is part of the Sahara Desert. More than half the population is composed of nomadic Arab tribes, Moslem in faith, while the rest are Black Africans.

In 1925 with the settlement of Paul Metzler, Baptist Mid-Missions (BM-M) extended its mission work northward from its base in Oubangui-Chari (now the Republic of Central Africa). At Balimba near Fort Archambault (today Sahr), Metzler first built a temporary home of grass mats with a thatch roof and then later one of brick. A shelter with a grass roof served as the first chapel. The work was concentrated in the southeastern part of the country and grew to five stations. In 1963 the BM-M separated its field in Chad from the one in the Central African Republic. In the same year the Association of Baptist Churches was formed.

Baptists suffered severe persecution because of their resistance in 1973 to pagan tribal initiation rites, which the government tried to enforce. The regime closed Baptist churches, executed thirteen pastors, and, except for medical personnel, expelled all Baptist missionaries. When the mission refused to cooperate with a newly formed Evangelical Church promoted by the government, it terminated its Koumra Medical Center, and the remaining missionaries left. With the overthrow of the military regime in 1975, the Baptist churches were reopened, and the pastors invited the missionaries to return. Only a few of the approximately thirty missionaries then in the country in 1973 re-entered, but new missionaries have come. In 1991 there were only seven missionaries on the field. The medical center was reopened in 1976 and provides medical training for Chadian young people. Bible schools provide training for church leaders. In 1993 Southern Baptists added Chad as a new mission field.

BIBLIOGRAPHY: For the work of BM-M, see Polly Strong, *Burning Wicks* (Cleveland: Baptist Mid-Missions, 1984), 111–16, 321, 363–64, 420–22, and *Field Surveys* (Cleveland: Baptist Mid-Missions, c. 1977), 9–10.

CONGO (1921)

	Members	Churches
Église Baptiste du Congo Populaire*	2,197	61

*It is today part of the Evangelical Church of Congo.

T he Republic of the Congo received its independence from France in 1960. From 1970 to 1990 it was a one-party Marxist state, but in the latter year democratic government was reinstituted. The Örebro Society in Sweden has been the only Baptist mission to establish a mission field in the country. In 1917 it sent missionaries to the Congo region, but it worked on the fields of other mission societies. In 1921 the French Governor General in Brazzaville granted the Society a concession at Matélé in the far north in the sparsely populated Sangha district. By 1953 three other stations were founded. A Bible school was established in 1954.

The work spread north to what is now the Central African Republic with both fields within the one mission. In 1961 the Congo field gained its own administration, and two years later all cooperation between the two fields ceased. In 1970 the churches joined the Federation of Christian Churches in the Congo. In 1978 the regime outlawed over thirty religious groups, including the Baptists, granting legal recognition to only seven. Today the Baptists are part of the Evangelical Church of Congo, by far the largest Protestant church in the country. Since 1978 there have been no missionaries of the Örebro Society permanently stationed in the country although the Society has continued financial assistance.

BIBLIOGRAPHY: Linné Ericksson, *I mänsklighetens tjänst* (Örebro: Libris, 1972), 85–87.

EQUATORIAL GUINEA (1843–1858, 1981–)

	Members	Churches
Southern Baptist Mission	154	(9)

T he Republic of Equatorial Guinea, a former Spanish possession, includes Rio Muni, an enclave between Cameroon and Gabon on the west coast of Africa and the island of Boiko (formerly Fernando Po). In its attempt to penetrate Cameroon, the Baptist Missionary Society established with Jamaican settlers a Christian community on Fernando Po, but most of the Jamaicans returned home, and the Spanish regime expelled the remaining Baptists in 1858.

The efforts of the Las Palmas Baptist Church in the Canary Islands to provide food and clothing to the needy inhabitants again brought Baptists to the country. In 1981 Southern Baptists sent an agricultural missionary to the Rio Muni sector and in the following year gained from the government permission to begin a mission. Work has begun both on

Boiko, from which Baptists were expelled about 125 years before, and Rio Muni. In 1991 the church in Malabo, the capital of Bioko and also the national capital, dedicated a new church building. Theological Education by Extension (TEE) and correspondence courses from the Baptist seminary in Madrid provide theological instruction. Bible studies for adults and Vacation Bible Schools for children have been means of evangelistic outreach.

In 1992 the Cameroon Baptist Convention, which traces its history to the Baptists who first came to Boiko (Fernando Po) in 1843, appointed its first missionary couple, Ilija Jam and his wife, to the island. Cameroonian Baptists are now returning the spiritual favor they received 150 years before.

BIBLIOGRAPHY: For early Baptist activity on Fernando Po, see Dalvan M. Coger, "An Early Missionary Enterprise: The Baptists at Fernando Po, 1840–1860," *American Baptist Quarterly*, 9 (1990): 158–66, and Solomon Nfor Gwei, *History of the British Baptist Mission in Cameroon, with Beginnings in Fernando Po, 1841–1886* (B.D. treatise, Baptist Theological Seminary, Rüschlikon, 1966), 1–32. For current Baptist activity, see *Your Guide to Foreign Missions*, 1992–1993, 43.

ZAIRE (1878)

	Members	Churches
1. Communauté Baptiste du Flueve Zaire (1972)	274,092	(221)
2. Communauté Baptiste du Zaire Ouest (1946)	252,000	(600)
3. Communauté des Églises Baptistes de Bandundu	24,371	(30)
4. Communauté Baptiste du Bas-Uélé (1964)	27,000	(219)
5. Communauté des Églises Baptistes du Zaire-Est	52,977	(196)
6. Communauté Baptiste au Kivu (1964)	93,800	(274)
7. Communauté des Églises Baptistes Indépéndantes Evangéliques (1932)	10,592	(226)
8. Communauté Evangélique Zairoise (1927)	4,537	(72)
9. 48th Communauté des Églises Baptistes Autonomes (1949)	15,000	(22)
10. Communauté Union des Églises Baptistes du Kwilu (1953)	2,383	(35)
11. Communauté Baptiste Mission de Sud-Kwango (1961)	833	(15)
12. Communauté Fidēles Protestants (1957)	8,000	(141)
13. African Baptist Assembly	n/a	n/a
	765,585	(2,051)

STATISTICS: Most statistics are from BWA, *Yearbook*, 1993–1994, 95–96, and David B. Barrett, ed., *World Christian Encyclopedia*, 762–763.

*I*n 1885 the Berlin Congress approved the establishment of the Congo Free State under the control of King Leopold II of Belgium. In 1908 the Free State became Belgian Congo, under the colonial administration of Belgium. Belgium granted independence in 1960, and in 1971 the country took its present name. After the USA, India, and Brazil, there are more Baptists in Zaire than any other nation. Aside from the Roman Catholic Church and the independent Kimbangu Church, Baptists are the largest religious community in the country, although divided into a number of bodies. Baptists were among the first Protestants to enter, bringing not only the Christian gospel but providing many social services.

With the exploration of the Congo basin in 1870s, the Christian world became aware of the opportunity of spreading the Christian faith and bringing the fruits of Western civilization into the heart of Africa. Upon the promise of one thousand pounds from Robert Arthington, the Baptist Missionary Society (BMS) in London approved the establishment of a Congo mission. In January 1878 Thomas Comber and George Grenfell, who had already served in Cameroon, made an exploratory trip on the lower Congo River and inland to São Salvador. In July 1879 H. E. Crudgington and W. Holman Bentley established a base station at São Salvador, which became part of Portuguese Congo (Angola), but in the Congo itself Grenfell began to establish a station at Musuki at the end of 1880, which in 1882 was moved to present-day Matadi and called Underhill.

Less than one hundred miles inland, rapids impeded navigation up the Congo River, blocking the way into the interior except by a tiresome journey of 250 miles over hill and valley until reaching Stanley Pool where today Kinshasa (formerly Leopoldville), the capital, is located there. With the desire to penetrate the upper Congo, the BMS approved Arthington's offer to provide a steamer. It was shipped from Liverpool in eight hundred sections and then brought by carrier across the 250 miles to Stanley Pool where it was reassembled under Grenfell's supervision. The *Peace* was launched in June 1884, and within two years Grenfell had chartered 3,400 miles of the Congo River system, receiving in 1887 the Founder's Medal of the Royal Geographical Society. Between 1886 and 1890 the BMS founded four stations on the upper river, and extension up the river continued with a station at Yakusu in 1896, located near Stanley Falls. Before World War I, BMS went even beyond Stanley Falls, but missions there were later relinquished. Nevertheless, the BMS established a remarkable string of stations more than 1,200 miles—a geographical feat unequaled by most other missions.

At first converts were few and missionary deaths were high. Thirty years after beginning, over fifty men and women of the mission had died, not including young children. In the absence of primary education and as a means of evangelization, the BMS established an extensive system of primary schools as well as secondary schools. The government provided funds for Roman Catholic schools but none for Protestant schools, a discriminatory policy which was not removed until 1948. BMS opened its first hospital in 1912 at Bolobo and opened three others in addition to cooperating with American Baptists and other missions in establishing a hospital at Kimpese. The mission opened a seminary at Yakusu and two Bible schools and has provided TEE. It has also engaged in women's literacy programs and agricultural projects. In 1893 the mission published the New Testament in Kikongo and by 1918 had produced literature in eleven languages. Even with strict discipline related particularly to strong drink and marital ties and despite defections, the membership of the mission has grown remarkably since World War I.

With the coming of independence, the BMS transferred its work to three regional Baptist churches—The Baptist Church of the Lower River, the Baptist Church of the Middle River, and the Baptist Church of the Upper River. In a move for unity and national identity, the government decreed that all Protestant bodies must become communities of a Church of Christ (which had been created in 1970) for legal recognition. Besides becoming a member of this church, the three Baptist bodies now became one body, the Baptist Community of the Zaire River (CBFZ), with a fourth region, Kinshasa, created from the Lower Region. BMS turned over its assets to CBFZ, terminating its legal existence. Its missionaries were now responsibile to the new body.

Simultaneously with the BMS, the Livingstone Inland Mission (LIM) entered the Congo. It established its first two stations, Palabala (1878) and Matadi (1880), shortly before the BMS formed its first one on the Congo River. Alfred Tilly, a member of the BMS Committee who believed the BMS would confine its mission activity on the coast, formed LIM as an interdenominational mission, gaining many of its mission recruits from the East London Institute for Home and Foreign Missions led by Henry Grattan Guiness. By 1883 LIM had recruited fifty missionaries, established seven stations stretching over seven hundred miles up the Congo, and formed seven stations, taking the lead in mission work. The mission became the responsibility of Guiness, who, in 1884, was glad to turn it over to the American Baptist Missionary Union (ABMU), since his interests were in Christian education rather than missionary administration. The ABMU took over six of the seven stations and retained nine of the twenty-six missionaries. The ABMU complemented the work of the BMS, with the stations of the two missions to some degree alternating.

Through the ministry of Henry Richards, a revival movement broke out in 1886 at Banza Manteke, which has been called the "Pentecost of the Congo." Within a short time more than a thousand Africans professed faith in Christ, placing their fetishes at the feet of the missionary. The revival spread to other stations. As their counterparts in the BMS, the missionaries exercised strict discipline, excluding members for polygamy, witchcraft, drunkenness, improper dances, and other pagan practices, with inquirers often in training for years before baptism. At the turn of the century, the mission began to extend east of Leopoldville (Kinshasa) into the Bandundu Region. In 1909 the ABMU and BMS opened the Kimpese Evangelical Training Institution to train evangelists and teachers. Today called the Evangelical Center of Cooperation, it operates a number of schools and receives support from two other non-Baptist bodies. As a result of a report of a Commission which had come to study educational conditions, the mission attempted in the early 1920s to improve its educational program, including better administration of its primary schools. In 1951 a Bible Institute was founded at Kikongo, today the Pastors' School, and with it a Women's School for the wives who came with their husbands. The mission has also engaged in TEE and cooperated with other denominations in the Theological Institute of Kinshasa and the Zaire Protestant Seminary. In the early 1920s the mission was operating six small hospitals and in 1937 opened a leprosy camp. In the 1960s the mission changed its medical program from healing to preventive health care.

In 1946 the missionaries and representatives of the churches founded the Convention of Baptist Churches. In 1960 the convention changed its name to the Association des Églises Baptistes du Congo Ouest with the mission separating itself from it. Six years later the mission turned over its responsibilities and assets to the Association, which took the name of Église Baptiste du Congo Ouest. Today it is called the Communauté Baptiste du Zaire Ouest (CBZO), a charter member of the Church of Christ.

Scandinavian Baptists also have had an interest in the Congo. The Swedish Baptist Missionary Society sent E. W. Sjöblom, its first missionary in 1892; he worked with the ABMU until his death in 1903. In 1919 the Society established its own work in the Bandundu, north of the American Baptist field, which has led to the formation of the Community of Baptist Churches of the Bandundu with about twenty-five thousand members. Norwegian Baptists established themselves in 1922 in the Uélé district in the very north of the country, territory released by the Heart of Africa Mission. Bernhard Aalbu, who already had entered the Congo in 1919, and Frithjov Iversen were the pioneers. Besides evangelism, the mission engaged in educational and medical work. In 1964 the governnment recognized the church body formed from the mission, the Église Baptiste du Bas-Uélé, now known as the Communauté Baptiste du Bas-Uélé.

In 1946 the newly formed Conservative Baptist Foreign Mission Society (today the CBI) took over the field of the Unevangelized Africa Mission in the Kivu province in eastern Congo. Paul Hurlburt, Sr., had established the mission in 1928, carrying on with his wife without furlough and with little missionary assistance. At this time the mission had 2,600 members, about 750 bush schools, a station school, and a leprosy clinic. As other missions, CBFMS engaged in evangelism, primary and secondary education, medical work, and in producing and distributing literature. In 1948 the mission established Rwanguba Bible Institute and later regional Bible schools.

Serious political turmoil and conflict in this region during the 1960s caused the CBFMS to evacuate its missionaries on at least four occasions. The CBFMS faced also a serious challenge from the Synod group, dissidents with nationalist aims who sought control. As a result the Association of Baptist Churches of Kivu, the organized church body on the field, lost a number of members, but in spite of outside ecclesiastical pressure it would not unite with the dissidents. In 1970 the government granted the Association legal recognition and, with the government's demand to join the Church of Christ, changed its name in January 1973 to the Community of Baptist Churches of Kivu, which since 1989 has taken the name of the Community of Baptist Churches of Eastern Zaire.

Because of its opposition to merge with the Church of Christ, Baptist Mid-Missions (BM-M) no longer has missionaries in the country, but during its stay did establish the Association (now Communauté) des Églises Baptistes Indepéndantes Evangéliques. Missionaries of the Canadian Baptist International Ministries came to Zaire first to work with Angolan refugees but continue to serve on the American Baptist field. Southern Baptists entered only in 1987; today they work with various Baptist congregations in Kikwit and Kinshasa.

Tensions have arisen between missionaries and national leaders, and Baptist ranks have been divided. Several Baptist groups have separated from the work of the established missions. The 48th Communauté des Églises Baptistes Autonomes (1949) separated from the Swedish Baptist mission; the Communauté des Fidèles Protestants (1957) from the Norwegian Baptists; and the Union des Églises Baptistes du Kwilu (1953) separated from Baptist Mid-Missions (BM-M). The Baptists on the Conservative Baptist field also divided. Those who are loyal to the missionaries cooperate in the Community of Baptist Churches of Eastern Zaire, while the dissidents are in the Baptist Community in Kivu.

The most spectacular division occurred with the appearance of the Church of Jesus Christ on Earth Through the Prophet Simon Kimbangu, today the largest independent church in Africa with three million adherents. One of the missionaries of the BMS had baptized Kimbangu in 1915, but in 1921, after his rejection as evangelist by the Nkamba congregation, he claimed through a vision that he had received divine authority to be a prophet with miraculous powers. Missionaries rejected his claims, and the Belgian government tried to suppress his movement by force, sentencing Kimbangu to death but then sending him to prison for life. With this, the Kimbangu movement took on a life of its own as an expression of African independence, gaining thousands of members.

There has been a remarkable degree of cooperation between the various Baptist missions, not only among themselves but with other evangelical groups. With other Protestant denominations all Baptist bodies are now communities within the Church of Christ, but each body retains its own autonomy in faith and practice and may work with its respective mission.

Baptists in Zaire have faced and continue to face many problems. During Belgian rule they and other Protestants experienced strong opposition from the Roman Catholic Church, discrimination from the regime, and beginnings of defection to prophet movements. Since independence because of civil conflict, there have been serious threats to the lives of the missionaries and often evacuation. With decline of the economy and the infrastructure of the nation, a very difficult load has been placed on the work. But through it all, Baptists have made significant contributions to the nation. In the early days, they helped to open up the country geographically. The ABMU and BMS also protested the inhuman labor practices of King Leopold. Besides their widespread evangelistic endeavors, their contributions in education, medicine, literacy, and other social services have been incalculable.

BIBLIOGRAPHY: The work of Brian Stanley, *The History of the Baptist Missionary Society 1792–1992* (Edinburgh: T&T Clark, 1992), 117–39, 336–68, 439–50, 458–66, and the centennial brochure, *One Hundred Years of Christian Mission in Angola and Zaire* (London: BMS, 1978), provide excellent material on the work of the BMS. Helpful accounts of the work of the American Baptists may be found in Robert Torbet, *Venture of Faith* (Philadelphia: Judson Press, 1955), 318–30, 562–79, and Dean R. Kirkwood, ed., *Mission in Mid–Continent: Zaire* (Valley Forge: International Ministries ABC/USA, c. 1982). For Norwegian Baptist work, see Arne J. Holte, (B.D. treatise, Baptist Theological Seminary, Rüschlikon, 1964). For Conservative Baptist work, see *Founded on the Word: Focused on the World* (Wheaton: CBFMS, 1978), 76–93; Hans W. Finzel, ed., *Partners Together* (Wheaton: CBFMS, 1993), 52–57; and Jack E. Nelson, *Christian Missionizing and Social Transformation* (New York: Praeger, 1992).

BAPTIST AND BAPTIST-RELATED MISSIONS

1. CAMEROON   UkBMS (1845–1886), GerMF (1891–1941), NABC (1935), EuEBM (1954), NBCA (1977–1986), BGC (1979)

2. CENTRAL AFRICAN REPUBLIC BM-M (1921), SwO (1923), EuEBM

3. CHAD   BM-M (1925), SBC (1993)

4. CONGO   SwO (1914)

5. EQUATORIAL GUINEA UkBMS (1843–1858), SBC (1981)

6. ERITREA   SBC (1994)

7. ZAIRE   UkBMS (1878), ABC (1884), SwBU (1892), NorBU (1922), CBI (1946), BBFI (1957), CaCBIM (1961), SBC (1987), IFM (1988), BIMI (1991), PNBC

C. NORTH AFRICA

*T*he five North African nations bordering the Mediterranean Sea are strongholds of Islam. Only the ancient land of Egypt has a significant Christian minority. The other four—Libya, Tunisia, Algeria, and Morocco—are at least 98 percent Moslem. Baptists in Egypt and Algeria formed indigenous congregations, but Baptists in the other three countries have worked primarily among expatriates. Because of Moslem hostility and government restrictions, including prohibitions on missionaries and institutional ministries, the Baptist presence is very small. In spite of the difficulties, Baptist representatives today serve in Egypt and Morocco, and some contact continues with believers in Algeria, where Baptist missionaries were expelled in 1970.

Although today there is no organized Baptist work in Tunisia and Libya, in years past Baptists have also been present in these countries. It was reported at the European Baptist Congress in 1908 that an Italian Baptist church of seventy members had been in existence in the city of Tunis in Tunisia for three years. In 1962 in Libya, Baptists formed the First Baptist Church of Tripoli composed of American expatriates related to the military and the oil industry. For a short time a second church for the military also existed. In 1965 Southern Baptists sent Harold Blankenship and his wife to serve on the field. With the departure of the military in 1970 and all other Americans in 1981, all Baptist work ceased by the latter date.

	Members	*Churches*
1. Algeria	n/a	n/a
2. Egypt	670	12
3. Morocco	<u>145</u>	<u>3</u>
	815	15

ALGERIA (1950)

*A*t the congress of the Baptist World Alliance in 1911, it was reported that French Baptists were undertaking mission activity among Moslems in Algeria, but this work has not survived. Another Baptist effort was undertaken in 1950 when Evangelical Baptist Missions (EBM) sent John Aseltine and his wife. By 1956 two other missionary couples had joined them. The mission conducted work among the Berbers on the Haut Plateau and in the cities of Alger and Oran.

According to the *World Christian Encyclopedia*, edited by David B. Barrett, the mission at one point had four congregations and fifty members.

With Algerian independence from France in 1962 and the expulsion of the missionaries in 1970, Baptist work was affected seriously. Today believers have come under serious persecution. Some have fled to France and others have gone underground. With great discretion, EBM maintains some relations with the remaining converts and also seeks to minister to Algerians who live in France.

BIBLIOGRAPHY: William J. Hopewell, Jr., *The Missionary Emphasis of the General Association of Regular Baptist Churches* (Chicago: Regular Baptist Press, 1963), 110–11. "Fields of Evangelical Baptist Missions," a section of a typed mss. from EBM.

EGYPT (1931)

	Members	Churches
General Baptist Evangelical Convention of Egypt (1960s)	670	(12)

*I*n spite of a strong Moslem majority, about 17 percent or more of the population are adherents of the ancient Coptic Church. In addition there are smaller groups of Christians, including the Coptic Evangelical Church, begun by Presbyterians in 1854. The Baptists are a small body which began in 1931 when Seddik W. Girgis (d. 1980), a Copt who had been converted to the evangelical faith, returned to Egypt to preach. Girgis had first come in contact with Baptists when working with the YMCA in Jerusalem. Upon the recommendation of J. Wash Watts, he attended Southwestern Baptist Theological Seminary in Texas, graduating with a Th.M. degree, and also earned a B.A. degree from Texas Christian University. While in Texas he joined a Baptist church and was ordained.

As the only Baptist in Egypt, Girgis began preaching in his home town of Fayyoum sixty-five miles southwest of Cairo, winning converts one by one, including his parents. By 1963 he had established six churches with a membership of 250. Girgis began a magazine, *The Baptist Evangel*, which he published for many years. In the late 1960s he founded the General Baptist Evangelical Convention, which he controlled as president until his death.

After more than one appeal to the Foreign Mission Board (FMB) of the Southern Baptist Convention, the FMB adopted Egypt as a field in November 1956 and began providing financial support. For a number of years the FMB also sent fraternal representatives, but only in 1981 were resident missionaries able to enter the country. At first the Egyptian pastors looked upon the missionaries as a threat to their ministry, and it took time for trust to develop. The FMB has subsidized Egyptian work heavily, but the Egyptian churches are today moving toward greater self-support.

In their outreach, Egyptian Baptists are establishing cell groups in new satellite cities. Theological Education by Extension (TEE) is offered in four centers, and new Sunday School materials in Arabic are now available. Because of the difficulties in reaching

Moslems, which include a prohibition of proselyting them, it is not surprising that most Baptist converts come from a Christian background. Christians also face social and religious discrimination. About 1971 the government closed the church building in Fayyoum because the congregation had not gained permission to build it. In spite of problems of living in a Moslem society, Baptists continue to grow even though numbers are small. They now number 670 in twelve churches. In the past both the Baptist Bible Fellowship International and Baptist International Missions have had missionaries in Egypt but report none at present.

BIBLIOGRAPHY: For material on Baptists in Egypt, see *Commission*, August 1985, 20–30.

MOROCCO (1966)

	Members	Churches
Southern Baptist Mission	145	(3)

*I*n 1966 Southern Baptists began a ministry to Moroccans when Joseph and Nancy Newton settled in Melilla, a Spanish enclave on the North African coast. The Newtons worked there with the Spanish Baptist church and Moroccans and later moved to Rabat in Morocco itself. Other missionaries, Merrill and Arlene Callaway, entered Morocco in 1967. After leaving for a time to serve in Yemen, they returned and settled in Tangier, maintaining the work in Morocco from that city. A good portion of Southern Baptist work has been in English and with expatriates. Southern Baptists help lead international English-language congregations in Fēs, Tangier, and Rabat. In 1985 the government closed the English-language bookstore, which Southern Baptists had purchased from another mission, but allowed it to reopen three years later.

Moroccan law does not recognize a native Moroccan church. Christianity is considered a religion of Europeans, and Christian converts face serious social pressures. These conditions make evangelism difficult. Nevertheless, Southern Baptist missionaries/representatives continue a quiet witness. Radio broadcasts and correspondence courses from the Baptist Center for Mass Communications in Beirut as well as video-cassettes provide helpful support. In addition, a small group of Berbers in France conduct with discretion a mission among their own people.

BIBLIOGRAPHY: Baker J. Cauthen and others, *Advance* (Nashville: Broadman Press, 1970), 234–35. *Middle East and South Asia* (Richmond: FMB, SBC, 1978), 45. *Your Guide to Foreign Missions*, 1994–1995, 129.

BAPTIST AND BAPTIST-RELATED MISSIONS

1. ALGERIA EBM (1950-1970)

2. EGYPT   SBC (1954)

3. MOROCCO SBC (1967)

D. SOUTHERN AFRICA AND THE INDIAN OCEAN

*I*n comparison to other denominations, Baptists had a very weak start in Southern Africa and made little impact in the region until after World War II. Until that time the major Baptist mission agencies which had an interest in Africa, except for the FMB of the National Baptist Convention, concentrated on the west of the continent. As a result, Baptists in the territory of what later became the Republic of South Africa were forced to look after themselves. Leading churches were the established Anglican and Dutch Reformed Churches and the Methodists, who had strong outside assistance. Baptists were a small minority. They had no strong base in the south of the continent for a move northward. Except for limited mission work in Lambaland in Zambia, the South African Baptist Missionary Society undertook no mission work outside South Africa proper, and the churches north of the country that belonged to the Baptist Union of South Africa were few in number and composed of white settlers.

Baptists also faced other problems in the region. In spite of the good intentions of Joseph Booth, his unstable relationships got Baptists off to a shaky start in Malawi. The FMB of the National Baptists, as a Black mission from America, was looked upon with suspicion by the British authorities. It faced restriction in South Africa and for a decade was outlawed in Malawi because of the rebellion of one of its missionaries.

But a new day has dawned for Baptists. They are experiencing rapid growth in many areas. The faithful planting and nurturing of the gospel witness by the South African Baptist Missionary Society (SoBMS), the Foreign Mission Board (FMB) of the National Baptist Convention, the Scandinavian Independent Baptist Mission, and the non-denominational South African General Mission have brought into existence strong Baptist bodies in South Africa, Malawi, Mozambique, and Zambia. The entrance of Southern Baptists in the 1950s and their expansion to every country of Southern Africa have not only boosted the Baptist cause in general but have produced large and growing conventions in Malawi, Zambia, and Zimbabwe. The reentry of mission work by Seventh Day Baptists has also added to Baptist work.

In the islands of the Indian Ocean off the east coast of Africa, Baptists are a very weak minority. Southern Baptists have planted a Baptist witness in Mauritius and Réunion but their effort in the Seychelles was discontinued. A small but indigenous Baptist body has taken root in Madagascar, which has received assistance from several Baptist bodies abroad.

	Members	Churches
1. Angola	115,318	369
2. Botswana	501	15
3. Lesotho	330	11
4. Madagascar	1,337	39
5. Malawi	190,105	1,774
6. Mauritius	116	1
7. Mozambique	210,200	1,015+
8. Namibia	3,968	44
9. Réunion	25	1
10. South Africa	78,796	786
11. Swaziland	310	9
12. Zambia	55,800	597
13. Zimbabwe	<u>124,028</u>	<u>550</u>
	780,834	5,211

ANGOLA (1878)

	Members	Churches
1. Igreja Evangélica Baptista de Angola (1977)	34,558	55
2. Igreja Evangélica de Angola	50,000	200
3. Convencão Baptista de Angola (1940)	15,470	87
4. Igreja Baptista Livre em Angola (1986)	<u>15,290</u>	<u>27</u>
	115,318	369

*A*fter centuries of Portuguese rule, Angola gained its independence in 1975. During the last three decades, the country has been beset by war—first with guerilla warfare from 1961 to 1975 against the Portuguese, and then civil war between rival groups in their struggle for power. A Marxist regime gained control of the central government but could not gain control over the entire territory. Because of warfare, many Angolans, including many Baptists, have suffered serious deprivation. In spite of the problems, including the departure of most of the missionaries, four Baptist bodies have not only managed to survive but have even thrived.

In its attempt to enter the Congo region in 1878, the Baptist Missionary Society (BMS) from London established its first base station at São Salvador, the capital of the

Bakongo people. In 1881, when it appeared that a route along the north bank of the Congo River would be feasible for mission operations, the BMS considered abandoning São Salvador. Because of the entreaties of the king, Dom Pedro V, who did not wish a Roman Catholic presence, the BMS stayed at São Salvador while still establishing a work in Congo (Zaire). After the baptism of five men, a church was formed at São Salvador on December 4, 1887, ten years after entry.

In 1960 the BMS separated the field in Angola from its Congo mission. In 1961 thirty-one missionaries served at three stations, and membership had reached ten thousand. The mission operated a hospital at São Salvador and two dispensaries at other sites. It also had established primary schools in addition to trade schools at each of the stations. A printing press at São Salvador printed books for schools and churches. But the beginning of the revolt against the Portuguese proved devastating to the mission. The missionaries not only left, but almost 80 percent of the population of northern Angola fled to Zaire, where the BMS began a relief ministry. In 1968 Baptist refugees formed the Association of Baptist Churches in Exile. With Angolan independence, the refugees returned in 1975, and the BMS provided financial assistance. Civil war broke out almost immediately, and Baptists were now in two different jurisdictions with little communication possible between the two sides. Some Baptists again went into exile in Zaire.

In spite of the conflict, growth continued. In 1977 Angolan Baptists founded the Evangelical Baptist Church of Angola (IEBA), which became a member of the Angolan Council of Evangelical Churches. IEBA maintained rather cordial relations with the Marxist regime in Luanda, whose only significant restriction was the prohibition of open-air evangelism. Because of the disrupted state of the country, many pastors were unable to get theological training. In 1982 the first BMS missionaries returned to the field.

Because of war, a number of members of the IEBA had moved farther south and formed churches in Luanda. Although it was still composed primarily of Bokongo, IEBA began reaching other tribal groups. In spite of destruction of property, martyrdom of some of its leaders, and periods of exile, the IEBA increased in spiritual strength.

Matthew Stober, after visiting Angola in 1899 where he witnessed territory in need of evangelization, founded in 1901 an independent mission agency, the Angola Evangelical Mission. Stober directed it until his death in 1951, gaining support from interested individuals in Great Britain. The mission worked among the Bakongo, not in the cooler plateau region where the BMS served but in a northwestern coastal area directly south of the Congo River and in the enclave of Cabinda north of the river. At its top strength, the mission had seventeen missionaries.

In 1954 the Canadian Baptist Foreign Mission Board assumed responsibility for the mission, which, at the time of Stober's death, was supporting only one missionary couple who were nearing retirement. Between 1956 and 1958, twenty-four Canadians left for language study in Portugal and then for the field. The first new missionaries arrived in Angola in 1957; at this time membership was almost five thousand. The mission built a small hospital at Quimpando and upgraded the medical clinics. Because of the rebellion, all Canadian missionaries had been forced to leave by 1963. Canadian missionaries were nevertheless able to provide relief for exiles in Zaire. With the granting of Angolan independence in 1975, Canadians still were not able to regain entry. The Canadian board, however, continued to maintain fraternal relations. The churches of the field formed the Evangelical Church of Angola, which today has a membership of 50,000.

In 1929 Manuel Ferreira Pedras and his wife, Justina, began working in Angola, the first Portuguese Baptists to serve on a foreign mission field. Later the Portuguese Baptist Convention officially supported their work. The couple settled at Etunda, a village near Nova Lisboa and in time established eight small congregations. In 1940 a Baptist Convention was formed. In the early 1960s Pedras retired to Portugal, and the struggling churches remained without a pastor until the Portuguese Convention sent another couple in 1966.

In 1968, in an effort to assist the struggling work, Southern Baptists sent to Luanda Harrison and June Pike, who had served as missionaries in Brazil. Pike served as pastor of the First Evangelical Baptist Church of Luanda as well as the English-speaking Community Baptist Church, which he organized. Between 1969 and 1975 the Convention grew from five hundred members in nine churches to ten thousand members in thirty-three congregations and eighty-seven preaching points. With independence, however, missionaries were forced to leave, but in 1983 Southern Baptists were able to send another missionary couple. In June 1990 a medical clinic was opened in the province of Huambo, and in September a seminary was established in Luanda with an enrollment of ten students.

A fourth Baptist body, the Free Baptist Church in Angola, exists with over fifteen thousand members. Lourenço Estefanio Pedro led in its formation in 1986 from Angolans who had lived as exiles in Zaire, where they came in contact with missionaries from the American Baptist Churches of USA. Seven of its churches are in the Luanda district, twenty in the Uige district and two in Zaire. All Baptist bodies, except the Evangelical Church of Angola, are members of the BWA.

BIBLIOGRAPHY: Material on the work of the BMS in Angola may be found in the centenary brochure, *One Hundred Years of Christian Mission in Angola and Zaire* (London: BMS, 1978), and the volume by Brian Stanley, *The History of the Baptist Missionary Society 1792–1992* (Edinburgh: T&T Clark, 1992). For the Evangelical Church in Angola and Canadian Baptists, see Orville E. Daniel, *Moving with the Times* (Toronto: CBOMB, 1973), 207–19, and Harry A. Refree, *Heritage and Horizon* (Mississauga, Ont.: Canadian Baptist Federation, 1988), 310–12. For the Baptist Convention of Angola and Southern Baptist work, see Baker J. Cauthen and others, *Advance* (Nashville: Broadman Press, 1970), 178–79, and *Your Guide to Foreign Missions*, 1992–1993, 28.

BOTSWANA (1968)

	Members	Churches
1. Southern Baptist Mission	501	(15)
2. National Baptist Convention, USA, Inc.	n/a	n/a
	501	(15)

*B*otswana is a republic north of South Africa, which has prospered because of its mineral wealth. Unlike many other African nations, it has experienced stability since it gained independence from Great Britain in 1966. The great majority of the people are Tswana. Because of the notable work of the London Missionary Society, which sent Robert Moffat and David Livingstone to Africa, and other missions, Christianity has had a significant impact on the nation.

Herbert Neely, a Southern Baptist missionary, was stationed near the border of Botswana in Rhodesia (Zimbabwe). He brought to the attention of H. Cornell Goerner, Southern Baptist area secretary for Africa, the possibility of mission work in northern Botswana. Neely and his wife periodically journeyed into Botswana and noted the responsiveness of the inhabitants. In 1968 Southern Baptists sent their first missionaries, Marvin and Elizabeth Reynolds, who settled in Francistown. In 1970 Charles and Jane Bellenger arrived. Charles Bellenger opened a dental clinic in Francisville, serving as the only resident dentist in the nation.

The Southern Baptist mission is also established in Gaborone, the capital, where a Baptist Center has been set up to meet human needs. The Southern Baptist mission uses the Bible Way correspondence course, radio, and the *Jesus* film. In 1990 the mission launched a special effort to work among the Kalanga, an unreached people, which resulted in some baptisms. The FMB of the National Baptist Convention, USA, provides support for a mission at Mahalapya. Baptists are still a small group and have not organized as yet a national convention, but they are active in ministry and are increasing in number.

BIBLIOGRAPHY: Baker J. Cauthen and others, *Advance* (Nashville: Broadman Press, 1970), 176–77. *Your Guide to Foreign Missions*, 1992–1993, 28–29.

LESOTHO (1961)

	Members	Churches
1. Bantu Baptist Church	300	(10)
2. Southern Baptist Mission	30	(1)
	330	(11)

*T*he Kingdom of Lesotho, surrounded entirely by South Africa, gained its independence in 1966 after being a protectorate of Great Britain. The Sotho people make up 93 percent of the population. The majority of the people are Roman Catholic.

An independent Bantu Baptist Church was established, which in the early 1980s had three hundred members in ten congregations. It has ties with the African United National Baptist Church in South Africa and the National Baptist Convention, USA. Since 1961 the FMB of the National Baptist Convention, USA, has sent missionaries to the country. It supports the W. J. Harvey Seminary and Secondary School, which has a campus of nine buildings, with around twenty enrolled in the seminary and more than three hundred in the secondary school.

Southern Baptists have only recently entered the country. Four missionaries reside in Maseru, the capital, where there are two churches related to the mission. A third church has been formed in Nyakosoba, a mountain town.

BIBLIOGRAPHY: For a small bit of information on the Bantu Baptist Church, see David B. Barrett, ed., *World Christian Encyclopedia* (Nairobi: Oxford University Press, 1982), 455. See William J. Harvey III, *Bridges of Faith Across the Seas* (Philadelphia: FMB of the NBC, USA, 1989), 279–80, for a sketch of the W. J. Harvey Seminary and Secondary School. See *Your Guide to Foreign Missions*, 1992–1993, 31–32, for information on Southern Baptist work.

MADAGASCAR (1932)

	Members	Churches
Fiangonana Batista Biblika eto Madagasikara (Biblical Baptist Church of Madagascar) (1932)/Malagasy Baptist Association	1,337	(39)

*M*adagascar is a large island republic in the Indian Ocean off the southeast coast of Africa. Its native people are primarily of Malayan-Indonesian stock. In 1960 it gained its independence, after having been under French control since 1885.

Mr. and Mrs. Brinly Evans, missionaries from Scotland who left the London Missionary Society, founded the Fiangonana Batista Biblika eto Madagasikara (FBBM), or Biblical Baptist Church of Madagascar. In 1932 they planted a church in Antananarivo, the capital, which they called Mission Biblique (Bible Mission). They began a second church in Moramanga and soon had an additional four village churches north of Moramanga.

The Evanses left Madagascar in 1944, appointing Pastor Rabenja Ramiarison to lead the work. He became the first associational president and served until about 1978 when his third son, Pastor Andrianavalona Rabenja, was elected president. The current president is Pastor Rabenja Rakotoarisoa, the eldest son of the first president. As a result of a national rebellion against the French colonial government in 1947, only the church in Antananarivo remained by 1950.

Pastor Randriamora, an early convert and church leader, founded an evangelical newspaper, *Vaovao Mahafaly* (Good News) in 1951, which had a wide circulation until it ceased in 1964. He became a church planter after his retirement from the postal service in 1966, establishing churches in Finarantsoa and Antananarivo.

Evans and his wife received support from the fundamentalist Evangelical Association of French-speaking Baptist Churches. They had become acquainted with this body during their stay of more than a year in France. The French association has continued to provide support to Baptists in Madagascar, such as providing funds for overseas or Bible school education, although it has never sent mission personnel.

In spite of strong opposition from the French association, Conservative Baptists were able to enter Madagascar in 1966 to serve with the FBBM, thanks in part to the endorsement of Evans, the founder. Conservative Baptists found a very conservative and isolated group of Baptists with a fortress mentality. The first missionaries were Mr. and Mrs. William F. Hunter, who were followed in 1968 by Mr. and Mrs. Mikel Neumann. Although the Hunters left in 1969, by 1970 there were ten missionaries, including their wives, on the field.

Conservative Baptists financed a literature program, which included publication of books and tracts in Malagasy as well as a Bible correspondence school. Some work was done through Theological Education by Extension (TEE). For some years an evening Bible school operated at Antananarivo. In 1987 Malagasy Baptists opened a regular Bible school at Antsirabe whose personnel was entirely Malagasy. The French association and Conservative Baptists equally financed the acquisition of the campus.

Malagasy Baptists worked with Conservative Baptists in church planting and leadership training and with the Africa Evangelical Fellowship (AEF) to begin a medical work in the north. In 1987 Southern Baptists sent Fred Sorrells to work with Malagasy Baptists in an agricultural ministry.

From one church in 1950, Malagasy Baptist churches grew to five in 1960, eleven in 1979, thirteen in 1980, thirty-two in 1990, and forty in 1993. Some reasons for growth have been due to the political and economic turmoil under a Marxist regime which created spiritual openness; key leaders returning after their training in Europe and North America; the return of students who were converted in Communist countries where they had gone to study; and the Bible correspondence and small group ministries.

Mikel Neumann

BIBLIOGRAPHY: Mikel Neumann, *Factors Underlying Accelerated Growth Trends as Reflected in the History of the Malagasy Baptist Church* (Doctor of Missiology dissertation, Fuller Theological Seminary, 1990). Fiangonana Batista Biblika, *Fahatsiarovana ny Fahadimampolo Taona* (Fiftieth Anniversary Souvenir) (Antananarivo: FBBM, 1982).

MALAWI (1892)

	Members	Churches
1. African Baptist Assembly of Malawi, Inc. (1945)	55,516	(784)
2. Central African Conference of Seventh Day Baptists (1969)	9,574	(31)
3. African United Baptist Church (1946)	n/a	n/a
4. Baptist Convention of Malawi (1970)	77,313	(728)
5. Independent Baptist Church (1971)	29,000	n/a

6. Evangelical Baptist Church (1973)	14,878	(231)
7. Free Baptist Church in Malawi	<u>3,824</u>	<u>n/a</u>
	190,105	(1,774)

STATISTICS: BWA *Yearbook*, 1993–1994, 97; Marjorie Froise, ed., *World Christianity: South Central Africa* (Monrovia, Calif.: MARC, 1991), 56; Don A. Sanford, *A Choosing People* (Nashville: Broadman Press, 1992), 293.

*T*he small country of Malawi, nestled in south-central Africa, is composed of Bantu people of whom 90 percent are Chewa.

In 1891 the territory, then known as Nyasaland, became a British protectorate, but in 1964 became independent. It has a significant although divided Baptist constituency. The history of Baptist beginnings and early development is one of the most unusual of any nation.

All of the early Baptist work revolves around Joseph Booth (1851–1932), an English Baptist who was a strong advocate of African rights and equality. In his account of Seventh Day Baptists in Nyasaland, N. Olney Moore, who personally knew Booth, wrote, "While Mr. Booth was a sincere and earnest Christian worker, he was also a sort of religious hitchhiker, who was in the habit of seeking and accepting lifts from any organization that was going his way, and abandoning it when it suited him or felt that he could not work satisfactorily with it any longer." The government of South Africa deported him in 1915 as a political undesirable. He helped to bring in National Baptists and Seventh Day Baptists, besides the South African Churches of Christ, Seventh-Day Adventists, and Jehovah's Witnesses! Most, if not all, the Christian sectarian movements in southern Nyasaland can trace their history in some way back to Booth.

After first living in New Zealand and Australia, Booth went to Nyasaland in 1892 where he led in establishing a series of industrial missions, which were to be self-supporting and teach Africans special skills. Booth did not remain long with any of them. British Baptists helped to finance the Zambezi Industrial Mission (1892), which later became the Zambezi Evangelical Church and a synod of the United Evangelical Church; Australian Baptists assisted the Nyaza Industrial Mission (1893), today a synod of the United Evangelical Church; and Scottish Baptists helped the Baptist Industrial Mission (1895), later taken over by Churches of Christ. In 1897 Booth took John Chilembwe of the Yao tribe to America, where with National Baptist support he received an education at Virginia Theological Seminary and College at Lynchburg. Returning to Africa in 1900 under the FMB of the National Baptist Convention, Chilembwe began the Providence Industrial Mission, where he was joined by L. N. Cheek and Emma B. Delaney. One of Chilembwe's impressive achievements was completing around 1913 a large church, three bricks thick with twin towers, the pride of Baptists in Nyasaland as well as Black Baptists in America. In leading an uprising against British authority in 1915, Chilembwe was killed, which resulted in the colonial regime dynamiting his church and banning the Providence Mission for many years. Today an independent Malawi honors Chilembwe as one of its martyrs, and every year a two-hour drama is presented on his life.

While in America Booth joined the Seventh Day Baptists and persuaded them to establish a Sabbath Evangelizing and Industrial Association. Booth returned to Nyasaland in

1899 and established in 1900 Plainfield Mission, which soon proved to be a failure, and the property sold to the Seventh-Day Adventists at a serious loss. In 1910 Booth again entered the picture when he persuaded Seventh Day Baptists that there were about ten thousand Sabbath keepers in Nyasaland, gaining their support for himself in Cape Town and his work in the territory. An investigating committee of Seventh Day Baptists in 1912 found only two thousand Seventh Day Baptists and, because of a breakdown in relations with Booth, they severed their connections with him. When the government deported Walter Cockerill, an independent missionary, in 1915, Seventh Day Baptists in Nyasaland were left without supervision or support for several decades.

Despite these erratic beginnings, the Baptist cause survived. In 1926 the British allowed National Baptists to reopen the Providence Industrial Mission by Daniel S. Malekebu (c. 1890–1978), a convert of the mission who had received medical and Bible school training in America. Today it is the most successful field for National Baptists, which has included not only the establishment of churches but two hospitals and schools. In 1945 Malekebu led in the formation of the National Baptist Assembly of Africa, Nyasaland, today called the African Baptist Assembly of Malawi—it was patterned after the National Baptist Convention, USA. The Providence Mission has suffered two schisms—the African United Baptist Church in 1946 and the Independent Baptist Church in 1971.

Seventh Day Baptists in Malawi continued correspondence with Seventh Day Baptists abroad. In 1947 Ronald Barrar of New Zealand responded to their request of help, and in 1953 the Seventh Day Baptist Missionary Society assumed responsibility for the field, which also included medical work. Today the Central African Conference is one of the strongest units in the world family of Seventh Day Baptists.

As part of its Central African Mission, Southern Baptists entered Malawi in 1959 with two couples who had served in what today is Zimbabwe. From the beginning, the mission followed a policy of self-support for new congregations. The mission accepted a few indigenous groups that had been influenced by Baptists and began to organize its own churches, the first one at Ndlama in 1962. In 1964 a separate Malawi mission was organized, and in 1965 in Lilongwe a small Bible school and a publication center were formed. In 1970 churches in the mission established a Malawi Baptist Convention. The work has grown very rapidly with congregations in eight major people groups with efforts today in reaching the Yao, most of whose faith is a syncretistic mixture of Islam and folk religion. The mission maintains a media center, producing radio programs and cassettes, and a medical clinic at Senga Bay, and utilizes TEE and the Bible Way correspondence course.

As the result of the work of two evangelists in 1973, a small group of Moslems were converted in the village of Mowere in the Machinga District who at first did not declare publicly their faith for fear of their neighbors. They formed a Christian church, the first congregation of the Evangelical Baptist Church (ECB), and moved to Mbere in the same district. In 1979 Matthias Munyewe, who had received seminary training in Zambia, became chairman of the ECB when this group had only four churches and four hundred members. He had a vision of reaching his own people, the Yao. With an extensive use of lay leadership, the ECB has had a phenomenal growth, reaching both Yao and non-Yao peoples. It is one of the fastest growing groups in South Africa and possibly the most successful in gaining adherents from a previously unreached Moslem population.

BIBLIOGRAPHY: The best account of Joseph Booth and John Chilembwe is in the scholarly work of George Shepperson and Thomas Price, *Independent African: John Chilembwe*

and the Origins, Setting and Significance of the Nyasaland Native Rising of 1915
(Edinburgh: Edinburgh University Press, 1958), which also appeared in a paperback edition
in 1987. For information on Christian sects in Nyasaland and their relation to Booth, see
R. L. Wishlade, *Sectarianism in Southern Nyasaland* (London: International African
Institute, 1965). For an account of National, Seventh Day, and Southern Baptists, see Davis
Lee Saunders, *A History of Baptists in East and Central Africa* (Th.D. dissertation, Southern
Baptist Theological Seminary, 1973), 12–48, 119–44, 238–60. The work by William J.
Harvey III, *Bridges of Faith Across the Seas* (Philadelphia: FMB of the NBC, USA, 1989),
includes references to the Providence Industrial Mission. For additional material on Seventh
Day Baptists, see the typed mss. by N. Olney Moore, *Seventh Day Baptists and Mission
Work in Nyasaland, Africa*, 1950, with an appendix compiled by Leon R. Lawton, in pos-
session of the Seventh Day Baptist Historical Society, Plainfield, N.J., as well as Don A.
Sanford, *A Choosing People* (Nashville: Broadman Press, 1992), 291–93. For additional
material on Southern Baptists, see Baker J. Cauthen and others, *Advance* (Nashville:
Broadman Press, 1970), 163–65, and *Your Guide to Foreign Missions*, 1992–1993, 32. For
an account of the Evangelical Baptist Church, see "A People to Win: The Story of the
Evangelical Baptist Church of Malawi," in Larry D. Pate, *From Every People* (Monrovia,
Calif.: MARC, 1989), 63–89.

MAURITIUS (1978)

	Members	Churches
Southern Baptist Mission (1978)	116	(1)

*M*auritius is a small island republic five hundred miles east of Madagascar
in the Indian Ocean. About half the population is Hindu, followed by
Christians, who are predominantly Roman Catholic, and Moslems.
Southern Baptist work began in 1978 upon the invitation of a Chinese Christian fellowship. A church has been established at Curepipe with preaching points at other
locations. There has been growth among both Chinese and native Mauritians.

BIBLIOGRAPHY: *Your Guide to Foreign Missions*, 1992–1993, 30.

MOZAMBIQUE (1921)

	Members	Churches
1. Convencão Baptista de Moçambique (1957)	10,200	(15)
2. Igreja União Baptista (1968)	200,000	(1,000+)
	210,200	(1,015+)

STATISTICS: Statistics for Igreja União Baptista were gained from Marjorie Froise, ed.,
World Christianity: South Central Africa (Monrovia, Calif.: Marc, 1991), 92, and from
Action Africa, Jan.-Mar., 1995, 4.

*M*ozambique gained its independence from Portugal in 1974. Years of fighting, first with rebellion against the Portuguese and then after independence from civil war, has left much of the country devastated with great loss of life and thousands of refugees in squatter villages or living abroad. Until recently the central government espoused Marxist principles, now renounced in an effort to bring peace and stability. The Roman Catholic Church is the largest religious community, but Baptists are the largest Protestant denomination, although far behind Catholics in number.

In 1949 the Baptist Union of Portugal sent Luís Rodrigues de Almeida and his wife to Mozambique, the first Portuguese Baptist missionaries to the country. In 1957 ethnic Portuguese organized with two churches the Baptist Convention of Mozambique, but with independence they with other compatriots soon left the country. They first, however, elected in 1975 Bento Matusse as president of the convention and pastor of the First Baptist Church of Maputo, which was located in the capital but devoid of members. In spite of the serious loss of the Portuguese members and the restrictions of the Marxist regime which forbade evangelization and children in Sunday School, the convention survived. In 1974 it had only five hundred members, but today it is showing a healthy growth with over ten thousand members, fifteen churches, over one hundred preaching places, eighteen pastors, seven national missionaries and three Bible schools. Quelimane in the Zambezia province has become a particularly important center of outreach.

In spite of government restriction, the convention has received some limited mission assistance. In 1971 Brazilian Baptists sent Valnice Coelho, who was able to stay in the country in spite of the forced withdrawals of other missionaries. In 1973 Southern Baptists sent a couple, who had served in Brazil, as fraternal representatives, but a second couple who replaced them was forced to leave soon after arriving in 1975. In 1986 Southern Baptists returned, helping to provide Bible Way correspondence, TEE, and training programs.

A larger Baptist movement is the United Baptist Church, the product of the union of two missions, one in the south and the other in the north of the country. In 1913 the Presbyterian Church of Scotland established a mission at Mihecani, 250 miles inland from Quelimane, the first Protestant witness in northern Mozambique. In 1933 it turned the enterprise over to the Nyasa Mission which, lacking finances and personnel, transferred it in 1939 to the South Africa General Mission (SAGM), today the Africa Evangelical Fellowship (AEF). SAGM had already entered Mozambique in 1936 with a station on a tributary of the Zambezi River but now assumed this new responsibility. The center at Mihecani had a primary school, health center, and a well-organized church. In 1959 the Portuguese regime closed the mission and in the following year refused reentry to missionaries of the mission who had been on furlough. SAGM requested the Free Baptist Union in Sweden (FBU), or Scandinavian Independent Baptist Union, which had had a mission hundreds of miles to the south, to oversee the work.

The FBU had entered Mozambique in 1921 when it voted to take over a mission work which a South African lawyer named Mr. Baker had begun in Gaza province. Two years earlier, two evangelists, who represented believers from Baker's work and were acquainted with Free Baptist mission work in the mines in South Africa, had already requested help. Among the pioneer missionaries were Ernst and Anna Svensson (who served until 1961) and Anton and Signe Johansson. Work was undertaken also in Maputo, where a church and school were established. In 1968 the FBU mission assumed responsibility for the field of the SAGM in the north.

The period from 1975 to 1982 proved to be particularly difficult when the Marxist regime nationalized mission property, closed churches, confiscated Bibles, imprisoned leaders, and forbade Sunday Schools and distribution of Christian literature. Facing famine and civil war, the government changed policy in the early 1980s, and since then there has been religious freedom and an increase of missionary forces, including the return of missions forced to leave, even though serious economic and political problems remain.

The United Baptist Church, the church body of the united FBU and SAGM (AEF) mission effort, has had an explosive growth, numbering today around 200,000 with more than 100,000 in the Napula province alone. The expulsion of the missionaries in the north, instead of slowing the work, brought greater vitality. In addition, the persecution and civil war helped to spread believers to other parts of the country where churches were planted. New congregations are today appearing among the Muslims of the north. With the assistance of the Africa Evangelical Fellowship, the United Baptist Church has opened a seminary in Maputo.

BIBLIOGRAPHY: For material on the Baptist Convention of Mozambique, see Donald D. Martin, "Mozambique: Promises of Peace," *Commission*, Dec. 1992, 40–51. For the work of the United Baptist Convention and the South Africa General Mission, see Phyllis Thompson, *Life Out of Death in Mozambique* (London: Hodder and Stoughton, 1989). For the work of the Free Baptist Union, see Eric Hansson and Barbro Wennbergs, eds., *Mission genom hundra år* (Tidaholm, Sweden: Fribaptistsamfundets Förlag, 1991).

NAMIBIA (1963)

	Members	Churches
Baptist Convention of Namibia (1984)	3,968	(44)

*A*fter several decades as German South West Africa and then, as a result of the First World War, a mandate of South Africa, Namibia finally received its independence in 1990. Although there were some earlier attempts by Baptists to minister in South West Africa, nothing permanent was established until the early 1960s.

In 1961 Mr. and Mrs. Fritz Haus with Maurice Darroll, General Secretary of the Baptist Union of South Africa, surveyed the country and held meetings in Walvis Bay (a town still under South Africa) and Windhoeck. In Walvis Bay a Baptist family, who in 1959 had moved from South Africa, was already conducting a Sunday School. In Windhoek in 1961 transplanted South African laypersons began to hold Bible studies, a Sunday School, and worship services. This effort led to the formation in 1963 of the first Baptist Church in the territory with sixteen charter members. A church was later organized in Walvis Bay in 1975. Although the Baptist Union wanted to send a mission worker to the country, it was unable to do so.

In responding to its request for a pastor, Southern Baptists sent in 1968 Charles Whitson and his wife to pastor the Windhoeck church. Today the church has an African pastor and is self-supporting. Southern Baptists have sponsored the Bible Way correspondence course, produced radio programs, provided medical treatment with a mobile care unit, and distributed relief. There has been a strong evangelistic response among the Bushmen in the Caprivi Strip, hitherto an unreached people. In 1984 the Baptist churches formed the Baptist Association of Namibia. Today Baptists in Namibia have a convention with five associations which were accepted into the BWA in 1993.

BIBLIOGRAPHY: Sydney Hudson-Reed, *By Taking Heed...* (Roodepoort: Baptist Publishing House, 1983), 318–319. For Southern Baptist work, see *Your Guide to Foreign Missions*, 1992–1993, 33, and Craig Bird, "Namibia: The Quiet Invasion," *Commission*, Dec. 1989, 35–53.

RÉUNION (1989)

	Members	Churches
Bras Panon Baptist Church (1989)	25	(1)

T he island of Réunion, a dependency of France, lies east of Madagascar in the Indian Ocean. In 1985 Southern Baptists entered the field, whose population is predominantly Roman Catholic. Since the Southern Baptist mission did not have legal recognition, its missionaries worked at first with the Evangelical Church. In 1989 a Malagasy couple who were French citizens and Baptists in France, helped to begin in 1989 the Bras Panon Baptist Church, located thirty kilometers from the capital of St. Denis. In 1992 Stanley and Jan McFall, Southern Baptist missionaries, started a mission in their home in St. Denis. Attendance of the church and mission is seventy-five. In the early 1990s the government recognized the Southern Baptist mission.

SOUTH AFRICA (1820)

	Members	Churches
1. Baptist Union of South Africa (1877)	33,777	(340)
2. Baptist Convention of South Africa (1966)	35,000	(125)
3. Baptist Union of Transkei (1980)	6,355	(312)
4. Seventh Day Baptists (1906)	364	(3)
5. Independent Baptist Church (1976)	2,200	n/a
6. Transvaal Independent Baptist Church (1985)	500	n/a

7. Reformed Baptist Association (1990)*	600	(6)
8. Free Baptist Church	n/a	n/a
	78,796	(786)

*Also members of the Baptist Union of South Africa

STATISTICS: BWA, *Yearbook*, 1993–1994, 97; Don A. Sanford, *A Choosing People*, 312; Eric Hansson and Barbro Wennbergs, eds., *Mission genom hundra år*, 306; David B. Barrett, ed., *World Christian Encyclopedia*, 626.

*C*aught in the crowded crossroads of change, economic stringency, and industrial revolution, some 4,500 British emigrants left England in 1820 to start a new life in South Africa. Among these settlers were several Baptist families who, upon arrival in their adopted country, appointed one of their number, William Miller (1779–1856), to be their spiritual leader.

Although untrained theologically, he had an acute mind, a ready tongue, a dedicated will, and a strong sense of call. Miller can be regarded as the founder of Baptist work in South Africa. It was he who laid the foundation stone of the first Baptist chapel in Grahamstown, which was completed in 1823.

The early years of the Baptist church in Grahamstown were troubled with controversy centered around the Calvinist/Arminian conflict. William Davies, who was sent by the BMS in England, was the first ordained Baptist minister to come to South Africa. Despite being shipwrecked on the outward voyage and losing his son in the wreckage, he and his wife arrived in Grahamstown in 1832 and exericised a short but fruitful ministry which strengthened, remotivated, and united the Grahamstown church. Although the BMS supplied two missionary pastors for the Grahamstown Church from 1821 to 1843, the Society's interests were in the Congo, not South Africa, and Baptists in the territory had to fend for themselves.

The first extension work was established in the farming area of Kariega, sixteen miles from Grahamstown. A series of frontier wars between nomadic blacks moving southwards and the settlers interrupted this work. The Kariega bears two dates, that of its commencement in 1834 and its completion in 1854.

A second influx of settlers, immigrants from Germany, played an important role. They were soldiers to whom the British government allotted land for fighting in the Crimean War. This military settlement was followed by an agricultural contingent in 1858 and another in 1859. Once again it was a layman, Carsten Langhein, who established the first German church. The congregation which had grown to three hundred in 1861, the year he was ordained, was widely dispersed.

Upon a plea for help, Johann Oncken, the German Baptist leader, sent in 1867 his personal assistant, Carl Hugo Gutsche (1843–1926), who with his gifted wife exercised a formative ministry. He established twenty-five churches in twenty-five years, the buildings for which were all opened free of debt. The German churches formed their own *Bund*, or association, a more closely united body than found among their English brethren. Unlike the English who practiced open communion and open membership, the Germans observed close communion and membership. As late as 1938 almost one-fourth of the European membership of the Baptist Union of South Africa was German. Gutsche baptized J. D. Odendall, who in 1886 founded the first Baptist church among the Afrikaans-speaking (or Dutch-speaking) population. In 1938 this ethnic group, which then had over five hundred members, formed an association, which in 1944 took the name Die Afrikaanse Baptiste Kerk, operating as a language-union within the Baptist Union.

The immigration of Telugus, who were Baptists in India, to work in the sugar plantations of Natal led to an Indian Baptist work. In 1903 the Telugu Baptist Home Missionary Society sent John Rangiah to serve as pastor. An Indian association was formed which later joined the Baptist Union. In 1938 it numbered 574 members in four churches.

In 1877 when Baptists in the Cape came together to welcome the newly appointed minister of the Grahamstown church, G. W. Cross, the momentous decision was taken to form the Baptist Union of South Africa. There were only four English-speaking churches—Grahamstown with its extension at Kariega, Port Elizabeth, Alice, and the newly formed church in Cape Town— together with the German church at King William's Town. From this small beginning, the Baptist Union has grown to over 33,000 members in some 340 churches, comprising all sectors of the heterogenous South African population, including English, German, Afrikaner, Asiatic Indian, Portuguese, Chinese, Coloured, and Black churches.

The struggling Baptist churches and the premature union they had formed were held together by a threefold cord—their evangelical emphasis, their biblical doctrine, and their missionary concern. Growth was slow, funds were scarce, vast distances made communication difficult, but the annual assemblies were well attended. Through its executive the Baptist Union laid good foundations for its policy and practice. The South African Baptist Missionary Society (SoBMS) was formed in 1892, the centenary year of the BMS, and like the parent body was separate from the Baptist Union. In 1924 the SoBMS came under the wing of the Baptist Union, the same executive serving both bodies. The South African Baptist Women's Association played an important role, but the Men's Association functioned only sporadically.

Regional associations evolved but were limited in their scope and dependent on the dedication of their elected executives and service committees. Besides the territorial association, there were the ethnic associations—Afrikaans, Indian (which had two associations), and also Coloured for a short period. At this time all Black churches were accounted as part of the SABMS. Although the Baptist Union was open to all churches, its congregations and associations nevertheless reflected the prevailing ethnic, linguistic, and cultural divisions in society as a whole. On the other hand, the leadership of the Baptist Union, including C. M. Doke, who served as president, resolutely opposed attempts by the government to entrench such divisions in legal enactments either before or after the enforcement of discriminatory apartheid from 1948 onwards.

In 1927 the Black churches formed a Bantu Baptist Church, but they were still under the control of the Baptist Union through the SABMS. In 1966 a Baptist Convention of South Africa with powers of self-government replaced the Bantu Church. Many have felt that a golden opportunity was lost of uniting the Convention with the Baptist Union at that stage. Subsequent attempts to do this have so far proved to be abortive, although an increasing number of Black churches have elected to leave the Convention and join the Baptist Union. The Baptist Union today has its first Black president, George Motale Ngamlana.

In the late 1970s the Baptist Union began a process of devolution with the associa-

SWAZILAND (1971)

	Members	Churches
1. National Baptist Convention Mission (1971)	n/a	(3)
2. Southern Baptist Mission (1983)	310	(6)
	310	(9)

Swaziland is a kingdom which borders South Africa and Mozambique, gaining its independence from Great Britain in 1968. A number of Black South African Baptists migrated to this country. In 1971 Baptist work began when the FMB of the National Baptist Convention, USA, sent E. G. Ngubeni, a South African who had been educated in the USA. The Swazi government granted to the FMB four acres of land to start a mission church. In 1993 National Baptists have three churches—in Mbabane, the capital; Hlane; and Nhlangano—and preschools in Mbabane and Hlane. Roxanne Jones is the Director of Missions.

In March 1976 Theodore Pass, supported by the South African Baptist Missionary Society, began services for a group of South African expatriates who had formed an English-speaking Christian fellowship and an interdenominational Sunday School. Pass desired to form a Swazi congregation but, despite attracting a multinational constituency, gained few Swazis. In 1979 the Mbane Baptist Church was constituted but today is a non-denominational congregation.

In October 1983 Davis Saunders, Area Director for Southern Baptists, asked veteran missionaries Roy and Patsy Davidson to transfer from Botswana to Swaziland. They began by teaching a discipleship course in their home with twelve in attendance. During the first school holiday they conducted a Vacation Bible School with seventy in attendance. From their efforts the Mbabane International Baptist Church was formed, which today has an average attendance of one hundred fifty with fifteen nationalities represented. A preschool in conjunction with the church was started in 1985. A Baptist church was established in Manzini in August 1989, which today averages ninety in attendance. Since 1983 seven Southern Baptist career missionaries have joined the Davidsons in ministry.

The United Nations and the Swazi government established two refugee camps for Mozambicans. In the Malindza Camp, the Southern Baptist mission conducted a feeding program, gave cooking utensils, hoes, and tents, and financed a water system. From this effort Isaac Silvano, an Angolan Baptist and graduate of the Baptist seminary in Rio de Janeiro, was instrumental in March 1990 in forming a church and becoming its pastor. The church has an average attendance of three hundred and has begun two preaching points in the camp. Silvano is also employed by Trans World Radio and broadcasts sermons in Portuguese to Mozambique and Angola. Another church was started in the Ndzevane Camp in June 1992 and has an average attendance of eighty.

Members of the Southern Baptist mission conduct a prison ministry, home Bible studies, a weekday Bible club, and a discipling program. The mission began the Bible Way correspondence course in 1986 which today enrolls 2,530.

Linda W. Bradley

BIBLIOGRAPHY: For National Baptists, see *Bridges of Faith Across the Seas* (Philadelphia: FMB of the NBC, USA, 1989), 279, 324. Material on the activity of the South African Baptist Missionary Society may be found in Sydney Hudson-Reed, *By Taking Heed...* (Roodepoort: Baptist Publishing House, 1983), 320–21.

ZAMBIA (1905)

	Members	Churches
1. Baptist Union of Zambia (1976)	15,000	(145)
2. Baptist Convention of Zambia (1974)	40,200	(445)
3. Reformed Baptist Association (1993)*	600	(7)
4. African Baptist Assembly	n/a	n/a
	55,800	(597)

*Ties with Zambian Baptist Association which is a member of the Baptist Union of Zambia.

STATISTICS: BWA, *Yearbook*, 1993–1994, 98; David B. Barrett, ed., *World Christian Encyclopedia*, 766–67; Marjorie Froise, ed., *World Christianity: South Central Africa* (Monrovia, Calif.: MARC, 1991), 139–140.

Z ambia, formerly known as Northern Rhodesia, gained independence from Great Britain in 1964. In 1905 William A. Phillips and Henry Masters, missionaries of the Nyasaland Industrial Mission which Joseph Booth had founded in 1892, traveled in the Copperbelt to locate a site for a mission. They established among the Lamba people a station at Kafulafuta, ninety miles north of Broken Hill. Upon hearing of the financial plight of the mission, Joseph J. Doke, minister of the Central Baptist Church of Johannesburg, and his son, Clement, made an exploratory trip in 1913. On the journey Joseph Doke died from typhoid fever, but Doke's death along with a positive report of the field fired the imagination of the South African Baptist Missionary Society (SABMS), which voted to assume responsibility for the station.

Clement Doke and his sister, Olive, and William Phillips, continued the mission, gave most valuable service. Clement and William translated the New Testament into Lamba with Clement completing the entire Bible in 1960. The Lambaland Mission established a boarding school, Bible school, village out-schools, and hospital and obtained a printing press, a gift from England. Itinerant evangelists spread the gospel among the Lamba people. The mission suffered serious losses of membership to independent African churches and financial difficulties but gained some financial assistance from the Rhodesian Baptist Association. It also began to show some growth, attaining twelve hundred members in forty-one churches in 1962. In 1969 the Australian Baptist Missionary Society sent its first missionaries to the field, and in 1973 the SABMS withdrew. In 1972 a Lambaland Baptist Association was established.

Upon the invitation of the SABMS to assist in mission work in the Copperbelt, the Scandinavian Independent Baptist Mission, supported by the Free Baptist Union of Sweden, sent its first missionaries in 1931 to Lambaland. Its major station was at Mpongwe where a hospital and Bible school were established. In 1968 it had one thousand members. In 1974 the Mpongwe Baptist Association was founded.

English-speaking European Baptist groups began to appear, which resulted in the establishment of churches at Ndola (1952), Kitwe (1957), Luanshya (1957), Lusaka (1960), Chingola (1960), and Broken Hill (1963). Its churches became members of the Rhodesian Baptist Association, formed in 1948, which in 1959 became the Baptist Union of Central Africa (BUCA), affiliated with the Baptist Union of South Africa. In 1961 the BUCA began to organize indigenous African congregations. Today its churches, which at first were White, are now predominantly Black. In 1971 a Zambian Baptist Association was established within the BUCA. In 1976 three Baptist bodies formed the Baptist Union of Zambia, including the Zambian Baptist Association of the BUCA, the Northern Association of the Australian Baptists, and the Mpongwe Association of the Free Baptist Union.

In 1959 Southern Baptists entered Zambia by sending Tom and Mary Small, who were transferred from Zimbabwe, and a new missionary couple, Zeb and Evelyn Moss. The first center was Kitwe in the Copperbelt, but the work moved to other Copperbelt towns. The mission entered Lusaka and then spread to Eastern Province with Chipata as a center. David Moffat, who was a Baptist and a great-great-great grandson of Robert Moffat, gave the mission a farm of 3,400 acres at Serenje, where there is today a training center and agricultural work. Southern Baptists established a seminary at Lusaka in 1967 and have used TEE and the Bible Way correspondence course. There is also a publishing center and a radio-television studio in Lusaka. In 1974 the Baptist Convention of Zambia was formed. The Southern Baptist work has grown rapidly with a membership today of forty thousand.

As an extension of its work in Malawi, the African Baptist Assembly also has some work in the country. Within the Baptist Union of Zambia, a Reformed Baptist movement among English-speaking churches has begun to take root. In 1990 four churches adopted the 1689 Baptist Confession of Faith. In 1993 Reformed Baptists formed an association with the future possibility of breaking their ties with the Baptist Union.

BIBLIOGRAPHY: Material on the beginnings and development of Baptist work in general in Zambia may be found in Davis Lee Saunders, *A History of Baptists in East and Central Africa* (Th.D. disssertation, Southern Baptist Theological Seminary, 1973), 48–62, 144–70, 260–72. The work by Sydney Hudson-Reed, *Channels for 100 Years of Missionary Endeavour* (n.p.: South African Baptist Historical Society, 1992), 10–16, contains an account of the Lambaland Mission of the SoBMS. Reed's work, *By Taking Heed...* (Roodepoort: Baptist Publishing House, 1983), 340–49, provides helpful information on the churches and work of the Zambian Baptist Association. For the work of the FBU of Sweden, see Eric Hansson and Barbro Wennberg, eds., *Mission genom hundra år* (Tidaholm: Fribaptistsamfundets Förlag, 1991), 196–243.

ZIMBABWE (1920)

	Members	Churches
1. Baptist Union of Zimbabwe (1959)	5,433	(33)
2. Baptist Convention of Zimbawe (1963)	110,482	(451)
3. United Baptist Church of Zimbabwe (1973)	6,000	(43)
4. National Baptist Convention of Zimbabwe (1989)	2,000	(23)
5. African Baptist Assembly	n/a	n/a
6. Seventh Day Baptists	113	n/a
	124,028	(550)

*A*s a British colony, Zimbabwe was called Southern Rhodesia, but in 1965 a government controlled by the White minority unilaterally proclaimed an independent Rhodesia. In 1980 Zimbabwe gained independence with Black majority rule.

German Baptists, who had trekked from their homes in South Africa to Somabula, twenty-four miles south of Gwelo (today Gweru), established in August 1920 the first Baptist church in Zimbabwe. In 1928 W. Martin, a recent graduate of Spurgeon's College in London, began to work in the territory with support from the Baptist Union of South Africa. White settlers constituted churches at Bulawayo and Salisbury (today Harare) in 1929. In 1948 four congregations, two from Salisbury and one each from Bulawayo and Gwelo, formed the Rhodesian Baptist Association, which in 1959 became the Baptist Union of Central Africa. Today this body is the Baptist Union of Zimbabwe with a predominantly Black membership which is integrated with Whites. Its appeal is more to the upper classes with services in their churches generally in English.

Zimbabwe was the first field which Southern Baptists entered in their expansion in Africa after the Second World War. The pioneer missionary was Clyde J. Dotson (1905–1982). In 1930 he began serving with his wife, Hattie, under the South Africa General Mission because the FMB of the SBC lacked funds to support them. Because of his opposition to this mission's policy of accepting both immersion and sprinkling as proper modes of baptism, he resigned in 1949 to become an independent missionary. In the following year, the FMB of the SBC appointed him and his wife as its first missionaries in Southern Rhodesia. By late 1952 ten additional missionaries were on the field, a hospital had been established at the Sanyati Reserve, and a central primary school and five out-schools were in operation. In 1955 a seminary opened near Gweru.

In 1963 messengers from the churches formed a Baptist Convention of Central Africa. When the mission began to reduce subsidies for pastors in the 1960s, a break in fellowship between the mission and the convention occurred, which was later overcome. In 1960 the mission appointed a couple to give their entire time to publications, and in 1967 a Baptist Publishing House was opened. Additional assistance to the work came from the establishment of a Bible Way correspondence course, the opening of

Baptist bookstores, and the formation of a Woman's Missionary Union and a Baptist Men's Fellowship. In 1985 the Baptist Convention assumed control of the Sanyati hospital. With a strong emphasis on evangelism, growth has been very rapid in both membership and churches.

The United Baptist Church of Zimbabwe is the product of the work of the South Africa General Mission (SoGM), which entered the country in 1897. To shed its interdenominational character, congregations of the SoGM formed in 1973 the United Baptist Church, indicating by its name it was uniting its congregations into one fellowship. Unlike most other Baptist bodies, the head of this body carries the title of bishop.

Because of its members who sought employment in Rhodesia, the Providence Industrial Mission of the National Baptist Convention, USA, extended an arm to Salisbury (Harare). In 1934 Daniel Malekebu, head of the mission, held meetings in the city and thereafter visited periodically. In the mid 1950s there were fourteen congregations with the two larger ones at Salisbury and Umtali. These Baptists are part of the African National Assembly centered in Malawi.

Seventh Day Baptist work began in Zimbabwe in 1968 with Lameck M. Vumah. Earlier in the year, Vumah, reared in a Seventh-Day Adventist home but converted under Baptists, had gone twice to Malawi where he was interviewed, instructed, and ordained by Seventh Day Baptists. A small work emerged from his efforts.

The most recent Baptist group is the National Baptist Convention of Zimbabwe, whose members were excluded in 1988 from the Baptist Convention for Pentecostalism. In 1989 they formed their convention which, despite its name, is not related to the National Baptists in the USA. This body practices speaking with tongues and divine healing. It began with four churches but today has twenty-three. In 1993 it was accepted into the BWA.

In 1992 four of the Baptist bodies—Baptist Union, Baptist Convention, United Baptist Church, and National Baptist Convention—formed the Baptist Heads of Denominations, comprised of the president and general secretary of each group. In 1993 this body hosted the General Council of the BWA and helped sponsor the Baptist World Youth Conference, both of which met in Harare. It is considering other opportunities of cooperation.

BIBLIOGRAPHY: For material on the Baptist Union, Southern Baptists, Providence Industrial Mission, and Seventh Day Baptists, see Davis Lee Saunders, *A History of Baptists in East and Central Africa* (Th.D. Dissertation, Southern Baptist Theological Seminary, 1973), 62–69, 73–119, 272–84. For additional information on the Baptist Union, see Sydney Hudson-Reed, *By Taking Heed...* (Roodepoort: Baptist Publishing House, 1983), 323–40, 343–46.

BAPTIST AND BAPTIST-RELATED MISSIONS

1. ANGOLA   UkBMS (1878), CaCBIM (1954), SBC (1968), BrB

2. BOTSWANA SBC (1968), NBC, BrB

3. LESOTHO   NBC (1961), SBC (1987)

4. MADAGASCAR   FrEA (1932), CBI (1966), SBC (1987)

5. MALAWI NBC (1900), SDBMS (1953), SBC (1959)

6. MAURITIUS SBC (1978)

7. MOZAMBIQUE SwFBU (1921), BrB (1971), SBC (1973–1975, 1986), EuEBM (1993), BrNB

8. NAMIBIA SBC (1968)

9. RÉUNION SBC (1985)

10. SOUTH AFRICA SwFBU (1892), NBC (1894), BIMI (1968), IFM (1975), SBC (1977), ABWE (1980), BBFI (1980), BrB (1980), EBM (1981), BWM (1988), ABC (1990)

11. SWAZILAND NBC (1971), SBC (1983)

12. ZAMBIA SoBMS (1913–1973), SwFBU (1931), SBC (1959), AuBMS (1969), BBFI (1989), BM-M (1991)

13. ZIMBABWE SBC (1950), IFM (1992), BrB, NMBC

NON-DENOMINATIONAL MISSION

1. MOZAMBIQUE SoGM (AEF) (1936)

6. Ghana	42,404	326
7. Guinea	67	4
8. Guinea-Bissau	—	—
9. Liberia	59,522	250
10. Mali	154	5
11. Niger Republic	600	8
12. Nigeria	629,586	4,837
13. Senegal	425	4
14. Sierra Leone	4,430	58
15. Togo	<u>11,600</u>	<u>186</u>
	775,673	6,171

BENIN (1966)

	Members	Churches
1. Convention Baptiste du Benin (1990)	1,806	(25)
2. Evangelical Baptist Mission	<u>300</u>	<u>(7)</u>
	2,106	(32)

*T*he small country of Benin, formerly called Dahomey and located between Nigeria and Togo, received independence from France in 1960. In 1966 Mr. and Mrs. Earl Watson, working with Evangelical Baptist Missions (EBM), began ministering in the coastal city of Cotonou, where the mission now has two churches. In the extreme north, EBM has engaged in bush evangelism and literacy ministries where it also has organized a number of churches and a Bible institute.

In 1970 Southern Baptists sent their first missionaries, Neville and Emma Claxton, to Contonou. Before their arrival, Yorubas from Nigeria already had established eight Baptist congregations in the country. In 1972 the Southern Baptist mission organized the first French-language Baptist church in Contonou, and since then two have been organized elsewhere. The Yoruba churches have formed two associations, and several congregations use a local language. A Baptist convention was formed in 1990. In outreach, the mission uses Theological Education by Extension (TEE), Bible correspondence, and films and also engages in medical work and agricultural projects.

BIBLIOGRAPHY: For Southern Baptist work, see *Your Guide to Foreign Missions,* 1992–1993, 42.

BURKINA FASO (1959)

	Members	Churches
Burkina Faso Baptist Convention (1977)	10,597	(113)

*T*he landlocked country of Burkina Faso, formerly called Upper Volta, gained independence from France in 1960. The country is predominantly animist with a strong Moslem presence and a small Christian minority (10 percent).

In 1959 officials of the FMB of the Southern Baptist Convention, visiting the country for possible entry of Southern Baptist missionaries, met with a small Yoruba congregation that had been established in Ouagadougou. The church requested mission help, and a missionary from northern Ghana began visiting the church at least twice yearly. In 1971 J. Bryant and Ina Durham settled in Ouagadougou as the first resident Southern Baptists. In 1977 twelve churches formed what is known today as the Burkina Faso Convention.

In Ouagadougou the Southern Baptist mission operates a Bible correspondence school and media center. The mission has established a dental clinic in another center and also engages in literacy and public health work. The Rural Training Center at Koudougou provides instruction in agriculture and other trades. The mission also produces Christian literature in the Moré language.

BIBLIOGRAPHY: For Southern Baptist work, see *Your Guide to Foreign Missions*, 1992–1993, 42–43.

CAPE VERDE (1955)

	Members	Churches
Baptist Church of Mindelo (1955)	43	(1)

*T*he Republic of Cape Verde, consisting of fifteen islands, lies about 285 miles off the western tip of Africa. In 1975 Cape Verde received its independence from Portugal. Most of the inhabitants are Roman Catholic with a few evangelical believers.

As a young man Manuel Ramos (b. 1915), who was converted in 1932 under the street preaching of a Nazarene missionary, became pastor of a church in Mindelo on the island of São Vicente. After reading about Baptists, he accepted Baptist beliefs and convinced 70 percent of his church to do the same. The church now considered itself Baptist. Individual Baptists provided some financial help but, since far more funds were needed, Ramos sent out an appeal in 1952 for help. The Baptist Missionary Association (BMA) responded but insisted that Ramos must first receive baptism on

Baptist authority. In 1955 he went to Portugal, where he was immersed by Joaquim Oliveira and ordained by a council of three ministers. Thereupon the BMA elected Ramos as its missionary.

Although Ramos has baptized many converts, his church at Mindelo remains small, partly because of emigration and death. With assistance from the USA, a church building was built in 1961. At present the church has a Sunday School of fifty pupils and three missions in the suburbs. Although Ramos has visited other islands, because of the expense of travel no permanent work has been established there.

BIBLIOGRAPHY: John W. Duggar, *The Baptist Missionary Association of America* (1950–1986), (Texarkana, Tex.: Baptist Publishing House, 1988), 99, 132–33, 259–60. "Cape Verde," *The Gleaner*, April, 1992, 4.

CÔTE D'IVOIRE (IVORY COAST) (1927)

	Members	Churches
1. Nigerian Baptist Convention (1930)	1,400	(22)
2. Union des Églises Evangéliques du Sud Ouest	2,772	(192)
3. Association des Églises Baptistes Evangéliques (1965)	4,500	(20)
4. Association des Églises Baptistes Libres (1992)	2,265*	(15)
5. Union des Églises Evangéliques Baptistes Meridionales (1984)	3,061	(95)
	13,998	(344)

*Average attendance

*C*ôte d'Ivoire, located on the south coast of West Africa between Liberia and Ghana, gained its independence from France in 1960. Before 1985 it was known as the Ivory Coast. About a third of the population is Christian, a quarter Moslem, and the rest tribal religionists. It has been one of the most stable and prosperous nations on the African continent.

Baptists were present before World War II. In 1927 the independent Tabernacle Baptist Church of Paris founded the Mission Biblique (MB) to provide support for an independent missionary and his wife. The mission grew and in 1960 had thirty-nine missionaries and eleven stations and published a bi-monthly paper. As a result of its work, a Union of Evangelical Churches of the Southwest has been formed. The Baptist General Conference (BGC) from America, deciding not to begin a Baptist body of its own, cooperates with the Union and encourages the churches it plants to affiliate with it.

In 1930 Yoruba Baptist traders from Nigeria began to establish congregations in Abidjan, the capital, and neighboring villages, gaining converts from the native population as well. These congregations became members of the Nigerian Baptist Convention. In 1993 the Home and Foreign Mission Board of the Nigerian Baptist Convention adopted the Côte d'Ivoire as a mission field for work among these churches.

After World War II, the newly formed Conservative Baptist Foreign Mission Society (CBFMS, today CBI) began to occupy in 1947 a field of more than one hundred square miles in northern Ivory Coast, inhabited primarily by Senufo and the Moslem Julas. The Christian and Missionary Alliance, unable to serve the entire field allotted to it, offered this area to CBFMS. Early work was very difficult, and the first baptism of seven young men did not occur until 1952. Missionaries undertook village evangelism, conducted Sunday School classes, provided limited medical services, and started to translate the Bible into several Senufo languages. In 1962 the mission established a hospital at Ferkéssédougou.

At the beginning of the 1960s, there were more than six hundred believers, two organized churches, and forty preaching points, but only about fifty believers had received baptism. In 1965 an Association of Evangelical Baptist Churches was formed. Because Senufo students were migrating to Abidjan, the mission extended its work to this city, far from its field in the north. A Senufo church was formed, which today is extending support to other groups in the suburbs. The mission now plans to follow Senufo people to other urban areas. Because of its success in launching a French-language magazine for children, CBI and other missions established an inter-mission Evangelical Publications Center. It is directed today by a CBI missionary to produce literature for Francophone Africa. With the help of teachers from other evangelical agencies, CBI operates the International Christian Academy, primarily a school for the children of missionaries. The mission also sponsors the Korhogo Bible School (1965) and the Bethel Bible Institute (1989), a French-speaking school.

The Free Will Baptist mission works primarily in the northeastern corner of the country, east of the Komoe River. In 1958, Lonnie and Anita Sparks arrived as the first Free Will Baptist missionaries, and two years later were joined by Bill and Joy Jones. In 1961 Dr. LaVerne Miley and his wife, Lorene, established a medical clinic in Doropo, which engages in an extensive medical ministry. The mission also has started a Bible institute program in Bouna. In 1992 the churches of the mission formed an Association of Free Baptist churches.

Southern Baptists did not enter until 1966. The first missionaries, John and Virginia Mills, were welcomed by the Yoruba churches, but their main purpose in coming was to work among the indigenous population by using French as the means of communication. By 1984 the work had grown to eleven churches when a Union of Southern Baptist Evangelical Churches was formed at Abidjan. The mission uses TEE and the Bible Way correspondence course and has established literature and media centers in Abidjan. It also engages in literacy and agricultural programs and has established a dental clinic at Bouaké. Because of the civil conflict in neighboring Liberia, many refugees have fled to the Côte d'Ivoire, which has opened the door for a relief ministry among them. Just inside the border Liberian refugees have formed eleven Baptist churches.

BIBLIOGRAPHY: For a reference to the Bible Mission of the Tabernacle Baptist Church of Paris, see Alexander de Chalandeu, *The History of the French-Speaking Countries of Europe* (Th.D. dissertation, Northern Baptist Theological Seminary, 1960), 117–18. For the work of CBI, see *Founded on the Word: Focused on the World* (Wheaton: CBFMS, 1978), 127–42, and Hans W. Finzel, ed., *Partners Together* (Wheaton: CBFMS, 1993), 24–29. For the beginning of Southern Baptist work, see Baker J. Cauthen and others, *Advance* (Nashville: Broadman Press, 1970), 173–74. For current Southern Baptist activity, see *Your Guide to Foreign Missions*, 1992–1993, 45–46.

THE GAMBIA (1979)

	Members	Churches
1. Association of Baptists for World Evangelism Mission	n/a	n/a
2. Southern Baptist Mission	141	(3)

*G*ambia is a sliver of a nation extending on both sides of the Gambia River within the heart of the country of Senegal. It received its independence from Great Britain in 1965. Its population is about 90 percent Muslim with less than 6 percent Christian, most of whom are Roman Catholic. Illiteracy is very high.

In 1979 Mel and Ruby Pittman, missionaries of the Association of Baptists for World Evangelism (ABWE) entered The Gambia, first settling in Banjul, the capital, but after a short time moved into the interior to Ndungu Kebbeh on the north bank of the Gambia River. In 1982 a medical center was opened but, after assistance from construction teams from the USA which renovated and enlarged the facilities, the new Ndunga Kebbeh Medical and Literacy Center was dedicated in 1989. Literacy work is in the Wolof language.

In 1982 Southern Baptists sent their first missionary couple, Ronald and Anita Hunt, who immediately engaged in the study of the Mandinka language. In November 1983 the mission opened in a suburb of Banjul a Baptist Community Center that provided crafts, sewing, cooking, sports, vocational training, Bible study, and correspondence courses. A community center also has been set up at Kanifing and a dental clinic at Farafenni. In its outreach, visual aids are important with the use of filmstrips, now translated into Mandinka, Wolof, and Fula, and the *Jesus* film, translated into Mandinka. Several churches, including the Glory Baptist Church in Banjul, have been established. The mission needs literature for Sunday Schools, correspondence work, and literacy programs.

BIBLIOGRAPHY: For material on the work of the ABWE at Ndungu Kebbeh, see Harold Amstutz, *Valued Heritage and Veritable Harvest* (Cherry Hill, N.J.: ABWE, c. 1991), 159–62. For the Southern Baptist mission, see *Your Guide to Foreign Missions*, 1990–1991, 19, and 1992–1993, 43–44.

GHANA (1918)

	Members	Churches
1. Ghana Baptist Convention (1947)	30,216	(289)
2. Ghana Association of Regular Baptist Churches	188	(15)
3. National Baptist Convention of America Mission	12,000	(22)
	42,404	(326)

After more than a century of control by Great Britain, Ghana, formerly known as the Gold Coast, was the first Black African nation to receive independence in 1957. More than 60 percent of the population is Christian with most members in the Roman Catholic, Methodist, Presbyterian, and Anglican churches. Baptists are a small but growing minority.

One early Baptist effort was the work of Mark C. Hayford, a Ghanaian, who received his call and ordination to the ministry while working in Nigeria. By 1926 Hayford had planted about forty-five churches, but after his death in 1935 they began to die.

Immigrant Yoruba Baptists from Nigeria began to enter the country to trade, establishing their first congregation in 1918. By 1920 they had grouped themselves into churches in all the major trading towns across the country. Because of the exclusive use of the Yoruba language, the churches made no impact on the Ghanaian community. In 1935 the churches formed the Yoruba Baptist Association, affiliated with the Nigerian Baptist Convention. On February 17, 1947, the first Southern Baptist missionaries, Homer and Ossie Littleton, arrived from Nigeria to work with the association, while the Nigerian Baptist Convention also sent John Idowu and his wife. Both couples settled in Kumasi where a church soon was organized. In the next year churches were established in Tamale and Sekondi. The first indigenous Ghanaian church with a continuous history was not formed until 1952. The Ghana Baptist Mission established a hospital at Nalerigu (1958), a training center (now a seminary at Abuakwa) and a training center at Tamale.

In 1947 the Yorubu association became the Gold Coast Baptist Conference and continued its affiliation with the Nigerian Convention until 1963. In 1964 it changed its name to Ghana Baptist Convention. In 1969 the Ghana government instituted a new aliens immigration policy that forced most of the Yorubas to leave the country, adversely affecting Baptist work. Most church buildings were left empty, and the convention lost its leaders.

With the cooperation of missionaries of the Ghana Baptist Mission, the convention was reorganized and registered with the government in 1973. From then on a truly indigenous Ghanaian Baptist work began to emerge and growth was rapid in membership, churches, seminary graduates, and ministry. In 1986 the convention suffered the misfortune of a split by the convention's call for a change in structural relationships with the Ghana Baptist Mission. In August 1992 a reconciliation of the two convention factions and the Ghana Baptist Mission was achieved through an agreed structure for single work.

At present the convention has fourteen associations, three hundred fifty churches and preaching stations, a membership of thirty thousand, one hundred thirty ministers, and a budget of about $45,000. Ghanaian Baptists remain conservative evangelicals, committed to soul winning and church planting. They also are committed to ministries that help meet physical and socioeconomic needs through nurseries, schools, adult literacy classes, and agricultural ventures. Direct evangelism is the responsibility of the local church, while the association takes care of home missions. Christian education is conducted mainly through the Sunday Schools and church training organizations. The main auxiliary groups are the Men's, Women's, Youth, and Adult Fellowships as well as student unions.

More than half of the members are between twenty-five and thirty-five years of age. About 40 percent is within the middle-wage income group; about 20 percent has an educational background of senior high school and above, while the majority of membership comes from urban tradesmen and rural peasants.

Worship services are conducted in various Ghanaian languages with English in some urban churches. The form of worship has evolved from traditional Southern Baptist pattern to one with Ghanaian cultural inflections. The service may include a period of hand-raising, singing, and mass prayer. Music may include hymns and local choruses with clapping and dancing to the tune of drums and guitar.

The convention is a member of the Christian Council of Ghana, an affiliate of the World Council of Churches, through which the convention also relates to the government on national issues. The convention has no direct relation with other Baptists in the country. It publishes a quarterly magazine, *The Baptist News*.

Kojo Osei-Wusuh

Other Baptists: Since Ghana's independence, National Baptists from the United States have provided some assistance. The FMB of the National Baptist Convention, USA entered in 1958, providing financial assistance to three churches, which were practically deserted with the Yoruba exodus. The FMB of the National Baptist Convention of America, which entered in 1980, is supporting an expanding Baptist work whose major centers are in Accra, Kumas, and Obusai, which is the site of the James Carl Sams Children's Center.

Baptist Mid-Missions has been in Ghana since 1946 from whose work a Ghana Association of Regular Baptist Churches has been formed. The churches of this mission are primarily on the coast around Accra and Tema and in the extreme northwest in the Upper Region. A Baptist Bible Institute has been established at Wa. The mission is engaged in literacy work and is supporting an effort to translate the New Testament and part of the Old Testament in the Wali language.

A Ghanaian, who had accepted the seventh day as the Sabbath, wrote in 1898 to a Seventh Day Baptist church of Richburg, New York (believing from its name it was wealthy), requesting financial assistance for two Africans to go to America to study. The publication of the letter stirred an interest among Seventh Day Baptists. After investigating the field, the Missionary Board of the denomination sent Peter Velthuysen to the field in 1902, but he died from tropical fever three months after arrival. In the 1960s there was a group of Seventh Day Baptists in the country who communicated with European Seventh Day Baptists, but Seventh Day Baptists have never again been able to send a missionary, nor have they incorporated the group into their World Federation.

BIBLIOGRAPHY: The work by Baker J. Cauthen and others, *Advance* (Nashville: Broadman Press, 1970), 154–57, contains material on the early history of the Southern Baptist mission. *Field Surveys* (Cleveland: Baptist Mid-Missions, c. 1977), 11–14, provides an account of the work of Baptist Mid-Missions. The pamphlet by Emmanuel Dorbadzi, "Focusing on Ghana, West Africa," (Dallas: FMB of the NBC of America), provides data on the Baptist work which the FMB of the National Baptist Convention of America is helping to finance. An account of Seventh Day Baptists may be found in Don A. Sanford, *A Choosing People* (Nashville: Broadman Press, 1992), 293–96.

GUINEA (1988)

	Members	Churches
Southern Baptist Mission	67	(4)

G uinea was a French territory until 1958 when it declared its independence. It is heavily Moslem (around 69 percent) with an extremely small Christian minority of a little more than 1 percent. In 1988 Southern Baptists sent a mission couple to Conakry, the capital, where they began language study. In 1990 the government of Guinea granted the Southern Baptist mission a protocol, or official recognition. A French/Susu church has been formed, and expatriates from Sierra Leone maintain two small churches and a preaching point. In October 1991 a Baptist center was opened which offers English classes. The mission opened another station in 1993 at Forecariah. The Baptist work is still in its infancy but has an open door in a predominantly Moslem land.

BIBLIOGRAPHY: For information on the Southern Baptist mission, see *Your Guide to Foreign Missions*, 1992–1993, 44–45; 1994–1995, 46–47.

GUINEA-BISSAU (1993)

T he little country of Guinea-Bissau, sandwiched in between Senegal and Guinea, gained independence from Portugal in 1974. About half the inhabitants are traditional tribalists, while 38 percent are Moslem and 10 percent Christian, mostly Roman Catholic. In December 1992 a Southern Baptist couple, Michael and Lynn Hutchinson, made an exploratory trip, and early in the following year established residency. There are only two other Protestant missions which have missionaries assigned to the country.

BIBLIOGRAPHY: For Southern Baptist work, see *Your Guide to Foreign Missions*, 1994–1995, 47.

The assassination sent shock waves through the Baptist community in Liberia and abroad, but Baptist work adjusted to new conditions. In 1989 civil war broke out and then resumed in 1992 with an attack on Monrovia itself, causing much disruption with many thousands dead or fleeing as refugees. Baptist Relief Services, coordinated by the Southern Baptist mission and the United Nations, provided humanitarian assistance. Ricks Institute reopened in 1991, and the Liberia Baptist Theological Seminary, the only seminary now operating in the country, resumed work in 1992. In spite of chaotic conditions, Baptist work continues. As one example, the historic Providence Baptist Church, although closed for six months in 1990, has grown from 1,200 members in 1989 to 2,700 at present.

BIBLIOGRAPHY: A very helpful survey of both Southern Baptist and National Baptist work in Liberia from a Virginia perspective is Nan F. Weeks and Blanche Sydnor White, *Liberia for Christ* (Richmond: Woman's Missionary Union of Virginia, 1959). Leroy Fitts has written, *Lott Carey: First Black Missionary to Africa* (Valley Forge: Judson Press, 1978), which includes an account of the work of the Lott Carey Baptist Foreign Mission Convention in Liberia and other fields. For additional information on Black Baptist involvement in Liberia, see William J. Harvey III, *Bridges Across the Seas* (Philadelphia: FMB of the NBC, USA, 1989), which relates the work of the National Baptist Convention, USA, and Walter L. Williams, *Black Americans and the Evangelization of Africa* (Madison: University of Wisconsin Press, 1982). The work of Baptist Mid-Missions may be found in *Field Surveys* (Cleveland: Baptist Mid-Missions, c. 1977) and Joseph Conrad Wold, *God's Impatience in Liberia* (Grand Rapids: William B. Eerdmans, 1968), 69–72. For Southern Baptist work, see Baker J. Cauthen and others, *Advance* (Nashville: Broadman Press, 1970), 136–40, 169–72. A very perceptive article on the close relations of church and state in Liberia is by a former Southern Baptist missionary in Liberia, William A. Poe, who wrote, "Not Christopolis but Christ and Caesar: Baptist Leadership in Liberia," *Journal of Church and State*, 24 (winter 1982): 535–51.

MALI (1951)

	Members	Churches
1. Evangelical Baptist Mission	100	(2)
2. Southern Baptist Mission	54	(3)
	154	(5)

*M*ali is a large landlocked country in the Sahel. The climate is hot and dry and only 2 percent of the land is arable. The population is more than 80 percent Moslem with a Christian minority of around 2 percent. In 1960 Mali gained independence from France.

Between 1925 and 1938 the Christian and Missionary Alliance undertook mission work in the area of Gao and Tombouctou (Timbuktu), cities located in the center of the nation near or on the big loop of the Niger River. In 1950 the Alliance turned over its missionary concession to Evangelical Baptist Missions (EBM). In 1951 Daniel Zimmerman and his wife went to the fanatically Moslem city of Gao where in time a Baptist church was formed. In 1952 Mr. and Mrs. David Marshall went to the fabled city of Tombouctou, which many popularly think of as the end of the earth. There was not a native Christian in more than a hundred miles in any direction, but eventually a church was founded here also. The members of both churches came primarily from other areas. Besides these congregations, the mission also has a church in the making at Dire and several other stations. The three congregations have national pastors, all converts from Islam.

In 1960 EBM acquired a houseboat to visit villages on the Niger River. One of the most effective means of outreach has been bookstores or reading rooms. The mission peddles Christian literature in markets or other commercial areas and also provides some medical and dental services. In an effort to reach Tauregs, the mission started a water project in Tombouctou in 1985. A Bible school has been established in Gao.

After learning of a development project conducted by Southern Baptists in Burkina Faso, the ambassador of Mali to the USA requested Southern Baptists to enter the country. Since at the time Southern Baptists already were considering Mali as a potential field from a survey conducted in 1982, the FMB of the Southern Baptist Convention immediately accepted the request, transferring a missionary couple from Burkina Faso to the western part of the country. In 1988 the mission opened a Baptist center in Bamako, the capital, and in 1990 a church was organized in the city. Another station, which reaches out to the Malinke people, is at Kéniéba where a church has been organized and several preaching points established. The mission uses film, the Bible Way correspondence course, and TEE.

BIBLIOGRAPHY: For the beginnings of the work of the Evangelical Baptist Mission, see William J. Hopewell, Jr., *The Missionary Emphasis of the General Association of Regular Baptist Churches* (Chicago: Regular Baptist Press, 1963), 108–10. For Southern Baptist work, see *Your Guide to Foreign Missions*, 1992–1993, 46–47.

NIGER REPUBLIC (1929)

	Members	Churches
Evangelical Baptist Missions and independent expatriate churches	600	(8)

*T*he Niger Republic is another landlocked country with a hot climate and little arable land. It received its independence from France in 1960. About 90 percent of the population is Moslem, and Christians are a tiny minority. Under the auspices of Evangelical Baptist Missions (EBM), Mr. and Mrs. McCaba and Mrs. A. G. Ollis entered the field in 1929, settling in Niamey on the Niger River, the capital of the territory. The mission is confined to the southwest corner of the country and has worked primarily among the Zarma tribe, which lives in the Niger valley.

McCaba translated a large part of the New Testament into the Zarma language, and in 1990 the mission completed the entire Bible in that language. In spite of a number of losses of missionary personnel through sickness and accident, EBM has been able to continue its work. It engages in evangelism and church planting, continues Bible translation, conducts literacy programs, and operates an elementary school and an evening Bible school.

EBM has two churches among the Zarma tribe—in Niamey and in Dosso—and three among the Gourma—one in Niamey and two in the villages. In Niamey there is a French church, an English church, and a Yoruba church, all occupying the same building, primarily ministering to expatriates.

Southern Baptist personnel entered Niger Republic in 1973, transferring from Nigeria. In 1990 the mission gained a protocol or legal recognition. After engaging in famine relief, it now concentrates on evangelism through cassettes and literature. It is cooperating with the EBM and Sudan Interior Mission (SIM) to translate the *Jesus* film into the Zarma language. The mission conducts a Baptist center which houses a library and offers English classes. No permanent church as yet has resulted from its work. Another mission, Baptist International Missions, has been working since 1966 among a predominantly nomadic people, finding the work difficult and slow.

BIBLIOGRAPHY: For the early work of Evangelical Baptist Missions, see William J. Hopewell, Jr., *The Missionary Emphasis of the General Association of Regular Baptist Churches* (Chicago: Regular Baptist Press, 1963), 105–08. For the work of Southern Baptists, see *Your Guide to Foreign Missions*, 1992–1993, 47, and 1994–1995, 49.

NIGERIA (1850)

	Members	Churches
1. Nigerian Baptist Convention (1919)	608,400	(4,656)
2. Mambilla Baptist Convention (1973)	18,046	(170)
3. Nigerian Conference of Seventh Day Baptists (1975)	2,140	(9)
4. United African Baptist Church (1938)	n/a	(n/a)
5. Benin United Baptist Mission of Nigeria (1942)	1,000	(2)
6. Gospel Baptist Convention (1950)	n/a	(n/a)
7. Evangelical Baptist Convention	n/a	(n/a)
8. Christ Temple Baptist Church	n/a	(n/a)
9. Calvary Association of Baptist Churches	n/a	(n/a)
	629,586	(4,837)

W ith a population of more than eighty-eight million, Nigeria is Africa's most highly populated country. It is a nation of many tribes with about 50 percent of the population Christian and 45 percent Moslem. Christians prevail in the south but Moslems dominate in the north. Great Britain granted Nigeria independence in 1960, but since then Nigeria has had a difficult time in establishing democratic rule.

Baptists have been in Nigeria nearly one hundred fifty years and constitute one of its largest denominations. The FMB of the Southern Baptist Convention established the work. The pioneer missionary, Thomas Jefferson Bowen of Jackson County, Georgia, landed at Badagry on August 5, 1850, and then proceeded to Yorubaland in Western Nigeria.

The work was slow at first because of weather conditions, the language barrier, inadequacy of missionary personnel, poor transportation, the hostility of some of the traditional rulers, the resilience of the traditional religion, and the threat of Islam. The pioneer period also coincided with the period of fratricidal civil wars in Yorubaland which was compounded by the Civil War in the USA which cut off funds. Between 1869 and 1874, Southern Baptists had no missionary in Nigeria, except Mrs. Sarah Harden, widow of a missionary who served without mission status.

Because of disputes between the missionaries and African leaders, the mission experienced a schism in 1888 when two hundred Nigerians left the Lagos church to form the Native Baptist Church, leaving only twenty-four in the original church. Although this episode was regarded initially as a tragedy, it was significant in many respects. It was the first expression in Nigeria of African initiative and nationalism in church life. The mission and the Native Baptist Church also now worked with greater zeal in establishing churches and preaching stations over the whole of southern Nigeria.

In 1914 the two bodies reunited under the umbrella of the Yoruba Baptist Association—1,646 members and fourteen churches came from the Native Church, while 1,234 members and seventeen churches from the churches cooperating with the mission. Five years later, the Yoruba Baptist Asssociation metamorphosed into the Nigerian Baptist Convention. The convention was essentially missionary in nature, and it drew the churches closer together for organized effort.

Since the 1930s Nigerian Baptists have enjoyed rapid growth. In 1937 the convention reported 211 churches and preaching stations and 21,214 members. While most of the churches were concentrated in the southwest among the Yorubas, churches began to spring up in the eastern and northern parts. At the end of 1970 there were 75,988 members, 455 churches, 934 mission points, and 539 trained pastors. Today there are more than 600,000 members and 4,600 churches, and about 1,550 trained pastors of various grades. In 1970 there were 216 missionaries but only around one hundred today, indicating the increasing national character of the work. The most important Baptist center in the country is at Ogbomosho, where the Nigerian Baptist Theological Seminary, Baptist Medical Centre, a nursing school, Kersey Children's Home, and Baptist Media Centre are located. In this area there are more than a hundred Baptist churches, and their members have scattered all over Nigeria planting Baptist work.

The Women's Missionary Union (WMU) is very strong, an indispensable auxiliary to the Nigerian Baptist Convention. Despite the negative attitude to women's role and a relative trivialization of their worth in traditional Nigerian society, the WMU has demonstrated in practical ways women's capabilities with grace and dignity. With its own budgets and leadership, the WMU seeks to draw out Nigerian Baptist women for practical evangelistic and missionary efforts. Special emphases include giving instruction in Bible and mission study, Christian service, prayer, and systematic giving. It also has established clinics, camps, classes in child and home care, and literacy work. WMU also includes the Lydia Auxiliary, Girls' Auxiliary, and Sunbeam Band. The Men's Missionary Union (MMU) also seeks to draw men together for practical evangelistic effort, but in many churches the MMU is less active than the women's organization. MMU also includes Royal Ambassadors for boys.

Baptist Convention (Ibadan: Baptist Press, 1975). J. A. Atanda, ed., Baptist Churches in Nigeria, 1850–1950 (Ibadan: University Press, 1988). Carlton F. Whirley, The Baptists of Nigeria: A Story to Tell (Nashville: Convention Press, 1988). Samuel Ade Ajayi, The Origin and Growth of Baptist Mission Work in Yorubaland, 1850–1960 (Ph.D. dissertation, University of Ibadan, 1992). Travis Collins, The Baptist Mission of Nigeria, 1850–1993 (Ibadan: Associated Book-Makers Nigeria Limited, 1993). For data on independent Baptist groups, see David B. Barrett, ed., World Christian Encyclopedia (Nairobi: Oxford University Press, 1982), 530–531.

SENEGAL (1962)

	Members	Churches
1. Conservative Baptist Mission	202	(1)
2. Southern Baptist Mission	223	(3)
	425	(4)

Senegal, on the extreme western tip of Africa, gained independence from France in 1960. More than 90 percent of the population is Moslem with 5 to 6 percent Christian, including an insignificant number of Protestants. When Baptist missionaries entered the territory, they had to start from scratch, gaining converts one by one. Although the work has been slow, both Baptist missions have shown progress in a very difficult field.

Conservative Baptists entered Senegal in 1962 because of civil conflict in Zaire. After a period of language study, Donald and Peg Penney moved to Thiès to begin a mission to the Wolof people. The first convert was won in 1965, who with two others was baptized in 1965. In 1980 the Evangelical Baptist Church of Thiès was formed. In 1971 Conservative Baptists moved farther inland to Diourbel to work among the Serere. The mission opened an Evangelistic Center in Thiès in 1966, which included a bookstore and reading room. Today there are nine groups, each with lay leaders who preach and teach. Conservative Baptists contributed to the translation of the New Testament in Wolof, which was ready for the public in 1988. The mission also began a witness among Mares from Mauritania, but in 1989 Senegal expelled the Maures, and the promising contacts with them were lost.

Southern Baptists entered in 1969 and have concentrated their work in Dakar, the capital, a city with a French and African blend and the gateway to Western Africa. In 1970 the mission opened a Baptist center, starting with a reading room and youth center. It later began another center at Bignona. The mission sponsors well-baby clinics and a radio ministry, which is also heard in Mauritania. Today the mission has three Baptist churches in the city—the International Baptist Church (English), Jungu Baptist (Wolof), and Église Baptiste de Dakar (French).

BIBLIOGRAPHY: The work of Conservative Baptists may be found in Founded on the Word: Focused on the World (Wheaton: CBFMS, 1978), 233–43, and Hans W. Finzel, ed., Partners Together (Wheaton: CBFMS, 1993), 44–47. For Southern Baptist efforts, see Your Guide to Foreign Missions, 1992–1993, 48–49, and 1994–1995, 50–51.

SIERRA LEONE (1792)

	Members	Churches
1. Baptist Convention of Sierra Leone (1974)	4,230	(36)
2. Emmanuel Baptist Conference (1993)	200	(22)
	4,430	(58)

*I*n 1787 Great Britain established Sierra Leone as a refuge for former slaves. After remaining a British colony for almost 175 years, Sierra Leone gained independence in 1961. As in Liberia, an elite class of former slaves, or Creoles, gained a dominant social position in the territory. Today only 10 percent of the population is Christian, while 50 percent is traditional religionists and 40 percent Moslem.

Among the early settlers were Black Baptists who in 1792 migrated from Nova Scotia in Canada with their pastor David George (1743–1810). George had been born in Virginia from parents who had been enslaved in Africa. After fleeing to Georgia and joining the first all-Black Baptist Church of Silver Bluff, South Carolina (formed c. 1773–1775), George was evacuated to Nova Scotia by the British in 1782, near the end of the American Revolutionary War.

The Baptist chapel which George established in Freetown in 1792 and which merged with the Church of God Baptist is the oldest Baptist church on the African continent. Because of the vicissitudes of Baptist life in the country, the comparatively small number of Baptists who first settled, and the lack of sustained Baptist interest in the territory until just recently, it is almost miraculous that Baptists have such an old congregation, antedating the next oldest by thirty years.

The effort of the Baptist Missionary Society (BMS) to begin a mission in Sierra Leone in 1794 ended in a fiasco with the expulsion of its missionary in 1797 for interfering in colonial affairs. Beginning in 1855 Southern Baptists included Sierra Leone with their field in Liberia, but the mission was small in effort, and disrupted by the American Civil War. After the war the mission was discontinued because of the interest in Nigeria. Of the three independent chapels established among the early settlers— Methodists, Countess of Huntingdon's Connexion, and Baptists—the Baptists were the smallest in number, and after George's death were lowest in social standing and associated with poverty.

By 1838, if not before, William Jenkins had established an African Baptist Church in Goderich Street in Freetown, a congregation of Ibos, separate from the old Baptist body which met on Rawdon Street. Some years after Jenkins' death in 1858, the church joined the other Baptists. In 1853 J. J. Bowen, Southern Baptist missionary to Nigeria, and two associates visited Freetown and ordained two men for the ministry. In 1859 there were only two Baptist churches related to Southern Baptist work—the church in Freetown with seventy-two members and one in Waterloo with thirty-four, which later transferred its membership to the Freetown congregation.

In spite of lack of mission funds, the Freetown Church continued for some years. By 1902, if not earlier, its members joined the Church of God, a free-will denomination of Baptist sentiments which John McCormack, a longtime resident of Sierra Leone, had established in Freetown. McCormack, on a trip to Liverpool in 1852, was converted to this denomination and on his return held services in his home. Upon his death in 1865, he left money to construct a building on Regent Road for his church. For many years the church was led by a son of a paramount chief, William Thomas George Lawson, and in turn by his son.

For many years the Baptist Commonwealth and Colonial Society (BCCS), incorporated within the BMS, provided funds annually to the Church of God Baptist from a trust which a friend of McCormack had established. During his tour of inspection from 1954 to 1957, F. C. Morton, treasurer of the BCCS, helped to settle problems in the Church of God Baptist. He also helped to bring to completion the building of the Robert Street Baptist Church, a congregation of Bassa from Liberia which Mrs. Mary Snowball had founded in 1921 in her home. Beginning in 1957 the BMS and BCCS began to provide missionary assistance, but the Church of God Baptist catered only to the Creoles and showed no interest in evangelistic outreach. In 1966 the BCCS cut off all financial aid to it.

Clifford Gill, BMS missionary in Sierra Leone who had earlier served in Zaire, entered work in Freetown but was discouraged with the prospect of outreach from the Church of God Baptist. In an effort to reach out, he requested the paramount chief, a Moslem, to allow him to commence Christian work in Mambolo. Instead of refusal, the chief recognized the educational and medical benefits of a Christian mission and gave his approval. Because the BMS felt unable to assume financial responsibility, the European Baptist Mission (EuEBM) accepted the field in 1965 with the BMS seconding Gill and his wife to the EuEBM. In 1968 the mission opened a secondary school and a dispensary. In 1971 the first nine Moslem converts were baptized.

In 1974 the Sierra Leone Baptist Convention was formed with headquarters today at Lunsar, seventy-six miles from Freetown. Lunsar not only includes the Baptist office but also the Baptist Eye Hospital (1975), a training center, and a radio recording studio. The convention operates a primary school and two secondary schools and, besides maintaining the training center at Lunsar, also helps to support the Sierra Leone Bible College.

Since the Second World War, several other Baptist missions have also entered Sierra Leone. In 1984 the Southern Baptists sent veteran missionaries from Nigeria, Albert H. and Ruth Dyson, to work with the Sierra Leone Baptist Convention and EBM. The National Baptist Convention, USA, has had an interest in Sierra Leone since 1950, providing support for the Roosevelt-Vine Memorial Secondary School in Freetown. In 1961 the Home and Foreign Mission Board of the Nigerian Baptist Convention sent F. P. Boyo and I. O. Badejogbim to begin work in Bumbuna in northern Sierra Leone. In 1972 the mission had only one church but today has twenty-two. Although members of the Nigerian Baptist mission were invited to join the Sierra Leone Baptist Convention, they have remained separate and in 1993 organized the Emmanuel Baptist Conference.

BIBLIOGRAPHY: For a general history of Baptist work, see S. J. Valcarcel, *A Short History of Baptists in Sierra Leone, 1792–1984* (Bad Homburg, Germany: European Baptist Mission, 1984). Baptist work in the nineteenth century may be found in Christopher Fyfe, "The Baptist Churches in Sierra Leone," *The Sierra Leone Bulletin of Religion*, 5 (1963): 55–60. A very helpful biography of David George is the work by Grant Gordon, *From Slavery to Freedom: The Life of David George, Pioneer Black Baptist Minister* (Hantsport, N.S., Canada: Lancelot Press, 1992). It includes in its appendices valuable documents, including letters of David George from Sierra Leone that appeared in the periodical edited by John Rippon in London, *Baptist Annual Register*, 1 (1790–1793) and 2 (1793–1797). Also see James W. St. G. Walker, *The Black Loyalists* (New York: Africana Publishing Company, 1976), 195–202, 289–91, 347–48, 369–73, for material on Baptists in the country in the nineteenth century.

TOGO (1959)

	Members	Churches
1. Convention Baptiste du Togo (1988)	11,600	(180)
2. Association of Baptists for World Evangelism Mission	n/a	(6)
	11,600	(186)

*T*ogo is a small country between Benin and Ghana. Britain and France, after gaining Togo from Germany during World War I, held it as trusteeships until the British sector joined Ghana in 1957 and the French sector became the independent Republic of Togo in 1960. Togo's population is about 30 percent Christian, 20 percent Moslem, while the rest are traditional religionists.

In a visit to Togo in 1958, a Southern Baptist missionary from Ghana found about six Baptist congregations already founded by Yoruba traders. The congregation in the capital city of Lomé, however, became the first formally organized Baptist church in 1959 and associated with the Baptists of Ghana. Upon the request for missionaries, Southern Baptists in 1964 sent G. Clayton and Helen Bond, the first Southern Baptist missionaries in a French-speaking land in Africa. They established a Baptist Center in Lomé, and in 1967 work was begun about 200 miles north in Sokodé. In 1971 a pastors' school was organized in Lomé, the Baptist School of Theology for West Africa. In 1988 the Togo Baptist Convention was formed, which has joined the Association of Evangelicals of Africa and Madagascar.

The mission conducts a film ministry, literature distribution, literacy programs, TEE, and the Bible Way correspondence course. It also operates an experimental farm.

The Association of Baptists for World Evangelism sent Dal and Kay Washer in 1974 to Lomé as its first missionaries. The mission has established a Blind Center, which teaches Braille, located now in Kpalime, and also the Karolyn Kempton Memorial Christian Hospital. The mission maintains a Baptist Publication Center, which publishes material in the Ewe langauge, and conducts Bible institutes at Kpalime and Lomé.

BIBLIOGRAPHY: For Southern Baptist work, see the booklet, *West Africa*, (Richmond: FMB, SBC, 1973), 22–27, and *Your Guide to Foreign Missions*, 1994–1995, 52–53. For the work of the ABWE, see Harold T. Commons, *Heritage & Harvest* (Cherry Hill, N.J.: ABWE, 1981), 85, and other literature on Togo from the ABWE.

BAPTIST AND BAPTIST-RELATED MISSIONS

1. BENIN   EBM (1966), SBC (1970), BWM (1991)

2. BURKINA FASO SBC (1971)

3. CAPE VERDE   BMA (1956)

4. CÔTE D'IVOIRE FrMB (1927), CBI (1947), FWB (1958), SBC (1966), BIMI (1970), EBM (1971), BM-M (1974), BGC (1977), BBFI (1988), NiNBC (1993), SBIC (1994)

5. THE GAMBIA ABWE (1979), SBC (1982)

6. GHANA   BM-M (1946), SBC (1947), NBC (1958), BIMI (1976), WBF (1977), NBCA (1980), ABWE (1992)

7. GUINEA   SBC (1988)

8. GUINEA-BISSAU SBC (1993)

9. LIBERIA   ABMU (1822–1856), SBC (1846–1875, 1960), NBC (1882), LC (1897), BM-M (1938), NBCA (1959), BIMI (1985), PNBC

10. MALI   EBM (1951), SBC (1983)

11. NIGER REPUBLIC   EBM (1929), BIMI (1966), SBC (1973)

12. NIGERIA   SBC (1850), NABC (1961), LC (1962), PNBC (1963), ABA (1976), BIMI (1982), EBM (1985), BBFI (1987), BWM, MBM

13. SENEGAL   CBI (1962), SBC (1969), BIMI (1975)

14. SIERRA LEONE   SBC (1855–1861, 1984), NBC (1950), NiNBC (1961), EuEBM (1965)

15. TOGO   SBC (1964), ABWE (1974)

II. Asia and Oceania

The continent of Asia and Oceania include about three million persons in all Baptist bodies. Asia witnessed the earliest foreign mission efforts of British and American Baptists and includes some of their most productive fields. Even though it was here the Christian faith was born, Asia has been one of the most resistant areas to the Christian gospel with its strong Moslem, Hindu, and Buddhist majorities and with millions more who are adherents of syncretistic faiths. In most nations of Asia, Christians of all kinds number 10 percent or less of the total population, with some countries having practically no Christians within the native population. Only the Philippines, Korea, and the countries of Oceania have a high percentage of Christians.

Asia's three billion people include more than half the world's population. The three million Baptists (one person in a thousand) seem a small minority indeed. On the other hand, except in Moslem Southwest Asia, Baptists are rather well located throughout the continent. They have a significant concentration of strength in southern India and have created practically a Baptist belt extending from northeast India across Burma into northern Thailand. There are also large numbers of Baptists in the Philippines and Indonesia. They have become indigenous within a number of groups who are willing to evangelize their own people with some of them now crossing international boundaries. Increasingly, Asiatics themselves are assuming responsibility for mission work. In China, where there is no recognized Baptist body, Baptist principles without the Baptist name are followed widely.

In 1927 there were about 375,000 Baptists in Asia and Oceania, including fifty-five thousand in China. As recently as 1965, Baptists, excluding those in China who could no longer be counted, were approaching a million. Today, a generation later, Baptists have three times as many members, which indicates that much future growth for Baptists will probably come from this part of the world.

Region	Countries	Members	Churches
A. East Asia	6	439,515	2,625
B. Oceania	11	129,541	1,640
C. South Asia	6	1,419,474	8,704
D. Southeast Asia	8	971,772	9,639
E. Southwest Asia	9	3,468	68
	40	2,963,770	22,676

A. EAST ASIA

*B*aptists from the West have put some of their largest mission investment into East Asia, particularly in territories inhabited by the Chinese. Baptists entered China early, and after their separation both Northern and Southern Baptists from the USA continued their mission involvement in the country, developing a number of important fields. British and Swedish Baptists also played a role. With the closing of mainland China to Christian mission work, the surrounding areas became significantly enhanced for mission service. Japan, a country where Baptists lagged far behind others in converts, received greater attention, Hong Kong became a major mission center, and Taiwan was entered. Ironically, Korea, a territory which Baptists had practically ignored until after World War II and which was dropped suddenly into the lap of Southern Baptists with the appeal of a church body for help, has become by far the most productive field for Baptists.

In spite of the control of much of the territory by Communist regimes in China and North Korea, Baptists continue to be lured to East Asia. Numerous conservative evangelical Baptist missions have sent missionaries to the area, particularly to Japan and Taiwan. Baptists now use nontraditional methods to provide a Christian witness in the Communist world, especially in China, and have even attempted to probe North Korea. The most recent country in East Asia accessible to Baptists is Mongolia—a nation until recently under firm Communist control and closed to all Christian work.

	Members	Churches
1. China	—	—
2. Hong Kong/Macao	47,113	94
3. Japan	47,967	620
4. Korea	323,750	1,713
5. Mongolia	17	1
6. Taiwan (Republic of China)	20,668	197
	439,515	2,625

CHINA (1836)

*T*he Chinese Empire, regarding itself as the Middle Kingdom, the center of the world, and proud of its ancient heritage, resisted Western encroachment. Although Nestorians had brought Christianity to China as early as the seventh century, it had died out twice before the Jesuits were able to reestablish it for a third time in the sixteenth century. In the eighteenth century the government expelled the Catholic missionaries, except those who continued to serve as astronomers, and periodically persecuted the Christian minority. At the beginning of the nineteenth century, the Christian presence was weak. Most Christians were Roman Catholic, with a very small contingent of Russian Orthodox in Peking. There were no Protestants. Although the regime prohibited Christian missionaries and the spread of the Christian faith, Robert Morrison, a Presbyterian appointed by the London Mission Society, was able to settle in Canton in 1807. He engaged in literary work while also serving as translator for the British East India Company.

Although arriving some years after Morrison, Baptists were among the pioneers in the 1830s who sought to reach the Chinese with the gospel. The Triennial Convention appointed William Dean as a missionary to the Chinese but, as China was still closed, Dean first settled in 1836 in Bangkok in Siam (Thailand). There in 1837 he formed the first Protestant Chinese church in all Asia, a Baptist congregation which still exists. The Triennial Convention appointed a second missionary, John Lewis Shuck (1814–1863), a native of Virginia, for the Chinese mission. He and his wife, Henrietta (1817–1844), after studying Chinese for five months in Singapore, arrived in 1836 in Macau, a Portuguese enclave on the Chinese mainland. Henrietta was the first female American missionary in China. A third Baptist missionary, Issachar J. Roberts (1802–1871), a native of Tennessee, went out independently, supported by his own Roberts Fund Society, and arrived in Macau in 1837. Although restricted in public evangelism, Shuck baptized in 1837 a Chinese who soon left the Christian faith. Henrietta established a school for both Chinese boys and girls and wrote articles on Chinese life, which were later published in a book.

During the First British War (or Opium War), Great Britain seized Hong Kong Island in January 1841. In the following year China was not only forced by treaty to recognize the British possession of Hong Kong but also was required to open to trade and foreign settlement five ports—Canton, Amoy, Fuchou, Ningpo, and Shanghai. In 1856 a Second British, or Opium War, which France also joined, resulted in the Treaties of Tientsin of 1858. This action opened eleven more ports, extended toleration to Christians, and permitted missionaries and other foreigners to travel into the interior. Baptists now took advantage of the concessions which the Western powers had imposed on a reluctant China. In 1842 Shuck and Roberts (who in 1841 became a missionary of the Triennial Convention) settled in Hong Kong, where they were joined by Dean, who had left Bangkok. In May 1842 Shuck formed the Queen's Road Baptist Church, and a year later Dean established the Tie Chiu Church, a Swatow congregation. The formation of these churches, the first Baptist congregations in the Pacific basin, preceded the formation of the first Baptist church on the West Coast of America—the West Union Baptist Church in Oregon in May 1844.

The separation of Northern and Southern Baptists in 1845 also divided the American Baptist mission. Dean remained with the Northern Baptists, which changed the Triennial Convention into the American Baptist Missionary Union, later called the American Baptist Foreign Mission Society (ABFMS). Shuck and Roberts, as Southerners, transferred their services to the new Foreign Mission Board of the Southern Baptist Convention (SBC). Both the Northern and Southern missions opened a number of fields throughout China and were joined by other Baptist missions from Great Britain, Sweden, and the United States.

Albert W. Wardin, Jr.

It was of little consequence that missionaries and other foreigners often were referred to as "foreign devils," but the insult thrown at Chinese Christians and others who worked for foreigners as "running dog of the foreigner" cut deeply. The antiforeign element in China in the late 1880s and again in the 1920s came from the understandable frustration of being abused by the Western powers. This resulted often in many Chinese Christians taking the brunt of the frustrations of the local population.

In general, the missionaries disliked the special protection they received from the unequal Western treaties following the Opium Wars. The Christian missionary and message, like it or not, was identified with the gunboat diplomacy that had opened China to the West. With the demise of the Qing dynasty and the floundering republicanism, the tide began to turn against any kind of foreign control. Communism in China met needs there because a small group of enthusiastic men and women lived out and expressed the bitterness and sorrow of the masses in a way that Confucianists, Christians, and Buddhists alike failed to do.

An underlying goal of all Baptist mission work had been to develop Christian leadership that could take the lead, direct the programs of evangelism, and meet the needs of the society far better than the foreign missionary. The primary concern during the 1914 Baptist Missionary Centennial celebrations in China was the training of the people to pick up the reins as the missionary moved on to other tasks.

American Baptist Foreign Mission Society.

The churches related to the American Baptist Foreign Mission Society (ABFMS) were located in South (Guangdong Province), East (Zhejiang, Jiangsu, and Anhui), and West (Sichuan) China. In 1900 there were eighteen ABFMS churches in China, but in 1927 they had grown to 164. Due to the political climate, the 1920s were a time of reexamination and regrouping. The summer of 1927 was one of the most difficult for Christian missions in China primarily because of antiforeign feeling. During these years the ABFMS churches began to form their local conventions and distance themselves a bit from foreign supervision. In 1922 the China Baptist Council, an autonomous body representing the three ABFMS conventions, was formed. This national body of five Chinese and three missionaries met in 1927 in Shanghai and recognized that their greatest need was not money or personnel but a deepening of the spiritual life of the Chinese Christians.

Gideon Chin helped develop a China-wide Five-Year Movement that conceived of Christianity in China as a movement to lead men and women to a more abundant life. Christians were to apply Christian standards of life in daily economic matters and uplift the toiling masses from their poverty and ignorance to a better life—both spiritual and material.

South China. In the eastern part of Guangdong, southern Fujian, and Jiangxi Provinces, ABFMS missionaries had some of their most fruitful work. The growth of the churches in the Swatow (Shantou) area of Guangdong was a result of the local believers and the help of many of their families living abroad. Across the bay from the city of Swatow on the island of Kakchieh, Baptists had one of their most outstanding mission efforts. In the city of Kityang, two physicians, C. B. Lesher and Clara C. Leach, extended the Christian witness through a Baptist hospital.

Political turmoil continued and, with the shooting of students by foreign troops in Shanghai in 1925, the churches in the South declared their independence from foreign direction. Graduates of the University of Shanghai and other American-style Baptist-related colleges led in the formation of the Ling Tong Baptist Council. Out of this step of faith came some of the best indigenous work Baptists ever accomplished in China.

East China. Toward the end of the nineteenth century, ABFMS missionaries began work in the three provinces of Jiangsu, Anhui, and Zhejiang. The churches organized the Zhejiang-Shanghai Baptist Convention. In the ancient port city of Ningpo, Esther

Ling gave leadership to the Riverside Academy, while in Huzhou Dr. Charles D. Leach directed the Baptist hospital. Dr. F. W. Goddard was in charge of another hospital in Shaoxing. In the city of Hangzhou, E. H. Clayton was principal of the Wayland Academy.

Pastor Dzin, who died in 1927, was a tower of strength even as far back as the Boxer Uprising of 1900. Four times he stopped invading armies from commandeering his church building. His daughter, Chen Mae-Dsin, was one of the first women doctors in East China, specializing in gynecology and obstetrics.

The ABFMS cooperated with other denominations, in education. With the SBC it organized the University of Shanghai. It worked with the West China Union University, the University of Nanjing, and the Ginling (Jinling) College for Women in Nanjing.

West China. ABFMS began work in Sichuan Province in 1888. Here again medical work was used to give a positive opening for the gospel. The Suifi Hospital and work of C. E. Tompkins as well as Chinese medical students from the Union Hospital in Chengdu set a standard for Western hospitals in China. The churches formed the Sichuan Baptist Convention in 1928. At the time the American Consulate was urging missionaries to leave the interior due to antiforeign feeling. While most missionaries left for a time, the work nevertheless continued to prosper.

Foreign Mission Board of the Southern Baptist Convention.

South China. The first mission field of the FMB of the Southern Baptist Convention was China. In 1845 it appointed S. C. Clopton and George Pearcy as its first missionaries to China; they arrived in Canton in 1846. In 1846 the FMB appointed J. L. Shuck and I. J. Roberts, who had served under the Triennial Convention. Henrietta Shuck, however, had died previously in November 1844. In the summer of 1844 Roberts had already moved to Canton, where he started a Baptist congregation. In April 1845 Shuck, accompanied by Dr. and Mrs. Thomas Devan, recently coming to China, also settled in Canton. They immediately formed the First Baptist Church of Canton.

With his eccentricities, Roberts did not associate well with the other missionaries, and in 1852 the FMB terminated his services. Roberts' primary claim to fame was his influence on one of his students, Hong Xiuquan, who founded the Taiping Heavenly Kingdom. This movement incorporated heterodox Christian beliefs, which in its rebellion from 1850 to 1864 proved to be a serious threat to the Qing dynasty. Although Roberts refused to baptize Hong in 1847, he supported the rebellion during much of its existence and then turned strongly against it.

The mission spread to the northern part of the province among the Hakka peoples and west to the province of Guangxi. The churches organized themselves into the Leung Kwang (Liang Guang or "two guangs") Baptist Convention.

P. H. Anderson served many years as teacher and president of the Graves Theological Seminary in Canton. The seminary later gained a Chinese president, a first for Southern Baptist missions. The Pui Ching Middle school for boys and the Pui To School for girls gave Baptists some outstanding leaders. David Y. K. Wong, grandson of one of the earliest Bible women to work in Guangxi Province, graduated from Pui Ching and became the first Chinese president of the Baptist World Alliance. Wong's father was a physician who worked in the Stout Memorial Baptist Hospital in Wuchow (Wuzhou) with missionaries Bill Wallace and Sam Rankin. Robert E. Beddoe had developed the hospital, which became the largest Baptist hospital in China. During the expulsion of the missionaries by the Communist regime, Wallace was arrested in December 1950 on the charge of being a spy. Two months later he died in prison.

Central China. The cities of Shanghai, Zhenjiang, and Yangzhou were the main centers of outreach in East China. Upon his return from America to China in 1847, Shuck with his second wife, Eliza, settled in Shanghai. Shortly before, Matthew T. and Eliza Yates and Thomas and Isabella Hall Tobey had arrived already to assist in the work. On November 6, 1947, Shuck and the others formed the first Baptist church of Shanghai, Old North Gate Church, which continued to grow until the Communist regime closed it in 1958. After the death of his second wife in 1851, Shuck returned to the United States. In spite of the short terms of other missionaries, Yates continued for forty-one years until his death in 1888.

David Wells Herring and R. T. Bryan were to carry Yates' message into the twentieth century. Chang Wen-kai, editor of a Baptist publication that reached every province as well as Chinese overseas, produced more Chinese Christian literature than anyone before him. In the late 1920s in Shaghai, Chang was instrumental in constructing the True Light Building, a headquarters for China Baptists. At the end of 1948 the China Baptist Convention was organized to promote the work of Baptist churches begun by the Southern Baptist mission. L. W. and Nellie Pierce began a Baptist hospital in Yanzhou; their daughter, Ethel, later joined them as a medical missionary.

North China. The port cities of Dengzhou (now Penglai) and Yantai were opened to the Baptist message in 1860 by missionaries J. Landrum Holmes, T. P. Crawford, J. B. Hartwell, C. W. Pruitt, and Lottie Moon (1840–1912). By 1912 Pingdu County pastor-evangelist Li Shouting had baptized 1,400 persons, and this area had become perhaps the greatest evangelistic center Southern Baptists ever had in China. Li was the first head of a home mission board established by Chinese Baptists. Princeton Hsu, longtime Baptist editor, called Li "the Apostle Paul of China" because Li baptized more than five thousand converts.

Lottie Moon, who studied village life and lived among the people, was convinced that the people must first be won as friends before they can be reached as believers. She increasingly adopted a Chinese lifestyle. The newly formed Women's Missionary Union adopted her suggestion of a Christmas offering for missions, raising in the first year, 1888, a little more than $3,300, which provided three assistants for her. Today the annual Christmas offering is named in her honor and currently raises more than eighty million a year, the single largest foreign mission offering of any denomination anywhere.

The pioneering days toward the close of the century brought differing approaches to reaching the Chinese. T. P. Crawford with several others withdrew from the mission and established in 1893 the Gospel Mission. It denied authority to mission boards in the appointment and direction of missionaries, advocated direct mission support from the churches, opposed remuneration for native Christians, and for some in the movement, the adoption of Chinese dress, housing, and food. The Gospel Mission sought its own field farther west in Shandong Province and about 1920 changed its name to the Baptist China Direct Mission. It maintained good relations with the Southern Baptist mission and continued until the establishment of the Communist regime.

The North China missionaries and churches of Shandong (Shantung) experienced revival in the late 1920s and early 1930s. Spiritual renewal came through the confession of sin and mutual forgiveness among missionaries and Chinese church and school leaders—a renewal never before experienced, which spread to the village and town churches in that part of China. Although the revival was primarily a Baptist phenomenon, other churches were touched in the process. Dr. T. W. Ayers established the first Baptist hospital in Shandong. He was ably assisted by Dr. Chu Pao-chin.

Interior China. W. W. Lawton and Eugene Sallee moved in 1904 from the Central China Mission to begin work farther inland. The area chosen was along the Yellow River, where ancient Chinese civilization began. They launched their efforts from Kaifeng, a former capital, and Zhengzhou, the present provincial capital. A Baptist convert, Dr. Chang Run Ming, and his wife, Wang Mei Jen, began the clinic that became the Huamei Baptist Hospital. Other pioneers of this area were Katie Murray, Wilson and Maude Fielder, and David and Alice Herring.

Manchuria. In 1924 Southern Baptist missionaries moved to Harbin, and in 1937 formed a separate mission.

British Baptist Missionary Society (BMS)

The BMS began work in the two mountain provinces of Shandong and Shanxi (the "shan" means "mountain": Shandong is east of a mountain range and Shanxi is west of one). Later Shanxi Province, west of Shanxi, also became a center for the work of the BMS. In 1870 the lone BMS missionaries, Mr. and Mrs. R. F. Laughton, were joined by Timothy Richard. Richard, as the Laughtons, was an advocate of self-supporting congregations, a bold move at the time. Richard later influenced the Presbyterian missionary John L. Nevius, who communicated the ideal of a self-governing, self-propagating, and self-supporting church. Richard was a forerunner of the idea of "cultural uplift," or changing the cultural values of the people. He aimed his message at those who apparently were seeking religious truth and could influence public opinion.

Alfred Jones reinforced the BMS work, and by the time of his first furlough there were forty-two self-supporting churches in Shandong Province. J. S. Whitewright began a pastor training institute in Chingzhou, emphasizing self-support from the beginning.

The BMS suffered the greatest losses among Baptists during the Boxer Rebellion of 1900, when hordes of peasants set out to cleanse China of the foreigner. Among the two thousand Protestant martyrs were twelve BMS missionaries and three BMS missionary children. The mission lost its entire mission force in Shanxi. At least seventy-two Chinese Baptists also were killed in the province.

Baptists and Educational Needs

In 1906 a remarkable effort of cooperation between the ABFMS and the FMB of the SBC occurred with the establishment of the University of Shanghai (first called Shanghai Baptist College and Seminary) to train future leaders. The university was constructed on swamp land near the Huangpu River far from the city center. In 1913 the school graduated its first two students, C. C. Chen and T. C. Wu, who went abroad for graduate study and returned to teach and preach in China. In that year there was not a single Chinese Baptist with the equivalent of a college education. By the late 1920s, the picture of Chinese Baptist leadership had changed completely. In

1927 there were more than one hundred Chinese college graduates serving as pastors, principals, teachers, and doctors of Baptist-related institutions.

The University of Shanghai became coeducational in 1920. In 1928 it gained its first Chinese president, Herman C. E. Liu, who took the school to new heights of usefulness. He recognized the need of trained Chinese leadership to reach China for Christ. The school had the highest percentage of students in Christian ministry in China. Even the voluntary chapel services were well attended by believers and nonbelievers. During the Japanese occupation of Shanghai during the Sino-Japanese War, Liu was assassinated in 1938 as he was waiting for a bus. He was too much of a Chinese nationalist for the Japanese to tolerate. In the late 1980s the People's Republic of China declared him a martyr of the revolution, and his statue graces the present campus, today called the East China University of Technology.

Britt E. Towery, Jr.

Other Baptist Missions

Other smaller Baptist missions have served in China also. In 1847 Seventh Day Baptists initiated a mission to China by sending Solomon and Lucy Carpenter and Nathan and Olive Wardner. In July 1850 the Shanghai Seventh Day Baptist Church was organized, and Mrs. Wardner began a day school. In 1949 the Shanghai Church, the largest Seventh Day Baptist church in the world at the time, had 670 members, but the work of the mission was terminated with the establishment of the Communist regime. The first Swedish Baptist missionary, Karl A. Vingren, arrived in China in 1891. A mission was formed in 1893 in Shandong Province. In 1916 the mission reported fourteen missionaries, four congregations, and 815 members. From 1934 to about 1941 the Convention of Regular Baptists of British Columbia maintained a North Manchuria Baptist Mission, which started five churches before the Japanese ended its work with the imprisonment of its last remaining missionary.

Several conservative evangelical Baptist missions entered China after the war, but their stay was brief because of the victory of the Communist regime a few years later. The Association of Baptists for World Evangelism (ABWE) began work in China in 1946 with the arrival in Luichow Peninsula in southeastern China of Mr. and Mrs. Victor Barnett, who had previously served in the area. By 1950 the seven missionaries of the mission had been forced to leave the country. The Conservative Baptist Foreign Mission Society (CBFMS) sent a party of ten missionaries, who arrived on the last day of 1946 in Shanghai. Several went to Jiangsi Province to serve in an orphanage while seven of them, joined in time by eleven others, went to the western portion of Sichuan Province in an attempt to reach the Nosu people. Before the missionaries were forced to leave, two churches were established which still function today. During evacuation one of the missionary wives contracted spinal meningitis and died, while veteran missionary Levi Lovegren was incarcerated from 1951 to 1955 on the charge of spying. Baptist Mid-Missions appointed as its first missionary, Violet LeFevre, who formerly had worked in China. By 1951 all five of the mission's missionaries, including two other women and a Chinese national, had left the country.

The Christian Situation Today

The Communist leadership which gained control of all of mainland China in 1949, proclaiming the People's Republic of China, was determined to revolutionize the nation socially and economically according to Marxist principles. In a comparatively short time the regime forced all foreign missionaries to leave and nationalized all mission enterprises, including schools and hospitals.

With the blessing of the government, the Three-Self Movement was formed in 1951. It advocated the earlier mission goals of self-government, self-propagation, and self-support of the churches, used now, however, not as a means of furthering the welfare of the churches but to cut them off entirely from Western ties and money. The regime demanded church leaders to give full political support. In 1958 the government began also to reduce greatly the number of churches in the towns, forcing their consolidation and eliminating all denominational lines, and many rural churches closed as well. In 1964 the government forbade teaching religion to anyone under eighteen years of age. Between 1966 and 1976, the years of the Cultural Revolution, when there was the attempt to eliminate all vestiges of the capitalistic past, the Christian community particularly suffered with the imprisonment of Christian leaders and the closing of all churches except one in Beijing. In 1949 there were about 170 Protestant denominations with 1,295,000 Protestant adherents, including 123,000 Baptists who made up about 10 percent of the total, but in the 1960s there were no more denominations and the surviving Christians had to meet secretly, if at all. Since there was no longer visible functioning Baptist bodies, the Baptist World Alliance dropped its Baptist figures for China. After more than one hundred years of heavy investment in both labor and finances with much sacrifice, it appeared that the mission investment had come to naught. Would Christianity be eliminated from China for a third time?

In the 1970s China began to change course and open to the West. In 1979 China changed its religious policy by allowing the reopening of churches and toleration of religious belief. It was discovered that the Christian church had survived. During the years of suppression, thousands of house churches functioned, and the Christian faith had grown to include millions of adherents. Today in Shandong Province alone, it is estimated there are five hundred thousand to eight hundred thousand Protestant believers. The government has permitted the recovery of church property and allowed the establishment of the Nanjing Union Theological College as well as a number of regional seminaries to meet the great need of trained leadership since the churches were left with a decreasing number of aging leaders.

An Amity Foundation has been formed as a channel for Western cooperation in social programs in the country. The Foundation received from the United Bible Societies a modern printing press on which it publishes Scripture and other Christian literature. Victims of past oppression were rehabilitated also. Matthew Tong of Dongshan Church in Canton; Stephen Wang of Shandong; Han Chongyi of Kaifeng, Henan; and Qi Qingcai of Shandong and Shanghai and others were leaders of integrity in their respective areas. All of these, along with many of their coworkers, had suffered during the antirights campaigns of the 1950s or the Cultural Revolution. A Chinese hymn with the opening words, "The winter is past," is now widely sung because it speaks of the Christians' hope for the future.

Although the status of the Christian churches is better than in 1958, the Communist regime is determined to maintain strict political control and expects support from the churches. It would like to eliminate the independent house churches and induce all believers to attend the registered churches. But in spite of government restrictions, including lack of access to the public media and prohibition of public evangelism and youth work, the Christian churches continue to grow. The churches are now living in a post-denominational age, but the majority of the worship services are much like Baptist or other evangelical services in the West. Within a number of congregations charismatic influences are strong, including speaking in tongues and divine healing.

The Protestant churches are, by and large, congregations of committed believers— they have passed through a "baptism of fire." The regime's official disfavor of all religion still makes Christianity an unpopular option for personal advancement. The government opposes the practice of infant baptism, and all Protestant congregations practice believer's baptism (by immersion or sprinkling). In practice they probably approximate more closely the Baptist ideal than many Baptist churches in the West with the Baptist name. Incidentally, there is one group of Baptists which has been discovered recently in China. An Australian Baptist missionary visited Lahus in southern China where he found about 17,000 Baptists who are served by two pastors.

Baptists from abroad, including the Baptist World Alliance and the Southern Baptist Convention, seek to cultivate relations with the Christian community in China. Missionaries, of course, are prohibited, but through Cooperative Services International, an office of the FBM of the SBC, numbers of Baptists have undertaken teaching positions in China, thereby providing a quiet Christian witness from abroad. In addition, Southern Baptist colleges and universities who are members of Cooperative Services International Education Consortium (CSIEC) have more than fifty educational exchange programs with China.

Albert W. Wardin, Jr.

BIBLIOGRAPHY: Valuable material on the efforts of the American Baptist Foreign Mission Society may be found in Dana M. Albaugh, *Between Two Centuries* (Philadelphia: Judson Press, 1935), 164–201, and Robert G. Torbet, *Venture of Faith* (Philadelphia: Judson Press, 1955), 288–317, 512–37. For information on Southern Baptists, see Winston Crawley, *Partners Across the Pacific* (Nashville: Broadman Press, 1986); Mary K. Crawford, *The Shantung Revival* (Shanghai: China Baptist Publication Society, 1933); and Catherine B. Allen, *The New Lottie Moon Story* (Nashville: Broadman Press, 1980). For Seventh Day Baptists, see Don A. Sanford, *A Choosing People* (Nashville: Broadman Press, 1992), 181–84. See Brian Stanley, *The History of the Baptist Missionary Society 1792–1992* (Edinburgh: T&T Clark, 1992), 175–207, 303–35, for information on British Baptists. Material on the work of the Gospel Mission which separated from the Southern Baptists may be found in T. L. Blalock, *Experiences of a Baptist Faith Missionary for 56 Years in China* (Fort Worth: Manney Printing Co., 1949). Information on the Swedish Baptist mission to 1916 may be found in J. Byström, *Sådd och Skörd* (Stockholm: Swedish Baptist Missionary Society, 1916), 116–229. On the work of conservative evangelical missions after World War II, consult William J. Hopewell, Jr., *The Missionary Emphasis of the General Association of Regular Baptist Churches* (Chicago: Regular Baptist Press, 1963), 97–98; *Founded on the Word: Focused on the World* (Wheaton: CBFMS, 1978), 27–34; and Polly Strong, *Burning Wicks* (Cleveland: BM-M, 1984), 243–47. On the current status of Christians in China today, see Britt E. Towery, Jr., *The Churches of China*, 3d ed. (Waco: Baylor University, 1990), Jonathan Cao, ed., *The China Mission Handbook* (Hong Kong: Chinese Church Research Center, 1989), and Alan Hunter and Kim-Kwong Chan, *Protestantism in Contemporary China* (New York: Cambridge University Press, 1993).. For a perceptive article on the impact of Protestant revivalism on the Taiping movement, see William R. Doezema, "Western Seeds of Eastern Heterodoxy," *Fides et Historia*, 25, no. 1 (1993): 73–98.

HONG KONG/MACAU (1836/1842)

	Members	Churches
1. Baptist Convention of Hong Kong (1938)	45,605	(68)
2. Fellowship of ABWE Churches	240	(10)
3. Hong Kong Conservative Baptist Association	518	(8)
4. Association of Baptist Churches of Macau	750	(8)
	47,113	(94)

*I*n 1842 China ceded Hong Kong Island and the peninsula of Kowloon to Great Britain and in 1898 leased for ninety-nine years additional territory on the mainland, the New Territories. In 1997 the Crown Colony of Hong Kong, which includes the New Territories, will become part of China but is to retain special autonomy for fifty years. Hong Kong, with a population of more than 5.5 million, possesses a dynamic capitalist economy and is a center of world trade. The port of Macau has been a Portuguese colony since 1557 but will revert to China in 1999, also with a guarantee of autonomy for an extended period.

Both Macau and Hong Kong were stepping stones for Baptist missionaries who sought entry into the Chinese Empire. John Lewis Shuck arrived in Macau in 1836 and baptized his first Chinese convert the following year but moved to Hong Kong in 1842 and Canton in 1845. Issachar J. Roberts settled in Macau in 1837, transferred to Hong Kong in 1842, then in 1844 moved to Canton. William Dean, who had ministered to Chinese in Bangkok, also settled in Hong Kong in 1842. Although Dean wished to retain Hong Kong as a permanent station, the American Baptist Missionary Union (ABMU) in 1860 shifted its South China headquarters from Hong Kong to Swatow. Even though leaving, both Shuck and Dean had organized Baptist churches in Hong Kong. Shuck established on May 15, 1842, the Queen's Road Baptist Church, and on May 28, 1843, Dean formed the Tie Chiu Baptist Church, composed of Swatow-speaking laborers. These congregations were the first Baptist congregations not only in Hong Kong but in the entire Pacific basin.

Although no more Baptist missionaries were stationed in Hong Kong until after World War II, Hong Kong was not completely neglected. Missionaries would visit, and laypeople helped to keep the work alive. After 1881 Baptist work in Hong Kong became part of the Southern Baptist mission in Canton and the Leung Kwong Baptist Convention. In 1938 the Hong Kong Baptist Association (now Convention) was organized with three churches and three chapels. In 1910 Macau again became a Southern Baptist mission when John and Lillian Galloway, with other missionaries who were members of an independent mission, became Southern Baptist appointees.

With the closing of China to Christian missionaries and the influx to Hong Kong and Macau of many refugees, including a number of Baptists, both territories became important mission centers. In 1949 Southern Baptists began to station missionaries in Hong Kong, and in 1951 American Baptists started work among Swatow-speaking refugees. With a strong Baptist base, a growing population, a large contingent of missionaries, and the establishment of numerous institutions, Baptist growth was rapid. In the mid-1950s

Southern Baptists sponsored six day schools with six thousand students enrolled through high school. In addition they had organized Hong Kong Baptist Theological Seminary (1951) and Hong Kong Baptist College (1956). In 1955 Dr. Sam Rankin established a Baptist clinic, which became the Hong Kong Baptist Hospital in 1963. The Baptist Press, founded in 1952, served as a regional publishing center for Southeast Asia. Today the Hong Kong Baptist Convention is one of the largest denominational bodies in the territory. In 1954 American Baptists formed the Joint Committee of Swatow Baptist Churches, whose congregations, however, are members of the convention.

The Association of Baptists for World Evangelism (ABWE) started work in Hong Kong in 1951 with Mr. and Mrs. Victor Barnett, who had served under the Association in China. The first effort was in the establishment of two rooftop schools in Kowloon. The work expanded to include children's clubs, kindergartens, English classes, tract distribution, medical clinics, and social service centers. ABWE has engaged also in church planting. A Fellowship of ABWE Churches has been formed, which includes more than fifteen congregations—more than ten are autonomous. The mission also established China Baptist Theological College, which includes an evening school for lay leaders.

Baptist Mid-Missions began its work in Hong Kong with the coming of Ernest Loong, a native Chinese, who left China in 1951, settled first in Indonesia, but then moved to Hong Kong in the following year. In 1952 he began a bimonthly publication, *A Witness*, continuing publication work which he already had started in China. In 1961 Loong established the Witness Baptist Church and, for a time, operated a primary day school.

Conservative Baptists sent their first missionaries to Hong Kong in 1963. The mission developed chapels/churches in housing developments and expanded its ministry through primary schools, study centers, and a social service center. They also began work in Macau in 1986.

BIBLIOGRAPHY: For a careful work on all Baptist missions in Hong Kong, see Paul Yat-Keung Wong, *The History of Baptist Missions in Hong Kong* (Ph.D. dissertaion, Southern Baptist Theological Seminary, 1974). For an additional source on Southern Baptist work, see Baker J. Cauthen and others, *Advance* (Nashville: Broadman Press, 1970), 106–10. For additional material on Conservative Baptists, see Han W. Finzel, ed., *Partners Together* (Wheaton: CBFMS, 1993), 62–65, 86–89.

JAPAN (1873)

	Members	Churches
1. Japan Baptist Convention (Nippon Baputesuto Renmei) (SBC) (1947)	31,039	(228)
2. Japan Baptist Union (Nippon Baputesuto Dōmei) (ABC) (1958)	4,809	(57)
3. Association of Baptists for World Evangelism (ABWE) (Bankoku Baputesuto Fukuin Dendo Kyōkai)	240	(9)

4. Baptist International Missions, Inc.	n/a	(60)
5. Baptist Mid-Missions (BM-M)	100	(7)
6. Conservative Baptist Association (Hoshu Baputesuto Dōmei) (1964) (CBI)	2,019	(46)
7. Gospel Baptist Association (Fukuin Baputesuto Kyōdan) (FWB)	203*	(8)
8. Japan Baptist Association (Nippon Baputesuto Rengō) (ABA)	300	(10)
9. Japan Baptist Church Association (Nippon Baputesuto Kyōkai Rengō) (BGC) (1965)	2,000	(47)
10. Japan Baptist Bible Fellowship (Nippon Baputesuto Baiburu Feroshippu) (BBFI)	2,000	(69)
11. Japan Baptist Conference (Nippon Baputesuto Senkyōdan) (1967) (NABC)	402	(7)
12. Japan Evangelical Churches Association (SwO)	1,563	(25)
13. Fellowship of Evangelical Baptist Churches (Nippon Fukuin Baputesuto Senkyōdan) (CaFEBC)	200	(9)
14. Okinawa Baptist Convention (Okinawa Baputesuto Renmei) (SBC/ABC) (1955)	3,092	(38)
	47,967	(620)

*Average attendance

*W*ith the arrival in 1859 of the first Protestant missionaries, Protestants have now been laboring in the Japanese Empire for more than one and a third centuries. A little more than 1 percent of the population is Protestant. The addition of Roman Catholics and indigenous Japanese bodies brings the Christian population to about 2.5 percent. With a closely knit homogeneous population that is wedded culturally to traditional family values and the Buddhist and Shinto faiths, Japan has strongly resisted the Christian faith. For many Japanese, religion does not mean a personal faith or commitment but an identification with traditional beliefs and rites. Although Japan has adapted remarkably well to the modern world of technology, science, and business, its acceptance of Western culture has proved to be most selective.

Baptists were among the pioneers in bringing the Christian faith to Japan, but their efforts were weak and faltering. Only after World War II have Baptists come in force. But even with the large increase of Baptist missions and growth of missionary personnel and expenditure, the results have been disappointing. Only two Baptist bodies have more than 4,000 members; the other groups, excluding Okinawa, have around 2,000 or less. As with other Protestants, congregations remain small with limited attendance.

The average size of a Baptist church is about eigthy-five members. In spite of the difficulties, Baptist missions, even with the high cost of living and high price of land, continue to be committed to an aggressive program of evangelism, hoping someday for a spiritual breakthrough.

On the flagship of the fleet of ships led by Commodore Matthew Perry in 1853, who forced Japan to open to the West, was a Baptist marine, Jonathan Goble, who wanted to discover the possibilities of mission work in the country. Goble returned to the United States with a Japanese castaway, called Sam Patch, who was converted, becoming the first Japanese Baptist. With the signing of a treaty between Japan and the USA in 1859 which allowed entry of missionaries, Jonathan and Eliza Goble settled in Japan in 1860 under the American Baptist Free Mission Society, an organization which favored the abolition of slavery. The FMB of the Southern Baptist Convention was also eager to enter the field and sent in the same year John and Sarah Rohrer. Unfortunately, the Rohrers never reached their destination because the boat on which they sailed disappeared on the high seas. In addition, the Civil War in America broke the momentum of a Southern Baptist effort for some years to come.

In 1872 the American Baptist Missionary Union (ABMU) accepted the Japanese field of the Free Mission Society and appointed both the Gobles and Nathan Brown. Brown was a former missionary to Burma and Assam and sixty-six years of age when he arrived on the field, with his new wife, Lottie, thirty-three years of age. On March 2, 1873, the Gobles and Browns formed in Yokohama the First Baptist church in Japan, the four composing the charter membership. Because of violence and slander against others, the ABMU dismissed Goble, who remained as an independent missionary until 1882. Brown, however, remained and translated the New Testament into Japanese. From 1874 to 1877 Australian Baptists had a short-lived mission, and the Baptist Missionary Society from London sent its first missionary in 1878 but gave up in 1890 in favor of the ABMU. By 1888 Baptists had 900 members but were far behind the Episcopalians, Congregationalists, Presbyterians, and Methodists. They were slower than other denominations in opening schools and a theological seminary. In 1898 the mission launched a gospel ship, donated by a shipowner in Scotland. Under the command of Luke W. Bickel, it sailed for many years on Japan's Inland Sea, visiting the many towns and villages of the area. Another innovative ministry was the establishment in 1908 of an institutional church in Tokyo, the Tabernacle. The church was primarily a project of William and Lucinda Axling, who served fifty-four years as missionaries to Japan. William Axling was made an honorary citizen of Tokyo before he and his wife left for the USA in 1955.

In 1889 Southern Baptists made a second attempt to enter Japan by sending two couples—John and Drucilla McCullum and John and Sophia A. Brunson. According to a comity agreement with the ABMU, Southern Baptists were allotted southwestern Japan. The two mission families established themselves in 1892 at Kokura on the northern tip of Kyushu, the southernmost of Japan's four major islands. The Brunsons, however, soon resigned. In 1893 the Moji Baptist church, the first in Kyushu, was organized, and in 1905 the first periodical, *Seiko*, was published. In 1916 the mission established in Fukuoka a middle school for boys, Seinan Gukuin, which later added a theological department and became a university with schooling from kindergarten through university. In 1922 Seinan Jo Gakuin, a school for girls, was started at Kitakyushu, which later included a junior college division. By the latter date the mission had eleven churches and 1,208 members. In 1918 Southern Baptists reorganized their Southwestern Association into the West Japan Baptist Convention, while in the same year Baptists related to the American Baptist mission formed the East Baptist Convention. At this time Southern Baptists terminated their comity agreement with the American Baptists, and in 1919 sent a missionary couple to Tokyo.

With fear of control by the totalitarian regime, the two Baptist unions united in 1940 to strengthen their position in relation to the government. The united convention had 6,863 members and eighty-nine churches, far behind the other major denominations. In 1941 the regime required the formation of the Kyōdan, or United Church of Christ, to unite all Protestants. Failure to join meant loss of legal status, and the Japan Baptist Convention joined as bloc four, in 1942, however, the government eliminated all blocs. War broke out between Japan and the United States in December 1941, and the remaining missionaries were interned and repatriated. The war brought destruction to church and school property. Southern Baptist educational institutions survived, but American Baptists were less fortunate. In Yokohama Soshin Jo Gakko, its school for girls, lost all its buildings, and at Kanto Gakuin, its boys' school, only one building remained.

After the war the churches in relation to the American Baptist mission stayed within the United Church but at the same time attempted to keep their identity, calling themselves the New Life Fellowship (Shinsei Kai). Axling strongly advocated remaining within the United Church and later became a general evangelist for it. A number of churches, however, were uncomfortable in the United Church, functioning as part of a quasi-denominational body. Twelve of them withdrew from the United Church in 1952, and three newly formed churches did not enter it. In 1953 the New Life Fellowship formally organized with churches both inside and outside the United Church.

In 1958 Baptists outside the United Church formed the Japan Baptist Union, but it has not grown in membership. In 1969 the Union established the Japan Baptist Overseas Mission Society, which has supported mission work in India, Bangladesh, and Philippines. The Union is a member of the National Christian Council of Japan and the BWA. Besides support for its own schools, including four secondary schools and five colleges, the Union and the American Baptist mission are strongly committed to the ecumenical movement and are related to such ecumenical institutions as the Tokyo Woman's Christian University and the International Christian University. On a different level, the churches of the Union, as other Baptists, sponsor many kindergartens, an effective ministry. The Swedish Baptist Missionary Society cooperates with the American Baptist work.

Sixteen churches related to the Southern Baptists withdrew from the United Church, and in 1947 they formed a new Japan Baptist Convention. The Southern Baptist mission greatly increased its missionary force and embarked on an aggressive program which sought to establish churches throughout the nation. By 1974 the convention had more than 250 churches and a membership of 23,000. The mission expanded the educational program of its two schools in Kyushu and launched Jordan Press (1949), a hospital at Kyoto (1955), and an assembly. The convention is the largest Baptist body in Japan and includes about two-thirds of all Baptists on the main islands. It is a member of the National Christian Council of Japan and the BWA.

After World War II, many other Baptist missions, primarily from the USA, entered Japan. At least sixteen of them continue today. Even though they have experienced some growth, none has reached any great size. Most of the post-war missions and their respective Baptist bodies may be divided into two groups.

One group, including the Conservative Baptist Association, Japan Baptist

Conference, Japan Baptist Church Association, and Japan Evangelical Churches Association cooperate with other evangelical Christians and are members of the Japan Evangelical Alliance. Conservative Baptists have concentrated their work on northern Honshu Island and Tokyo and have engaged in an outstanding publication ministry. The North American Baptist Conference (NABC) initiated work at Ise and Kyoto on Honshu, and its work led to the formation of the Japan Baptist Conference, which is a member of the BWA. The Japan Baptist Church Association is a body which developed from the work of the Baptist General Conference (BGC), whose ministry also has been on Honshu, mainly in the Kanto and Kansai regions. This body has a strong church planting ministry, and between 1971 and 1990 has grown from seven hundred members to two thousand. It, too, has sent missionaries to the Philippines. The Örebro Society from Sweden began working in the Osaka area on Honshu and today is in partnership with the Japan Evangelical Churches Association. The mission of the Fellowship of Evangelical Baptist Churches from Canada is in ideological agreement with the above-mentioned Baptists but is not a member of the Japan Evangelical Alliance. The Fellowship assumed the work of the Regular Baptist Mission from British Columbia, which began in 1952 in Toyama Province and today has nine churches.

The remaining missions and their respective bodies in the second group are, by and large, strongly fundamentalist and most, if not all of them, practice second-degree separation, rejecting cooperation with fellow Baptists and other evangelicals who may associate with individuals whom they consider liberal. Most of them strongly emphasize local church independence. One of the most aggressive and successful of these missions is the Baptist Bible Fellowship, which currently has twenty-nine missionaries under appointment and churches in seven local associations throughout the nation. Between 1971 to 1990 it doubled its membership from 930 members to about 2,000. Baptist Mid-Missions (BM-M) has work in both Fukushima Prefecture on Honshu and on Shikoku Island, while the Association of Baptists for World Evangelism (ABWE) started on Kyushu Island but has entered the Kobe-Osaka area in central Honshu. Baptist International Missions, Inc. (BIMI), entering Japan in 1964, has established about sixty churches and the Kansai Independent Baptist Bible School. The churches of this mission have formed the Japan Independent Baptist Mission Society, whose missionaries serve in Japan and abroad. Free Will Baptists center their work in Sapporo, the capital of the northern island of Hokkaido, and in Tokyo.

There is little unity and practical cooperation among the Baptist missions and church bodies. Before World War II, American and Southern Baptists maintained fraternal relations but today, except in the Ryukyu Islands, go their separate ways. The BGC, NABC, and CBI have had some cooperative endeavors in theological education or publication work, but they maintain separate Baptist organizations. In 1970 the Japan Baptist Convention, Japan Baptist Union, and Japan Baptist Church Association served as hosts for the meeting of the BWA in Tokyo.

Baptists in the Ryukyu Islands have organized their own Okinawa Convention. In 1891 the ABMU sent Michinosuke Hara of the East Japan Baptist Convention to serve in the islands. His support came from Mrs. Robert Allen of Glasgow, Scotland, who was interested in seeing work started there. Before World War II, Baptists had organized four churches—the first one in Naha in 1904. In 1955 the American Baptist Foreign Mission Society began to send missionaries, who were joined by workers from the Japan Baptist Convention (related to Southern Baptists) and later in 1960 by Southern Baptist missionaries. American and Southern Baptists on Okinawa cooperate here with one Baptist convention.

BIBLIOGRAPHY: Two helpful sources on Baptist bodies in Japan are F. Calvin Parker, "Baptist Missions in Japan, 1945–73: A Study in Relationships," *Japan Christian Quarterly*, 40, no. 1 (winter 1974): 32–41, and Kumazawa Yoshinobu and David L. Swain, eds., *Christianity in Japan, 1971–90* (Tokyo: Kyo Bun Kwan, 1991), 281–85, 304–5. A very fine account of the work of the American Baptist mission to the 1950s may be found in Robert G. Torbet, *Venture of Faith* (Philadelphia: Judson Press, 1955). A volume which concentrates on American Baptist-related work after World War II and the contributions of the Japanese themselves is Dean R. Kirkwood and Glenn G. Gano, eds., *Followers of the "Son"* (Valley Forge, Pa.: International Ministries, ABC/USA, 1974). A well-written and detailed history of the Southern Baptist mission is the work by F. Calvin Parker, *The Southern Baptist Mission in Japan, 1889–1989* (Lanham, Md.: University Press of America, 1991). A good survey of Japan as a mission field with an emphasis on Southern Baptists, but including other Baptists, is the mission study by W. Maxfield Garrott, *Japan Advances* (Nashville: Convention Press, 1956). For the work of various Baptist missions which entered Japan after World War II, see the following: Hans W. Finzel, ed., *Partners Together* (Wheaton: CBFMS, 1993), 76–81, for Conservative Baptists; David Guston and Martin Erikson, eds., *Fifteen Eventful Years* (Chicago: Harvest, 1961), 100–106, for the mission of the BGC; *Opening Doors in Japan* (Forest Park, Ill.: Roger Williams Press, c. 1963), on the mission of the NABC; L. K. Tarr, *This Dominion His Dominion* (Willowdale, Ont.: FEBC, 1968), 161–63, on the Japan Regular Baptist Mission; and William J. Hopewell, Jr., *The Missionary Emphasis of the General Association of Regular Baptist Churches* (Chicago: Regular Baptist Press, 1963), 99–100, on the beginnings of the BM-M and ABWE in Japan. For work in the Ryuku Islands, see Ed Bollinger, "Baptist Work in the Ryukyu Islands," *Japan Christian Quarterly*, 30, no. 1 (Jan. 1964), 30–32.

KOREA, REPUBLIC OF (1889)

	Members	Churches
1. Korea Baptist Convention (1949)	323,750	(1,548)
2. Korea Baptist Bible Fellowship	n/a	(160)
3. Missionary Baptists (ABA)	n/a	(5)
	323,750	(1,713)

*A*lthough Protestantism has been in Korea only a little more than a century, Korea has been the most fruitful mission field in Asia for evangelical Christians. In South Korea alone, about one-third of the population is Christian, including Protestants and Roman Catholics. Some of the largest Protestant churches in the world are in the country. As a result of the introduction of the Nevius plan—the emphasis of self-support, self-government, and self-propagation—the Korean "Pentecost" of 1907, the importance of prayer in the life of the churches (daybreak prayer, overnight prayer, and prayer mountains), and a commitment to evangelism,Korean Christians of various denominations have become a mighty force for the evangelical cause in Korea and in other parts of the world.

The Christian churches experienced persecution under the Japanese, who occupied the country from 1910 to 1945, and under Communists, who caused many Christians to flee south because of their control of North Korea after World War II. The Korean War (1950–1953) brought great suffering to the population as a whole and also initiated another influx of Christians from the north. The Republic of Korea, which was organized in 1948 in the southern part of the Korean peninsula, previously occupied by American troops, has become one of the economic powers of East Asia since the war. The Democratic People's Republic in North Korea, a totalitarian Communist regime, has practically prohibited the Christian faith, though one or two showcase churches remain open in Pyongyang.

Except for a short period in the late nineteenth and early twentieth centuries, there was no Baptist body as such in Korea before 1949. The Christian group, which later became the Korea Baptist Convention, called itself by other names, although others referred to it as Baptist. Malcolm C. Fenwick (1863–1935), a native of Canada who was probably of Presbyterian stock but with no particular denominational affiliation, went to Korea in late 1889, five years after the first missionaries had arrived. In 1893 he returned to Canada where in the following year he established the Corea Itinerant Mission, an interdenominational faith mission, with himself as director. Two years later he returned to Korea, settling in Wonsan in the north where he had once resided previously.

In 1895 members of the Clarendon Street Baptist Church of Boston, pastored by Adoniram Judson Gordon, a promoter of missions, founded the Ella Thing Memorial Mission, an independent mission which sent missionaries to Korea who eventually settled in areas one hundred fifty miles south of Seoul. When the last missionaries of the mission, Mr. and Mrs. Frederick W. Steadman, left in 1901, the mission was turned over to the Corea Intinerant Mission. While serving as a missionary in Japan, Steadman visited Korea several times and baptized converts. In 1905 Steadman estimated there were about three hundred Baptists in the country.

By 1905 the work had grown to thirty-one congregations, which led Fenwick to form in that year the Church of Christ in Corea. The church was considered a single body and given an authoritarian structure. Fenwick was its head until 1914. In doctrine the church stressed the second coming of Christ and the indwelling of the Holy Spirit. During the Japanese occupation, the name of the church was changed several times because of the political implication of the name or to distinguish the church from others. The church expanded outside the borders of Korea into China, including Manchuria, as well as southern Siberia, numbering more than 254 congregations in 1940. Japanese authorities imprisoned thirty-two leaders of the church in 1942 because of their insistence on the Lordship of Christ at His second coming. Two years later the regime formally dissolved the church.

After the liberation of Korea, the church reestablished itself with a convention organization and took one of its earlier names, the Church of Christ in East Asia. With a desire to develop a relationship with some Christian body in the USA, contact was made with Southern Baptists. After Baker J. Cauthen, then Secretary for the Orient of the FMB of the Southern Baptist Convention, met at the church's convention in 1949, the church decided to become a Baptist body and requested missionaries. The first Southern Baptist missionaries, John and Jewell Abernathy, arrived in February 1950 just before the outbreak of the Korean War.

During the war some Baptists were killed, including four pastors, and many church buildings were damaged seriously or destroyed. Southern Baptists sent large amounts of relief of food and clothing. Baptist chaplains in the U.S. armed forces also helped to support the Baptist cause. In 1954 the mission established the Korea Baptist Theological Seminary in Taejon, which in 1992 moved to a new campus near Yusong.

Two years later the Bill Wallace Memorial Hospital in Pusan was begun, which had developed from an earlier medical ministry. A Publication Department was formed in 1958 in Pusan which, after moving to Taejon, settled in 1961 in Seoul. In 1965 the mission opened a Baptist Building for its work.

In 1951 the Korean convention reported a membership of twelve thousand but in 1958 only a little more than four thousand. Refugees who joined the Baptists when relief was available now left to rejoin their former churches, and others dropped out because of poor pastoral leadership. Because of internal rivalries within the convention and conflict and lack of trust between some of the leaders in the convention and the missionaries, who controlled much of the finances, the convention split in 1959 into two bodies. Even though the International Council of Christian Churches (ICCC) provided financial support for the body which was not in cooperation with the mission, the division was healed in 1968. In spite of these difficulties, the united convention in 1969 reported 378 churches and a membership of more than fifty thousand.

Growth in the last quarter century has been phenomenal even though in 1990 it excluded a church of 20,000 members for its toleration of shamanistic beliefs. The convention includes some large congregations, but none compare with the largest Christian congregation in the world—the pentecostal Yoido Full Gospel Church—which had over 600,000 members in 1990 and is located across the street from the Baptist Building. In 1990 Korean Baptists were hosts of the meeting of the Baptist World Alliance in Seoul, which used the Olympic Stadium for the opening session. Just before the Congress and during its sessions, ten thousand were baptized in the Han River in two baptismal services. As the Republic of Korea in 1988 proclaimed its coming of age in the world community with its sponsorship of the Olympic Games, Korean Baptists now proclaimed their growing importance in the Baptist world community.

With other Korean Christians, Korean Baptists also are making their contribution to missions outside Korea. A Korean Baptist Overseas Mission Society and a South East Asia Baptist Mission Society have been formed. The large Kang Nam Joon Ang Baptist Church of Seoul with more than ten thousand adult members supports mission work in both Ghana and Taiwan. Koreans in other countries are making their mark as well. In the USA Korean Baptists are probably the fastest growing Baptist body among ethnics, while in the former USSR Koreans have formed churches in Uzbekistan and Kazakhstan.

Unlike Japan, Baptists in Korea, by and large, are united in one Baptist body and work with one Baptist mission. There are, however, 160 churches related to the Baptist Bible Fellowship in Korea, a work begun by Mr. and Mrs. Isaac Foster, and which also supports foreign mission work. The Baptist Bible Fellowship in America has at present twelve missionary families appointed to the field. Baptist Faith Missions sent Louis Carver in 1971 who organized a church in Seoul in the following year and two others by 1979. The American Baptist Association has organized a few Missionary Baptist churches and missions. Several other fundamentalist Baptist missions also have missionaries in the country.

Although North Korea continues to be sealed off from the West and the Christian world, Baptists have been able to make a few contacts. A delegation of Korean-American pastors visited Pyongyang in 1989, attending services at the Bongsu Church, the only Protestant church building in the country at the time. A little later representatives of Cooperative Services International (CSI), a Southern Baptist aid organization, visited Pyongyang in an attempt to develop ties with the country. Early in 1994 Billy Graham visited the president of the country.

BIBLIOGRAPHY: Malcolm C. Fenwick, the founder of the Corea Intinerant Mission, wrote, *The Church of Christ in Corea* (New York: George H. Doran, 1911; reprint, Seoul: Baptist Publications, 1967), which describes his work in the country. A carefully written history by a Korean Baptist from a Korean perspective is the work by Timothy Hyo-Hoon Cho, *A History of the Korea Baptist Convention: 1889–1969* (Th.D. dissertation, Southern Baptist Theological Seminary, 1970). For an account of the visit of representatives of the CSI to North Korea, see Mike Chute, "North Korea: A 'Socialist Paradise' Reaching Out," *Commission*, Feb./Mar. 1990, 6–33.

MONGOLIA (1994)

	Members	Churches
Baptist Church, Ulaanbaatar (1994)	17	(1)

*T*he country of Mongolia, an independent nation since 1921, was controlled by a totalitarian Communist regime until 1992. The country has long been Buddhist, but the regime suppressed most religious expression. With the coming of democratic reform and an opening to the West, Christianity found an opportunity for entrance.

Southern Baptists began to send teachers and medical workers to Mongolia. Gary and Evelyn Harthcock, who went to Mongolia in 1992 to teach English under the International Service Corps of the FMB of the Southern Baptist Convention, gathered a group for Bible study. As a result of this effort, more than forty Mongolian citizens requested the government to grant recognition to the formation of a Baptist church in Ulaanbaatar, the capital. On February 1, 1994, the government granted the petition, the first in Mongolia's history to a Christian church, though at the same time denying requests from as many as ten other Christian groups. Seventeen Mongolian Christians organized the church on February 14. At present it meets in the National Sports Center.

BIBLIOGRAPHY: Martha Skelton, "Mongolia: On Its Own," *Commission*, April 1993, 6–39, and "Mongolia: Land of Journeying Spirits," *Commission*, May 1993, 56–77. "Mongolian Baptists Recognized," *Commission*, Mar.-Apr. 1994, 3.

TAIWAN (REPUBLIC OF CHINA) (1948)

	Members	Churches
1. Chinese Baptist Convention (1954)	17,162	(152)
2. Baptist Bible Fellowship	1,440	(15)

3. Conservative Baptist Association (1959)	1,691	(24)
4. Baptist Missionary Association	<u>375</u>	<u>(6)</u>
	20,668	(197)

*W*ith the establishment of the People's Republic of China on the Chinese mainland in 1949, the Nationalist government of China with two million mainland Chinese fled to Taiwan, an island one hundred miles off the southeast coast of China. Since then it has maintained a separate Chinese regime. Christian missionaries soon found mainland China closed to them, but Taiwan was an open field.

Shortly before the influx of Chinese from the mainland, the China Baptist Convention in 1948 sent Yang Mei-tsai to Taiwan, who was accompanied by Bertha Smith, a Southern Baptist missionary who had been forced to leave Shandong. Services were held in Smith's home in Taipei, and a church was formed in August 1949. By the end of 1951 Southern Baptists had ten single women and two families at work in six cities. After rapid growth, membership leveled off in the middle 1960s. The increasing prosperity of Taiwanese society and a resurgence of traditional Chinese religion served as barriers to further expansion. Since then there has been additional growth, but it has fallen far short of early projections.

In 1952 the mission opened the Taiwan Baptist Theological Seminary. The missionaries at first concentrated on the Mandarin-speaking population, but in 1958 two chapels for native Taiwanese were established in Taipei. For mass communication, the mission prepared radio programs, published literature, and started bookstores and reading rooms. On Taiwan, Southern Baptists did not develop educational or benevolent institutions for the general populace but concentrated on evangelism. In 1954 the Chinese Baptist Convention was formed. In 1960 it sent its first missionary abroad to Bangkok, Thailand, and shortly afterward a couple to Korea. In 1984 the convention sent a missionary to American Samoa to minister to Chinese seamen. It also has sought to work among the Hakka minority and mountain tribal people on the island.

Taiwan has attracted other Baptist missions. The Baptist Bible Fellowship International (BBFI) has been present since 1950. Two of its earliest missionaries, Mr. and Mrs. William F. Logan, who had served in China, formed the Taipei Baptist Tabernacle. Today BBFI has eight couples in the country.

Conservative Baptists were the next to enter in 1952, sending both veteran Chinese missionaries and new appointees. Since other missions already were located in the large cities, the Conservative Baptists went to secondary cities in the south- central area and used both Mandarin and Taiwanese. Conservative Baptists founded a Conservative Baptist Bible College and a Literature Center, which produced some notable publications. In 1959 a Conservative Baptist Association was organized. Missionaries Ralph and Ruth Covell produced a Bible translation of the New Testament for the Sediq, a mountain people. In the mid-1960s missionaries changed their strategy by moving to the large urban centers. Through evangelistic services conducted by a Conservative Baptist missionary in 1959, Lee Teng-hui became a Christian; this man became president of the Republic of China in 1988.

The Baptist Missionary Association has a small work. Its first missionaries were Jack Bateman, born in China who spoke Chinese as a native, and his wife, LaTrell. Bateman formed the Gospel Baptist Church in Taipei. Two other mission couples joined the mission, and other congregations were formed. Today the mission is served by one missionary couple and two nationals. Baptists from Korea also have instituted some mission work in the country.

BIBLIOGRAPHY: For Southern Baptist work, see Baker J. Cauthen and others, *Advance* (Nashville: Broadman Press, 1970), 103–6; W. Carl Hunker, *Taiwan: Unfinished Revolution* (Nashville: Convention Press, 1970); Murray A. Rubinstein, "American Evangelicalism in the Chinese Environment: Southern Baptist Convention Missionaries in Taiwan, 1949–1989," *American Baptist Quarterly*, 2 (1983): 269–89, and Michael Chute, "Church Planting: The Challenge of Taiwan," *Commission*, May 1993, 6–53. The booklet, *What God Hath Wrought!* (Springfield, Mo.: BBF, 1957), 2:36–38, provides some data on the work of the BBFI. For Conservative Baptists, see Hans W. Finzel, ed., *Partners Together* (Wheaton, Ill.: CBFMS, 1993), 102–7. See John W. Duggar, *The Baptist Missionary Association of America (1950–1986)* (Texarkana, Tex.: Baptist Publishing House, 1988), 89, 135–36, 261, for the work of the BMA.

BAPTIST AND BAPTIST-RELATED MISSIONS

1. CHINA ABC (1836–1952), SBC (1845–1951), SDBMS (1847–1950), SwBMS (1891–?), Gospel Mission/Baptist China Direct Mission (1893–?), CaRegular Baptists (1934–c. 1941), ABWE (1946–1950), CBFMS (1946–1951), BM-M (1947–1951)

2. HONG KONG ABC (1842–1860, 1951), SBC (1949) BBFI (1950), ABWE (1951), BM-M (1952) CBI (1963)

2a. MACAU SBC (1910), CBI (1986)

3. JAPAN ABC (1872), SBC (1889), CBI (1947), BGC (1948), BM-M (1949), BBFI (1950), SwO (1949), NABC (1951), SwBMS (1952), ABWE (1953), BMA (1953), FWB (1954), ABA (1962), BIMI (1964), BWM (1964), CaFEBC (1965), MBM (1969), EBM (1983)

4. KOREA SBC (1950), BBFI (1958), BFM (1971), ABA (1972), BIMI (1978), BWM (1979), LIB (1980)

5. MONGOLIA SBC (1991)

6. TAIWAN (REPUBLIC OF CHINA) SBC (1948), BBFI (1950), CBI (1952), BMA (1953), BM-M (1972), BIMI (1979), MWBM (1987), KoSEABMS

B. OCEANIA

O ceania is a vast territory stretching across the Pacific Ocean from Australia and New Guinea on the west to the Americas on the east. The area includes the island states of Australia and New Zealand, countries which are related to the highly developed Western world. Oceania also includes thousands of other islands, all of which, except for New Guinea, are extremely small and may be regionally grouped based on their native populations, such as Micronesia, Melanesia, and Polynesia.

Baptists were very late in arriving in Australia and, although they were among the first settlers in New Zealand, they had a slow start there. In both Australia and New Zealand, as in other former British dominions, Baptists have always been poor cousins to the far better established Anglicans, Methodists, Presbyterians, and Roman Catholics. Elsewhere in Oceania, except for Guam, there was practically no Baptist presence until after World War II. Congregationalists, Methodists, and Mormons entered these islands early and undertook extensive mission work, but Baptist mission interests were elsewhere.

Baptists are now beginning to compensate a bit for past neglect. The most dramatic increase in Baptist numbers has been in Papua New Guinea, which Baptist missionaries entered less than fifty years ago. But even with the increase in recent years of Baptist missions and missionaries and their entry into new areas, Baptists are still far behind other major denominations in the area. In addition, there are no Baptist bodies in such territories as French Polynesia, the Cook Islands (which belongs to New Zealand), and Palau (a possession of the USA) or the small independent states of Kiribati, Marshall Islands, Nauru, Tonga, and Tuvalu.

	Members	Churches
1. Australia	64,662	836
2. Fiji	666	14
3. Guam	769	8
4. Micronesia (Chuuk Islands)	—	—
5. New Caledonia	—	—
6. New Zealand	24,636	214
7. Northern Mariana Islands	350	1
8. Papua New Guinea	38,250	525
9. Samoa (American and Western)	208	6

10. Solomon Islands	n/a	35
11. Vanuatu	n/a	1
	129,541	1,640

AUSTRALIA (1831)

	Members	Churches
1. Baptist Union of Australia (1926)	64,560	(785)
2. Association of Baptists for World Evangelism	n/a	(6)
3. Australian Baptist Independent Fellowship	n/a	(n/a)
4. Baptist Bible Fellowship International	n/a	(7)
5. Faith Baptist Churches Fellowship of Congregational Churches	n/a	(22)
6. Missionary Baptists (ABA)	n/a	(5)
7. Reformed Baptists	n/a	(4)
8. Seventh Day Baptists	78	(3)
9. Strict and Particular Baptist Churches	24	(4)
	64,662	(836)

NOTE: Except for the Baptist Union of Australia, Missionary Baptists, Seventh Day Baptists, and Strict and Particular Baptists, information on the various Baptist bodies was gained from David B. Barrett, ed., *World Christian Encyclopedia*, 156.

The first Baptist service of worship in Australia was held in Sydney on April 24, 1831, more than four decades after the British penal colony had begun in 1788. The first preacher was John McKaeg who conducted the first baptisms in Wolloomooloo Bay in 1832. While he gathered a motley group around him, a grant of land was received and plans for a chapel were made. Regrettably, he ended in jail, a social and economic disgrace, a drunkard and a bankrupt.

Faced with this tragic situation, a group of Sydney Baptists asked the Baptist Missionary Society (BMS) for assistance. They responded by inviting John Saunders to accept the post. A man of devotion, integrity, and with an undeniable missionary vocation, Saunders proved to be an outstanding leader. A chapel was built in Bathurst Street, and a church formed in 1836. Saunders became highly respected in the community, honored for his compassion toward convicts and aborigines, his opposition to transportation of convicts, and especially his leadership in the temperance movement. He established a strong church in the colony and became a leader for Baptists scattered through the other colonies.

The first Australian Baptist church actually had been formed in the southernmost colony of Van Diemen's Land (Tasmania from 1853). Henry Dowling, a strict

Calvinist, had led a small group to form a church in Hobart Town in 1835. This church was later dissolved. Dowling was revered widely as a father figure, traveling constantly between Launceston and Hobart, ministering to the convicts in what was probably the harshest penal colony. He also nurtured the few Baptists scattered about the colony.

The story of Australian Baptists during the early nineteenth century is generally one of unplanned beginnings, internal squabbles, lack of pastoral leadership, and very little support from the Baptists "back home" in Britain. Beginning so late in the colony's development meant that many Baptists had already identified with established churches of other denominations. Debates were fierce and unrelenting, especially about Calvinism, open membership, and open communion. These often led to divisions. The story is duplicated in each state, although the regional variations reflected in part the fortunes of those colonies. Even after the federation of the colonies into the Commonwealth of Australia in 1900, Baptist organization and economic strength remained with the individual states.

In New South Wales the early foundation laid by Saunders was threatened by lack of leadership. Parramatta was founded in 1851 with William Hopkins Carey (grandson of the famous missionary) as first pastor, but he died in 1852 at the age of twenty-two. A Baptist association was formed in 1868, later known as the Baptist Union.

In Tasmania the work initiated by Dowling was later to be strengthened by the generosity of William and Mary Ann Gibson. They were enthusiasts for the ministry of Charles Haddon Spurgeon and were inspired by the visits to the colony of his son Thomas. The Gibsons built fifteen chapels, many manses, and brought out young men from Spurgeon's Pastors' College—in 1885 his graduates occupied every pulpit in Tasmania. Spurgeon's influence was significant in all the Australian colonies, especially in Tasmania and New South Wales. The best known pastor to come to Australia from Spurgeon's college was the distinguished preacher and essayist F. W. Boreham, who had pastorates in Hobart and Melbourne. The Baptist Union of Tasmania was formed in 1884.

The situation of dissenters in South Australia, founded in 1836 with free settlers and no convicts, was different. But here, too, Baptist beginnings were marred by the same squabbles, even though the Scotch Baptist David Maclaren (father of the famous preacher and expositor Alexander) was a leading figure in the South Australian Company. Church services were held from 1837, but the coming of Silas Mead in 1861 marked a new and enlarged identity for Baptists in Adelaide. He established the Flinders Street Church which in ten years grew from 26 to 411. Mead, an advocate of open membership, was a pronounced Baptist who also worked harmoniously with others. His church was a model for many others, and numerous suburban churches were commenced by his people. The Baptist Union in this state was formed in 1863.

The first Baptist services were held in Melbourne (in what was to become Victoria after its independence from New South Wales) in 1837. With the coming of John Ham in 1843 and the formation of the Collins Street Church, the work in Victoria assumed a more stable identity. This church, like Sydney and Hobart, had accepted Crown grants of land. This raised another contentious issue for Baptists because the propriety of accepting state aid was generally rejected and seen as a compromise of Baptist beliefs. The discovery of gold in Victoria during the 1850s brought a boom growth to Victoria, which increased its population from 76,000 to 540,000 in a decade. Baptists

Johnson (Terry Colson's father), Paul Hartman, and his wife, Ruth, who was a dentist, made the journey to Puluwat, four thousand miles southwest of Hawaii. In 1993 the Colsons and a missionary from Australia, Hub Corbett, undertook an evangelistic trip to Satawan Island with plans for a continuing ministry there. Another mission, Independent Faith Mission, has two missionaries serving in the Chuuk Islands.

BIBLIOGRAPHY: For the work of Baptist Mid-Missions in the Chuuk Islands, see *Harvest*, winter 1994, 14–15.

NEW CALEDONIA (1989)

N ew Caledonia, a possession of France located between Australia and Fiji is predominantly Roman Catholic. A couple from the FMB of the Southern Baptist Convention arrived on the island in 1989 but left after two years. The FMB has appointed another couple to serve.

BIBLIOGRAPHY: *Your Guide to Foreign Missions*, 1994–1995, 103.

NEW ZEALAND (1851)

	Members	Churches
1. Baptist Union of New Zealand (1882)	23,936	(201)
2. Baptist Mid-Missions (BM-M)	40	(1)
3. Bible Baptists (BBFI)	400	(6)
4. Landmark Missionary Baptists (ABA)	140	(2)
5. Seventh Day Baptists	50	(2)
6. Baptist World Mission (BWM)	70	(2)
	24,636	(214)

T he treaty of Waitangi in 1840 between the indigenous Maori people of New Zealand and the British Crown marked the beginning of New Zealand as a nation. Baptists were among the early settlers, but it was not until 1851 that the first Baptist church was founded at Nelson. This pioneering work paved the way for other congregations in the scattered settlements. In early census returns Baptists represented about 2 percent of the population, a percentage that has hardly changed to this day.

In 1882 the twenty-two Baptist churches then in existence formed the Baptist Union of New Zealand to foster unity, joint action, an adequate ministry, and church growth. Unity has been advanced through annual assemblies and the monthly *New Zealand Baptist*, which today has a circulation of eleven thousand. Significant joint action began with the formation of the New Zealand Baptist Missionary Society (NzBMS) in

1885. Within a year the society sent its first missionary, Rosalie MacGeorge, to India. Since then the society has served in India, Bangladesh, Fiji, Indonesia, Zaire, France, Papua New Guinea, and Hong Kong.

The work of home missions and evangelism has included the appointment of national evangelists, church extension organizers, the development of a church growth school, and a variety of outreach efforts—the sponsorship of Billy Graham Crusades and, with the help of Southern Baptists, the introduction of the all-age Sunday School. Until the 1960s, following the British pattern, Sunday schools were for children only. For about a decade they operated with considerable success and then faded out under the pressure of social changes and the charismatic movement.

The charismatic movement aroused considerable suspicion initially. Gradually the churches began to accept its more positive aspects. By the 1980s the influence of the movement was particularly noticeable in changed patterns of worship, which became more spontaneous, usually led by lay leaders with pastors preaching. Instead of hymnals, most churches use overhead projectors with a variety of hymns, songs, and choruses. These changes may have gone too far—now there is considerable discussion about worship and its appropriate forms.

Early ministry was supplied largely from England. By the 1890s indigenous pastors began to be trained, but it was not until 1926 that the Baptist Theological College was established in Auckland. Today this school, renamed Carey Baptist College, has thirty-eight students.

Although the first four missionaries overseas were women, it was not until 1908 that women participated in the assemblies of the Baptist Union. Men monopolized the diaconate, committees, and the ministry. In 1984 Dame Vivian Boyd was elected president of the Union, the first woman to hold the office. Although a number of women have been trained as pastors, only two have held pastorates where they were in sole charge. Other women serve as chaplains, educators, and pastoral assistants. An increasing number of women also participate in church life as deacons, elders, and worship leaders.

New Zealand Baptists were founding members of the National Council of Churches (NCC) in 1941 and the World Council of Churches (WCC) in 1948. The NCC disbanded in 1985 to make way for a new ecumenical body. After much debate the Baptist Union decided not to affiliate with it but remains in the WCC, the Christian Conference of Asia, and local ecumenical bodies. Since Vatican Council II and the emergence of the charismatic movement, the traditional fear of Roman Catholicism has dissipated, and there is now a more open attitude. Separation of church and state remains a feature of New Zealand life, but in social service work Baptists regularly cooperate with the state for the benefit of the wider community.

Baptist life in New Zealand is becoming more multicultural. Apart from the important Maori ministry, work is developing among Chinese, Koreans, and immigrants from the Pacific Islands. Theologically, New Zealand Baptists are predominantly conservative evangelicals without the extremes of fundamentalism on the one hand or so-called modernism on the other. New Zealand Baptists, mainly a middle-class people, are in the process of rethinking their mission and worship. Denominational loyalty is not as strong as in the past, the working classes remain outside the churches, and witness in an increasingly secular and materialistic culture is demanding deeper understanding and commitment.

In addition to the churches of the Baptist Union, there are two congregations of Seventh Day Baptists, one formed in 1940 at Auckland on the North Island and another in 1943 at Christchurch on the South Island. In the last couple of decades, several fundamentalist Baptist groups of American origin have arrived. So far they have shown little readiness to cooperate with other Baptists.

Angus H. MacLeod

BIBLIOGRAPHY: Paul Tenson, J. Ayson Clifford, G. T. Beilby, and S. L. Edgar, *A Handful of Grain: A Centenary History of the Baptist Union of New Zealand,* 4 vols. (Wellington: New Zealand Baptist Historical Society, 1982–1984). John Laird, "History of New Zealand Baptists," *Chronicle,* 1 (1938): 115–21, 124.

NORTHERN MARIANA ISLANDS (1947)

	Members	Churches
Saipan Community Church (1967)	350	(1)

*T*he Commonwealth of the Northern Mariana Islands is a territory in political union with the USA. The Commonwealth includes fourteen islands, six of which are inhabited. Most inhabitants live in Saipan, the center of government and commerce. The native population is primarily Chamorro with immigrants from other islands. The majority of the population is Roman Catholic.

Upon the request of a U.S. navy chaplain for a missionary, the General Baptist Foreign Mission Society (GBFMS) sent Edward and Gertie Stevens to Saipan in 1947, thus initiating the Saipan Baptist Mission, the first Protestant work in the area. Stevens served as well on the neighboring island of Tinian, working among the lepers of the Tinian Leprosarium, and on Chi Chi Jima, far to the north in the Bonin Islands. In 1967 the Saipan Baptist Mission was reorganized, changing its name to the Saipan Community Church Affiliated with General Baptists. At this time it was primarily a congregation of civil service workers serving the United States government and composed of people from many denominations but including no General Baptists. With the influx of Christians from other islands in Micronesia as well as Filipinos, the congregation has now become increasingly cosmopolitan. With support from the GBFMS, the General Baptist churches in Guam, and the Saipan Church, Benito Porcadilla arrived in 1976 from the Philippines to work among Filipinos. The average attendance of the church is six hundred. The church is a member of the Marianas Association of General Baptists.

The Saipan Church assumed control of the Saipan Community School, constructing a building for it with money received from the Far East Broadcasting Corporation (FEBC). FEBC gave the funds in gratitude for the church's leasing to it some of its land for a broadcasting center. In 1976 a breakthrough in denominational cooperation occurred when the Saipan Church and Roman Catholics cooperated in distributing to every home *The Way*, a Living Bible version of Scripture, copies of which were provided by the World Home Bible League.

BIBLIOGRAPHY: For a detailed account of the General Baptist work on Saipan, see Charles L. Carr, *Seed, Soil, and Seasons* (Poplar Bluff, Mo.: GBFMS, 1988). Also see Leonora Mosende Douglas, ed., *World Christianity: Oceania* (Monrovia, Calif.: MARC and MARC Europe, 1986), 201–2.

PALAU (BELAU) (1981)

*P*alau (or Belau) is a self-governing territory in association with the USA, located in the Caroline chain. The population is only 15,000 with only eight of of its more than two hundred islands permanently populated. In 1981 two veteran missionary couples who had served in Liberia with Baptist Mid-Missions (BM-M), Karl and Marion Luyben and Floyd and Frances Holmes, moved to Koror, the capital of Palau which contains two-thirds of the population. They engaged in personal evangelism and a radio ministry. Today, however, BM-M has no mission work in the territory.

BIBLIOGRAPHY: Polly Strong, *Burning Wicks* (Cleveland: BM-M, 1984), 413.

PAPUA NEW GUINEA (1949)

	Members	Churches
1. Baptist Union of Papua New Guinea (1977)	35,500	(325)
2. Independent Baptists	2,750*	(200)
a. ABWE	500	(n/a)
b. BBFI	2,250	(60)
c. BIMI	n/a	(n/a)
d. BWM	n/a	(n/a)
e. MBM	n/a	(n/a)
	38,250	(525)

*As one might note, membership of Independent Baptists is incomplete.

*P*apua New Guinea occupies the eastern half of the island of New Guinea. In 1905 Australia acquired the southern half of eastern New Guinea from Great Britain and gained the northern half from Germany as a result of World War I. Papua New Guinea became an independent nation in 1975. The inhabitants are divided in numerous tribes, speaking many distinct languages. They lived as primitive people isolated from the rest of the world until the beginning of Western penetration in the last half of the nineteenth century. The population today is largely Christianized, one of the great success stories of missions in the modern era.

Because of the interest of Australian army chaplains who saw New Guinea as a possible mission field during their service in World War II, Australian Baptists opened a

(Literature Committee, National Council of Churches, Bangladesh/Bangladesh Baptist Sangha, 1987), and Brian Stanley, *The History of the Baptist Missionary Society* (Edinburgh: T&T Clark, 1992), 401–7, 431–34. The mission activity of the Australian Baptists may be found in Jess Redman, *The Light Shines On* (Victoria: Australian BMS, 1982), and of the New Zealand Baptists in S. L. Edgar and M. J. Eade, *Toward the Sunrise* (Wellington, New Zealand: New Zealand Baptist Historical Society, 1985). For Southern Baptist beginnings, see Baker J. Cauthen and others, *Advance* (Nashville: Broadman Press, 1970), 236–38. Material on the work of the ABWE is in Harold T. Commons, *Heritage & Harvest* (Cherry Hill, N.J.: ABWE, 1981), 127–41. For the medical work of Viggo B. Olsen, see his book, *Daktar* (Chicago: Moody Press, 1975).

BHUTAN

The small kingdom of Bhutan in the eastern Himalayas, located between India and China, is predominantly Buddhist with a Hindu minority. The government permits no missionary activity, and there is only one Roman Catholic parish and no organized Protestant church in the country. The Ao Baptist Churches Association of Nagaland, India, has some work in the country among the Hindu.

BIBLIOGRAPHY: Lary D. Pate, *From Every People* (Monrovia, Calif.: MARC, 1989), 148.

INDIA (1793)

	Members	Churches
A. North (Hindustan)		
1. Association of Oriya Baptist Churches (1922)	2,901	(61)
2. Baptist Union of North India (1948)	n/a	(n/a)
3. Bengal Baptist Fellowship (1979)	1,200	(44)
4. Bengal Baptist Union (1935) (BMS)	3,800	(39)
5. Bengal Baptist Union (1935)	n/a	(n/a)
6. Christian Service Society (Bengal Orissa Bihar Baptist Convention)	7,994	(69)
7. Conference of Free Will Baptists (1952)	2,048*	(12)
8. Cuttack and Sambalpur Dioceses of the Church of North India (1970)	25,562	(n/a)
9. Fellowship of Free Baptist Churches of North India (1950s)	915	(33)
10. Original Free Will Baptists (1975)	n/a	(48)
11. Sora Association of Baptist Churches (1950)	4,000	(200)
12. Utkal Baptist Churches Association (1922)	2,500	(12)
	50,920	(518)

B. Northeast (Assam and Neighboring States)

    Council of Baptist Churches in North

East India (1950)	549,800	(4,262)
13. Assam Baptist Convention (1914)		
14. Garo Baptist Convention (1875)		
15. Karbi Anglong Baptist Convention (1990)		
16. Manipur Baptist Convention		
17. Nagaland Baptist Church Council (1937)		
18. Association of Regular Independent		
Baptist Churches of India	2,329	(58)
19. Baptist Church of Mizoram (1903)	48,000	(300)
20. Lower Assam Baptist Union	12,597	(157)
21. North Bank Christian Association (1950)	39,559	(585)
22. Tripura Baptist Christian Union (1938)	<u>25,000</u>	<u>(350)</u>
	677,285	(5,712)

C. Northwest

23. Northwest India Baptist Association (1977)	<u>20,000</u>	<u>(80)</u>
	20,000	(80)

D. South (Dravidian)

24. American Baptist Association Mission (1973)	n/a	(9)
25. Baptist Bible Believers Association (1968)	250	(5)
26. Convention of Baptist Churches of		
the Northern Circars (1947)	125,000	(125)
27. India Association of General Baptists (1982)	9,400	(81)
28. Independent Bible Baptist Convention (1987)	5,000	(99)
29. India Seventh Day Baptist Conference	38,024	(258)
30. Karnataka Baptist Convention (1977)	13,000	(105)
31. Malankara Seventh Day Baptist Church	83	(3)
32. Samavesam of Telugu Baptist Churches (1897)	431,832	(835)
33. Telugu Baptist Churches (Independent) (1968)	1,000	(20)
34. Tamil Baptists (Strict Baptists)	1,100	(70)
35. Tamilnod Association of Free Will		
Baptist Churches (1967)	<u>n/a</u>	<u>(4)</u>
	624,689	(1,614)

E. South Central (Maharashtra State)

36. Baptist Bible Fellowship (1955)	n/a	(n/a)
37. Baptist Christian Association (1957)	2,369	(29)
38. Baptist Missionary Association		
of Maharashtra (1975)	n/a	(n/a)
39. Convention of Baptist Churches of Maharashtra	7,420	(37)
40. Separate Baptists in Christ	<u>1,200</u>	<u>(3)</u>
	10,989	(69)
Grand Totals	1,383,883	(7,993)

*The membership, representing average attendance and not baptized members, also includes the Tamilnod Association of Free Will Baptist Churches.

STATISTICS: There are at least two other small bodies, Baptist Christian Churches and New Testament Baptist Christian Association, both members of the International Council of Christian Churches (ICC), which are unlocated. The names of Baptist bodies and missions and the statistics have come in part from David B. Barrett, ed., *World Christian Encyclopedia*, 377–80; BWA, *Yearbook*, 1993–1994, 98; and *Mission Handbook*, 1993–1995, 344–48. The editor gained additional information through correspondence and interview.

*A*lthough India possesses an ancient civilization, it has been independent only since 1947 when Great Britain granted it the status of a self-governing dominion. Three years later India became a republic. Its territory of more than one and a quarter million square miles includes most of the Indian subcontinent and extends from the lofty Himalayas in the north across the Ganges Plain to the Deccan Peninsula in the south. With a population of around 900 million, which continues to grow at a high rate, India is one of the most populous countries in the world with many diverse languages and cultures. India is a federal union of twenty-six states and nine union territories, whose boundaries coincide rather closely to the major linguistic divisions of the nation. The Hindus predominate and include about 79 percent of the population, but there is a strong Moslem minority of 11 percent and a smaller Christian community of 4 percent.

India became the first Baptist foreign mission field with the arrival in 1793 of William Carey (1761–1834) and Dr. John Thomas in Bengal. Carey is not only one of the great heroes of the Baptist faith but, because of his manifesto for Christian missions, *An Inquiry into the Obligation of Christians, to Use Means for the Conversion of the Heathens*, and his example on the mission field, he also has been called the father of modern missions. His accomplishments in evangelism, training, translation of Scripture, establishment of schools, and social reform continue to be inspiring monuments to his work. In November 1993 in Calcutta more than 3,500 Indian Baptists and their guests celebrated the bicentennial of Carey's arrival. Before the celebration, 150 Indian leaders attended an Evangelism and Mission Conference, sponsored by the Asian Baptist Federation and the BWA.

Although the government of India has reduced greatly the number of Western missionaries in the country, Baptist missions continue financial support, assisting Baptist work through the few remaining missionaries or increasingly through national work-ers. Today, by and large, Indian Baptists control the Baptist work and are responsible for much of the evangelism. In an effort to increase the pace of evangelism and church planting, Southern Baptists organized in 1982 National Indian Ministries for the train-ing and support of Indian nationals, a program which seeks to work nationally with various Baptist groups.

After two hundred years of Baptist activity, India, with a membership of around 1,400,000 Baptists, has more Baptists than any other nation, except the USA. Baptists are the largest Protestant body in India. The country possesses a great diversity of Baptist groups which vary in size. The Baptist Union of India, which sought to coordinate Baptist work, never became a viable organization. As in the USA, Baptists are spread unevenly throughout the country. They exhibit great strength among the tribal hill peo-ple of the northeast and among the Telugus of the south, but in Hindustan, the tradi-tional heartland of India, and in the north and northwest the Baptist presence is weak.

BIBLIOGRAPHY: Over fifty biographies have been written on the life of Carey. One stan-dard biography is S. Pearce Carey, *William Carey, D.D. Fellow of Linnean Society* (London: Hodder and Stoughton, 1923, 2d ed., and New York: George H. Doran, 1923). For recent biographical studies of William Carey and his coworkers, see Timothy George, *Faithful Witness: The Life and Mission of William Carey* (Birmingham, Ala.: New Hope, 1991), and the well-illustrated issue of *Christian History*, 11, no. 4. Although a number of volumes have been written on various Baptist missions in India, there is no one comprehensive history of Baptists in the country. Henry C. Vedder, *A Short History of Baptist Missions* (Philadelphia; Judson Press, 1927), 1–86, and Jasper L. McPhail, *Beneath the Himalayas* (Nashville: Convention Press, 1966), provide, however, general surveys of Baptist work. The June/July 1992 issue of *Commission* contains valuable articles on the current status of Baptist work in India from a Southern Baptist perspective.

A. NORTH INDIA (HINDUSTAN)

Baptists of North India Historically Related to the Baptist Missionary Society

India was the first mission field selected by the Baptist Missionary Society (BMS), which was formed by a group of English Particular (Calvinistic) Baptists in 1792. India was thus the first non-Western country in which churches of a Baptist faith and order were planted. The pioneering BMS missionaries, William Carey and John Thomas, landed in Bengal on November 10, 1793. The earliest Baptist churches were formed at Serampore, where the first Indian baptist, Krishna Pal, was baptized in December 1800, and in Calcutta, where a Baptist service of worship began in 1803, leading to the opening of Lall Bazar Baptist chapel in 1809. Under the leadership of Joshua Marshman, the missionaries invested heavily in education—from elementary schools upwards to Serampore College, which was founded in 1818 to train Indian nationals to evangelize their fellow countrymen. By 1837, BMS work had spread within West Bengal to other centers, such as Katwa and Suri; and beyond it to East Bengal (mod-ern Bangladesh), to Monghyr in the state of Bihar, and to Allahabad, Agra, and Delhi in northwestern India. By 1843 the BMS churches recorded a total of 454 church mem-bers in Bengal and a further 465 in northern India. About half of these members, how-ever, were of European origin. In addition, the General Baptist Missionary Society (GBMS) of England, formed in 1816 by the General Baptist New Connexion, had begun in the state of Orissa in 1822. GBMS had about two hundred converts by 1842.

The slow progress of church growth among the Hindu population of northern India was a discouragement which the BMS and GBMS shared with all other Protestant missions working in the same area. The primary obstacle was the caste system, which dictated that any Hindu who professed conversion to Christianity became a literal "outcaste" from society, deprived of normal means of livelihood and consequently dependent on the mission community for financial support and protection. Most of the Baptist churches which developed in nineteenth-century-India were accordingly weak in number, social status, and resources of finance and leadership. In 1868 only two or three of the 130 native agents employed by the BMS in India were not supported wholly by BMS funds or by funds collected from Europeans in India. Over the next half-century, this depressing picture was modified to some extent, especially in the stronger churches of the Barisal district of East Bengal. By 1913 forty-seven Indian pastors and thirty evangelists were supported by the churches. Nevertheless, the essential problem remained. When promising Christian leaders did emerge, the poverty of the people appeared to dictate that these should become not pastors of Indian congregations but "Indian home missionaries" employed and paid by the BMS. This trend lies at the root of the relative weakness of the Baptist churches in northern India today.

The main exceptions to this picture of relative weakness and dependency were among tribal and low-caste peoples, who were the focus of an increasing amount of missionary attention from the 1880s onwards. The Mundas and other aboriginal peoples of West Orissa, the Santals of northern Bengal, and the inhabitants of the Chittagong Hill Tracts, and the Lushai of Mizoram (in the far northeast) responded in large numbers. The Mizoram mission in northeastern India, commenced in 1903, yielded a self-supporting Baptist church by 1913. In Orissa, the story of Baptist church growth among tribal peoples has continued to the present. From 1956 the tribal peoples of the Kond Hills turned to Christ on a scale which no missionary had dared to anticipate.

It was in the tribal areas of BMS work in India, where conversion took place on a suffcent scale for self-sustaining churches, that the most rapid progress toward genuinely autonomous Baptist churches was made. The first fully autonomous church body to be formed in the BMS India mission was the Utkal Central Church Council established in Orissa in 1933. It drew its numerical strength from the tribal animistic people of West Orissa. In Bengal and northern India, on the other hand, where the problems of dependency were more acute, the transfer of power from mission to church proved harder to implement. The process began in Bengal in 1931, but it was only in 1935 that the Bengal Baptist Union began to secure substantial autonomy from the BMS. In northern India the Baptist Union of North India was not formed until 1948.

India stood in the vanguard of the movement toward Protestant church union which gathered strength in the wake of the World Missionary Conference at Edinburgh in 1910. The Church of North India (CNI), formed in November 1970, is unique among modern church unions in its successful inclusion of Baptist Christians among a pedobaptist majority. Not all BMS-related churches, however, elected to join. The Baptist Church of Mizo District had withdrawn at an earlier state from the CNI negotiations, partly on theological grounds and also because of the prospect of a separate church union in northeast India, which has not yet been realized. Neither the Bengal Baptist Union nor the Baptist Union of North India was able to reach a united decision either for or against the CNI: their member churches made individual decisions to join or stay out. By 1975 about three quarters of the former Baptist churches of West Bengal and about half of the churches of Bihar, Delhi, Baraut, and Simla had entered. In both parts of northern India a small offshoot of Baptist churches remained, out of fellowship with those churches that had entered. Church union has sadly left the churches of a Baptist tradition in northern India more divided rather than less divided.

Both in Bengal and in northern India the baptistic Christian community remains small and relatively weak in resources. Only in Orissa have Baptists entered the CNI in sufficient numbers to exert a decisive and creative influence on the united church. The Cuttack diocese was one of the largest in the CNI at its formation, extending more than three hundred miles from east to west, and containing 25,562 members, many of them Baptists in the Kond Hills. The Orissa Baptist leader, J. K. Mohanty, became the first Bishop of Cuttack. In 1972 the diocese split in two, and a separate diocese of Sambulpur was created in West Orissa.

Perhaps the most noticeable change in Indian Baptist church life discernible from the late 1960s onwards was the decreasing role played by foreign missionaries. In 1955 there were 138 BMS missionaries serving in the country. From 1966, the picture changed rapidly as government opposition to the involvement of expatriates in the Indian Church hardened. In 1994 there are only four missionaries. On the other hand, the assumption of mission responsibility by the Indians themselves, such as Mizoram in the northeast, more than compensates for this loss.

Brian Stanley

BIBLIOGRAPHY: E. Daniel Potts, *British Baptist Missionaries in India 1793–1837: The History of Serampore and its Missions* (Cambridge: Cambridge University Press, 1967). Brian Stanley, *The History of the Baptist Missionary Society 1792–1992* (Edinburgh: T&T Clark, 1992).

Baptists of North India Historically Related to the American Baptist Churches in the U.S.A.

Christian Service Society (CSS). Missionary work by American Baptists in the Bengal-Orissa-Bihar region commenced at the same time as in southern and northeastern India, but at first the work was under the Free Will Baptist Missionary Society. In 1911 the twenty-three churches with 1,621 members came under the American Baptist Foreign Mission Society when Free Will Baptists in the North joined with the Northern Baptist Convention (now American Baptist Churches, USA).

Members of CSS churches are found in the area where the three states of Bengal, Bihar, and Orissa come together. They speak four major languages—Bengali, Hindi, Santali, and Oriya. In some urban centers of Orissa, Telegu-speaking people are also members of the churches. This mission never experienced the large-scale movements that took place in Andhra and among the hill tribes of the northeast, partly because of the problems of linguistic diversity. Always a small church, it was difficult to build leadership at the denominational level or maintain institutions established by the mission.

The mission placed its main institutional emphasis on education. Free Will Baptists established the Balasore Industrial School in 1906. There were also high schools for both boys and girls at Balasore; the schools at Bhimpore primarily served the Santal community. It was among the Santals, a tribal people, that the evangelistic work was most effective during the twentieth century.

Frederick S. Downs

Other Baptists in North India

As already indicated, there are serious divisions among Baptists in northern India. While many Baptists entered the Church of North India, a number of Baptists in both the Baptist Union of North India and the Bengal Baptist Union retained their identity. In the separation, Baptists who refused to join went to court to retain their church property. To add to the confusion, there are two Bengal Baptist Unions, one which relates to the BMS and the other which receives Southern Baptist support.

The historic Carey Baptist Church in Calcutta, where Adoniram Judson and Luther Rice were immersed, remains independent. In 1955 J. William Cook, a Conservative Baptist pastor of the Carey Church, established Calcutta Bible College, which adjoins the church. The school, which receives financial support from Conservative Baptists and Southern Baptists, seeks to work with various Baptist groups and trains pastors and church planters.

In 1905 Canadian Baptists sent J. A. and Eva Glendinning to work in the hilly eastern Ghats in the state of Orissa. Early on, work among the Oriyas, a Hindu people, made good progress. In 1910 a church was organized at Buradingi. In 1922 four churches formed an Association of Oriya Baptist Churches (later known as Utkal Baptist Churches Association). In 1929 the mission opened a hospital. In spite of defection, persecution, and loss of missionary personnel, the work, although small, survived. Canadian Baptists also extended their work to the Soras, an animistic tribe, who lived interspersed among the Oriyas. The first Sora was baptized in 1928, and an association organized in 1950, which was reconstituted in 1958. The missionaries put the Sora language into writing and produced a Sora New Testament, which was published in 1965.

The work of the Örebro Mission Society from Sweden commenced with the arrival of C. E. Sjogren in 1908. Although Sjogren died two years later, the work continued with other arrivals, including Lydia Magnusson and Helga Modig, who settled in the Deoria district on the Ganges Plains in Uttar Pradesh Province. The work also branched out into the Gorakhpur district and into Bihar and West Bengal. In the 1950s a Fellowship of Free Baptist Churches in North India was formed, which today is a member of the Evangelical Fellowship of India.

In 1947 the National Association of Free Will Baptists from the USA opened a work with Paul Woolsey and his wife. The work developed primarily in Bihar and West Bengal, and today has only one missionary on the field. A Conference of Free Will Baptists was formed in 1952. The Board of Foreign Missions of the Convention of Original Free Will Baptists of North Carolina opened work in 1975. A headquarters church is in Bareilly in Uttar Pradesh Province. In 1992 the mission had forty-eight congregations and twenty-eight elementary schools with an enrollment of four thousand students.

At Bishnupur in 1979 native Indian Baptists under the leadership of K. K. Santh and Pallab Ray formed the Bengal Baptist Fellowship. It is a member of the BWA and is independent of any foreign Baptist mission.

Albert W. Wardin, Jr.

B. NORTHEAST INDIA (ASSAM AND NEIGHBORING STATES)

Baptists of Northeast India Historically Related to the American Baptist Churches in the USA

Council of Baptist Churches in North East India (CBCNEI). One of the most successful mission fields of the American Baptist Churches, USA, has been the area encompassed by the CBCNEI. The members of CBCNEI churches live in the five northeastern Indian states of Assam, Arunachal Pradesh, Manipur, Meghalya, and Nagaland. They speak about fifty different languages. Because no language is understood by all members, the work of the CBCNEI as a whole is done in English, the medium of higher education in India.

The missionaries who began work in the northeast in 1836 were first attempting to find a route over the mountains into the Shan territories of northern Burma and southern China. Finding that impractical, they turned instead to the plains-dwelling Assamese, where the first convert, Nidhi Levi, was baptized in 1841. The first church was organized in 1845 with three branch congregations at Sibsagar, Nagaon, and Guwahati.

At the turn of the century, Baptists were found mainly among the tea garden laborers of Upper Assam and the Garos of Mehalaya. It was not long, however, before the Christian movement gained momentum in Nagaland and Manipur. During the second decade of the twentieth century and continuously since, the movement in Nagaland has grown in strength, beginning with the Ao Nagas and gradually being introduced among the many other tribes. Today Baptists are the leading religious body in Nagaland with 270,000 members, 1,272 churches, and nineteen tribal associations and include large churches with up to four thousand members. In Manipur, similarly, the small band of student-converts at the Ukhrul mission school was the beginning of a large-scale movement that began after World War I and was accelerated as the result of a charismatic revival. The mission, local congregations, and associations appointed evangelists for work among the hill areas, but it was mainly laypeople who spread the faith.

Inasmuch as all of the hill tribes did not have a written language, the missionaries undertook the work of reducing their languages to written form—eventually using the Roman script for the purpose. Consequently, it was among these peoples that Christians produced the first literature, often portions of the Scriptures in addition to the grammars and other learning tools needed for their schools.

In the plains areas there were a number of schools in rural and urban centers, but the most important institutions were the cluster known as the Jorhat Christian schools, established at Jorhat in Upper Assam in the early part of the century. Graduates of the high school at Jorhat assumed important positions in Assamese professional, economical, and political life. It was in the hills, however, that the most extensive educational work was done since the British government gave to the mission responsibility for the entire educational system in the Garo Hills, Nagaland, and the hill areas of Manipur. Higher-level training schools produced teachers for the network of village schools that were supported partly by government grants but mainly by the contributions of the people themselves. In due course the mission established Bible schools in the major language areas. Later the English-language central Bible school at Jorhat was upgraded to a theological seminary, Eastern Theological College. Regional seminaries were instituted at Mokokchung in the Ao Naga area and at Kangpokpi in Manipur.

During the nineteenth century, missionaries had often provided medicine and elementary health services, but it was not until the twentieth century that systematic medical work was begun. The first hospital was built at Tura in the Garo Hills, followed by others.

The churches in the northeast are organized into structures which superficially resemble those of Baptists elsewhere but which actually represent adaptation to the context. Local congregations, each with its own pastor, are grouped in various ways. There are mother-daughter church complexes, or circles. The most important group is the association. The association initially represented a single language group, though larger groups are broken down into several associations. These associations are in turn grouped together into five regional conventions: Assam, Garo, Karbi Anglong, Manipur, and Nagaland. The five conventions are members of the Council of Baptist Churches in North East India (CBCNEI), formed in 1950. At that time the American Baptist mission turned over its mission responsibilities to this body. With a restructuring of the Council in 1992, each body was encouraged to apply separately for membership in the Baptist World Alliance (BWA), which three have now done. Membership of the CBCNEI in the BWA is now terminated.

From the time of its creation in 1950, the CBCNEI sent missionaries to unevangelized parts of the northeast and has participated in the United Mission to Nepal, besides sending teams of medical workers to serve refugees in Southeast Asia. Even earlier associations and individual congregations began to send evangelists or missionaries to work among other tribes. The Nagas alone have more than one thousand missionaries serving in Myanmar, Nepal, and India.

Various insurgencies in the northeast affected the CBCNEI during the second half of the century. They accelerated the departure of foreign missionaries and disrupted the normal activities of the churches in Nagaland and Manipur. In both those areas Christians played a significant role in movements to bring peace. In three states in which CBCNEI churches are found—Meghalaya, Nagaland, and Manipur—Christians have come to occupy positions of political, social, and economic dominance. This gave status to the Christian community and led to considerable increase in its material resources.

Theologically, the CBCNEI reflects the ethos of mainline evangelicalism that the founding missionaries represented. Because of this, it has embraced the conciliar and cooperative institutional ecumenism of their parent denomination. The CBCNEI is related to the National Council of Churches in India, the regional constituent council of the area in which it is located, the Baptist Council on World Mission, the BWA, and several Asian Baptist and ecumenical organizations. Although it does not belong to the World Council of Churches, it participates in a number of its programs. Generally, it represents a comprehensive ecumenism that relates them to the WCC and the National Christian Council of India on the one hand and the Evangelical Fellowship of India on the other. Until after World War II there were no significant theological divisions among the Indian members of the churches. After that, such differences have appeared, largely due to the influence of American-based fundamentalists. In no case has this led to the division of the churches, though it has contributed to the reluctance of at least some of them to enter into church unions. By and large, contextual issues like linguism, tribalism, and castism have been more important than theological issues in creating tensions with the churches.

Frederick S. Downs

BIBLIOGRAPHY: Dana M. Albaugh, *Between Two Centuries: A Study of Four Mission Fields, Assam, South India, Bengal-Orissa, and South China* (Philadelphia: Judson Press, 1935). Victor Hugo Sword, *Baptists in Assam* (Chicago: Missionary Press, 1935). Robert G. Torbet, *Venture of Faith* (Philadelphia: Judson Press, 1955). Joseph Puthenpurakal, *Baptist Missions in Nagaland* (Calcutta: Firma KLM, 1984). Milton S. Sangma, *History of American Baptist Mission in Northeast India, 1836–1950*, 2 vols. (New Delhi: Mittal Publications, 1987–1992). Frederick S. Downs, *The Mighty Works of God: A Brief History of the Council of Baptist Churches in North East India: The Mission Period 1836–1950* (Gauhati: Christian International Centre, 1971); "Social Influences on Nineteenth-Century Baptist Missionaries in India," *American Baptist Quarterly* 8, no. 4 (1989): 247–56; *History of Christianity in India*, vol. 5, part 5, *North East India in the Nineteenth and Twentieth Centuries* (Bangalore: Church History Association of India, 1992).

Baptists Historically Related to the Baptist Missionary Society

Baptist Church of Mizoram. In 1903 the BMS sent J. H. Lorrain and F. W. Savidge, who had worked formerly under other missions in northeast India, into southern Mizoram—territory released by the Welsh Calvinistic Methodists. The Mizo people were animists and former headhunters. With the beginning of revival in 1907 and the establishment of the all-age Sunday School, by 1913 the Mizo Baptist community had become self-supporting and self-propagating. The mission provided training for church leaders as well as general education for both boys and girls. This helped to make Mizoram one of the most literate states in India. With the Presbyterian church in the north, it is said that Mizoram today is 85 percent Christian.

In 1968 the Baptist Church of Mizoram formed the Zoram Baptist Mission, which has reached out beyond its own people. The mission began working among Chakma and Riang immigrants in western Mizoram. With the withdrawal of the Australian BMS from the Goalpara district of Assam and upon its invitation, the Zoram Baptist Mission in 1968 began working among the Rabha people in the Goalpara district of Assam. In similar manner, the mission also took up work with the Tripura Baptist Christian Union when the New Zealand BMS withdrew. Including their missionaries in other parts of India and Thailand, the Baptists of Mizoram, with a membership of around 41,000 in 1989, were supporting 581 full-time pastors and other church workers. In Mizoram the vision of the younger churches becoming the pioneers of mission within Asia in the post-colonial age is already a reality.

Brian Stanley and Albert W. Wardin, Jr.

BIBLIOGRAPHY: Brian Stanley, *The History of the Baptist Missionary Society 1792–1992* (Edinburgh: T&T Clark, 1993), 269–76, 426–27.

Other Baptist Bodies

After consultation with the American Baptist mission in Assam, in 1947 American Baptists released the Goalpara district in southern Assam to the Australian Baptist Missionary Society (ABMS). The pioneer missionaries were Wilf and Gwen Crofts, who began work among the Boro people. The mission extended its work to the Rabhas and the Garos, a people related to the Garos in Bangladesh among whom the ABMS was already working. Three unions were formed—Goalpara Boro Baptist Church Union, Rabha Baptist Church Union, and North Golpara Garo Baptist Union—which today are part of the Lower Assam Baptist Union.

For some time the New Zealand Baptist Missionary Society (NZBMS) had an interest in Tripura state which adjoined its work in East Bengal (Bangladesh). It was not until 1938 that the maharaja of Tripura granted permission to missionaries of the society to enter. The North East General Mission had already engaged in some mission work in the area but withdrew, leaving the entire field to the NZBMS. In December 1938 the Christians who were already in the state formed the Tripura Baptist Christian Union. In spite of periodic persecution, growth has been rapid, increasing from 300 believers in fourteen congregations in 1940 to twenty-five thousand today. By the time the last missionaries of the NZBMS were forced to leave in 1973, the Tripura Union was completely autonomous. During their service, the missionaries had estabished a 35-bed hospital, two district dispensaries, Tripura Theological School, Bible and Training School, Christian Literature Society, Christian Welfare Society, Women's Society, St. Paul's (a high school), and village schools.

With the establishment by the Baptist General Conference (BGC, then known as the Swedish Baptist Conference of America) of its own Board of Foreign Missions and its cutting of ties with the American Baptist Foreign Mission Society (ABFMS), the conference sought a field in Assam where its missionaries had worked under the ABFMS for years. The ABFMS granted the North Bank, north of the Brahamaputra River, a plain which was 250 miles in length and thirty to sixty miles in width. In 1945 the first four missionaries began work in a field which at that time had 121 churches in three associations. The mission engaged in evangelism, education, and medicine; this included opening a hospital at Tezpur in 1954, a lying-in hospital, a medical center for lepers, a mobile medical unit, and dispensaries. The last missionary left in 1980. At that time the work had 275 churches, but today there are 585. The churches on the field formed the North Bank Christian Association, which has five associations, each with its own language. The work is completely self-supporting. The BGC, however, continues to serve as a partner in training, literacy work, medicine, and church planting. The association is a member of the Evangelical Fellowship of India.

The work of Baptist Mid-Missions (BM-M) began in 1935 with Dr. and Mrs. G. G. Crozier, veteran missionaries who formerly had served under the ABFMS and the Northeast India General Mission. They began work among Manipuris who had migrated to the Cachar district of southern Assam. The mission established a hospital at Alipur, a leprosy colony at Makunda, and a Christian Literature House, Christian Press, and the Northeast India Baptist Bible College at Silchar. The work was extended to other tribes. By the mid-1970s the mission had forty-eight churches and more than 2,300 members in three fellowships—Fellowship of Baptist Churches in Assam with work in more than ten languages, the New Testament Baptist Churches Association among the Simte people in southern Manipur, and the Fellowship of Mizo New Testament Baptist Churches among the Mizo.

Albert W. Wardin, Jr.

BIBLIOGRAPHY: For work of Australian Baptists, see Jess Redman, *The Light Shines On* (Hawthorn, Victoria: Australian BMS, 1982), 115–16, 121–33, and for New Zealand Baptists, see S. L. Edgar and M. J. Eade, *Toward the Sunrise* (Wellington: New Zealand Baptist Historical Society, 1985), 143–244. For the early work of the BGC on the North Bank of Assam, see David Guston and Martin Erikson, eds., *Fifteen Eventful Years* (Chicago: Harvest Publications, 1961), 84–100. For the work of BM-M, see *Field Surveys* (Cleveland: BM-M, c. 1977), 29–36.

C. NORTHWEST INDIA

North West India Baptist Association

There is only one Baptist body in northwest India—the North West India Baptist Association. This Baptist group had its beginning in 1977 when Nazir Masih, a native Indian resigning as a translator and distributor of literature for Every Home Crusade, began preaching in the city of Chanigarh. Although baptized as a believer and believing Baptist principles, he knew nothing of Baptists until John Wardle, a Southern Baptist pastor visiting from Florida, encouraged him to begin evangelistic work.

Masih first formed a house church and, with Southern Baptist financial assistance, constructed a church building, which required $200,000 to meet the government's specifications. Masih is engaged in an aggressive church planting ministry in the states of Chanigarh and Punjab. By 1992 he and twenty-two church planters had established 120 churches and 250 preaching points with a membership of twenty thousand.

Albert W. Wardin, Jr.

BIBLIOGRAPHY: Michael Chute, "India: Baptist in Head and Heart in Chanigarh," *Commission*, June/July 1992, 30–37.

D. SOUTH INDIA (DRAVIDIAN)

Baptists of South India Historically Related to the American Baptist Churches in the USA

Samvesam of Telegu Baptist Churches (STBC). The work in Andhra Pradesh and northeast India was started by American Baptist missionaries in the same year—1836. For a period of four years, members of the missionary family assigned to southern India moved from one place to another until they finally settled at Nellore in 1840. This has been the headquarters of the mission and the church ever since. The first church was established there with eight members in 1844. With one family and one station for many years, the South India field came to be known as the Lone Star mission.

The first significant movement to Christianity associated with the work of American Baptist missionaries and their Telugu colleagues began in 1866 when John E. Clough established a station at Ongole. A number of Madigas, an outcaste community, began to become Christians. The best-known movement among the Madigas began after the great famine of 1876. Within a period of six months, 9,606 persons were baptized, 2,222 of them on a single day. The most distinctive feature of Clough's leadership was his conviction that Western patterns of church life should not be imposed upon the Telugus. As much as possible Clough encouraged the Christians to remain in their traditional social environment rather than forming separate Christian ghettoes.

Between 1925 and 1935 there was a significant movement of caste Hindus (Sudras) to Christianity—some thirty thousand in the decade. This was unique insofar as the primary evangelism among them was undertaken by persons of a Lait (outcaste) background. The principal growth, however, continued to be among the Dalits. Unlike other fields, the South India Mission almost exclusively related to members of one language—Telugu—which enabled it to develop literature, programs, and institutions for the entire constituency.

Because its members came from among the very poor, the mission placed its educational emphasis upon primary and technical education. Nevertheless, it opened important high schools for both boys and girls. At the collegiate level, ecumenical institutions like the Women's Christian College in Madras and the coeducational Madras Christian College were supported. Health ministries were more extensive in the South India Mission than in any other field of American Baptist missionary activity. By the third decade of the twentieth century, the mission had established seven hospitals with the two at Nellore and Hanamakonda being the most important continuing to provide medical service. The STBC churches also have been connected closely with the ecumenical Christian Medical College and Hospital in Vellore, Tamil Nadu.

Andhra Baptists took a leading role in the development of theological education. The seminary at Ramapatnam, founded in the 1870s, is the oldest American Baptist-related ministerial training institution in India. With other denominations, the mission helped to form the Andhra Christian Theological College, now located in Hyderabad.

The Telugu churches did not find the transition from mission to church as easy as did the churches of the northeast. There were numerous problems at the denominational level that resulted in litigation and struggles for leadership. Since the Baptists in Andhra came primarily from an outcaste background, they were accustomed to dependency. Only gradually are these problems being resolved. There, however, continues to be considerable vitality at the level of the local church. One example of Indian initiative is the work of the Hyderabad Baptist Church, one of the fastest growing congregations in the country. Under the leadership of Pastor G. Samuel, the church, organized only in 1969, today includes more than 5,000 members, has established 36 new churches, and has ministers working in 75 villages.

The STBC is a members of the World Council of Churches, the National Council of Churches in India, and its regional constituent council. It is also a member of the BWA, the Baptist Council on World Mission, and several Asian Baptist and ecumenical organizations.

Frederick S. Downs

BIBLIOGRAPHY: John E. Clough, *From Darkness to Light: A Story of the Telugu Awakening* (Philadelphia: American Baptist Publication Society, 1882), and *Social Christianity in the Orient* (New York: Macmillan, 1914). Dana M. Albaugh, *Between Two Centuries: A Study of Four Mission Fields, Assam, South India, Bengal-Orissa, and South China* (Philadelphia: Judson Press, 1935). For information on the Hyderabad Baptist Church, see Michael Chute, "India: Hyderabad Church—Attempting Great Things," *Commission*, June/July 1992, 50–57, and Bachan Cannady, "The Village Mission of G. Samuel," *American Baptists in Mission*, Summer 1993, 4–5.

Other Baptist Bodies

Most Baptists in southern India are members of the Samevsam of Telugu Baptist Churches, but there are a number of smaller bodies. One of the largest of these is the Convention of Baptist Churches of the Northern Circars, a product of the mission work of Canadian Baptists. In response to an appeal in 1873 from Indian evangelist Thomas Gabriel for mission help among the Telugus of the northern districts, Baptists in Ontario and Quebec sent John and Mary McLaurin to Kakinada in 1874. The couple had been working under the ABMU in Ongole. In 1947 the Convention of Baptist Churches of the Northern Circars was formed; so-named because its field covered the northern circars, or districts, of Andhra State. By the 1960s Canadian Baptists had developed an array of institutions in education—a theological college at Kakinada, training schools, and high schools—and in medicine—seven hospitals, two leprosaria, and dispensaries. They also were engaged in literacy work, the care of orphans, and the Bible training of women.

In 1975 P. Suvarna Raj, who began his own indigenous movement after the Canadian missionaries left in the early 1970s, wrote to the General Baptist Foreign Mission Society (GBFMS) in Missouri concerning a possible affiliation. In 1982 the General Association of General Baptists accepted the Indian group for a probationary period of three years and then in 1985 as a permanent member. A partnership between the GBFMS and the India Association of General Baptists has developed with some financial contribution to mission projects by the GBFMS and an exchange of visits between the two groups. The India Association of General Baptists is a member of the BWA.

The largest Seventh Day Baptist body in the world is in Andrha. In 1950 a former priest of the Roman Catholic Church, B. John V. Rao, formed a Telugu Seventh Day Baptist Mission. Through correspondence, contact was made with Seventh Day Baptists in the United States. Later the group was accepted into the Seventh Day Baptist Federation. In 1988 the India Seventh Day Baptist Conference reported 37,980 members, 258 churches, 60 field evangelists, 5 social service teams, and 2 medical centers. In 1985 a Malankara Seventh Day Baptist Church in Kerala State was organized and accepted in 1989 into the Seventh Day Baptist Federation. At that time it had 3 churches and 2 other groups with 170 members.

Another group in Kerala State is the American Baptist Association Mission which began in 1973. In 1992 it reported nine churches and three missions. Another work, which is primarily in Kerala, receives support from churches of the Baptist Bible Fellowship in America. It is headed by K. C. Thomas and assisted by his sons, Paul and Sam, Indians who graduated from the Baptist Bible College of Springfield, Missouri. After his graduation from the college in 1968, Thomas returned to India the following year and started his first church, Bethel Baptist in Chathannoor. Today there are ninety-nine churches with about five thousand members. He also has founded four Bible institutes, including the Baptist Bible College of Chathannoor, a woman's institute in Kerala, one in Hyderabad, and one just across the border in Tamil Nadu. Since 1987 an annual fellowship meeting, called the Independent Bible Baptist Convention, is held in Chathannoor. Most of the work is among the Malayalam people, but some is conducted among other peoples, including Tamils.

In Tamil Nadu Province near Coimbatore, Free Will Baptists from America have a small mission. In 1935 Laura Belle Barnard, the first commissioned missionary of the National Association of Free Will Baptists, entered the field. In 1967 the Tamilnod Association of Free Will Baptist Churches was formed, which today has four churches, all with native pastors. Since 1861 the Grace Baptist Mission, supported by Strict Baptists in England, has supported a mission among the Tamils in Tamil Nadu. It was this mission's only work for one hundred years. The work is today indigenous and growing. The mission is engaged in medical and literature work, which includes translation of books into Tamil. A Tamil magazine appears monthly, and a Tamil hymnbook has been published recently.

Southern Baptists were unable to enter India until 1962 when the Indian government permitted a Southern Baptist surgeon to serve the Christian Medical College at Vellore in Karnataka Province. The government then invited Southern Baptists to begin a medical ministry in Bangalore, where the Bangalore Baptist hospital was opened. With the reduction by 1981 to only one missionary at the hospital, Dr. Rebekah Naylor, who had come in 1974, and her uncertainty of being able to remain, the FMB of the Southern Baptist Convention turned over the management of the hospital in 1989 to the Vellore Medical College with continuing subsidies until 1993. In the meantime Southern Baptists provided about $500,000 for a new wing to the hospital and work on a new outpatient clinic. Because of the Southern Baptist witness, Baptist churches began to be formed in the area. In 1976 a Karnataka Baptist Convention was formed, which in early 1980 had 17 churches, 4 schools, and 1,997 members. Today it has 105 churches and 13,000 members and is a member of the BWA.

Albert W. Wardin, Jr.

BIBLIOGRAPHY: Material on the Canadian Baptist mission may be found in Orville E. Daniel, *Moving with the Times* (Toronto: Canadian Baptist Overseas Mission Board, 1973). For Seventh Day Baptists, see Don A. Sanford, *A Choosing People* (Nashville: Broadman Press, 1992), 307–8, 312–13. Material on the work of K. C. Thomas may be found in *Baptist Bible Tribune*, Oct. 1993, 22. For the work of the Grace Baptist Mission among the Tamils, see the booklet, *Other Sheep of the Tamil Fold*, published by the mission, as well as its publication, *Herald*, Jan./Mar. 1992, 2. Information on Southern Baptists is in Baker J. Cauthen and others, *Advance* (Nashville: Broadman Press, 1970), 238–39, and Michael Chute, "India: Change Blows Across Bangalore," *Commission*, June/July 1992, 18–23.

E. SOUTH CENTRAL INDIA (MAHARASHTRA STATE)

*T*he Baptists in Maharashtra State are small in number but are showing growth, particularly in the area of Bombay. Owen Cooper, a former president of the Southern Baptist Convention, established Universal Concerns Foundation which supported the planting of churches in Calcutta, Orissa, and Bombay. Through this effort seven churches were founded in Bombay. In 1985 G. Krupananda, an associate director of National Indian Ministries, an agency to expand Southern Baptist work in India, settled in Bombay. By 1992 he was supervising thirty-four congregations in the city and the work of six church planters, four volunteers, and a Bible woman. He centered his work on suburban slum areas to which people were migrating. A Convention of Baptist Churches in Maharashtra has been organized, which is a member of the BWA.

In 1945 missionaries of the Conservative Baptist Foreign Mission Society (CBFMS, today CBI) arrived on the field of the Korku and Central India Hill Mission (K&CIHM), a British mission in central India. In 1944 CBMS had agreed tentatively to take over this work. Albert Norton had begun the work in Achalpur in 1874 and later formed the K&CIHM for support, but it was now facing a reduction of finances and missionaries. In 1947 CBFMS formally took over its operation.

There were five language groups in the area, but the CBFMS missionaries concentrated on Hindi-Korku and Marathi. The mission engaged in evangelistic work as well as institutional ministries, including support for the Achalpur Christian Hospital, Boys' Christian Home, Girls' Christian Institute, and Kothara Leprosy Hospital. A special effort was made to reach the Korkus, an almost unreached animistic tribal people, but it would take twenty-seven years before the first Korku church was formed. In 1957 a Baptist Christian Association (BCA) was organized. In 1971 CBFMS turned over its work to it. In 1991 BCA had thirteen evangelists on the field and also cooperated with several Indian missions in reaching the Korkus. At that time only two Conservative Baptist missionaries remained on the field.

In 1955 the Baptist Bible Fellowship International (BBFI) approved support for Mr. and Mrs. Edward Jelley, who worked about two hundred miles east of Bombay. Today BBFI continues to support three members of the Jelley family.

The Baptist Missionary Association (BMA) in America helps to support two Indian nationals, Sumitra Borde and his nephew, Pradeep Borde, in Maharashtra State in the area of Aurangabad-Pune. Both of them, after attending the seminary of the Baptist Missionary Association in Jacksonville, Texas, returned to their homeland and were elected as national workers by the BMA. In 1992 it was reported that the work had more than forty-five missions. The BMA also supports a third national worker, Prakash Guruputra, who also received training in the USA, and who resides in Gulbarga, Karnataka State.

Albert W. Wardin, Jr.

BIBLIOGRAPHY: For Baptist work in Bombay, see Michael Chute, "India: Taking a Hint in Bombay," *Commission*, June/July 1992, 38–43. For the work of the CBFMS, see *Founded on the Word: Focused on the World* (Wheaton: CBFMS, 1978), 11–15, and Hans W. Finzel, ed., *Partners Together* (Wheaton: CBFMS, 1993), 66–69. For a short reference to the work of the BBFI, see Fred S. Donnelson, ed., *What God Hath Wrought!* (Springfield, Mo.: BBF, 1957), 2:46–47. Material on the Baptist Missionary Association of Maharashtra may be found in John W. Duggar, *The Baptist Missionary Association of America* (1950–1986) (Texarkana, Tex: Baptist Publishing House, 1988), 262, and *Gleaner*, July 1992, 6, 22–23.

NEPAL (1989)

	Members	Churches
1. Nepal Baptist Church Council (1993)	1,500	(15)
2. Original Free Will Baptists (1991)	n/a	(1)
	1,500	(16)

*T*he kingdom of Nepal, a Hindu nation between India and China in the Himalayas, has been closed to the Christian gospel until recently. In 1954 Nepal allowed the United Mission to Nepal (UMN), an interdenominational Christian agency, to provide educational and medical services but prohibited direct evangelism. In 1991 the UMN was supervising the work of 382 missionaries, representing thirty-eight Christian groups. The Baptist Missionary Society (BMS) provided a nursing sister in 1962 and formally joined the mission in 1968. In 1983 Southern Baptists sent its first couple who served at a UMN hospital in Tansen. Other Baptist missions also participated in the UMN. As a result of Christian witness, an indigenous Nepalese church, the Church of Christ in Nepal, was founded in 1966, and a Nepal Christian Fellowship in 1969. After the shift in Nepal in 1990 from an autocratic to a democratic regime, the number of Christians has increased rapidly.

About 1989 Nepalese Baptists from Nagaland in India returned to Nepal and began to preach and form their own congregations. Under the leadership of H. B. Gurung and other pastors, the Nepal Baptist Churches Fellowship was founded with Gurang as general secretary. In December 1993 the Nepal Baptist Church Council was established. Today there are 15 churches and 35 fellowships with a constituency of 1,500 believers.

In 1991 the Original Free Will Baptists from the USA opened Nepal as one of its fields with workers from India. In the same year a congregation was founded.

BIBLIOGRAPHY: For the work of the BMS with the UMN, see Brian Stanley, *The History of the Baptist Missionary Society 1792–1992* (Edinburgh: T&T Clark, 1992), 434–38. For Southern Baptist participation in UMN, see Michael Chute, "Nepal: No Christian 'Shangri-La,'" *Commission*, June/July 1991, 48–79. For indigenous Baptist work in Nepal, see *BWA News*, April 1993, 3; Jan. 1994, 3; Mar. 1994, 3; and *Sword and Trowel* 2 (London, 1993), 6–7.

PAKISTAN (1954)

	Members	Churches
Sindh Evangelical Baptist Association (1980)	1,500	(25)

*W*ith the division of India in 1947, Pakistan became an independent state. With a Moslem majority of 97 percent, it has been a difficult field for Christian missions. In 1954 the Conservative Baptist Foreign Mission Society (CBFMS, now CBI), entered a field in northwest Sindh Province, which the Church Missionary Society, an Anglican Society, then understaffed, had released to it. The first missionaries—Ray and Jean Buker, Polly Brown, Warren and Shirley Webster, and Charles and Elaine Raub—first settled in Larkana, about three hundred miles north of Karachi. They commenced working in the four western districts of Sindh Province—Jacobabad, Shikarpur, Larkana, and Dadu—and found small pockets of nominal Christians in each district center. The recent ancestors of these people had migrated into Sindh from Punjab Province where there had been a mass movement to Christianity from among some outcaste Hindus. There was also a small Anglican church in Larkana which the Anglican bishop turned over to the Baptists in 1955.

The Baptist missionaries taught personal faith in Christ and discipleship. In 1961 the Larkana Church called a pastor and assumed his full support. In 1964 a congregation was formed at Jacobabad, and in 1966 the Shikarpur Church adopted a preliminary organization. The first generation of Baptist missionaries did not confine themselves to the Punjabi nominal Christians. They also reached out to the majority Muslim community and the small Hindu minority through Scripture distribution, Bible correspondence courses, and radio programs broadcast from outside the country. They spearheaded the translation of the Bible in everyday Sindhi and produced other literature. In medicine, they cooperated with the Holland Eye Hospital in Shikarpur, which the government forced to close in 1974 because of its evangelistic impact, and also established a hospital for women and children in the city, which is now being transformed into a general hospital.

One exciting event was the conversion of a leader in a Hindu tribe called the

Marwaris. In 1963 a Baptist missionary baptized him and six family members. This was the beginning of a movement that has brought hundreds to Christ and the formation of small congregations.

In 1969 the Fellowship of Evangelical Baptist Churches (CaFEBC) Canada sent a nurse to serve in the Shikarpur Hospital and has since sent other medical personnel, teachers, and church planters to work with the Conservative Baptist mission. In 1984 Southern Baptists also began to send personnel to work with the two missions, first concentrating in Karachi, the large port city in southern Sindh. An International Baptist Church has been established in the city.

Recently, Baptists are beginning to form churches in the province of Punjab. During the building of a large dam at Mangla, a construction worker founded the first church there in the early 1960s. In 1989 Southern Baptist missionaries began to help him train leaders in New Testament church principles. One leader from Islamabad, the capital, who attended some of the training sessions accepted believer's baptism and returned to his city, forming several Baptist groups of worshipers. There are a few isolated Baptist churches in other parts of Punjab. Southern Baptist missionaries are locating them and are conducting leadership training seminars in various areas.

About 1954 the Baptist Bible Fellowship International (BBFI) also began a ministry in Pakistan. Charles Coleman and his wife settled in Karachi. Following the same pattern as its Baptist counterparts in the interior, this mission also started Baptist churches among the nominal Punjabi Christians. Coleman helped to constitute the Sher Shah Baptist Church in Karachi, one of the first Baptist congregations in the country.

Conservative Baptists founded the Indus Christian Fellowship (Baptist), which is today the field conference of CBI and CaFEBC. Southern Baptists cooperate with the fellowship. With the encouragement of the missionaries of all four missions, Baptists in Sindh formed the Sindh Evangelical Baptist Association, which today has more than 1,500 baptized believers in twenty-five churches and fifty-six worshiping groups. There is no Baptist organization, however, in Punjab Province. There are a few small groups of Muslim converts who meet regularly in Larkana and Shikarpur but are not organized into churches as yet.

Hubert F. Addleton. Supplemented by Albert W. Wardin, Jr.

BIBLIOGRAPHY: Material on Conservative Baptists may be found in *Founded on the Word: Focused on the World* (Wheaton: CBFMS, 1978), 161–71, and Hans W. Finzel, ed., *Partners Together* (Wheaton: CBFMS, 1993), 90–95. For work of Southern Baptists, see *Your Guide to Foreign Missions, 1994–1995*, 103.

SRI LANKA (1812)

	Members	Churches
1. Sri Lanka Baptist Sangamaya	2,420	(22)
2. Revival Baptist Church (BBFI)	35	(1)
	2,455	(23)

Sri Lanka, formerly known as Ceylon, is an island off the southern tip of India. In 1948 Great Britain granted the island independence as a self-governing dominion. In 1972 Sri Lanka became a republic. More than two-thirds of the population is Buddhist with Hindu (15 percent), Christian (8 percent), and Moslem minorities (7 percent).

Baptist work in Sri Lanka began in the early nineteenth century as an indirect consequence of the unsympathetic attitude to nonconformist missionary work in India taken by the East India Company. James Chater, missionary of the Baptist Missionary Society (BMS) in Calcutta, having been deported from Bengal by the company authorities, went first to Burma and then to Ceylon in 1812. Chater found the Sinhalese population unresponsive but continued evangelistic and school work on the island until his death in 1829. Chater's successor, Ebenezer Daniel, built up the Baptist mission from a mere two churches in 1830 to ten mission stations, more than 500 church members, and about 1,200 school pupils by his death in 1844.

Nevertheless, the Baptist cause in Sri Lanka remained weak throughout the nineteenth century in comparison with the Methodist and Anglican missions which had followed in Chater's wake. Although the Baptist mission was served by some notable missionaries, such as the Sinhalese scholar, Charles Carter, it suffered from inadequate input of human and financial resources and a lack of facilities for training indigenous teachers and evangelists. In addition, the mission's strategic dependence on elementary education was challenged from the 1880s by a Buddhist revival which hotly disputed missionary control of schooling. Although the BMS resolved in the early 1900s to increase its allocation of resources to Sri Lanka, the Baptist denomination has remained one of the smallest Protestant communities. Baptist membership has grown from about 1,000 in 1913 to only about 2,400 today. Most of these members are drawn from the Sinhalese population; Baptists have done little work among the Tamil population in the north. Nevertheless, individual Baptist leaders, such as W. M. P. Jayatunga, C. H. Ratnaike, S. J. de S. Weerasinghe, and W. G. Wickramasinghe, have exercised influential roles in education, the Bible Society, and the National Christian Council. The devolution of power from the BMS to the indigenous churches began with the formation of the Ceylon Baptist Council in 1935 and was completed in 1974 when the Sri Lanka Baptist Sangamaya (the successor to the Council) assumed control of all property formerly held by the missionary society.

Brian Stanley

From 1959 to 1964 the Conservative Baptist Foreign Mission Society had a short-lived mission served by Bruce and Esther Ker and Jim Cook (son of J. William Cook who served in Calcutta) and his wife, Sylvia. For a time Cook was coach of the basketball team of the University of Sri Lanka. During their stay they founded Sri Lanka Youth for Christ and in 1963 began the Colombo Bible College. When the government failed to renew their visas because of opposition from certain Christian leaders, they were forced to leave the country. In 1977 Southern Baptists began to send personnel who worked with the Sri Lanka Sangamaya. In 1991 Terry Unruh of the Baptist Bible Fellowship International (BBFI) entered the country and in 1992 established the Revival Baptist Church near Colombo. It is led by a national pastor, Gamini De Silva.

Albert W. Wardin, Jr.

BIBLIOGRAPHY: H. J. Charter, *Ceylon Advancing* (London: Carey Kingsgate Press, 1954). Brian Stanley, *The History of the Baptist Missionary Society 1792–1992* (Edinburgh: T&T Clark, 1992). For the Conservative Baptist mission, see Hans W. Finzel, ed., *Partners Together* (Wheaton: CBFMS, 1993), 170–71. For the BBFI, see, "Pastors Visit India and Sri Lanka," *Baptist Bible Tribune*, Oct. 1993, 22. For a survey of Sri Lankan Baptists and Southern Baptist activity, see Michael Chute, "Sri Lanka: Going `Door to Door,'" *Commission*, May 1992, 52–75.

BAPTIST AND BAPTIST-RELATED MISSIONS

1. BANGLADESH UkBMS (1795), AuBMS (1882), NzBMS (1886), ABWE (1957), SBC (1957), SwO (1970)

2. BHUTAN —

3. INDIA UkBMS (1793), ABC (1836), UkGBM (1861), CaCBIM (1874), SwO (1908), BM-M (1935), FWB (1935), NzBMS (1938), CBI (1945), BGC (1946), AuBMS (1947), SBC (1962), LC (1963), ABA (1973), SDBMS (1974), BMA (1975), OFWB (1975), BIMI (1978) BWM (1989)

4. NEPAL UkBMS (1962), SBC (1983), OFWB (1991), ABC, InCBCNEI, NorBU, SwO

5. PAKISTAN BBFI (1954), CBI (1954), SwO (1960), CaFEBC (1969), SBC (1984)

6. SRI LANKA UkBMS (1812), SBC (1977), WBF (1985), BBFI (1991)

D. SOUTHEAST ASIA

Southeast Asia, stretching from Myanmar (Burma) to Indonesia, is a territory of peninsulas and archipelagoes. The area includes almost one million Baptists, although half of them live in one country, Myanmar. Myanmar was entered in 1813—the first mission field for American Baptists and their most successful. Except for the Philippines, which was entered in 1900, Baptists neglected most of the territory for the next 135 years. It was only after the closing of China after World War II and the appearance of new Baptist missions that Baptists began to cultivate the territory systematically. They not only reentered Thailand but also began mission activity in Indonesia, Malaysia, Singapore, and even Vietnam and Laos. Success has been primarily among tribal peoples.

	Membership	Churches
1. Brunei	n/a	2
2. Indonesia	118,500	1,190
3. Malaysia	7,100	88
4. Myanmar (Burma)	497,731	3,528
5. Philippines	314,207	4,514
6. Singapore	7,000	29
7. Thailand	27,234	287
8. Vietnam	n/a	1
	971,772	9,639

BRUNEI (1950S)

In the tiny state of Brunei, a sultanate located on the north coast of Kalimantan (Borneo), Baptists have been present in small number. In the late 1950s an Australian missionary began evangelistic work. The Baptist Convention of Hong Kong continued the work until its missionary could no longer obtain a resident permit. A Southern Baptist missionary in Singapore began to visit Brunei monthly. Then in 1981 he moved with his family to the capital, Bandar Seri Begawan, assisting a Baptist church in the city as well as one in Seria, more than one hundred miles away. Because of visa restriction, there are at present no Southern Baptist representatives in the country.

BIBLIOGRAPHY: *Your Guide to Foreign Missions*, 1994–1995, 106.

INDONESIA (1951)

1. Union of Indonesian Baptist Churches		
(Gabungan Gereja Baptis Indonesia) (1971)	50,000	(625)
2. Convention of Indonesian Baptist Churches		
(Kerapatan Gereja Baptis Indonesia) (1951)	7,000	(214)
3. Evangelical Baptist Association of Indonesia		
(Gereja Perhimpunan Injili Baptis Indonesia)		
(1956)	5,500	(119)
4. Independent Baptists of Indonesia (Gereja		
Baptis Independent di Indonesia) (1986)	5,000	(56)
5. Jakarta Synod of the Baptist Christian Church		
(Sinode Gereja Kristen Baptis Jakarta) (1952)	2,000	(6)
6. Fellowship of Irian Jaya Baptist Churches		
(Persekutuan Gereja-Gereja		
Baptis Irian Jaya) (1966)	<u>49,000</u>	<u>(170)</u>
	118,500	(1,190)

*I*ndonesia, an archipelago of seventeen thousand islands stretching from Malaysia in the west to New Guinea in the east and including Sumatra, Java, Sulawei (Celebes), Kalimantan (most of Borneo), and Irian Jaya (the western half of New Guinea), is the fourth most populous country in the world. God worked through unusual people and strange events to bring into being six distinct groups of Baptists in a strongly Moslem or syncretistic Moslem nation.

A stubborn Saxon from the Reformed Church who became English Baptists' outstanding missionary and Bible translator in Java; a self-styled Dutch-American doctor who paved the way for a Baptist hospital in western Kalimantan; an Indonesian Christian youth who flew away from his home early one morning (still in his pajamas!) and returned many years later to become a leader among Baptists; a transplanted Chinese Baptist from Hong Kong—these are a few of the unusual people.

An attempted Communist coup and its bloody aftermath; a tribal massacre of new believers in the interior; a breakaway group from an old-line Protestant denomination that became convicted about personal faith and believer's baptism; a meeting, apparently by chance, bringing together two groups of Baptists started separately on the same island—these are some of the strange events.

The Napoleonic Wars saw the Dutch colonial empire in the East Indies shift temporarily into British hands. Starting in 1813, English Baptists used this window of opportunity to send some twenty missionaries to Java, Sumatra, and the Moluccas. Among them were a son of William Carey and a nephew of William Ward, Carey's Serampore colleague.

But the outstanding Baptist missionary to Indonesia in those early days was Gottlob Bruckner, a stubborn Saxon. Like Adoniram Judson and Luther Rice, he became a Baptist on the mission field. Serving faithfully among the Javanese from 1814 to 1857,

Bruckner made the first translation of the New Testament into one of Indonesia's hundreds of tribal languages. Twentieth-century Baptists have continued in the Bruckner tradition, producing Scriptures both in area dialects and in modern-language versions of the national language, now called Indonesian.

Strange to say, no lasting Baptist work developed from the sacrifices made by those pioneers. The Dutch took over the Indies again and drove out British missionaries. Not until well into the twentieth century did Baptists begin to take root in Indonesian soil. And they did so in widely different places and strangely different ways, as this brief review of bodies will show:

Union of Indonesian Baptist Churches (Gabungan Gereja Baptis Indonesia) (GGBI)

The closing of China to foreign missionaries in 1949 sent Southern Baptists (USA) looking for other fields in Asia. On Christmas day 1951 three "old China hands" landed in Jakarta, capital of Indonesia. One of their first Indonesian coworkers was Pastor Ais Pormes, who as a youth had flown away from his native Moluccas after helping rescue the crew of a downed American warplane. Getting an education in Australia and America, he then came back to plant what soon became a large Baptist church in the capital city.

During the 1950s and 1960s Southern Baptist missionaries started many institutions in Java: a seminary, a publishing house, a hospital, and several student centers. Yet Baptist church growth remained relatively slow and weak until the aftermath of the failed Communist coup in 1965. Then Baptists, like other denominations, capitalized on a phenomenal turning to Christ—in Java and on other islands as well.

The union was established in August 1971. It has continued to work with Southern Baptists and also with Baptist missionaries from Japan, Korea, and elsewhere. Another hospital and a rural development model have been established on Sumatra, a university in eastern Java, and several more theological schools in various places. Baptist churches have been planted on Java, Sumatra, Bali, Ambon, Ceram, Kalimantan, Sulawesi, Timor, and Moa. By the mid-1990s, the union's evangelism coordinator estimated 50,000 baptized believers in 625 congregations.

Convention of Indonesian Baptist Churches (Kerapatan Gereja Baptis Indonesia) (KGBI)

In the late '30s and '40s, several young people from the old-line Protestant Reformed denomination of Minahasa (northern Sulawesi) studied at a Christian and Missionary Alliance Bible school in southern Sulawesi. Becoming convicted about personal faith and believer's baptism, they returned home to bring new spiritual life to needy churches. But church leaders did not welcome this new movement. These young evangelicals then formed a new denomination in October 1951.

Several young people from the new group studied at the Baptist seminary in Semarang, Java. Gradually they came to realize that they were, in fact, Baptists and began to use that name in 1979. Characteristically missionary in outlook, they began to reach out to other parts of Sulawesi, to the Sangir-Talaud islands, to Halmahera, to several areas in Java and Sumatra, and especially to western Kalimantan.

Both Canadian Baptist and Southern Baptist missionaries work with this convention, especially at its seminaries—one in Manado (northern Sulawesi) and another in Pontianak (western Kalimantan). By the mid-1990s the convention claimed 7,000 baptized believers in 214 congregations.

Evangelical Baptist Association of Indonesia (Gereja Perhimpunan Injili Baptis Indonesia) (GPIBI)

About 1925 a hardheaded Dutch-American named John G. Breman began evangelizing among the Dayaks of western Kalimantan. Basically a Baptist, he led the way toward a national convention, organized in 1956 and first designated as Baptist in 1965. A self-styled doctor, he laid the groundwork for Conservative Baptist missionaries from the USA who arrived in 1961 and established Bethesda Hospital at Serukam, an outstanding medical institution. Other ministries of Evangelical Baptists include youth hostels, Bible schools, and TEE, with teachers of village pastors arriving by airplane.

By 1984 this group also began working outside Kalimantan, especially in cooperation with the large nondenominational Evangelical Theological Seminary in central Java. By the mid-1990s they had 5,500 baptized believers in 119 congregations on Java, Sumatra, and Kalimantan, with home mission work on Bali as well. Evangelical Baptists have not joined the Baptist World Alliance (BWA) but cooperate through the Baptist Fellowship of Indonesia.

Independent Baptists in Indonesia (Gereja Baptis Independent di Indonesia) (GBII)

Independent Baptist missionaries began to arrive in Indonsia in 1970, sent by World Baptist Fellowship, Baptist Bible Fellowship International (USA), Baptist Bible Fellowship (Japan), Baptist International Missions, Macedonia World Baptist Missions, and other groups. Indonesian government policy forced them all to establish a common organization in 1986.

Independent Baptists' greatest strength is in Jakarta, the capital, where a Bible school was started in 1971. There are, however, also churches and branch Bible schools in western and central Java and in northern Sumatra. By the mid-1990s Independent Baptists estimated five thousand baptized believers in fifty-six congregations. They have not joined the BWA but cooperate through the Baptist Fellowship of Indonesia.

Jakarta Synod of the Baptist Christian Church (Sinode Gereja Kristen Baptis Jakarta) (SGKBJ)

In 1952 a small group came out of a Mandarin-speaking congregation in Jakarta. Through the influence of Ernest Loong, a pastor who moved from Hong Kong, these believers became Baptists in 1953. Later an American missionary supported through Baptist Mid-Missions assisted them.

Like many other Asian evangelicals, these Indonesians of Chinese descent consider themselves one church with several congregations. By the mid-1990s they reported two thousand members—in Jakarta and also on Belitung and Sumatra. They assist twenty-eight home missionaries in Java and Irian Jaya, and since 1980 they have published a quarterly magazine. Jakarta Synod Baptists have not joined the BWA, but they cooperate through the Baptist Fellowship of Indonesia.

Fellowship of Irian Jaya Baptist Churches (Persekutuan Gereja-Gereja Baptis Irian Jaya) (PGBIJ)

After colonial forces had been driven out by Indonesian freedom fighters from 1945 through 1949, the Dutch held on a while longer in New Guinea. Baptists from Australia worked in the eastern half of the island (now the independent country of Papua New Guinea), and in 1955 they also began to survey the possibility of working among primitive tribes in the western half, now Irian Jaya (a province of Indonesia).

Evangelization among the Dani (or Lani) of the Baliem Valley began in 1956. God's good timing brought a people movement, as Danis piled up their fetishes for burning. The first converts were baptized in May 1962. Four months later animists attacked and massacred many believers; but the blood of the Makki martyrs became the seed of the church. By 1982 Baptists were baptizing seven thousand Danis in a single year.

Meanwhile the Fellowship of Irian Jaya Baptist churches had been established in December 1966. In December 1977 a fellowship leader met many Baptists he was unaware of at a Christmas celebration of university students in Jayapura, the provincial capital. These students came from the Bird's Head region of northwestern Irian; they were spiritual heirs of Dutch Mennonite missionaries who labored there from 1950 to 1963, leaving when Indonesia gained control of Irian.

The two groups merged and later spread into other areas of Irian and to at least one other island. The Indonesian government, by moving homesteaders from overcrowded Java, has opened new home mission fields for the fellowship. By the mid-1990s there were 49,000 baptized believers, besides potential baptismal candidates, in 170 congregations. Among their ministries are a theological college, two Bible schools, a hospital, and an agriculture/forestry center.

William N. McElrath

BIBLIOGRAPHY: For the beginnings of the Southern Baptist mission, see John Irvin Nance, *A History of the Indonesian Baptist Mission: 1950–1960* (M.A. thesis, Baylor University, 1969). For the work of Conservative Baptists, see Hans W. Finzel, ed., *Partners Together* (Wheaton: CBFMS, 1993), 70–75. For a short historical survey of Independent Baptists, see Tom Crawford, "Indonesia and Independent Baptists," *Baptist Bible Tribune*, March 1994, 18–19. For the Australian Baptist mission in Irian Jaya, see Jess Redman, *The Light Shines On* (Hawthorn, Victoria: Australian BMS, 1982), 167–98.

MALAYSIA (1938)

	Members	Churches
1. Malaysia Baptist Convention (1953)	7,000	(83)
2. Reformed Baptists	100	(5)
	7,100	(88)

*T*he state of Malaysia was created in 1963. It included Malaya (a territory on the tip of southeast Asia to which Great Britain had granted independence in 1957), Singapore, and British territories in northern Borneo. With a Chinese majority, Singapore separated in 1965, leaving the Malays in control. The religious configuration of the country is diverse with about half the population Moslem (predominantly Malay), about a fourth traditional Chinese, and the rest Hindu and Buddhist (13 percent), Christian (6 percent), and animist (4 percent).

In October 1938 Chinese Baptists organized the first Baptist church in Malyasia— the Oversea-Chinese (Swatow) Baptist Church of Alor Star. The church survived the Japanese occupation during World War II but needed assistance as did the two Chinese

Baptist churches in Singapore. With the closure of China to missionaries, Southern Baptists were ready to enter Singapore and Malaysia. In 1951 Miss Jessie Green, who since 1936 had worked with Cantonese Chinese in China, settled in Kuala Lumpur. In December 1952 eighteen charter members formed the Kuala Lumpur Baptist Church. Members who attended the English-language services of the church formed the First Baptist Church of Petaling Jaya in 1957.

In 1952 the Southern Baptist mission was formed with stations at Kuala Lumpur and Singapore. In 1964 the mission sent a team to investigate mission work in East Malaysia on the island of Borneo. The first missionary couple entered Sabah (North Borneo) in 1964; in March 1965 they led in forming the Jesselton Baptist Church. In 1970 the first missionary couple entered Sarawak.

In 1954 in Penang the mission opened the Malaysia Baptist Theological Seminary with English- and Chinese-language sections. It also established a Baptist bookstore in the same city and an assembly on the west coast. In 1953 the Malaya (today Malaysian) Baptist Convention was formed. By the mid-1960s the missionaries were working or planning to work in several languages—Malay, Tamil, English, and four Chinese dialects—and were ministering to Chinese, Indians, and tribal people. The work among the Chinese made the most progress, followed at a slower pace by work among the Indians. Because of government regulation and social pressure, opportunity for ministry among the Moslem Malay population was extremely limited.

Reformed Baptists began with the work of Poh Boon Sing, a Malaysian citizen of Chinese descent who had studied in Liverpool, England. The Belvidere Road Baptist Church in Liverpool commissioned him for mission service. In 1982 he formed a Reformed Baptist church in Serang, which was followed by four other congregations in the next eleven years, all in the area of Kuala Lumpur. A Malaysia Reformed Ministers' Conference was begun in 1987. In October 1987 the government imprisoned Sing for eleven months, charged with evangelizing Malays. The five congregations which Sing established have one hundred members.

BIBLIOGRAPHY: Lillie O. Rogers, ed., *A History of Baptists in Malaysia and Singapore* ([Singapore]: n.p., 1971).

MYANMAR (BURMA) (1813)

	Members	Churches
1. Myanmar Baptist Convention (1865)	496,961	(3,513)
2. Myanmar Seventh Day Baptist Conference (1965)	770	(15)
3. Fundamental Baptist Churches of Myanmar (1979)	n/a	(n/a)
	497,731	(3,528)

*T*he nation of Myanmar, known until 1989 as Burma, gained its independence from Great Britain in 1948. Since the early 1960s the country has followed a rather isolationist course with a military regime today holding power. The ethnic Burmese with the Shan peoples are predominantly Buddhist, a religion which includes about 85 percent of the population. There is, however, a strong and growing Christian minority of more than 5 percent, whose members come primarily from the many hill people in the country.

Myanmar has been one of the most successful Baptist mission fields. Baptists were the first Protestants to enter Myanmar and are the largest Christian denomination in the country. The BMS made the first attempt to enter in 1807, but its effort soon ceased. Adoniram Judson (1788–1850) and his wife, Ann, were the forerunners of Baptist work. At the same time they were the first American Baptists to serve as missionaries abroad. The Judsons are two of the most heroic, if not revered, figures in Baptist mission annals. The story of their becoming Baptists after arrival on the field, the trials on the field (including imprisonment), the six years of patient ministry before the baptism of the first convert, the faithful work and early death of Ann, and the monumental achievement of producing grammar and a Burmese Bible (which is still a standard version) were all events which have inspired Baptists and other evangelicals for more than 150 years. It is not surprising that probably more Baptist churches and schools carry the name "Judson" than any other.

After their arrival in India in 1812 under the auspices of the American Board of Commissioners for Foreign Missions, the Judsons adopted believer's baptism and were baptized by William Ward, a British Baptist missionary in Calcutta. Another colleague, Luther Rice, also followed the same course. With their resignations from the American Board, Judson and Rice sought Baptist support from the USA. Rice returned home, never to return again to the field. In 1814 he led in the formation of the Triennial Convention, an organization to support missions, the first national Baptist body in the country. With the refusal of the British authorities to allow the Judsons to remain in India, they settled in 1813 in Rangoon in the Burmese Empire.

In 1828 George Boardman and his wife, who had arrived on the field two years earlier, opened a station at Tavoy, taking with them Ko Tha Byu, a Karen convert, who had been a notorious convict. Byu became an outstanding evangelist among his tribal people who were animists, and with Boardman initiated a great ingathering of Karen converts. Today the Karen Baptist Convention is the largest of the constituent bodies within the Myanmar Baptist Convention (organized in 1865). The Karen Convention with the Zomi Convention (Chins) and the Kachin Convention compose more than three-fourths of the Baptist membership, although many other peoples, including ethnic Burmese and Shans, are also adherents. In addition to two churches independent of any regional convention, the Myamar Convention included fourteen constituent bodies in the 1980s.

The mission established many primary and secondary schools. In addition, it formed in 1871 Rangoon Baptist College (later called Judson Baptist College), which was nationalized after World War II. The mission formed a Burman Theological Seminary in 1836, the Karen Theological Seminary in 1845, and later a number of Bible schools for various ethnic groups. In 1963 there were eighteen theological schools and seminaries conducted in six different languages with 741 students of which 281 were women. Five of the institutions were located on Seminary Hill in Rangoon. The mission also established hospitals and dispensaries. At Namkham in northeast Myanmar near the Chinese border, Dr. Gordon S. Seagrave developed an outstanding medical ministry—remembered in part for his books, which included, *Tales of a Waste-Basket Surgeon* (1938) and *Burma Surgeon* (1943).

Translation and publication of literature has always had high priority. The Baptist Mission Press was established in 1816 in Rangoon with the gift of a printing press from the British Baptist missionaries in Serampore, India. In its first one hundred years, the press had published the entire Bible in five languages and portions of the Bible in a sixth language.

The occupation by the Japanese during World War II brought disruption to mission work as well as much destruction of property, but with financial assistance from abroad the work was renewed. In spite of the expulsion in 1966 of the missionaries, the nationalization in 1965 and 1966 of Christian properties—hospitals, dispensaries, and schools—and tribal insurgency, Baptists continue to grow at a phenomenal rate. At the time of Judson's death in 1850, there were 7,904 members; in 1963, the sesquicentennial of the mission, the membership was 216,000; today it is around 500,000, more than doubled in the last thirty years. In December 1977, in observance of the centennial of mission work among the Kachins, almost 100,000 Kachins gathered for the celebration, and 6,215 converts were baptized in one day in the Irrawaddy River. Between 1953 and 1960 the mission transferred full responsibility of the work to the Burmese Baptists. The Baptist Convention is a member of the Myanmar Council of Churches, the World Council of Churches, and the BWA.

In 1960 two natives of the country began a Seventh Day Baptist mission, which led in 1965 to the organization of a Burma Seventh Day Baptist Conference. It joined the Seventh Day Baptist World Federation and also the BWA but withdrew from the latter body in 1993.

BIBLIOGRAPHY: A classic in mission biography is the work by Courtney Anderson, *To the Golden Shore: The Life of Adoniram Judson* (Boston: Little, Brown and Company, 1956; Garden City, N.Y.: Dolphin Books, 1961). A very fine account of Baptist work in Myanmar to the mid-1950s may be found in Robert G. Torbet, *Venture of Faith* (Philadelphia: Judson Press, 1955). The book, *Baptist Bible Chronicle*, with book one written by Maung Shwe Wwa and book two edited by Genevieve and Erville Sowards, (Rangoon: Board of Publications, Burma Baptist Convention, 1963), provides much helpful material. For the development of Kachin Baptists, see Herman G. Tegenfeld, *A Century of Growth: The Kachin Baptist Church of Burma* (South Pasadena, Calif.: William Carey Library, 1974). For Seventh Day Baptists, see Don A. Sanford, *A Choosing People* (Nashville: Broadman Press, 1992), 308–9. David B. Barrett, *World Christian Encyclopedia* (Nairobi: Oxford University Press, 1982), 201–4, provides helpful data.

PHILIPPINES (1900)

	Members	Churches
1. Convention of Philippine Baptist Churches (1935)	89,316	(677)
2. Association of Fundamental Baptist Churches in the Philippines	42,347	(901)

Southern Baptists:	89,031	(1,673)
3. Luzon Convention of Southern Baptist Churches		
4. Mindanao Baptist Convention of Southern Baptist Churches		
5. Visayan Baptist Convention		
6. Chinese Baptist Convention		
7. Baptist Conference of the Philippines (1954)	10,315	(172)
8. Conservative Baptist Association of the Philippines (1961)	21,351	(142)
9. General Baptist Church of the Philippines (1980)	13,558	(227)
10. Free Will Baptist Church	432	(24)
11. Independent Baptist Churches in the Philippines (1975)	3,075	(75)
12. Baptist Bible Fellowship of the Philippines	26,960	(337)
13. Bumila Fellowship of Baptist Churches (1951)	700	(32)
14. Association of Baptist Churches in Luzon, Visayas, and Mindanao (1965)	6,283	(61)
15. International Baptist Missionary Fellowship of the Philippines (c. 1976)	6,650	(70)
16. Missionary Baptists	3,330	(90)
17. Seventh Day Baptist Philippine Conference (1981)	392	(14)
18. Reformed Baptist Fellowship of Churches (1986)	420	(17)
19. Primitive Baptists (1994)	47	(2)
	314,207	(4,514)

STATISTICS: The corresponding editor gained data on Baptist missions, bodies, and statistics primarily from BWA, *Yearbook*, 1993–1994, 99; *Dawn 2000: Nationwide Survey Report* (Colorado Springs, Co.: OC International, 1982); A. Leonard Tuggy and Ralph Toliver, *Seeing the Church in the Philippines* (Manila: O.M.F. Publishers, 1972); Brian T. Ellis, "A Brief History of Baptist Work in the Philippines," typed mss., 1993; and *Mission Handbook*, 1993–1995, 385–89. The editor did not list groups for which he had no information, such as the Association of Central Baptist Churches in the Philippines, Baptist Missionary Alliance of Panay Island, Independent Fundamental Baptist Association of the Philippines, and Negros Fundamental Fellowship (Baptist).

*I*n 1898 the United States wrested the Philippines from the control of Spain and in 1946 granted independence. The country consists of a maze of seven thousand islands with Luzon in the north, the largest and most populated island, followed in the central area by a collection of islands called the Visayan Islands, and then by Mindanao, a large island in the south. Although the population is predominantly Roman Catholic (83 percent), the Philippines has a significant minority of indigenous and Protestant congregations. Baptists were one of the first Protestants to enter the Philippines after the American occupation and today, including all Baptist groups, are one of the largest Protestant denominations in the country. Baptists continue to grow rapidly and are found in all parts of the country. They have particular strength in the metropolitan area of Manila, Western Visayas, and Mindanao. Practically every type of Baptist has been imported from the United States—ecumenical mainline, conservative evangelical, independent fundamental, Landmark Missionary Baptist, as well as Seventh Day, Free Will, and Primitive Baptists. Philippine Baptists are like a jigsaw puzzle whose pieces are difficult to fit together. Much of the Filipino Baptist work is today indigenous, and at least three of the Filipino Baptist bodies have sent missionaries abroad.

Convention of Philippine Baptist Churches

The Baptist pioneer in the Philippines was Eric Lund (1852–1933), a native of Sweden. After serving with the American Baptist Missionary Union (ABMU) in Spain, Lund and a Filipino convert, Braulio Manikin, opened in 1900 a mission of the ABMU at Jaro, three miles from Iloilo on the island of Panay in the Visayas, where a church was organized in February 1901. Lund was a noted linguist; he wrote or edited in Spanish, Visayan, and English and translated the Bible into Panayan, a subdialect of Visayan, and the New Testament in two other subdialects.

The mission began the Jaro Industrial School (1905), which in 1923 became Central Philippine College and in 1953 Central Philippine University, an outstanding educational institution. Other institutions included a Bible school (1905–1912), a Baptist Missionary Training School for women (1908–1938), Home School at Capiz in 1906 (which became Filamer Christian College), and a Girls' Academy (1910–1918). The mission also engaged in hospital work at Capiz and Iloilo. After World War II the Convention Baptist Bible School and the North Negros Baptist Bible College were begun and TEE introduced. In 1935 a Convention of Philippine Baptist Churches was formed.

The Japanese occupation of the Philippines during World War II brought destruction of mission property as well as internment and death to missionaries. On December 1943, the Japanese executed on Panay Island eleven American Baptist missionaries and the thirteen-year-old son of a missionary couple after discovering their hiding place.

Since the 1950s the convention has shown significant growth and today includes about 28 percent of all Philippine Baptists. In 1969 it began to send missionaries abroad, including Indonesia, Japan, Laos, Thailand, Germany, and the USA, and in 1978 formed a Commission on Overseas Mission and Evangelism. Although the convention rejected overtures to join the United Church of Christ in the Philippines, it has strong ties with the National Council of Churches in the Philippines, the only Baptist body which is a member. The convention today is in partnership with both the Board of International Ministries of the American Baptist Churches, USA, and the Australian Baptist Missionary Society.

Association of Fundamental Baptist Churches (and separating bodies)

A break in Baptist ranks occurred in 1927 when Dr. Raphael C. Thomas, who served at the Baptist hospital at Jaro, refused to give up his evangelistic field trips and confine his work to the hospital. Upon the resignations of Thomas and his wife, Norma, Mrs. George W. Doane called a meeting at her home which led to the formation of what became known as the Association of Baptists for World Evangelism (ABWE), a mission agency which was fundamentalist in conviction and separatist in ecclesiastical relations. One of the strong supporters of the new venture was Mrs. Henry W. Peabody, Thomas' mother-in-law, who was very prominent in Northern Baptist Convention circles but now resigned all her positions in that body. Thomas settled in Manila in 1928 where he established the First Baptist Church of the city.

With an emphasis on evangelism and church planting, the mission, not accepting comity agreements as the Philippine Convention, soon began work in all parts of the nation. This included areas outside of Manila on Luzon, the Visayas, Mindanao, and even Palawan, a group of almost one hundred islands far to the west. The Presbyterians, who had been allotted Palawan were willing to release this area to the new mission. The mission used a gospel ship, earlier used by the ABFMS in Japan, for work in the area. The mission established evangelistic institutes in Manila (today the Baptist Bible Seminary and Institute) and Iliolo (today the Doane Baptist Bible College). The mission engages in medical work and aviation evangelism and at present is stressing urban evangelism.

After World War II, the mission followed a strict indigenous policy which demanded self-support. Besides establishing regional associations, the churches formed the Association of Fundamental Baptist Churches. In 1957 they organized a Philippine Association of Baptists for World Evangelism, a foreign mission agency, which sought to send its first missionaries to Borneo. In 1964 it sent a missionary to Thailand; by 1979 four churches had been formed among the Chinese.

Several groups with roots in the work of ABWE exist as separate entities. One body is the Bumila Fellowship of Baptist Churches, with which International Missions is in cooperation. A second group is the Association of Baptist Churches in Luzon, Visayas, and Mindanao (ABCLVM). Under the leadership of Antonio F. Ormeo of the First Baptist Church of Manila and other pastors, a division occurred within the Association of Fundamental Baptist Churches in 1965. The schism was over the issue of ecclesiastical separation, which was complicated further by personal differences with some of the missionaries. The dissenting group, taking a stronger stand on separation than the parent mission, formed the ABCLVM. A third body is the International Baptist Missionary Fellowship (IBMF). One of the dissidents in the ABCLVM, Gavino Tica, went to the USA to study but returned around 1976 under the auspices of Baptist International Missions, Inc. (BIMI) to begin a new work, IBMF. Tilca, however, broke with BIMI and is entirely independent.

Southern Baptists

With the closure of China to Southern Baptist missionaries, the FMB of the Southern Baptist Convention entered the Philippines with an aggressive evangelistic program. Today four conventions relate to Southern Baptist work—the Luzon Convention, Visayan Convention, Mindanao Convention, and Chinese Convention with a membership which includes about 28 percent of all Filipino Baptists. The first missionaries arrived in 1948 and initially worked among the Chinese, but their ministry was soon extended to native Filipinos. One area of rapid development was in Mindanao where Baptists had migrated from the Visayas but were not followed up by the Philippine Convention because of comity. The mission opened the Philippine Baptist Theological Seminary in 1952 at Baguio, and it also opened a Bible school (today Southern Philippines Baptist Theological Seminary) at Davao in Mindanao. The mission put a strong emphasis on literature and radio ministries. It has established a Philippine Baptist Refugee Ministry and a Mindanao Rural Life Center, which provides programs

Testament. Dean arrived in 1835 and, working among Chinese in the Teochiu, or Swatow, dialect, founded the Maitrichit Baptist Church in Bangkok in 1837—the first Protestant church in Thailand, indeed the first in east Asia. It continues today as a strong Chinese congregation. In 1861 a Siamese Baptist Church was formed, but the mission formally closed its work among the Siamese in 1868.

Many early missionaries saw Thailand as a back door to China; when that vast land opened up, missionaries gravitated toward it. Dean served in China from 1842 to 1864 and then returned to Thailand, finally retiring in 1884 to the USA. Only one American missionary remained, L. A. Eaton, who served from 1882 to 1893. The field in Thailand was left an orphan. The one Chinese church, however, continued faithfully with only periodic encouragement by the Ling Tong Convention in China and occasional visits by American missionaries. At one point the church had 500 members and five outstations in places like Chon Buri and Chacheungsao. In 1934 the Maitrichit Church and the Hua Kun Chao Church (formed in Chon Buri in 1931) joined with other Protestants in the formation of the Church of Christ in Thailand, thereby becoming part of a Chinese district in the new church. Today there are 32 Chinese Baptist churches in the 12th District with more than 2,600 members. In 1978 the Maitrichit Church formed the Maitrichit Church Mission, which has supported several missionaries.

Baptist missionaries returned to Thailand after the Communist government in China expelled all missionaries. Southern Baptists arrived in 1949 and American Baptists in 1952. American Baptists have worked with the Chinese churches of the 12th District and also with Karen, Lahu, Akha, and Lisu peoples. Later Swedish, Australian, and British Baptists joined the American Baptists in their mission work.

Karen Baptists from Burma first sent missionaries to the Karens in Thailand in 1880, and soon two churches were established. The Karen work grew to twenty churches with 800 members by 1954. Since then, American Baptist and other cooperating missionaries have helped the Karen churches in agricultural, educational, evangelistic, and medical work and in training leaders. They have established several hostels, two hospitals, a school for children from several tribes, and a Center for the Uplift of Hilltribes, which trains young people in agricultural and biblical skills. A Karen Baptist Convention and a Lahu Baptist Convention have been organized, both showing significant growth and engaging in extensive programs of ministry.

The Southern Baptist missionaries who transferred to Thailand from China began work among the Chinese. While continuing in Chinese work, they eventually concentrated their major effort on the Thai population. Their primary purpose was evangelism and establishing churches. In its effort to strengthen the churches and to reach the Thai people, the mission began the Thailand Baptist Theological Seminary (1952), Baptist Christian Education (for publications), the Christian Conference Center at Pattaya, Baptist Student Center, Baptist Mass Communications, and Bangkla Baptist Hospital. The mission also has established two other ministries to meet human needs and for evangelism—Thai Country Trim to assist rural Thai women to increase their income at home and Thailand Baptist Rural Life Development Center.

In 1964 Baptists from the Philippines, representing the Philippine Association for World Evangelism (a mission agency of the Association of Fundamental Baptist Churches) began mission work among the Chinese. By 1979 they had four churches with seventy-four members. As ecclesiastical separatists, they do not cooperate with other Baptists.

The churches growing out of Southern Baptist work formed the Thailand Baptist Churches Association (TBCA) in 1971. Increasingly accepted by the churches, it became a partner with the Thailand Baptist Mission. By the early nineties, the TBCA was filling a more independent role in overseeing and planning the work. It challenged the churches with a strong program of outreach, and in 1993 it was supporting eleven home missionary families.

In 1976 representatives of Chinese, Thai, Karen, and Lahu Baptist churches formed the Thailand Baptist Convention. After a few years of regular fellowship meetings, the various language groups have focused their work mainly in their own conventions; today the Thailand Baptist convention no longer exists.

Ronald C. Hill. Supplemented by Albert W. Wardin, Jr.

BIBLIOGRAPHY: A very helpful survey of Baptist work in Thailand—including American, Southern, and Philippine Baptist mission efforts as well as material on Chinese, Karen, and Lahu Baptists—is in Alexander Garnett Smith, *A History of Baptist Missions in Thailand* (M.Div. research paper, Western Evangelical Seminary, 1980). For the history of the Maitrichit Church, see Samuel Kho, *150 Years of Thankfulness: A History of the Maitrichit Baptist Church, 1837–1987* (Bangkok, 1987). For the work of American Baptists, see Russell E. Brown, *Doing the Gospel in Southeast Asia* (Valley Forge: Judson Press, 1968), 38–63. For a popularly written mission study on early Southern Baptist work, see Frances E. Hudgins, *Temples of the Dawn* (Nashville: Convention Press, 1958). Another Southern Baptist mission book is Ronald C. Hill, *Bangkok: An Urban Arena* (Nashville: Convention Press, 1982).

VIETNAM (1962)

	Members	Churches
Grace Baptist Church, Ho Chi Minh City	n/a	(1)

*V*ietnam is a Communist state with a Christian minority of around 10 percent. Most Christians are adherents of the Roman Catholic Church, while most of the small Protestant community belong to the Evangelical Church of Vietnam, a product of the mission work of the Christian and Missionary Alliance.

After the defeat of French forces, Vietnam was divided between north and south in 1954. A Communist regime took control in North Vietnam, while a noncommunist government assumed power in South Vietnam. With the determination of North Vietnam to unify the country, civil war began immediately and dragged on until 1975. Even though from 1961 to 1973 the United States was directly involved militarily, its effort to save South Vietnam from Communist control failed. After the conquest of South Vietnam by North Vietnam in 1975, a unifed Vietnam was proclaimed in the following year.

In 1959 Southern Baptists sent their first missionary couple, Herman and Dottie Hayes. In March 1962 the first converts were baptized, and in the following November in Saigon the first Baptist church was organized. The Southern Baptist mission embarked on a program of church planting. In 1962 it established a Department of Publication, which produced literature in Vietnamese, and in 1963 a Baptist Bible Institute was founded, which was superseded by a seminary program in 1967. A Radio and Television Commission, established in 1965, sought to use radio, television, and visual aids in reaching the public. In spite of the dangers of the war, which necessitated missionaries' flying between cities, the mission continued to grow. At the beginning of 1970 Southern Baptists had thirty-nine missionaries on the field at seven stations. There were six churches with a membership of 917.

The collapse of South Vietnam and the withdrawal of all Americans in 1975 brought the mission to an end. The Communist regime closed all Baptist churches, except the Grace Baptist Church in Ho Chi Minh City (the former Saigon), or used their facilities for other purposes. Le Quoc Chanh, the pastor of the church in 1975 and the mission's first convert in 1961, gave his exit pass to a friend and has continued to serve the church. In spite of the hardships of political and social change, the church has flourished with crowded services with about 350 adults and numerous children, daily early morning prayer sessions, youth meetings, and a choir program. Some Baptists, however, who lost their church buildings continue to meet in homes. Both Roman Catholic and Protestant churches have shown significant growth since 1975. Under Cooperative Services International, a Southern Baptist agency, Southern Baptists reentered Vietnam in 1989 by working in agricultural projects.

Beginning in 1971 Southern Baptists had a short-lived mission in Laos, bordering Vietnam. In 1971 they sent their first couple; two more couples and a journeyman joined in 1974. On Easter 1973 the first baptismal service was held. The Convention of Philippine Baptist Churches also sent a couple of missionaries to Laos, one in 1971 and another in 1973. Because of the establishment of a Communist regime in 1975, there is apparently no Baptist work in the country today.

BIBLIOGRAPHY: For the work of the Southern Baptist mission to 1970, see Baker J. Cauthen and others, *Advance* (Nashville: Broadman Press, 1970), 132–34. For information on Baptists and particularly the Grace Baptist Church after 1975, see *Northwest Baptist Witness*, June 6, 1989, 6, and October 14, 1994, 12, and *Baptist and Reflector*, Sep. 29, 1993, 4.

BAPTIST AND BAPTIST-RELATED MISSIONS

1. BRUNEI   —

2. INDONESIA UkBMS (1813–1847), SBC (1951), AuBMS (1955), CBI (1961), WBF (1970), BIMI (1971), BBFI (1973), CaBIM (1973), NzBMS (1979), MWBM (1980), JnBBF, JnBC, PhCBA

3. MALAYSIA SBC (1951), RBMS

4. MYANMAR (BURMA) ABC (1814), BIMI (1984), BWM (1991)

5. PHILIPPINES ABC (1900), ABWE (1928), SBC (1948), BBFI (1950), BGC (1950), CBI (1955), GBFMS (1957), ABA (1961), OFWB (1969), BIMI (1970), BMA (1974), SDBMS (1974), BFM (1980), BM-M (1980), CLF (1981), NABC (1986), AuBMS (1988), LIB (1989), IFM (1991), RBMS, UkGBM

6. SINGAPORE SBC (1950), ABC (1967–1990), BBFI (1968), BIMI (1982), CBI (1983), BWM (1988)

7. THAILAND ABC (1833–1893, 1952), SBC (1949), AuBMS (1971), PhABWE (1964), PhCPBC (1974), SwBU (1976), BIMI (1979), BWM (1980), BBFI (1983), BGC (1988), UkBMS (1988), SwO

8. VIETNAM SBC (1959–1975)

E. SOUTHWEST ASIA

*T*he territory of southwest Asia, known also as the Middle East if Egypt is included, stretches from the Mediterranean Sea to Afghanistan on the border of the Indian subcontinent. The area is the home of the three monotheistic faiths of Judaism, Christianity, and Islam. Judaism predominates in Israel; Christianity prevails in Cyprus as well as maintains a strong minority in Lebanon and important Christian communities in Israel, Jordan, Syria, and Iraq. In the remaining countries, Islam holds nearly universal sway.

With the rising tide of Moslem fundamentalism, Islam—always resistant to the Christian gospel—has become increasingly intolerant. In Islamic nations, Christian evangelism or proselyting is prohibited, and Moslems who convert face ostracism, if not worse penalties. Since the word "missionary" has a strongly negative connotation, mission workers prefer some other designation, such as representative.

Small Baptist communities and mission efforts exist in the Bible lands of Israel, Jordan, Lebanon, and Syria. Some Baptist work is conducted in Cyprus, Turkey, United Arab Emirates, Bahrain, and Yemen. In the other nations, such as Saudi Arabia, Oman, Qatar, Kuwait (in the Arabian peninsula), and Iraq, Iran, and Afghanistan, there is no recognized Baptist community or official mission presence. Although in a country such as Saudi Arabia, the protector of Islam's holiest cities, there may be no public evidence of a Christian church, yet work is conducted unofficially with discretion among expatriates.

Doors to mission opportunities are often barred or, if once open, are closed. In 1990 the pastor of the Baptist church in Amman, witnessing a revival among evangelicals in Baghdad, considered opening Baptist work in the city but was refused by the government. During the occupation of Kuwait by Iraq in 1990, one Southern Baptist representative, Maurice Graham, who had gone to work with the National Evangelical Church of Kuwait, was held as a hostage for a time. His release ended Southern Baptist representation in the country.

Today in Iran there are no Baptist churches, even though there have been congregations in the past. Before World War I two Baptist missions worked among the Nestorians in the northwest of Persia, as Iran was then known. Yonan H. Shahbaz, beginning in 1898 and with private help from Northern Baptists in the USA, established within the next decade three congregations with about 140 members at Geogtapa and other sites. Beginning in 1904 with independent support of Southern Baptists, Dr. Ismael N. Yohanan, trained in medicine and theology, also started mission work. These missions did not survive. In 1968 a Southern Baptist couple, George and Joan Braswell, entered Iran, and for a time Braswell taught at the faculty of Islamic theology of the University of Tehran. In 1972 Americans, attracted by the oil industry, formed an English-language Baptist church in Tehran, which also established missions in three other cities. Baptist work, however, ceased with the departure of all Americans by 1979 because of the anti-American policies of the Shiite Islamic regime.

In spite of past failure, the traditional hostilities between the three monotheistic faiths, military conflict, militant fundamentalism, restrictions on mission activity, and the numerical weakness of the Baptist communities, Baptists maintain a very active presence in the region. Through personal witness, mass communication, and institutional ministries, they not only have won converts, even though numbers may be small compared to other fields, but also have extended the benefits of Western medicine and education to thousands.

BIBLIOGRAPHY: For a general survey of Baptist work among Arabs in the Middle East, see J. D. Hughey, "Baptist Foreign Mission Work in the Middle East," *Baptist History and Heritage*, 4 (1969): 106–11, and Finlay M. Graham, *Sons of Ishmael: How Shall They Hear?* (Nashville; Convention Press, 1969). For a description of Baptist work among the Nestorians in Persia, see J. Heinrichs, "Persisch-Baptistische Missionsglocken," *Der Sendbote*, Jan. 22, 1908, 57–58, and Jan. 29, 1908, 73.

	Members	Churches
1. Cyprus	n/a	2
2. Israel	700	8
3. Jordan	1,296	18
4. Lebanon	1,000	28
5. Palestine (West Bank, Gaza and East Jerusalem)	212	6
6. Syria	190	4
7. Turkey	n/a	1
8. United Arab Emirates/Bahrain	—	—
9. Yemen	70	1
	3,468	68

CYPRUS (1985)

	Members	Churches
1. Baptist International Missions	n/a	(1)
2. Macedonia World Baptist Missions	n/a	(1)
	n/a	(2)

B aptist work in Cyprus is recent. Two independent Baptist missions—Baptist International Missions and Macedonia World Baptist Missions—serve in the country. Each one has two missionaries and has established a church, while the latter mission also supports a small Bible school. Because of conflict in Lebanon, Southern Baptists have used Cyprus as a base where the Arab Theological

Seminary has operated more than once. Southern Baptists, however, have not formally established Cyprus as one of their fields, although they have worked among Kurdish refugees in the area of Larnaca, and another Southern Baptist assigned to Lebanon is working in a sports program.

BIBLIOGRAPHY: For Southern Baptist work, see *Your Guide to Foreign Missions,* 1994–1995, 128–29.

ISRAEL (1911)

	Members	Churches
1. Association of Baptist Churches in Israel (1965)	677	(7)
2. Reformed Baptists	23	(1)
	700	(8)

*B*aptists entered Palestine in 1911, then under Turkish control with the coming of Shukri Musa, who had been baptized by George W. Truett at the First Baptist Church of Dallas. With the support of Baptists of the Illinois Baptist State Association, Musa began in Zefat (Safad). He baptized here his first convert, but soon opened a mission in Nazareth where he started a church. In 1897 and again in 1900 and 1919, the Southern Baptist Convention expressed great interest in establishing work in Palestine, but it was not until Southern Baptist missionary couples arrived in Jerusalem in early 1923 after Palestine had become a British mandate that Southern Baptist work began. One couple soon left because of health problems, but J. Wash Watts and his wife, Mattie, remained, living first in Jerusalem and then in Tel Aviv. The ministry of Watts and his wife was primarily directed toward winning Jews, but the mission did not neglect Arab evangelism. Besides the church in Nazareth, which also had a day school (1937), congregations were established in Jerusalem (1925) and Haifa (1936).

With the disruption of World War II and the withdrawal and resignation of missionaries, Baptist work almost disappeared and had to be renewed with the reentry of missionaries in 1944. In 1948 the new state of Israel was proclaimed and, in spite of Arab attack, it survived. Although in 1950 there were only two churches—one in Jerusalem and the other in Arab Nazareth—and twenty members, Baptist work took on new life in Israel. New missionaries, including Robert L. Lindsey, an important leader of the work who produced a Hebrew translation of Mark, and his wife, Margaret, strengthened the mission. In 1948 the mission reopened the elementary school in Nazareth and added a high school several years later. The Nazareth school, the top Arab school in Israel, today has an enrollment of more than seven hundred students and a waiting list. In 1955 the mission purchased a farm near Petah Tiqwa, which is the largest camp and conference center in Israel. The mission also began publication work and operated two bookstores. In 1964 Dwight Baker launched a Christian Service Training Center in Haifa for Arab believers. In 1964 five churches with 181 members formed the Association of Baptist Churches in Israel.

Today there are about seven hundred Baptists in Israel, including both Jewish and

religious population of Europe/Eurasia. However, the difference in strength is not as great as it appears when it is realized that these churches include in their statistics masses of people baptized as infants who rarely attend church.

On first appearance, it appears that European Baptists are remarkably well distributed. While they have pockets of strength, there are very few Baptists in a number of parts of Europe/Eurasia, particularly in Roman Catholic countries, which are represented in five of the above regions, the Balkans south of the Danube River, and Moslem areas in Central Asia. On the other hand, Baptists have important constituencies in the United Kingdom, northern Germany, and Sweden, in addition to a belt of strength across Hungary, Romania, Moldova, and Ukraine.

With the large number of American servicemen and their families, a new dimension to European Baptist life was added in the 1950s with the appearance of English-language churches, generally led by Southern Baptists. Even though these churches are members of a European Baptist Convention, most also affiliate with the Baptist union of their country. With the decrease in military personnel, these churches are increasingly becoming international churches, reaching out to the larger community.

Baptists grew rapidly from the middle of the nineteenth century to World War I, but in the following decades European Baptists have been affected seriously by the two World Wars, the growing secularization of western and central Europe, and the seven decades of Communist control in the USSR and four decades of this control in the rest of eastern Europe. The number of Baptists in Europe today is a bit less than in 1927. Baptists in the British Isles and northern Europe have suffered decline. Those in central and southern Europe have registered gains, but because of the growth of Baptists in Romania, southeastern Europe has had the most spectacular increase. In Eurasia, the former territory of the USSR which experienced more than two generations of Communist rule, there are surprisingly about as many Baptists today as there were in 1928, if both Baptists and Evangelical Christians are included. In fact, Baptists at present are experiencing their greatest growth in former Communist lands, particularly Russia, Ukraine, Moldova, and Romania.

In spite of theological differences, European Baptists are united; most of them belong to the European Baptist Federation (EuEBF) and the Baptist World Alliance (BWA). Many Baptists are pietists, moderately conservative, such as those in Germanic and Scandinavian lands. Others are strongly conservative or fundamentalist, particularly in Eastern Europe and Ireland. Except in England, theological liberalism has found little acceptance, but even there most Baptists would identify with broad evangelical affirmations. There is a divide between Baptists in eastern Europe and western Europe over issues of personal morality with the former holding to a more rigid and separatist puritanical code than is found in Western Europe.

Only the Baptist Unions of Great Britain, Denmark, Italy, Hungary, and Russia are members of the World Council of Churches, while a rather large number of unions relate to the Conference of European Churches. In addition to those who are in the World Council of Churches, membership and leadership are widespread in national councils of churches, free church organizations, and Evangelical Alliances. Baptists in southeastern Europe, recently freed from Communist control, have become leaders in a number of national Evangelical Alliances.

European Baptists still maintain their heritage of a believer's church with a concern for evangelism. Composed of the common people, Baptist churches have given a spiritual home as well as social mobility to hundreds of thousands. As a minority advocating separation of church and state, they have been pioneers in the struggle for religious liberty.

BIBLIOGRAPHY: The history of Baptists in Europe may be found in the standard Baptist histories of Robert G. Torbet or H. Leon McBeth, or in histories of Baptists in individual countries. Books on European Baptists as a whole, however, are generally restricted to surveys. J. H. Rushbrooke wrote or edited several helpful volumes on Baptists on the continent, excluding the British Isles—*The Baptist Movement in the Continent of Europe* (London: Carey Press/Kingsgate Press, 1915), a second volume of the same name (London: Kingsgate Press, 1923), and *Some Chapters of European History* (London: Kingsgate Press, 1929). Rushbrooke also wrote with Charles A. Brooks, *Baptist Work in Europe* (London: Baptist Union Publication Department, 1920). Helpful surveys also include J. D. Franks, comp., *European Baptists Today*, 2d rev. ed. (Rüschlikon-Zürich: Author, 1952); Irwin Barnes, *Truth Is Immortal* (London: Carey Kingsgate Press, 1955); H. Cornell Goerner, *Hands Across the Sea* (Nashville: Convention Press, 1961); Erik Rudén, *Baptismen i Europa* (Stockholm: Westerbergs Forlag 1964); Dean R. Kirkwood, ed., *European Baptists: A Magnificent Minority* (Valley Forge: International Ministries, American Baptist Churches/USA, 1981); J. D. Hughey, *Baptist Partnership in Europe* (Nashville: Broadman Press, 1982); and G. Keith Parker, *Baptists in Europe: History and Confessions of Faith* (Nashville: Broadman Press, 1982). For a history of the early years of the European Baptist Convention, see Lewis M. Krause, *Scattered Abroad* (Heidelberg: Author, 1966); for its present work, see Mike Creswell, "English-language Churches: Changing with the Times," *Commission*, December 1992, 56–59.

A. BRITISH ISLES

*E*ngland is the cradle of the Baptist movement, producing two Baptist traditions—almost simultaneously in the first decades of the seventeenth century General Baptists and the Particular or Calvinistic Baptists. Before 1660 Baptists had appeared also in Wales, Scotland, and Ireland, but they were extinguished in Scotland until replanted in the eighteenth century and barely survived in Ireland until they were rejuvenated in the nineteenth century. Baptists from Britain also helped to plant the Baptist witness in the British colonies of America and in time took it to other British dominions. With William Carey in the forefront, English Baptists in 1792 initiated the modern missionary movement which today encompasses the globe.

Their confessions of faith helped to establish the doctrinal standards of Baptists. English Baptists not only practiced believer's baptism, recovered by the continental Anabaptists a century before, but were the first denominational group in modern times to practice believer's baptism by immersion as the general norm. Because of their experience with military associations during the Puritan revolution, English Baptists adopted the association for cooperation and fellowship among the churches. They were also leaders in establishing schools for pastoral training. With their American brethren, British Baptists were in the forefront of developing international Baptist ties through the Baptist World Alliance.

	Members	Churches
1. England	156,540	2,278
2. Ireland	8,778	113
3. Scotland	15,287	177
4. Wales	37,463	729
	218,068	3,297

ENGLAND (1612)

	Members	Churches
1. Baptist Union of Great Britain (1813)*	138,512	(1,787)
2. Grace Baptist Assembly	10,000	(260)
3. Gospel Standard Strict Baptists	6,400	(156)

4. Reformed Baptists	n/a	n/a
5. Old Baptist Union (1880)	663	(18)
6. Seventh Day Baptists	55	(2)
7. Jesus Fellowship Church (Baptist)	910	(49)
8. Progressive National Baptists	n/a	(6)
	156,540	2,278

*The total membership of the Baptist Union in Great Britain 1991 was 160,431 (2,121) which includes 12,079 (185) in Wales, 9,552 (146) in dual affiliation with the Baptist Union of Wales, and 288 (3) in dual affiliation with the Baptist Union of Scotland.

 nglish Baptists, with a continuous history from the early seventeenth century, have the longest history of any group of Baptists in the world. Initially there were two streams of Baptist life: General Baptists and Particular Baptists.

The General Baptists were so called because they believed that the benefits of saving grace were available to all. John Smyth (c. 1750–1612), a former Fellow of Christ's College in the University of Cambridge, and a group of Lincolnshire Puritans, under threat of persecution in the early years of James I's reign, sought refuge in the Netherlands. There Smyth and his followers encountered the Mennonites and came to the conviction that only believer's baptism was valid. Accordingly, early in 1609 Smyth rebaptized himself and then proceeded to baptize those of his company who sought believer's baptism. Smyth died in the Netherlands in 1612. In the same year, Thomas Helwys (c. 1550–c. 1616), whom Smyth had baptized, published *The Mistery of Iniquity*, a very early plea for religious toleration. Helwys returned to England in 1612 after disagreeing with Smyth over relationships with the Mennonites. Helwys founded the first Baptist church on British soil at Spitalfields, London, in 1612.

By 1638 at the latest, there were also Baptist congregations holding a Calvinist theology in London. These were formed by members of older Independent churches who came to practice believer's baptism. Committed to the concept of the church as the fellowship of believers, they judged only believer's baptism appropriate to such an understanding. Since they believed in a particular salvation for the elect only, they came to be known as Particular Baptists. Initially, both groups baptized by sprinkling, but by the 1640s they were agreed that immersion was the right mode.

The extent to which these early Baptists were influenced by continental Anabaptism has been contested vehemently. The links of the early General Baptists with Dutch Mennonites are clear, but it is equally apparent that the Particular Baptists arose out of a conscientious search among the English Separatists for the paradigm of an apostolic church. This, they believed, could only be discovered in the pages of the New Testament.

Very soon these infant churches were hurled into all the fury of the debate about the proper relationship of church and state as the controversy with the king developed in the latter years of Charles I's reign and the turmoil of the Protectorate and Commonwealth. Few Baptists were prepared to serve within the Puritan state church in the Cromwellian period; most continued to work with gathered congregations outside the parish structure.

Toward the end of the Commonwealth period, there were other threats to Baptist life. Millenarian speculation was common among Puritans at this time. Fifth Monarchism was not so much a sect but as a view that a number of Baptists, among others, came to adopt. Some Baptist leaders, such as Vavasour Powell (1617–1670), carried many church members with them with some becoming active plotters against the state. The Quakers also secured a large following among former Baptists with their emphasis on the inner witness of the Spirit versus the outward rules of church membership or indeed the written Word of Scripture. Whole congregations transferred their allegiance.

Patterns of worship among early Baptists might seem rather uninspiring to late twentieth-century Baptists, for initially there was hostility both to hymns and to congregational singing. Even when hymns became accepted, verses had to be lined out before books became common. The basic diet, therefore, was the reading of the Psalms and other portions of Scripture, prayers embracing the praise of God, confession of sin together with petition and intercession, and preaching. By contrast, the ordinances of baptism, very often conducted in the open air, and the Lord's Supper introduced dramatic visual and participatory elements, including at least an annual pledging of the membership to the church covenant, the basis of their corporate life.

It has been estimated that by 1660 there were roughly three hundred Baptist churches within the two traditions. The Restoration heralded a quarter century of intermittent persecution by the state. The "Glorious" Revolution of 1688 and the accession of the Protestant sovereigns, William and Mary, brought only limited toleration. Oppressive laws remained on the statute book, though Protestant dissenters of Trinitarian faith who subscribed to the main points of the Thirty-Nine Articles were sometimes exempted from the penalties prescribed.

With toleration there came, among churchmen and dissenters, both a less intense commitment and a tolerance for a wider range of theological views. Some of the General Baptists, alongside many of the Presbyterians, fell prey to the spread of Arianism, that is, a denial of the divinity of Christ. By the end of the eighteenth century many General Baptist congregations had adopted a full-blown Unitarianism. By contrast, many Particular Baptists, especially those who looked to the London leadership of John Gill (1697–1771) and John Brine (1703–1765), overreacting against theological liberalism, adopted a hyper-Calvinist position, which so stressed the sovereignty of God that it threatened both individual moral action and evangelism. Churches within the orbit of Bristol College, on the other hand, never deviated from a more open evangelical Calvinism.

This meant that Baptists were not in a position immediately to benefit from the new life born of the Great Awakening. But several initiatives brought the impact of the Awakening to bear upon Baptist life. First, a group of village laborers in Leicestershire, who had been evangelized by a servant of the Countess of Huntingdon, came independently to Baptist convictions in 1755 with Samuel Deacon (1714–1812) as their leader. Dan Taylor (1738–1816), a Yorkshire miner converted among the Methodists, similarly came to Baptist convictions through his own study of the Scriptures. He sought out the General Baptists of Lincolnshire to be baptized, but eventually both the Leicestershire group and Dan Taylor's church, together with those General Baptist churches that remained orthodox, formed the New Connexion of General Baptists in 1770—they could not live with the doctrinal latitude of the old General Baptists. The New Connexion established a more tightly knit denomination centered in the emerging industrial communities of the East Midlands and north into Yorkshire. The Old Connexion of General Baptists continues to exist as a group of Unitarians.

New life came to the Particular Baptists at the end of the eighteenth century through a particularly creative partnership between three Northamptonshire ministers. John Sutcliff (1752–1814) called his fellow ministers to more urgent prayer; William Carey (1761–1834) invited them to consider wider horizons of mission; and Andrew Fuller (1754–1815) gave a new defense for moderate Calvinism. In 1792 the Particular Baptist Missionary Society for Propagating the Gospel among the Heathen was founded, and the following year William Carey with a physician, John Thomas, arrived in India. The new society not only committed British Baptists to mission overseas but also revived the ailing fortunes of the churches at home. Within five years the Baptist Itinerant Society was founded to accomplish mission work in rural areas. This ushered in a period of church growth. Particular Baptist churches increased from about four hundred in 1789 to more than a thousand by 1835.

After founding the missionary society, British Baptists also began thinking nationally. In 1813 a Baptist Union was established, although within twenty years it was refounded to allow for General Baptist membership. A process of growing together was begun which was completed in 1891 with the uniting of General and Particular Baptist work. Robert Hall (1764–1831) with others began to advocate open communion, while others strongly opposed the new trend. Until 1809 Baptists had been content to get their religious intelligence from the *Evangelical Magazine*, but in that year a separate monthly *Baptist Magazine* came into being. Many other magazines came and went, but from 1855 *The Freeman* offered Baptists a weekly paper, which was taken over by the Baptist Union to become *The Baptist Times and Freeman* in 1899.

Bristol College had been reorganized in 1770 for the training of the ministry, and new institutions were established at Horton in Bradford, Yorkshire, in 1805 and at Stepney in East London in 1810. Charles Haddon Spurgeon founded a rather different college in south London in 1856 which sought to produce preachers of the gospel. Ten years later a new college in the northwest, which moved to Manchester in 1873, was also established, initially to provide for close-communion churches of the Northwestern Association.

Until 1828 Baptists in Britain were second-class citizens living under the limitations of the Test and Corporation Acts; they were unable to participate in local government or to hold office under the Crown, though for a number of years no penalties had been imposed. In addition, Baptists had to pay rates for the upkeep of the local church when the local vestry required it until 1868, and it was not until 1871 that religious tests were removed in the ancient universities. Therefore, campaigning for full civil liberties consumed much Baptist energy. Along with other free churchmen, Baptists came to exhibit what was known as the "nonconformist conscience" with its concerns not only for issues of private morality—Sunday observance, sexual license, temperance, gambling, and other forms of amusement which offended against an inherited Puritanism—but also broader structural issues concerning slavery in the colonies, poverty, employment, housing, and education.

British Baptists grew in the nineteenth century in number, in influence, and in the development of denominational institutions. When the Baptist Union was relaunched in 1833, the reported membership of associated churches was not much more than 40,000; allowing for a known short-fall on churches reporting, the figure could be as high as 70,000. Membership peaked in 1906, when a figure for England and Wales of those churches listed in the *Handbook* yielded just short of 411,000 members in 2,811 churches with a Sunday School enrollment of almost 570,000. Compared with other Protestant denominations, the Baptists were stronger among the lower classes.

In 1991 the Baptist Union had declined to 160,000 members in 2,121 churches with 136,000 young people associated in youth groups of different kinds. These figures, however, are not wholly comparable to the 1906 figures since the earlier figures included many Strict and independent Baptist congregations never in membership with the Union as well as Welsh and Scottish churches which, for reasons of nationalism, no longer affiliate with it. In addition, because of theological issues and the Union's ecumenical involvement, some churches had left the Baptist Union and joined the Federation of Independent Evangelical Churches. There is, however, a new spirit of outreach today. Church attendance exceeds membership; 125 are in worship for every one hundred members.

From the end of the eighteenth century, the life of the local church became much more varied with Sunday worship, now confidently embracing hymn-singing but still climaxing in the sermon, supplemented by Sunday Schools. Generations of Baptist leaders gave the work of the Sunday School the highest priority, further spawning a range of societies concerned with the training and welfare of young people. More broadly, any description of Baptist life would be incomplete if it failed to give proper attention to Christian philanthropy, extended to all in need from orphans through slum dwellers to the elderly.

Superficially, the two most prominent Baptist preachers of Victorian Britain, Charles Haddon Spurgeon (1834–1892) and John Clifford (1836–1923), might seem to represent the unresolved tensions between General and Particular Baptists. Yet Spurgeon, while vigorously defending inherited understandings of the faith, was well aware of the need to woo new worshipers. His Metropolitan Tabernacle, a great center of evangelism, was also an institutional church insofar as it supported a battery of agencies and organizations to meet the social and spiritual needs of the people of south London. John Clifford held "advanced" views in many areas of theology, wrote socialist tracts for the Fabian Society, and led the movement of "Passive Resistance" in opposition to the government's determination to give rate aid to denominational schools at the beginning of the twentieth century. But for all their differences, both were committed totally to personal evangelism.

In more recent years, English Baptists have emerged as a bridge denomination occupying a mediating position between the mainstream denominations and evangelical sectarianism. Thus they have been fully involved ecumenically as founding members of the British Council of Churches and the World Council of Churches. Denominational agencies are more developed with, in particular, a superintending ministry that cares for ministers and churches on a regional basis. Worship patterns have changed with the denomination open to charismatic influences and enriched by them.

Seventh Day Baptists, who arose in the 1650s, have only two small churches whose members came from Seventh Day Baptists in Jamaica and do not descend from the original English churches. The Old Baptist Union (founded in 1880) is rather centrally organized with an evangelical Arminian basis of belief. Most of its churches now belong to a non-geographical association in membership with the Baptist Union.

Strict Baptists arose in the nineteenth century because of their opposition to Fuller's moderate Calvinism and open communion and open membership. They are divided into three groups. The Grace Baptist Assembly links together churches which, in former years, subscribed to *Earthen Vessel* and the *Gospel Herald* but which since 1970 publish the magazine *Grace*. This first group consists of about 260 churches and has become more open and willing to share in evangelistic outreach, leading some to form isolated Reformed Baptist congregations. Another group of Strict Baptists, similar to Reformed Baptists, is sometimes known after one of their leading ministers as Gadbyites but more frequently by the name of their periodical, *The Gospel Standard*. A third group adheres to the magazine *The Christian's Pathway*.

The Jesus Fellowship Church (Baptist) was formerly the Bugbrooke Baptist Church in Northamptonshire. Following a directive policy over its members and its planting of congregations in competition to existing Baptist churches, its membership of the Baptist Union was terminated as earlier it had been expelled from the Evangelical Alliance.

Some Southern Baptist congregations, which originally served personnel on American military bases, have become indigenized, especially with the reduction of American military personnel. The movement of population has brought Progressive Baptist congregations to England, which minister among the Black population and are seeking affiliation to the Baptist Union as a non-geographical association. There are also other expatriate Baptist churches.

Separatist fundamentalist missions from America have entered, bringing their own brand of evangelicalism with American trappings. They have found England a difficult field. Beyond these groups there are a number of "baptistic" groups among congregations that have come into being during the last forty years with which associations of the Baptist Union are willing to collaborate.

John H. Y. Briggs

BIBLIOGRAPHY: For a well-written history, see A. C. Underwood, *A History of the English Baptists* (London: Carey Kingsgate Press, 1947). The Baptist Historical Society is producing an excellent series on the history of English Baptists under the general editorship of B. R. White, which includes the followng works: B. R. White, *The English Baptists of the Seventeenth Century* (London: Baptist Historical Society, 1983); Raymond Brown, *The English Baptists of the Eighteenth Century* (London: Baptist Historical Society, 1986); J. H. Y. Briggs, *The English Baptists in the Nineteenth Century* (London: Baptist Historical Society, 1994); and W. M. S. West, *The English Baptists in the Twentieth Century* (in preparation). H. Wheeler Robinson, *The Life and Faith of the Baptists*, rev. ed. (London: Kingsgate Press, 1946), is an excellent study of English Baptist origins and principles. For historical material on Strict Baptists, see Kenneth Dix, "Particular Baptists and Strict Baptists," The Strict Baptist Historical Society, *Annual Report and Bulletin*, 1976, no. 13. The article by Wayne Detzler, "A Wave of Separatist Baptists Engulfs Britain, Then Recedes," *Christianity Today*, April 24, 1981, 46–47, reviews the work of independent fundamentalist missions in England.

IRELAND (1640)

Republic of Ireland

	Members	Churches
1. Baptist Union of Ireland (1895)	405	(11)
2. Grace Baptist Assembly	70	(2)
3. Independent churches	<u>150</u>	<u>(6)</u>
	625	(19)

Northern Ireland

	Members	Churches
1. Baptist Union of Ireland (1895)	8,083	(91)
2. Independent churches	<u>70</u>	<u>(3)</u>
	8,153	(94)

Total membership in Ireland is 8,778 in 113 churches.

STATISTICS: Baptist Union of Ireland, *Assembly Handbook*, 1991, and *Irish Christian Handbook* in *European Churches Handbook*, pt. 2 (London: MARC, 1991), 31.

*T*he Baptists of Ireland are one of the oldest Baptist bodies, arising almost contemporaneously with the Particular (Calvinistic) Baptists of England. In 1653 there were ten Baptist congregations with nine of them in the south— Dublin, Waterford, Clonmel, Kilkenny, Cork, Limerick, Galway, Wexford, and Kerry, and one in the north near Carrick Fergus. Today the Baptist constituency is reversed with most members in the north.

The arrival of Baptists in Cromwell's army in 1649 gave the Baptist cause a boost. In 1653 the Baptist brethren in Ireland requested correspondence from Baptists in Britain and some assistance. With the collapse of Cromwell's regime, the Baptist cause, which was located in areas of Roman Catholic dominance and attracting an English and not an Irish membership, declined seriously.

Baptist fortunes in Ireland began to revive with the formation of the Baptist Society for Propagating the Gospel in Ireland. This society was formed in London in 1813 with an auxiliary in Dublin, formed in 1814. It was organized in response to an appeal of nine young men in Dublin, who began mission activity in 1812, as well as a call from two English ministers who had visited Ireland on deputation for the BMS. The new organization practically served as an extension of the BMS in Ireland. In 1888 the society became the Irish Baptist Home Mission when it came under the Irish Baptist Association, which had been organized in 1862. Although emigration as a result of the Great Famine of 1847 affected Baptist membership, the Ulster Revival of 1859 helped to bring renewed strength. The outstanding Irish minister in the nineteenth century was Alexander Carson (1776–1844) of Scottish-Irish ancestry. Carson developed the largest Baptist congregation at the time at Tobormore and wrote a classic work on baptism.

In 1895 Irish Baptists replaced the Irish Baptist Association with the Irish Baptist Union. They severed their ties with the BMS and formed in 1924 the Irish Baptist Foreign Mission. In 1977 this organization united with Irish Home Mission to become Baptist Missions, which exists as a department of the Baptist Union of Ireland. In addition, Irish Baptists maintain a Women's Fellowship, Baptist Youth Fellowship, Orphan Society, and an Irish Baptist Historical Society and publish *The Irish Baptist*. Because of the benevolence of John D. Rockefeller, Sr., an Irish Baptist Training Institute was established in 1892, which today is the Irish Baptist College, located in Belfast. In 1991 it had an enrollment of thirty-six full- and part-time students.

Under Hugh D. Brown, a pastor in Dublin, Irish Baptists supported Charles Haddon

Spurgeon in the Downgrade Controversy and adopted in 1888 a conservative statement which has since been expanded and must be accepted by churches, pastors, and new members. Because of their conservative theology, Irish Baptists are not members of either the EBF or BWA. On the other hand, they will cooperate with other Baptists, as in the Fellowship of Evangelical Baptists in Europe or in mission work with Conservative Baptist International (CBI) from the USA.

Unlike most Baptist unions in northern Europe, Irish Baptists have experienced a steady, although not spectacular, rise in membership. In 1888 there were 18 churches, rising to 58 in 1938, and today totaling more than 100. Within the Irish Union there is a Northern Association for Northern Ireland, which is part of the United Kingdom, and a Southern Association for the Republic of Ireland. The Irish Union thereby represents Baptist work in both Irelands even though they are under separate political jurisdictions. The Northern Association includes about 90 percent of the churches and 95 percent of the members, indicating that Irish Baptists have had far more success among the Scottish-Irish Protestant population in the north than among the Irish Catholic population in the south. Since World War II several independent Baptist missions from America have entered Ireland with CBI, cooperating with and not working apart from the Irish Union.

In line with the historical Irish reputation for missions, in evidence as early as the fifth century, Irish Baptists, though few in number, maintain their part of the tradition. In 1991 about 150 men and women from Irish Baptist churches were serving in fields outside of Ireland, many under evangelical nondenominational missions. As part of their own mission effort, Irish Baptists have had a field in Peru since 1927 and in France since 1977, where they work in cooperation with Conservative Baptist International.

BIBLIOGRAPHY: For a most valuable document from Irish Baptists in 1653, see B. R. White, ed., *Association Records of the Particular Baptists of England, Wales and Ireland to 1660*, pt. 2 (London: Baptist Historical Society, 1971–1974), 110–124. For a centennial history of the Irish Baptist Home Mission, see *Celebrating 100 Years* (Belfast: Baptist Union of Ireland, 1988). For other material, consult Frank H. Forbes, "Ireland," in J. D. Franks, comp., *European Baptists Today*, 2d rev. ed. (Rüschlikon-Zürich: Author, 1952), 45–48, and Leon McBeth, *The Baptist Heritage* (Nashville: Broadman Press, 1987), 312–16, 536–39. For a contemporary view of Irish Baptists, see Martha Skelton, "Ireland: Baptist Witness and Ministry," *Commission*, May 1989, 8–59, 62–63. Joshua Thompson is writing a centennial history of the Irish Baptist Union, which is to be published in 1995.

SCOTLAND (1750)

	Members	Churches
1. Baptist Union of Scotland (1869)	14,407	(169)
2. Non-Union churches	880	(8)
	15,287	(177)

*B*aptist beliefs first arrived in Scotland with the troops of Oliver Cromwell in the mid-seventeenth century, but the small churches they founded soon disappeared. The earliest surviving congregation, at Keiss in Sutherland, was created in 1750 by Sir William Sinclair, "the preaching knight," who convinced a number of his tenants of the rightness of believer's baptism. More influential were the so-called Scotch Baptists, begun in Edinburgh in 1765 by Robert Carmichael, a former Presbyterian minister. Archibald McLean, originally a Glasgow bookseller, joined Carmichael in the following year. Having previously been swayed by the Glasites, McLean adopted the convictions that faith is a matter of rational assent and that New Testament church order should be imitated rigorously. Accordingly, the Scotch Baptists, in contrast to the established church in Scotland, insisted on weekly communion (a practice that has remained normal in Scotland ever since), and a plurality of elders in each congregation rather than a single trained minister.

Another stream of Baptist life flowed from the evangelism of the Haldane brothers, Robert and James, who adopted Baptist views in 1808. In the same year Christopher Anderson constituted Charlotte Chapel in Edinburgh with himself as the single pastor according to the "English order," which gradually prevailed in Scotland. The Haldanes and Anderson promoted several organizations to spread the gospel in the Highlands, where some of the gems of nineteenth-century Gaelic literature were hymns by Baptist preachers. Meanwhile in the Shetland Islands, Baptist convictions arose independently. In 1815 Sinclair Thomson accepted believer's baptism as a result of personal study of the Scriptures and founded a series of Baptist congregations. By 1844 in the whole of Scotland there were 91 churches with 5,500 members, some 1,000 of whom were Gaelic speakers.

A spontaneous revival movement that swept much of Scotland in 1859 and succeeding years, together with the organized missions of Americans Dwight L. Moody and Ira D. Sankey in 1874, gave fresh impetus to the churches. The revival fervor eroded the prevailing Calvinism and encouraged the introduction of organs, hymnbooks, and choirs. After two earlier unsuccessful attempts in 1827 and 1835 through 1856, a Baptist Union of Scotland was formed in 1869 and launched *The Scottish Baptist Magazine* as a monthly in 1874. From the 1870s district associations were created, and in 1893 a Baptist Theological College was established in Glasgow. A Women's Auxiliary linking the women's fellowships began in 1909, though a Baptist Men's Movement had to wait until 1947. Sunday Schools, together with uniformed Boys' Brigade units and Christian Endeavour branches, became large organizations in the growing cities. In addition, there were often Bands of Hope, training the young in total abstinence, a popular cause. Wealthy laymen were generous to philanthropic schemes with William Quarrier, the founder of a children's home at Bridge of Weir, being the most celebrated. Baptists generally supported the Liberal Party, although from 1917 to 1921 they supported an early leader of the Labor Party, William Adamson, a Fife miner.

Scottish Baptists were bound together by support for the BMS and also, for a few years from 1895, of the Baptist Industrial Mission in Malawi. They contributed to several faith missions which, together with premillennial doctrine and the holiness teaching of the Keswick movement, fostered conservative theological tendencies in the early twentieth century. During the 1940s, denunciation of alleged modernism in the Theological College led to the temporary establishment of a rival conservative body. Ecumenical relations caused further tension. In 1955 Scotch Baptists withdrew from the World Council of Churches and in 1989 declined to join the new ecumenical body, Action of Churches Together in Scotland. A few churches, including the largest, Charlotte Chapel in Edinburgh, left the Baptist Union because of its earlier ecumenical links, some of them forming a loose network of Reformed Baptists. There has been, however, enthusiastic cooperation with other evangelicals, especially in support of the evangelistic missions of Billy Graham.

By 1984 Baptists, with 3 percent of adult church attenders, enjoyed the highest ratio of attendance to membership in Scotland. Their greatest strength was in the Central Belt embracing Glasgow and Edinburgh; their members, who had traditionally been chiefly working class, included a larger proportion drawn from the middle classes. Although the Reformed emphasis on the preaching of the Word was common, charismatic renewal, leading to informal worship and patterns of team ministry, have come to dominate several growing congregations and to influence many others. A number of separatist Bible Baptist churches with pastors sent from the United States appeared in the 1970s, but churches in the Baptist Union received at least as much support from the Southern Baptist Convention.

The Baptist Union, which had been served by a full-time secretary since 1920, acquired a separate superintendent in 1983. With other union officials, the superintendent cooperates closely with the Baptist Union of Great Britain, which includes a few Scottish churches. In contrast to most English churches, the great majority in Scotland restrict membership to baptized believers and also, probably in imitation of Presbyterian elders, allow deacons to serve for life. The Baptist Union decided in 1985 not to accept women as candidates for ministerial training, but the churches remain free to call anyone of their choice. The Baptists of Scotland continue to cherish congregational self-government as well as zeal for the gospel.

David W. Bebbington

BIBLIOGRAPHY: For a standard history of Scotch Baptists, see D. W. Bebbingon, ed., *The Baptists of Scotland: A History* (Glasgow: Baptist Union of Scotland, 1988). For an earlier history, see Derek B. Murray, *The First Hundred Years: The Baptist Union of Scotland* (Glasgow: Baptist Union of Scotland, 1969), as well as his article, "Baptists in Scotland Before 1869," *Baptist Quarterly*, 23 (April 1970): 251–65. Another earlier history is George Yuille, ed., *History of the Baptists in Scotland from Pre-Reformation Times* (Glasgow: Baptist Union Publications' Committee, 1926).

WALES (1849)

	Members	Churches
1. Undeb Bedydd wyr Cymru (Baptist Union of Wales) (1866)*	25,384	(544)
2. Baptist Union of Great Britain (1813) (Churches in the East Glamorganshire, Gwent, and West Wales Associations)	11,236	(171)

3. North Wales English Baptist Union (1879)
   (These churches are also part of the Lancashire
   and Cheshire Association of the Baptist Union
   of Great Britain)   <u>843</u>   <u>(14)</u>

                                                37,463   (729)

*There are 146 churches with a membership of 9,552 in the Baptist Union of Wales which have dual membership with the Baptist Union of Great Britain.

STATISTICS: BWA, *Yearbook*, 1993–1994, 101, and Baptist Union of Great Britain, *Directory*, 1993–1994, 159.

O ne of the most fruitful European fields for Baptists before World War I was Wales with the highest density of Baptist meetinghouses in Europe. Welsh Baptists have had a long and noble history, contributing to the spread of the Baptist faith in the British Isles and even in America. Their precipitous decline in the twentieth century, however, is unparalleled in Baptist history.

One of the first Baptists to preach in Wales was Hugh Evans, a General Baptist who began work about 1646 and soon gained the assistance of Jeremy Ives, a General Baptist minister in London. The true founder of Baptist work was John Miles (1621–1683), who began mission activity in Wales in 1649 with Thomas Proud on behalf of Particular (Calvinistic) Baptists of London. Miles and Proud founded a church at Ilston near Swansea with others soon to follow. In 1650 the Ilston Church with two other congregations held the first general meeting of Particular Baptists in the country. Miles accepted appointment and financial support from Cromwell's government.

After the restoration of Charles II in 1660, Welsh Baptists faced persecution. In the early 1660s Miles with other members of the Ilston congregation settled in Massachusetts, establishing near Swansea the first Baptist congregation in the state. Welsh Baptists identified themselves with the Particular Baptists in England, accepting the Second London Confession of Faith of 1677. They followed the strict Puritan morality of the typical dissenter of the day. They observed close communion, a practice generally observed to the present day except by churches in Wales belonging to the Baptist Union of Great Britain.

One of the outstanding Baptist evangelists of the nineteenth century was Christmas Evans (1766–1838) who traveled throughout the country. The typical Welsh Baptist pastor used a popular style in preaching. Baptists grew so rapidly that by 1900 they numbered more than 100,000 with their strength primarily in the south. They and other dissenting denominations, such as the Congregationalists and Calvinistic Methodists, had more adherents than the Church of Wales (Anglican), which was soon disestablished.

Welsh Baptists developed strong associations and, in spite of their reservations concerning centralization, they finally formed in 1866 a national union. In 1912 they established a Baptist Bookroom, which became the Publication Department of the union. The department publishes in both English and Welsh, including the Welsh paper *Seren Cymru*. To accommodate both the Welsh-speaking and English-speaking churches, a Welsh Assembly and an English Assembly were formed within the union, each with its own officers. Independent of the Welsh Union, three colleges were founded, two of which survive—South Wales Baptist College (1807), now at Cardiff, and North Wales Baptist College (1862), now at Bangor.

In 1950 the Welsh Baptist Union numbered 89,000 in 740 churches but dropped to 600 churches in 1982 with 400 still Welsh-speaking. With still a total of more than 500 churches, the membership of the union is only 25,000 with 9,500 also holding dual membership in the Baptist Union of Great Britain. In addition, the Baptist Union of Great Britain includes three associations in the south of Wales and a group of churches in the north, totaling 12,000 members. The average size of all Baptist churches in Wales is only a little more than fifty.

Why the serious decline? The closing of coal mines with forced migration and the secularization of society, which no longer looks to the chapel as the center of life, have taken their toll. In addition, Welsh Baptists have been holding on to chapels with a handful of people and an aging membership which cannot provide a significant program of nurture and outreach. Although English is almost universal and Welsh is the native tongue of only one-fourth of the population, yet many churches hold on to Welsh even though it is increasingly difficult to get trained pastors who speak Welsh. Only time will tell whether the situation can be reversed or even stabilized for a community which, in the past, has played such an important role in Baptist life.

BIBLIOGRAPHY: For early records of Welsh Baptists, see B. R. White, ed., *Association Records of the Particular Baptists of England, Wales and Ireland to 1660*, pt. 1 (London: Baptist Historical Society, 1971–1974), 1–17. On early Welsh history, also see B. R. White, "John Miles and the Structures of the Calvinistic Baptist Mission to South Wales 1649–1660," in Mansel John, ed., *Welsh Baptist Studies* (Cardiff: South Wales Baptist College, 1976), 35–76. For a standard history of Welsh Baptists, see T. M. Bassett, *The Welsh Baptists* (Swansea: Ilston House, 1977). For additional material, see Ifor Evans, "Wales," in J. D. Franks, comp., *European Baptists Today*, 2d rev. ed. (Rüschlikon-Zürich: Author, 1952), 83–85, and Leon McBeth, *The Baptist Heritage* (Nashville: Broadman Press, 1987), 316–21, 526–31.

BAPTIST AND BAPTIST-RELATED MISSIONS

1. ENGLAND   BIMI (1970), BBFI (1971), BM-M (1972), BWM (1974), EBM (1976), ABWE (1984), IFM (1984), MWBM (1989), MBM, ABA, PNBC

2. IRELAND   WBF (1961), BBFI (1977), BM-M (1977), BIMI (1978), CBI (1992)

3. SCOTLAND   SBC (1977), BM-M (1979), BBFI (1983), BWM (1984), RBMS (1988), IBFI (1994)

4. WALES   BBFI (1981), SBC (1991)

B. CENTRAL EUROPE

The primary impulse of the Baptist movement in continental Europe came from Germany, spreading not only throughout central Europe but also north and east. Beginning in 1834 and using the heritage of pietism and earlier evangelical awakenings, the great German leader Gerhard Oncken (1800–1884) developed a dynamic missionary movement. Although Oncken sought relations and support from other evangelicals, his own movement was exclusive and sectarian, proclaiming "One Lord, one faith, one baptism." He developed a sense of corporate unity among the churches—the need to belong to a *Bund*, or union, as well as a local association, which would bring both support and coordination. In 1847 German Baptists adopted a confessional statement with a Calvinist orientation. This document became a model for many Baptists outside Germany.

This missionary thrust, energized by the motto "every Baptist a missionary," was aided by revivalism. Itinerant missionaries, colporteurs (peddlers of Christian literature), as well as artisans and other laypersons, spread the faith. German Baptists did not organize a church unless it reached a certain level of strength and could establish preaching stations, which reached out to scattered members and spread the gospel even further. Oncken recognized the importance of training and in Hamburg organized a training course, which became a seminary in 1889, attracting students from all over Europe. As a former colporteur, Oncken recognized the importance of literature and launched an effective publication ministry.

The Baptist movement spread rapidly across Germany and then to neighboring lands in the west, to the north into Scandinavia, as well as to the east where the numerous German settlements proved to be a bridge for introducing the Baptist faith. The German *Bund* itself became international, not only including churches in neighboring Switzerland and Austria, but also, for a time, churches in Denmark, the Netherlands, and the Russian Empire (to 1887), as well as Hungary, Romania, and Bulgaria.

Despite the successes of the German Baptist movement, it also had its limitations. With the exception of Orthodox populations in Transylvania and Ukraine, it was successful only among peoples of a Protestant Lutheran or Reformed background, but not among the Roman Catholic population. Current Baptist statistics in the Catholic areas of Austria, Czech Republic, Slovakia, and Poland still reflect this fact. Even though the Baptist witness spread to non-Germanic peoples, it was as much, if not more, these peoples' reaching out to Baptists than Baptists reaching out to them. German communities in other lands were often self-contained and failed to breach the cultural barriers. In addition, German Baptists were often insensitive to the desire of non-German Baptists for recognition and control of their own work, particularly in Hungary, Bulgaria, and Latvia. Despite these deficiencies, the Oncken movement is still one of the greatest stories of mission achievement in Baptist annals.

The conflict of World War II which brought death, destruction, and dislocation to millions, particularly in central and eastern Europe, took a toll on European Baptist life. Although in the 1940s, Baptist refugees augmented Baptist strength in the west, at the same time flourishing areas of German Baptist work were lost in the east with the shift of boundaries and the deportation of populations, while many churches in Germany itself were destroyed. Moreover, German Baptists had been forced to live under a Nationalist Socialist regime which undermined Christian values and then, as a result of World War II, to see a part of its constituency live in another German state under Communist control for more than four decades. Even though Germany is now reunited, German Baptists today face a post-Christian population, particularly in the northern areas of its traditional strength where western materialism and Communist atheism have penetrated deeply. Nevertheless, the southern area of Germany, which is more open to religious influences, is now the greatest area of potential growth. In addition, thousands of German-Russians have flooded into the country, providing Baptists with another important constituency.

Outside of Germany and the Netherlands, Baptist work in Central Europe is small, facing not only the resistance of traditional Roman Catholic populations but also the secularization of much of European life. The attempt in the 1960s to plant an English-language church at Luxembourg City failed when the American personnel departed. On the other hand, with a numerically strong constituency within a reunited German Baptist Union, Baptists of central Europe are again in a strategic position to play a leading role.

	Members	*Churches*
1. Austria	1,059	19
2. Czech Republic	2,221	38
3. Germany	114,231	702
4. Netherlands	14,972	120
5. Poland	3,770	67
6. Slovakia	1,843	15
7. Switzerland (German-Speaking)	1,393	16
	139,489	977

AUSTRIA (1846)

	Members	Churches
1. Union of Baptist Churches in Austria (1953)	942	(15)
2. Free Baptists in Austria (1978)	117	(4)
	1,059	(19)

*I*n 1528 Balthasar Hübmaier, an Anabaptist, was burned at the stake in Vienna. Because of his views on church and state, Baptists have identified more closely with him than with any other Anabaptist leader of the sixteenth century. When the Baptist movement began in Austria in the middle of the nineteenth century, the Austrian regime was still strongly opposed to free church principles, and Baptists had to meet secretly. Even though Austria today guarantees religious freedom, Baptist beliefs continue to face strong resistance in a country where the majority of the people are Roman Catholic.

Joseph Marschall and another compatriot known as Hornung, upon completing their work in Hamburg after the Great Fire of 1842, were sent by Johann Oncken back to their native land in 1846 to distribute Bibles and tracts and hold services. In 1847 the first couple was baptized in Vienna, and in the following year Oncken visited Vienna twice. But in the reactionary period after the revolutions of 1848 through 1849, the small group of Baptists met with difficulty. In 1849 the regime expelled J. L. Hinrichs, who had just begun serving as pastor and in 1851 raided a Baptist meeting, imprisoning four of the leaders for three weeks and expelling those not born in Vienna.

Fortunately for the suppressed group, Edward Millard (1822–1906), a Baptist born in Bath, England, arrived in 1851 to direct the work of the British and Foreign Bible Society in the Austrian Empire. Even though he was forced to leave between 1852 and 1863, he returned to Vienna and on December 20, 1869, formed a Baptist church with twenty members. For a number of years, Millard served as pastor, but the congregation continued to face opposition and was forced to move from place to place. Baptist mission points appeared in Ternitz, Steyr, and Graz, where a church was organized in 1882 but did not survive. In 1885 an Austria-Hungarian Association was founded and continued until the turn of the century.

With the help of German Baptists from North America (later named North American Baptists) and Swedish Baptists, the first Baptist chapel in the country was dedicated in 1922 at the Ternitz mission and a second one at the end of 1924 for the Vienna congregation. Austrian Baptists also received pastoral assistance through the work of Carl Füllbrandt, who from 1925 to 1954 headed the Danubian mission of the North American Baptist Conference. After World War II and until 1966, this conference also provided financial assistance, handing over administrative responsibility for the Austrian work to the Baptist Union of Germany in 1963. When a church was founded in Salzburg in 1948, the Vienna congregation was the only other Baptist church in the country. Another church was formed at Bad Ischl in 1950. In 1953 Austrian Baptists founded a Union of Baptist Churches. From 255 members in 1928, Austrian Baptists grew to 750 in 1965 and today have around 1,000.

Since World War II, a number of other North American Baptist missions have entered the field, but they, too, have found the work slow and difficult. An early one was Baptist Mid-Missions, which conducted evangelistic meetings and Bible clubs for children. The Conservative Baptist Foreign Mission Society (CBFMS, but now CBI) entered in 1970, establishing an International Baptist Chapel, which became an independent church. At first CBFMS cooperated with the Austrian Union, but because of doctrinal differences CBFMS began working in the southern province of Carinthia and then later worked with the Free Baptist Church in the Vienna area. In 1965 the FMB of the Southern Baptist Convention sent fraternal representatives to serve with the Baptist Union.

In 1977 after an evangelistic campaign in Vienna, a number of Baptists and Mennonite Brethren desired ties of closer cooperation. This interest then led in 1981 to the formation of the Arbeitsgemeinschaft Evangeliker Gemeinden in Österreich (Working Group of Evangelical Churches in Austria) on a platform of biblical inerrancy and believer's baptism. Today the Working Group has a membership of forty churches, besides observers. Although Baptists in the Austrian Union cooperate with the Evangelical Alliance, only some of its churches hold membership in the Working Group while others are simply observers.

BIBLIOGRAPHY: For Baptist work in Austria, particularly its beginnings, see Rudolf Donat, *Wie das Werk begann* (Kassel: Oncken, 1958), 421–27, 431–34, 437–39, and J. H. Rushbrooke, *The Baptist Movement in the Continent of Europe* (London: Kingsgate Press, 1923), 49–53. Richard Rabenau, "Austria," in J. D. Franks, ed., *European Baptists Today*, 2d rev. ed. (Rüschlikon-Zürich: Author, 1952), 11–14, provides a general survey. For recent developments, see *Austrian Christian Handbook* in *European Churches Handbook*, pt. 2 (London: MARC Europe, 1992), 22, 24, 37, 40, 55–57.

CZECH REPUBLIC (GERMANS, 1867; CZECHS, 1877)

	Members	Churches
Ustredi Bratrske-Jednoty-Baptistu (Baptist Unity of Brethren) (1919)	2,221	(38)

As early as the 1860s, Baptists appeared on the territory that formed the unified state of Czechs and Slovaks from 1918 to 1992, known as Czechoslovakia. Until the end of World War I, this territory was part of Austria-Hungary. In 1858 Magnus Knappe, a preacher from Germany, began to travel regularly from his home to the Broumov region of northern Bohemia, where he preached to the German-speaking minority. On August 3, 1867, Knappe performed the first baptism on Czech soil. Another missionary was August Meereis, who was of Czech descent but born and converted in Volhynia, Russia, and who served as a colporteur of the BFBS in central Bohemia. On April 13, 1877, Meereis baptized the first Czechs in Brandys and Orlici. Associated with these believers were also a few people who had been baptized in Vienna.

After meeting Meereis, Henry Novotny (1846–1912), preacher of the Free Reformed Church in Prague, was baptized in Lodz, Poland, by Karl Ondra. Novotny became pastor of the first Baptist congregation in Bohemia, organized on March 15, 1884, at Hledsebe near Prague. With sixteen members, the church shortly moved to Prague, calling itself the Prague Congregation of Christians Baptized in Faith. The church received aid from the German Baptist Union and within ten years had a membership of 180 and several active mission stations.

State authorities hampered local mission activity since only the Roman Catholic Church and, to a lesser extent, the Reformed and Lutheran Churches were recognized as state churches. Baptists had no right to own their places of worship. In fact, their very worship services were illegal and had to be held under the protective name of another organization. Novotny constructed a church building in his own backyard; when discovered even that was boarded up by the police. Baptists were the target of public insult and slander as well as court investigation. Baptisms could be held only in strictest secrecy.

World War I, while it took its toll on the Baptist community, brought forth the new state of Czechoslovakia. In 1919 in the Slovakian village of Vavrišovo, Baptists formed the Unity of Brethren of Chelčicky, naming the union after a Hussite leader of the fifteenth century. The new union included fifteen Bohemian, Moravian, Slovakian, German, and Hungarian congregations. For several years after the war, the reaction against the former domination of the Roman Catholic Church benefited Baptist growth. The American Baptist Foreign Mission Society and British Baptists provided support. In 1921 a seminary was opened in Prague and two magazines, *Chelčicky* and *Rosievač*, began circulation with the latter still published today.

After a certain degree of stagnation before World War II, due to a struggle with theological liberalism, and during the war itself, a new upsurge of activity occurred from 1945 to 1947, largely coming from immigrants returning from exile. Neither Czech nor Slovak Baptists, however, have as yet fully recovered from the paralysis following the extensive campaign by the Communist regime against Baptist preachers and laymen during the 1950s. No other church, except the Roman Catholic, suffered as much. The regime sentenced many preachers to long years in prison, from which several never returned, and also forbade those who did survive to work in the church after their release.

In the 1960s the Baptists, who by now had dropped "Chelčicky" in favor of simply "Baptist" in their name, formed two regional groups: Bohemian-Moravian and Slovakian. This reflected the division of the country into two republics in federal union. The number of congregations in both republics roughly corresponded to that of the population with a ratio of two to one in favor of the Czech churches, while the membership of about four thousand, which remained stable for decades, was about equal in both regions. Although each area had its own administration and annual conferences, a federal administration was maintained for education, missions, music, and women's ministry. State-wide conferences on a federal level met annually but never adopted a binding confession of faith.

With the closure in the 1950s of the Baptist seminary, pastors studied at the Protestant theological faculties in Prague and Bratislava and, in exceptional cases, for short periods abroad. Later a correspondence course was developed, also open to the laity. The Communist regime greatly limited publication activity and for many years until 1968 even forbade *Rosievač*. Other publications were negligible with the exception of an annual collection of daily devotions, *Slova života* (Words of Life).

Toward the end of the 1980s, the religious situation began to improve, and previously little-used possibilities opened up with the November revolution of 1989. In 1992 a Bible school specializing in diaconal ministries was founded in the old Moravian capital of Olomouc. The impact, however, of certain groups of enthusiasts as well as parachurch groups have unfortunately left some adverse effects on Baptist life.

Relations with the BWA and EBF were never severed although they were always the object of careful observation and control by state police and the Ministry of Culture. Membership of ecumenical organizations never occurred beyond the domestic context. With the division of Czechoslovakia into two independent states in January 1, 1993, a corresponding division also has occurred in the Baptist Union.

Peter and Harriet Macek

BIBLIOGRAPHY: The book by Joseph Novotny, *The Baptist Romance in the Heart of Europe* (New York: Czechoslovak Baptist Convention in America and Canada, 1939), is primarily a work on the life of Henry Novotny, pastor of the first Baptist church in the Czech Republic. A very good account of Czech and Slovak Baptists in both Czechoslovakia and America before World War II is the work by Vaclav Vojta, *Czechoslovak Baptists* (Minneapolis: Czechoslovak Baptist Convention in America and Canada, 1941). Also see, J. H. Rushbrooke, *Some Chapters of European Baptist History* (London: Kingsgate Press, 1929), 104–18.

GERMANY (1834)

	Members	Churches
1. Bund Evangelisch-Freikirchlicher Gemeinden (Union of Evangelical Free Church Congregations) (1849)	86,956	(591)
2. Vereinigung der Heimgekehrten Evangeliums-Christen Baptisten Brüdergemeinden (Association of the Returned Evangelical-Christian Baptist Brethren Congregations) (1978)	10,000	(50)
3. Bund Taufgesinnter Gemeinden (Union of Baptism-Minded Congregations) (1989)	3,275*	(11)
4. Bruderschaft (Brotherhood)	14,000*	(50)
	114,231	(702)

*Three Mennonite Brethren churches with 1,540 members belong to the Bund Taufgesinnter Gemeinden, and 21 Mennonite Brethren churches with about 7,500 members belong to the Bruderschaft.

Union of Evangelical Free Church Congregations

The German Baptists arose out of the early nineteenth-century Awakening. The first German Baptist congregation was founded by Johann Gerhard Oncken (1800–1884), generally regarded as the father of the Baptist movement on the European continent. Born in the Lutheran town of Varel in Oldenburg in northern Germany, Oncken lived in abject poverty until 1814 when he was apprenticed to a Scottish merchant and went to Britain. He lived for a while in a Reformed Presbyterian home in Scotland and then in England. In both places he came to know people whose Christian faith was quite different from the rationalistic piety that prevailed in Germany.

Converted in a Methodist chapel in 1820, Oncken began working three years later as a missionary for the interdenominational Continental Society for the Diffusion of Religious Knowledge over the Continent of Europe. He was assigned to Hamburg, where he engaged in preaching and Bible and tract distribution. Such activities were illegal, and state church officials did everything they could to hinder his work. Desirous of a more satisfactory spiritual home for his converts than the established Lutheran church, Oncken investigated the possibility of a believer's church. The result was the formation of a Baptist congregation. On April 22, 1834, Barnas Sears, an American theology professor who was then studying in Germany, baptized Oncken and six other persons in the Elbe River. On the following day Oncken was ordained as the elder of the new church in Hamburg.

In the ensuing years Oncken conducted missionary work in close contact with American and British mission societies which gave him moral and financial support. He traveled around Europe, gathering awakened and newly converted people into congregations structured on a New Testament basis. Since religious liberty was virtually unknown in those times, Baptists suffered discrimination and oppression. Still the movement spread in Germany, which was not yet politically unified, and in the neighboring lands, especially to the east.

Oncken's operative principle was a missionary understanding of the priesthood of all believers, and he bestowed this legacy upon the continental Baptists. A tireless fundraiser, he was once asked by an English friend as to how many missionaries he was actually supporting. Oncken immediately gave him the total number of members, for: "We consider every member a missionary." Before long, the phrase "every Baptist a missionary" became the watchword of the movement. Manual laborers (craftsmen) played an especially important role in spreading the word and planting new congregations.

Other significant figures in the continental endeavor were Gottfried Wilhelm Lehmann (1799–1882), a Berliner who was the founder of the Baptists in Prussia, and Julius Köbner (1806–1884), a Jewish Christian from Denmark who worked in Hamburg, Barmen, and Copenhagen. During the revolutionary year 1848 Köbner issued "The Free Primitive Christianity's Manifesto to the German People," which energetically called for religious liberty. The Union of Baptist Congregations was formed in 1849. At the time of Oncken's death thirty-five years later, the number of congregations had swelled to 165 in more than a dozen countries with a membership exceeding 30,000. In addition, an untold number had emigrated to North America for socioeconomic reasons or to escape oppression.

A conflict over the structure of the common endeavor overshadowed the last years of Oncken's life. The result was that the local congregations acquired greater independence but also had to take more responsibility for missions and their internal operation. Boards of elders, which included pastors employed by the congregations, now provided leadership. Sunday Schools for children played a key role in the spread of the Baptists since they often were the core group for "stations," that is, branch congregations. By the end of the century, American-style protracted evangelistic meetings with special speakers were utilized to foster church growth.

After World War I, the Weimar Republic viewed the free churches more favorably than the former Empire. In 1930 Baptists were granted legal equality with other religious confessions. They now could use new means, such as tent meetings, but still suffered discrimination.

During the period of the Third Reich, the German Baptist leaders above all wished to avoid endangering what they had gained and to continue their evangelistic work. Thus they kept their distance from the *Kirchenkampf* (Church Struggle), but this involved compromises which, viewed from hindsight, were rather questionable. The Baptist World Congress met in Berlin in 1934 and commemorated the centenary of the founding of the German Baptists, an occasion of great importance for this minority church. The National Socialist state, however, shamelessly portrayed the Congress as proof of "the religious tolerance of the German nation" despite the fact that the mainline Protestant church was at that very moment under severe pressure. Fifty years later in 1984 at the Hamburg meeting of the European Baptist Federation, the German Baptist Union issued a statement acknowledging its errors in the Nazi period: "We did not publicly join the strife nor the sufferings of the Confessing Church and failed to withstand more consciously the violations of the divine commandments and injunctions. We, the German Baptist Union, are humbled by having been subordinated often to the ideological seduction of that time, in not having shown greater courage in acknowledging truth and justice."

By 1936 all denominations were experiencing the essentially anti-Christian thrust of National Socialist religious policy. Bowing to official pressure, the Baptist Union in 1938 accepted the Elim Congregations, a Pentecostal body, and in 1942 the German branch of the Plymouth Brethren. The united body was named the "Union of Evangelical Free Church Congregations," the title which it retains today. After World War II, most Elim congregations left the union as well as many Brethren assemblies. The Brethren who remained maintain their own distinctive spiritual and structural characteristics as a subgroup and are in fellowship with Brethren groups outside the Union. Since Baptists were clearly in the majority, the Union not give up its close ties with the world Baptist movement. The dream of many people of a new Evangelical Free Church, composed of many groups but possessing a common identity, failed to materialize.

During World War II about five thousand Baptists lost their lives, and after 1945 about 40,000, a third of the membership, were forced to flee their homes. The Union lost 145 congregations and 407 branches that lay beyond the Oder-Neisse line, the new eastern boundary of Germany. With the generous assistance of Baptists around the world, especially those in Scandinavia and North America, congregational life in West Germany experienced a new beginning. The many refugees, particularly the East Prussians, helped in founding new congregations, but many of them emigrated to North and South America.

As a result of the political division of Germany, the churches located east of the Elbe River in the German Democratic Republic found themselves in a new dictatorship. For an entire generation the Communist regime kept them under political and ideological pressure. Compared to other Communist countries, Baptists in the German Democratic Republic were permitted to conduct traditional congregational work relatively undisturbed. They, however, had to put up with numerous restrictions, particularly in youth and educational work. From time to time there were also obstacles to evangelistic and publication activities, and the construction of new church buildings and other facilities was always extremely difficult. The regime also compelled them to cut their organizational ties with the Baptist Union in West Germany.

The totally different political and social conditions in the east and west produced contrasting ways of thinking and behaving, a fact which became increasingly obvious after the fall of the Berlin Wall and the reunification of Germany. Nevertheless, the common Baptist heritage and overriding sense of mission greatly eased the task of reunion. In spite of Cold War pressure, contacts between Baptists in the East and West were always maintained, even though in divided Germany two separate unions existed from 1969 to 1991.

In the years since 1960 new social and religious developments have confronted the German Baptists, such as secularization, an increasingly multicultural society, the indifference of the population to the church, new religious movements, and the general decline of values. German Baptists have had to respond to these problems through increased efforts in home mission work, such as the founding of new congregations, new forms of evangelization, better biblical training for members, which has included congregational Bible schools for adults, better training for pastors and other church workers, and numerous social services.

Congregations and special initiative groups are engaged in peace work. They have produced a sensitivity to responsibility for political and social developments in their own country and the Two-Thirds World and for global ecology. In all congregations the commitment to world missions remains as deep as ever, and great efforts are being devoted to furthering church growth in eastern Europe.

The theological positions of Oncken and his associates were spelled out in the Confession of 1847, which with some minor changes was followed until World War II. Apart from the specific articles on the church and baptism, it was basically a Calvinist-leaning Reformation statement. Some Lutheran accents, such as the work of God in baptism, came from Lehmann. Strongly influenced by the spirituality of the Moravian Brethren at Herrnhut, Lehmann also introduced pietistic elements into German Baptist life, such as the love feast and Moravian hymns. As a result, German Baptists were in many respects different from Anglo-Saxon Baptists, including a different outlook on political involvement. Until recent times, a pietistic-revivalist devotion was the hallmark of German Baptists, which meant an exclusive dependence on the Bible in all matters of faith and practice (including congregational structure), a strong missionary orientation, a personal piety with an emphasis on conversion and witness, and a provincial mentality that the congregation was "Zion," which grew out of its minority status.

The distinctive character of Baptist piety can be seen in its hymnody. The first generation utilized Lutheran chorales, Herrnhut hymns, and some songs written by Baptists, including those by Köbner who even edited a hymnbook called *Glaubensstimme* (Voice of Faith). At the end of the nineteenth century, gospel songs were added, many of which were translated by the well-known German-American Walter Rauschenbusch. He produced a German edition of Ira Sankey's *Gospel Hymns* that went through many editions and is still used today in Germany and in German-speaking congregations in eastern Europe. The recently published official Baptist hymnbook, *Gemeindelieder* (Songs for the Congregation), contains approximately 30 percent of its hymns from the twentieth century, 22 percent from the nineteenth-century Awakening, 23 percent from eighteenth-century pietism, and 25 percent from classical chorales and hymns from Luther to Paul Gerhardt. A supplementary collection, *Neue Gemindelieder* (New Songs for the Congregation), was published in 1993, which contains a rich cross section of contemporary musical styles and modern evangelical spirituality.

Until World War II, German Baptists observed close communion, that is, only immersed believers were allowed to participate. As a result of the spiritual community that Baptists developed with other Christians from the trials of the Nazi era and the war, including the military captivity of many pastors, and through postwar ecumenical contacts, most Baptists moved away from this practice by the beginning of the 1960s. Still all congregations hold to the principle that membership must be restricted to those who are "baptized believing Christians."

In 1977 the Executive Board of the Union (*Bundesrat*) recommended to the congregations a new confession of faith called the *Rechenschaft vom Glauben* (Statement of Faith, a term patterned after 1 Peter 3:15), which an international commission of Baptists from Switzerland, Austria, and the two German states prepared. It is clear from the text that the authors had utilized many ideas found in the new Word of God theology. The main references to Scripture were from Romans and 1 Corinthians in contrast to the Oncken confession which drew heavily from Acts.

Although early twentieth-century Pentecostalism had a minimal impact on the Baptists, some Holiness emphases found their way into the churches. The charismatic movement has had a noteworthy influence on some individuals and congregations, particularly in worship and hymnody. The contemporary conservative evangelical theological trend, such as that represented in the Lausanne movement, has exercised some influence, but the great majority of German Baptists regard the "new fundamentalism" as too aggressive and insufficient in answering the burning theological questions of the day. At times intense debates have occurred over interpretation of Scripture and the place of women in the pastoral ministry. The Executive Board decided in 1992 that it was up to each congregation whether it wished to call a woman as pastor. Because of the many new influences and questions, German Baptists today are engaged in a lively discussion about their identity. The earlier homogeneity is now a thing of the past.

The oldest agency of the union is its publishing house. Oncken founded it in 1828, and it has belonged to the union since 1879, when it was reorganized by Philipp Bickel (1829–1914). Oncken Verlag in Kassel publishes the weekly denominational magazine *Die Gemeinde* (The Congregation), an evangelistic leaflet *Friedenbote* (Herald of Peace), and periodicals for all areas of church life. It also runs a mail-order book service. The book publishing branch is in Wuppertal. Its output is aimed not only at Baptists but also at all German-speaking Protestants. It is particularly well known as the German publisher of the works of Charles H. Spurgeon.

The theological seminary was established in Hamburg in 1880. It offers a five-year course of study for men and women. A one-year course qualifies people for the ministry who have already studied theology in the public universities. Many feel that, despite internal tension, the reason German Baptists have never split denominationally is because almost all pastors have been trained at the same institution. Baptists in neighboring countries also send students; before World War II 25 percent of the student body was from eastern and southeastern Europe. In 1994 it was decided to relocate (prospectively in 1997) the seminary to a larger campus near Berlin to be able to provide training for other church workers as well as pastors.

In 1949 a youth department was added to the Hamburg seminary to train voluntary workers in children's and youth work. The union maintains a Bible school in Berlin which offers a one-year course. Many Baptists also attend an older Bible school which the Brethren assemblies operate in Wiedenest. Within the union are separate training programs for volunteers who engage in ministries to women, men, and senior citizens.

In the latter part of the nineteenth century, Baptists began engaging in social ministries. The oldest of these is the Bethel Deaconess Institution in Berlin, founded by Eduard Scheve (1836–1909). Currently it operates ten hospitals as well as numerous senior citzens' centers, nursing homes, social assistance offices, holiday and training centers, kindergartens, and other diaconal enterprises, including the highly-regarded Christian Homes for the Handicapped in Schmalkalden.

Various agencies coordinate the denomination's missionary work. The office of home missions, located at the Baptist Union's headquarters in Bad Homburg, is responsible for congregational development, tent missions, church planting, congregational Bible school programs, home circles, singles' ministry, and work among foreigners in Germany. The European Baptist Mission, also located in Bad Homburg, is a cooperative venture which coordinates foreign missionary work by the Baptist unions of Germany and ten other countries. It has fields in four South American and five African countries. The first German Baptist missionaries went to Cameroon in 1891; today they work in partnership with Baptists there. German Baptists also have a diaconal enterprise in India.

Oncken was the only German delegate who did not belong to the established church who participated in the founding of the Evangelical Alliance in London in 1846. Since then German Baptists have always participated in the Alliance. Because most of its congregations were not in sympathy with the goals and programs of the World Council of Churches, the union did not become a member. It did join, however, the German Association of Christian Churches in 1948, an agency which fosters ecumenical contacts and helps solve interconfessional conflicts. It also belongs to the Conference of European Churches and the Association of Evangelical Free Churches. The Christian Singer's Union, a free church choral association to which most Baptist church choirs belong, provides training and assistance for choirs and their leaders.

German Baptists have been vitally involved in the Baptist World Alliance (BWA) and the European Baptist Federation (EuEBF). Gerhard Claas (1928–1988) was general secretary of the EuEBF from 1976 to 1980 and then served in the same post with the BWA. Karl-Heinz Walter was chosen general secretary of EuEBF in 1989, and its headquarters are now located in Hamburg.

The six hundred congregations of the German Baptist Union are organized into fourteen regional associations and possess 87,000 members. Although about 2,500 baptisms occur each year, membership has remained stagnant for some years. Only a portion of the German-speaking Baptists who have immigrated from eastern Europe have joined churches of the union since the cultural and spiritual differences are considerable. German-Russians within the union have formed a special grouping. Baptists sponsor services in twenty-one foreign languages in 143 cities and towns. This is a reflection of the challenge which today faces the German Federal Republic and the German Baptist churches.

Günter Balders. Translated from the German by Richard Pierard.

BIBLIOGRAPHY: The two works by Rudolf Donat, *Wie das Werk begann* (Kassel: Oncken, 1958) and *Das wachsende Werk* (Kassel: Oncken, 1960), provide a wealth of detail. In 1984 the German Baptist Union produced a 150th anniversary history, *Ein Herr, ein Glaube, eine Taufe* (Wuppertal and Kassel: Oncken, 1984; 1989, 3d ed.), edited by Günter Balders with chapters contributed by various authors. The German Union has produced *Der Bund Evangelisch-Freikirchlicher Gemeinden in Deutschland* (Wuppertal and Kassel: Oncken, 1992), a beautifully illustrated work on Baptists in Germany today. For biographies of J. G. Oncken, see Hans Luckey, *Johann Gerhard Oncken und die Anfänge des deutschen Baptismus* (Kassel: Oncken, 1934; 1958, 3d ed.), and Günter Balders, *Theurer Bruder Oncken* (Wuppertal and Kassel: Oncken, 1978; 1984, 2d ed.). For a biography of Lehmann, see Hans Luckey, *Gottfried Wilhelm Lehmann und die Entstehung einer deutschen Freikirche* (Kassel: Oncken, 1939). For accounts of the German Baptists and the National Socialist regime, see Paul Schmidt, *Unser Weg als Bund Evangelisch-Freikirchlicher Gemeinden in den Jahren 1941–1946* (Stuttgart: Oncken, 1946); Klaus Bloedhorn, Jr., *Untertan der Obrigkeit?* (Witten-Stockum: Verlag am Steinberg, 1982); and Andrea Strübind, *Die unfreie Freikirche: Der Bund der Baptistengemeinden im Dritten Reich* (Neukirchen-Vluyn: Neukirchener, 1991). For a study of church growth among German-speaking Baptists, see William L. Wagner, *New Move Forward in Europe* (South Pasadena: South Carey Library, 1978).

German-Russian Baptists in Germany

With greater freedom for Germans in the USSR to emigrate to the West in the 1970s, later accelerated by the collapse of Communism and the Soviet Union itself, the Baptist population has been enhanced greatly by the influx of ethnic Germans from the former Soviet Union. For many years as the only recognized body for Protestants, Russian Baptist churches in Kazakhstan and Central Asia attracted many Germans who had been deported east, particularly people with a Baptist, Mennonite Brethren (closely related to Baptists), Mennonite, or Lutheran background. In time the regime allowed Germans to form their own churches. Some Baptists and Mennonites with a German heritage were also members of churches in Siberia.

Since 1950 more than 500,000 German-Russians have settled in Germany with 15 percent claiming to be Baptists and another 10 percent Mennonite and Mennonite Brethren. Today in Germany there are possibly around 100,000 individuals, including children, who at present or in the past have had ties with the Baptist and Mennonite Brethren communities from the former Soviet Union. Although they came with high expectations of improved economic conditions and freedom, they were often shocked by the materialism and secularism of German society. With a tradition of separation from worldly activity, including a prohibition of the use of alcohol and tobacco, as well as wearing only plain dress, differences in worship, such as standing or kneeling in prayer instead of sitting, and use of lay preachers, it is not surprising that they organized their own congregations. They also brought with them the division between registered and non-registered Baptists in the USSR.

Although some German-Russians or their churches joined the German Baptist Union, the majority belong to their own fellowships, which include both Baptist and Mennonite Brethren antecedents. The Association of Evangelical-Christian Baptist Brethren, which, including their children, claims a constituency of twenty thousand, is largely composed of Reform Baptists, those who broke with the official Russian Baptist Union. Members of the association also formed a mission society, Missionswerk Friedensstimme, which supports work in the former USSR. The Union of Baptism-Minded Congregations and the Brotherhood, a loose fellowship of churches, include both Baptist and Mennonite Brethren churches. Other German-Russians have joined a purely Mennonite Brethren fellowship, while still others remain entirely independent.

Albert W. Wardin, Jr.

BIBLIOGRAPHY: For articles on the German-Russian immigrants, see Alexander Neufeld, "Issues in Church Life and Polity in Germany," *Direction*, 20 (fall 1991), 143–46; Jakob Janzen, "Die Deutschen in der baptistischen Bewegung der UdSSR/Bundesrepublic Deutschland," in *Referate der Kulturtagung der Deutschen aus Russland/UdSSR* (Stuttgart: Landsmannsachaft der Deutschen aus Russland, 1990), 90–101; and John N. Klassen, "The Recent Russian German Emigres of Germany: A Survey Report," *Mennonite Historian*, 20 (March 1994), 1–2. For a book on the German-Russian immigrants, see Johannes Reimer, *Aussiedler sind anders*, 2d ed. (Wuppertal and Kassel: Oncken, 1990).

NETHERLANDS (1845)

	Members	Churches
1. Unie van Baptisten Gemeenten (1881)	12,386	(85)
2. Broederschap van Baptistengemeenten	2,500	(26)
3. Seventh Day Baptists (1877)	31	(2)
4. Baptist Mid-Missions (1954)	<u>55</u>	<u>(7)</u>
	14,972	(120)

The Baptist movement in the Netherlands has no direct continuity with the congregation of English refugees pastored by John Smyth, who baptized himself and other members of his group by affusion around 1609. The current Baptist movement began in 1845 when Julius Köbner, one of the early leaders of the Baptists in Germany, immersed Johannes Elias Feisser (1805–1865) at Gasselternijveen and six others. Feisser had been a minister of the Dutch Reformed Church who, after being suspended for not baptizing an infant of non-practicing parents, came to believe that baptism should be limited to believers. Feisser's group soon moved to Stadskanaal in Groningen Province, which developed into an important Baptist center.

Another early Baptist leader was H. Z. Kloekers, a former missionary in Shanghai, China, where he accepted Baptist tenets and joined the Baptist Missionary Society. In 1881 he led in the formation of a Union of Baptist Churches with seven congregations. Congregations under the influence of Peter Johannes de Neui, who came from East Friesland in Germany, accepted the strong Calvinistic orientation of the German Baptists and did not join. In 1882 the Union began *Christen* (The Christian), which continues as the Union's periodical. During one period in its history, the Dutch Union was a member of the German Baptist Union, but it always retained its independence.

Even though Dutch Baptists were influenced by both German and British Baptists with half of their ministers studying at the Hamburg Seminary for many years while the other half studied in England, America, and Scandinavia, Dutch Baptists are nevertheless an indigenous movement. In comparison to other European areas, they have received little mission aid. Despite difficulties during World War II when some ministers were arrested or deported, Dutch Baptists have had steady growth. In 1908 there were 1,200 members in 17 churches in the Union and 7 churches with about 400 members outside it. In 1932 membership was more than 4,000 and today about 15,000, including all Baptists. Dutch Baptists started a strong youth program in 1925, which has helped to maintain their numerical strength. Baptist strength is in the north, not in the Roman Catholic south of the country.

Dutch Baptists formed a Deaconess House and, after an earlier failure, established a seminary, "De Vinkenhof," in Utrecht Province in 1958. Before World War II, Dutch Baptists cooperated with the British Baptist Missionary Society (BMS) in Zaire, but today they work through the European Baptist Mission (EBM). In 1945 the union became a member of the Ecumenical Council of Churches in the Netherlands and three years later joined the World Council of Churches. With criticism of liberalism in both organizations, the union left both councils in 1963 to avoid a split in its ranks.

In 1981 Henk G. Koekkoek led in founding the Brotherhood of Baptist Churches, which brought together churches independent of the union. The Brotherhood operates on a narrower theological base than the union. In 1877 the Seventh Day Baptists established their first church in Haarlem but today have only two small congregations. Independent Baptist missions have had only a limited impact. The first one, Baptist Mid-Missions (BM-M), began work in 1954 with the arrival of Mr. and Mrs. Herbert Boyd. The work of Southern Baptists is limited: two representatives work with the International Baptist Church at Eindhoven.

BIBLIOGRAPHY: For two very helpful articles, see Jan A. Brandsma, "Johannes Elias Feisser and the Rise of the Netherlands Baptists," *Baptist Quarterly*, 16 (Jan. 1955): 10–21, and Jannes Reiling, "Baptists in the Netherlands," *Baptist Quarterly*, 28 (April 1979): 62–68. Also see J. H. Rushbrooke, *The Baptist Movement in the Continent of Europe* (London: Kingsgate Press, 1923), 54–60.

POLAND (1858)

	Members	Churches
1. Union of Christian Baptists (1922)	3,335	(56)
2. Sabbath Day Christian Church (1933)	435	(11)
	3,770	(67)

*B*y 1795 Poland was divided and occupied by three neighboring countries: Russia, Germany, and Austria. Poland disappeared as a sovereign state until 1918. In the Russian part of Poland (Congress Poland), Gottfried Alf (1831–1898), a German who was a village teacher as well as a cantor in the Lutheran Church, began Baptist work in Adamow near Warsaw. On November 28, 1858, Wilhelm Weist, crossing the border from Germany, baptized Alf and eight others, followed on the next day by seventeen more. In 1861 the first church was founded at Adamow, followed almost immediately by one at Kicin. Despite severe persecution, including many imprisonments, Alf continued to lead the work, which spread in Poland and by migration into Volhynia in Russia. Although some Slavic people were gained, most of the members at this time were German. A Russian Poland Association was founded in 1877, which became part of the Union of Baptist Churches in Russia, organized by German Baptists in 1887. A Slavic congregation, formed in the village of Zelow, near Lodz in 1872, is considered the mother church of Slavic Baptists in Poland.

With the independence of Poland in 1918, which acquired West Prussia and Posen from Germany in the west and territory from Russia in the east, the Baptist situation was changed radically. Because of cultural differences, the Germans in 1928 formed a Union of the Baptist Churches of the German Language, which included the German association in central Poland, the Posen-Pommerellian Association, which had been in Germany, and an association in Polish Volhynia. In 1939 it had eight thousand members in thirty-eight churches. In 1922 Slavic Baptists formed a Union of Slavic Baptists in Poland, which included Polish, Russian, Ukrainian, Belorussian, and Czech congregations. The Slavic work grew rapidly, especially in the Ukrainian and Belorussian areas, from 936 members in 10 churches in 1922 to 7,700 members in 1939. But World War II drastically changed the situation. With the migration of the Germans, the German Union ceased and, with the Soviet annexation of eastern Poland, most of the Slavic Baptists were also lost, leaving no more than 1,500 Polish members.

After the war, Polish Baptists refused to enter the United Evangelical Church, which included the free church denominations, because they feared the presence of Pentecostals in it. They therefore remained a tiny minority, living not only in a predominantly Roman Catholic culture but subject to Communist control for more than four decades.

With the collapse of the Communist regime, Polish Baptists are now taking advantage of new opportunities. In 1992 the churches of the Polish Union baptized 241, an excellent ratio to membership. The work of the Baptist Union includes departments of youth, children, women, evangelism, education, radio, music, and church building. It supports several full-time youth and children's workers. Besides Sunday Schools and youth meetings in the churches, Polish Baptists also conduct children's camps every summer and winter, gathering thousands of children from both Baptist and non-Baptist homes. Since 1927 the Baptist Union has maintained a home for the elderly at Bialystok.

The Polish Union publishes a monthly, *Slowo Prawdy* (The Word of Truth), issued from 1925 to 1939 and then again from 1957 to the present. Since 1957 the union has published about one hundred books, including volumes by William Barclay and Billy Graham. Under the Communists, censorship was strong, and Baptists could publish only for the Baptist community with paper rationed according to Baptist membership.

A Baptist seminary existed before and after World War II, but the school has never had a permanent home. Today the seminary is at the Baptist church in Wroclaw with twenty students enrolled. Pastors also receive training at the Christian Theological Academy in Warsaw, a predominantly Lutheran school. Twice a year the union sponsors a week of training sessions for pastors and lay preachers. At present the Baptist Union is constructing an educational center at Radosc near Warsaw for theological education, leadership training, and conferences.

Mission work is generally through the local church. Some churches conduct evangelistic services in public places, such as theaters, clubs, and parks, and also services in prisons. For some time under the Communists, new church buildings were prohibited but when later permitted were generally allowed only on back streets. In 1961 the regime, however, allowed Baptists to build a beautiful and commodious sanctuary and church center in Warsaw.

The most important part of the service in a local church is the sermon, which is expository. In larger churches the choir may sing several times. Worshipers sit to sing but kneel to pray. Many young pastors use a period of twenty minutes before the service for the singing of choruses. Most preaching is in Polish except in the eastern part of the country where Russian may be used.

During the Communist era, Baptists were denied promotion to positions of leadership in society or appointment as teachers. Today in the larger churches, members include office workers and medical personnel, but most members in the smaller churches are unskilled workers or farmers.

The Polish Union is a member of the EBF and BWA. It maintains good relations with the other churches of the country, including the Roman Catholic Church, even though government officials consult this church on matters which also affect Baptist church life. With the dissolution of the United Evangelical Church in 1989, one of its members, the Evangelical Christian Union with about seven hundred members in twenty-two churches, remains as an independent body. Although Evangelical Christians united with Baptists in Russia and for a short time in the 1920s with Baptists in Poland, they now remain a distinct body, no longer seeking any other alliances.

In 1933 a separation occurred among Seventh-Day Adventists which, after assuming different designations, adopted in 1961 the name Sabbath Day Christian Church. Soon afterwards Seventh Day Baptists made their first official contact with the group. In 1984 it became a member of the Seventh Day Baptist World Federation.

Konstanty Wiazowski and Albert W. Wardin, Jr.

BIBLIOGRAPHY: For a standard history on Baptists in Poland before World War II, see Eduard Kupsch, *Geschichte der Baptisten in Polen 1852–1932* (Zdunska-Wola: Author, 1932). A very fine work in Polish, much of it based on government archives, is Henryk Ryszard Tomaszewski, *Baptiyści w Polsce w latach 1858–1918* (Warsaw: Slowo i Zycie, 1993). For a helpful article, see M. S. Lesik, "The Baptists in Poland," *Baptist Quarterly*, 7 (April, 1934): 79–84.

SLOVAKIA (1888)

	Members	Churches
Baptist Unity of Brethren (1919)	1,843	(15)

When Baptists entered Slovakia, it was part of the kingdom of Hungary, a constituent member of the dual monarchy of Austria-Hungary. While the work in Bohemia and Moravia (today part of the Czech Republic) was oriented toward Germany, Slovak Baptists were influenced largely by Baptists in Hungary.

The pioneer of the work was August Meereis, a former colporteur of the British and Foreign Bible Society (BFBS), who had served in Bohemia but, from 1888 to 1902, served as a Baptist missionary in Slovakia. As early as 1878 Meereis began to minister in Kežmarok, where he formed a German Baptist church on July 15, 1888, the first in

Slovakia. Another center for Baptist work developed at Liptovsky Sväty Mikuláš where Vaclav Brož of Czech descent settled about 1880, beginning meetings in his home. Because of his witness, Baptist views spread to neighboring villages. In 1882 Heinrich Meyer, the Baptist leader in Budapest, baptized eighteen believers in the Vah River in Brož's home village. Meereis also visited Bratislava, where he baptized converts as early as 1889. In 1897 Baptists formed an independent church at Vavrišovo, followed soon by two others. In 1900 the four churches which then had been organized had about two hundred members.

With the establishment of an independent Czechoslovakia, Czech and Slovak Baptists formed a Baptist union in Vavrišovo. In the 1960s Czech and Slovak Baptists established regional conferences within the union but, with the division of Czechs and Slovaks in 1993, Slovak Baptists now have an independent union.

Baptists continue to be a small minority in a predominantly Roman Catholic country. Although suffering recently from a Pentecostal defection, the Baptist church in Bratislava, today the capital, is one of the leading congregations. There also exists a Slovakian Baptist community in the Vojvodina region of Serbia.

BIBLIOGRAPHY: Vaclav Vojta, *Czechoslovak Baptists* (Minneapolis: n.p., 1941).

SWITZERLAND (GERMAN-SPEAKING) (1847)

	Members	Churches
Bund der Baptisten-Gemeinden (1924)	1,393	(16)

In addition, there are 560 French-speaking Baptists in fifteen churches.

*T*he founder of German Baptists, Johann G. Oncken, influenced the origin of the Baptist churches in Switzerland. During his visit to Switzerland (August-November 1847), Oncken met a number of "Baptist" groups. In Hochwart, near Wattwil in the Toggenburg region, he discovered the first of such groups and there baptized several believers. Three years earlier in Hamburg, Oncken had baptized Friedrich Maier, a citizen of Altheim near Üblingen on Lake Constance, who fled to Switzerland in 1849. In the same year Maier was instrumental in starting the Baptist church in Zürich, which became a center of mission activity in Switzerland and continues to the present day to be the largest Baptist church in the country.

In 1870 the Swiss churches joined the German Baptist Union. In 1924 they founded a separate Union of Baptist Churches, first as an association within the German Baptist Union but since 1948 as an independent body. Before World War II, there was a close association with German Baptists, including the exchange of pastors and subscription to German Baptist publications, but today the Swiss are more independent.

Although some new churches appeared after World War II, for decades Swiss Baptists have shown little growth. In the Baptist Union in 1992 there were 16 churches with 1,364 members in German-speaking Switzerland and one church with 29 members in Ticino, the Italian-speaking canton or state. The German-speaking churches were concentrated along the Protestant northern border, leaving the Catholic cantons untouched. There are also fifteen French-speaking churches who maintain their own association, not cooperating with the Baptist Union nor belonging to the EuEBF or BWA.

Bible study and prayer groups, choirs, women's groups, and youth groups are important aspects of Swiss Baptist church life. Since 1930 the Diakonissenhaus Salem (Salem Deaconess House) has provided an opportunity of ministry for Baptist women. Although it now plans to relocate, the International Baptist Theological Seminary has existed in Rüschlikon on Lake Zürich since 1949, providing theological education for students and pastors from many lands.

The official publication of Swiss Baptists is *Der Gemeindebote* (Church Messenger), a monthly publication. The Baptist Union of Switzerland cooperated with the German and Austrian Baptist Unions in formulating a *Rechenschaft vom Glauben* (Statement of Faith), which in 1977 was recommended for use in the churches—a confession which contains the basic beliefs of Swiss Baptists. The Swiss Baptist Union cooperates with the European Baptist Mission Society and is a member of the EBF and the BWA. It also belongs to the Swiss Council of Churches and the Council of Free Churches and Communions in Switzerland.

Thorwald Lorenzen

BIBLIOGRAPHY: For a fine basic history, see Kaspar Schneiter, *Geschichte des Baptismus in der Schweiz 1847-1978* (Zürich: Author, 1979). Also see Schneiter's article in English, "Switzerland (German-Speaking)—in J. D. Franks, comp., *European Baptists Today*, 2d rev. ed. (Rüshlikon-Zürich: Author, 1952). For beginnings in Switzerland, see Theodor Bächtold, *Johann Gerhard Oncken and Baptist Beginnings in Switzerland* (B.D. thesis, Baptist Theological Seminary, Rüschlikon, 1970).

BAPTIST AND BAPTIST-RELATED MISSIONS

1. AUSTRIA   SBC (1965), BM-M (1967), CBI (1970), BBFI (1984), BIMI (1984), MWBM (1984), SwO (1987), MBM, UkGBM

2. CZECH REPUBLIC   BBFI (1992), CBI (1992), LIB (1992), SBC (1992), CBF (1993), BGC, RBS

3. GERMANY   BM-M (1950), BGEA (1954), SBC (1961), BWM (1968), BIMI (1969), BBFI (1970), EBM (1977), CBI (1981), MBM (1981), MWBM (1984), LIB (1986), FWB (1988), ABWE (1989), ABA

4. NETHERLANDS   BM-M (1954), BBFI (1979), CBI (1985), BIMI (1978), SBC (1988)

5. POLAND   SBC (1990), BIMI (1992), CBI (1992), MBW, R-UEBU, UMBS

6. SLOVAKIA   BGC

7. SWITZERLAND (GERMAN-SPEAKING)   SBC (1948), BBFI (1987), CBF (1992)

C. EURASIA (COMMONWEALTH OF INDEPENDENT STATES)

*I*n the great land mass which stretches east to west from the borders of Poland to the Pacific and north to south from the Arctic Ocean to southern Asia, known today as the Commonwealth of Independent States (CIS), live 300,000 Baptists (or Evangelical Christians-Baptists). Except for Mennonites who entered the Russian Empire in the late eighteenth century, Baptists were the first free church to establish congregations in the Empire. Within the twelve republics of the CIS, Baptists are not only the leading evangelical free-church denomination but also the leading Protestant body except in Belarus and Armenia, where Pentecostals have greater strength, and possibly Kazakhstan where German Lutherans are decreasing because of emegration, may still be supported by larger numbers.

CHURCH LIFE AND MORALITY

*W*ith their strict adherence to the authority of Scripture, personal piety, rigorous personal morality, revivalism, missionary witness, and the demand of clear evidence of repentance and faith before baptism as a believer, Baptists in the CIS have maintained, unlike many Baptists in the West, the standards of nineteenth-century Baptist life. Because of their isolation with roots in the rural areas and working classes and years of suppression under both Czars and Soviet commissars, it is not surprising that they, like the Russian Orthodox Church, have preserved a traditional morality and theology which many Baptists in the West would consider too restrictive.

Membership standards are strict, and church discipline with possibility of exclusion is practiced. One needs to be at least fourteen years of age before baptism, and a baptismal candidate is put on probation for a half year if not longer before acceptance. Baptism by immersion is a great event, often held in the open where it also serves as a witness to the outside world. After baptism, the candidate is given flowers. As a sign of separation from the world, churches strictly forbid the drinking of alcoholic beverages and the use of tobacco. Such activities as dancing and attendance at theaters/cinemas are considered harmful to a believer's spiritual life. Female members should not appear as women of the world and are to eschew jewelry and use of cosmetics; married women wear a head covering, generally a scarf, in services.

One of the distinguishing features of Baptist life in the CIS is the worship in their churches, called prayer houses. In the front of the sanctuary, the words "God Is Love" or other Scripture are often prominently displayed. Services are at least two hours long and include several biblical sermons from three or four preachers and a number of choir anthems if not also special musical numbers. The intensity of worship, similar to the reverence found in an Orthodox church, is very serious and personal. Prayer requests are written on slips of paper that are passed to the pulpit where they are read before the congregation. A service will include several periods of spontaneous prayer with men or women leading out in turn with the congregation praying with them, whispering in a quiet undertone. As in the Orthodox Church, prayer is done by standing or kneeling. When a visitor extends greetings, the congregation may shout out in unison a greeting in return. As in Russian tradition, Easter is the most important Christian holy day and, when the minister speaks the words "Christ is risen," the congregation responds with great fervor, "Christ is risen indeed!" Unlike the Orthodox Church, which provides no seats for worshipers, Baptists have benches or pews. But with insufficient seating in a crowded church, it is common for worshipers to stand during an entire two-hour service. Men and women are generally segregated in worship, and among their own sex they may practice the kiss of peace.

Russian Baptists have developed an outstanding hymnody. Although they might borrow an Easter hymn from the Orthodox, they generally sing gospel hymns, brought in from the West or hymns of their own composition. Christian rock is not acceptable. In Orthodox style, the tempo is slow but, unlike the Orthodox, Baptists use musical instruments, such as pianos or organs, and may use a guitar but oppose saxophones or drums, which they consider inappropriate for a proper spirit of worship.

Like German Baptists, Russian Baptists were slow to organize small groups of believers into independent congregations. They preferred to keep them as mission stations of a mother church until they become self-sustaining. A mother church would develop a number of preachers who could serve the church and its stations. Even today a congregation, besides its senior pastor or elder, will have a number of preachers who share in the pastoral ministry.

BAPTISTS IN THE RUSSIAN EMPIRE (1855–1917)

*W*hen Baptists began penetrating the Russian Empire, it included, by and large, not only the present CIS but also Finland, the Baltic states of Estonia, Latvia, and Lithuania, and Poland. What later became the united body of Evangelical Christians and Baptists had its origins in three distinct movements, all arising in the middle of the nineteenth century. First, a German stream with a Swedish rivulet established congregations among Germans, Swedes, Latvians, and Estonians. A second stream arose in the south with one source among Ukrainian peasants, known as stundists, and a second source in the Caucasus in Georgia, primarily among Russian Molokans. A third stream appeared among the Russian aristocracy of St. Petersburg, begun by a British nobleman, whose later adherents became generally Evangelical Christians, although some became Baptists. During the period of the Empire, each movement established its own union—the Russian Baptist Union (1884); the Union of Baptist Churches of Russia (1887), composed of Germans and Baltic peoples; and the All-Union Council of Evangelical Christians (1909).

German and Other Non-Slavic Baptists

In 1855 a tailor, C. Plonus, moved to St. Petersburg from Memel in Germany, where he distributed tracts, gathering a circle about him. More important for the German work, however, was the baptism in 1858 in Poland of Gottfried Alf (1831–1858), a Lutheran school teacher, who became the founder of Baptist work in Poland and helped to foster German Baptist work in Volhynia in the western Ukraine, where some

Baptists had settled. In May 1864 the first two Baptist churches in the Ukraine were founded—one at Horzcik and the other at Soroczin. Before World War I German Baptist work also appeared in Kherson Province in southern Ukraine, the Volga, Caucasus, western Siberia, and in the Tashkent area. German Baptists expanded among German stundists—people who met for an hour (in German, *Stunde*) of devotions. Revivals among the German population also helped to pave the way for the establishment of the Baptist witness.

Through the agency of the Baptist church in Memel, Germany (today in Lithuania), Baptist work spread among Germans and Latvians in what is today Latvia. German Baptists from St. Petersburg and Latvia also began to gain Estonians. In return, Latvians and Estonians established congregations in St. Petersburg. German Baptists also contributed to the rise of Ukrainian Baptists in Kherson Province and to Russian Baptists in the Caucasus. German Baptists contributed their confessional standards, polity, mission organization, and hymnody to both Baltic and Slavic Baptists.

German Baptists experienced strong opposition from the Lutheran clergy and persecution, but in 1879 the Russian government granted them recognition and thus toleration. But toleration was not extended to Russian or Ukrainian Baptists, who as Orthodox were forbidden to leave the state church. German Baptists formed associations, the first in 1872, and in 1887 they established the Union of Baptist Churches of Russia, thereby formally separating from the Baptist Union of Germany. In 1901 the union had five associations with 22,244 members, including 8,000 Latvians and Lithuanians. The German Baptists developed their own publications and from 1907 to 1910 operated a preachers' school in Lodz, the first Baptist school in the Empire, until closed by the government. In spite of heavy migration to America, with evangelistic zeal and some financial support from abroad, German Baptists in the Russian Empire continued to grow.

German Baptists also influenced the rise of Mennonite Brethren in Ukraine in 1860, who differed from German Baptists only by their advocacy of nonresistance and footwashing as an ordinance. Under Baptist influence, two of their leaders immersed each other, thus beginning in their group believer's baptism by immersion. Mennonite Brethren, in turn, contributed to the rise of the Ukrainian Baptist movement.

Swedish Baptists as early as 1856 had formed a small congregation in the Åland Islands, between Sweden and Finland, the first Baptist church in the Russian Empire. Their movement later extended itself to Swedes in Finland and entered St. Petersburg, where a congregation was founded. Their work, however, was largely confined to Finland, which separated from Russia in 1917; therefore, their impact on Russia was very limited.

Russian/Ukrainian Baptists

Although borrowing from others, Russian/Ukrainian Baptists were an indigenous movement. Colporteurs of the British and Foreign Bible Society spread the Scripture and helped to prepare the way for the reception of evangelical teaching among the Slavic population. In addition, the stundist movement among the Germans had an impact. Ukrainian peasants, at times employed by Germans, were attracted to the devotional hours of the German stundists. About 1860 some of them began to remove their icons and declined to attend the Orthodox church. Some also began to be attracted to believer's baptism, a step which was illegal for those reared as Orthodox. In 1869 a Ukrainian, Efim Tsymbal, secretly slipped into a baptismal line and was baptized by a pastor of the Mennonite Brethren, thus beginning a Baptist movement among the Ukrainians. In the next year Tsymbal baptized Ivan Ryaboshapka (1831–1900), who then baptized Mikhail Ratushnyĭ (1830–c.1915) in 1871. Ryaboshapka and Ratushnyĭ were two of the greatest evangelists in the Ukraine. At first not all Ukrainian stundists accepted believer's baptism, but in time Ukrainian stundism as a whole became a Stundo-Baptist movement. The first Ukrainian congregation was at Lyubomirka in Kherson Province. With the encouragement of the Orthodox Church, the authorities severely persecuted the movement, especially in the 1880s and 1890s.

In 1862 a German Lithuanian, Martin Kalweit (1833–1918), settled near Tiflis (today Tbilisi), Georgia, in the Caucasus. A year later he moved to the city itself, where he held services for his immediate family and others who might come. In 1867 Kalweit baptized the first Russian convert, Nikita I. Voronin (1840–1905), a member of the Molokans, a proto-Protestant Russian group that rejected the sacraments of the Orthodox Church. At first there were services in both German and Russian, but German services ceased after the Germans left the area. In 1880 the Tiflis church was formally organized, and the Baptist movement spread to other areas of the Caucasus and up the Volga Valley and to Molokan communities in both Azerbaijan and the Don Region. From the Molokans in the Caucasus came some of the most gifted Baptist or Evangelical Christian leaders: Vasiliĭ G. Pavlov (1854–1924), who, after studying under Johann Oncken at Hamburg, launched a most successful missionary career and became a leading figure in the Baptist movement; V. V. Ivanov-Klyshnikov, a great evangelist who suffered much for the faith; Deĭ I. Mazaev, for many years president of the Russian Baptist Union; his brother, Gavriel; and Ivan S. Prokhanov, although becoming a Baptist, he was later the leader of the Evangelical Christians. Another outstanding figure was Johann (Ivan) Kargel (1849–1937), baptized at Tiflis and a student at Hamburg, who became a noted teacher and theologian among Baptists and Evangelical Christians.

The movement in Ukraine and the movement in the Caucasus coalesced. Under the leadership of Johann Wieler, a member of the Mennonite Brethren, a Russian Baptist Union was founded in 1884, which appointed itinerant missionaries. The government refused to recognize the legality of the union, although it periodically held congresses. After toleration was granted in 1905, Russian Baptists, in spite of continuing problems with church and state, undertook an extended missionary and publication ministry, including the issuing of the *Baptist*. William Fetler (1883–1957), a graduate of Spurgeon's College in London and of Latvian and Baltic German parentage, established in 1908 in St. Petersburg a dynamic church, *Dom Evangeliya* (House or Temple of the Gospel). Russian-Ukrainian Baptists grew rapidly from about 20,000 in 1908 to more than 65,000 in 1912.

Pashkovites/Evangelical Christians

In 1874 Lord Radstock, a British nobleman and an evangelical in the Church of England with ties to the Plymouth Brethren, began to hold meetings in St. Petersburg in the homes of Russian aristocrats, preaching justification by faith alone. The movement attracted Colonel Vasiliĭ A. Pashkov (1831–1902), a wealthy nobleman, who became the movement's primary benefactor, and Count Modest M. Korff (1842–1931), both later exiled. Pashkovites established a publication society which distributed tracts and other literature, but the government disbanded it. Through the

Pashkovites, evangelical ideas not only spread among aristocrats but also among the lower classes both inside and outside of St. Petersburg. Pashkovism at first was a spiritual movement within the Orthodox Church and not schismatic, even though some of its adherents, such as Pashkov, accepted believer's baptism.

The regime attemped to suppress the movement, but it survived primarily because of the faithfulness of a group of aristocratic women. It gained the support of two Baptists—Johann Kargel, who had become pastor of the German Baptist church of St. Petersburg, and Ivan S. Prokhanov (1869–1935), at that time an engineer who received part of his education at Bristol College, Britain's first Baptist theological college. With the Toleration Act of 1905, the Pashkovite movement assumed the name, Evangelical Christian. Two Evangelical Christian churches emerged in St. Petersburg, one under Prokhanov and a second under Kargel.

In 1903 the Russian Baptist Congress accepted the Pashkovites and took the name, Union of Evangelical Christians-Baptists. Prokhanov, a strong leader in his own right and opposed to the Baptist leadership, however, began to form in 1908 his own organization. He called a congress in Odessa and in the following year established in St. Petersburg an All-Russian Union of Evangelical Christians with himself as president. In 1911 the Baptist World Alliance accepted Prokhanov, electing him one of its vice-presidents. With its own publishing activity and later a training school, the Evangelical Christian Union became a serious rival to the Baptists. Prokhanov, a talented writer of hymns, in 1902 issued a very popular hymnal, *Gusli*, as well as other hymnals. Prokhanov, although basically Baptist in faith and practice, rejected formal ordination as unnecessary, observed open communion, and opposed what he considered was the rigid sectarianism of the Russian Baptists. Both before and after the First World War, he did not hesitate to reach out abroad to non-Baptists for financial support. Evangelical Christians numbered around 8,500 in 1914.

BAPTISTS AND EVANGELICAL CHRISTIANS IN THE USSR (1917–1991)

*W*ith the overthrow of the Czarist regime in 1917, evangelicals believed a new day had come with the proclamation of full liberty by the Provisional Government. The seizure of power by the Communists in November, although bringing separation of church and state, ushered in a regime whose ultimate aim was to establish an atheistic socialist state. The new government initiated a program of atheistic indoctrination and propaganda and brought religious restrictions, such as closing Sunday Schools, and persecution. After the initial period of War Communism, Baptists and Evangelical Christians experienced a period of comparative freedom and very rapid growth under the New Economic Policy (1921–1928). In 1928 the Russian Baptist Union claimed 200,000 members with 5,000 preaching places but only 1,200 buildings either owned or rented. Evangelical Christians made extravagant claims of membership but probably had less. The Baptist World Alliance (BWA) made strenuous efforts to bring the Baptists and Evangelical Christians into one union, but the effort failed and the two continued as serious rivals, each with its own mission programs, publishing activity, and training schools. Under government pressure, both unions professed their loyalty to the Soviet state by approving military service for their members.

With the loss of territory in the west by the Russian state, the Union of Baptist Churches of Russia was reduced in size and confined to German churches. The government, not wishing to deal with them as Germans, forced them to join the Ukrainian Baptist Union, even though half their churches were outside Ukraine. In the 1920s they also experienced revival, for a time published their own paper, and in 1926 reported 11,746 members in fifty-one churches with many more adherents who were not yet baptized.

The inauguration in 1928 under Joseph Stalin of a series of Five-Year Plans, which sought to transform the USSR into a fully Communist state with industrialization and collectivization of agriculture, brought serious consequences to all religions. By the late 1930s most churches were closed. The regime charged pastors and other leaders with espionage, among other things, and sent them to prison and exile with many not surviving. The Russian Baptist Union ceased to exist in 1935, while the Evangelical Christian Union barely survived. German Baptists not only lost their churches, but in 1941 during World War II many were deported to the east, while others, who fell under German control fled to the west toward the end of the war.

Feeling pressure for change during the conflict with Nazi Germany, Stalin instituted a program of limited toleration for certain recognized religious bodies but co-opted them for the regime's political purposes. The regime demanded full political loyalty and support for its foreign policy, particularly its peace program. In 1944 the government allowed Baptists and Evangelical Christians to form the All-Union Council of Evangelical Christians-Baptists, which served as an umbrella group for all evangelical bodies accepting believer's baptism. The government refused registration to any congregation not joining. In most cases, the regime would register not more than one evangelical congregation in any city or rural site. In 1945 Pentecostals joined, accepting the August Agreement, which included the provision that worshipers would abstain from speaking in tongues in general meetings and that footwashing would be discouraged. In 1947 an agreement was made with the Oneness Pentecostals, and other groups were absorbed also. In 1963 the All-Union Council recognized Mennonite Brethren as part of the Baptist Union and in time a number of their groups were registered. Although the All-Union Council strenuously attempted to maintain unity, there were defections, especially among Pentecostals, but also among Baptists.

The All-Union Council, with headquarters in Moscow, was for years until their deaths under the steady leadership of two former members of the Evangelical Christians—Jakov I. Zhidkov (1885–1966), who served as president, and Aleksandr V. Karev (1894–1971), serving as general secretary. The All-Union Council issued a journal, *Bratskiĭ vestnik*, and in 1968 inaugurated correspondence courses for pastors. In 1979 a separate administration for the Russian Republic was established apart from the All-Union structure. Eleven senior presbyters supervised the work in each of the republics or combination of republics. In Russia, Ukraine, and Belarus there were also deputy presbyters and senior presbyters who administered in various regions. In 1955 Russian Baptists again participated in a congress of the Baptist World Alliance, the first since 1928. With other Russian religious bodies, the All-Union Council joined the World Council of Churches in 1962.

Despite prohibition of Sunday Schools, youth work, or public evangelism and despite a severe shortage of Bibles and other Christian literature, Russian Baptists maintained a faithful witness and theological integrity under intense political pressure. Under Nikita Khrushchev the regime forced the All-Union Council to issue in 1960 new statutes and a letter of instruction, limiting the evangelistic outreach of the churches. This action resulted in a schism in 1961 which led to the formation in 1962 of an Organizing Committee, superseded in 1965 by a Council of Churches of Evangelical Christians-Baptists.

The new group, known as *Initsiativniki*, or Reform Baptists, claimed that the All-Union Council was collaborating too closely with the regime and violating the Baptist principle of separation of church and state. The president of the new council was Gennadiĭ K. Kryuchkov, who, after serving a prison term, spent much of his time underground in hiding. The secretary, Georgi P. Vins, was twice imprisoned. In an exchange for spies, worked out through the offices of President Jimmy Carter of the USA, the Russian government deported Vins to America in 1979. Because the Reform Baptists refused registration and conducted a vigorous evangelistic program, including Sunday Schools, youth work, and an underground press, the government used its resources to stamp it out by fines and imprisonment. Women in the Reform Baptist movement formed a Council of Prisoners' Relatives and appealed to the West for relief. Their oppression produced among them a theology of suffering. Although in 1963 a congress of the registered Baptists repealed the statutes and letter of instruction and the Baptist leadership later repented of issuing the documents, the breach has never been healed between the two groups. The government began to register autonomous Baptist churches not aligned with either the All-Union Council or the Council of Churches, thereby creating a third group of Baptists.

The reforms of Gorbachev helped to bring religious freedom. Russian Baptists began in 1988 (the year of the 1000th anniversary of the Christianization of Russia) to open new churches, construct buildings, form Sunday Schools, and to enter the field of mass evangelization. Russian Baptists met in 1990 in their 44th All-Union Congress, made changes in leadership, and adopted a new charter. In 1989 an independent Baptist paper, *Protestant*, appeared to promote new initiatives. Its publishers have also begun publishing *Khristianin* and *Baptist*, reviving by name two renowned periodicals of the Evangelical Christians and Baptists of an earlier age. The Union, while continuing *Bratskiĭ vestnik*, began issuing in 1989 a sprightly paper, *Khristianskoe slovo*. About 1992 the correspondence courses were transformed into a Bible Institute. With the departure of the Pentecostals in 1989, the membership of the union fell significantly, numbering 204,000 members in 2,260 churches at the beginning of 1990. At the end of 1988, the last of the Reform Baptists in prison were released. In 1989 the Reform Baptists, probably then numbering about 42,000, held for the first time a congress without molestation.

EVANGELICAL CHRISTIANS-BAPTISTS IN THE CIS (1991–)

*W*ith the collapse of the USSR and the emergence of independent states, which in late 1991 formed the Commonwealth of Independent States (CIS), the Baptist Union was again transformed, becoming in 1992 the Euro-Asiatic Federation of Unions of Evangelical Christians-Baptists. The Federation incorporated ten independent Baptist unions. In 1993 Russian Baptists opened in Moscow a five-story building, serving not only as an administrative center but as a home for the Moscow Baptist Theological Seminary, which opened in October with seventeen students. The Federation and the Russian Baptist Union cooperate in maintaining the seminary and the Federation's two journals. The Federation not only plays an important role in providing a degree of institutional unity for Baptists of the CIS but also provides assistance to the very weak unions which at present have not elected to enter the Baptist World Alliance as individual entities. Because of a great surge in evangelism, establishment of new congregations, and church construction, the Federation as a whole is registering significant growth. Unfortunately, however, the Baptist unions in the Caucasus and Central Asia have suffered severe losses because of the emigration of many German and Russian believers.

In October 1993 the Reform Baptists, known today as independent or non-registered Baptists, held a congress in Tula with 350 delegates representing more than 50,000 members. With twelve associations, Reform Baptists are also embarking on an aggressive program, including an attempt to win adherents among non-Slavic minorities. The autonomous churches, a mediating group between the other two bodies, continue a separate existence with possibly 25,000 members in more than 100 churches.

With the new freedom have come great opportunities of preaching in public places, campaigns and rallies, distribution of literature, and establishment of Sunday Schools. Baptists also have entered the previously prohibited field of social service and today minister in psychiatric hospitals, boarding schools, and prisons and work among refugees. On the other hand, there also are problems. On top of economic and political dislocation has come a bewildering new world. Cults from the West are now competing for converts, and the secular lifestyles and the products of the West are a great lure to a society which had been protected from them for a long time. With a rigid morality and ingrown traditions, Russian Baptists now also face the daunting task of meeting these new challenges and winning people, many are open to religious values but have been reared in a secular atheistic society. Evangelicals from the West, many representing not only Baptist but also parachurch organizations with different lifestyles, mission methods, and music, appear at times more of a threat than a help.

With assistance from Baptists in the West and other evangelical agencies of like mind, Russian Baptists are nevertheless trying carefully to make right choices while taking advantage of the new opportunities. Even before the demise of the USSR, a number of nondenominational agencies greatly assisted Baptist work, notably Licht im Osten in Germany and the Slavic Gospel Association in America. In addition the Billy Graham Evangelistic Association and Luis Palau Evangelistic Association, both headed by Baptists, also have conducted preaching campaigns, with the former organization establishing an office in Moscow.

BIBLIOGRAPHY: For an extensive bibliography on Baptists and other evangelicals in the Russian Empire and USSR, see Albert W. Wardin, Jr., *Evangelical Sectarians in the Russian Empire and the USSR: A Bibliographic Guide* (Metuchen, N.J.: Scarecrow Press, 1995). An excellent study on Baptists is the work by Paul Steeves, *The Russian Baptist Union, 1917–1935* (Ph.D. dissertation, University of Kansas, 1976). For more contemporary developments, see Walter Sawatsky, *Soviet Evangelicals Since World War II* (Kitchener, Ont. and Scottdale, Pa.: Herald Press, 1981), a work of meticulous scholarship. On Baptists in the Russian Empire, see Samuel J. Nesdoly, "Baptists in Tsarist Russia," in *The Modern Encyclopedia of Religions in Russia and the Soviet Union* (MERRSU), 3:202–11. German Baptists are covered in two articles by Albert W. Wardin, Jr., "Baptists (German) in Russia and USSR," *MERRSU*, 3:192–202, and "Mennonite Brethren and German Baptists in Russia: Affinities and Dissimilarities," in Paul Toews, ed., *Mennonites and Baptists: A Continuing Conversation* (Winnipeg, Man., and Hillsboro, Kans.: Kindred Press, 1993), 97–112. For a scholarly study of Baptists and Evangelical Christians before World War I from a Marxist perspective, see A. I. Klibanov, *Istoriya religioznogo sektantstva v Rossii* (Moscow: "Nauka," 1965), which was later translated into English by Ethel Dunn and published by Pergamon Press in 1982. Michael Bourdeaux, *Religious Ferment in Russia* (London and New York: St. Martin's Press, 1968), provides a helpful account of the beginnings of the Reform Baptist movement. On the Pashkovite movement, see Edmund Heier,

Religious Schism in the Russian Aristocracy 1860–1900 (The Hague: Martinus Nijhoff, 1970). For Evangelical Christians, see the scholarly work by Wilhelm Kahle, Evangelische Christen in Russland und der Sovetunion (Wuppertal and Kassel: Oncken, 1978). A few years ago, the Russian Baptists themselves issued their own comprehensive history, Istoriya evangel'skikh khristian-baptistov v SSSR (Moscow: All-Union Council of Evangelical Christians-Baptists, 1989), primarily a narrative account stressing the indigenous character of the Baptist movement.

	Members	Churches
1. Armenia	790	23
2. Azerbaijan	497	15
3. Belarus	9,927	135
4. Georgia	4,000	34
5. Kazakhstan	14,545	203
6. Kyrgyzstan	3,460	20
7. Moldova	17,800	225
8. Russia	98,848	1,255
9. Tajikistan	347	7
10. Turkmenistan	112	3
11. Ukraine	160,481	1,400
12. Uzbekistan	3,500	25
	314,307	3,345

ARMENIA (1890)

	Members	Churches
Union of Evangelical Christians-Baptists	790	(23)

*A*rmenians, an ancient Christian people with their own Gregorian Apostolic Church, have remarkably preserved their traditions despite control by Russians and massacre by Turks. In addition to a large diaspora, Armenians again have an independent republic in the Caucasus which, except in the north, is surrounded by predominantly Moslem populations.

From the mission activity between 1822 and 1835 of Count Felician Zaremba and other missionaries of the Basel Mission, a Protestant society in Switzerland, some Armenians became evangelical believers. This movement divided into two brotherhoods—one centered in Shemakha in Azerbaijan, where in 1866 a Lutheran church was formed, and the other, the Ararat Brotherhood, which included adherents in the Karabakh region, now fought over by Armenia and Azerbaijan. From the latter brotherhood, a Baptist congregation of fifty members was formed in 1890 in Susha. Other groups appeared in Stepanakept in Karabakh and in Kumayri in Armenia proper.

Under the Stalinist persecution of the 1930s, all congregations were closed, but with a new religious policy in 1944 the situation changed for the better. In Yerevan, the capital, Baptists along with other Armenian evangelicals who had returned to their homeland but baptized as infants formed a congregation. After discussion with the Baptist leadership, the group accepted believer's baptism as the norm, and the congregation of 110 members was accepted in 1947 into the Union of Evangelical Christians-Baptists of the USSR.

At the end of 1991 it was reported that Armenia had six congregations with Yerevan, the mother church, numbering about 480 members. The congregation in Yerevan and the one in Kumayri were the only two with prayer houses. With their new freedom, Baptists in Armenia have undertaken a vigorous evangelistic program. With Bibles and other Christian literature supplied by Bible societies and Armenians from abroad, they are engaged in an extensive program of distribution. Evangelistic work is conducted not only in the churches but also in hospitals, prisons, and schools. With numerous homeless, widows, orphans, and refugees, Baptists are also engaged in charity work. Today there are twenty-three churches and missions, a significant increase in two years. Armenian Baptists today have their own Baptist union, a member of the Euro-Asiatic Federation but not of the BWA.

BIBLIOGRAPHY: *Istoriya evangel'skikh khristian-baptistov v SSSR* (Moscow: All-Union Council of Evangelical Christians-Baptists, 1989), 306–7, 497–98. *Khristianskoe slovo*, Nov. 1991, 2, and March 1994, 8, 10.

AZERBAIJAN (1873)

	Members	Churches
Union of Evangelical Christians-Baptists	497	(15)

*L*ike neighboring Armenia, Azerbaijan was also incorporated into the Russian Empire in the early nineteenth century. Unlike the Armenians, however, most Azeris are Turkish-speaking Moslems. Consequently, the Baptist work in this territory has been primarily among Russians and Ukrainians, not the indigenous population.

In 1873 Vasiliĭ V. Ivanov-Klyshnikov (1846–1919), a Molokan who had been baptized two years before in the Baptist church in Tiflis in Georgia, began preaching in present-day Azerbaijan and gaining converts. In 1876 the great Baptist missionary leader, V. G. Pavlov, visited the same territory, and a church was organized in Lenkoran on the Caspian Sea. In 1879 the Tiflis Church sent Ivanov to Baku Province, where he converted a number of Molokan families. In the following year he was the first Baptist to preach in the town of Baku, beginning there a church which he later served as pastor from 1900 to 1917.

The Baku church has survived, and in 1989 was one of six registered Baptist churches in the country. At this time it was meeting in a reconstructed house. With the collapse of the USSR and the establishment of an independent Azerbaijan, Baptists today have their own union, which is a member of the Euro-Asiatic Federation but not a member of the BWA. At the beginning of 1991 Baptists had sixteen churches with 620 members but two years later they had only 497 members, reflecting loss through emigration because of the difficult political situation in the country. Russian and native Azeris attend the Baku Church where a portion of the service, including preaching and some of the hymns, are in the Azeri language. There are Azeri congregations in Shemakha.

BIBLIOGRAPHY: *Istoriya evangel'skikh khristian-baptistov v SSSR* (Moscow: All-Union Council of Evangelical Christians-Baptists, 1989), 76–78, 307, 498, 527. *Khristianskoe slovo*, March 1994, 8, 10. See Jim Forest, *Religion in the New Russia* (New York: Crossroad, 1990), 144–46, 196, for a visit to the Baku Church at the end of the 1980s and an assessment of the religious situation in Azerbaijan by the head of the Council for Religious Affairs in the territory.

BELARUS (1877)

	Members	Churches
Union of Evangelical Christians-Baptists (1990)	9,927	(135)

*B*elarus received evangelical impulses from both Ukraine and St. Petersburg. Among the first Belorussians to accept the Baptist faith were peasants who had gone to southern Ukraine for work, were converted, and then returned to their homes. One such individual was Dmitriĭ P. Semenstov, who, after joining the Baptists in Odessa, returned in 1877 to the village of Usokh, where he gained other adherents. By 1882 there were nineteen and in 1885 the number had grown to ninety-five. The Baptist cause was assisted by the visits of V. G. Pavlov and V. N. Ivanov. Support also came from the Pashkovites in St. Petersburg.

Colporteurs also helped to spread evangelical teaching. One of them was Gerasim S. Andryukov, who led B. S. Cheberuk to the faith. Cheberuk became the first pastor of the Baptist congregation which started in Minsk in 1912, the capital of Belarus. Today the Minsk Church is the leading Baptist congregation in the republic with 1,150 members.

With the annexation of eastern Poland by Soviet Russia in 1939, Belarus extended westward. This incorporated many evangelical believers into the Union of Evangelical Christians-Baptists of the USSR (formed in 1944). The Union not only united Evangelical Christians and Baptists but also included a substantial number of Pentecostals, embracing a mainline group and a "Jesus Only" body, as well as members from the Union of Churches of Christ. The majority of the members were Belorussian, but Russians, Poles, and even Gypsies were included.

At this time most members worked in agriculture. Believers began to move to the cities where they, although still working class, began to occupy skilled positions in offices, factories, and transport. Government restrictions and harassment in the 1960s closed a number of churches, including the church in Brest. Yet Baptists continued to maintain a vital witness and were also able to retain a significant number of their youth.

With the increased religious freedom under Gorbachev, Baptists found new opportunities for growth but lost the Pentecostals, who today are probably the leading evangelical group in the republic. In 1989 there was only one Baptist church in Minsk; today there are six. Baptists have begun constructing buildings and have developed new programs of outreach and ministry, including work in prisons and hospitals. As in earlier years the strength of Baptists and other evangelicals today is in the west of the country, and therefore Baptists have begun a special ministry in the north of the country where evangelicals are few. Ninety students are now enrolled in its Bible Institute. The Baptist union, established in 1990, is a member of both the Euro-Asiatic Federation and BWA. Southern Baptists have sent a missionary couple to assist the Union. There are also some independent Baptists in the country.

BIBLIOGRAPHY: *Istoriya evangel'skikh khristian-baptistov v SSSR* (Moscow: All-Union Council of Evangelical Christians-Baptists, 1989), 380–96. M. Ya. Lensu and E. S. Prokoshina, eds., *Baptism i Baptisty* (Minsk: "Nauka i tekhnika," 1969), 13–38. Paul D. Steeves, *The Russian Baptist Union, 1917–1935* (Ph.D. dissertation, University of Kansas, 1976), 22–23. For a history of the Minsk Church, see "Minsk," *Bratskii vestnik*, no. 1 (1988): 93–94. For the current status of Baptists in Belarus, see Mike Crewsell, "Belarus: The Panters Lend a Hand," *Commission*, Jan. 1993, 38–65, and *Khristianskoe slovo*, March 1994, 6–7, 10.

GEORGIA (1862)

	Members	Churches
Union of Evangelical Christians-Baptists (1990)	4,000	(34)

G eorgia, a republic in the Caucasus, then part of the Russian Empire, was settled in the nineteenth century by a number of German emigrants. In September 1862 a German Lithuanian, Martin Kalweit (1833–1918), a simple artisan born in Kovno Province near the German border but a member of a German Baptist congregation at Ickschen in East Prussia, settled near Tiflis (now Tbilisi). After a year, he moved into the city where, fearful of his Russian neighbors, he held worship for his family and other Germans who might attend. Jakov Delyakov, a colporteur, but himself not yet a Baptist, directed Nikita I. Voronin (1840–1905), a Russian and member of the Molokans, to the group. Voronin was searching the Scriptures and seeking baptism. On August 20, 1867, Kalweit baptized him in the Kura River, a historic date because it marked the beginning of the Baptist movement among the Russians in the Russian Empire.

Because of the mission activity of Kalweit and Voronin, the Tiflis congregation grew with services in both German and Russian. Voronin gained converts in the Molokan community, notably Vasiliĭ G. Pavlov (1854–1924), who was baptized in 1871. From 1875 to 1876 Pavlov studied in Hamburg, Germany, under Johann Oncken, who ordained him for missionary service. Pavlov became the foremost Baptist leader until his death. The Baptist movement spread north into Russia proper in the northern Caucasus and up the Volga River and east into Azerbaijan. The Tiflis Church, formally organized in 1880, became a model for the entire Russian/Ukrainian movement. It also supported a united work with the Stundo-Baptists in Ukraine and was the site in 1879 of the first Russian Baptist conference. The Tiflis Church suffered much persecution. For a time in the early part of the century it was troubled by the Pentecostal movement, which was then entering Russia. From 1937 to 1944 the church was closed. Shortly after reopening, it united in 1945 with the Evangelical Christian congregation in the city.

Armenians became members of both the Baptist and Evangelical Christian churches in Tiflis, and around 1924 a separate Armenian Evangelical Christian congregation was formed and two years later a Baptist one. After the oppression under Stalin, Armenian groups reappeared in both the Baptist and Evangelical Christian congregations and then became part of the united church in 1945.

About 1912 the Tiflis Church also began to receive native Georgian believers, the first being Alekseĭ Z. Khutsishvili and his mother. Preaching in the Georgian language commenced only in 1919 with services on Saturday. With the evangelistic activity of Il'ya M. Kandelaki and Zakhariĭ Patsiashvili, groups of believers began appearing in some of the villages. In 1925 a collection of twenty-one Georgian hymns was published, translated from the Russian primarily by Kandelaki, but it was later expanded to include four hundred songs, most of which were composed or translated by Ekaterina A. Kutateladze. Evangelical Christians also formed a Georgian congregation in Tiflis and one in a neighboring village. In 1945 all the Baptist and Evangelical Christian Georgians in Tiflis became part of the united Tiflis Church. Another ethnic group which joined the church was the Ossetians, who formed their own fellowship within the church in 1965.

In 1988 the Tbilisi Church, as it became known with the change in name of the city in 1935, was composed of 2,450 members: 1,500 in the Georgian congregation, 550 in the Russian, 150 in the Armenian, and 250 in the Ossetian. Each group had its own pastors, services, and choirs. This church was one of the most remarkable multilingual congregations anywhere.

After the proclamation of a Georgian Republic in 1918, the Tiflis Church took the initiative to form a Trans-Caucasus Union of Baptists in 1919. But after Georgia was incorporated in 1921 into the Soviet Union, it became part of the Russian Baptist Federation. In 1944 Georgian Baptists came under the All-Union Council of Evangelical Christians-Baptists and a senior presbyter who administered the three Caucasian republics. With the collapse of the Soviet Union, Georgian Baptists in March 1990 formed their own union, which is a member of both the Euro-Asiatic Federation and the BWA.

In 1990 the Georgian Baptist Union had 5,320 members but in a period of economic and political disruption, it claimed only 3,600 at the beginning of 1993. The Georgian Union has rebounded today to 4,000 members in thirty-four churches. Recently a Kurdish Baptist Church was organized and joined the Georgian Union. Georgian Baptists publish two journals, *Bifleem* and *Golos Bozhiĭ,* and in 1993 formed a theological school at Gurdzhaani. They conduct services not only in their churches but also evangelistic services in prisons, factories, and other public places. Seventeen missionaries are active in all parts of the country.

BIBLIOGRAPHY: For the beginnings of Baptists in Tbilisi, see Martin Kalweit's letter of July 10/22, 1869, in *Missionsblatt*, Sep. 1869, 129–32 (translated into English in *Baptist Missionary Magazine*, Jan. 1870, 19–21). *Istoriya evangel'skikh khristian-baptistov v SSSR* (Moscow: All-Union Council of Evangelical Christians-Baptists, 1989), 74–79, 305–6, 496–97, contains historical accounts of Baptists in Georgia. For a history of the Tbilisi Church, see A. Belousov, "Yubileinaya tserkov v Tbilisi," *Bratskiĭ vestnik*, no. 4 (1967): 22–32, which includes material on the work among Armenians and Georgians. A comparatively recent account of the Tbilisi Church is in the article by Martha Skelton, "Tbilisi: Four-Part Harmony," *Commission*, Sep. 1988, 40–47. For recent data on Baptists in Georgia, see *Khristianskoe slovo*, Sep./Oct. 1993, 9, and March 1994, 8, 10.

KAZAKHSTAN (1908)

	Members	Churches
1. Union of Evangelical Christians-Baptists	10,495	(170)
2. Independent (Reform) Baptists	3,600	(30)
3. Korean Baptist churches	450	(3)
	14,545	(203)

STATISTICS: *Khristianskoe slovo*, March 1994, 10. Patrick Johnstone, *Operation World*, (Grand Rapids: Zondervan, 1993), 328.

Kazakhstan is a large country of more than one million square miles, located in the heart of Asia between Russia and China. In 1991 it became an independent state with a population of seventeen million. The Kazakhs themselves, previously a nomadic people, are nominally Moslem and speak a language related to Turkish. They, however, compose only 40 percent of the population, while the remainder is mainly Russian with large Ukrainian and German minorities. Baptists entered the territory with the migration of German and Slavic settlers.

Probably the first Baptist congregation formed in Kazakhstan was at Petropavlosk in the northern tip of the territory, where a church was established in 1908 through the influence of Gavriel I. Mazaev. Mazaev was a wealthy sheep farmer and brother of the president of the Russian Baptist Union. He had moved in 1905 to the area of Petropavlovsk, then considered part of Siberia. He was the church's first pastor. With the arrival of Baptist settlers from Ukraine and Orenburg in Siberia, a church of ten members was formed far to the south at Alma-Ata in 1917. In 1920 Baptists established a congregation at Dzhambul and in 1931 a second church in Alma-Ata.

German Baptists also were present in the early twentieth century. The German Baptist paper, *Der Hausfreund*, reported in 1908 that the German Baptist church in Omsk in Siberia had a station at Semipalatinsk. In 1909 it was reported that another church in Siberia, Hoffnungstal (organized in 1907), had a station at Akmolinsk (today Tselinograd). Both stations were in the northern part of present-day Kazakhstan.

With the deportation of many Germans to the East in 1941, the German population in Kazakhstan was greatly augmented, which brought strength to the Baptist churches in the territory. Since at that time Germans could not form their own churches, a number of Germans, including not only Baptists but also Lutherans and Mennonites, began to attend Baptist congregations which then added German in their services or established separate German sections. At a congress in Moscow in 1963 of Evangelical Christians-Baptists, Mennonite Brethren, who were very closely related to German Baptists, were recognized as part of the Baptist Union with the result that many of their fellowships received registration from the government. Although a number of Mennonite Brethren congregations joined the Baptists, others, remained independent of them. The coal-mining city of Karaganda in northern Kazakstan became a very important center of religious life as it included not only large Catholic and Lutheran churches but a Baptist church of one thousand members and a large independent Mennonite Brethren congregation.

A revival in the late 1970s among the German members had a strong impact upon their youth and spread to the Russian believers. At that time half of all Baptists in Kazakhstan were German. Germans began to receive Bibles and hymnals in their own language. Baptists recognized the importance of the German element when in the 1970s two of their members were appointed assistant senior presbyters for Kazakhstan. In addition, a number of German Baptists/Mennonites played an active role in the separatist Reform Baptist movement. With the exodus of many Germans to Germany in recent years, Baptists and Mennonites have suffered loss with the closure of some churches. On the other hand, with the strong evangelistic outreach of Baptists in the country, others are replacing them. Germans still play an important role, and the current president of the Baptist Union in Kazakhstan is German.

In 1963 in Kazakhstan, Baptists had twelve registered congregations and about eighty small groups. At the beginning of 1994 they claimed 170 churches and groups and 10,495 members. In spite of emigration, they continue to grow. Today Almaty (formerly Alma-Ata) has four churches in the Baptist Union with the Central Church reporting 1,150 members. In 1992 the church at Chimket, with a membership of 700, dedicated a new building, built on a hill in the center of the city.

Baptists in Siberia in the 1920s made an attempt to evangelize native Kazakhs. But Baptists have done little to reach them from that time until recently. Today Baptists have freedom to evangelize, and the Kazakhs themselves, many not particularly attached to their own Moslem heritage, are more open to the Christian gospel since the collapse of Communism. Licht im Osten, with an office in Almaty, sends Kazakh radio broadcasts and distributes Kazakh Christian literature. Southern Baptists are attempting to develop relationships with the Kazakh community; for example, in 1991 they sponsored a Kazakh-American festival, and Baptist personnel serve in Kazakh educational institutions. In 1993 the wife of a Southern Baptist professor produced, with the assistance of translators, the first Kazakh collection of Christian hymns, entitled *Kazaktyn Kudaïdy Madaktau Enderi* (Kazakh Praise Songs to God). Korean Baptists, financed from Korea, have come to serve as missionaries for life. They immerse themselves in Kazkah culture; as Asiatics they find it much easier to identify with Kazakhs than individuals from the West. Through the efforts of Korean and Southern Baptists as well as Russian Baptists who reside in the country, a number of Kazakh fellowships have been formed. Kazakh Baptist services are very informal with no limit on time. Kazakhs worship on rugs, sitting in a circle or against the wall, and partake of refreshments, placed on a table or rug.

Baptists in Kazakhstan are a remarkably diverse body, not only including Russians, Ukrainians, and Germans as in the past, but Koreans and Kazakhs have now been added to the mixture. They have their own union, which is a member of the Euro-Asiatic Federation and the BWA.

BIBLIOGRAPHY: *Istoriya evangel'skikh khristian-baptistov v SSR* (Moscow: All-Union Council of Evangelical Christians-Baptists, 1989), 498–504. "Petropavlovsk," *Bratskiĭ vestnik*, no. 5 (1988): 92–96. *Der Hausfreund*, Feb. 6, 1908, 45, and Jan. 7, 1909, 5.

KYRGYZSTAN (1912)

	Members	Churches
Union of Evangelical Christians-Baptists	3,460	(20)

K yrgyzstan is a country of high mountains and wide valleys, nestled between Uzbekistan, Kazakhstan, and China. The Kyrgyz, a people of Turkic Mongolian heritage and nominally Moslem, predominate with Uzbeks following in number. Until recent years, Kyrgyzstan has also had a significant Slavic and German minority.

In 1912 Rodion G. Bershadskiĭ and his wife, converts to the Baptist faith, moved from Orenburg Province to Bishkek (for many years called Frunze under the Soviet regime). They were accompanied by the Marudin family. Bershadskiĭ conducted services in the Marudin home; even when he and his wife returned to Orenburg Province, meetings continued. In 1919 the group of believers divided between Baptists and Evangelical Christians. In 1945 the congregation, which now united both groups, had eighty-three members, but with the rapid growth of membership to eight hundred a second prayer house was opened in 1946. Other congregations also appeared with many members entering the churches who had a German Mennonite background.

In recent years Baptists in Kyrgyzstan have lost members because of the emigration of German and Russians members, yet their work continues to thrive. They have taken advantage of their new freedoms, holding services in the opera house, theaters, stadiums, culture palaces, schools, hospitals, prisons, and the open air. They have not only formed new churches but in their outreach have engaged in literature, radio, and television.

An important factor in the growth of Baptists has been the establishment in 1990 in Bishkek of the mission Ray of Hope, led by Heinrich Voth, a Baptist working with the German mission Licht im Osten. Before its formal organization, it had worked secretly for many years. The Ray of Hope Mission works not only in Kyrgyzstan but also in Uzbekistan and Turkmenistan, attempting to reach both Russians and Kyrgyz. Today it has a missionary force of more than twenty-five with 200 to 300 volunteers. In April 1993 it opened a Bible school in Bishkek, which had an enrollment of twenty-four.

One of the most encouraging aspects of Baptist work today has been the outreach to the native Kyrgyz—the most successful of any to a Moslem people in Central Asia. In the mid-seventies a Kyrgyz believer was killed; ten years later church elders cautioned another convert to await baptism until he was strong enough to face persecution. The situation has changed. In 1992 the Bishkek church immersed 311 believers, including thirty Kyrgyz. By early 1993, two hundred had been converted with fifty baptized. Churches of Kyrgyz believers have been formed in Bishkek and Naryn. Eleven students in the Bible school are Kyrgyz. Reasons for this success have been the activity of the Ray of Hope Mission and the personal witness of individual Baptists; some of them have even moved to Moslem villages to live there as Christian witnesses.

The Baptists in Kyrgyzstan have their own Baptist union, a member of the Euro-Asiatic Federation, but the Kyrgyz Baptist Union does not independently belong to the BWA.

BIBLIOGRAPHY: V. I. A., "Kratkaya istoriya vozniknoveniya i razvitiya Obshchiny evangel'skikh khristian-baptistov v g. Frunze" (A Short History of the Origin and Development of the Church of Evangelical Christians-Baptists in the City of Frunze), *Bratskiĭ vestnik*, no. 2, (1955): 59–62. For current information on Baptists in Kyrgyzstan, see *Khristianskoe slovo*, Oct./Nov. 1992, 13; Feb. 1993, 8; and March 1994, 7, 10. For information on outreach to the Kyrgyz and Ray of Hope Mission, see *Light in the East News*, June 1985, 11–12; Sep. 1992, 10; Dec. 1992, 9; and Mar. 1992, 5–9.

MOLDOVA (GERMANS, 1876; RUSSIANS/UKRAINIANS, 1908)

	Members	Churches
Union of Evangelical Christians-Baptists (1991)	17,800	(225)

*M*oldova, located between Romania and Ukraine, has been an independent republic within the CIS since 1991. The majority of its population is Romanian (Moldavian), but there are a large Ukrainian minority and other nationalities. Moldova was formerly known as Bessarabia; its boundaries were the Dnester and Prut Rivers when it was part of the Russian Empire (1812–1917) and of Romania (1918–1940, 1941–1944). With its incorporation into the USSR, however, it became the Moldavian Republic with altered boundaries, losing its southern region but acquiring some territory along the east bank of the Dnester River.

German Baptists started the first Baptist work in Bessarabia in Turtino in 1876 with the baptism of nine believers. In 1879 a congregation was formed which became independent in 1907 from its mother church in Ukraine. In the same year the three German Baptist churches, then in Bessarabia, formed an association. By 1940 German Baptists had thirty congregations with a constituency of 1,185. Since the forced repatriation of the Germans in 1940, these congregations came to an end, and the site of the first church is today in Ukraine.

In 1908 a Russian Baptist congregation appeared in Kishinev. In 1912 an evangelical Russian congregation was formed at Cetatea Alba (Akkerman), today also in Ukraine. At the beginning of 1918 there were only two Russian Baptist churches which, with their mission stations, had 254 members. Romanian Baptists, scattered over the territory, numbered only forty. A Russian-speaking Bessarabian Baptist Union was formed in 1920, and in the 1930s a Russian-Romanian journal, *Svetil'nik* (The Lamp), was published in Kishinev.

Between the First and Second World Wars, Southern Baptists, who took responsibility for Baptist work in Romania, provided some financial assistance for pastors and chapels. In addition, Walter E. and Hazel Craighead, first serving under the Russian Missionary Society and then with Southern Baptists, did notable work from 1921 to 1939 among the Ukrainian population. In spite of poverty and persecution, Baptists in Bessarabia carried much of the responsibility for their own work. The Baptist cause among Ukrainians and Romanians grew rapidly and included adherents from Jews, Bulgarians, and Gagauz. The growth from 254 members in two churches to 18,000 in 347 churches by 1942 was almost unprecedented.

Under Soviet control, Baptists in the Moldavian Republic suffered the same religious restrictions and atheistic propaganda as other religious groups in the USSR. Under the All-Union Council of Evangelical Christians-Baptists, they had their own senior presbyter and council of presbyters. There was some activity by Reform Baptists who broke with the All-Union Council.

With religious freedom in an independent Moldova, Baptists in the republic have embarked on a vigorous evangelistic effort with rapid growth again in members and churches. They have built many new prayer houses and in 1993 had thirty-four missionaries at work. The republic has been divided into seven regions with a missionary responsible for the formation of new congregations. They evangelize on the streets and in parks, stadiums, hospitals, and culture palaces. Thirty Baptists conduct Bible lessons for children in the public schools. In addition, there are congregations with the same beliefs as Baptists which are independent of any union. In 1991 the Baptists in Moldova again organized an independent union, which became a member of the BWA, whose head is now called bishop instead of senior presbyter.

BIBLIOGRAPHY: Mrs. Peter Trutza, "A Short History of Roumanian Baptists," *Chronicle*, 5 (1942): 12–13. A. I. Mitskevich, "Vospominaniya o vozniknovenii Dela Gospodnego v Moldavii" (Reminiscences on the Origin of the Cause of the Lord in Moldavia), *Bratskiĭ vestnik*, no. 2; (1955): 53–57. Charles A. Brooks and J. H. Rushbrooke, *Baptist Work in Europe* (London: Baptist Union Publication Department, 1920), 51–52, 59. *Istoriya evangel'skikh khristian-baptistov v SSSR* (Moscow, 1989), 219–333. Walter E. Craighead, "The Gospel in Bessarabia," *Home and Foreign Fields*, April 1935, 10–11. *Der Wahrheitszeuge*, Nov. 3, 1929, 351–52, and Nov. 13, 1932, 367–68. For the current status of Baptists in Moldova, see *Khristianskoe slovo*, Apr. 1992, 8, and Sep./Oct. 1993, 2.

RUSSIA (GERMANS, 1855; RUSSIANS, 1874)

	Members	Churches
1. Union of Evangelical Christians-Baptists (1979)	78,848	(1,050)
2. Reform (non-registered) Baptists	10,000	(125)
3. Autonomous congregations	10,000	(80)
	98,848	(1,255)

STATISTICS: Statistics for the Union of Evangelical Christians-Baptists are from *Khristianskoe slovo*, March 1994, 10. Statistics of the Reform Baptists and autonomous congregations are from Patrick Johnstone, *Operation World* (Grand Rapids: Zondervan, 1993), 467.

*R*ussia, the largest republic in the CIS, contains a Baptist constituency of 100,000, the strongest Protestant group in the country. Baptist churches stretch west to east from Kaliningrad to Kamchatka Peninsula with congregations in European Russia, Siberia, and the Far East. Although Baptist churches are found everywhere, they are distributed unevenly with comparatively less strength in the central Russian provinces.

The German Baptists were the first to enter Russia proper. In 1855 C. Plonus moved to St. Petersburg (then the capital of the Russian Empire) and gathered a small group around him. From this small beginning, a German Baptist church was organized in 1880, which acquired its own premises only in 1912. Other non-Slavic Baptists also formed congregations—Swedes in 1889 (including Finnish-speaking members), Latvians in 1895, and Estonians in 1902. Beginning in 1874 under the ministry of Lord Radstock in St. Petersburg, the Pashkovites, named after Vasiliĭ Pashkov, began among the Russian aristocracy. This evangelical movement spread to the lower classes and other parts of Russia but was suppressed by the government. After toleration in 1905, the Pashkovites became known as Evangelical Christians, while some of their adherents became Baptists. After coming to St. Petersburg to serve the Latvian Baptist Church, William Fetler established in 1908 *Dom Evangeliya*, a strong Baptist congregation.

Evangelicals also entered Moscow, a citadel of the Orthodox faith. In the 1880s a loose evangelical group with ties to the Pashkovites appeared, from which an Evangelical Christian congregation developed after 1905. Before World War I, Fetler also planted a Baptist congregation in Moscow.

A very important center of the Baptist faith developed in Tiflis (Tbilisi) in Georgia, where in 1867 the first Russian Baptist was baptized. This movement moved from Transcaucasia northward into Russia proper and up the Volga River. It also joined with the Stundo-Baptist movement, which had begun in the 1860s in Ukraine. In 1884 Russian/Ukrainian Baptists formed a Russian Baptist Union, which included Baptists in Ukraine and the Caucasus.

The Baptist faith also crossed the Ural Mountains into Siberia. An early center was Novosibirsk, where evangelical believers began meeting in 1903. Soon after 1900 German Baptists were widely scattered over western Siberia. One important center was at Hofnungstal, where a church was formed in 1907. Another church was formed at Omsk. In 1889 Yakov Delyakov (1829–1898), an outstanding missionary/colporteur, began a Baptist work among the Molokans in eastern Siberia at Blagoveshchensk. In the Far East, evangelical meetings began in 1913 in Vladivostok and in 1917 in Khabarovsk. A Far East Baptist Union was formed in 1913, which extended into eastern Siberia. In the Far Eastern Republic, which existed until 1922, German and Swedish Baptist missions from America engaged in a fruitful ministry.

After World War I, Moscow became the headquarters of the Russian Baptist Union. St. Petersburg remained the center of the Evangelical Christian Union until 1931, when it also was established in Moscow. Both Baptists and Evangelical Christians flourished in the 1920s, but under Stalinist oppression from 1928 to the early 1940s the regime closed most churches and exiled or imprisoned the leadership with many leaders never surviving.

A new day dawned for Baptists in Russia with the formation in 1944 in Moscow of the All-Union Council of Evangelical Christians-Baptists. With the headquarters of the Council on its premises, the Moscow Central Church of Evangelical Christians-Baptists, the largest in the USSR with five thousand members and the only evangelical church in the city, became the center of Baptist life for the entire Soviet Union. With its large building, which the Evangelical Christian congregation had acquired from the German Reformed in 1922, it was a showplace for visitors from abroad who attended its packed services. Leningrad (the former St. Petersburg) also remained an important center, which in this period had a congregation of three thousand members. In the 1930s *Dom Evangeliya* lost its building, but the regime later gave to the Evangelical Christian-Baptist congregation a large Orthodox building on the outskirts of the city.

In 1979 a separate administrative structure, apart from the All-Union structure, was established for the Russian Republic. It continues today as the Union of Evangelical Christians-Baptists of Russia, a member of the Euro-Asiatic Federation of Unions, formed in 1992. With the collapse of Communism and the Soviet regime, Baptists in the Russian Republic are again growing rapidly with many new churches and Sunday Schools in Moscow and other areas of the country. Moscow Baptists are not only engaged in an extensive evangelistic ministry but a social ministry as well. Reform, or non-registered, Baptists and autonomous Baptist congregations also augment Baptist numbers.

BIBLIOGRAPHY: The Russian Baptist history, *Istoriya evangel'skikh khristian-baptistov v SSSR* (Moscow: All-Union Council of Evangelical Christian-Baptists, 1989), includes a wealth of information on Baptists in the Russian Republic, including material on leading churches. For a current appraisal of Baptists in the Russian Republic by the president of the Russian Union, V. E. Logvinenko, see *Khristianskoe slovo*, Oct./Nov. 1992, 12. For other material, see the bibliography at the end of the introductory section on Baptists in the CIS.

TAJIKISTAN (1929)

	Members	Churches
Union of Evangelical Christians-Baptists of Central Asia	347	(7)

STATISTICS: See *Khristianskoe slovo*, March 1994, 7.

*T*ajikistan is a small mountainous republic which borders Uzbekistan, Kyrgyzstan, China, and Afghanistan. Tajiks compose more than 50 percent of the population, followed by an Uzbek minority of 23 percent. The population is nominally Moslem with a Christian presence among the decreasing Slavic and German minority.

The beginning of the Baptist church in Dushanbe, the capital, was a result of the deportation of two Baptist elders and their families because of their religious faith. Other Baptists settled there as well, and in 1930 the congregation chose I. Ya. Danilenko as its first pastor. Evangelical Christians also formed a congregation, but the two congregations united in 1936. From 1937 to 1943 the authorities closed the church. When the government registered the church in 1944, there were thirty-five left to attend. In 1989 the church had more than 800 members with almost half of them German and with services in both Russian and German. The congregation included as many as sixteen national groups. In addition to the Dushanbe Church, Baptists formed other congregations in the territory.

The collapse of the Soviet Union, instead of bringing increased opportunity for expansion in Tajikistan, has brought nothing but tragedy. Civil war has left death and destruction. Many Russians and Germans have emigrated, greatly weakening the churches. With empty churches and with Christians meeting secretly, the future appears dim. The independent Reform Baptist Church in Dushanbe, which recently had 150 members, now has only 59 but still continues. Only time will tell whether the evangelical community will survive and eventually attempt to reach the Tajiks, an unreached Moslem people. Baptists in Tajikistan do not have their own union but belong to the Union of Evangelical Christians-Baptists of Central Asia.

BIBLIOGRAPHY: *Istoriya evangel'skikh khristian-baptistov v SSSR* (Moscow, 1989), 507–8. For a description of problems in Tajikistan, see the article, "Tadschikistan vom Krieg zerrissen," in *Nachrichten von Missionsfeldern im Osten*, no. 2 (1993): 8–11.

TURKMENISTAN (1890)

	Members	Churches
Union of Evangelical Christians-Baptists of Central Asia (1992)	112	(3)

*T*urkmenistan is a territory of vast deserts and few population centers. Most of the population is composed of Turkmen and a minority of Kazakhs, both groups nominally Moslem. Christianity of any type, much less the evangelical faith, has had little impact in the territory. As in the other republics of Central Asia, the work has been primarily among the western European population.

Evangelical activity began in 1890 through the witness of I. K. Savel'ev, who settled in Ashkhabad from Vladikavkas, and the arrival from Samaria Province of F. S. Ovsyannikov, a convert of the Mennonite Brethren. In 1892 they, with others, established a settlement, later known as Kuropatkinsky, twenty kilometers from Ashkhabad, where a church was formed and continued into the twentieth century. In time a Russian congregation was organized in Ashkhabad itself. In 1913 there were 410 Baptists and 220 Evangelical Christians in the territory.

From 1937 to 1944 the regime suppressed the Ashkhabad congregation, and a number of believers left. The church revived and in 1983 dedicated its church building, a house which it had renovated. In the early 1990s the church had thirty-nine members, including three Turkmen but no elder and was led by an older woman of the congregation. There was another congregation at Nebitdag with fifty members and a third in Krasnovodsk with eighteen. Five Baptists lived in Mary. The Central Asian Christian Mission, a Baptist mission in Tashkent, has undertaken evangelistic and welfare work in the republic. In addition, Licht im Osten provides literature in the Russian and Turkmen languages and supports missionaries at work in the country. The few Baptists are members of the Union of Evangelical Christians-Baptists of Central Asia.

BIBLIOGRAPHY: For a review of Baptist work in Turkmenistan, see *Istoriya evangel'skikh khristian-baptistov v SSSR* (Moscow, 1989), 508–9. For material on evangelical sectarians in Turkmenistan, see A. M. Chiperis, "Sovremennoe sektantstvo v Turkmenskoĭ SSR (Contemporary Sectarianism in Turkmen SSR), Turkmen Academy of Sciences, *Izvestiya*, no. 5 (1964): 74–82, and A. A. Zav'yalov, "Proniknovenie khristianskogo sektantstva v Zakaspiĭskuyu oblast'" (Penetration of Christian Sectarianism in the Trans-Caspian Region), Turkmen Academy of Sciences, *Izvestiya*, no. 1 (1973): 72–75. For a recent account on Baptists in Turkmenistan, see the report by B. N. Serin in *Khristianskoe slovo*, Jan. 1992, 3.

UKRAINE (GERMANS, 1864; UKRAINIANS, 1869)

	Members	Churches
1. Union of Evangelical Christians-Baptists (1992)	106,581	(1,301)
2. Reform (non-registered) Baptists	38,900	n/a
3. Autonomous congregations	15,000	n/a
	160,481	(1,400)

STATISTICS: Patrick Johnstone in *Operation World* (Grand Rapids: Zondervan, 1993), estimates 162,000 members in 1,400 congregations for the three Baptist groups (p. 551). Statistics for the Union of Evangelical Christians-Baptists are from *Khristianskoe slovo*, March 1994, 10. The editor has estimated the membership of the Reform Baptists by subtracting their memberships in Kazakhstan and Russia, as reported in *Operation World*, from the total membership represented by delegates at the Reform Baptist conference in Tula in 1993. The editor has estimated the membership of the autonomous congregations by subtracting their membership in Russia, as reported in *Operation World*, from the membership as reported in Sabrina Petra Ramet, ed., *Protestantism and Politics in Eastern Europe and Russia* (Durham and London: Duke University Press, 1992), 274.

*W*ithin the CIS, Ukraine has more evangelical believers than any other republic and includes half of the Baptists. About 1859 and 1860 three movements appeared simultaneously, each interacting on each other, helping to produce the present body of Evangelical Christians-Baptists.

The first movement occurred in 1859. German Baptists began to settle in Volhynia in the western Ukraine, where in May 1864 they established two congregations at Horczik and Soroczin, the first Baptist churches in the territory. In 1869 German Baptists also established a congregation farther east at Neu-Danzig. In 1860 a Mennonite Brethren movement arose, breaking from other Mennonites upon their insistence of a regenerate church membership. Because of Baptist influence, two of their members in the same year immersed each other, introducing this baptismal mode into their ranks. The third movement happened about 1860 when Ukrainian peasants, influenced by German stundists, began to meet for devotions. In 1869 a member of the Mennonite Brethren immersed one of them, an action which began a Ukrainian Stundo-Baptist movement. In 1884 Ukrainian Baptists, with support from Baptists in the Caucasus, formed a Russian Baptist Union. In spite of serious persecution in the nineteenth century, Baptists continued to grow.

After the Communist revolution, Ukrainian Baptists formed an All-Ukrainian Baptist Union, holding its first congress in Kiev in 1918. From that date to 1928 they held five congresses and in 1926 began to publish their own journal. During the years of famine and religious persecution in the 1930s, Ukrainian Baptists suffered heavily. With a change in religious policy in the 1940s, they gained greater freedom, although still under government control. Despite their membership in the All-Union Council of Evangelical Christians-Baptists, they had their own senior presbyter, deputy presbyters, and presbyters for various regions.

Today Ukrainian Baptists have a modern headquarters in Kiev. Since 1989, they have published their own Ukrainian journal, *Khrystyyans'ke zhyttya*, besides a paper in Russian. In 1992 they formed an independent Baptist union, which is a member of the Euro-Asiatic Federation and the BWA. The Ukrainian Union is growing rapidly, registering in 1993 a gain of more than one hundred new congregations. In Kiev today there are more than ten Baptist churches. The union sponsors fifty missionaries, and evangelism is conducted in educational institutions, military units, and prisons. Preaching is in eleven languages. There are also important bodies of Reform (non-registered) and autonomous Baptists. While Pentecostals are stronger than Baptists in western Ukraine, Baptists lead overall and are the stronger body in the central and eastern sections.

Baptist missions from abroad have entered the Ukraine, including several Russian/Ukrainian agencies from North America, in addition to many nondenominational groups. The Light in the East Mission from Germany is a partner of the Light of the Gospel Mission, a Ukrainian mission which works throughout the CIS.

Ukrainian Baptists sponsor a theological seminary in Kiev, a Bible school in Odessa, and Bible institutes with extension programs in seven centers. The Euro-Asian Federation has established a seminary in Odessa. Denver Conservative Baptist Seminary cooperates with the Light of the Gospel Mission in sponsoring the Light of the Gospel Bible College in Rovno, Ukraine.

BIBLIOGRAPHY: See *Istoriya evangel'skikh khristian-baptistov v SSSR* (Moscow, 1989), 52–73, 297–301, 482–96, for material on Baptists in the Ukraine. L. Zabko-Potapowicz wrote a Ukrainian work, *Khrystove svitlo v Ukraïni* (Winnipeg, Man., and Chester, Pa., 1952), which suggests 1852 as the origin of Ukrainian Baptists. For a recent report on Ukrainian Baptists by Ya. K. Dukhonchenko, late president of the Ukrainian Union, see *Khristianskoe slovo*, Oct./Nov. 1992, 12.

6. Lithuania	320	6
7. Norway	5,652	66
8. Sweden	<u>49,862</u>	<u>722</u>
	76,704	1,028

DENMARK (1839)

	Members	Churches
Danske Baptistsamfund (Danish Baptist Union) (1849/1888)	5,805	(45)

*B*aptists in Denmark arose in the 1830s from a religious awakening within the Lutheran state church. They were to become instrumental in the realization of religious liberty in Denmark in the Constitution of 1849. Previously, Baptist infants were baptized by compulsion, and Baptists were fined and imprisoned. Baptist work first began when Julius Köbner, a Danish Jew and coworker with J. G. Oncken, the German Baptist leader, visited Denmark in 1839 and met with individuals who already had Baptist views. Oncken baptized the converts and established the first church in Copenhagen in 1839.

The Danish Baptist Union was part of the German Baptist Union from 1849 to 1888, when they oriented themselves westwards, partly because 25 percent of the Danish Baptists emigrated to the USA before 1900. The Danish Baptist Union, reconstructed in 1888, accepted the New Hampshire Confession instead of the German Confession of 1847, and for a generation Danish Baptist pastors were educated at Morgan Park Seminary near Chicago. Because of these roots, Danish Baptists have always had an international perspective and have always participated in international Baptist life—the BWA since 1905 and EBF since 1948. The New Hampshire Confession never became important to Danish Baptists, and today their constitution has no confessional basis. Gradually their profile has become less Calvinistic, more Lutheran and ecumenical, moving from a "closed" Baptist tradition to an "open" style with open communion since the 1930s. Since the 1980s they occasionally have accepted membership from infant-baptizing traditions. Since 1918 Danish Baptists have had their own theological seminary.

Danish Baptists have always been a small minority—one Baptist for almost 1,000 Danes, with about 6,000 members today, but their influence has been more significant than such figures suggest. In the last fifty years, they have played an active role in the national ecumenical movement, participating in the Danish Bible Society, Dan Church Aid, the Danish Mission Council, and the Danish *Kirchen Tage*. They have tried to bring together the Lutheran state church (which claims 88 percent of the population), the other small denominations, and the Roman Catholic Church, having good relations with all Christians in a secularized and post-Christian society. Internationally, Danish Baptists have been a member of the World Council of Churches since 1948 but have also participated in the Lausanne Movement and have been inspired by the charismatic movement.

In this multi-faceted spiritual situation, they seek their identity as an open, cooperating, evangelical Baptist movement. This is partly done by church planting both as a union and as local congregations, especially since the beginning of the 1980s. In the last decade five new churches have been established, but membership has declined over the past twenty-five years. Today the Danish Baptist Union numbers forty-five congregations. Since they are a little more than 150 years old, tradition is important in Danish Baptist life, but they are also concerned about their transformation for the future. Tensions inevitably appear, but annual conferences, engagement in mission, and an open dialogue among the pastors have prevented schisms.

The mission of the church has developed along traditional lines. In home missions, the local congregations dominate. This work, which includes an evangelistic dimension, involves the nurture of children, youth groups, and scouts. In foreign missions, Danish Baptists since 1928 have directed their efforts to Burundi and Rwanda in Africa, where they have cooperated with the new African Baptist unions since 1960. Since Denmark has been receiving different ethnic and religious groups from abroad, Danish Baptists now need to orient themselves to minister in a multicultural society. In education, Danish Baptists formed primary schools because of malice from the Lutherans, but today they maintain only two folk high schools, one at Rebild and another at Tølløse, which is also the location of the seminary. They have issued a weekly paper since 1854 as well as other literature.

In earlier years Baptists came from the lower classes of agricultural and urban workers, but most Baptists today belong to the upper middle class. Danish Baptists participate in the political and cultural life of the country. Two Baptists are presently members of the Danish parliament, and a Dane, Knud Wümpelmann, was elected president of the BWA in 1990.

Bent Hylleberg

BIBLIOGRAPHY: See Bent Hylleberg and Bjarne Moller Jorgensen, *Et kirkesamfund bliver til: Danske baptisters historie gennem 150 år* (Brande, Denmark: Føltveds Forlag, 1989), for a 150th anniversary history of Danish Baptists. For an article in English by the president of the Danish Baptist Theological Seminary at that time, see Johannes Norgaard, "The Rise of the Baptist Churches in Denmark," *Chronicle*, 10 (1947): 146–60.

ESTONIA (1884)

	Members	Churches
1. Union of Evangelical Christians-Baptists (1896)	6,511	(84)
2. Seventh Day Baptists (late 1920s)	60	(1)
	6,571	(85)

*T*he small republic of Estonia, predominantly Lutheran in religious heritage, regained its independence in 1991 after its annexation by the USSR in 1940. When Baptists entered the country in the nineteenth century, it was then part of the Russian Empire.

As a result of a revival brought by Swedish missionaries in the 1870s, beginning on the island of Worms and spreading to the mainland, some individuals began to baptize believers by sprinkling. After discovering Baptists in St. Petersburg, they invited Adam R. Schiewe (1843–1930), pastor of the German Baptist church of St. Petersburg, to visit them. On February 23, 1884, he immersed fourteen believers in the Baltic Sea at Haapsalu. Two days later, in spite of threats, Schiewe baptized thirteen others and two more the next day, making a total of twenty-nine. For some years Schiewe undertook mission journeys into Estonia, including visits to Tallinn (then called Reval) and the islands of Vormsi and Dagö. At the same time, Julius Herrmann, pastor of the German Baptist church in Riga, went to Pärnu in southern Estonia and on August 31, 1884, at midnight baptized seven believers, products of the same awakening, who had also heard about Baptists.

In spite of persecution, Estonian Baptists began forming independent congregations with the first three in 1894 at Haapsalu, Kärdla, and Tallinn, and establishing in 1896 an association that belonged to the Union of Baptist Churches in Russia, composed primarily of Germans. In 1904 a paper, *Teekäija* (The Pilgrim), edited by Andres Teterman, appeared. By 1908 there were 2,435 members in twenty churches. The First World War, however, brought suffering with the closure of churches and exile of pastors.

With Estonian independence in 1918, the association became the Estonian Baptist Union. With the assistance of British Baptists and Northern Baptists in the USA, Estonian Baptists continued to make progress. Between 1922 to 1929 a seminary at Keila (Kegal) operated with Adam Podin (b. 1862), a Latvian, as rector. Earlier in his career, Podin had ministered to inmates in Russian prisons and continued his ministry to prisoners and lepers in Estonia. In 1931 a new seminary opened in Tallinn. In 1939 Estonian Baptists numbered 7,508 in fifty-one churches.

During the first Soviet occupation of Estonia (1940–1941), the regime closed a number of churches and exiled Baptist ministers and lay members. The Soviets returned after the German occupation (1941-1944), but five to six hundred Estonian Baptists fled the country, including a number of ministers. Because of the warfare, a number of church buildings were destroyed.

Under political pressure, Estonian Baptists joined in 1945 the All-Union Council of Christians-Baptists in the USSR as did also the Evangelical Christians, Evangelical Christian Free, and Pentecostals. In 1950 the regime compelled the merger of most of the free-church congregations in Tallinn; at the same time, the union congregation was given Oleviste Cathedral, a German Lutheran structure which had been built in the thirteenth century. It could seat two thousand but four thousand or more could crowd in. Under the outstanding leadership of its pastor and theologian, Oswald Tärk (1904–1984), the Oleviste Church became a dynamic evangelical center, known throughout the Soviet Union. It held both youth and healing services and was under strong Pentecostal influence from Finland. Tärk prepared correspondence courses for pastors. In their union with other groups, Baptists maintained their numbers rather well. They reported 8,273 members in 84 churches in 1968, including 1,400 in the

Oleviste Church, despite the decline in the small rural churches and restrictions imposed by the Soviet regime, especially in evangelism and youth work.

With the renewal of Estonian independence, Baptists again have full religious freedom. As early as 1989 they again published *Teekäija*, which had been suspended since 1940, and again operated a small seminary in Tallinn. Although comparatively few, Estonian Baptists, even after the separation of the Pentecostals, are the largest free church in the country. The Estonian Baptist Union includes both Estonian and Russian congregations. As in earlier years, they are undertaking a vigorous program of outreach, including the use of radio.

Seventh Day Baptists have one congregation in Estonia, organized in the late 1920s, at Rakvere. Since 1990 they have published a monthly paper in Rakvere, *Hüüdja Hääl*.

BIBLIOGRAPHY: For a bibliography of Estonian Baptists, see Albert W. Wardin, Jr., *Evangelical Sectarians in the Russian Empire and the USSR: A Bibliographic Guide* (Metuchen, N.J.: Scarecrow Press, 1995), nos. 2248–277, 5024–64, 5808–35. Estonian Baptists produced a twenty-fifth anniversary history, *Eesti Baptisti koguduste ajaloolik Album* (Tallinn: J. Felsberg and A. Tetermann, 1911), and a fiftieth anniversary history by Richard Kaups, *Viiskümmend aastat apostlite radadel, 1884–1934* (Tallinn: Publishing House of the Estonian Baptist Union, 1934). For the beginnings of Estonian Baptist work, see *Der Wahrheitszeuge*, April 15, 1884, 85; May 1, 1884, 96; Feb. 15, 1885, 37; and *Der Sendbote*, Jan. 14, 1885, 14–15. For a contemporary view of Estonian Baptists, see Martha Skelton, "Estonian Baptists: Keeping Up with Opportunities," *Commission*, Jan. 1991, 28–43. For a recent report, see *Khristianskoe slovo*, March 1994, 9.

FINLAND (SWEDISH, 1856; FINNISH, 1870)

	Members	Churches
1. Baptist Union of Finland (Swedish) (1892)	1,594	(21)
2. Finnish Baptist Union (1904)	668	(10)
3. Seventh Day Baptists (1980s)	35	(2)
	2,297	(33)

*T*he Lutheran state church of Finland claims more than 85 percent of the population of the country. Despite Lutheran opposition, the Baptist message came to Finland during the 1850s. In 1856 Swedes founded the first Baptist church in the Åland Islands at a time when Finland was part of the Russian Empire. The first Swedish-speaking church on the mainland was founded in 1870 at Jakobstad (Pietarsaari), with the first baptism performed the year before. Also in 1870, as a result of the preaching of a Finnish sailor by the name of Henriksson, a Finnish-speaking church was established at Luvia with nine members. The Finnish-speaking work developed, however, primarily through Swedish-speaking Baptists.

In 1889 the American Baptist Missionary Union accepted Finland as a mission field, and Baptists in Sweden also sent financial assistance. The status of the Baptist churches improved in 1889 when a law was passed allowing them to register as their own entity. In 1892 Baptists founded a district union in Jakobstad. In the same year I. S. Osterman started *Finska Månadsposten* (Finnish Monthly Mail) for Swedish readers; in 1896 Veikko Palomaa began *Totuuden Kaiku* (Echo of Truth) for Finnish readers. The foremost pioneer in Finnish Baptist work among both Swedes and Finns was Erik Jansson (1848–1927), a Swedish-speaking Finn.

Partly because of language problems, a division occurred between Swedish and Finnish-speaking Baptists. The Finns formed their own conference in 1904. The two language groups still maintain separate unions. Both unions have suffered losses of membership. At its peak the Swedish-speaking union had more than 2,500 members and the Finnish 1,300. The impact of World War I and the rise of Pentecostalism both brought decline.

The two Baptist unions differ theologically to a certain extent. The Finnish-speaking Baptists represent a more fundamentalistic outlook, practice close communion, and may be classified as Pentecostal in piety. The Swedish-speaking Baptists practice open communion and ordain women, while one church has open membership. Charismatic elements are also found among its congregations. There is little cooperation between the two unions, primarily because of language and geography, but also because of differences of emphasis.

Both unions have organized women's, children's, and youth work. Focus is on the worship service, but weekly Bible study and prayer meetings are common. Music is especially important among the Swedish-speaking Baptists. Outreach is mainly by the promotion of evangelistic campaigns. In some areas Baptists are active in local radio work. Finnish-speaking Baptists support itinerant home mission workers who mainly visit the churches. Theological education has developed little. The Finnish-speaking Baptists conduct a Bible institute; Swedish-speaking personnel are trained either at an ecumenical institute, the Åbo Academy, or abroad. Both unions suffer from a lack of pastors.

The Finnish Baptist Union has a publishing house which issues a monthly magazine and occasionally a children's periodical. Recently it has published a computerized version of the Bible. Swedish-speaking Baptists have issued a periodical for more than a hundred years, at present a tabloid which appears every three weeks.

Baptists in Finland conduct foreign mission work through different channels. The Finnish Baptist Union is a member of the European Baptist Mission, while the Baptist Union of Finland cooperates with both Swedish and Danish Baptists and has sent missionaries to Africa, Asia, and South America. An important aspect of more recent mission activity has been projects in the Baltic states, especially in Estonia.

Baptists in Finland, particularly Swedish-speaking, have been active in education and social work. They also have been influential in political life, mainly on a local basis. Members of both Baptist unions represent the middle class, are predominantly female, with the age structure leaning toward the older generation. Leaders and members of the mission boards are late middle age or older; the mission board of the Finnish Baptist Union is solely male.

From the beginning, Baptists in Finland were forerunners for the concept of a free church. With the Free Evangelical, Methodist, and Pentecostal churches, Baptists have formed Free Church Councils for both language groups. These councils serve as forums for matters of common interest and form a united free-church front. The

Swedish-speaking Baptist union is also a member of the Finnish Ecumenical Council, whose General Secretary in 1994 was a Baptist pastor.

In the 1980s a Seventh Day Baptist group began meeting in Turku as a result of the witness of Thomas McElwain, a professor at the University of Turku who was married to a Finn. A second church at Helsinki was organized around 1988. Finnish Seventh Day Baptists publish a paper, *Euroopan Vapaa Sana*, and have formed a Baltic Convention with the Seventh Day Baptist church in Rakvere, Estonia.

Mai-Britt Vehkaoja and Albert W. Wardin, Jr.

BIBLIOGRAPHY: The work by David Edén, *Svenska baptisterna i Finland historia 1856–1931* (Vasa: A. B. Frams, 1931) is a comprehensive 75th anniversary history of Swedish Baptists in Finland. For Finnish-Speaking Baptists, see Euvo Aaltio, *A History of the National Baptists in Finland* (B.D. thesis, Baptist Theological Seminary, Rüschlikon, Switzerland, 1958), and Markku Niskanen, *The Finnish-Speaking Baptists 1896–1922* (B.D. treatise, Baptist Theological Seminary, Rüschlikon, Switzerland, 1984). For an article on Baptists in Finland, see Alfons Sundqvist, "The Baptist Movement in Finland," *Chronicle*, 11 (1948): 3–16. For a recent account on Baptists in the Finnish Baptist Union, see Mike Creswell, "Finland: A Mission Field?" *Commission*, June/July 1988, 10–37.

ICELAND (1962)

	Members	Churches
1. First Baptist Church of Njardvik (1982)	190	(attendance)
2. Baptist Bible Fellowship Mission (1984)	7	(attendance)
	197	

*M*ost Baptist work in Iceland has been among the American military and their families. In February 1962 Wally Rice, a Southern Baptist navy serviceman, and his wife began an English-language Baptist work at the Keflavik base, which was organized as the Keflavik Baptist Church in 1964. Rice served as first pastor of the group. Southern Baptists sent R. W. Terry and his wife to serve the congregation in December 1963; they left three and a half years later. Independent Baptists then assumed responsibility, but the church dissolved.

The Baptist church in Njardvik began in 1982 when another serviceman, John Opferman, an independent Baptist, formed the United Baptist Church of Njardvik and served as its first pastor. It was called "United" since it was formed from three different Baptist Bible study groups on the base at Njardvik but later changed its name to First Baptist Church. The thriving congregation is independent of any Baptist mission abroad. It operates its own radio station and is planning to build a church structure.

These two congregations attempted to witness to native Icelanders but with little success, partly because of the language barrier. With the appointment in 1982 of Mr. and Mrs. Richard M. Smith, the Baptist Bible Fellowship began a mission to reach the native population. The Smiths arrived in 1984 and today lead a small mission which averages a weekly attendance of six or seven. In 1991 Smith baptized the first Icelander, Einer Arnarsson, in a public pool in Njardvik.

BIBLIOGRAPHY; Richard Smith, "Spiritual Coldness Abounds in Iceland," *Baptist Bible Tribune*, June/July, 1993, 24–25. Albert W. Wardin, Jr., gained additional information from correspondence with Richard Smith and telephone conversations with Baptists who had lived in Iceland.

LATVIA (1860)

	Members	Churches
Union of Baptist Churches (1879)	6,000	(70)

*B*efore the existence of an independent Latvia in 1918, most Latvians lived in the provinces of Courland and Livonia in the Russian Empire. The German Baptist church in Memel in East Prussia in Germany (today Klaipeda, Lithuania) became the mother church or "Antioch" of the Baptist movement in these provinces. The first Latvian Baptist, Frizis Jekabsons (Jacobson), was baptized in this church in 1855; at the close of the Crimean War he settled in Libau (today Liepaja). German members of the Memel church also settled in Libau as well as in Grobin, and because of their witness a Latvian Baptist movement took root. Another center was at Windau (now Ventspils), where a group, meeting for prayer and Bible study, adopted Baptist beliefs. After crossing the border in a farmer's cart, Adam Gertners (Gaertner) (1829–1876), his wife, and nine others were baptized in September 1860 in Memel. In 1861 two other groups traveled by sea to avoid the border crossing. In September of the same year, Gertners baptized seventy-two believers, the first on Latvian soil.

Despite harsh persecution, including beating and imprisonment, the Baptist movement grew rapidly in Courland and also spread to Livonia. In 1865 the Russian government in Courland granted freedom to the Baptists, but the Lutheran Church, to which the majority of Latvians belonged, continued its strong opposition. At first all Baptists in Latvia were members of the Memel church with the Latvian congregations as mission stations. In 1875 this church and its twenty-seven stations had 2,780 members, the majority of whom lived in a foreign country! Beginning in 1876 and several years following, the Memel church began to grant independence to its stations, starting first with the one in Riga. In 1879 the Prussian Association granted Latvian Baptists authorization to form the Baltic Association. In 1881 it had 3,944 members.

Unfortunately, relations between the German Baptists and Latvian Baptists deteriorated with the latter resenting their subordination in the German Baptist Union (*Bund*). Jekabs Rumbergs (Jacob Rumberg) (d. 1923), after his exclusion from the Riga church in the mid-1880s, led in the formation of the Baltic Association of Latvian Baptist Churches in Russia with 2,500 members. In 1889 the earlier Baltic Association joined the predominantly German Union of Baptist Churches in Russia. In 1893 the schism was healed when the two Baltic associations united.

Rumbergs began an outstanding tradition of publication in Latvia by establishing his own publishing house. He edited *Ewangelists* from 1880 to 1885, published a hymnal of 647 hymns, and in 1882 wrote *Atbilde* (A Reply), an answer to a Lutheran polemical work. John A. Frey (1863–1950), one of the foremost leaders in Latvian Baptist life, established in the late 1880s a publication house which produced abundant amounts of evangelical literature. William Fetler (1883–1957), noted revivalist of Latvian and German Baltic ancestry, organized congregations in St. Petersburg and Riga, edited Latvian papers and published many Latvian titles before and after World War I.

By 1913 Latvian Baptists had 8,500 members in ninety churches and were giving to home and foreign missions. But World War I brought disruption, including property damage, the closing of Baptist churches, and the banishment of three Baptist pastors, including Frey. In 1917 Latvian Baptists from various parts of Russia replaced their association with a Latvian Baptist Union.

With Latvian independence in 1918, Latvian Baptists now had full freedom but suffered losses with the migration of members to Brazil as well as defection to the Pentecostals. In 1923 delegates at a congress of the Latvian Baptist Union refused to seat Fetler, who headed his own Russian Missionary Society and who was considered uncooperative. This action led Fetler to establish a Second Latvian Baptist Union, a division which continued until 1934. Despite these difficulties, Latvian Baptists continued to grow, assisted by Northern Baptists from the USA and British and Canadian Baptists. They opened a seminary in 1922 and completed in 1934 a five-story Baptist Church House for the Latvian Union and the seminary. In 1929 Oswald J. Smith of Toronto formed the Russian Border Mission, which began mission work in Latgalia, a predominantly Roman Catholic area.

In 1940 Baptists numbered 11,931 in 104 churches. Much hardship resulted from the annexation of Latvia by the Soviet Union in that year, the occupation of the Germans from 1941 to 1944, and the reoccupation by the Soviets until the renewal of Latvian independence in 1991. In 1940 the Soviet regime confiscated the Church House and closed the seminary, publication work, and a number of churches in addition to deporting Baptist leaders. With the return of the Soviets in 1944, a Baptist community of three thousand fled the country. In 1945 Latvian Baptists became members of the All-Union Council of Evangelical Christians-Baptists, maintaining, however, an administrative center in Riga, headed by a senior presbyter who bore the title of bishop. Membership declined to 4,500.

With the reforms under Gorbachev and the reestablishment of Latvian independence, Latvian Baptists are now experiencing renewal. They have regained lost properties, such as the Church House and Fetler's large Salvation Temple in Riga. They have opened a seminary and resumed publication work, issuing a calendar and several journals, including *Lāba Vēsts* (Good News). They also continue their outstanding choral tradition.

In 1988 Vadim Kovalev, minister of the Russian congregation in Riga, began the Latvian Christian Mission, a nondenominational agency, the first in the Soviet Union under the Gorbachev reforms. This mission engages in a ministry of evangelization, religious instruction, and welfare as well as mission work in other parts of the former Soviet Union. Important Latvian Baptist communities also exist in Brazil, Canada, and the USA.

BIBLIOGRAPHY: For a bibliography of Latvian Baptists, see Albert W. Wardin, Jr., *Evangelical Sectarians in the Russian Empire and the USSR: A Bibliographic Guide*

(Metuchen, N.J.: Scarecrow Press, 1995), nos. 1852–59, 2159–247, 4944–5008, 5789–806. For a comprehensive history of Latvian Baptists before the First World War, see Janis Riss (Riess), *Latweeschu baptistu draudschu iaszelschanās un winu tahlakā attihstiba* (Riga: Latweeschu baptistu draudschu apgahdibâ, 1913). To commemorate the Latvian Baptist centennial, the Latvian Baptist Union of America produced in 1960 a valuable volume by many authors, *Dzīvības Celš* (The Way of Life), edited by Fridrichs Čukers, R. Ekšteins, and A. Mēters. For a contemporary picture of Latvian Baptists, see Martha Skelton "Latvian Baptists: Reclaiming and Rebuilding," *Commission*, Jan. 1991, 12–27. Also see the reports of Yanis Eisans, Bishop of the Latvian Baptist Union, in *Khristianskoe slovo*, Oct./Nov. 1992, 12–13, and Sep./Oct. 1993, 9.

LITHUANIA (1867) (LATVIANS, 1867; GERMANS, 1889; LITHUANIANS, 1921)

	Members	Churches
1. Union of Free Evangelical Churches (1923)	320	(6)
2. Reform (non-registered) Baptists	n/a	(1)
	320	(6)

*T*he first Baptist church in the present territory of Lithuania was the German Baptist church of Memel (today Klaipeda): it was the first one in East Prussia, organized in 1841 and the mother church of Latvian Baptists. Since this church was in German territory until annexed in 1923 by Lithuania, its history rightly belongs to Germany. Baptist work in Lithuania therefore begins in the provinces of Kovno and Vilna, part of the Russian Empire to 1917.

German Baptists in East Prussia were successful in their work among Protestant Lithuanians in their midst, baptizing the first Lithuanian in 1851. German Baptists sent Karl Albrecht to work among them in 1854, and they also produced Lithuanian tracts and a hymnal. They were very unsuccessful, however, in gaining adherents among the largely Roman Catholic population across the border in Russia. The first Baptists to form congregations there were persecuted Latvian Baptists from Courland, who settled near the border in Kovno Province, establishing their first congregation in 1867 and later three more.

The German Baptist church of Eydtkuhnen in East Prussia proved to be another base. It extended its work through mission stations across the border into Russia, which included forming a mission in Kovno. Through the efforts of August H. Stoltenhof, who moved to the city in 1886, a German Baptist church was organized on February 23, 1889. Even though its members were scattered during World War I, the church survived, gaining assistance from German Baptists in North America. The congregation also worked among Russians and gained a few Lithuanians.

Lithuania gained its independence in 1918 and in 1923 annexed Memelland. The annexation significantly added to the Baptist community in Lithuania, which at the time had only 220 members. Memelland had 300 Lithuanian Baptists in four congregations and 420 German Baptists, including the historic German Baptist church of Memel. German Baptists also published their own paper, *Missionsklänge*. They were now the predominant group in Lithuania among the Latvian, Russian, and Lithuanian believers. Work among native Lithuanians in the former provinces of Kovno and Vilna, however, was still in its infancy. With the assistance of British Baptists and Northern Baptists from the USA, Teodoras Gerikas (1891–1947), of Lithuanian and Latvian parentage, began serving as a missionary/colporteur in Memelland in 1921 and then in Lithuania itself. He established a preaching center in a small hall in Šiauliai, where he organized a church in 1927. After moving to Kovno (Kaunas) in 1932, Gerikas formed a church there. Two years later he organized a Russian congregation in Kaunas. In January 1924 he began issuing *Tiesos Draugas* (Friend of Truth), a Lithuanian Baptist paper which continued until 1940.

In 1923 a Joint Committee of Cooperation was formed to coordinate Baptist work among the various nationalities with German Baptists continuing their membership in the Baptist Union of Germany. In 1924 there were ten churches and 1,094 members. In Memel in 1933, Baptists in Lithuania formed their own union, which still did not include all congregations.

The annexation of Memel by Germany in 1939, the later departure of the German population from the rest of Lithuania, and the incorporation of Lithuania into the Soviet Union in 1940 severely affected the Baptist cause but it survived. In 1945 Lithuanian Baptists, joined by Pentecostals, became part of the All-Union Council of Evangelical Christians-Baptists of the Soviet Union with their own senior presbyter. In the late 1980s there were only four registered Baptist churches, and these included many Pentecostal members. There was an active church in Vilnius, a union in 1948 of the Baptist and Pentecostal congregations, which conducted preaching in Lithuanian, Polish, and Russian; a Lithuanian church in Klaipeda, organized in 1968; a Latvian congregation in Ilakyaĭ; and a fourth church in Biržai, which arose from people with Lithuanian Reformed antecedents.

With the renewal of Lithuanian independence, Baptists face a new future. Pentecostals in 1991 formed their own union, leaving Baptists with only 160 members. At a conference in June 1992, Baptists resumed their existence as an independent union—the Union of Free Evangelical Churches–Baptist in belief and polity. They applied for reinstatement into the BWA. Today they number 320 members in six churches and in 1993 baptized about 100 converts. They engage in Sunday School and youth work as well as in a prison ministry. Preaching is conducted in Lithuanian, Latvian, and Russian, but Russian believers are a small minority. There is an unregistered Baptist church in Klaipeda. Since Lithuanian Baptists lack a Bible school, they organize short-term seminars to train leaders. Recently, Baptist Bible Fellowship International has appointed missionary personnel to the country, and the FMB of the Southern Baptist Convention is considering doing the same.

BIBLIOGRAPHY: For a bibliography of Baptists in Lithuania, see Albert W. Wardin, Jr., *Evangelical Sectarians in the Russian Empire and the USSR: A Bibliographic Guide* (Metuchen, N.J.: Scarecrow Press, 1995), nos. 1441–42, 1860–68, 4923–39, 5781–88. For a short historical account, see *Istoriya evangel'skikh khristian-baptistov v SSSR* (Moscow: All-Union Council of Evangelical Christians-Baptists, 1989), 372–79. For material in English, see J. H. Rushbrooke, *Some Chapters of European Baptist History* (London: Kingsgate Press, 1929), 72–79. For a recent report by Albert Latuzhis, the president of the Lithuanian Union, see *Khristianskoe slovo*, Sep./Oct. 1993, 9, and March 1994, 9.

NORWAY (1860)

	Members	Churches
1. Det Norske Baptistsamfunn (Norwegian Baptist Union) (1877)	5,577	(64)
2. Independent churches (ABWE) (1978)	<u>75</u>	<u>(2)</u>
	5,652	(66)

*I*n 1837 a young Norwegian, Enoch Richard Haftorsen Svee, went to Copenhagen in Denmark to prepare for foreign mission work. There he became a Baptist and in 1842 returned to Norway, supported by American Baptists through Johann G. Oncken of Hamburg. Svee died the following year before his labors resulted in the establishment of a Baptist work.

The founder of Baptists in the country was a former Danish sailor, Frederick Ludvig Rymker. He worked in Norway from 1857 to 1862 and established several Baptist churches. The first was the Baptist Church of Porsgrund and Solum (now Skien), formed on April 22, 1860. During the following years, Baptist work spread to most parts of Norway, especially through such men as the Norwegian Gottfried Hübert, supported by the Baptist Missionary Society of England, and a former Swedish blacksmith, Ola B. Hansson, who led revivals in several places and became the great leader of Baptist work in northern Norway for twenty-five years.

Norwegian Baptists formed their first district association in 1872 and a Baptist union in 1879. In 1876 there were 14 churches and 511 members. Twenty years later there were 26 churches with 2,132 members, a remarkable growth in a country with a strong confessional Lutheran state church.

In 1904 Mons A. Öhrn predicted in a lecture that in the next twenty-five years the number of Baptists would quintuple. This did not happen. Until 1920 the work grew, even though the new Pentecostal movement attracted many Baptists. In one year the Southern District Association lost almost a third of its membership but even so experienced net growth! The 1920s were years of slower growth and organizational consolidation. From 1932 to 1937 some churches experienced exceptional growth, and during World War II the denomination attracted new members. In 1948 the Baptist Union reached a peak in membership with 7,436 members. Since 1948 there have been ebbs and flows. In the 1950s and again in the 1970s there was a slight increase in some years. On the whole, however, the Baptist Union has declined over the last forty years by some 2,000.

The Baptists of Norway have always enjoyed a closely knit fellowship. No major divisions have taken place, although a handful of churches have left the union, either to identify themselves with the Pentecostal movement or to become independent. At present there are three English-language churches. One is the North Sea Baptist Church in Stavanger in cooperation with the Union. Two other small congregations, attracting few Norwegians, cooperation with the Association of Baptists for World Evangelism (ABWE) in the USA.

In the beginning Norwegian Baptists were recruited from the working class: industrial workers, tenants, fishermen, farmers, and the like. Due both to upward social mobility among Baptists and a general transformation of the population, the majority of Baptists today belong to the middle class.

Local churches have carried on the national ministry through church planting and lay evangelism. The Baptist Union and district associations, however, have employed trained evangelists. From 1970 to 1975 a German Baptist minister worked as National Secretary of Evangelism, partly supported by the Southern Baptists. Four Baptist churches have Vietnamese groups, sponsoring worship services and educational programs in the Vietnamese language. During the summer, a few churches conduct worship in English, although not on a regular basis.

Sunday Schools traditionally have been for children up to the age of fourteen. Between 1966 and 1973 a serious attempt was made to introduce the all-age Sunday School; program material was produced and courses for teachers and other personnel were held. Even though several churches started such work, none was established on a permanent basis. Bible study groups and meetings on weekdays proved to be far more attractive.

In 1922 Norwegian Baptists established the Norwegian Baptist Youth Association. This organization is now the most important agent for evangelization. Some Baptist churches have held men's meetings from time to time, but no organized men's work exists. On the other hand, women's societies in local churches with a special interest in foreign missions have been a feature of Baptist life from the beginning. In 1916 the Norwegian Baptist Women's Association was formed.

After supporting and sending out missionaries to Africa through the American Baptist Missionary Union, beginning in 1892, the Baptist Union formed its own foreign ministry in 1915. In 1918 it sent Bernhard Aalbu, who opened a field in the Belgian Congo (now Zaire) in 1920. Since 1946 a seamen's church in San Francisco has been supported as a joint project with other Scandinavian Baptist unions and the American Baptist Churches in the USA (ABC). In more recent years Norwegian Baptists have sent missionaries to Nepal. They also engage in relief and evangelistic work in the former Soviet Union.

Norwegian Baptists began a theological seminary in 1910. In 1971 it added a one-year Bible school course and since 1988 a two-year extension course for lay leaders. The number of students during the last decade has varied from fifteen to forty-five. Many Baptist ministers have continued their theological education at the Baptist seminary in Rüschlikon, Switzerland. In 1958 they began a folk high school. Both the seminary and high school receive some government grants. In theology Norwegian Baptists might best be described as open conservative.

Both on a local and a national level, Norwegian Baptists have participated in ecumenical projects and organizations, often pioneering such initiatives. This applies, for example, to the National Free Church Sunday School Association, the Free Church Council, the Norwegian Faith and Order Forum, and the National Council of Churches. Relations with the Church of Norway (the Lutheran state church) have changed from conflict in earlier years to mutual respect, dialogue, and cooperation at present. The Baptist Union is not a member of the World Council of Churches but has very close ties with Baptists in Scandinavia and within the EuEBF and the BWA. Two Norwegian Baptists, Arnold T. Ohrn and Josef Nordenhaug, both served long terms as general secretaries of the BWA.

Peder A. Eidberg

BIBLIOGRAPHY: A good reference in English is Peder Stiansen, *History of the Baptists in Norway* (Chicago: The Blessing Press, 1933). For a Norwegian work, see Peder A. Eidberg, *Baptisterne—tro og liv* [The Baptists—Beliefs and Ethos] (Oslo: Norsk Litteraturselskap, 1976). On church-state issues, see Frederick Hale, "The Norwegian Baptist Quest for Toleration," *Foundations* 20 (1979): 293–305.

SWEDEN (1848)

	Members	Churches
1. Svenska baptistsamfundet (Baptist Union of Sweden) (1857)	20,124	(318)
2. Fribaptistsamfundet/Helgelseförbundet (Free Baptist Union/Holiness Union) (1872/1887)	7,000	(150)
3. Öbrebromissionen (Örebro Mission) (1892)	22,738	(254)
	49,862	(722)

One of the early successes of the Baptist movement on the continent of Europe was in Sweden. Baptists were beneficiaries of a religious awakening, influenced by revivals in England and the United States. Pietists appeared, whose members were called *läsare* (readers) because in their own circles or at home they read the Scripture and other devotional material. The state Lutheran Church, fearing division, opposed the revival movement. State authorities used the Conventicle Placard of 1726 to break up pietistic circles and punish their adherents.

The Swedish Baptist movement began inauspiciously. On September 21, 1848, A. P. Förster, a Danish Baptist preacher, sent by the German Baptist church of Hamburg, Germany, baptized five converts at Vallersvik, south of Göteborg. At the baptism was Frederick O. Nilsson (1809–1881), a Bible colporteur. Nilsson, through the influence of G. W. Schroeder, a sea captain, had accepted Baptist views and had already been baptized by J. G. Oncken in 1847 in Hamburg. One of the baptismal candidates was Nilsson's wife and two were his brothers. That evening in the home of Bernhardt N. Nilsson the first Baptist church in Sweden was constituted with six members. In the following spring, F. O. Nilsson went to Hamburg for ordination but soon after his return was tried before the church consistory. In 1851 Baptists formed the first Sunday School in the country.

The Baptists suffered intense persecution, and in 1851 the authorities forced Nilsson's banishment. At that time there were only fifty-six Baptists in scattered localities. After two years in Copenhagen, Nilsson and his wife settled in the USA, where he did pioneer mission work. Upon receiving a pardon from King Charles XV, Nilsson returned to his native land in 1860, serving the newly formed church at Göteborg from 1861 to 1868 but soon afterwards returned to the USA.

The struggling Baptists were most fortunate to gain Anders Wiberg (1816–1887), a priest of the Lutheran state church, who became the foremost Swedish Baptist leader in the nineteenth century. He became an adherent of the revival movement and at first opposed believer's baptism but later wrote a book defending it. On a trip to the USA in 1852, Nilsson baptized Wiberg in Copenhagen. In America he was ordained and employed by the American Baptist Publication Society (ABPS), writing and translating. Upon his return to Sweden in 1855 with the support of the ABPS, he became pastor of the Baptist church in Stockholm and wrote the first Swedish Baptist confession of faith, which was widely adopted. In 1856 Wiberg began editing a periodical called *Evangelisten* and formed a mission society, which sent out colporteurs supported by the ABPS. Through his initiative, Swedish Baptists began to hold general conferences, which helped to bring unified action. The Swedish Baptist movement grew rapidly. By the time of the third conference in 1861 there were almost five thousand members in 125 churches, including a congregation in the Åland Islands, located between Sweden and Finland and under the rule of the Russian Empire. Unlike the German pattern which organized only churches which had reached a certain strength and could mother mission stations, Swedish Baptists formed the smallest groups into organized congregations.

After a stay in the USA from 1863 to 1866, Wiberg returned to Sweden, accompanied by K. O. Broady and J. A. Edgren who came as missionaries. In 1866 the ABPS transferred its support of the Swedish work to the American Baptist Missionary Union (ABMU). The general conference of 1866 approved the support of the ABMU and the establishment of a seminary (Betelseminariet). It also elected Broady as president of the school, with Wiberg, Edgren, and two others as members of the faculty. The ABMU continued support until almost the end of the century. It was not until 1889 that the general conference formed a Swedish Baptist Union, whose work was executed by five committees, including one for home missions and one for foreign missions. In 1867 a second publication, *Nyhetsbladet*, appeared, which changed its name in December 1868 to *Vecko-Posten*. In 1919 it came under the control of the Union. In 1880 Swedish Baptists published their first hymnal.

Although persecution began to abate, Baptists as dissenters from the church did not get any significant relief until 1873 when an act which included civil marriage was passed. It was not until 1952, however, that Swedish Baptist pastors could officially preside at a marriage and Swedish Baptists could leave the state church without forfeiting any civil rights. Swedish Baptists continued to grow rapidly. In 1874 there were 225 churches and more than 10,000 members; in 1914 there were 635 churches, 21 district associations, and more than 54,000 members. Swedish Baptists established a number of institutions, which included a Baptist Young Peoples' Association (1905), Publication Society (1919), folk high school at Sjövik (1921), Nurses' and Deaconesses' Association (1922), orphanage for boys (1932), and hostel for young men (1951), besides homes for the aged and musical and mission associations. Swedish Baptists helped to encourage Baptist work in Norway and supported mission work in the Russian Empire in Finland, Estonia, and St. Petersburg. They also extended assistance to missionaries in Spain, China, the Congo (Zaire), and later aid to India, Japan, Thailand and several European countries.

At the general conference of 1858 the issue of close versus open communion was debated with the German representatives arguing for close communion while the English representatives supported the latter view. The conference decided to allow each church to follow its own practice, but close communion became the prevailing practice. Today, however, there has been a shift to open communion. Since the 1950s Swedish Baptists began to accept women pastors.

Swedish Baptists suffered a small defection when the Free Baptist Union was formed in 1872 under the leadership of Helge Åkesson. There were doctrinal differences over reconciliation, justification, and sanctification. Although Free Baptists have remained a small group, they nevertheless developed a successful foreign mission program with fields in South Africa, Mozambique, Zambia, China, Hong Kong, and more recently in Portugal. Free Baptists merged in 1993 with the Swedish Holiness Union.

The entry of the Pentecostal movement into Sweden in the early twentieth century caused Swedish Baptists further division. One of the pastors who accepted Pentecostalism was Lewi Pethrus of the Filadelfia Church of Stockholm. In 1913 the Baptist district association excluded the church ostensibly over its practice of open communion, but its adherence to Pentecostalism was the basic issue. Pethrus, who helped to imprint Baptist polity upon Pentecostalism in Scandinavia, made the Filadelfia Church the flagship of the Pentecostal movement in this part of the world. In the 1930s Swedish Baptists suffered further division from the Örebro movement. John Ongman, pastor of the Filadelfia Church of Örebro, founded the Örebro Mission in 1892, which not only developed an independent mission program but also became favorably inclined toward Pentecostalism. During his life Ongman remained loyal to the Swedish Baptist Union, but after his death in 1931 new leaders wanted to follow an independent course. They criticized leaders of the Swedish Union for their participation in the ecumenical movement and opposition to Pentecostalism. In 1936 the Filadelfia Church left the union, which was followed by other congregations. There are cordial relations today between the Swedish Union and the Örebro Mission with many on both sides feeling that the division should never have occurred. Today the two groups share a publishing house, Lilris, and cooperate in other ventures. Both organizations are about equal in size, but together they number more than eleven thousand less than the membership of the Swedish Union eighty years before. In spite of the division and loss of members, both the Baptist Union and the Örebro Mission continue as vigorous Christian bodies. The Örebro Mission has developed an outstanding record in foreign missions, establishing work in Latin America, Asia, and Africa.

The Swedish Baptist Union was a charter member of the Baptist World Alliance in 1905. In 1913 it hosted a European Baptist congress and in 1923 and 1975 two world congresses of the BWA. All three Swedish Baptist groups are members of the Swedish Free Church Council, while the Baptist Union and Örebro Mission are also members of the Swedish Evangelical Alliance. The Swedish Union belongs to the Swedish Ecumenical Council but not the World Council of Churches.

BIBLIOGRAPHY: For a detailed and well-illustrated centennial history of Swedish Baptists, see George Fridén, ed., *Svensk baptism genom 100 år* (Stockholm: Baptistmissionens Bokförlag, 1948). For a history of Swedish Baptist foreign mission work to 1916, see J. Byström, *Sådd och Skörd* (Stockholm: Ernst Westerbergs, 1916). For a centennial history of Free Baptists, see *Fribaptistsamfundet 100 år* (Habo: Fribaptistsamfundets Forlag, 1972), and the mission work of the Free Baptists, see Eric Hansson and Barbro Wennberg, eds., *Mission genom hundra år* (Tidaholm: Fribaptistsamfundets Förlag, 1991). For a 75th anniversary history of the Örebro Society, see *"...men Gud gav växten"* (Örebromissionens Förlag, 1967), and for a centennial history see G. Sundströn, *100 år i ord och bild, Örelromissionen 1892–1992* (Örebro: Lilris, 1992).. For helpful material in English, see Mrs. M. F. Anderson, *The Baptists in Sweden* (Philadelphia: American Baptist Publication Society, c. 1860); H. Danielson, "Swedish Baptist Union," in *Baptist Work in Denmark, Finland, Norway and Sweden* (Stockholm: Baptistmissionens Bokförlag, 1947); Nils Sundholm, "Baptists in Sweden," *Baptist Quarterly*, 15 (Oct. 1953): 182–87; and Magnus Lindvall, "Anders Wiberg: Swedish Revivalist and Baptist Leader," *Baptist Quarterly*, 32 (Oct. 1987): 172–80.

BAPTIST AND BAPTIST-RELATED MISSIONS

1. DENMARK   SBC (1990), ABA

2. ESTONIA SBC (1993)

3. FINLAND BM-M (1980), SBC (1984), SDBMS (1987)

4. ICELAND BBFI (1984)

5. LATVIA   SBC (1993), CaUSC, GerMF, RBS, R-UEBU, UkRAD

6. LITHUANIA BBFI (1991), RBS

7. NORWAY   BBFI (1971), BIMI (1973), ABWE (1978), SBC (1982), BMA, MBM

8. SWEDEN EBM (1974), RBMS

NONDENOMINATIONAL MISSION

1. LATVIA   GerLIO in cooperation with the Latvian Christian Mission

E. SOUTHEASTERN EUROPE

Baptists had difficulty entering southeastern Europe. In this territory, stretching from the Danubian basin in Hungary through the Balkans to the Aegean Sea, live numerous nationalities, generally divided between the Roman Catholic and Orthodox faiths with Protestant and Moslem minorities. Except for Hungary and Romania, Baptists are small, struggling minorities. In territory south of the Drava and Danube Rivers there are, with the exclusion of Dobruja, only five thousand Baptists. On the other hand, Baptists are the largest free-church group in Romania and one of the most vigorous Baptist bodies in all of Europe.

Baptists of the area reflect the diverse multiethnic character of the region with even the smallest Baptist bodies including various nationalities. Before World War II, German settlers were an important factor in planting the Baptist witness. Equally important was the work of colporteurs of the British and Foreign Bible Society (BFBS) who, through their witness and distribution of Scripture, helped to plant the gospel. Because of the influence of Edward Millard, a British Baptist who was the representative of the BFBS in Vienna, and Baptist colporteurs who served with him, Baptist ideals were spread. Other Baptist colporteurs worked farther east in Bulgaria and Turkish-held territory. Reported aggressiveness of the Baptist colporteurs caused the BFBS to send an investigator in the 1870s. He reported that Millard exercised no undue bias in selecting Baptists, since of the forty-nine colporteurs under him only fourteen were Baptists, who were probably appointed because they were more ardent in seeking converts. This report nevertheless shows that Baptists, as small as they were in Continental Europe at this time, had a significant number in colportage and were already known for their zeal.

Except for a few agencies, Baptists from abroad have shown little interest in southeastern Europe until recently. Baptists in Germany provided some financial assistance before World War I. Between the First and Second World Wars German Baptists of North America supported a Danubian mission, while Southern Baptists entered Hungary, Romania, and Yugoslavia. The four decades of Communist control of the area brought great injury, and some Baptist leaders, particularly in Romania and Bulgaria, underwent great suffering for their faith. Baptists today are showing vigor and, with assistance from abroad, are engaged in an extensive program of evangelization. Besides Southern Baptists and North American Baptists (the former German Baptists of North America), a number of independent conservative/fundamentalist Baptist missions are now present. In the former Yugoslavia, Baptists are also engaged in extensive relief efforts.

In an effort to present a united front before their governments and to gain cooperation from other evangelicals, Baptists have led in forming Evangelical Alliances in their respective countries. These alliances relate to either the European Evangelical Alliance or the World Evangelical Fellowship, if not both. At present Baptists are in leadership positions in Evangelical Alliances in Romania, Bulgaria, and Albania.

	Members	Churches
1. Albania	67	3
2. Bosnia	40	1
3. Bulgaria	2,500	30
4. Croatia	2,030	30
5. Greece	184	1
6. Hungary	11,161	252
7. Macedonia	39	2
8. Romania	109,043	1,422
9. Slovenia	130	4
10. Yugoslavia (Serbia/Montenego)	1,368	51
	126,562	1,796

ALBANIA (1937)

	Members	Churches
1. Korçë Church (1890/1937)	30	(1)
2. Tirana Baptist Church (1994)	37	—
3. Sarande Church (1993)	n/a	(1)
	67	(2)

B ecause of its mountainous terrain, underdeveloped economy, centuries of Turkish rule, and decades of control by an oppressive Communist regime, Albania has been one of the most isolated areas of Europe. In 1967 the Communist government closed all places of worship, declaring Albania to be the world's first atheist state. Since the seventeenth century Albania has had a nominal Moslem majority—about 70 percent before World War II—with the rest divided between Roman Catholic and Orthodox.

The BFBS and the American Board of Commissioners were the only Protestant agencies to work in Albania before World War I. In 1890 Gerasim Quiris (or Kyrias), a convert of the American Board and ordained as an evangelist, moved to Korçë in southeastern Albania where he conducted worship services and began a Sunday School. In 1921 the American Board withdrew from Albania, which left two of their Presbyterian missionaries, Phineas and Violet Kennedy, without support. In 1923 the Kennedys founded the Albanian Evangelical Mission, which continued as the only Protestant mission in the country but received some support from the American

European Fellowship. In 1932 Edwin and Dorothy Jacques, Baptists and graduates of Gordon College of Theology and Missions, joined the mission.

With the retirement of the Kennedys at the end of 1936, Edwin Jacques introduced believer's baptism. In 1937 a convert was baptized in a newly built baptistry. By 1938 thirty-four converts were under instruction for baptism, but local authorities stopped a planned baptismal service by imprisoning three candidates and seizing the one who had been baptized the year before, mistaking him for another candidate. It was not until after the Italian occupation in April 1939 that two of the candidates were finally baptized in a river. Because of World War II and the Italian occupation, all missionaries of the mission were forced to leave. Although Jacques and his wife attempted to return in 1945, deeding the mission property over to the newly formed Conservative Baptist Foreign Mission Society (CBFMS), the recently established Communist regime ended all possibility of mission work. In later years, however, the FMB of the Southern Baptist Convention supported a daily Albanian radio broadcast.

With the opening in 1991 of Albania to the West and the fall of the Communist regime, evangelical missions and missionaries are now flooding into the country, which before had practically been ignored by all Protestants. After forty-seven years of absence, the CBFMS (now CBI) is resuming work with two veteran missionary couples and Korçë as a center. Evangelical work at Korçë had survived miraculously with a few believers who continued to meet in homes. One of them was Ligor Çina, who had been baptized by Jacques in 1939 and was imprisoned a number of times for his witness. Another agency is the Albanian Evangelical Trust (AET), founded in 1986 in Wrexham, Clwyd in Wales, by David Young, a Strict Baptist minister. This mission sent to Korçë Mike Brown, a Baptist who earlier had served among Albanians in Kosovo; AET also supports two non-Baptist missionaries in Tirana.

In 1992 the BWA with other Baptist agencies provided economic aid to Albania and gained permission to open a Baptist center in Tirana, which is operated by the European Baptist Federation and BMS. The BMS sent to Albania two of its medical missionaries—Chris and Mairi Burnett, Scottish Baptists. In September 1993, the center began worship services with preaching by Saverio Guarna of Italy, who baptized seven converts two weeks later. Besides the BMS, a number of other international Baptist organizations cooperate with the center, including the Italian Baptist Union, FMB of the Southern Baptist Convention, Canadian Baptist International Ministries, and Cooperative Baptist Fellowship. With the signing in 1994 of a covenant by Albanian believers in Tirana and Bregu, the center is now forming itself into a church. In 1993 Darvie F. Fenison, a missionary in cooperation with the ABA, began working in the extreme south at Sarandë.

In 1993 an Evangelical Brotherhood, which is seeking membership in the European Evangelical Alliance, was formed to represent the interests of evangelical missions and churches in Albania. Its first president is Ligor Çina, the Baptist who survived the many years of Communist oppression.

BIBLIOGRAPHY: See Edwin E. Jacques and Pavlos Katershosh, *The Awakenings at Korça and Vagia* (Wrexham, Clywd, UK: Albanian Evangelical Trust, 1992), for the mission work of the American Board and the Albanian Evangelical Mission. For a good survey of Protestantism in Albania, see Jacques, "Protestantism in Albania," mss., 1993. For recent developments, see Mike Creswell, "Albania Emerges from Darkness," *Commission*, June/July 1992, 74–79, and European Baptist Press Service, Jan. 13, 1994, 3-4; July 4, 1994, 3; July 19, 1994, 1.

BOSNIA (1863)

	Members	Churches
Sarajevo Baptist Church	40	

The state of Bosnia with a large Moslem population, beset by civil war and facing division between Serbs and Croats, has had only a limited Baptist presence. It was in Bosnia, however, that Baptists established their first fellowship and observed their first baptism in what later became Yugoslavia, a country which at one time incorporated Bosnia, Serbia, Croatia, Macedonia, Montenegro, and Slovenia. The first Baptist work was predominantly German.

In 1863 Franz Tabor, a former member of the Nazarene group, and his wife, both baptized in the previous year in the German Baptist congregation in Bucharest, moved to the predominantly Moslem city of Sarajevo. Tabor served as a colporteur of the BFBS in Bosnia-Herzegovina. With adherents coming from the independent Irby Educational Mission and German settlers, a Baptist congregation formed around Tabor. He was later succeeded in Sarajevo by two other Baptist colporteurs, Adolf Hempt, baptized in Novi Sad in 1875, and Edward Millard. The first baptism in Bosnia occurred at Lukovac, near Tuzla, fifty miles north of Sarajevo, where August Liebig baptized two brothers on June 20, 1863. By 1890 there were four mission stations in Bosnia, including Sarajevo, with a total membership of only nineteen.

Between the First and Second World Wars, the German Baptist Conference in North America provided assistance to German Baptist work in Yugoslavia, including Bosnia. The work included at least two small congregations of which one was at Petrovo Polje. With the departure of the German population as a result of World War II, the German Baptist work ceased. The congregation in Sarajevo joined the German Conference during the 1930s, but after the war only a remnant of the church survived. By the time of the outbreak of civil war in Bosnia in 1992, a new Baptist congregation had been started in Sarajevo, pastored by Boris Karceravic. However, because of the fighting, he and his family migrated to Germany. Only time will tell to what extent Baptist work has survived when peace is restored.

BIBLIOGRAPHY: See the bibliography for Yugoslavia.

BULGARIA (1880)

	Members	Churches
Union of Baptist Churches (1908)	2,500	(30)

*L*ocated in the southeastern end of the Balkans, Bulgaria has been an arduous field for Baptist work. As one Bulgarian pastor wrote years ago, this field has been a Baptist "stepchild." With great difficulty and under much persecution, Baptists have survived, living first under the Bulgarian monarchy and then under a Communist regime which almost eliminated them. With the collapse of Communism, Bulgarian Baptists are now facing a new day with growth and evangelistic outreach.

Because of the witness of a Baptist colporteur of German extraction, Bulgarians in Kazanlik who accepted Baptist principles appealed many times for a Baptist pastor to visit them. In 1880, Johann Kargel, who had just completed service at the German Baptist congregation in St. Petersburg, Russia, moved to Bulgaria for mission work, supported by V. A. Pashkov. In the company of Martin Heringer, a Baptist colporteur of German heritage who served as interpreter, Kargel made the difficult trip across the Balkan Mountains and baptized five candidates on September 17, 1880. Kargel made Ruse on the Danube River the center of his work, organizing a church there in 1884, considering Kazanlik a station. Bulgarian Baptists in Kazanlik later resented this status; they considered themselves an independent congregation even though they had no settled pastor.

Baptists formed churches in Lom (1896), Sofia (1899), Chirpan (1903), and other locations. Before World War I, the work was multinational—Bulgarians, Germans, and Russians provided pastoral service and mission activity among Bulgarians, Germans, Russians, Hungarians, and Gypsies. Believers in the village of Golintsi near Lom established the first Gypsy Baptist congregation anywhere. In 1899 three Bulgarian churches petitioned the American Baptist Missionary Union (ABMA) for assistance. They complained that the Baptists in Germany neglected them, failing to give pastoral support, help with building chapels, and assistance in printing Bulgarian literature, while refusing entry of Bulgarian students into the Hamburg seminary. In 1908 Bulgarian Baptists formed a Baptist Union, which in 1918 numbered sixteen churches. Between the First and Second World Wars, the Baptist Union tripled their numbers with the financial assistance from the German Baptist Conference in North America, which supplied pastoral aid and finances for chapels.

After the establishment of a Communist regime in the 1940s, Bulgarian Baptists went through four decades of woe. Cut off from the West, their work continued under strict surveillance and restriction with no publications or public evangelism permitted. The regime in 1949 placed five Baptist pastors and other Protestant ministers on public trial, forcing them under psychological pressure and physical torture to confess to espionage and other crimes. The regime also imprisoned other Baptist leaders. Eventually all Baptists were released, but the regime with these and other measures seriously weakened the small Baptist group.

Under the leadership of Theodor Angelov, Bulgarian Baptists have taken on new life. The largest church, located in Varna, completed a new structure in 1991, the first new building in five decades. Later the Baptists regained their building in Ruse, which the regime had confiscated. Pentecostals are by far the largest Protestant group in Bulgaria today. However, Baptists, despite their small size and the current attacks by the Orthodox Church, continue to add their strength to the Protestant minority in the country. At the recently founded Evangelical Alliance of Bulgaria in 1993, composed of Baptists and four other denominations, Angelov was elected president.

BIBLIOGRAPHY: Albert W. Wardin, Jr., "The Baptists in Bulgaria," *Baptist Quarterly*, 34 (Oct. 1991), 148–59, is a study of Bulgarian Baptists from their beginnings to the present, using German, Bulgarian, and English sources.

CROATIA (1883)

	Members	Churches
Union of Baptist Churches (1991)	2,030	(30)

T he strongly Roman Catholic country of Croatia declared its independence from Yugoslavia in 1991. Baptists have had a presence there for more than a century. In 1883 Filip Lotz, converted and baptized in Vienna, returned to his home in Daruvar in Slavonia. Through his witness, individuals were converted and baptized. At first the work was among Germans, but it soon became a Croatian and Czech ministry. About 1890 another fellowship appeared in Zagreb when Ivan Zrinscak returned from Budapest, where he had become a Baptist. The Baptist witness spread to other centers.

In 1921 in Daruvar, Baptists formed a Serbo-Croatian Conference and organized the Zagreb church which, in some respects, became a competing Baptist center to the one in Novi Sad in Serbia. On the invitation of Croatian Baptists, Vinko Vacek, of Czech ancestry and pastor of a Serbo-Croatian church in Detroit, USA, arrived in 1922 to lead Yugoslav work. At this time there were only about 115 Serbo-Croatian Baptists. In 1923 Vacek began to edit a journal, *Glas Evandjelja*. In 1924 Yugoslav Baptists formed a Baptist Union with which the Serbo-Croatian Conference cooperated and elected Vacek as president. In 1948 there were about nine hundred Baptists in Croatia and Slovenia.

During World War II, a Croatian state was established under Fascist control. All Baptist churches were prohibited, but Baptists met secretly. The work of the Baptist Union resumed after the war. In 1957 Josip Horak, pastor of the Zagreb church, became president of both the Serbo-Croatian Conference and the Baptist Union, and in 1961 he began to preach in Croatian on Radio Monte Carlo.

After the collapse of Communism and the dissolution of Yugoslavia, Baptists in Croatia formed their own union in 1991. Because of the civil war and numerous refugees, Croatian Baptists have received relief supplies, including assistance from Canadian Baptists, Southern Baptists, and the Baptist World Alliance, and have formed their own relief organization. Because of their relief work, Baptists have now gained a certain degree of recognition which they did not have previously. In spite of the chaotic times, Baptists in Croatia are also engaged in extensive evangelistic activity among refugees and other inhabitants, reaching out as well to the Serbian population in the territory.

BIBLIOGRAPHY: See the bibliography for Yugoslavia.

GREECE (1836)

	Members	Churches
Southern Baptist Mission (1972)	184	(1)

D espite mission activity, Greece is practically the only European country where Baptists have had almost no success in gaining converts from the native population. In 1836 missionaries from the American Baptist Mission Union, Horace T. Love and Cephas Pascoe, settled at Patrai in the northern Peloponnesus, where they preached, distributed Scripture, and established a mission school. In the face of Orthodox opposition, the work was most difficult. From 1840 to 1851 the main center of the mission was on Corfu (then part of the Ionian Islands), a state under British protection. The first Greek convert, named Apostolos, was baptized in August 1840. For a time he served as an associate in the mission. The mission also attempted work at Piraeus and Athens.

With no mission workers, the mission was suspended between 1857 and 1871 until the appointment of Demetrius Z. Sakellarious, a former mission worker who had graduated from Newton Theological Institution. Although he and his wife worked diligently, the effort produced practically no results. In 1881 the church in Athens reported seven members. By 1886 the mission had ended.

Among the American military in Athens, a Baptist fellowship developed in the 1960s, which led to the formation of Trinity Baptist Church. In 1972 the FMB of the SBC sent missionary assistance to the church. With the departure of American personnel, the Trinity Church has become an international congregation. It cooperates with a small Greek Baptist congregation in Athens and also extends work among Filipino domestics, a work which has the potential of becoming a church. BIMI has work among women and children in Katerini.

BIBLIOGRAPHY: G. Winfred Hervey, *The Story of Baptist Missions in Foreign Lands from the Time of Carey to the Present Date* (St. Louis: Chaney R. Barnes, 1886), 820–30, provides an account of the work of the ABMU. For more recent Baptist activity, see G. Keith Parker, *Baptists in Europe: History and Confessions of Faith* (Nashville: Broadman Press, 1982), 185, and *Your Guide to Foreign Missions, 1992–1993*, 112.

HUNGARY (1846)

	Members	Churches
Baptist Union of Hungary (1920)	11,161	(252)

*T*he Baptist movement in Hungary has played an important role in the spread of the Baptist faith throughout the Danubian lands. Hungarian Baptists not only maintain a union in Hungary, where they have the largest free-church constituency, but also a union in Transylvania, Romania, and another in the USA.

In the 1840s a number of craftsmen from the Austrian Empire (which then included Hungary) came to work in Hamburg after the Great Fire, where they were converted and baptized. In 1846 J. G. Oncken, the German Baptist leader, sent three of them—John Rottmayer, Karl Scharschmidt, and Johann Woyka—to return to Hungary to distribute Scripture and spread the gospel. Three others from Germany, including F. Oncken, joined them. Work was started in Fünfkirchen (today Pécs), and F. Oncken held services in Rottmayer's apartment in Pest (now part of Budapest). But opposition was intense, and the work barely took root.

A new day arrived in 1873 when Henrich Meyer (1842–1919), a German citizen, settled in Budapest as a colporteur for the BFBS. In spite of Catholic and Protestant opposition, the German Baptist church in Budapest was revived. Because of Meyer's mission activity, he was compelled to relinquish his position as colporteur. Through his energetic efforts along with faithful coworkers, the Baptist faith spread not only in present-day Hungary but through the kingdom of Hungary of that day which included Slovakia, Transylvania (today in Romania), as well as Vojvodina (today in Serbia). In 1885 an Austria-Hungarian Association was founded within the German Union with only one church in Hungary—the Budapest church with forty-two stations and a membership of 652. At the end of 1893, the church reported 2,088 members.

Upon their return from the seminary in Hamburg, Lajos Balogh and Andreas Udvarnoki, two Hungarians, began in 1893 a movement away from the autocratic control of Meyer—a man who never learned Hungarian and who retained all the mission congregations as stations of his church. Hungarians began to organize the stations as independent churches and formed their own union, which received state recognition in 1905. The new union included most of the Hungarian and Slovak Baptists, while Meyer's group included the German Baptists, 85 percent of the Romanian Baptists, and some Hungarians. Although state recognition removed certain disabilities, the new union adopted statutes which compromised Baptist polity by transforming the Baptists into a centralized body. The state could interfere in church affairs, such as in the election of pastors and the setting of educational standards for them. State recognition placed Meyer's group, who called themselves Free Baptists, in a vulnerable position; they were looked upon by others as "unrecognized." At the end of 1907 an arbitration committee of the Baptist World Alliance, composed of British Baptists but unfortunately with no German member, suggested that the statutes be changed and a new union be formed to include both groups. Although a new union was organized in 1908, it failed to bring unity.

The German Baptist church in Budapest developed a publication center, which issued five Hungarian papers before World War I, including *Bekehirnök* (Messenger of Peace), still published today, a German paper, two Romanian papers, besides a small weekly paper. Baptists in Hungary also established an orphanage and two homes for the aged. The attempt to found a seminary in 1906 ended, however, in failure when it closed because of lack of finances.

In 1920 a conference finally brought unity with the formation of a new union. At that time the Free Baptists were reduced to about four thousand since, as a result of World War I, their Romanian members were in Romania, while the Hungarian body, most of whose members continued to live within Hungary, had about ten thousand. After the war the Baptist World Alliance and Hungarian Baptists in the USA sent relief. As a result of the London Conference, Hungary was assigned to Southern Baptists as a mission responsibility. They provided relief and money for chapels but sent no missionaries until the mid-1930s. With Southern Baptist assistance, a seminary was established in 1920 in Budapest, which received a spacious building through the gift of a Southern Baptist woman, Varina Brown. German Baptists from the USA assisted German work, resenting the attempt of Southern Baptists, who considered Hungary their own preserve. Between the First and Second World Wars, Hungarian Baptists doubled their numbers and new leaders appeared, such as Imre Somogyi, who died in 1951.

During the four decades of Communist rule, which began in 1947, Baptists faced serious challenges. According to Kornel Gyori, who published a remarkable document in 1989, "*Vizsgáljuk meg útjainkat!*" ("Let Us Examine Our Ways!"), Baptists took a mediating position. They cooperated with the regime in the hope of preserving as much freedom as possible. On the one hand, they did not fight the regime by going underground nor, on the other hand, did they become propagandists for the Party. Despite government manipulation, loss of preaching licenses, and denial of building permits, Hungarian Baptists preserved a vital spiritual life, maintaining Sunday Schools and youth programs, even if it meant changing the nomenclature and disregarding various directives which sought to limit them. With some financial help from Southern Baptists, Hungarian Baptists constructed seventy-two church buildings.

With the collapse of the Communist regime, Hungarian Baptists face a new period of opportunity. More people attend their services than are on the membership rolls. In Budapest an International Baptist Lay Academy has been founded, which attracts students from neighboring countries. Hungarian Baptists are members of both the World Council of Churches and the Hungarian Evangelical Alliance.

BIBLIOGRAPHY: For the beginnings of Baptist work in Hungary, see Rudolf Donat, *Wie das Werk begann* (Kassel: Oncken, 1958), 421–23, 427–28, 434–38. For Hungarian Baptists before World War I, see C. T. Byford, "The Movement in Hungary: Progress and Difficulties," in J. H. Rushbrooke, ed., *The Baptist Movement in the Continent of Europe* (London: Carey Press/Kingsgate Press, 1915), 99–112. The work by Barnabas Somogyi, *Emléklapok a Magyarországi Baptista Egház 125 éves jubileumáról* (Budapest: Hungarian Baptist Union, 1972), commemorates the 125th anniversary of Hungarian work. For a discussion of Hungarian Baptists during the Communist period, see Kornel Gyori "*Vizsgáljuk meg útjainkat!*" ("Let Us Examine Our Ways!") (Budapest: Author, 1989). For a contemporary account, see Martha Skelton, "Hungary: Eastern Bloc, Western Style," *Commission*, Feb./Mar. 1988, 22–49.

MACEDONIA (1928)

	Members	Churches
1. Union of Baptist Churches (1991)	35	(2)
2. Reformed Baptists	4	—
	39	(2)

*M*acedonia, one of the republics attempting to maintain its independence following the dissolution of Yugoslavia, is a small republic, tucked between Bulgaria, Greece, Albania, and Serbia. It is predominantly Orthodox with an Albanian Moslem minority. When the American Board withdrew from Macedonia at the end of 1921, Methodists attempted to assume responsibility for the work in Radoviš, where a Congregational church had been established. Since the Methodists had no legal recognition, unlike the Baptists, the Radoviš congregation joined the Baptists in 1928. In the same year in Skopje, Vinko Vacek, president of the Baptist Union of Yugoslavia, baptized three converts and began a mission station there. In 1936 the Baptist church in Belgrade assumed responsibility for Macedonia.

Today there are two small Baptist churches and one small fellowship. The Radoviš church has its own structure, and the church in Skopje has a building which it shares with the Congregationalists. In 1991 the Baptists in Macedonia formed their own union. Because of the disturbing conditions in the country, the Baptist pastor of the two churches, an alumnus of Southwestern Baptist Seminary, left in October 1992 with his family for America. In Biota there is a small group of four Baptists of the Reformed Baptist persuasion. They are not organized yet, now meeting with the Methodists.

BIBLIOGRAPHY: John David Hopper, *A History of Baptists in Yugoslavia: 1862–1962* (Ph.D. dissertation, Southwestern Baptist Theological Seminary, 1977), 149–50. *Baptist Press*, Nashville, Tenn., Feb. 17, 1993, 7–8. *RBMS Reports*, Feb. 1993, 1.

ROMANIA (GERMANS, 1856; HUNGARIANS/ROMANIANS, 1875)

	Members	Churches
1. Baptist Union of Romania (1919)	100,000	(1,323)
2. Union of Hungarian Baptist Churches (1990)	9,043	(99)
	109,043	(1,422)

*O*ne of the most successful and effective Baptist bodies in Europe is in Romania. Despite persecution under monarchical regimes and suppression under Fascist and Communist rule, Baptists have become the largest evangelical free church in Romania. Three ethnic groups—Germans, Hungarians, and Romanians—each made their contribution.

Romanian Baptist history is complex in that Baptists began at different times in separate areas under different jurisdictions, not finally brought together until 1919 in a united Romanian state. Germans made the first contribution when Carl Scharschmidt, a carpenter, settled in Bucharest in 1856, where in 1863 August Liebig founded a church, which still continues today on Popa Rusa Street as a Romanian congregation. German Russians, who had been exiled in 1864 from Ukraine, formed a congregation at Cataloi in the Dobruja in 1869, at the time still under Turkish rule. A third center for Germans was a congregation at Tarutino in Bessarabia (its site today in Ukraine). This church began in 1875, and became independent in 1907, sponsoring many mission stations. In the early 1930s Germans had ten churches but less than one thousand members. Because of emigration, the German work today is almost extinct.

Another Baptist thrust came from Hungary into Transylvania and Banat, territories which then were part of Hungary. A Baptist colporteur of the BFBS from Budapest, Anton Novak, discovered a group of Hungarians of the Reformed faith who wished to study the Scriptures. In 1875 Henrich Meyer, Baptist leader in Budapest, baptized them and formed a church in Salonta Mare, the first in Transylvania. Among the eight who were baptized was Mihai Cornya. He became a dynamic evangelist, a man of the people, preaching to both Romanians amd Hungarians. Transylvania now holds by far the largest number of Romanian Baptists, particularly near the western border, as well as a separate Hungarian Baptist Union. In Oradea the First Baptist Church (Hungarian) has 1,100 members, while the Second Baptist Church (Romanian) has three thousand, the largest Baptist church in Europe outside of Russia. The latter congregation maintains Emanuel Bible School, a high school, an orphanage, and is building a large sanctuary.

The penetration of Baptists among Romanians into the Old Kingdom of Romania was, however, comparatively late. In spite of Orthodox opposition, a church was formed in 1909 in Jegalia. C. Adorian (1882–1954), a Romanian who had joined the German church in Bucharest and studied at the seminary in Hamburg, began a separate Romanian work in Bucharest in December 1912.

With Romania united, Romanian Baptists under Adorian's leadership formed the Baptist Union of Romania in 1919. Each ethnic group, however, had its own special interests, making cooperation difficult. The Germans possessed their own association, and in 1920 the Hungarians in Transylvania and the Russians/Ukrainians in Bessarabia formed their own unions. Beginning in December 1919 Romanian Baptists published a small paper. In 1921 they established a seminary in Transylvania, which moved to Bucharest in the following year. As a result of the London Conference, Southern Baptists assumed mission responsibility for Romania, sending their first missionaries in 1923. One year earlier, Southern Baptists bought property in Bucharest for a seminary on which a building was erected. In 1929 they opened a Baptist Missionary Training School for women.

With their evangelistic zeal, Baptists in Romania continued to grow rapidly, numbering forty-five thousand by 1930. Along with their evangelism, they followed a strict Puritan code of rejecting alcohol and tobacco, adornment for women, as well as supporting strict Sunday observance. Relations with the state were at times difficult, particularly up to 1928 and then again from 1937 to 1944. From December 1938 to April 1939 all Baptist churches were officially closed.

With the fall of the Fascist regime, Baptists in 1944 received legal recognition and took advantage of the freedom they enjoyed in the immediate post-war period. In 1946 they began issuing, *Îndrumătoral Creștin Baptist* (The Christian Baptist Guide), its current journal, and the seminary flourished. Beginning in 1955, however, the Communist regime began a campaign to limit religion, and Baptists faced discrimination, harassment, closure of churches, threats and attacks on ministers, removal of licenses for preaching, prohibition of youth and Sunday School work, and manipulation of the leadership. Baptists continued their witness under stressful circumstances. Because of the published protest of Joseph Tson, a Baptist pastor who had studied in Great Britain, the government was forced to make some concessions.

With the overthrow of the Communist regime in December 1989, Baptists in Romania again found a climate of freedom. Despite economic hardship, Romanian

Baptists are vigorously engaged in evangelistic activity, teaching in public schools, and using radio and television. Hungarian Baptists in Romania once again have their own union. Baptists have taken the lead in forming an Evangelical Alliance of Romania with Paul Negrut, a Baptist, as president. Southern Baptists for a second time along with many other Baptist missions have entered Romania. One of the most active is the Romanian Missionary Society under the leadership of Tson, which was formed in 1968 by Romanians outside the country.

BIBLIOGRAPHY: The work by Alexa Popovici, *Istoria Baptiştilor din România*, 2 vols. (Chicago: Author, 1980–1989), is a comprehensive history written by a Romanian Baptist who migrated to the USA. The first volume covers 1856 to 1919 and the second one from 1919 to 1944. Ion Bunaciu, who served as president of the seminary in Bucharest in the Communist period, wrote *Istoria raspîndirii credinţei Baptiste în România* (Bucharest: Baptist Union of Romania, 1981). Mrs. Peter Trutza, "A Short History of Roumanian Baptists," *Chronicle*, 5 (1942): 9–21, provides a general survey. For a well-documented article, see R. E. Davies, "Persecution and Growth: A Hundred Years of Baptist Life in Romania," *Baptist Quarterly* 33 (April 1990): 265–74.

SLOVENIA (1923)

	Members	Churches
Union of Baptist Churches of Slovenia (1991)	130	(4)

*I*n a territory between Croatia, Austria, and Italy, the predominantly Roman Catholic republic of Slovenia, which declared its independence from Yugoslavia in 1991, contains a small group of Baptists. As the result of the witness of Martin Hlastan, a member of the Free Brethren who had served as a colporteur of the BFBS before World War I, Jurij Cater was converted. By 1923 Cater was holding meetings in his home in Hrastnik. From the group meeting in his home, the first Baptists were baptized. Meetings were shifted to Trbovlje, and Slovenians who had returned from Russia as Baptists increased their number. In 1927 the work in Slovenia came under the Zagreb church. When Slovenian Baptists held their first conference in 1938, Baptist groups existed in several places, including the Trbovlje area, Celje, Ljubljana, Maribor, and Kranj. In the latter two locations, German Baptists also participated.

At the time of the Italian occupation of Slovenia during World War II, Baptist congregations were closed and some Baptists imprisoned. One Baptist leader disappeared and another Baptist was sent to the concentration camp at Dachau. After the war, Baptists in Slovenia made little progress. With the collapse of a united Yugoslav state, Slovenian Baptists formed their own union.

Today there are four churches in the Slovenian Baptist Union with a membership of 130 and an attendance of 100. The pastor of the largest church has had some formal training, but the other congregations are led by lay leaders. In 1992 Conservative Baptist International (CBI) sent Mel and Patty Davis to Slovenia, who were joined by a second couple in 1994. The Davises started in 1994 a group which consists primarily of young Christians. In 1993 the FMB of the Southern Baptist Convention appointed a couple to serve in the country, who are now in language study.

BIBLIOGRAPHY: John David Hopper, *A History of Baptists in Yugoslavia: 1862–1962* (Ph.D. dissertation, Southwestern Baptist Theological Seminary, 1977), 77–80, 133–37, 160. *Your Guide to Foreign Missions*, 1994–1995, 119. Correspondence of Patty Davis with the editor, July 14, 1994.

YUGOSLAVIA (SERBIA/MONTENEGRO) (1875)

	Members	Churches
1. Baptist Union of Yugoslavia (1992)	1,368	(51)
2. Union of Evangelical-Christian Baptists	n/a	n/a
	1,368	(51)

Yugoslavia today includes only the two states of Serbia and Montenegro since the dissolution of the country in 1991. The strongest Baptist work in Serbia has always been in Vojvodina and Western Banat, a multinational territory in the north, which belonged to Hungary before the end of World War I. Baptists first took root there among the Germans (1875), then the Hungarians (1899), Slovaks (1900), Romanians (1922), and finally among the Serbs (1925). Baptist work in the rest of Serbia has always been very weak.

On November 16, 1875, Heinrich Meyer, the leader of Baptist work in Budapest, baptized Adolf Hempt and three others in Novi Sad, followed by two more three days later. These candidates were members of the Nazarenes, a pacifist group, located largely in Hungary, which at that time practiced believer's baptism by sprinkling. Baptist work spread to other centers. Although it was predominantly German, Slavic and Hungarian names began to appear in the membership records. In 1891 the church in Novi Sad became an independent congregation and was led for the next thirty-one years by Julius Peter, who also attended the church's stations and extended the work. German Baptists formed an association, which included work in Croatia, Slovenia, and Bosnia. The association ceased in 1944 with the forced emigration of the German population. At that time they had more than five hundred members in seven churches.

In 1898 Meyer baptized in Budapest a Slovak, Josip Turoci, who moved to Bački Petrovac the following year and began witnessing. The work grew to such an extent that Slovak Baptists formed in 1909 an organization for elders which developed in 1918 into a Slovak conference. The Slovak work was primarily a lay movement. In moving to another village, Slovak Baptists would frequently begin a Bible study. They grew from 283 in 1922 to 1,400 in 1959 but since have declined because of emigration and lack of evangelistic outreach.

The Hungarian work in Serbia was at first an extension from Hungary. In 1900 five believers were baptized in Bajmok, forming a station of a church in Hungary but becoming independent in 1903. In 1922 there were 117 Hungarian Baptists and 263 in 1962 with Svilojevo as their main center. Straža in Western Banat became the first center of Romanian work when a convert returned from Romania in 1922; through his witness, the first baptism occurred in 1924. Up to the end of World War II, Hungarian Baptists in Serbia associated with the Slovak conference, which assisted them. In 1961 they had 362 members.

In the kingdom of Serbia a German Baptist fellowship had developed in Belgrade by the 1890s. The multiethnic congregation was rather unstable and did not get a firm Slavic base until 1926. In Vojvodina a Serb-Slovak mission began in 1925 at the German church in Novi Sad and a Serb work in 1933 at the German church in Kikinda.

A few years after the formation of Yugoslavia in 1918 (which at that time also included Croatia, Slovenia, Bosnia, and Macedonia), Yugoslav Baptists formed a Baptist Union in 1924 with Vinko Vacek as president. The London Conference had assigned Yugoslavia to Southern Baptists, who encouraged the formation of a union, provided finanical assistance, and in 1938 sent John A. and Pauline Moore to the country as missionaries. In 1940 John Moore opened in Belgrade a small seminary, but because of World War II the Moores were forced to leave and the seminary closed. The Yugoslav Baptist paper *Glas Evandjelja* also stopped publishing.

After the war, the Baptist Union was revived. The seminary was started anew in 1954 in Zagreb, then moved to Daruvar, and in 1957 to Novi Sad, where it has done outstanding work in educating Baptist ministers as well as students from other denominations. In 1959 a new paper, *Glasnik* (Herald), made its appearance. After the war, Adolf Lehotsky reconstituted the important church at Novi Sad, now left without its German members, but becoming a multiethnic congregation with as many as seven different nationalities in attendance. Under Communist rule Baptists in Yugoslavia suffered less and were under less strict control than Baptists to the east. Yugoslav Baptists were even allowed to conduct Sunday Schools.

Baptists south of Belgrade have always been few and far between. Today there is a small church in Peć in Kosovo Province, reduced in size because of emigration, and another in Niš, which was begun about 1985. Baptists are also very scarce in Montenegro, where there is only one Baptist church.

The dismemberment of Yugoslavia and the outbreak of civil war in 1991 has also brought an end to the Yugoslav Baptist Union, as Baptists in each republic have established their own unions. On March 21, 1992, the Baptist Union of Serbia was formed and then accepted into the Baptist World Alliance (BWA). In 1994 it changed its name to the Baptist Union of Yugoslavia. A second group, the Union of Evangelical-Christian Baptists, receiving recognition by the government, has also applied to the BWA for membership. In 1990 Southern Baptists reentered Yugoslavia and are engaged in a relief ministry in Serbia.

BIBLIOGRAPHY: A very helpful work which describes in great detail the beginnings and development of Baptist churches in each ethnic group is John David Hopper, *A History of Baptists in Yugoslavia: 1862–1962* (Ph.D. dissertation, Southwestern Baptist Theological Seminary, 1977). Also see Hopper's article, "Baptist Beginnings in Yugoslavia," *Baptist History and Heritage*, 17 (1982): 28–37. The work by Mile Imerovski, *Baptist Origins during the Nineteenth Century in Present-Day Yugoslavia* (B.D. treatise, Baptist Theological Seminary, Rüschlikon, Switzerland, 1986), provides valuable information on Baptist-Nazarene relations and the activity of Baptist colporteurs. For an article by a Yugoslav, see Franjo Klem, "Yugoslavia," in J. D. Franks, comp., *European Baptists Today*, 2d rev. ed. (Rüschlikon-Zürich: Author, 1952), 86–92.

BAPTIST AND BAPTIST-RELATED MISSIONS

1. ALBANIA UkAET (1991), CBI (1992), EuEBF (1992), UkBMS (1992), ABA (1993), CBF (1993), CaCBIM, UkLA/LR

2. BOSNIA —

3. BULGARIA NABC (1920–1941, 1992), OFWB (1991), SBC (1991), LPEA

4. CROATIA SBC (1990), R-UEBU

5. GREECE ABMU (1836–1886), SBC (1972), BIMI (1973)

6. HUNGARY SBC (1921–1948, 1988), BBFI (1990), BIMI (1992), CBI (1992), LIB (1992), ABWE, BWM, MBM, RBS, UkBMS

7. MACEDONIA —

8. ROMANIA SBC (1921–1948, 1990), RMS (1968), BBFI (1990), BIMI (1992), CBI (1992), ABA, ABWE, BWM, EBM, IBFI, LIB, LPEA, MBM, RBS, UkHIM, UkLA/LR

9. SLOVENIA CBI (1992), SBC (1993)

10. YUGOSLAVIA (SERBIA/ MONTENEGRO) SBC (1921–1941, 1990), SwO

F. SOUTHERN (LATIN) EUROPE

*L*atin Europe, dominated by the Roman Catholic Church, has been the most unresponsive field in Europe for Baptists. Only thirty-five thousand Baptists reside in these lands in churches with an average membership of sixty. In their rejection of the Roman Catholic Church, people are more apt to move toward secularism, not to evangelical Christianity. The limited Baptist results are certainly not due to a limited mission effort since Baptists entered all these countries in the nineteenth century; in fact, France had the first Baptists on the continent. It is also not due to lack of sustained effort, because Baptists have maintained missions here throughout the entire period with missionaries coming from both America and other parts of Europe. Besides, Baptist interest in the field has greatly increased in the last several decades, with almost an avalanche of Baptist missions, many of them independent missions from America. There are as many Baptist mission agencies here as one would find anywhere in the Third World.

Although Baptist beginnings in the French-speaking areas were often indigenous, much of the Baptist work, unlike other areas of Europe, is the result of the work of the foreign missionary, looked upon as an outsider with a heretical creed whose cultural values often proved to be a barrier to the message he or she proclaimed. Even after work was planted, there have been very few periods of even moderate growth. A good portion of current growth comes from converts among foreigners who have moved into the area, not from the indigenous population. Baptists also have been hindered by controversy and division in their own ranks.

Despite its problems, the tenacious witness of many missionaries along with local believers has established a credible evangelical testimony in an indifferent environment. Baptists today are as energetic, if not more so than ever before and are seeing some results to their labors.

	Members	*Churches*
1. Belgium	1,058	20
2. France	8,965	172
3. Italy	5,032	102
4. Malta	54	3
5. Portugal	5,500	98
6. Spain	13,182	169
7. Switzerland (French-Speaking)	560	15
	34,351	579

BELGIUM (1892)

	Members	Churches
1. Union des Églises Evangéliques Baptistes (1922)	855	(13)
2. Association Evangélique des Églises Baptistes de Langue Française (1924)	63	(2)
3. Baptist Bible Fellowship International (BBFI) (1962)	140*	(5)
	1,058	(20)

*Attendance

*B*elgium, a small country with a Roman Catholic heritage, has been a difficult field for Baptists. The country is divided between two major groups—French and Flemish—with Baptist work almost entirely among the French.

Baptists entered Belgium as an extension of Baptist work in northern France. A congregation was founded in Ougree near Liege in 1892 after two workmen, who had been converted, returned to their home. Another early center was at Peruwelz, which was due to a couple, converted in Denain, France, who moved there before the 1880s. Through their witness, a group of believers began to meet in homes, then gained in 1895 their first regular pastor and in 1904 their own church building. A third congregation appeared in 1904 at Mont-sur-Marchienne near Charleroi. They dedicated a building the following year. Baptists also founded a church in Brussels, which joined the fundamentalist Association Evangélique des Églises Baptistes de Langue Française in 1924. Two years earlier the other Baptist churches in Belgium formed their own Union of Evangelical Baptist Churches.

After the devastation of World War I, the American Baptist Foreign Mission Society provided financial assistance to Belgian Baptists as well as after the Second World War. Even with outside assistance, Belgian Baptists, however, showed little growth. Besides a mission in Brussels, the union in 1958 had only nine churches and mission stations and 280 members, including a Polish Baptist church, formed in 1954. The churches were small, lacking ability to support a pastor full-time, often losing their young people who moved elsewhere. As a French-speaking body, the union made little attempt to reach the Flemish population. Finally, in 1954 the first Baptist church in Flanders was founded at Gent, which joined the Baptist Union.

In the last two decades, the Baptist Union has grown from 300 to 850 members, due largely to the addition of two English-speaking international Baptist churches in Brussels and Antwerp. The union also includes German-speaking churches on the frontier. It is now receiving mission assistance from Southern, Canadian, and British Baptists. In 1992 the Baptist Union observed the centennial of Belgian Baptist work.

Baptist missions from North America have also augmented Baptist strength. Since its entry in 1962, the Baptist Bible Fellowship International (BBFI) has baptized more than four hundred believers and organized five French-speaking churches, which currently have an attendance of around 140. Tom and Donna Duniho, missionaries from the Belgium Congo (Zaire), founded the first church in 1964. In addition, churches of the Fellowship of Evangelical Baptist Churches in Canada began supporting a Flemish Baptist work. This mission includes work in Antwerp and Gent and has now extended its activity to French-speaking Belgium. Baptist International Missions, Inc. (BIMI) works among the American military.

BIBLIOGRAPHY: Alexander de Chalandeau, *The History of the Baptist Movement in the French-Speaking Countries of Europe* (Th.D. dissertation, Northern Baptist Theological Seminary, 1960), 81–84, 130, 144–46, provides material on the work among French-speaking Belgians. The account by A. H. Deelstra, "Belgien," in European Baptist Federation, *Congress*, 1958, 205–6, provides material on Flemish Baptist work. Maurice S. Entwistle, "Belgium," in *European Baptists: A Magnificent Minority* (Valley Forge, Pa.: International Ministries, American Baptist Churches/USA, 1981), 168–72, provides a general survey, while the article by Tom Duniho in *Baptist Bible Tribune*, April 1992, 21, describes the work of the BBFI.

FRANCE (1820)

	Members	Churches
1. Federation des Églises Evangéliques Baptistes (1911)	5,600	(93)
Cooperating missions: SBC (1960); NzBMS (1981); SwO (1982); BGC (1987); UkBMS (1988)		
2. Association Evangélique des Églises Baptistes de Langue Française (1921)	910	(24)
3. Tabernacle Baptist Church, Paris (1921)	207	(1)
4. Baptist Mid-Missions (1948)	657	(14)
5. Evangelical Baptist Mission (1956)	420	(12)
6. Églises Baptistes Indépendantes	510	(11)
Cooperating missions: SEE (1956); BBFI (1970); ABWE (1984)		
7. Alliance Baptiste Evangélique de Paris-Est et Nord (1983)	457	(9)
Cooperating missions: CBI (1962); CaFEBC (1985); IrBM (1977)		
8. Free Will Baptists (1966)	154*	(3)
9. Baptist International Missions, Inc. (BIMI) (1969)	<u>50</u>	<u>(5)</u>
	8,965	(172)

*Attendance

STATISTICS: See *French Christian Handbook* in *European Churches Handbook*, pt. 1

(MARC Europe, 1991), 31, for French Baptist statistics except for the Federation, which
were gained from BWA, *Yearbook*, 1993–1994, 101, and the Alliance, which were gained
from CBInternational (CBI).

*E*xcept for the later part of the nineteenth century, France has been an inhospitable field for Baptists. France is proud of its culture, which includes a heritage of Roman Catholicism and rationalism, and has been increasingly de-Christianized, thus continuing to be a formidable challenge to evangelicalism. France is also the most divided Baptist field on the European continent. It has been beset by personal rivalry, liberal-fundamentalist conflict, and the entry of numerous Baptist missions which often simply stake out their own territory. But with a renewed stress on evangelism by the Federation of Evangelical Baptist Churches and the activity of more than twenty Baptist missions which have entered France since World War II, Baptists are showing more strength than they have had in many decades.

An early source for the Baptist movement came from believers in the village of Nomain in northern France who had been influenced by their own study of the Bible and an article on William Carey. In 1820 Henry Pyt, a missionary of the Continental Society, immersed members from this group, thereby creating the first Baptist church. Because of Pyt's activity and assistance by the Continental Society, other small Baptist congregations appeared. From this circle of believers would later come such outstanding Baptist leaders as Joseph Thieffry and Jean-Baptiste Crétin.

Formal Baptist work did not begin, however, until 1832, when the Baptist General Convention (Triennial Convention) in the USA sent Ira Chase with Casimir Rostan, a Frenchman who had studied at Newton Theological Institution, to survey the field. Rostan began preaching and lecturing in Paris but died of cholera in December 1833. The Trienniel Convention then sent Isaac Willmarth in 1834, who served for three years, and D. Newton Sheldon and Erastus Willard in 1835, with Sheldon staying five years and Willard serving twenty-one. Willmarth organized a church of ten members in Paris on May 10, 1835. In 1836 Willmarth and Willard moved to Douai near Nomain and established a school which provided training for a number of early French leaders until its demise in 1839. Willard also established in 1838 at Douai a mixed French and English church. The American missionaries extended assistance to the Baptist congregations already existing in the north, which they found weak in number and lacking in Baptist organization and discipline. The American mission also provided support for native preachers and colporteurs. By 1838 there were seven churches with 148 members.

In 1849 French Baptists formed their first association. Though progress was slow, Baptist work developed in the north, the Aisne and Oise Valleys, as well as in a few large cities such as Paris, Lyons, and Saint-Etienne. At this time French Baptists were often harassed. They did not gain their religious freedom until after the establishment of the Third French Republic in 1871, nor were they guaranteed full rights until 1881. From the birth of the Republic until the end of the century, Baptists experienced unprecedented growth. New pastors joined the ranks—Philemon Vincent (1860–1927), the first French pastor to earn a theological degree; Ruben Saillens (1855–1942), the son-in-law of J. B. Crétin who had served with the MacAll Mission and an outstanding writer of hymns; Paul Besson, who went to Argentina as a missionary; Charles Ramseyer; and others.

French work spread into neighboring Belgium and Switzerland. In 1900 there were thirty Baptist churches with two thousand members with churches not only in the north but also in Marseille and Nice in the south. With American help, Baptists in Paris built in 1873 a large chapel on Rue de Lille. Saillens formed in the late 1880s a second church on Rue Saint-Denis, and Philémon Vincent established in 1899 a church on Rue de Maine. A paper, *L'Echo de la Vérité*, was founded in 1879, and Philémon Vincent and his brother Samuel published *La Pioche et la Truelle*, a paper for evangelism with a circulation of twelve thousand a month.

Beginning in 1892 a strong rivalry developed between two gifted pastors, Ruben Saillens and Philémon Vincent, which also affected the large Vincent family. The quarrel divided French Baptists into two camps. Partly because of it, French Baptists lost their momentum which they have regained only in recent years. In spite of the conflict, French Baptists formed a French Baptist Union in 1907 which included two associations—Franco-Belgium, whose adherents generally had a Roman Catholic background, and Franco-Swiss, largely with Huguenot antecedents. In 1911 the Franco-Belgium Association became the Federation des Églises Evangéliques Baptistes du Nord, and in the same year the Vincents formed the Baptist Evangelical Mission of Paris, which helped to continue the conflict. As most of the Federation's churches were in the area of battle during World War I, many of its members scattered and suffered serious loss in life and property.

After the war, French Baptists formally divided. As a result of the decision of the French Union in 1920 to reject the establishment of a school on strict conservative principles, Saillens and his son-in-law, Arthur Blocher, left the union. Blocher, who was pastoring at Rue de Lille, was forced to leave this church and in 1921 formed the Tabernacle Baptist Church, which continues to this day to be independent. Later Blocher's son, Jacques, became its pastor. Since 1927 the church has had its own mission work in the Côte d'Ivoire, the Biblical Mission, and maintains a camp, nursing home, and publishing interests, including the publication of *Le Bon Combat*. The church has close ties with the Nogent Bible Institute, founded in 1921 by Saillens, and the Evangelical Theological Seminary.

In 1921 six churches, also objecting to the theological latitude of the French Union, formed under the leadership of Robert Dubarry what today is called the Association Evangélique des Églises Baptistes de Langue Française. Besides churches in France, it includes fifteen in Switzerland and another in Belgium. It publishes *Lien Fraternel* and conducts a correspondence course. After a short period of cooperation with the Conservative Baptist Foreign Mission Society (CBFMS) after the Second World War, the association maintains fellowship with more separatist fundamentalists, such as the Association of Regular Baptist Churches of Canada.

With the two defections, the Federation dropped "du Nord" from its title and sought to be a national body. It continued to gain assistance from Northern Baptists in the USA. In 1926 the Federation assumed responsibility for the Baptist work in Brittany, which Welsh Baptists in Glagmoran had started in 1834 but which had been taken over in 1843 by the BMS of England. In 1937 it formed a home mission board. The Society of Baptist Publications was organized in 1944; it publishes Sunday School materials and distributes Christian literature through its bookstore, which now has two branches. Its monthly paper is *Croire et Servir*. Under the umbrella of the Association Baptiste pour l'Entraide et la Jeunesse, it has developed an orphanage, a home for youth in trouble, a home for the aged, social work centers, and youth camps. In Massy, south of Paris, it opened, with assistance from Southern Baptists, a center

Faculty of Theology in Rome or at the International Baptist seminary at Rüschlikon. Women are organized into an Evangelical Baptist Women's Movement. By only one vote, the union decided not to partipate in a program whereby taxpayers could designate a portion of their taxes to the denomination of their choice.

Italian Baptists cooperate closely with the Waldensians and Methodists in the country, developing a reciprocal relationship with them, even to the extent of sharing pastors. Each congregation, however, maintains its own tradition. The three bodies, beginning in 1993, are issuing a joint publication called *Reformation*.

The Baptist Union is a founding member of the Federation of Evangelical Churches in Italy, and through it conducts work with young people and Sunday Schools. It is also an associate member of the World Council of Churches, the Conference of European Churches, as well as the European Baptist Federation and BWA.

Churches are members of two regional associations and are located not only on the mainland but also in Sicily and Sardinia. Within the union are about 120 preaching points and fifty pastors, who are assisted by lay preachers. Pastors and lay preachers may be either men or women.

In the past, the Baptist cause has been weakened seriously by emigration to America, but today Baptists in Italy are finding new opportunities of witness. In 1992 the Baptist Union accepted two English-speaking churches and one Chinese congregation in Milan for which the union is calling a pastor from China. Ethnic ministries are conducted among Americans, Germans, and Spanish.

The Conservative Baptist Foreign Mission Society (now CBI) began its work in 1947 at Catanzaro at the southern toe of Italy. In 1951 the mission formed in Naples a Centro Biblico, a Christian literature and publishing center. Conservative Baptists have established their own association. The American Baptist Association Missionary Committee (ABA) has work in Sicily.

In spite of a long and sustained mission effort and the entry of numerous other Baptist missions, Italy remains a difficult field. Even though membership is low, the community strength of Italian Baptists is five times as much.

Franco Scaramuccia and Albert W. Wardin, Jr.

BIBLIOGRAPHY: For a work by a pastor of the Baptist church in Rome, see Peter Chiminelli, *The Baptists in Italy* (Nashville: Sunday School Board/SBC, 1923). The son of George B. Taylor, George Braxton Taylor, has written *Southern Baptists in Sunny Italy* (New York: Walter Neale, 1929). A very valuable article is by Salvatore Mondello and Pellegrino Nazzaro, "The Origins of Baptist Evangelism in Italy, 1848–1920," *American Baptist Quarterly*, (1988): 110–27.

MALTA (1984)

	Members	Churches
1. Baptist Bible Fellowship International Mission	n/a	(2)
2. Independent Baptist Church of Malta	<u>54</u>	<u>(1)</u>
	54	(3)

*T*he small republic of Malta consists of several islands which lie in the Mediterranean Sea between Italy and North Africa. The population is predominantly Roman Catholic. Baptist work in the country is very new.

In 1984 the Baptist Bible Fellowship International (BBFI) in the USA sent Joe and Jenny Mifsud who began a mission in 1985, which today is the Bible Baptist Church of Sliema. Because of problems with health, the Mifsuds left in 1993.

Another pioneering couple from BBFI were Ray and Wanda Hoover, who served for four years after arriving in 1984. The Hoovers worked with a house group, which a non-Baptist missionary from Norway had started in the early 1970s, but then led by Edwin Caruana, a native Maltese. The work was organized as the Independent Baptist Church of Malta. It continues under Caruana's leadership, who in 1994 represented the church at the congress of the European Baptist Fellowship in Lillehammer, Norway. A third church was organized in Zejtun, served by Paul Mizzi, a Maltese Baptist pastor, since its founding in 1991.

BIBLIOGRAPHY: Correspondence of Ray Hoover with the editor, Sep. 30, 1994. European Baptist Press Service, Aug. 25, 1994, 1.

PORTUGAL (1888)

	Members	Churches
1. Convenção Batista Portugesa (1920)	4,000	(59)
2. Associação de Igrejas Batistas Portuguesas (1955)	1,000	(19)
3. Independent churches	n/a	(20)
	5,500*	(98)

STATISTICS: According to Norman Harrell (see bibliography), the total Baptist membership is about 5,500. For other statistics, see David B. Barrett, ed., *World Christian Encyclopedia*, 577, and BWA *Yearbook*, 1993–1994, 101.

*T*he Baptist work in Portugal has always been small. It has had a checkered and complex history, suffering from division and experiencing the impact of various Baptist missions, holding inconsistent mission philosophies and often sporadic in support. Since World War II, however, Portuguese Baptists have become a movement of growing vitality.

Joseph Charles Jones (1848–1928) organized on September 6, 1888, in Oporto the first Baptist church, an open-communion congregation. Jones, who served as pastor, was a merchant of Welsh descent who had been born in Oporto but baptized in the Metropolitan Tabernacle in London. In 1908 Robert Young, an independent missionary who arrived in 1906 in Oporto, established a congregation, simply known as Christian, which in 1908 became Baptist. In September of the same year excluded members of this church formed their own congregation under Jeronomio Sousa and appealed to Brazilian Baptists for affiliation.

In December 1909 Zachary C. Taylor, a Southern Baptist missionary from Brazil, organized in Oporto the first "regular" Baptist church, which later became known as the First Baptist Church or the Baptist Tabernacle. The church practiced close communion. Taylor formed the church from individuals who had been excluded from the congregation which Robert Young had established and required their rebaptism. In 1912 First Baptist Church received Jones with his small congregation without rebaptism. In 1920 Portuguese Baptists formed the Portuguese Baptist Convention with Jones as its first president.

One of the important pioneers was João J. de Oliveira (1883–1958), a native of Portugal and a graduate of Southwestern Baptist Seminary in Texas. After a ministry in Brazil, he arrived in 1911 as the first missionary of the Foreign Mission Board of Brazil to Portugal. In his long career in ministering in Portugal and to Portuguese in America, he affiliated at one time or another with ten different organizations, nine of them Baptist, and diligently sought funds from abroad. Besides serving as pastor, he organized a number of the early churches, engaged in publishing, including the issuing of two journals.

With the encouragement of Oliveira, Mr. and Mrs. Albert W. Luper, supported by the Baptist Missionary Association of Texas (BMAT), arrived in 1922. In the same year Oliveira became a missionary of this group and resigned from the Brazilian Board in an effort to free funds for another missionary. In 1926 a complete rupture occurred on the field between Oliveira and António Maurício, another missionary. In that year the Portuguese Baptist Convention decided to affiliate only with the Brazilian Board and established a new Baptist journal, *O Semeador Batista*. In 1928 Oliviera and his supporters founded the Portuguese Baptist Alliance in Viseu. In 1927 the BMAT turned over its responsibilities to the American Baptist Association (ABA): however, with the coming of the Great Depression, ABA was forced to cease sending funds. Oliveira migrated in 1930 to the USA, where he worked under the Northern Baptists among Portuguese in Rhode Island, and the Lupers returned to Texas in 1931. By 1932 the alliance ended as well as Oliveira's two journals.

During the difficult years of the Depression, Brazilian Baptists continued financial support but reduced the amount. Mr. and Mrs. William Hatcher, volunteer Southern Baptist missionaries, arrived in 1933 and reopened the seminary, which had been established in 1922. In 1935 the Portuguese Baptist Convention reported having thirteen churches, twelve missions, and 432 members.

A new era began in 1945 when Oliveira returned to Portugal at the age of sixty-two under the sponsorship of the newly formed Conservative Baptist Foreign Mission Society (CBFMS, today CBI). With Oliveira's support, the Baptist Union of Portugal was formed in 1946 but ceased in 1956. Under the direction of Samuel Faircloth, the CBFMS opened a seminary in Leira in October 1950, which provided training for a significant number of pastors until it closed in 1962. Conservative Baptists also provided limited pastoral support, directed particularly to the beginning of new work, and engaged in correspondence and literature programs. In 1954 the Baptist Missionary Association (BMA, then known as the North American Baptist Association), a Landmark body which separated from the American Baptist Association, began to provide funds for Portuguese pastors, starting with four of the churches. In January 1955 churches in fellowship with the BMA formed the Association of Portuguese Baptist

Churches, which printed its own paper, *A Mensagem Batista*. In 1962 there were eighteen churches in cooperation. In this year the association established a seminary in Oporto, which moved near Lisbon and then to Leira before ceasing in the 1970s.

In the meantime Brazilian Baptists continued their interest in the field, sending a new missionary couple in 1953. In 1959 the Foreign Mission Board of the Southern Baptist Convention (FMB) surveyed the field and in the following year sent Grayson and Betty Jean Tennison as its first permanent missionaries. Southern Baptist missionaries have assisted in evangelism, communications, publications, theological education, and music. The FMB-SBC has cooperated with the Portuguese Baptist Convention in providing funds for church buildings, a communication studio, a radio ministry (1967), and a bookstore (1968). In 1969 the Portuguese Baptist Convention with Southern Baptist assistance opened a seminary. Several independent fundamentalist missions have entered the field in recent years.

The Portuguese Baptist Convention is a member of the BWA. In spite of their divisions, Portuguese Baptists have held several joint meetings, or "national encounters," three in 1975 and a fourth in 1990. Portuguese Baptists have engaged in a limited way in foreign mission work in the former Portuguese possessions in Africa. In 1931 the Portuguese Baptists commissioned Mr. and Mrs. Manuel Pedras to serve in Angola, and in 1949 the Baptist Union of Portugal sent Mr. and Mrs. Luís de Almeida to Mozambique.

BIBLIOGRAPHY: The best comprehensive history with an excellent bibliography in both Portuguese and English is by Norman Lynn Harrell, *Beginnings of Baptist Work in Portugal 1808–1928* (M.A. in Missiology thesis, Southwestern Baptist Theological Seminary, 1991), on which much of the above article is based. In spite of the title, Harrell's work goes to 1991. For the Portuguese Baptist situation around 1950, see the article "Portugal," by Fernando de Macedo in J. D. Franks, comp., *European Baptists Today*, 2d rev. ed. (Rüschlikon-Zürich: Author, 1952), 57–61. For accounts of the work of Brazilian Baptists, see A. R. Crabtree, *Baptists in Brazil* (Rio de Janeiro: Baptist Publishing House of Brazil, 1953), 135–37; of the Baptist Missionary Association of Texas and the American Baptist Association, see Conrad N. Glover and Austin T. Powers, *The American Baptist Association, 1924–1974* (Texarkana, Tex.: Bogard Press, 1979), 127ff.,160ff.; of the Baptist Missionary Association, see John W. Duggar, *The Baptist Missionary Association of America 1950–1986* (Texarkana, Tex.: Baptist Publishing House, 1988), 95ff., 131–32, 203; and of the Conservative Baptists, see *Founded on the Word: Focused on the World* (Wheaton, Ill.: CBFMS, 1978), 37–45, and Hans W. Finzel, ed., *Partners Together* (Wheaton, Ill.: CBFMS, 1993), 138–41.

SPAIN (1869)

	Members	Churches
1. Unión Evangélica Bautista Española (U.E.B.E.) (1929)	7,700	(65)
2. Federación de Iglesias Evangélicas Independientes de España (F.I.E.I.) (1957)	4,400	(62)
3. Asociación de Iglesias Evangélicas Bautistas Independientes de España (A.I.E.B.I.) (Strict Baptists)	200	(5)

4. Comunión Bautista Independiente
   (Fundamental Baptists)   825   (36)

5. Free Will Baptists   57   (1)

6. Other Baptists   n/a   n/a

                                                13,182   (169)

STATISTICS: According to the *Spanish Christian Handbook* in the *European Churches Handbook*, pt. 2 (MARC Europe, 1991), 16, there were 12,993 Baptists in 198 churches in 1990. For statistics of U.E.B.E., see BWA, *Yearbook*, 1993–1994, 101. For F.I.E.I. and Fundamental Baptists, see the *Spanish Christian Handbook*, 16. For A.I.E.B.I., see David B. Barrett, ed., *World Christian Encyclopedia*, 631. Free Will Baptists supplied their own statistics.

*W*ith Spain's strong Roman Catholic heritage, Spanish Baptists generally experienced only toleration, if not outright oppression, from the 1860s until the 1960s. Before the passage of the Law of Religious Liberty in 1968, true religious liberty existed for only short periods of time.

A revolution in Spain in 1868 opened the door for William I. Knapp, an American, to begin mission work. At first he cooperated with Presbyterians, thinking it to be a more practical course, but on August 10, 1870, he formed the First Baptist Church of Madrid. Appointed by the American Baptist Missionary Union (ABMU) as its missionary, Knapp also established work in other areas. After the first interest in Protestantism evaporated, progress was very slow. In 1876 when Knapp resigned, in part because of political instability and lack of funds from the ABMU, there were 250 Baptists in the country.

Knapp left the work in the hands of native pastors, but all of the churches and missions from Knapp's endeavors disappeared. His work, however, was not in vain since the seed of future work had been sown. The Baptist cause was saved with the arrival of Eric Lund, a Swede, who had begun working in Galicia in 1877 but soon moved to Figueras in Catalonia where a church was formed in 1881 by Cifre, a Spanish coworker. In the same year the Swedish Baptist Union (SwBU) appointed Lund and his wife as missionaries, but by mutual consent of the American and Swedish bodies they became missionaries of the ABMU. In 1883 Lund formed a church in Barcelona. The SwBU appointed other missionaries and the ABMU provided assistance to Spanish coworkers. But with the church in Barcelona practically dead because of the migration of its members to South America and decreases in other points, Lund decided in 1891 to try another strategy and go to the villages. In 1896 there were ten churches and 115 members. Unfortunately, the cities were neglected and converts were not adequately nurtured. Lund himself left Spain in 1900 to open a new Baptist field in the Philippine Islands.

As a result of the London Conference in 1920, which assigned Baptist mission responsibility in Europe, Southern Baptists were given Spain and other areas. The ABMU, SwBU, and an independent foreign mission committee of Swedish Baptists in Chicago now came under the administration of the FMB of the Southern Baptist Convention. Under the direction of Everett Gill, Sr., European superintendent for the FMB-SBC, the work was reorganized and expanded. In 1922 a training school in Barcelona opened, which continued until 1929. In 1922 Spanish Baptists founded the Unión Evangélica Bautista Española, but in 1929 established the more permanent

Spanish Baptist Convention, which later in 1953 took the same name as the earlier union. In 1923 a paper, *El Mensajero Bautista*, began publication; it later took the name, *El Eco de la Verdad*, the name of an earlier Baptist paper that had ceased some years before. By 1930 Baptists had grown to around one thousand members in twenty-one churches.

Although there was more freedom under the Republic, founded in 1931, Baptists stagnated. Unfortunately, Spanish Baptists were not as yet self-supporting, and the continued decrease of funds from the FMB, which had already begun before the Great Depression of the 1930s, reduced the number of pastors and mission activity. As a result of a devastating three-year civil war (1936–1939), which led to the establishment of a Fascist regime under Francisco Franco, about a fourth of the members either died or fled the country, many going to France. In addition, most Baptist and other Protestant churches were now closed, and from 1939 to 1945 the church in Madrid was the only Baptist congregation which could maintain anything like a normal program. After 1945 there was more toleration but oppression continued with closure of churches, imprisonment and fines for evangelistic activity, persecution of evangelicals in the armed services, and prohibition of signs which indicated Protestant churches or services. In addition, the teaching of the Roman Catholic faith was mandatory in the schools. In 1956 the Spanish Baptist Union helped to form with other denominations a Committee of Evangelical Defense, which elected Jose Cardona, a Baptist pastor, as executive secretary, to petition the government for more freedom. In spite of the difficulties, Baptists grew by 1958 to more than 2,200 members in forty-two churches.

The 1960s witnessed greater freedom with all closed churches open by 1963 and permission in 1966 for a bookstore. In 1967 a Law on Religious Liberty was passed, but the Baptist Union, believing the law kept Protestants in a secondary status, directed its churches not to register under the law. Some churches, however, broke rank and registered, which caused much controversy in the Union. In 1980 the government finally approved a new law which gave Protestants full rights.

In 1947 the FMB sent John David Hughey, the first Southern Baptist missionary to arrive after World War II. In 1975 the FMB had thirty-five missionaries on the field, a number which increased eight years later to fifty. The FMB provided funds for buildings and church planting as well as money for theological education, a conference center, a correspondence course, a radio recording studio, and a pastors' pension fund. At the same time there was an increase in self-supporting churches. The number of pastors grew with many receiving theological training either at the seminary in Barcelona, which reopened in 1948 and later moved to Alcobendas, near Madrid, or the International Baptist Seminary in Switzerland.

Since 1975 the Spanish Baptist Union has become practically independent, assuming greater responsibility for the direction of its cooperative work and raising more of its own funds. In addition the FMB turned over its properties that were used by Spanish Baptists either to the Baptist Union or the churches. Missionaries play a more supportive than directive role today.

In the early 1920s most of the Baptist work in Spain was consolidated under Southern Baptists and remained so until after the Second World War. In 1949, however, a schism occurred when the Southern Baptist mission informed Samuel Vila, president of the Baptist Convention, that he and his church could no longer continue in the convention because of funds received from another mission. Two churches with four hundred members immediately left the union. This defection led in 1957 to the for-

IV. *Latin America and the Caribbean*

Baptists have come a long way in Latin America and the Caribbean during the last two generations. From around ninety-five thousand in 1927, Baptists are now two million. Before World War I, much of the Baptist work was limited to certain areas. Through the Baptist Missionary Society from England and Jamaican Baptists, a rather extensive work had developed among English-speaking Blacks in the Caribbean. In addition, Baptist work among Latin peoples was taking some root in Argentina, Chile, and Brazil in South America and in Cuba, Mexico, and Puerto Rico in Middle America, but elsewhere it was very weak or non-existent. Today, however, Baptists may be found in every country and in growing numbers.

Baptists have ministered to many ethnic groups in this territory. Black Baptists appeared not only in the English-speaking British islands of the Caribbean but also in Belize, Honduras, Nicaragua, Panama, Guyana, and Colombia. The first Baptists in Chile were German; the first in Argentina were Welsh and French; the first in Brazil were North American; the first in Venezuela were Caribbean Blacks; the first in Guyana were Chinese; and the first in Suriname were Javanese! Baptists today have large English, French Creole, Spanish, and Portuguese-speaking constituencies with work among indigenous Indian tribes also. Although most of their members have come from the economically deprived classes, Baptists are found among other classes as well.

Latin America and the Caribbean beckon as a great mission challenge. The field is diverse from primitive Indian tribes to the masses in the rapidly growing urban centers. With the rapid growth of evangelicalism, which is providing the lower classes with dignity and self-identity, the potential for growth appears unlimited. After years of slow development, Baptists are now in a position to reap rich dividends from earlier efforts.

BIBLIOGRAPHY: An excellent bibliography on Spanish-speaking Baptists is, Ernest Edwin Atkinson, *A Selected Bibliography of Hispanic Baptist History* (Nashville: Historical Commission/SBC, 1981). It includes a wide range of books, articles, and other materials.

Regions	Countries	Members	Churches
A. Caribbean	24	399,612	1,905
B. Middle America	8	196,307	2,080
C. South America	<u>13</u>	<u>1,387,491</u>	<u>8,741</u>
	45	1,983,410	12,726

A. CARIBBEAN

Baptists in the Caribbean have had a checkered history. They have experienced both victory and suffering and have faced numerous problems. The honor of bringing the Baptist witness to the area belongs to freed Black slaves from the USA who settled in Jamaica, Turks and Caicos, the Dominican Republic, and Trinidad. Missionaries of the Baptist Missionary Society (BMS) did not arrive until twenty-seven years later in Trinidad, thirty-one years later in Jamaica, and over a half century later in the Bahamas.

The Baptist mission in Jamaica appeared to be a victory for the rapid development of work on indigenous principles. In 1842 Jamaican Baptists became self-supporting and also formed their own Jamaican Baptist Missionary Society (JaBMS). But a weak economic base and the lack of trained pastors and lay leaders turned advance into decline. The decision of the BMS in 1892 to withdraw almost entirely from the Caribbean left a serious void in finances and leadership. At the same time, the BMS and JaBMS failed to enter the English-speaking islands in the Leewards and Windwards.

Another difficulty was the relationship between the missionaries of the BMS who were trained in a Western European culture. They attempted to minister to the existing Baptist population, which was largely preliterate and whose faith was mixed with pagan survivals. It is not surprising that the history of Baptists in Jamaica, the Bahamas, and Trinidad is also a story of misunderstanding and division.

The waning and disappearance of Spanish power in the Caribbean in the late nineteenth century opened new fields for Southern and Northern Baptists from the USA. The Southern Baptists entered Cuba and the Northern Baptists entered both Cuba and Puerto Rico. In comparison to other Protestants, Baptists have been relatively successful in these two islands. Another field which has opened substantially to Baptists with Northern (American) Baptists taking the lead is Haiti, where mass movements have occurred. Since World War II, mission agencies from the USA, including Southern Baptists, National or Black Baptists, and independent evangelical conservative Baptist missions, have now entered every political entity in the Leeward and Windward Islands.

In comparison to the established Anglican and Roman Catholic Churches, Baptists are few, but they have made great progress since the 1920s when they had only around fifty thousand members. Today they cover the region and are the leading Protestant denomination in the Bahamas, Turks and Caicos, and Haiti. Baptists along with Pentecostals are in the forefront for Protestants in Cuba as well. Their first members came from the lowest economic classes, many of them slaves or recently freed, but today they are increasingly taking their place in the higher ranks of society. Baptists also have been able to plant an effective witness among the various language groups, whether they be English, Spanish, or French.

Although Caribbean Baptists are somewhat fragmented, there is some cooperation.

schools are merged as the Jordan-Prince Williams Baptist School. The convention also operates the Bahamas Baptist Bible Institute (1972) and Bahamas Baptist College (1988).

In 1951 Southern Baptists sent their first missionary couple, Henry and Lelia McMillan, and two years later John and Mildred Mein. Because of problems of health, the McMillans left, but the Meins, seeing the great need for training, opened the Bahamas Baptist Institute in their home in 1953. At first it included a training school and then a theological division; both, however, closed in 1967. Southern Baptists helped to develop in the 1960s the "Baptist Hour," a weekly radio program, and also established in Nassau the Caribbean Media Center, which in 1987 moved to Florida. Baptist International Missions, Inc. (BIMI) has sent a number of missionaries to the Bahamas, where they established churches and the Nassau Christian Academy.

In 1968 Bahamian Baptists formed a United Baptist Choir. In an effort at greater unity, the Bahamas Convention adopted a new constitution, which was accepted in 1971 by six Baptist groups and the Pilgrim Baptist Church. The associations, which are not organized geographically, have greater strength than the convention and wield a strong influence over the churches which each has developed. About four-fifths of the Baptist churches now belong to the convention. In 1977 the first issue of *Bahamas Baptist Gazette* was published.

Baptists in the Bahamas have come a long way. Colonial society despised the Black inhabitants, but Blacks readily received the Baptist message as did their brethren in the USA. Baptists are the largest denomination in the Bahamas. They have made great social and educational strides. The present prime minister of the Bahamas, Hubert Ingraham, elected in 1992, has joined the Zion Baptist Church of Nassau. Before independence, Baptists had no recognition at government functions, as the Anglicans and Roman Catholics, but today they are seventh in protocol.

BIBLIOGRAPHY: A standard history is Michael C. Symonette and Antonina Canzoneri, *Baptists in the Bahamas* (El Paso, Tex.: Baptist Publishing House, 1977). Additional information may be found in Peter Brewer, "British Baptist Missionaries and Baptist Work in the Bahamas," *Baptist Quarterly*, 32, no. 6 (April 1988): 295–301, and Philip Rahming, "Baptists in the Bahamas," *Our Christian Heritage, 1492–1992* (Nassau, 1992), 15–16.

BARBADOS (1905)

	Members	Churches
1. Barbados Baptist Convention (1974)	421	(4)
2. National Baptist churches	*n/a*	(4)
	421	(8)

*T*he island of Barbados received independence from Great Britain in 1966. It is predominantly Protestant with Anglicans the leading denomination.

The beginning of Baptist work in Barbados has been documented insufficiently. The National Baptist Convention in the USA recorded in its 1908 *Journal* that it had two missionaries in Barbados, A. S. Phillips and T. E. Smith, and there were three churches—at St Thomas (formed in 1905), Bridgetown (1907), and St. Johns (1908)—with a membership of 105. In 1977 the FMB of the National Baptist Convention, USA, reentered the field by appointing as superintendent for its work, Sinclair Rudder, pastor of the Packers and Cleveland Baptist Churches. In the early twentieth century, a Free Baptist Association existed, which was in fellowship with Free Will Baptists in the northern states of the USA.

In 1972 Southern Baptists entered Barbados with the arrival of William and Elba Womack. They established the Windward Islands Mission to include Barbados and the Windward Islands. In 1974 two churches, formerly known as Bethany Christian Churches, and one congregation which separated from First Baptist Church of Bridgetown formed the Barbados Baptist Convention. In 1977 the mission began the Barbados Baptist College, which provides theological training for church leaders in Barbados and other Caribbean islands. A number of other conservative evangelical Baptist missions have also entered Barbados since the Second World War.

BIBLIOGRAPHY: For work of the National Baptist Convention, USA, see William J. Harvey III, *Bridges of Faith Across the Seas* (Philadelphia: FMB/NBC, USA, 1989), 287–89. For Southern Baptists, see William W. Graves, *Baptist Trade Winds* (Nashville: Convention Press, 1979), 75–79, and *Your Guide to Foreign Missions, 1994–1995,* 66.

BERMUDA (1932)

	Members	Churches
Bermuda Baptist Fellowship (1981)	336	(4)

*A*lthough Bermuda, a dependency of Great Britain, is not in the Caribbean, this group of islands in the Atlantic is classified with the Caribbean region because of its Caribbean ties. The Emmanuel Baptist Church in Hamilton, formed in 1932, is the oldest congregation. It started when a Baptist woman who moved to Bermuda from the USA helped to provide for a pastor from Jamaica to begin the church. In 1956 a group of American service personnel formed the First Baptist Church of Devonshire with ties to Baptists in Texas and, for a short time, with Baptists in South Carolina. In 1966 Southern Baptist missionaries arrived to work with the church, which today is an interracial congregation. A Bermuda Baptist Fellowship has been formed, consisting of four churches, which is a member of the BWA.

BIBLIOGRAPHY: Mike Creswell, "Bermuda!" *Commission,* August 1985, 50–63.

CAYMAN ISLANDS (1885)

	Members	Churches
1. Cayman Baptist Association, Cayman Brac	400	(n/a)
2. First Baptist Church, Grand Cayman	<u>151</u>	<u>(1)</u>
	551	(n/a)

T he three Cayman Islands, lying south of Cuba, are a dependency of Great Britain. The Jamaica Baptist Mission Society (JaBMS) showed an interest in the Cayman Islands with the visit in 1885 by J. H. Sobey, who found the people ready for a missionary. The JaBMS sent a succession of missionaries until 1933, when the last one returned in the aftermath of a destructive hurricane. As a result of the work, at least four churches were established on Cayman Brac and one on Little Cayman.

In 1977 a Southern Baptist missionary couple arrived, who found in existence a Cayman Baptist Association composed of churches on Cayman Brac. Through their mission work, the First Baptist Church of Grand Cayman was organized. Today Southern Baptists have a worker who serves among the youth.

BIBLIOGRAPHY: Inez Knibb Sibley, *The Baptists of Jamaica* (Kingston: Jamaica Baptist Union, 1965), 28–29. *Your Guide to Foreign Missions*, 1994–1995, 61.

CUBA (1886)

	Members	Churches
1. Convención Bautista de Cuba Occidental (1905)	7,627	(113)
2. Convención Bautista de Cuba Oriental (1905)	8,844	(138)
3. Convención Bautista Libre de Cuba (1943)	1,040	(16)
4. Fraternidad de Iglesias Bautistas de Cuba (1989)	<u>2,400</u>	<u>(12)</u>
	19,911	(279)

D uring the Ten Years War (1868–1878) against Spanish domination, many Cuban exiles became members of Protestant churches in the USA. One of them, Albert J. Díaz, returned in 1882 to Cuba after joining a Baptist church in New York City. In the following year Díaz organized an independent congregation, Iglesia Getsemaní, in Havana. A Cuban lady named Adela Fales and Pastor F. W. Wood, both working with Cuban exiles in Key West, Florida, heard of the work of Díaz. Wood encouraged Southern Baptists to send missionaries to Cuba, and in 1885 Díaz was ordained as a Baptist minister in Key West. In 1886 Díaz led his congregation in Havana to become a Baptist church and immersed believers in the Havana harbor. In the same year, Wood went to Cienfuegos under the Jamaica Baptist Missionary Society (JaBMS), which had been interested in Cuba since 1884 when George Henderson visited the country. For some years, JaBMS sustained a mission interest in the island. Florida Baptists also provided some funds for Díaz and Wood. Beginning in 1886, the Home Mission Board (HMB) of the Southern Baptist Convention officially entered the field for Southern Baptists with Díaz serving as its first general missionary.

In 1886 the Spanish regime granted religious toleration. In the following year, Díaz bought land for a cemetery and purchased the Jané theater, which became the head-quarters of Baptist work. In this early period, Baptists preached in Havana, Cienfuegos, Regla, Batabanó, Guanabacoa, and Trinidad. During the new War of Independence (1895–1898), however, Protestants were accused of helping the inde-pendence forces. Díaz was imprisoned until the U.S. State Department obtained his release. The Spanish-American War of 1898 ended Spanish rule and, after several years of occupation, the USA recognized Cuban independence in 1902. In November 1898 the HMB of the Southern Baptist Convention transferred the eastern half of the island to the America Baptist Home Mission Society (ABHMS) for mission work while retaining the four western provinces.

A number of exiled Cuban pastors returned after the war, and Díaz resumed his work in Havana. In January 1901 Southern Baptists, lacking confidence in Díaz, sent C. D. Daniel as superintendent of the work, which precipitated Díaz's resignation. In 1905 Daniel helped to organize the Western Baptist Convention of Cuba. Nathaniel McCall, who arrived in 1905, soon succeeded Daniel and remained for forty-two years as leader of the work. In 1905 he began theological training in Havana. Southern Baptists founded in Havana the Colegio Bautista. In 1907 Baptists in western Cuba started a periodical, *Sion*, later renamed *La Voz Bautista*.

J. R. O'Halloran, a missionary of the HMB of the SBC, began working in eastern Cuba in 1898, establishing work in Santiago de Cuba and Guantánamo. In October 1899 Harwell Robert Moseley became the first superintendent for the ABHMS and Teófilo Barocio, a Mexican pastor, took charge of the church in Santiago. Moseley with others founded the Eastern Baptist Convention of Cuba in 1905. Robert Routledge from Canada and Oscar Rodríguez from Puerto Rico also served as super-intendents. In 1907 American Baptists established Colegios Internacionales in El Cristo near Santiago, which became one of eastern Cuba's most prestigious private schools. In 1904 Baptists in eastern Cuba began the publication of *El Mensajero*.

Thomas and Mabel Willey, Free Will Baptists who had served in Panama and entered Cuba in 1941, laid the foundations for the work of the Free Baptist Convention. In February 1943 Willey organized the Free Will Baptist Association of Pinar del Río. In the same year a Bible institute, "Cedars of Lebanon," was organized. The churches of the Free Baptist Convention are primarily in Pinar del Río and Havana. Today the Convention maintains a small theological school and publishes *El Mensajero Fiel*.

In 1989 three Baptist churches organized La Fraternidad de Iglesias Bautistas de Cuba. The Western Convention had excluded this group for its involvement in the political sphere, its practice of open communion, and its less restrictive policy on bap-tism. One of its leaders, Raúl Suárez, pastor of the Emmanuel Baptist Church of Havana and for many years president of the Ecumenical Council of Cuba, is also a member of Parliament. Today this body has ties with American Baptists and with the Alliance of Baptists, an independent group of Southern Baptists in the USA.

When Fidel Castro, who established a Communist regime in Cuba, gained power in 1959, there were Baptist churches all over the country. Baptists also operated two seminaries, schools, homes for the aged, and retreat centers. In 1961 the government nationalized the schools, but most churches and the two seminaries remained open. Cuban Baptists continue to maintain organizations for men, women, youth, and children. Sunday Schools are well organized and growing, and youth work is strong. The Cuban conventions have no foreign mission boards but in the past have supported missionaries in Colombia and Central America. Today mission work is conducted among Haitians and other Caribbean peoples living in the country.

Before the revolution, most Baptists were from the working class, a few from the middle and professional classes, and none from the upper class. Some Baptists were elected to positions in local government and to Parliament. Other Baptists, however, were active in the revolution, and a prominent Baptist teacher, Frank País, became the second most important leader of the movement that brought Castro to power. País was killed during the struggle and became a national hero. After the revolutionary government proclaimed itself Marxist-Leninist in 1961, a number of Baptists, including pastors and missionaries, left the island. In April 1965 the government arrested forty-eight Baptist leaders in the Western Convention, including Herbert Caudill, superintendent of the HMB since 1947, and his son-in-law, David Fite, who served as a missionary. Almost all of them, including Caudill and Fite, were sentenced to prison, accused of currency violations and cooperation with the CIA. Caudill and Fite could not leave until 1969. During the 1980s the regime became less restrictive on religion.

Cuban Baptist work is self-governing and self-supporting, although Baptist agencies from abroad may send money for special projects. In 1988 the FMB of the SBC agreed to take responsibility for Cuba from the Home Mission Board. The Western and Eastern Conventions are members of the BWA and also the Free Baptist Convention, the only Free Will Baptist body in the world which belongs to the Alliance. Relations with other denominations are usually friendly, but most Baptists are not ecumenically oriented. Only the Free Baptist Convention and La Fraternidad are members of the Ecumenical Council.

Cuban Baptists are conservative in theology although some are familiar with contemporary theological thought. The charismatic movement, though not strong among Baptists, is making inroads in some areas. Music style is traditional, but contemporary and national music is becoming fashionable in some churches. Only Fraternidad churches ordain women as pastors.

Baptists and Pentecostals are the two largest Protestant denominations on the island. In spite of a Marxist regime which imposes some restrictions and denies almost completely access to mass communications, Baptist churches, in the face of growing economic problems in the country, are experiencing revival. Churches are full, attracting many young people as well as some professionals. In some areas attendance has doubled in the last three years. Local congregations are organizing hundreds of house churches (*casa culto*).

Marcos A. Ramos

BIBLIOGRAPHY: Material on the Western Convention may be found in A. S. Rodríguez, *La Obra Bautista en Cuba Occidental* (Havana: Imprenta Bautista, 1930), and Harold

Edward Greer, *History of Southern Baptist Mission Work in Cuba 1886–1916* (M.A. thesis, University of Alabama, 1963). For the Eastern Convention, see Samuel Deulofeu, *Cronologia de la Obra Bautista en Cuba Oriental* (Palma Soriano, 1983). A Baptist pastor and historian who formerly lived in Cuba, Marcos A. Ramos, has written two important studies on Protestantism in Cuba, which includes much valuable information on Baptists— *Panorama del Protestantismo en Cuba* (Miami: Editorial Caribe, 1986) and *Protestantism and Revolution in Cuba* (Coral Gables, Fla.: North-South Center for the Research Institute for Cuban Studies, University of Miami, 1989). For the work of the Jamaica BMS in Cuba, see Inez Knibb Sibley, *The Baptists of Jamaica* (Kingston: Jamaica Baptist Union, 1965), 26–27. For Free Will Baptists, see Mary Wisehart, ed., *The Fifty–Year Record of the National Association of Free Will Baptists 1935–1985* (Nashville: Randall House Publications, 1988), 60–61.

DOMINICAN REPUBLIC (1843)

	Members	Churches
1. Dominican National Baptist Convention (1968)	1,292	(20)
2. Baptist Mid-Missions	118	(3)
3. Dominican Conservative Baptist Fellowship (1987)	n/a	(n/a)
4. Iglesia Bautista Misionera Haitiana (1987)	1,000	(21)
5. Asociación Bautista Vida Eterna (1983)	225	(6)
	2,635	(50)

T he Dominican Republic, a Spanish-speaking nation with more than 95 percent of the population nominally Roman Catholic, includes the eastern two-thirds of the island of Hispaniola. Its neighbor to the west is Haiti, a predominantly Black French-speaking country.

The first Baptist work was English-speaking. Former American slaves had settled at Puerto Plata, a town on the north coast which had an English community that fellowshiped with the English-speaking Grand Turk Island to the north. In 1843 William Littlewood, a missionary of the Baptist Missionary Society (BMS) who was appointed to the Bahamas, visited Puerto Plata and organized a church among the American Black Baptist community. Because of the War of Independence in 1844, the church was dispersed but was reconstituted by W. K. Rycroft, another missionary of the BMS, when he settled there in 1852. There was still a small English-speaking group of three churches in existence as late as 1930.

A more important Baptist work has developed among French-speaking Haitian immigrants. There is evidence of Baptist work among these immigrants in the nineteenth century, but the oldest Baptist work among them today started in the 1920s when they immigrated into the country during the sugar boom. The first church, La Ramona, was established in 1922. In 1929 Haitian Baptists began to support missionaries to work among the Haitian migrants. In 1987 the Haitians gained autonomy and formed an association. The Haitian Association developed ties with the Board of International Ministries (BIM) of the American Baptist Churches, USA (ABC). The work of the churches in the Association includes two vocational centers, a craft cooperative, medical clinics, and food distribution centers.

Since 1949 Baptist Mid-Missions (BM-M) has had a small work. Three couples who were serving in the Dominican Republic resigned from an interdenominational mission when its leadership became Pentecostal. They then turned to BM-M, which appointed them. The first work was in Hato Major where a church was formed in 1953. By 1977 there were three congregations.

In 1962 Southern Baptists entered the Dominican Republic with the arrival of Howard and Dorothy Shoemake, missionaries who transferred from Ecuador. In 1964 the Central Baptist Church of Santo Domingo was started, and by 1970 there were five churches. The mission has extended its outreach by forming mission points, training nationals, and starting student work, clinics with local churches, and a deaf ministry. In 1968 a Dominican National Baptist Convention was organized. The work is supplemented by a Dominican Baptist Seminary and a small home for the aged for Haitians. The Convention has purchased a site in La Vega for a Baptist conference center.

In 1985 the Conservative Baptist Home Mission Society (CBHMS) appointed a national Dominican, Joaquin Vargas, to serve. Two years later a Dominican Conservative Baptist Association was formed and a program of TEE instituted. In 1992 the mission established the Las Caobas Baptist Church and Community Center, which provides a number of family services.

The Vida Eterna Association is a result of the work of a church in Puerto Rico which sent evangelists to the country in 1980. In 1983 five of the churches from this work broke from the control of the mother church, formed their own association, and became associated with the BIM of the American Baptist Churches, USA. The churches extend their outreach through grade schools, a vocational training center, literacy programs, and medical services.

BIBLIOGRAPHY: For a general survey of Baptist work from the beginnings to the 1960s, see Horace O. Russell, *The Baptist Witness* (El Paso, Tex.: Carib Baptist Publications, 1983), 146–48. For the activity of the Baptist Missionary Society, see Brian Stanley, *The History of the Baptist Missionary Society 1792–1992* (Edinburgh: T&T Clark, 1992), 93. For the work of Baptist Mid-Missions, see Polly Strong, *Burning Wicks* (Cleveland: BM-M, 1984), 274–76. For Southern Baptist work, see *Your Guide to Foreign Missions*, 1994–1995, 61. On the work of the Conservative Baptist Home Mission Society, see *The Challenge*, Sep. 1987, 4, and spring 1992, 1–2. For information on the associations related to the American Baptists, see the brochure, "Dominican Republic," in the Caribbean Mission Study Packet, "Caribbean Connections," of International Ministries, ABC/USA.

HAITI (1836)

	Members	Churches
1. Convention Baptiste de' Haiti (1964)	83,000	(104)
2. Églises Ebenezer et Tabernacle	45,000	(50)
3. Mission Baptiste (BM-M)	530	(n/a)
4. Baptist Haiti Mission	36,820	(105)

5. Mission Evangélique Baptiste du Sud-Haiti	60,000	(282)
6. Union Evangélique Baptiste d'Haiti	10,113	(100)
	235,463	(641)

STATISTICS: It is not easy to obtain reliable statistics on Baptists in Haiti. Older statistics understate Baptist strength, while current statistics tend to inflate it. Statistics, as found in David B. Barrett, ed., *World Christian Encyclopedia*, 350, are outdated, but Barrett's figures for membership of Mission Baptiste and Union Evangélique Baptiste were used as the best available. Statistics for the Convention Baptiste were gained from the Board of International Ministries, ABC/USA, and statistics for Mission Evangélique Baptiste du Sud-Haiti from WorldTeam. Sem Marseille provided the membership and number of churches for Mission Baptiste Conservatrice and for the membership of Églises Ebenezer. There are also independent Baptist groups which are not included in the above figures.

T he second oldest republic in the Americas is Haiti, which proclaimed its independence from France in 1804. Its population is predominantly Black and French-speaking. Although the majority of the populace is Roman Catholic, voodoo is strongly intertwined. Haiti is mountainous, overpopulated, limited in resources, and is the poorest nation in the Western hemisphere. Besides their evangelistic work, missions have provided the country with a broad range of social services.

The Protestant minority is rapidly growing, and Baptists are the largest Protestant body in Haiti. As late as 1938 there were only eight thousand Baptists, but since World War II the growth has been explosive. In a number of places there has been a mass movement to the Baptist faith, and for some time Protestants were simply known as Baptists. As with other evangelicals in other parts of Latin America and the Caribbean, people who accept the Baptist faith gain a new status, feeling they are full members of society.

For such an important Baptist field, it is surprising that Baptist work in Haiti was so sporadic for so long. For a century, from 1823 to 1923, there were fits and starts but no comprehensive Baptist work until the coming of the American Baptist Home Mission Society (ABHMS). The Massachusetts Baptist Missionary Society sent Thomas Paul in 1823, who preached and distributed Scripture for six months, but there was no follow-up. In 1835 the Triennial Convention sent to Port-au-Prince William C. Monroe, a Black who offered his services. In January of the following year, he organized a church composed of English-speaking Blacks, but he resigned in 1837. A more lasting work came from the efforts of the American Baptist Free Mission Society, an abolitionist group which was attracted to the country because it was a free Black republic. It sent William M. Jones to Port-au-Prince in January 1845. Several others joined the mission, including Mr. and Mrs. William L. Judd, who arrived in 1847 and remained for about twenty years. In 1890 Lucius Hippolite, a Haitian who was one of Judd's converts and was educated abroad, became pastor of Judd's church in Port-au-Prince in 1890 and served it until his death in 1928. Its membership was small.

British and Jamaican Baptists also made some efforts, which proved to be limited. From 1845 to 1885 the Baptist Missionary Society sent a number of missionaries, and then it turned over its mission to the Jamaica Baptist Missionary Society (JaBMS). Work was established at Jacmel in the south, but the work was limited in personnel and resources. Jamaican Baptists sent their first missionary couple to this field in 1883. They continued to provide support for some years, including assistance to Nosirel

L'Herrison, an educated Haitian who became pastor of the Jacmel Church in 1894. Some thirty-five years later it was reported that the church had 1,200 members with a constituency of more than 3,000 and twelve missions. Jamaican Baptists also had interests in other areas. In 1874 they sent George Angus, a graduate of Calabar College, to St. Marc on the west coast and Daniel Kitchen to Port-de-Paix in the north, who later settled at Cap-Haitien.

Jemima Straight, a teacher who supported herself, began another work in the north. She went to teach at Ste. Suzanne near Trou-de-Nord. From her appeal for mission help, Elie Marc, a French student at Newton Theological Institution, then came to Haiti in 1894 and became pastor of the church at Trou-de-Nord (which Daniel Kitchen had founded) and supported himself. Marc evangelized the surrounding areas and entered the interior. He also trained a few men for pastoral service.

Entry of the American Baptist Home Mission Society in 1923 began a new day in Baptist missions in Haiti. When A. Groves Wood arrived, there were only about 1,200 scattered Baptists and eight pastors. The two main centers of Baptist work were in the extreme north, led by MARC, and in the extreme south, led by L'Herrison. Wood felt the greatest need was in the north; so he established the mission at Cap-Haitien in 1924 and also gained MARC's cooperation. Spreading the gospel, Wood traveled primarily on horseback at first but later journeyed by car. Wood trained Haitian pastors and organized numerous primary schools. In 1942 Edith Robinson, a Haitian who was appointed as a missionary, founded the College Pratique de Nord, which developed into an outstanding secondary school. The mission provided funds for schools at the churches for members eager to learn to read. The mission established a seminary at Limbé (1947), Good Samaritan Hospital (1953), four miles from the seminary, and an Eye Center at Cap-Haitien (1989). In addition, the mission has several clinics, two agricultural centers, and about eighty-five schools with twenty-seven thousand students. The mission also has dug more than 120 artesian wells to supply drinking water. In 1964 the Baptist Convention of Haiti was formed and is a member of the BWA. In 1977 the responsibility of American Baptist mission work in the country was transferred to the Board of International Ministries, ABC.

In 1916 the Lott Carey Baptist Foreign Mission Convention (LC) entered the country by providing support for pastors/teachers already on the field. One missionary who received support was Boaz Harris, who had a successful work on the island of Gonâve. In 1975 the Lott Carey Convention terminated its work.

A nondenominational mission which has been very successful in Haiti is WorldTeam (WT). As the Cuba Bible Institute, it found a field among Haitians who had been converted by Baptists when they worked in the Cuban sugar fields. In 1936 three missionaries opened the field, today known as the Evangelical Baptist Mission of South Haiti. In the following year the mission organized a Bible school in Les Cayes. Since then the mission has established a seminary, a hospital, and a radio network and has engaged in community development and programs for child care. There are 284 churches with more than 60,000 members and 183 schools with 23,000 students related to the mission. Another nondenominational mission which works with a group of Haitian Baptists is UFM International (UFMI), known as Evangelical Crusade Mission when it entered the field in 1943. It took over a work which another missionary had started in 1928. In 1977 the churches of the mission formed the Evangelical Baptist Union of Haiti. The mission maintains a seminary, a Bible school, and a hospital.

Another very successful mission has been the Baptist Haiti Mission, founded in 1946 by John and Rhoda Turnbull, who were accompanied by their son, Wallace. Two years later the mission was turned over to Wallace, who continues to administer the work. The mission began in the mountains of Kenscoff, a needy area suggested by the president of Haiti, Elie Lescot. For a time the mission was associated with the Conservative Baptist Home Mission Society but today is entirely independent. It has spread to five provinces and includes 308 churches and missions with 120,000 in attendance as well as 185 Christian day schools with 44,500 students. The mission's medical ministry includes a hospital and a clinic as well as six satellite clinics. In its self-help programs, it trains families in crafts and marketing and distributes trees for reforestation. In relief work, it distributes food and builds homes for the destitute. The Baptist Haiti Mission is a member of the BWA.

An independent group of Baptists is the Ebenezer Baptists who suffered division in 1937 with the establishment of the Tabernacle Baptist Church. The two groups are located in southeastern Haiti. Since World War II, a number of other Baptist missions have entered the country, including the National Baptist Convention of America and the Progressive National Baptist Convention.

Sem Marseille and Albert W. Wardin, Jr.

BIBLIOGRAPHY: For general surveys of Baptist work in Haiti, see Charles S. Detweiler, *The Waiting Isles* (Philadelphia: Judson Press, 1930), 91–120; George A. Bowdler, *Baptist Missions in the West Indies* (Th.D. dissertation, New Orleans Baptist Theological Seminary, 1948), 62–69, 126–33; and Horace O. Russell, *The Baptist Witness* (El Paso: Carib Baptist Publications, 1983), 133–39. Material on the work of the BMS may be found in Brian Stanley, *History of the Baptist Missionary Society 1792–1992* (Edinburgh: T&T Clark, 1992), 93–95, 100; for the Lott Carey Mission, see Leroy Fitts, *Lott Carey* (Valley Forge: Judson Press, 1978), 121–29; and for the Baptist Haiti Mission, see Mildred Anderson, *Beyond All This* (Grand Rapids: Baptist Haiti Mission, 1979). For current material on the work of American Baptists, see the brochure, "Haiti," in the mission packet, "Caribbean Connections," of International Ministries, ABC/USA.

JAMAICA (1783)

	Members	Churches
1. Jamaica Baptist Union (1849)	43,000	(293)
2. Seventh Day Baptist Conference (1923)	1,415	(26)
3. Association of Independent Baptist Churches (1963) (BM-M)	1,000	(40)
4. Fellowship of Independent Baptist Churches (1961) (Reformed Baptists)	2,000	(15)
5. Fellowship of National Full Gospel Baptist Churches of Jamaica	3,200	(35)
6. Jamaica Association of General Baptists (1963)	440	(12)
7. Jamaica Fellowship Baptist Convention	n/a	(31)
	51,055	(452)

B aptists came to Jamaica with George Leile (c. 1750–1828), who sailed from Savannah, Georgia, to Kingston, Jamaica, in 1782. Upon the reverses of the British in the War of American Independence, Liele, a freed slave, left with the British forces, armed with a letter of recommendation to the acting governor of Jamaica. With this introduction, he secured work in Spanish Town, the capital. He preached at the Kingston Race Course and in December 1783 formed a church in Kingston.

Despite some setbacks, he established work throughout the island aided by able preachers and deacons, some of whom had been migrants like himself. One of these was Moses Baker, who organized a witness in Montego Bay and was encouraged to write to the Baptist Missionary Society (BMS) of London for help. Another correspondent to the BMS was Nicholas Sweigle. In 1814 the BMS sent John Rowe (1788–1816) to initiate a fraternal association, which has continued to the present. Despite the hostility of the plantocracy and the inhospitable environment due to the presence of disease, over the next twenty years the BMS sent out more than sixty missionaries, most of them couples.

In December 1831 a slave insurrection broke out, which involved some Baptists and was soon named "the Baptist war." The planters blamed Baptists and other dissenters for the revolt. Although the missionaries were exonerated, White citizens destroyed Baptist and Methodist chapels, which unwittingly helped to bring an end to slavery itself. In England William Knibb, Thomas Burchell, and James Phillippo, missionaries from Jamaica, were very effective in attacking slavery before committees of Parliament.

With the abolition of slavery (1833) and full emancipation (1838), Baptists began to consolidate their work. In 1837 with the help of Joseph Sturge (1793–1859), the Jamaica Education Society was established as an agency to promote education to the secondary level without government grants. About this time William Knibb, James Phillippo, and John Clark pioneered in organizing free villages whereby each freed slave would own a plot of land sufficient to produce food for his family and also ensure him a vote for the National Assembly. In 1842 the Western and Eastern Unions declared their independence of the BMS, founded the Jamaica Baptist Missionary Society (JaBMS), and approved establishing Calabar Theological College, which opened in the following year. The JaBMS sent missionaries to Africa in 1843 and started missions in Haiti (1879), Panama (1894), and Nicaragua (1904). JaBMS also developed ties with San Andrés Island, Colombia, and Free Town in Sierra Leone. In 1847 the *Jamaica Baptist Reporter* was founded to facilitate the merger of the Western and Eastern Unions, which was accomplished in 1849 with the formation of the Jamaica Baptist Union.

In 1860 a revival broke out which revitalized the churches, and its effect was to last a generation. There was an increase in membership, and Baptists began to exert their influence on the national scene. This led in 1865 to confrontation with the government over oppressive fiscal policies and discrimination in the use of land. As a result of the Morant Bay Rebellion, the government executed William Gordon, a legislator with Baptist sympathies, and Paul Bogle, a Baptist deacon, and arrested and incarcerated several Baptist pastors. Today Jamaica honors Gordon and Bogle as national heroes.

Baptists divided on the question of violence, the role of representatives of the BMS in national affairs, and color, which had increasingly become an issue with the presence of African-Americans who had migrated to the island in significant numbers. A

Native Baptist Church was established in 1866. There were also misgivings with the British liturgical tradition and this led to several schisms. A split in the Brown Town Church over divine healing led to the formation of the Tabernacle Church (1876) and a division in the Westmoreland churches produced the Christian Catholic Church (1884).

At first, Baptists adhered to voluntarism in education, refusing to accept help from the Negro Education Grant (1844), established by the British Parliament. Baptists abandoned this policy in 1870 when Calabar College moved to Kingston and grants were accepted to fund the large network of elementary schools attached to the churches. Calabar now trained school teachers and added a regular school. In 1912 a boys' school was established and now continues as Calabar High School. A girls' school was later developed at Westwood.

Sunday Schools were of two kinds—those with a general education curriculum and those created specifically for Bible knowledge and moral training. A Sunday School Society was formed in 1869, whose mandate included the education of indentured laborers from India and the development of a mission agenda in the churches. The work among the Indians became the special responsibility of the St. Mary Baptist Association, which began in earnest in 1873.

In 1892 the BMS withdrew all subsidies except salaries for missionaries who taught in the theological school. With a weak economic base; migration to Panama, Cuba, and Costa Rica; a lack of sufficient pastors and trained lay leaders; and controversy over Calabar College; membership began to decline, dropping to less than twenty-two thousand in 1942. The introduction of critical biblical studies at the college and opposition to the influence of the college's president in denominational affairs led to the exodus of many Baptists to other communions.

Jamaican Baptists established several important denominational institutions in the third and fourth decades of the twentieth century. They included a Jamaica Baptist Women's Federation (1922), the Laymen's Movement (1934), a Youth Department (1934), the Spiritual Rearmament Conference (1938), and the Gordon Somers Society (1940) for students in higher education.

Some financial relief was provided with the formation of a sustentation fund, financed by the BMS, American Baptist Foreign Mission Society, and Jamaican Baptists; it aided the most poorly paid pastors but was inadequate to meet all the needs. In the 1950s a more sufficient central fund was established with assistance from the BMS, Canadian Baptists, and, for a time, by Southern Baptists. Southern Baptists also taught stewardship and provided pastors for evangelistic campaigns and students for Vacation Bible Schools.

In 1966 Calabar College merged into the newly formed United Theological College of the West Indies, which in the following year operated on a new campus adjacent to the University of the West Indies. In spite of emigration, Baptist membership again increased in the 1950s and, although there was another decline in the latter half of the 1980s, it has again shown recovery.

The Jamaica Baptist Union is a charter member of the BWA, the only Baptist body on the island to belong. In 1910 it formed an Evangelical Council with Anglicans, Presbyterians, and Methodists.

In polity, the basic unit is the local church. Churches belong to circuits—voluntary units that share a pastor and cooperate in ministry. Circuits are grouped to form area

6. St. Martin/St. Maarten (1986)

Southern Baptist Mission	785	(9)

7. U.S. Virgin Islands

a. Baptist General Conference	630	(6)
b. Baptist International Missions, Inc.	500	(n/a)
c. Southern Baptists	n/a	(4)
d. Virgin Islands Baptist Mission	n/a	(2)
e. Other congregations	n/a	(2)
	1,130	(14)

GRAND TOTALS	3,750	(43)

T he Leeward Islands, located on the northern end of the Lesser Antilles, extend from the U.S. Virgin Islands in the north to Guadeloupe in the south. The United States possesses the U.S. Virgin Islands, while Great Britain still controls the British Virgin Islands, Anguilla, and Montserrat. Guadeloupe and more than half of St. Martin/St. Maarten are an overseas department of France, while the Netherlands possesses the remainder of St. Martin/St. Maarten, Saba, and Saint Eustatius. There are two independent nations—Antigua, which also includes Barbuda, and the Federation of St. Kitts and Nevis. The Anglican, Roman Catholic, and Methodist churches with roots in the colonial period predominate. Baptists have a presence, but it is weak in part because of their late entry. The first Baptist mission did not arrive until the 1960s.

One early center of work has been on St. Kitts. After a trip to New York City in 1963, William Connor, an Anglican layman, realizing he was Baptist in conviction, returned to the island and constituted Antioch Baptist Church from a fellowship and Sunday School he had already begun. Since then a Baptist association has been established. Southern Baptist missionaries and laypeople from the USA have given personal support to the work.

As a result of a survey of the Caribbean by the Foreign Mission Board of the Southern Baptist Convention in 1961, it was decided that work should begin, among other places, in the French West Indies. The first Southern Baptist missionaries, William and Violet Cain, entered Guadeloupe in 1964. Today there are seven churches, including a Haitian congregation and a Dominican English-speaking congregation. In 1986 the Baptist Federation of Guadeloupe was organized, and the missionaries work under this body. The work includes a bookstore and a film library. Property has been purchased for a camp.

In 1968 Southern Baptist missionaries in Trinidad began to visit Antigua weekly to minister to Baptists on the island. Earlier, at the beginning of the 1960s, a missionary who was a member of the General Association of Regular Baptists had organized the First Baptist Church of Antigua, but it was short-lived. Around 1965, another congregation, Central Baptist Church, was formed from a mission Sunday School of the extinct church. In 1969 Southern Baptists sent to Antigua their first resident missionaries, Vernon and Carolyn Sydow, who had served in Brazil. In 1980 three churches formed the Antigua Baptist Association. The churches also have established preaching points. Baptists are attempting to reach Haitians who have entered Antigua as refugees. In 1990 the Central Baptist Church adopted the 1689 Baptist Confession, thus adopting a Reformed Baptist position.

Southern Baptists from Antigua have assisted Baptist work in St. Kitts (where there is a Baptist association), Montserrat (where there is a church), and Tortola in the British Virgin Islands. On December 31, 1976, a Southern Baptist couple, Lester and Fonda Boyd, arrived in Tortola in the British Virgin Islands to assist the Mt. Carmel Baptist Church. Beginning in the 1960s, independent Baptists from the USA had started Mt. Carmel and five other churches. The Boyds turned their work over to a layman at the end of 1980, but today a missionary from St. Martin visits the island regularly for training lay members.

In 1986 Southern Baptists sent a couple to St. Martin/St. Maarten, and today missionaries live on both the Dutch and French sides of the island. The work includes an international Baptist church and a mission to Chinese seamen. Southern Baptists also have a monthly Bible study on Anguilla. In an effort to coordinate the work in the area, Southern Baptists formed the Leeward Islands Mission in 1972.

Baptist International Missions (BIMI) is the only independent fundamental Baptist agency listed as working today in the Leewards. In 1963 the mission entered the U.S. Virgin Islands, in 1968 Anguilla, and in 1975 Antigua. On Antigua it has established the Caribbean Radio Lighthouse, which broadcasts throughout the Caribbean and provides Bible correspondence lessons.

The Baptist General Conference (BGC) opened a mission on Montserrat with the coming of Mr. and Mrs. Norril Gumbs, who were sent by the First Baptist Church of Frederiksted, Virgin Islands. In 1969 the Calvary Baptist Church was organized, and ten years later it dedicated a new church building.

Several Baptist bodies are represented in the U.S. Virgin Islands. The National Baptist Convention of America ((NBC) has ties with the Virgin Islands Baptist Mission, which includes a church as well as the Virgin Islands Bible Institute on St. Thomas, a church on St. Croix, besides a few churches in Dominica and St. Vincent. The Progressive National Baptist Convention (PNBC) helps support a church on St. Croix. The Home Mission Board of the SBC assumes responsibility for Southern Baptist work, assisting two churches on St. Croix and two on St. Thomas. In 1960 the Home Mission Board of the Baptist General Conference approved Clifford and LeEllen Bubar, who had served under another mission, as missionaries at Frederiksted on St. Croix, where a Baptist chapel already was functioning. In 1962 the First Baptist Church of Frederiksted was formed. Today the BGC has five other congregations on St. Croix, including a Hispanic congregation. There is a Free Will Baptist church at Christiansted on St. Croix, and, as already noted, Baptist International Missions, Inc., also has work in the islands.

BIBLIOGRAPHY: For a general introduction to Baptist work in the Leeward Islands, see Horace O. Russell, *The Baptist Witness* (El Paso, Tex.: Carib Baptist Publications, 1983), 155–58. For additional material on Southern Baptists, see the brochure, *The Caribbean* (FMB/SBC, 1974); Lester E. Boyd, "Mission in Tortola, *Encyclopedia of Southern Baptists*, 4:2524; Mary E. Speidel, "St. Maarten! Port of Call," *Commission*, July/Aug. 1994, 4–33; and *Your Guide to Foreign Missions*, 1994–1995, 63–64. For the work of the Baptist General Conference, see David Guston and Martin Erikson, eds., *Fifteen Eventful Years* (Chicago: Harvest, 1961), 61–62, and Donald E. Anderson, ed., *The 1970s in the Ministry of the Baptist General Conference* (Arlington Heights, Ill.: BGC, 1981), 36–37.

NETHERLANDS ANTILLES (1983)

	Members	Churches
Southern Baptist Mission	240	(3)

*T*he Netherlands has a number of islands in the Antilles, including Curaçao and Aruba off the northern coast of South America. In 1983 Southern Baptists entered Curaçao as a joint project of the Baptist Convention of Venezuela and the FMB of the Southern Baptist Convention. It was the first foreign mission endeavor of the Venezuelan Convention and the first joint venture of the FMB with a Baptist convention outside the USA. In 1983 Calvary Baptist Church was organized with two other congregations formed since then. In 1992 Southern Baptists sent a missionary couple to Aruba, and Venezuelan seminary students have canvassed the island to discover interest for Bible studies. The mission has translated materials into Papiamento, the most commonly used language, which is a combination of European, Indian, and West African languages.

BIBLIOGRAPHY: *Your Guide to Foreign Missions*, 1994–1995, 64–65.

PUERTO RICO (1899)

	Members	Churches
1. Convention of Baptist Churches of Puerto Rico (1902)	19,175	(79)
2. Puerto Rico Baptist Association (1965) (SBC)	5,128	(45)
3. Puerto Rico Baptist Association (CB)	93	(4)
	24,396	(128)

*P*uerto Rico, acquired in 1898 by the USA as a result of the Spanish-American War, is a self-governing commonwealth. It is predominantly Roman Catholic with, however, a vigorous Protestant minority of 8 to 9 percent of the population. Its culture is primarily Hispanic.

The Baptists were the first Protestant denomination to send missionaries to Puerto Rico. In 1898 William H. Sloan, an American Baptist missionary from Mexico, after preaching at several sites, recommended to the American Baptist Home Mission Society (ABHMS) that it enter the island. In 1899 the ABHMS sent Hugh P. McCormick and A. B. Rudd, both natives of Virginia and former missionaries to Mexico, while the Woman's American Baptist Home Mission Society sent Ida Hayes and Jeanne P. Duggan. Other denominations quickly followed, and they and the Baptists divided the territory by comity but left the main cities of San Juan and Ponce open to all missions. Baptists gained a central territory along the former Spanish military highway from San Juan in the north to Ponce in the south.

McCormick opened a preaching station in Río Piedras in the north and in June 1899 baptized his first converts, Mr. and Mrs. Manuel Lebrón. Lebrón became the first Puerto Rican Baptist minister. On July 9, 1899, a church was organized at Río Piedras, the first Protestant congregation in Puerto Rico. The Baptist witness spread into neighboring towns.

In the meantime Rudd began work in the south. On November 21, 1899, the First Baptist Church of Ponce was formed. Baptists also spread from here to other areas, both along the coast and into the interior. In 1902 an association was formed which later became the Convention of Baptist Churches of Puerto Rico. In 1907 a theological school was instituted in the Ponce Church, later moving to other sites, but in 1919 becoming part of the newly formed interdenominational Evangelical Seminary of Puerto Rico. The Baptist Academy was established at Barranquitas. Growth has been steady; in 1919 there were 5,000 members in the convention, but today there are more than 19,000.

Southern Baptist work first started among the U.S. military. Between the mid-1950s and 1964 congregations appeared in Aguadilla, Puerto Nuevo, Ponce, and Ceiba. Services began to be conducted in both English and Spanish and attracted Puerto Ricans. In 1964 the Home Mission Board of the Southern Baptist Convention entered the field. In 1965 a Puerto Rico Baptist Association of five churches and five missions was formed. In 1970 the Association had grown to five Spanish-speaking and four English-speaking congregations besides a number of missions. Today it numbers more than 5,000 members.

Since World War II a number of other Baptist missions also have entered the field. One of these is the Conservative Baptist Home Mission Society which works in western Puerto Rico. The Conservative Baptists have a small association of four churches.

BIBLIOGRAPHY: For a general survey of Baptist work, see Horace O. Russell, *The Baptist Witness* (El Paso, Tex.: Carib Publications, 1983), 148–53. For a history of American Baptist work, see Charles S. Detweiler, *The Waiting Isles* (Philadelphia: Judson Press, 1930), 19–60; Tómas Rosario Ramos, *Historia de los Bautistas de Puerto Rico*, 2d rev. ed. (Santo Domingo: Editora Educativa Dominicana, 1979); and Jose L. Delgado, "Brief History of the Baptist Mission in Puerto Rico, *Chronicle*, 2, no. 4 (1939): 160–70. For the activity of Southern Baptists, see Dallas M. Lee, "Missions in Puerto Rico," *Encyclopedia of Southern Baptists*, 3:1927–28.

TRINIDAD AND TOBAGO (1816)

	Members	Churches
1. Baptist Union of Trinidad and Tobago	3,450	(23)
2. Fundamental Baptist Mission	350	(8)
3. Trindad and Tobago Baptist Association	n/a	(n/a)
4. Union of Independent Baptist Churches	n/a	(n/a)
	3,800	(31)

*T*rinidad and Tobago gained independence from Great Britain in 1962. The country is located off the north shore of South America, close to Venezuela. About 36 percent of the population is Roman Catholic, while Protestants include about 30 percent, Hindus 25 percent, and Moslems 6 percent.

During the War of 1812 (1812–1815) in the USA, a number of Blacks escaped slavery by joining British marine regiments. After the war, the British government recompensed these soldiers by settling them and their families in the south of Trinidad in Savannah Grande. The villages which the settlers founded, called "The American Villages," often carried the name of the company in which the soliders had served, such as Fifth Company. A number of the settlers were Baptists and brought their faith with them. William Hamilton, who arrived in 1816, founded the Fifth Company Church, the first Baptist church in Trinidad, and remained its leader until his death in 1860.

In 1843 George Cowen, the first missionary of the Baptist Missionary Society (BMS) to serve in Trinidad, settled at Port of Spain in the north. John Law arrived in 1845 and settled in the south, working among the Blacks in the American Villages until his death in 1852 at the age of forty-two. He attempted to organize the work but met with hostility for his efforts to eliminate superstition, heathen customs, and disorderly practices. In 1892 the BMS withdrew from the field only to reenter in 1946. Churches in cooperation with the BMS formed the Baptist Union of Trinidad and Tobago in the 1860s.

In the early twentieth century a break occurred in Baptist ranks with the formation of the Union of Independent Baptist Churches, which has since divided into two parts. A number of Black Baptists resented the meddling and control of British Baptists, such as J. J. Cooksey, a missionary of the BMS who received his financial support from the government, and B. E. Horlick, pastor of the St. John's Church in Port of Spain who attempted to eliminate the all-night meetings and to control licenses to perform marriages.

Another Baptist group is the Fundamental Baptist Mission, formed by James Vincent Quamina (1879–1945), a native of Tobago who was forced to leave his earlier denomination after he accepted the doctrine of eternal security. In 1912 he began to preach independently. On a trip to the USA in 1921, he was able to organize the Fundamental Baptist Mission of Trinidad and Tobago for support. In 1991 a Canadian office was opened. In 1959 the Fundamental Mission began a primary school at Laventille. In Trinidad the work has always been under local leadership, although it continues to receive financial assistance and some mission personnel from abroad.

Southern Baptists sent their first missionary couple, Emit and Kathryn Ray, in 1962. At first Southern Baptists formed their own churches, and then in 1971 these congregations joined the Baptist Union. Tension, however, developed between the union and the Southern Baptist missionaries. When the union required the missionaries to become fully part of the union, they withdrew. Four churches which they had founded also left and established the Trinidad and Tobago Baptist Association.

Although the Baptists of Trinidad and Tobago are divided into five distinct groups, there is some cooperation among them. The Trinidad and Tobago Baptist Fellowship provides opportunity for special projects in ministry and training. There are also indigenous Baptist groups, the Spiritual Baptists and the Shouter Baptists. Their identification as Baptist is more in name only as their polity and practice do not reflect established Baptist traditions.

V. Anthony Cadette and Albert W. Wardin, Jr.

BIBLIOGRAPHY: For the work of the Baptist Missionary Society, see Sidney G. Poupard, "Baptist Beginnings in Trinidad," *Baptist Quarterly*, 14, no. 5 (Jan. 1952): 232–234; Peter Brewer, "Ministry in a West Indian Town: John Law in Port of Spain, 1845–1870," *Baptist Quarterly*, 33, no. 6 (Apr. 1990): 175–285; and Brian Stanley, *The History of the Baptist Missionary Society 1792–1992* (Edinburgh: T&T Clark, 1992), 94–95, 102–5, 251–54, 264–68. For the Fundamental Baptist Mission, see Ann Philip, *The History of the Fundamental Baptist Mission of Trinidad and Tobago from 1912 to 1973* (Thesis, University of the West Indies, 1974), which was published by the U.S. Board of the Fundamental Mission in 1990. For Southern Baptists, see the brochure, *The Caribbean* (Richmond: FMB/SBC, 1974), 10–14, and *Your Guide to Foreign Missions, 1994–1995*, 65–66.

TURKS AND CAICOS

	Members	Churches
Turks and Caicos Baptist Union	511	(13)

Τhe Turks and Caicos Islands, located at the southeastern end of the Bahamas chain, is a British colony with a population of about twelve thousand. The Baptists are the largest religious body in the territory.

Baptists began as an extension from the Bahamas. About 1830 Sharper Morris, a former slave from America who was residing in Nassau, visited the Turks where he helped to stop the persecution of Baptists and baptized fifty converts. Mr. and Mrs. Ebenezer Quant, missionaries of the Baptist Missionary Society (BMS), resided in the Turks from around 1835 to 1841 and helped to constitute the first Baptist church on Grand Turk with seventeen charter members.

J. Henry Pusey, a BMS missionary who served from 1880 to 1910, provided strong leadership. During his tenure, he led in the forming of the Turks and Caicos Baptist Union and gave to senior deacons ministerial responsibilities, which they continue to exercise. In 1892 the BMS turned the work over to the Jamaica Baptist Missionary Society, arranging for a four-year subsidy to ease the transition. In recent years, Southern Baptists have cooperated with the Jamaica Baptists in work on the islands, providing missionaries from 1982 to 1989, helping to train leaders, and providing workshops in stewardship and Christian education.

BIBLIOGRAPHY: For a general survey, see Horace O. Russell, *The Baptist Witness* (El Paso: Carib Baptist Publications, 1983), 109–11. For the work of the Jamaica Baptist Missionary Society, see Inez Knibb Sibley, *The Baptists of Jamaica* (Kingston: Jamaica Baptist Union, 1965), 29–30. For Southern Baptist activity, see *Your Guide to Foreign Missions, 1994–1995*, 68.

WINDWARD ISLANDS

	Members	Churches
1. Dominica		
Dominica Baptist Union (1982)	190	(5)
2. Grenada (1975)		
Grenada Baptist Assocation(1981)	250	(4)
3. Martinique (1946)		
Église Baptiste Indépendante	200	(6)
4. St. Lucia (1948)		
a. Baptist Mid-Missions	200	(11)
b. Southern Baptist Mission	<u>53</u>	<u>(2)</u>
	253	(13)
5. St. Vincent and the Grenadines (1947)		
a. Baptist Mid-Missions	300	(9)
b. St. Vincent Baptist Convention (1987)	<u>350</u>	<u>(5)</u>
	650	(14)
GRAND TOTALS	1,543	(42)

*T*he Windward Islands, stretching from Dominica in the north to Grenada in the south, include four independent nations in addition to Martinique, which is a French overseas department. As in the Leewards, the Anglican, Roman Catholic, and Methodist churches dominate religious life. In addition there is a strong Seventh-Day Adventist presence. Baptists did not arrive until after World War II and are comparatively weak.

Because of their work in other French-speaking lands, Evangelical Baptist Missions (EBM)was attracted to Martinique, sending its first missionary, Charles Shoemaker, in 1946. Today there are six churches related to the mission. In 1977 Southern Baptists sent missionaries to the island to work with national Baptists. Southern Baptists have no resident missionaries at present, but missionaries may visit the island from Guadeloupe.

The next mission to enter the area was Baptist Mid-Missions (BM-M). Eugene and Hilda McMillan arrived in 1947 and formed in the same year the Arnos Vale Baptist Church. In 1953 the Windward Islands Baptist Bible School was organized in the home of the missionaries and three years later moved to its own campus. It serves students from St. Vincent and neighboring islands. In 1948 BM-M sent James and Leah Wooster to St. Lucia, who settled in Castries. Soon after their arrival, much of the town was destroyed. As a result of the Wooster's relief work, the Baptist cause gained special respect. BM-M has nine churches on St. Vincent and eleven on St. Lucia.

Southern Baptists also work on St. Vincent and St. Lucia. Donald and Maudie

Overstreet started work in St. Vincent in January 1977 with a Bible study program, assisted by a man who had become a Christian while imprisoned in Grenada. In 1987 four congregations formed the St. Vincent Baptist Convention. In 1983 a Southern Baptist missionary couple, Jonathan and La Homa Singleton, moved to St. Lucia from Dominica. Two churches and a Baptist center have been established.

Southern Baptists entered Grenada with the coming in 1975 of Manget and Elaine Herrin, who had served in Guyana. Before their arrival Southern Baptists already had contact in the island with Leon Edwards—a man who was serving a life sentence for murder in Richmond Hill Prison but was converted by listening to the "Baptist Hour." The Radio and Television Commission of the Southern Baptist Convention filmed the story of his life, and prison officials allowed J. P. Allen of the Commission to baptize him in the Caribbean Sea before the film crew left. The mission includes prison and dental ministries. In 1981 four churches organized the Grenada Baptist Association. Several other Baptist missions also have entered Grenada. There are Spiritual Baptists with roots in Trinidad, whose faith is a mixture of Christian and pagan elements.

Before the arrival of Southern Baptists in Dominica, the Mt. Gerizim Baptist Church in the capital city of Roseau sought ties with Southern Baptists. The first missionary couple, Fred and Betty Walker, arrived in 1975, having previously served in Kenya. Soon the Mt. Gerizim Church severed its relation with Southern Baptists, but members of the church formed Deliverance Baptist Church, which maintained fellowship with the mission. In 1979 Hurricane David brought great destruction, and the missionaries, with help from the BWA and the Caribbean Baptist Fellowship, provided relief and also built and repaired homes. In 1982 three churches formed the Dominica Baptist Union. As in Grenada, the mission includes a prison ministry and dental services.

BIBLIOGRAPHY: For a general survey, see Horace O. Russell, *The Baptist Witness* (El Paso: Carib Baptist Publications, 1983), 159–62. For the work of Evangelical Baptist Missions on Martinique, see William J. Hopewell, Jr., *The Missionary Emphasis of the General Association of Regular Baptist Churches* (Chicago: Regular Baptist Press, 1963), 134–35. For the work of Baptist Mid-Missions, see *Field Surveys*, (Cleveland: BM-M, c. 1977), 107–11, and Polly Strong, *Burning Wicks* (Cleveland: BM-M, 1984), 279–82. For Southern Baptist work, see *Your Guide to Foreign Missions*, 1994–1995, 66–69.

BAPTIST AND BAPTIST-RELATED MISSIONS

1. BAHAMAS   UkBMS (1833–1931), NBC (1946), SBC (1951–1992), BIMI (1968), MWBM (1983), PNBC

2. BARBADOS   BBFI (1962), SBC (1972), NBC (1977), BIMI (1978), BM-M (1990), PNBC

3. BERMUDA   SBC (1966)

4. CAYMAN ISLANDS   JaBMS (1885–1933), BIMI (1960), SBC (1977)

5. CUBA   —

6. DOMINICAN REPUBLIC   BM-M (1949), SBC (1962), BIMI (1969), ABC (1980), CBHMS (1985), BWM (1986), BrB (1991)

7. HAITI   ABC (1923), BM-M (1932), BHM (1946), MWBM (1967), BIMI (1978), SBC (1978), BBFI (1982), BWM (1986), CBHMS (1992), NBCA, PNBC

8. JAMAICA SDBMS (1927), BM-M (1938), GBFMS (1961), BIMI (1971), NBC (1971), BBFI (1972), RBMS (1972), MWBM (1983), NBCA, PNBC

9. LEEWARD ISLANDS   BGC (1960), BIMI (1963), SBC (1964), NBCA, PNBC

10. NETHERLANDS ANTILLES SBC (1983)

11. PUERTO RICO BBFI (1955), CBHMS (1958), BM-M (1959), SBC (1964), BIMI (1965), BWM (1985), MWBM (1987), MBM

12. TRINIDAD AND TOBAGO UkBMS (1843–1892, 1946), FBT&T (1921), SBC (1962), BIMI (1974)

13. TURKS AND CAICOS JaBMS (1892)

14. WINDWARD ISLANDS   EBM (1946), BM-M (1947), SBC (1975), BIMI (1979), MWBM (1986), MBM

NONDENOMINATIONAL MISSIONS

1. HAITI   WT (1935), UFMI (1943)

B. MIDDLE AMERICA

*M*iddle America, the land bridge between the United States and South America, including Mexico and seven Central American nations, has a large mestizo population with important Indian and White minorities as well as a small Black population along the Caribbean coast. Until recently most people were Roman Catholic or adherents of folk religion mixed with Catholicism, but today the region is experiencing a religious revolution with large numbers converting to evangelical Christianity.

It is not surprising that Baptists in the USA would show an early interest in Mexico, a neighbor with a number of its people living in the USA. Baptists were among the first Protestants to enter the country, establishing in the country the first evangelical church for Mexicans.

For Central America, however, the Baptist story is much different. Except for very limited efforts among English-speaking Blacks on the Caribbean coast or off-shore islands, primarily by Jamaican Baptists, there was no other Baptist effort in the nineteenth century. Before the beginning of World War II, there was also practically no work among the Spanish-speaking populace except for Northern (American) Baptists serving in El Salvador and Nicaragua.

Since the beginning of World War II, Baptist missions from the USA have flooded the area. Southern Baptists, no longer confining themselves to Mexico and Panama, have entered every country, and conservative evangelical missions are also well represented. As recently as 1965, there were about fifty thousand Baptists, including forty thousand in Mexico. Today the number is probably around 200,000 if returns could be obtained from all Baptist missions.

National bodies related historically to American and Southern Baptists are members of the Baptist World Alliance and the Union of Baptists in Latin America, but a number of other groups are outside these organizations. Under the auspices of the BWA, Baptists from Mexico and Central America held in 1993 their first conference, which also included Conservative Baptists, who otherwise are not members.

	Members	Churches
1. Belize	1,237	10
2. Costa Rica	4,540	68
3. El Salvador	11,602	62
4. Guatemala	17,500	163
5. Honduras	17,089	311

6. Mexico	120,877	1,224
7. Nicarauga	13,154	131
8. Panama	<u>10,308</u>	<u>111</u>
	196,307	2,080

BELIZE (1822)

	Members	Churches
Baptist Association of Belize	1,237	(10)

T he little country of Belize, formerly known as British Honduras, located on the eastern coast of Central America and bordering Mexico and Guatemala, gained its independence from Great Britain in 1981. English is the official language, but Spanish and Creole dialects are spoken widely. About two-thirds of the population is Roman Catholic with a Protestant minority of about 28 percent.

Although Baptists were one of the first Protestant groups in the country, arriving in the early nineteenth century, they have always been small in number. The Baptist Missionary Society (BMS) worked in the country from 1822 to 1850, sending its first missionary, James Bourne. He arrived with the financial support of G. F. Angus, a wealthy shipowner and supporter of the BMS. During Bourne's tenure, he organized a church in Belize City, which had seven members by 1825. In 1835 Alexander Henderson, a man with strict communion views, replaced Bourne, who went to the Bahamas. By 1843 the mission included the church at Belize City with two hundred members, four mission stations, five schools, and three Sunday Schools. Conflict between Henderson and J. P. Butterfield, a General Baptist who came in 1844, led to the termination of Henderson's services with the BMS in 1846. Four years later the BMS withdrew from the field and sold its property. The Jamaica Baptist Missionary Society (JaBMS) assumed limited responsibility for the field until 1901.

After World War II, the Conservative Baptist Home Mission Society (CBHMS) entered Belize in 1960, followed in 1977 by Southern Baptists. Both missions work together and with the Baptist Association of Belize. Baptist membership in the Association has now risen to more than 1,200. The Baptist Bible Fellowship International (BBFI) entered in 1978 and has missionary couples at Orange Walk Town, Corozal, and near Belmopan.

BIBLIOGRAPHY: For a survey of the beginnings of Baptists in Belize, see Horace O. Russell, *The Baptist Witness* (El Paso: Carib Baptist Publicatons, 1983), 170–75. For Southern Baptist work, see *Your Guide to Foreign Missions*, 1994–1995, 56. For data on the activity of the Baptist Bible Fellowship, see Jack Foster, "The Wonderful World of Make Belize," *Baptist Bible Tribune*, April 1992, 20.

COSTA RICA (1888)

	Members	Churches
1. Convención Bautista de Costa Rica (1947)	3,500	(24)
2. Union Nacional de Iglesias Bautistas de Costa Rica (1981)	1,040	(17)
3. Asociación Bautista Costarricense (ABA)	n/a	(16)
4. Baptist Missionary Association of Costa Rica (BMA)	n/a	(11)
	4,540	(68)

Soon after gaining freedom from Spain in 1821, Costa Rica became a member of the United Provinces of Central America in 1823 but withdrew in 1838. Unlike other Central American states, the majority of the population of Costa Rica is of Hispanic background. There are mestizo and Black minorities but comparatively few Indians. About 95 percent of the populace is Roman Catholic.

Because many Jamaicans settled in the banana plantations of Costa Rica, the Jamaica Baptist Missionary Society (JaBMS) sent E. J. Hewett and J. H. Sobey to survey the area in 1888. Sobey relinquished his pastorate in Montego Bay and became the first resident missionary of the JaBMS in the country, serving until 1899. He established a chapel at Puerto Limón and also preached in the interior. Sobey ministered in English, but a second missionary, James Hayter, attempted to reach the Spanish-speaking population. JaBMS sent other missionaries but gave up responsibility for the field before World War I.

A Bible study which met in homes in San José was another Baptist source. In December 1943 the group formed the First Baptist Church of San José with forty-nine charter members. Aurelio Gutíerrez, who had studied at a Baptist school in Nicaragua, taught Baptist doctrine to the group. Upon the recommendation of Paul C. Bell, superintendent of Baptist work in Panama, the Home Mission Board of the Southern Baptist Convention extended aid to the church. In 1948 the HMB sent its first resident missionaries, Van Earl and Waurayne Hughes, who in the following year came under the auspices of the FMB of the Southern Baptist Convention. The Southern Baptist mission established in San José the Baptist Theological Institute (1950), a Baptist center, and a Baptist bookstore.

In 1947 four churches formed the Baptist Convention of Costa Rica with which Southern Baptists cooperated. In 1980, because of a dispute over a missionary, the convention became alienated from the Southern Baptist mission and severed its relationship with it. Churches who now withdrew from the convention and were willing to continue Southern Baptist ties formed the National Union of Baptist Churches in 1981. Southern Baptists today cooperate primarily with the National Union, while the International Board of American Baptist Churches cooperates with the convention.

A number of other Baptist missions have entered Costa Rica since World War II. The Conservative Baptist Home Mission Society (CBHMS) sent Vergil and Dorothy Gerber and Carrie Muntz to work with other evangelical mission agencies in forming L.E.A.L.

This effort facilitated the distribution of Christian literature in Latin America and published, *Verbo,* an evangelical magazine. Today First Baptist Church of Puerto Limón and Waldeck Baptist Church maintain fraternal relations with the Conservative Baptist Association of America.

Landmark Missionary Baptists are well represented in Costa Rica. American Baptist Association (ABA), which began in 1940, currently has sixteen churches and six missions. Its churches have formed the Costa Rica Baptist Association. The work of the Baptist Missionary Association (BMA) began in 1961 with the coming of Mr. and Mrs. Duane Heflin. The mission started a Bible training school, and by 1984 eleven churches had been established as well as the Baptist Missionary Association of Costa Rica.

BIBLIOGRAPHY: For the work of the Jamaica Baptist Missionary Society, see "*Glorious Liberty*" (London: BMS, 1914), 153–54. For beginnings of Baptist work in the 1940s and 1950s, see Charles W. Bryan, "Mission in Costa Rica," *Encyclopedia of Southern Baptists,* 1:325. For the early involvement of Conservative Baptists in Costa Rica, see CBHMS, *The Year 1958,* 8–9. For the mission of the Baptist Missionary Association, see John W. Duggar, *The Baptist Missionary Association of America (1950–1986)* (Texarkana, Tex.: Baptist Publishing House, 1988), 135, 204, 256. For information on the separation of the SBC from the Southern Baptist mission, see *Commission,* May 1981, 66.

EL SALVADOR (1911)

	Members	Churches
1. Asociación Bautista de El Salvador (1934)	5,402	(61)
2. National Baptist Convention churches	1,200	(n/a)
3. Independent church, San Salvador	5,000	(1)
	11,602	(62)

*E*l Salvador, a small but heavily populated country between Guatemala and Honduras, has a largely mestizo population. About 95 percent of the population are adherents of the Roman Catholic Church with many of them following a syncretic Catholic-Mayan faith. Baptists have always been a small body in the country with Pentecostals far more numerous.

In 1911 the American Baptist Home Mission Society entered the field. It appointed for a year William Keech, an English Baptist who had served as superintendent of the British and Foreign Bible Society in Central America, and Mr. and Mrs. Percy T. Chapman, who were already serving as self-supporting missionaries in Santa Ana where they had established a church and erected a church building. Chapman traveled to other parts of the country and formed other congregations, finding groups already prepared by the work of the colporteurs, peddlers of Christian literature, of the Bible societies. In 1915 the Woman's American Baptist Home Mission Society (WABHMS) sent its first two missionaries. This mission instituted Colegio Bautista in Santa Ana and a sister school in San Salvador, both institutions beginning as elementary schools but becoming high schools as well.

Aside from the churches in Santa Ana and El Salvador, much of the work has been in rural areas. The seminary which was established in the country was moved to Nicaragua and did not continue to serve El Salvador as was hoped. The work has been handicapped by a lack of trained leadership.

With the support of American Baptists, Southern Baptists sent a couple to develop a literature ministry in 1974, which led to the organization of a bookstore and a warehouse outlet for books. Today Southern Baptists have a small staff in the country which is involved in evangelism and church development, working with churches and missions outside the Baptist Association. The Baptist Missionary Society (BMS) in England has entered into an association with the Baptist Association, sending a missionary in 1988.

There are also National Baptist churches which have been served by National (or Black Baptist) missionaries from the USA. A large number of independent Baptist churches also exist. The largest one with five thousand members, which claims to be the largest Baptist church in Latin America, is located in San Salvador.

BIBLIOGRAPHY: For American Baptist work, see G. Pitt Beers, *Ministry to Turbulent America* (Philadelphia: Judson Press, 1957), 142–46, and Dean R. Kirkwood, *Renewal Amid Revolution* (Valley Forge: International Ministries/ABC/USA, 1980), 20–24. For Southern Baptist work, see *Your Guide to Foreign Missions*, 1994–1995, 74. For a reference to National Baptists, see David B. Barrett, ed., *World Christian Encyclopedia* (Nairobi: Oxford Press, 1982), 280.

GUATEMALA (1948)

	Members	Churches
Convención Bautista de Guatemala (1946)	17,500	(163)

*A*fter being part of the United Provinces of Central America from 1823 to 1839, Guatemala became a separate state. Many of its people are Mayan Indians with most of the rest mestizo. Although a majority of the people are members of the Roman Catholic Church, there is a rapidly growing Protestant population.

In 1928 an independent Christian movement began, which as early as 1931 started using literature from the Spanish Baptist Publishing House in El Paso. In 1939 its churches organized the Convention of Evangelical Independent Churches, later taking as their standard the *Baptist Manual for Baptist Churches* by Edward T. Hiscox. After making contact with Southern Baptists, three Southern Baptists visited them, including Paul C. Bell, superintendent of Southern Baptist work in Panama. Bell found most of the churches ready to identify themselves as Baptists. After Bell and the other two Southern Baptists baptized three hundred of their members, nine churches were formed which organized a Convention of Baptist Churches in 1946. In the following year the Foreign Mission Board (FMB) of the Southern Baptist Convention took over responsibility for the work, and in 1948 the first resident Southern Baptist missionaries, William and Carra Webb of the Mexican mission, settled in Guatemala City.

The work expanded swiftly in number of missionaries and churches, and by the early 1970s all churches were self-supporting. In Guatemala City the mission established a theological institute and a bookstore. In 1960 missionaries entered Quetzaltenango, the country's second city; four years later they entered Cobán to begin work among the K'ekchi' Indians. Today there is a Kekchi Indian Baptist Association.

The mission of the Baptist Missionary Association (BMA) began in 1964 with Mr. and Mrs. Glen Stroud working in Guatemala City, where they organized two churches and a clinic. After furlough, the Strouds moved into the highlands. In 1986 the mission reported three churches, five missions, two grade schools, and a correspondence Bible study which enrolled 600 people.

BIBLIOGRAPHY: For the beginnings of Baptist work, see Albert McClellan, *Rainbow South* (Nashville: Broadman Press, 1952), 64–90. For current work of Southern Baptists, see *Your Guide to Foreign Missions*, 1993–1994, 74, 76. For the work of the Baptist Missionary Association, see John W. Duggar, *The Baptist Missionary Association of America (1950–1986)* (Texarkana, Tex.: Baptist Publishing House, 1988), 134, 204, 256.

HONDURAS (1946)

	Members	Churches
1. Convención Bautista Hondureña (1958)	7,089	(96)
2. Conservative Baptist Association of Honduras	6,000	(120)
3. Miskito Baptist Association	4,000	(40)
4. Baptist Missionary Association	n/a	(19)*
5. Baptist International Missions, Inc.	n/a	(36)
6. Good Samaritan Baptists	n/a	(n/a)
	17,089	(311)

*Includes missions

After its membership in the United Provinces of Central America, Honduras became a separate nation in 1838. Most of the population is mestizo with an Indian minority. About 95 percent of the population is Roman Catholic, but there is a growing Protestant minority.

In 1920 the American Baptist Home Mission Society assigned Mr. and Mrs. Lance A. Mantle to Honduras. They settled in Tegucigalpa, the capital, and made short survey trips but resigned a year and a half later before formal work was established.

In January 1946 Paul C. Bell, superintendent of Southern Baptist work in Panama, visited a small independent congregation in Choluteca, which considered itself Baptist in belief and practice. Bell was accompanied by his son, Paul, Jr., and Aurelio Gutiérrez. During their brief visit, the believers were examined and baptized and a church organized. In 1947 the FMB of the Southern Baptist Convention took over the mission, making the work in Honduras first a part of the Mexican mission and then the Guatemala mission. The first resident Southern Baptist missionaries, Edward and Alice Hurst and John and Wynona Ratliff, settled in Tegucigalpa in 1954. The mission opened a theological institute, but since then theological education has undergone several stages of transition, resulting in a decentralized plan with classes in six cities. The mission also started a bookstore, a radio and television ministry, and began rural medical work.

In March 1958 five churches formed the Honduras Baptist Association, today the National Convention of Baptist Churches of Honduras. It currently has eleven associations with approximately seven thousand members. An encampment, called BAGOPE, on Lake Yojoa attracts thousands each year for retreats and camps. Associational camps also are being developed. In 1993 the convention sponsored Mr. and Mrs. Jacobo Rios as their first national missionaries.

Evangelism and church planting have been major thrusts of the convention's work. Natural and political crises, however, have given Baptists the opportunity to respond to human needs and enhance their witness as well. A vocational training center in Tegucigalpa provides short-term training in agriculture, domestic arts, and other specialites; the mission also has engaged in drilling wells. Churches sponsor schools and out-patient medical clinics.

The Mexican Baptist Convention supports a missionary couple, Mr. and Mrs. Javier Valenzuela, and several short-term volunteers. The Honduras Convention also has a fraternal relation with a Miskito Association of more than forty congregations and their four thousand members. These churches are the outgrowth of an independent ministry among the Miskito Indians in eastern Honduras by Mr. and Mrs. Landon Wilkerson of Southern Baptist antecedents who began work in Puerto Lempira in 1965.

Conservative Baptists started with the work of Mr. and Mrs. Lee Irons, who, in 1946, began an English-speaking mission in La Ceiba in the north and the Bay Islands off the northern coast. A century earlier a church was organized on Roatán in the Bay Islands, and the Belize mission, which had been instituted by the Baptist Missionary Society, sent Francis Curran to organize the work. Over the years some missionaries came from Belize or Jamaica but, when the Irons arrived, they found little trace of the earlier work. In 1951 the Conservative Baptist Home Mission Society (CBHMS) assumed responsibility. In 1986 it was reported that the Conservative mission had around 120 churches with about 100 rural churches on the north coast, eleven churches in the Bay Islands (eight English-speaking and three Spanish-speaking), and eight churches in Tegucigalpa. A Conservative Baptist Association of Honduras has been formed. Conservative Baptists have emphasized TEE with a center in La Ceiba. They also maintain four radio stations—two in Tegucigalpa, one in San Pedro Sula, and a new station in La Ceiba.

A third mission is the Baptist Missionary Association, which began work with the arrival of Mr. and Mrs. Bobby Bowman in 1976. Among this mission's ministry are a Bible institute, a hospital, and a Vocational Technical Institute. While most of its ministry is in Spanish, three congregations on the Caribbean coast are among the Garifuna, or Black Caribs, people of African descent who speak English. The mission has a total of nineteen churches and missions.

There are thirty-six Baptist churches which are a result of the work of Baptist International Missions, Inc. (BIMI). The Honduras Baptist Medical-Dental Mission, a volunteer organization formed in 1972, has aided this mission with short-term medical clinics in southern Honduras. The mission also has a Bible institute in Danli.

During the Sandinista Revolution in Nicaragua, many Nicaraguans sought refuge in southern Honduras. Among these refugees is a group known as the Good Samaritan Baptists, who had split from BIMI. They have begun several churches in Choluteca Department among both refugees and local residents.

Besides the above bodies, there are also other independent Baptist missions and churches. The total number of all Baptist congregations is probably between 425 and 450, and they cover most of the country.

Stanley D. Stamps and Albert W. Wardin, Jr.

BIBLIOGRAPHY: For Southern Baptist work, see Wayne Wheeler, "Honduras," in the booklet, *Middle America* (Richmond: FMB/SBC, 1974), 27–33, and *Your Guide to Foreign Missions*, 1994–1995, 76. For Conservative Baptists, see *The Challenge*, November 1986, 1–2, and the booklet by George Patterson, *Historia de los Bautistas Conservadores en Honduras* (La Ceiba: Instituto Bíblico de Extensión, c. 1983). For the early work on Roatán, see Horace O. Russell, *The Baptist Witness* (El Paso: Carib Baptist Publications, 1983), 173–74. For the Baptist Missionary Association, see John Duggar, *The Baptist Missionary Association of America (1950–1986)* (Texarkana, Tex.: Baptist Publishing House, 1988), 205, 257. For the work of Baptist Bible Fellowship International, see Pamela Rather, "Honduras: A People Struggling for Freedom," *Baptist Bible Tribune*, Dec. 1993, 19.

MEXICO (1864)

	Members	Churches
1. Convención National Bautista de Mexico (1903)	66,398	(888)
2. Baptist Bible Fellowship of Mexico (1952)	52,500	(233)
3. American Baptist Association	n/a	(36)
4. Baptist International Missions, Inc.	1,500	(29)
5. Conservative Baptist Association of Mexico	n/a	(27)
6. Seventh Day Baptists	479	(11)
	120,877	(1,224)

*T*he first Baptist church in Mexico was organized on January 30, 1864, at Monterrey. On that day James Hickey, Baptist colporteur of the American Bible Society, baptized Thomas Westrup, José Maria Uranga, and Arcadio Uranga. These three persons with Mr. and Mrs. Hickey constituted the first evangelical church in Mexico. Westrup and the two Uranga brothers organized six additional churches by July 1869. Thomas Westrup was a missionary of the American Baptist Home Mission Society (ABHMS) from 1870 to 1873 when the Panic of 1873 forced the ABHMS to suspend its work in Mexico.

John Westrup, brother of Thomas, organized three Baptist churches in northern Mexico by 1879. The FMB of the Southern Baptist Convention employed him as a missionary. He began his duties on November 1, 1880, but unidentified assassins ambushed him on December 21. The FMB sent William D. Powell to investigate. Burdened by an unfinished task, Powell and his wife, Mary, were named missionaries in July 1882. The ABHMS appointed W. T. Green later that same year. During the next two decades Northern and Southern Baptists each sent approximately fifty missionaries to Mexico. In 1884 churches from Powell's field organized the Coahuila Baptist Association in Saltillo, and in the following year churches in the Monterrey area organized the Nuevo Leon Baptist Association.

In 1901 Northern Baptists reported 43 churches and missions with 721 members; Southern Baptists reported 37 churches, 21 missions, and 1,189 members. Several Baptist churches were cooperating with the interdenominational National Sunday School Convention. Alejandro Treviño and missionaries John S. Cheavens and James G. Chastain proposed the organization of a National Baptist Convention. In September 1903 forty-three messengers and twenty Baptists without credentials met at the First Baptist Church, Mexico City, and after two days adopted a provisional constitution and laid foundations for missionary, theological, and publication work. This marked the beginning of the transition from missionary to national leadership. At the 1904 Convention, Trevino was named representative to the 1905 Baptist World Congress.

Baptist work accelerated greatly until its decimation by the Revolution of 1910–1917. Churches were destroyed, seminaries and mission schools closed, members were scattered, and some suffered martyrdom. After the 1911 meeting of the convention, corporate meetings were suspended. The postrevolutionary Mexican constitution of 1917 brought cautious hope to evangelical churches. The government promised separation of church and state but was committed to socialist principles. It nationalized church property, limited worship to the confines of church property, and allowed only native-born Mexican citizens to officiate.

The National Baptist Convention resumed its annual meetings in 1919 with fifty-four churches represented. It honored its dead and charted a course for reconstruction. A Woman's Baptist Missionary Union was organized that year, and the convention's mission board resumed work among indigenous peoples. In the USA the coming of economic depression slowed mission support, and few additional missionaries were appointed before 1938.

By the mid-1940s the National Baptist Convention operated through five permanent boards: Missions, Evangelism, Publications, Christian Education, and Stewardship. Later the organizational structure was enlarged. The convention gave major emphasis to evangelizing Mexico City and other urban centers. It cooperated with Baptists in Texas in a river ministry for evangelizing territory along the Rio Grande River.

In 1971 the duplication of association, convention, and mission programs was so great that coordination was imperative. Integration of evangelism and church development began in 1974. In 1977 the FMB of the Southern Baptist Convention delivered the property of the Mexican Baptist Theological Seminary near Mexico City and the ninety-two–bed Mexico-Americano Hospital in Guadalajara to the convention. The Mexican mission of the FMB pledged to work within the framework of the programs of the convention. By 1993 integration was considered a reality, and the convention was declared self-sustaining. In 1975 the convention reported 309 churches, but in nizing the first Cuna Indian Baptist church, located in the San Blas Islands. Recently, a work has started in the province of Chiriqui among the Guaymí Indians.

In 1959 Van Royen gathered four ethnic groups and ten small churches to form the Panama Baptist Convention. At the first of the year in 1975, the Foreign Mission Board of the SBC took over the mission responsibilities of the Home Mission Board. In spite of greatly reduced American personnel, the convention continues to grow and minister to a variety of ethnic groups. It has ten associations and includes, besides the small Canal Zone Association for North Americans (171 members in 2 churches); the Central Association, an English-speaking association for West Indians (1,310 in 8 churches); the Bocas del Toro Association which is mixed English and Spanish (358 members in 4 churches); the San Blas Association for Cuna Indians (2,198 members in 17 churches), while the other associations serve the rest of the Spanish-speaking constituency. Baptists in Panama maintain a seminary, four primary schools, a camp, and a bookstore. The convention issues a periodical, *El Eco Bautista de Panama.*

The first mission of Free Will Baptists in Panama resulted from the work of Thomas H. and Mabel Willey among Indian tribes in the interior. The National Association of Free Will Baptists, organized in 1935, endorsed the Willeys among their first missionaries. In 1941 they transferred to Cuba. In 1961 Thomas and Emma Ruth Willey and John and Barbara Willey Moehlman reopened the work. Today there are five churches with more than five hundred in average attendance with missionaries working primarily in the Las Tablas area and Panama City.

In 1978 Jim and Phyliss Childress arrived in 1978, initiating the work of the Baptist Bible Fellowship International (BBFI), forming the Maranatha Baptist Church. Today this mission includes four missionary couples working with seven churches and sponsors the Baptist Bible Fundamental Institute, which is located at the Maranatha Church. Baptist International Missions, Inc. (BIMI) has three missionaries who work among the U.S. military. This mission has two churches and a Christian school. In Chiriquí Province, Jim Willis, an independent Baptist missionary who is sponsored by the Miller Road Baptist Church of Garland, Texas, has developed his own mission since 1974, which today has eight churches. His son, Byron, serves with him.

The National Baptist Convention from the USA began work in Panama in 1907, but it was not continued. At present the FMB of the National Baptist Convention of America helps to support three churches with a membership of about two hundred.

Alcides Lozano and Albert W. Wardin, Jr.

BIBLIOGRAPHY: For data on the work of Jamaican Baptists in Panama, see *"Glorious Liberty"* (London: BMS, 1914), 152–53; Inez Knibb Sibley, *The Baptists of Jamaica* (Kingston: Jamaica Baptist Union, 1965), 17–28; and Horace O. Russell, *The Baptist Witness* (El Paso: Carib Baptist Publications, 1983), 198–99. For the beginnings of Southern Baptist work, see Loyd Corder, "Baptists in Panama and Canal Zone," *Encyclopedia of Southern Baptists*, 2:1068–70. For material on Free Will Baptists, see Mary Wisehart, ed., *The Fifty-Year Record of the National Association of Free Will Baptists 1935–1985* (Nashville: Randall House Publications, 1988), 67. Helpful information on the work of Baptist Bible Fellowship International and Baptist International Missions, Inc., and other independents was gained from a letter from Blaine Gaudette, Balboa, Panama, June 4, 1992.

BAPTIST AND BAPTIST-RELATED MISSIONS

1. BELIZE   UkBMS (1822–1850), JaBMS (1889–1900), CBHMS (1960), SBC (1977), BBFI (1978), NMBC

2. COSTA RICA   JaBMS (1888–?), ABA (1940), SBC (1948), CBHMS (1955), BMA (1961), BIMI (1968), BBFI (1970), ABC (1981), BrB (1991)

3. EL SALVADOR   ABC (1911), SBC (1975), UkBMS (1988)

4. GUATEMALA   SBC (1948), BMA (1964), WBF (1968), BIMI (1971), BBFI (1975), CLF (1977), IBFI (1984), CBHMS (1992), MBM

5. HONDURAS   CBHMS (1951), SBC (1954), BM-M (1955), WBF (1969), BIMI (1970), BFM (1972), BBFI (1974), BMA (1976), IBFI (1984), ABC (1991), MexB

6. MEXICO   ABC (1870), SBC (1880), BBFI (1950), BMA (1950), BGC (1951), CBHMS (1952), WBF (1953), ABA (1955), BM-M (1960), OFWB (1962), BWM (1964), BIMI (1965), MBM (1966), TIBM (1975), MWBM (1983), IBFI (1984), IFM (1985), LIB (1987), ABWE (1989), NABC (1992)

7. NICARAGUA   ABC (1916), NBC (1951), BIMI (1959), ABA (1963), BMA (1964), SBC (1990), UkBMS (1990)

8. PANAMA   SBC (1905), FWB (1935–1941, 1961), BBFI (1978), BIMI (1980), NBCA

gram in 1965. It has had a very successful mission among the Guaraní Indians. Missionaries of the Baptist General Conference arrived in 1957 under the sponsorship of the Conservative Baptists and worked in other sites in the northwest. The also have joined the convention.

In recent years some missionaries from independent North American groups have come, but their work remains isolated. One of them is the Baptist Bible Fellowship International, whose first missionaries were Mr. and Mrs. Jimmy Strickland who arrived in 1961. In the following year they formed the Bible Baptist Church of Castelar, a suburb of Buenos Aires. Today the mission has eleven churches, and six missions with a weekly attendance of more than 1,800.

Argentine Baptist churches are not characterized by significant distinctions, mainly due to the rather European orientation of the people. Educational work existed in former years, but a good public program has not made it a priority. By contrast, social work is developing as economic conditions have worsened in recent years. Churches have always promoted Sunday Schools as well as women's and youth work. The large International Baptist Seminary in Buenos Aires offers a high-level educational program; there are also several other training institutions in different parts of the country.

Central Baptist Church with 1,500 in attendance is the largest congregation. It was the first Baptist church in the country to ordain women, and five of its nine ministers are women. Its fifty-four deacons are responsibile for most of the pastoral care, and the church sponsors a medical clinic, dental office, food store, clothing room, and daily lunch program.

Spanish is generally used in worship; other European languages are being displaced quickly. There are relatively few Indians in the country, but there is a good missionary work among Indians, using their own language. Worship has been more or less traditional, although it has been changing in recent years. Some churches have been caught up in Pentecostal-type worship, which includes much emotionalism and falling in the Spirit. Argentine Baptists are producing their own music, using a variety of instruments.

Argentina has always been a liberal country, but Roman Catholic influence is felt in a number of ways. Since Besson, and through Varetto and Varetto's son-in-law, Santiago Canclini, Baptists have been leaders in matters of freedom of conscience, a fact recognized by all other evangelical or Protestant churches. In general, relations with other evangelicals have been good, although cooperation is not strong. There is no relationship with the Roman Catholic Church, which is more conservative than in other countries. The Argentine Convention is an active member of the Baptist World Alliance. The Alliance chose Buenos Aires to be the site of the tenth Baptist Youth World Congress in 1984 and selected the same site for the seventeenth Baptist World Congress in 1995.

Arnoldo Canclini. Supplemented by Albert W. Wardin, Jr.

BIBLIOGRAPHY: For a good survey of Baptist work in Argentina, see Arnoldo Canclini, ed., *Un Hombre, un Pueblo* (Buenos Aires: Asociación Bautista Argentina de Publicaciones, 1981). For an informative article on Besson, see Robert F. Elder, "Pablo Besson of Argentina," *Baptist Quarterly*, 7, no. 1 (Jan. 1934): 27–22. For the development of Southern Baptist work and the Argentine Convention, see Hugo H. Culpepper, "Mission in Argentina," and Santiago Canclini, "Argentine Baptist Convention," *Encyclopedia of Southern Baptists*, 1:59–60. For the work of Conservative Baptists, see Hans W. Finzel, ed., *Partners Together* (Wheaton: CBFMS, 1993), 150–55. For Baptist Bible Fellowship International, see Richard Todd, "Argentina, Land of the Gaucho," *Baptist Bible Tribune*, Jan. 1992, 20.

BOLIVIA (1898)

	Members	Churches
1. Unión Bautista Boliviana (1936)	12,075	(105)
2. Convención Bautista Boliviana	2,527	(31)
3. Baptist International Missions, Inc.	2,500	(13)
	17,102	(149)

*B*olivia, in the central Andes, has been independent since 1825. More than half of the population belongs to the Quechua and Aymara Indian tribes, while others are mestizo or European. More than 90 percent of the population professes the Roman Catholic faith. The largest Protestant body is Seventh-Day Adventist.

Protestants were late in arriving in Bolivia. After the Brethren Assemblies, Canadian Baptists were the first Protestants to send resident missionaries. Archibald Reekie established the Canadian mission in 1898 at Oruro on the eastern side of the Altiplano. He did not perform his first baptism until 1902 when he immersed an Englishman, a Scot, and the Scot's Bolivian wife. The wife was probably the first Bolivian to become a Protestant on Bolivian soil. Although religious freedom was proclaimed in 1905, results continued to be meager.

After abandoning the establishment of schools in 1908, the mission later reversed this policy and in Oruro in 1923 started a school with the lower primary grades, which today is an outstanding elementary and high school. The first two Protestant church buildings were built in 1924—the Baptist churches of La Paz and Cochabamba. On the initiative of the missionaries, a Bolivian Baptist Union was organized in 1936 when membership was 345. The mission instituted the Cochabamba Bible College (later Baptist Theological Seminary) in 1941 and also embarked in radio evangelism.

In 1949 a mob of Indians at Melcamaya, drunk and incited by a priest, stoned a truck with Baptists, killing eight of them, including the president of the Bolivian Baptist Union, a missionary, and a promising young pastor. Instead of creating further animosity toward evangelicals, the attack produced a wave of sympathy throughout the county, and attendance in the churches increased. In the same year the government permitted the mission to open the Southern Cross Radio Station in La Paz—the only Protestant station in the country—which gained a large cross section of listeners for its excellent broadcasting. Gaining converts continued to be difficult, but the mission was reaching not only middle-class mestizos but also Aymara and Quechua Indians. In 1950 there were 750 members, but today the total is 12,000.

In 1946 the Brazilian Baptist Convention entered the country when Mr. and Mrs. Waldomiro Mota went to Santa Cruz in eastern Bolivia. In this city the mission established the Instituto Bautista Boliviano and the Baptist Theological Seminary of Eastern Bolivia. In 1979 Southern Baptists entered the field to assist the Brazilian mission.

Mr. and Mrs. M. S. Arrington, representing the Baptist Missionary Association (BMA), entered Bolivia in 1967 and, after organizing a mission and completing language study in Santa Cruz, they went into the interior where they formed a station with a clinic and worked among the Yuras and Guaranis. Lloyd Marvin, a missionary pilot, and his wife moved to Santa Cruz and, with an airplane purchased by the BMA in the USA, was able to bring supplies regularly to the Arringtons. In 1962 the Maranatha Baptist Mission (MBM), led by John Gunther, started work in Samaipata and also in towns in the Cochabamba Valley. The Baptist Bible Fellowship International (BBFI) has a small work with three churches, one mission, and a Bible institute. In addition, there are Latvian Baptists at Rincón del Tigre. Baptist International Missions, Inc., which has been in the country about twenty-five years, has thirteen churches. Its senior missionaries in Bolivia are L. T. and Geraldine Everett, and the mother church of the mission, located in Santa Cruz, averages 460 in attendance.

BIBLIOGRAPHY: On the work of Canadian Baptists, see Orville E. Daniel, *Moving with the Times* (Toronto: Canadian Baptist Overseas Mission Board, 1973), 60–69, 98–106; Ada P. Stearns, "Dawn over the Bolivian Hills," *Missions*, Oct. 1961, 28–29; and C. Peter Wagner, *The Protestant Movement in Bolivia* (South Pasadena, Calif.: William Carey Library, 1970), 33–54. Wagner also has a small amount of data on Brazilian Baptists and the Maranatha Baptist Mission. For the work of the Baptist Missionary Association, see John W. Duggar, *The Baptist Missionary Association of America (1950–1986)* (Texarkana, Tex.: Baptist Publishing House, 1988), 134–35, 204. For the work of the Baptist Bible Fellowship International, see Paul Frizzell, "Bolivia—The Heart of South America," *Baptist Bible Tribune*, May 1992, 26.

BRAZIL (1871)/(1882)

	Members	Churches
1. Convenção Batista Brasileira (1907)	902,000	(4,810)
2. Convenção Batista Nacional (1967)	200,000	(900)
3. Convenção das Igrejas Batistas Independentes do Brasil (1952) (Örebro Society)	27,515	(204)
4. Associação Batista do Brasil (1954) (BMA)	n/a	(16)
5. Associação das Igrejas Batistas Livre do Brasil (1978) (FWB)	758*	(9)
6. Associação dos Batistas Evangelismo Mundial (ABWE)	n/a	(n/a)
7. Associação Nacional das Igrejas Batistas Regulares (BM-M)	30,000	(132)
8. Baptist International Missions, Inc.	2,700	(34)
9. Batistas de Fé (BFM)	3,925	(33)
10. Confraternidade Batista Mundial do Brasil (WBF)	4,650*	(26)
11. Igreja Batista do Sétimo Dia do Brasil (Seventh Day Baptists)	3,500	(100)

12. Igreja Batista Evangélica Restrita (Strict Baptists)	1,000	(16)
13. Igreja Cristã Batista Biblica (BBFI)	n/a	(135)
14. Reformed Baptists	<u>50</u>	<u>(1)</u>
	1,176,098	(6,416)

*Average attendance

*B*razil, the largest country in South America, occupying the eastern half of the continent, has a population of 158 million. It is a nation with great ethnic variety including Portuguese and other Europeans, Africans, mulattoes, mestizos, as well as smaller groups of Indians, Japanese, and other orientals. Although Roman Catholicism is the predominant faith, it is often mixed with spiritism and other pagan elements. Protestants or evangelicals are a rapidly growing segment of the population. After Pentecostals, which hold a commanding lead, Baptists are the largest and fastest growing Protestant body. Brazil has become one of the most productive fields for Baptists who have more than doubled their numbers since 1980. Since World War II, a flood of Baptist missions has entered the country, primarily conservative evangelical agencies from the USA, but several others have come from Canada, Europe, and Japan.

The first missionary Foreign Mission Board (FMB) of the Southern Baptist Convention, sent to Brazil was Thomas Jefferson Bowen, who had served in Africa. He labored for almost two years from 1859 to 1861, but poor health forced his return to the USA. After the American Civil War, a group of Southerners founded a colony at Santa Barbara, São Paulo, where they organized a church in 1871 and requested Southern Baptist missionaries. In 1881 the FMB sent William (1855–1939) and Anne (1859–1942) Bagby; William spent fifty-eight years and Anne sixty-one years in Brazil. All five of their children became missionaries, four of them in Brazil. Because of their foundational work and dedicated service, the Bagbys are one of the great missionary families in Baptist annals.

Zachary and Kate Taylor arrived the next year. The Bagbys and Taylors settled in Salvador, Bahia. On October 15, 1882, they formed the first Baptist church for Brazilians, which at the time included only one Brazilian, a former priest. In 1884 the Bagbys moved to Rio de Janeiro, forming there in the same year the First Baptist Church. At first the early believers faced much opposition and even persecution. In 1889 Emperor Pedro II was overthrown and a republic declared, which brought religious freedom. The work spread to other centers, including the Amazon Valley where Erik A. Nelson did pioneer work. After arriving in 1891, he soon married his fiancée, Ida, and in 1898 both became missionaries of the FMB of the Southern Baptist Convention.

In 1907 on the twenty-fifth anniversary of the founding of the first Brazilian church, the Brazilian Baptist Convention was formed in Salvador. The development by Brazilian Baptists of many denominational agencies has followed the organizational pattern of Southern Baptists on the national and state levels but with a Brazilian flavor. Two important bodies are the Foreign and Home Mission Boards. Today the Foreign Mission Board supports an expanded program with 132 missionaries in ten South American countries, four African nations, Canada, and a number of European countries. At present the Home Mission Board has 450 missionaries on the field. In 1908 a Woman's Missionary Union was formed, and in 1928 a relief and annuity board was organized. In 1960 the Brazilian Convention hosted in Rio de Janeiro the tenth Congress of the Baptist World Alliance (BWA).

The FMB of the Southern Baptist Convention continues to maintain a large staff in Brazil—270 missionaries in 1993. They are divided into three missions—North Brazil, South Brazil, and Equatorial Brazil. Although maintaining their own mission organization, the missionaries work within the structure of the Brazilian Convention and related agencies. Southern Baptists from the USA also contribute to Brazilian work through Southern Baptist state conventions in the USA, which have entered into partnerships, and volunteers—around 1,800 in 1993—who engage in teaching, construction, evangelism, and medical work.

Baptists have formed a number of schools which range from kindergarten to high school. In 1902 a seminary was established in 1902 in Recife for North Brazil and six years later one at Rio de Janeiro for South Brazil. Over the years the national and state conventions have opened other theological institutions.

Publishing has been a very important enterprise. In 1901 the Brazilian Baptist Publication Society was formed, and the Brazilian periodical, *O Jornal Batista*, was launched. In 1910 the Brazilian Convention merged its publication program with its newly created Sunday School Board. In 1940 the missionaries formed the Brazilian Bible Press, which became part of the Sunday School Board in the 1960s. Brazilian Baptists have published great quantities of Christian literature, including Bibles, books, tracts, and curricular materials. Because of their emphasis on studying and reading the Bible, in a number of places Baptists were known as *Bíblias* (Bibles). Brazilian Baptists also effectively use radio and television, and the convention has formed a Radio and Television Board. Both the missionaries and Brazilian Baptists carry on a wide range of ministries to meet human needs, including drug and alcohol rehabilitation, well-drilling, orphanages, and a ministry to street children. Their medical ministry includes a hospital at Fortaleza and numerous clinics.

Unlike most Baptist churches in the USA but like their brethren in Russia, Brazilian churches generally exercise strict discipline, which may even lead to expulsion. Believers are expected to maintain high standards of personal morality and are admonished to refrain from smoking, drinking, and dancing. Most churches also observe restricted (or close) communion.

Foreign ethnic groups, particularly Latvians and Germans, are also part of the Baptist mosaic. Latvian Baptists first arrived in 1890 and organized their first church in 1892. Another group of Latvian Baptists migrated to Brazil in 1922 and 1923, believing in the soon return of Christ. They settled as pioneers in the interior of the state of São Paulo. German Baptists, many of them originally from Russia, settled primarily in the state of Rio Grande do Sul, the southernmost state, where they have their own state convention within the Brazilian Convention.

For some years Brazilian Baptists have struggled with Pentecostalism, which has had a great impact on the religious life of the country. In spite of their opposition to Pentecostalism, a Pentecostal Holiness movement called Renovation developed within Baptist ranks, which engaged in lengthy prayer services, speaking in tongues, divine healing, and the seeking of a second blessing. A division occurred which led to the founding in 1967 of the National Baptist Convention, which the Baptist World Alliance later accepted into membership. The National Convention has grown rapidly and claims 200,000 members in 900 churches and 1,600 fellowships. It maintains its headquarters in Brasília, publishes its own literature including a periodical, and supports 200 missionaries in Brazil and missions in Uruguay, Paraguay, Bolivia, and Mozambique. The Board of International Ministries of the American Baptist Churches, USA, has entered into a fraternal relationship with the National Baptist Convention.

Aside from the FMB of the Southern Baptist Convention, a number of Baptist missions in Brazil work with the Brazilian Baptist Convention or with one or more of the state conventions. Among these are the Conservative Baptists, who entered northeastern Brazil in 1946 and have since moved to São Paulo State and to Brasília, where they work with seminaries. The Baptist Missionary Society from England, which now counts Brazil as its second largest mission field, began in 1953 in Paraná State but has moved subsequently to other areas as well. The Baptist General Conference entered in 1955, first wishing to establish an independent work, but today cooperates with the São Paulo State Baptist Convention and the Brazilian Baptist Convention. The North American Baptist Conference, entering in 1966, serves in Rio Grande do Sul. Other missions which cooperate with the Brazilian Convention are the Japan Baptist Convention, Canadian Baptist International Ministries, and European Baptist Mission.

Among missions which maintain independent work, the oldest is the Örebro Society from Sweden whose first missionary began working among Swedish colonists in Rio Grande do Sul in 1912. The work has expanded to Brazilians and other ethnic groups and to other areas. From this mission a Convention of Independent Baptist Churches was formed in 1952, which today not only has home missionaries but also missionaries in Portugal, Peru, and Paraguay.

In 1922 Boyce Taylor in western Kentucky led Baptists with Landmark Baptist antecedents to form the Amazon Valley Baptist Faith Mission, which sent its first missionary family to the Amazon in 1923. The mission continues as Baptist Faith Missions. From its work a number of Faith Baptist churches have been organized. In the 1950s Free Will Baptists began in São Paulo State but have moved to other states and include work among Indians in northern Brazil. The first missionary of the Baptist Missionary Baptist Association, a Landmark body, arrived in 1951 in Sao Paulo state. Three years later a national association was formed.

Beginning in 1935 but particularly after World War II, a large number of independent fundamentalist Baptist missions from the USA entered Brazil. Baptist Mid-Missions (BM-M) started to work in 1935 in Manaus and Juazeiro do Norte in the north and in 1951 in São Paulo in the south. Brazil is this mission's largest field, which includes 138 churches and 101 fellowships. In the southern region, the mission maintains a seminary, correspondence school, camp, and Regular Baptist Press. In 1942 Mr. and Mrs. Robert Standley, who had been working with a small independent mission, became the first missionaries of the Association of Baptists for World Evangelism (ABWE) in the northeastern state of Rio Grande do Norte. Work later expanded to the neighboring state of Pernambuco and then to São Paulo in the south, where today the mission cooperates with BM-M in the Regular Baptist Press. Additional fields today include Salvador in Bahia, Recife in Pernambuco, and the states of Minas Gerais and Amazonas. Brazil is also the largest field of the ABWE. In 1947 Jack Looney, sponsored by World Baptist Fellowship (WBF), entered Brazil under the auspices of ABWE. At present WBF has fifteen missionary couples and two single missionaries working in five states, located in the south, northeast, and the Amazon, and supports three Bible institutes. Baptist Bible Fellowship International (BBFI) began in the early 1950s and today works in thirteen states and sponsors a number of Bible institutes.

There are a number of other small Baptist groups. One is the Seventh Day Baptists—a group which in 1913 had withdrawn from the Seventh-Day Adventists, became Seventh Day Baptists in 1950, and four years later were accepted by the Seventh Day Baptist World Federation. There are also Strict Baptists and at least one Reformed Baptist church at São José dos Campos. David B. Barrett in *World Christian Encyclopedia*, p. 194, lists several other groups with the Baptist name for which there is no readily available data.

BIBLIOGRAPHY: A basic history in Portuguese on the Brazilian Baptist Convention is José dos Reis Pereira, *História dos Batistas do Brasil, 1882–1982* (Rio de Janeiro: JUERP, 1982). See also A. R. Crabtree and A. N. Mesquita, *História dos Baptistas do Brasil*, vols. 1 and 2 (Rio de Janeiro: Casa Publicadora Batista, 1937–1939). In English see A. R. Crabtree, *Baptists in Brazil* (Rio de Janeiro: Baptist Publishing House, 1953). The work by Lester C. Bell, *Which Way in Brazil?* (Nashville: Convention Press, 1965) is one of the finest in a series of study books on Brazil published by the FMB of the Southern Baptist Convention. For information on the work of pioneer missionaries, see Helen Bagby Harrison, *The Bagbys of Brazil* (Nashville: Broadman Press, 1954); Solomon L. Ginsburg, *A Wandering Jew in Brazil* (Nashville: Sunday School Board/SBC, 1922); and John Monroe Landers, *Eric Alfred Nelson* (Ph.D., Texas Christian University, 1982), which also includes material on the work of Baptist Faith Missions in the Amazon. For current work of the FMB of the Southern Baptist Convention in Brazil, see *Your Guide to Foreign Missions*, 1994–1995, 56–60. A comprehensive history of Latvian Baptists in Brazil is Osvaldo Ronis, *Uma Epopéia de Fé* (Rio de Janeiro: Casa Publicadora Batista, 1974).

For the work of Baptist missions, other than Southern Baptist, which cooperate with the Brazilian Baptist Convention, see Hans W. Finzel, ed., *Partners Together* (Wheaton: CBFMS, 1993), 156–63 for the CBFMS (CBI); Brian Stanley, *The History of the Baptist Missionary Society 1792–1992* (Edinburgh: T&T Clark, 1992), 471–501, for the BMS; Donald E. Anderson, ed., *The 1970s in the Ministry of the Baptist General Conference* (Arlington Heights, Ill.: BGC, 1981), 89–90, for the BGC; and Frank H. Woyke, *Heritage and Ministry of the North American Baptist Conference* (Oakbrook Terrace, Ill.: NABC, 1979), 407–08, for the NABC.

For materials on fundamentalist Baptist missions, see George Kircher, *Punching Holes in the Darkness* (Cleveland: BM-M, 1989) for BM-M; Harold T. Commons, *Heritage & Harvest* (Cherry Hill, N.J.: ABWE, 1981), 49–52, for the ABWE; and David Rohr, "Brazil a Land of Breathtaking Beauty, Unexplored Potential, Endless Opportunities," *Baptist Bible Tribune*, May 1992, 27, for the BBFI.

For the Örebro Society, see Linné Eriksson, *I mänsklighetens tjänst* (Örebro: Libris, 1972), 74–77; for Baptist Faith Missions, see *Mission Sheets*, July 1992, 1; for the Baptist Missionary Association, see John Duggar, *The Baptist Missionary Association of America (1950–1986)* (Texarkana, Tex.: Baptist Publishing House, 1988), 88–90, 95, 97–98, 132, 259, 269; for Free Will Baptists, see Mary Wisehart, ed., *The Fifty-Year Record of the National Association of Free Will Baptists 1935–1985* (Nashville: Randall House Publications, 1988), 63–64; and for Seventh Day Baptists, see Don A. Sanford, *A Choosing People* (Nashville: Broadman Press, 1992), 307.

CHILE (1892)

	Members	Churches
1. Convención Evangélica Bautista de Chile (1908)	26,723	(235)
2. Misión Chilena (Iglesia Bautista Nacional) (1940)	<u>5,600</u>	<u>(37)</u>
	32,323	(272)

*C*hile, a long narrow country stretching 2,600 miles along the western coast of South America, gained independence from Spain in 1818. Most of the population is either mestizo or European with an Indian minority. Although the country is predominantly Roman Catholic, more than 10 percent of the population are Protestants with the greatest number being members of indigenous Pentecostal bodies.

The government of Chile requested Oscar von Barchwitz, a Baptist pastor from Germany who had settled in Chile, to recruit German settlers. By 1884 a number of German families had settled in southern Chile, among whom were Baptists. A strong revival movement, led by Philip Maier, spread among the German colonists, and in 1892 the first German Baptist church was organized at Contulmo. Other churches followed at El Salto and Victoria. The revival also spread to Spanish-speaking Chileans. Henry Weiss, a Mennonite from Minnesota who arrived in 1897, helped organize the German work and also worked among the Chileans. In 1898 the Christian and Missionary Alliance provided financial support to Weiss and Albert E. Dawson, a Canadian missionary.

In the meantime in 1888, William MacDonald (1852–1939), a Baptist minister from Scotland, and his wife, Janet, settled in Chile. In 1899 he joined Weiss and Dawson in the work of the Alliance. MacDonald was a man of strong will and conviction. He wished to gain Baptist support from abroad, which caused supporters of the Alliance to charge him with disloyalty. Matters came to a head when he learned that a missionary of the Alliance had baptized an infant by sprinkling. With bitter debate on both sides, a break occurred which led to the formation in April 1908 of an Evangelical Baptist Union (later called Convention). The union started with less than five hundred members, composed of people with little education. The union chose MacDonald as superintendent, where he dominated, ruling like a bishop and moving pastors at will.

MacDonald traveled extensively and recruited workers to spread the gospel. He also provided short-term institutes for training and used *La Voz Bautista*, the paper he founded, to inculcate Baptist beliefs and practice. MacDonald gained support from several Latin American countries, and, beginning in 1914, Southern Baptists sent some finanical aid. Upon his request, the FMB of the Southern Baptist Convention sent its first missionaries in 1917, William and Mary Davidson, who were soon followed by others. In 1920 the FMB also appointed MacDonald as one of its missionaries, but the process of shifting from one-man rule to mission control took time. In 1917 the union had about eighteen churches and 1,250 members.

In a dispute in the 1930s over the transfer of a missionary to another area, Ismael Neveu, MacDonald's son-in-law, feeling the transfer unjust, left the convention. Within several years seven churches joined him, and in 1940 he led in founding the Chilean Mission or National Baptist Church, the only permanent division which the Baptist Convention of Chile has experienced. Today the Chilean Mission has 5,600 members in thirty-seven churches and recently has entered into partnership with the Board of International Ministries of the American Baptist Churches/USA.

Educational institutions have enhanced the work of the Baptist Convention. In 1922, one of the missionaries, Nora Graham, established the Colegio Bautista, a Baptist academy in Temuco, which with its high standards has brought prestige to Baptists in the area. A Baptist girls' home also has been organized in Temuco, which provides care for homeless girls. In 1939 in Santiago, the Chilean Baptist Theological

Seminary was instituted, and in 1948 a women's training school was added to the school. A Woman's Missionary Union was formed in 1923. In Antofagasta in the north, the mission opened a goodwill center that includes a medical clinic, which today offers a wide range of services.

It has taken years for Chilean Baptists to move toward self-support. By the 1970s most churches were self-supporting, but the convention was still subsidized by the FMB, and its offices were held jointly by Chilean nationals and the missionaries. Today missionaries no longer hold positions in the convention, and a plan of reducing the subsidy has been inaugurated.

The Brazilian Baptist Convention has sent a number of missionaries to work with the Baptist Convention. In addition, several independent Baptist missions have entered the country. In 1953 the Association of Baptists for World Evangelism (ABWE) arrived in Chile and has concentrated its work in Santiago, where it has established a Baptist Bible Institute. It has found Chile, however, to be one of its most difficult fields. In 1954 Baptist Bible Fellowship International (BBFI) began in Santiago with two missionary families and has now spread to other centers in the north and south.

BIBLIOGRAPHY: The work *Diamantes Bautistas* ([Santiago]: Convención Evangélica Bautista, c. 1983), is a seventy-fifth anniversary history of the Baptist Convention. A good survey is the work by James Henry Bitner, *A Critical Study of Baptist Church Growth in Chile* (Th.D. dissertation, Southwestern Baptist Theological Seminary, 1975). For informative articles, see R. Cecil Moore, "Mission in Chile," and "Chilean Baptist Convention," in *Encyclopedia of Southern Baptists*, 1:252–53. For data on German Baptist beginnings in Chile, see M. L. Leuschner, "The Spectacular South in South America," *Baptist Herald*, July 9, 1959, 10–12, 23, which includes a photograph of Oscar von Barchwitz. For the work of the Association of Baptists for World Evangelism, see Harold T. Commons, *Heritage and Harvest* (Cherry Hill, N.J.: ABWE, 1981), 119–25. For Baptist Bible Fellowship International, see David Lingo, "...He Decided to Create One Last Land...Chile!" *Baptist Bible Tribune*, Sep. 1992, 20–21.

COLOMBIA (1844)/(1916)

	Members	Churches
1. Convención Bautista Colombiana (1952)	12,045	(110)
2. Asociación de Iglesias Bautistas Evangélicas (1973) (CaFEBC)	n/a	(19)
3. Asamblea Evangélica Luz y Verdad (Reformed Baptists)	n/a	(n/a)
	12,045	(129)

C olombia, located in the northwest corner of South America, gained its independence from Spain in 1819. Roman Catholicism claims the allegiance of more than 95 percent of the population, and until recent decades Protestantism has faced much opposition, even persecution. Few Protestant missions entered the country before 1920. Although a concordat with the Vatican is still in force, evangelicals can now participate more actively in Columbian society and government. The atmosphere of unrest caused by guerilla and drug activity hampers the nation, but evangelicals, including Baptists, continue to grow.

In 1845 sea captain Philip Livingston (1814–1891) began Baptist work among former slaves on the English-speaking islands of San Andrés and Providence, Colombian possessions four hundred miles northwest of the country. In 1852 a church was formally organized. He founded a dynasty of preachers who produced stable churches and a Christian society.

Upon his return to Colombia in 1916, Miguel Del Real, a political refugee who had accepted Christ in Cuba, began preaching and started the First Baptist Church of Ciénaga and in 1919 the First Baptist Church of Barranquilla. Cuban Baptists later sent missionaries but were soon forced to leave. At the request of the few remaining Baptists, the FMB of the Southern Baptist Convention sent Henry and Dorothy Schweinsberg in 1941 to establish the work.

The mission set far-sighted strategies based on evangelism, church development, Christian education, preparation of leadership, and the use of music, radio, and the printed page. It set priorities for expansion into the major cities. The FMB and the Jarman Foundation provided funds for a church building in each city chosen as a center for expansion. Cartagena was entered in 1943, Cali in 1945, Bogotá in 1947, and Medellín in 1955.

Nine Colombian and three Venezuelan churches formed the Colombo-Venezuelan Baptist Convention in 1949, but it soon divided into two national conventions with Colombia forming its own convention in 1952. In 1993 the Colombian Convention reported 110 organized churches and 400 mission groups, some developed, others in beginning stages. Today there are nine regional associations. Baptist work has spread into the Andean and coastal regions and into two states of the sparsely populated Eastern Plains.

The convention works through departments of evangelism, missions, Christian education, Woman's Missionary Union, youth, and social action, among others. All are supported through the convention's cooperative program and mission offerings. The Board of Colombian Missions sends missionaries to Guajiro Indians, Armero volcanic disaster victims, teeming Bogotá, and the frontier territory of the Eastern Plains. Missionaries from Brazil cooperate with the Colombian Board. The Board also works through associations and churches and fosters a program of volunteer missions. The national youth organization, ANJOB, and the Woman's Missionary Union support the mission program in the churches. Missionaries of the Southern Baptist Convention cooperate with the convention in evangelism, church planting and development, institutions, and special projects.

The Baptist clinic, begun in Barranquilla in 1949 by Dr. Roy C. McGlamery, is now a modern sixty-bed hospital. It also works through clinics in poor areas of the coastal cities and through medical caravans to outlying areas in jungles, mountains, and plains.

The International Baptist Theological Seminary, opened in Cali in 1953, has had as its purpose the preparation of Christian workers for Colombia as well as other countries. In the intervening years, students from eighteen countries have attended and more than three hundred graduated. It averages seventy-five to eighty students in the resident institution with teaching by extension in other centers.

Baptist Communications in Cali, founded in 1970 by John Magyar, prepares radio and television programs, cassettes, and videos for Spanish-speaking Latin America. For the convention, it provides *TeleAmigo*, telephone lines with counseling for interested callers; the news magazine, *El Bautista Colombiano*; films; and other materials.

The initial work of the Association of Baptists for World Evangelism (ABWE) among Indian tribal peoples was the downstream extension to Leticia of the work established by Mr. and Mrs. William G. Scherer on the Amazon River in Peru. ABWE missionaries, however, did not settle in Leticia until 1942, and a church was formed there two years later. By means of aviation, the work was extended into the state of Amazonas. Because of government curtailment of work among the Indians in 1977, the aviation ministry was terminated, and ABWE transferred two of its mission families to Bogotá, where two years earlier it had already sent its first mission family. In 1973 Baptist Bible Fellowship International (BBFI) sent Craig and Fran Lingo as pioneer missionaries, and a small work has developed.

In 1970 the Fellowship of Evangelical Baptist Churches (CaFEBC) in Canada sent its first mission couple. The CaFEBC started with work already begun in the coastal state of Sucre by an independent Canadian Baptist mission. In 1973 an Association of Evangelical Baptist Churches of Colombia was formed. The mission shifted its primary interest to Medellín, purchasing a nearby farm and adjoining property on which it established a Bible institute (closed in 1980) and a missionary children's school, and where it is developing a conference center. There is also a small association of churches centered around San Gil in the state of Santander which is Reformed Baptist in principle. The Progressive National Baptists from the USA provide support for a primary and secondary school on San Andrés Island.

Crea Ridenour

BIBLIOGRAPHY: A standard volume on Colombian Baptist history is Crea Ridenour, *Up from Zero: A History of the Development of Baptist Work in Colombia* (Cali: Historical Commission/Colombia Baptist Mission, 1989). Its Spanish adaptation is called, *Un Pueblo con Futuro*. A Southern Baptist mission study book which provides helpful material is William R. Estep, Jr., *Colombia: Land of Conflict and Promise* (Nashville: Convention Press, 1968). For the work of the Association of Baptists for World Evangelism, see Harold T. Commons, *Heritage & Harvest* (Cherry Hill, N.J.: ABWE, 1981), 48–49, 52–55. For Baptist Bible Fellowship International, see Craig Lingo, "Lessons Learned: Twenty Years in Colombia," *Baptist Bible Tribune*, 21, Oct. 1992. For the work of Reformed Baptists, see *RBMS Reports*, November 1991. Loren C. Turnage in his work *Island Heritage* (Cali: Historical Commission/Colombia Baptist Mission, 1975) has written a detailed history of Baptists on San Andrés and Providencia.

ECUADOR (1950)

	Members	Churches
1. Convención Bautista del Ecuador (1972)	10,397	(118)
2. Misión Bautista del Compañerismo	n/a	(31)
	10,397	(149)

*E*cuador, located between Colombia and Peru and straddling the Andes Mountains, includes large mestizo and Indian populations. As its neighbors, it is predominantly Roman Catholic with a small but growing Protestant minority. Southern Baptists sent two missionary families in 1950, and work was started in Quito, the capital, where in 1952 the Central Baptist Church was organized. The mission entered Guayaquil in 1953, which became a leading center of Southern Baptist work. In 1954 two small independent churches in Guayas Province which followed Baptist practice became officially Baptist. A Baptist Convention was organized in 1972.

The mission today has a theological institute in Quito and a mass media center in Guayaquil. Five bookstores have been established. Four Baptist centers provide a number of programs in health care, literacy training, daycare, agriculture, and training in technical skills.

Independent Baptist missions are also well represented in Ecuador. The World Baptist Fellowship (WBF) was the first of these missions with the arrival of Charles and Juanita Bowen in 1971, followed in 1974 by Mel and Charlene Neill. The first church of the mission was formed in 1973. Under the sponsorship of the WBF, the first missionaries of the Baptist Bible Fellowship International (BBFI), Joe and Sylvia Wells, arrived in 1978, and under the same sponsorship the first missionaries of Baptist Mid-Missions (BM-M), Robert and Lena Meyer, arrived in 1988, who were soon followed by Jim and Alethia Lossing. Since WBF and BBFI had developed extensive work in Quito and its vicinity and Baptists were well established in Guayaquil, the missionaries of BM-M settled in Cuenca, the third largest city in the country with limited evangelical witness. The three groups cooperate in a Baptist Mission Fellowship which in 1993 listed thirty-one churches, eighteen missions, and seven Bible institutes.

BIBLIOGRAPHY: E. Gordon Crocker, "Mission in Ecuador," *Encyclopedia of Southern Baptists*, 1:385. For current Southern Baptist work, see *Your Guide to Foreign Missions*, 1994–1995, 85–86. For work of the Baptist Bible Fellowship International, see Currie Wells, "Making Christ Known in a Land Not Well Known," *Baptist Bible Tribune*, November 1992, 21, and for Baptist Mid-Missions see, "Arriving in Ecuador," *Harvest*, fall 1992, 14. The corresponding editor gained additional information on Independent Baptist work through correspondence with Mel Neill of WBF and Joe Wells of BBFI.

FRENCH GUIANA (1982)

	Members	Churches
Federation of Baptist Churches (1993)	375	(4)

*F*rench Guiana, located on the northeast coast of South America, is an overseas department of France. It is a small territory with only 100,000 inhabitants. The population is about 80 percent Roman Catholic with a very small Protestant minority. In 1982 Southern Baptists sent their first missionary couple, James and Jerene Darnell, who had experience working in the Côte d' Ivoire (Ivory Coast). Two years later a French-speaking congregation began meeting in the home of the missionaries in Cayenne, the capital. The group organized as the first Baptist church in the country and has now divided into two independent congregations—one French-speaking and the other English-speaking. Work was also started in Kourou. In 1993 four churches formed a Federation of Baptist Churches. TEE has been a helpful means in teaching Baptist principles to students meeting in both Cayenne and Kourou. Evangelical Baptist Missions has also entered the territory and at present has four missionaries under appointment.

BIBLIOGRAPHY: *Your Guide to Foreign Missions*, 1990–1991, 31, 33, and 1994–1995, 61–62.

GUYANA (1861)

	Members	Churches
1. Baptist Cooperative Convention of Guyana (1973)	1,237	(15)
2. Association of Baptist Churches of Guyana	500	(5)
3. Seventh Day Baptists	312	(6)
	2,049	(26)

G uyana, located between Venezuela and Suriname, gained independence from Great Britain in 1966. It is the only English-speaking country in South America. About half the population is East Indian, while 30 percent are African. Amerindian tribes live in the interior. The religious picture is as mixed as the population with more than one-third Hindu, more than one-third Protestant, more than one-sixth Roman Catholic, and a bit less than one-tenth Moslem.

Baptist work in Guyana has been varied, difficult, and sporadic. It is one field where Baptists of three different races have attempted to introduce or develop Baptist work. In 1861 Lough Fook, a member of the Baptist church in Canton, China, a product of Southern Baptist work, went as a worker to Guyana to minister to Chinese indentured servants. He settled in Georgetown (then Demerara). In 1878 he had a congregation of 156 members. The church sent Tso Sune to China as a self-supporting missionary. Fook died in 1884, and his work did not survive.

Because of Guyana's large Black population, the National Baptist Convention from the USA took an interest in Guyana. From records of the National Baptist Convention in the early twentieth century, it appears there were at least two Black Baptist churches in Georgetown—Bethel Baptist, founded in 1899, with a membership of 263, and Nazareth Baptist, founded in 1902, with forty-two members. A third church, Dalgin, Demerara River, established in 1904, had thirty-three members. Dr. Prowd, superintendent of the convention's work in South America, was pastor of the Bethel Baptist Church, and S. A. Richardson pastored the other two congregations. One of the converts of this mission was Josephine Straughn, who settled in the USA and for more than twenty years was a field agent of the FMB of the National Baptist Convention until her death in 1928.

National Baptists lost their ties with Guyana until the FMB of the National Baptist Conventon, USA, in 1936 started providing tuition for students in Georgetown. The FMB also began supporting local pastors, listing three of them in 1941, but this support ended by the early 1950s, if not earlier. Another Black Baptist mission agency, the Lott Carey Foreign Mission Convention, began providing support in 1970 for Dr. A. Carlyle Miller, a native of Guyana who was a minister and doctor who, after studying in the USA, had returned to his native land in 1946. The convention assisted Miller in his ministerial, medical, and educational work.

In 1954 Baptist Mid-Missions (BM-M) sent Mr. and Mrs. Walter Spieth, who formed a church in Georgetown. An East Indian worker in the mission formed a second church in the town. Between 1970 and 1989 BM-M abandoned the field but has since re-entered. The mission today has five churches, all members of the Association of Baptist Churches of Guyana.

When Otis and Martha Brady, missionaries of the FMB of the Southern Baptist Convention, arrived in 1962, they found the small work of BM-M but embarked on their own program. They led in organizing the Central Baptist Church in Georgetown in 1963, and within seven years the work had grown to 7 churches, 19 missions, and more than 750 members. The mission has utilized evangelistic meetings, a camping program, radio, and TEE.

Another Baptist group with an interest in Guyana has been Seventh Day Baptists. T. L. M. Spencer, a native of Barbados and a former missionary of the Seventh-day Adventists, after accepting Seventh Day Baptist doctrine, appealed to Seventh Day Baptists in the USA for support. In November 1913 he formed a Seventh Day Baptist Church. The Seventh Day Baptist Missionary Society (SDBMS) helped him acquire property, and the American Sabbath Tract Society enabled him to publish a paper, the *Gospel Herald*. In 1927 the SDBMS sent Mr. and Mrs. Royal Thorngate to Guyana. After investigation, the SDBMS dismissed Spencer for improper conduct, but when he left he took a large part of his congregation, which seriously weakened the mission. After Thorngate contracted malaria, he and his family returned to the USA in 1930, and SDBMS was unable to send another missionary couple until 1962. In 1988 the work reported six churches with around 300 members.

BIBLIOGRAPHY: For the work of the FMB of the National Baptist Convention, see National Baptist Convention, *Journal*, 1907, p. 50; 1908, p. 196; 1909, p. 106; and William J. Harvey III, *Bridges of Faith Across the Seas* (Philadelphia: FMB/NBC, USA, 1989), 109–10, 125–27, 141, 160. For the involvement of the Lott Carey Convention, see Leroy Fitts, *Lott Carey* (Valley Forge: Judson Press, 1978), 145–48. For data on the beginning of the work of Baptist Mid-Missions, see William J. Hopewell, Jr., *The Missionary Emphasis of the General Association of Regular Baptist Churches* (Chicago: Regular Baptist Press, 1963), 134. For the beginning of Southern Baptist work, see Mrs. Otis W. Brady, "Mission in Guyana," *Encyclopedia of Southern Baptists*, 3:1746, and William W. Graves, *Baptist Trade Winds* (Nashville: Convention Press, 1979), 41–46. For Seventh Day Baptists, see Don A. Sanford, *A Choosing People* (Nashville: Broadman Press, 1992), 297–99. Information on Chinese Baptists in Guyana was gained from Britt E. Towery, Jr., Waco, Texas.

PARAGUAY (1919)

	Members	Churches
1. Convención Evangélica Bautista del Paraguay (1956)	5,910	(85)
2. Asociación de Iglesias Cristianas Evangélicas y Bautistas Eslavas del Paraguay	950	(7)
3. Asociación Cristiana Evangélica y Bautista Ucraniana en el Paraguay	100	(3)
4. Iglesia Bautista Independiente "Maranata"	250	(3)
	7,210	(98)

STATISTICS: Except for the Baptist Convention, statistics were gained from Rodolfo Plett, *El Protestantismo en el Paraguay* (Asunción: Instituto Bíblico Asunción, 1987), 115–16.

P araguay is a landlocked country surrounded by Argentina, Brazil, and Bolivia. It gained independence from Spain in 1811. Much of the population is mestizo with both Spanish and Guaraní, an Indian language, widely spoken. Paraguay is a strong Roman Catholic country but contains a growing Protestant minority. One of the largest Protestant groups is the German Mennonites who, beginning in the 1920s, migrated from Canada and then from Soviet Russia, settling in colonies, and have gained converts from the native Indian population. Baptists and Pentecostals are two of the other larger Protestant bodies.

The Baptist work began as an extension from Argentina. In 1919 the Argentine Baptist Convention sent Mr. and Mrs. Maximino Fernández to Asunción where they led in forming the First Baptist Church in October 1920. Baptists in Argentina supported the mission until the FMB of the Southern Baptist Convention assumed responsibility in 1945 as part of its River Plate Mission. In 1952 a separate Paraguayan Mission was established. In 1956 Paraguayan Baptists formed their own convention. In Asunción the Baptist mission founded the Paraguay Baptist Theological Institute (1956), a bookstore, a goodwill center, and a mass media center. One of the outstanding achievements of the mission was the opening in 1953 of a hospital in Asunción, the first Baptist hospital in South America, with a school of nursing related to it today.

In 1930 Slavic Baptists migrated to Paraguay and formed the Association of Evangelical Christian and Slavic Baptist Churches of Paraguay. In 1956 a group separated and formed the Evangelical Christian and Ukrainian Baptist Association in Paraguay. In 1974 the Association of Baptists for World Evangelism (ABWE) began an independent Baptist work and created the Maranatha Independent Baptist Church in Stroessner, a suburb of Asunción. The mission has formed two other congregations. Three Brazilian Baptist missions also work in Paraguay.

BIBLIOGRAPHY: For Baptist beginnings in Paraguay, see Baker J. Cauthen and others, *Advance* (Nashville: Broadman Press, 1970), 265–66. For current Southern Baptist work, see *Your Guide to Foreign Missions*, 1994–1995, 86–87. See Rodolfo Plett, *El*

Protestantismo en el Paraguay (Asunción: Instituto Bíblico Asunción, 1987), 115–16, for information on Independent Baptists and Slavic Baptists. For additional information on Independent Baptists, see Harold T. Commons, *Heritage & Harvest* (Cherry Hill, N.J.: ABWE, 1981), 187–88.

PERU (1927)

	Members	Churches
1. Convención Evangélica Bautista del Peru (1966) (SBC)	9,708	(194)
2. Unión de Iglesias Bautistas de Sud Peru (Irish Baptists)	5,000	(130)
3. American Baptist Association	1,000	(5)
4. Association of Baptists for World Evangelism	n/a	(93)
5. Baptist Bible Fellowship	n/a	(66)
6. Baptist International Missions, Inc.	1,500	(28)
7. Baptist Mid-Missions	25,000	(200)
	42,208	(716)

*P*eru, located on the western coast of South America in the Andes, has a population that is almost half Indian—primarily Quechua and Aymara—with more than a third mestizo and the remainder primarily European. Peru's geography is most diverse with a narrow strip of desert along the coast, the high Andes, and the jungles of the Amazon Valley in the east. Roman Catholicism is the predominant faith and maintains a special status in the country, but Protestants may practice and propagate their faith and are a growing minority.

In comparison to a number of other missions, Baptists were late in entering Peru and have been in the country only two generations. Before World War II, four Baptist missions began to establish themselves—one in southern Peru, a second in both southern and northern Peru, and two in the Amazon Valley. Since the war, three of these missions have expanded to other parts of Peru, and other missions have joined them.

The first to enter Peru was the Irish Baptist Foreign Mission (today Baptist Missions) (IrBM) in 1927, who sent Mr. and Mrs. G. C. Oehring, who settled in Urubamba, Cuzco Department. The work of this mission, however, has been primarily in Puno Department among the Aymara Indians along Lake Titicaca. Some work also has been done in the adjoining department of Tacna, just north of Chile. In 1952 the Union of Baptist Churches of South Peru was formed. Most of the churches are around Lake Titicaca but at least nine of them are in the Tacna area.

The next mission, Amazon Valley Baptist Faith Mission (today Baptist Faith Missions) (BFM), entered Peru in 1935 with the arrival of Richard P. (1883–1964) and Mary Frances Hallum. They made their headquarters in Iquitos on the Amazon River but reached out to other areas. In February 1937 in Iquitos a Baptist church of eleven members was formed with three members of the Hallum family and eight nationals, probably the first Baptist church in the country. The mission continues to serve in the Amazon but also has work in Lima.

The third mission, Baptist Mid-Missions (BM-M), began its work in 1936 with the settlement of Mabel Walker in Urubamba in Cuzco Department, working alone for many years and unable to return home on furlough for eleven years because of World War II. The mission has worked in a number of other areas as well. In 1937 Mr. and Mrs. Elias Jones went into the Andes of Northern Peru; in 1944 Mr. and Mrs. Edward deRosset settled in Trujillo, three hundred miles north of Lima on the coast; in 1946 Mr. and Mrs. Dean Pittman went into the jungles from Cuzco, attempting to work among the Wachipairi and Maschco Indian tribes; in 1952 Mr. and Mrs. Paul Tanner settled in Cuzco; and in 1954 Mr. and Mrs. Charles W. Cook served in Lima. By the mid-1970s, the mission had sent out thirty-three missionaries and its work was concentrated in three general areas—Cuzco, which also included Quillabamba; the Greater Lima area; and northern Peru, incorporating the coastal area, including Sullana, near the border of Ecuador, Chiclayo, and Trujillo, in addition to work in the Andes. In 1972 the mission established a seminary in Lima, which it later moved to Trujillo. In the mid-1980s the mission had more than 50 churches, but today it has 200 churches with 25,000 members and 45,000 in attendance.

The fourth mission, the Association of Baptists for World Evangelism (ABWE), began its ministry in the Upper Amazon Valley in 1939 when it accepted Mr. and Mrs. William G. Scherer as its missionaries. The Scherers, after serving under the Inland South America Missionary Union in Brazil, worked for eight years as independent missionaries among the Indians in the Upper Amazon in Peru, in a territory stretching three hundred miles from Iquitos to the Brazilian border. Far from civilization, they established a station at Pevas on the Amazon River and undertook pioneer work, traveling often by canoe in the early days. Since then the mission has expanded several hundred miles upriver from Iquitos and eastward into Brazil. The mission opened a Bible institute in Iquitos. ABWE has now expanded into other areas of Peru—to Lima in the late 1950s; to Ica Department in the south, entering the city of Ica, where Baptist Bible Seminary has been established, and Nazca; and to Arequipa, capital of Arequipa Department.

In 1950 the FMB of the Southern Baptist Convention entered Peru with the arrival of Marion D. Oates and his wife, Clifford Belle. In August 1951 they led in establishing the Ebenezer Baptist Church in the Miraflores section of Lima. In 1952 First Baptist Church of Lima was formed in the heart of the city. Under the influence of a Baptist convert who returned to his home in Arequipa, a small group of believers agreed in 1954 to become a Baptist congregation. Roy and Martha Chamlee settled in Trujillo in 1956, where Southern Baptists had already acquired a small work. After returning it to its founder, the Chamlees organized a mission which in 1959 became Central Baptist Church, possibly the largest Baptist church in the country today. In 1966 the Evangelical Baptist Convention of Peru was formed. By the end of 1972, there were ten churches with more than 1,700 members, and Southern Baptists had established work in twelve of the departments of the country. At first Southern Baptist work was confined primarily to major cities in the coastal region, but it later began to penetrate the mountains, much of it carried by native believers. Work has also been organized in the Amazon region.

The Southern Baptist mission engaged in a radio ministry and opened a mass media center in Trujillo. Its institute, founded in Lima in 1959, is now the Baptist Theological

Seminary in Trujillo. The mission has opened bookstores and developed a camp near Lima. Five clinics have been established, and teams of volunteers from the USA and Peru engage in medical and dental programs.

The American Baptist Association (ABA) has worked in Peru since 1960. The current pastor of the First Missionary Baptist Church of Trujilio, Carlos Angullo, also serves a church in El Porvenir and nine missions. A Peruvian convert who studied in the USA, Ricardo Roldan returned to Peru and started four missions in Trujillo and the Andes and led them to establish seven additional missions. Five of the missions have become churches. Roldan also founded in Trujillo the Peruvian Baptist Institute.

In 1960 Baptist Bible Fellowship International (BBFI) commenced its work with Rudy Johnson in the metropolitan Lima area. A Bible institute began in 1965, today known as the Bible Baptist Seminary. About thirty-six congregations exist in the Lima area and thirty outside of Lima from north to south. Baptist International Missions, Inc. (BIMI), has twenty-eight churches as well as a deaf ministry in Lima, which includes a school for deaf young people and a deaf Bible Institute. Graduates of the Bible school have begun nine deaf churches which stretch from Iquitos on the Amazon River to Arequipa in the south. Among other Baptist missions from abroad, three are from South America itself—two from Brazil and one from Argentina.

With the presence of numerous Baptist missions and the expansion of the major ones, Baptists are penetrating all regions of the country with Trujillo becoming a rather important center for Baptists. Baptists gained a certain status when Carlos García, a former Baptist pastor, was elected second vice-president of Peru. After serving twenty months under President Alberto Fujimori, García has now left politics to reenter Christian work.

BIBLIOGRAPHY: Information on the beginnings of the Irish Baptist mission may be found in Newstie, May 1984, 1. For a historical survey of the work of Baptist Faith Missions in the Amazon, see Jim Orrick, "Pioneer in Peru," Mission Sheets, Sep. 1991, 1. Several sources provide material on Baptist Mid-Missions and the Association of Baptists for World Evangelism—William J. Hopewell, Jr., The Missionary Emphasis of the General Association of Regular Baptist Churches (Chicago: Regular Baptist Press, 1963), 127–31; Field Surveys (Cleveland: BM-M, c. 1977), 117–19; Polly Strong, Burning Wicks (Cleveland: BM-M, 1984), 271–74; and Harold T. Commons, Heritage & Harvest (Cherry Hill, N.J.: ABWE, 1981), 47–49. For Southern Baptists, see Robert Harris, "Mission in Peru," Encyclopedia of Southern Baptists, 2:1088; Baker J. Cauthen and others, Advance (Nashville: Broadman Press, 1970), 167–269; Keith D. Shelton, "Peru," in the brochure, South America (Richmond: FMB/SBC, 1975), 53–58; Anita Bowden, "Peru: Seeking Hope," Commission, Dec. 1986, 12–37; and Martha Skelton, "Peru," Commission, Jan. 1992, 6–41. For the American Baptist Association, see "Ricardo Roldan," in the ABA publication, Missions, May 1994, 9–10, and American Baptist Association, Yearbook, 1992, 470–72. Correspondence of the editor provided additional data on the work of the American Baptist Association, the Baptist Bible Fellowship International, Baptist Mid-Missions, and Baptist International Missions, Inc.

SURINAME (1888)

	Members	Churches
United Baptist Organization of Suriname (1981)	117	(4)

*F*ormerly known as Dutch Guiana, Suriname, located on the northern coast of South America, gained independence from the Netherlands in 1975. About 38 percent of the inhabitants are Creole (mulatto), but Asiatic Indians and Javanese are significant segments of the population along with minorities of Bush Negroes and native Indians. A large majority is Christian, but minorites of Muslims and tribal religionists exist.

In 1888 a native of Suriname, Solomon Bromet, after studying in England, returned home to work among Javanese immigrants, some of whom had already become Baptists in Indonesia. In 1907 the National Baptist Convention in the USA reported that C. P. Rier, a pastor in Paramaibo, needed more support. Rier was pastor of a church organized in 1898 which had sixty-nine members.

Nondenominational missions, such as the West Indies Mission (today WorldTeam USA) and Independent Faith Missions, have conducted work with a Baptist character. When Southern Baptists arrived in 1971, they found that the West Indies Mission had started two churches in Paramaibo and was working among Bush Negroes and Indians in the interior.

The first Southern Baptist missionaries, Harold and Martha Lewis, transferred from Trinidad and, after language study, established a Christian Life Development Center in Paramaibo in 1973. Other missionaries have followed. They not only have studied Dutch, the offical language, but also Hindi to reach East Indians and Sranangtongo, a widely used indigenous tongue. In 1991 four churches formed the United Baptist Organization of Suriname. In 1992 three pastors were ordained, the first in the country. Two of them served Dutch-language churches, while one pastored an English-speaking congregation.

BIBLIOGRAPHY: For general surveys of Baptist work, see William W. Graves, *Baptist Trade Winds* (Nashville: Convention Press, 1979), 69–75, and Horace O. Russell, *The Baptist Witness* (El Paso: Carib Baptist Publications, 1983), 176–77. For the work of C. P. Rier, see National Baptist Convention, *Journal*, 1907, p. 50, and 1908, p. 106.

URUGUAY (1911)

	Members	Churches
1. Convención Evangélica Bautista del Uruguay (1948)	3,928	(54)
2. Asociación Nacional de los Bautistas Libres (1986)	266*	(7)
3. Asociación Misionera Bautista de America en el Uruguay (1991)	125	(3)
	4,319	(64)

*Average attendance

*T*he small republic of Uruguay, located between Brazil and Argentina, possesses a predominantly European population. Although a majority of the people are nominally Roman Catholic, much of the population is indifferent to religion and a large segment consists of freethinkers and atheists, unusual for South America. In such a secular society, Baptist work has been slow, and Baptists remain a very small minority, even a minority among evangelicals.

Paul Besson, who founded Baptist work in Argentina, spent vacations in Montevideo and had contacts in the city, but no permanent Baptist work developed from his activity. In 1911 the Baptist mission in Argentina of the FMB of the Southern Baptist Convention sent James and Helen Quarles to Montevideo to open Baptist work. In August 1911 the two missionaries and a family from Rosario, Argentina, which included Epifania González and three of her children, formed the First Baptist Church of Montevideo. The church did not get a proper building until 1942. Its membership in 1944 was 186 of which less than 25 percent were men. For many years the involvement of the FMB was limited, and between 1922 and 1939 it sent no new missionaries. In 1925 the two Baptist churches in Montevideo formed an association, and in August 1934 a Uruguayan association was organized to include all six churches in the country. In January 1934 women formed the Federation of Baptist Women of Uruguay. Eleven churches formed the Evangelical Baptist Convention of Uruguay in 1948.

In 1954 five missionary couples of the FMB organized a Uruguayan Baptist Mission, separate from the River Plate Mission centered in Argentina. By 1965 the number of missionaries had risen to twenty-two. After operating a Bible institute with night classes from 1937 to 1940 in Montevideo, the mission opened the Baptist Theological Institute in the same city in 1956. In spite of some progress, the convention in 1970 included only twenty-four churches and 1,700 members. Today, however, there are fifty-four congregations and the membership is approaching four thousand. To assist the mission program, the FMB bought a farm at Mercedes to serve as a model to neighboring farmers on which an agricultural evangelist and his wife settled in 1990. The Brazilian Baptist Convention and the Baptist General Conference from the USA both assist the Uruguayan Convention.

In 1962 Bill and Glenda Fulcher and Paul and Amy Robinson, representing Free Will Baptists from the USA, settled in Rivera, across the border from Brazil, where they soon formed two churches and other preaching points. Walter and Marcia Ellison settled in 1982 in Montevideo where a congregation was started. Today Free Will Baptists have seven churches. In 1965 the Baptist Missionary Association (BMA) sent James and Allyne Poole to Uruguay who, in four years of service, led in establishing three churches. After their leaving in 1969, the work continued under native leadership. The next missionary family to serve, A. L. and Bonnie Jo Shipp, arrived in 1989. In 1991 a Baptist Missionary Association of America in Uruguay was formed, which today has three churches and one mission. In 1989 a Bible institute was established. Baptist Bible Fellowship International (BBFI) and Baptist World Mission (BWM) have small mission forces, and the National Baptist Convention of Brazil is also represented.

BIBLIOGRAPHY: Two studies on Baptists in Uruguay are Bailis William Orrick, *A History of Southern Baptist Missions in Uruguay* (M.A. thesis, Baylor University, 1965), and James W. Bartley, Jr., *A History of Uruguayan Baptists with Particular Reference to Church Growth* (Th.D. dissertation, Southwestern Baptist Theological Seminary, 1972). On current

work of Southern Baptists in the country, see Martha Skelton, "Uruguay: Crisis of Hope,"
Dec. 1991, 10–41. On Free Will Baptists, see Mary Wisehart, ed., *The Fifty-Year Record of
the National Association of Free Will Baptists 1935–1985* (Nashville: Randall House
Publications, 1988), 66–67. On the Baptist Missionary Association, see John Duggar, *The
Baptist Missionary Association of America (1950–1986)* (Texarkana, Tex.: Baptist
Publishing House, 1988), 134.

VENEZUELA (1924)

	Members	Churches
1. Convención Nacional Bautista de Venezuela (1951)	16,900	(179)
2. Conferencia de Iglesias Bautistas de Delta, Monagas y Guayana	4,000	(25)
3. Baptist International Missions, Inc.	400	(3)
4. Conservative Baptists	136	(1)
	21,436	(208)

*V*enezuela, on the northern Caribbean Coast of South America, became an
independent state in 1830 with its withdrawal from Colombia (New
Granada). It has a diverse population of mestizo, European, Black, and
Indian peoples. As in other Spanish-speaking lands, the Roman Catholic faith predominates, but Protestantism is growing.

In 1924 O. R. Covault, a Baptist pastor in Ohio who went as an independent missionary with his family to South America, began to minister in El Callao, Bolívar State,
in the Guayana region, located in a gold-mining area. Eighteen months later, a church
was formed, composed of English-speaking Blacks, many of whom were immigrants
from the Caribbean islands. Covault returned to the USA where he was accepted as a
missionary by Baptist Mid-Missions in March 1927. The work soon became Spanish-
speaking and, within a comparatively short-time, national leaders were assuming
responsibility. The mission expanded into other areas of Bolívar, including Ciudad
Guayana. In 1940 it entered the delta of the Orinoco River, a land of mestizos and
Indians, reaching communities on the channels by dugout canoe but later by motor
launch and a small airplane. In 1950 the mission entered Barrancas in Monagas State.
Three years later it gained permission from the government to work among the Warao
tribe living in Monagas. The first Warao church was formed in 1964. Today the mission has twenty-five churches, a bookstore, high school, day school, and Bible institute, and its work is largely in the hands of nationals.

Evangelicals who used literature from the Baptist Spanish Publishing House in El
Paso, Texas, helped to prepare the way for Southern Baptist entry. In 1945 the
Southern Baptist mission in Colombia began work in Venezuela through Julio Moros,
a minister in Caracas, the capital. The Central Baptist Church of Caracas was formed
in 1946. The FMB of the Southern Baptist Convention sent its first missionaries in
1949 when it transferred Thomas and Carolyn Neely from Colombia to Caracas. They

were followed in the next year by James and Ruth Moss, who transferred from Colombia to Barquisimeto. In 1949 five churches joined with churches in Colombia to form a convention for both Colombia and Venezuela, but in August 1951 six churches organized a separate National Baptist Convention of Venezuela. Two months later a monthly, the *Luminar Bautista*, began publication. By the mid-1970s the convention had grown to include more than 2,500 members in 45 churches and 60 mission points. Four churches, composed of members from North America, were English-speaking. Today there are almost 17,000 members in more than 179 churches and 160 preaching points. At present the FMB of the Southern Baptist Convention has seventy-one missionaries in the country.

In 1970 the mission established a seminary in Los Teques. Today six Bible institutes and numerous centers for TEE provide additional opportunities for training. As part of their evangelistic witness and health-care ministry, Venezuelan Baptists opened in 1991 a walk-in clinic in Caracas, and volunteers from the USA have assisted in the Caracas clinic as well as in special evangelistic clinics.

Some additional Baptist missions have entered Venezuela and, except for Baptist Bible Fellowship International, have come within the last fifteen years and maintain comparatively small staffs. The Brazilian Baptist Convention has also entered the country.

BIBLIOGRAPHY: For the work of Baptist Mid-Missions, see Polly Strong, *Burning Wicks* (Cleveland: BM-M, 1984), 123–25, and *Field Surveys* (Cleveland: BM-M, c. 1977), 121–23. For Southern Baptists, see Charles B. Clark, "Mission in Venezuela," and "Venezuelan Baptist Convention," *Encyclopedia of Southern Baptists*, 2:1443, and *Your Guide to Foreign Missions*, 1994–1995, 88–89.

BAPTIST AND BAPTIST-RELATED MISSIONS

1. ARGENTINA   SBC (1903), CBI (1947), BGC, (1955) BBFI (1961), EuEBM (1969), EBM (1974), BrB (1976), BWM (1978), ABWE (1978), BIMI (1983), BM-M (1987), MBM

2. BOLIVIA   CaCBIM (1898), BrB (1946), MBM (1962), BMA (1967), BIMI (1969), BBFI (1978), SBC (1979), ABC (1986), EuEBM (1992), BrNB

3. BRAZIL   SBC (1881), SwO (1912), BFM (1923), BM-M (1935), ABWE (1942), CBI (1946), WBF (1947), BMA (1951), BBFI (1952), UkBMS (1953), BGC (1955), FWB (1958), JnBC (1963), BWM (1965), NABC (1966), BIMI (1967), IBJM (1968), EuEBM (1969), CaCBIM (1975), MWBM (1978), IBFI (1984), ABC (1991), MBM

4. CHILE   SBC (1917), ABWE (1953), BBFI (1954), MBM (1963), BM-M (1993), BrB

5. COLOMBIA   SBC (1941), ABWE (1942), WBF (1968), CaFEBC (1969), ABA (1971), BBFI (1973), RBMS (1974), BrB (1983), BIMI (1990), MBM, PNBC, UkGBM

6. ECUADOR   SBC (1950), WBF (1971), BBFI (1978), BrB (1982), BM-M (1988), BIMI (1990)

7. FRENCH GUIANA   SBC (1982), EBM (1984)

8. GUYANA BM-M (1954–1970, 1989), SBC (1962), LC (1970), CaFEBC (1990), BIMI (1991)

9. PARAGUAY SBC (1945), BrB (1964), ABWE (1974), BBFI (1980), BrIB, BrNB

10. PERU　　IrBM (1927), BFM (1935), BM-M (1937), ABWE (1939), SBC (1950), ABA (1960), BBFI (1960), MBM (1964), BIMI (1967), EuEBM (1980), BrB (1983), MWBM (1987), ArEBC, BrIB

11. SURINAME　IFM (1967), SBC (1971)

12. URUGUAY SBC (1911), BBFI (1959), BWM (1962), FWB (1962), BMA (1965), BrB (1975), BGC (1991), BrNB

13. VENEZUELA BM-M (1924), SBC (1949), BBFI (1966), BrB (1977), BIMI (1980), CBI (1986), CaFEBC (1990), MBM

NONDENOMINATIONAL MISSION

1. SURINAME WT (1956)

v. *Northern America*

D espite the great disparity between the strength of Baptists in Canada and the United States of America, it is logical to place them in one region not just because they are neighbors. Both groups, although influenced by European Baptists, created their own Baptist identities in a New World which spanned a whole continent. Although both groups are predominantly Anglo-Saxon, they nevertheless have had extensive ministries among numerous ethnic minorities. Both American and Canadian Baptists have experienced serious theological controversy and division.

There are similarities in viewing the pattern of Baptist life in both nations. The comparative homogeneity and moderate stance of Baptists in the northeast of the United States is comparable to Baptist life in the Atlantic Provinces of Canada. The theological and ethnic diversity in the Great Lakes region of America is somewhat comparable to the Central Provinces of Canada, and the ethnic presence in the American Great Plains is even stronger in the Canadian Prairies. In both countries conservative evangelicalism is a particularly strong force on the Pacific Coast.

One great difference, however, is the relative position of the two bodies in their respective countries. In the USA, Baptists are the largest Protestant body and, because of their dominance in the South, act almost like an established church in the region. Because of the dominance of the Roman Catholic, Anglican, and United Churches, Baptists in Canada are almost pushed out of their status as a denomination forcing it to compete with other evangelicals in the remaining religious market.

Countries	Members	Churches
1. Canada	231,007	2,070
2. United States of America	28,156,504	89,115
	28,387,511	91,185

NORTHERN AMERICAN—CANADA (1783)

Countries	Members	Churches
1. Canadian Baptist Federation (CBF) (1944)	133,607	(1,120)
2. Fellowship of Evangelical Baptist Churches in Canada (CaFEBC) (1953)	58,670	(525)
3. North American Baptist Conference (NABC) (1865)	17,698	(118)
4. Canadian Convention of Southern Baptists (CCSB) (1985)	6,852	(70)
5. Baptist General Conference of Canada (BGCC) (1981)	6,465	(92)
6. Baptist Bible Fellowship International (BBFI)	n/a	(61)
7. Ukrainian Evangelical Baptist Convention of Canada (1950)	3,200	(25)
8. Free Will Baptists (FWB) (1874)	1,875	(17)
9. Association of Regular Baptist Churches (ARBC) (1958)	1,500	(10)
10. Fellowship of Fundamental Baptist Churches (FFBC) (1960)	600	(11)
11. Union of Slavic Churches of Evangelical Christians and Slavic Baptists of Canada (1958)	500	(11)
12. Missionary Baptists (ABA)	n/a	(7)
13. Reformed Baptists (RB)	n/a	(2)
14. Seventh Day Baptists (SDB)	40	(1)
	231,007	(2,070)

REGIONAL DISTRIBUTION:

Atlantic: Newfoundland, Prince Edward Island, New Brunswick, Nova Scotia

	N.F.	P.E.I.	N.B.	N.S.
a. CBF	253 (7)	2,199 (22)	31,947 (254)	31,866 (272)

b. FEBC		n/a (1)	1,545 (5)	744 (12)
c. FFBC			n/a (7)	n/a (4)
d. BBFI	n/a (2)			n/a (1)
e. RB	—	—	n/a (1)	—
	253 (9)	2,199 (23)	33,492 (267)	32,610 (289)

Central: Quebec, Ontario

	Que.	Ont.
a. CBF	3,333 (40)	43,349 (360)
b. FEBC	6,375 (85)	38,352 (272)
c. NABC		1,794 (12)
d. CCSB	573 (11)	277 (6)
e. BGCC	151 (3)	311 (8)
f. BBFI	n/a (6)	n/a (22)
g. MB		n/a (5)
h. RB	n/a (1)	—
	10,432 (146)	84,083 (685)

Prairie: Manitoba, Saskatchewan, Alberta

	Man.	Sask.	Alta.
a. CBF	1,897 (24)	2,978 (22)	7,333 (61)
b. FEBC	585 (9)	440 (5)	1,508 (26)
c. NABC	2,438 (16)	1,342 (15)	7,838 (50)
d. CCSB	370 (5)	938 (13)	1,636 (15)
e. BGCC	1,316 (15)	741 (14)	1,703 (19)
f. BBFI	n/a (2)	n/a (3)	n/a (7)
	6,606 (71)	6,439 (72)	20,018 (178)

Pacific/Territories: British Columbia, Northwest Territories, Yukon Territory

	B.C.	N.W.T.	Y.T.
a. CBF	8,234 (55)	147 (2)	71 (1)
b. FEBC	9,072 (108)	49 (1)	n/a (1)
c. NABC	4,286 (25)		

d. CCSB	3,058 (20)		
e. BGCC	2,243 (23)		
f. BBFI	n/a (17)		n/a (1)
g. MB	n/a (2)	—	—
	26,893 (250)	196 (3)	71 (3)

(Some small Baptist groups were not included in the regional distribution because of a lack of data on the exact location of their churches.)

STATISTICS: The statistics for the first six Baptist bodies and the Missionary Baptists and Reformed Baptists came directly from official sources, including yearbooks, periodicals, or correspondence. Statistics on the Free Will Baptists, Association of Regular Baptist Churches, and Seventh Day Baptists were gained from David T. Priestley, "Canadian Baptists in National Perspective," *Baptist Quarterly*, 32, no. 7 (July 1988), 308. Membership of the Ukrainian Evangelical Baptist Convention, Union of Slavic Churches of Evangelical Christians and Slavic Baptists of Canada, and Fellowship of Fundamental Baptist Churches was obtained from Arthur Carl Piepkorn, *Profiles in Belief* (New York: Harper and Row, 1978), 2:454–55, 459–60.

*C*anadian Baptists have been significantly affected, not only by immigration and Anglo-American intrusion, but also by regionalism, ethnicity, and a variety of indigenous religious movements. Consequently, the spectrum of those carrying the Baptist name in Canada has been disconcertingly wide, frustratingly complex, and numerically weaker as the twentieth century has unfolded. In 1871 it was estimated that 6.7 percent of all Canadians were Baptists; by 1911 the percentage dropped to 5.3, in 1941 to 4.2, and in 1992 to 3.4.

In 1880 I. E. Bill, the aging Baptist leader of Maritime Canada, remarked that "there is a future for Baptists" in this country because they have "a past that has laid foundations broad and deep upon which they may go on to build." These great expectations were not shared by those original New England settlers who established the original Baptist churches in Canada, nor are they shared by most Canadian Baptists today.

More than a century before Bill recorded his optimistic outlook, the first Baptist churches in what is now Canada were planted in 1763 at Sackville, Nova Scotia (now in New Brunswick), and Horton, Nova Scotia, in 1765. Both congregations ceased to exist, although the church in Horton was reconstituted in 1778. If it had not been for the Great Awakening in Nova Scotia (1776–1784) led by Henry Alline, the charismatic preacher from Falmouth, it is unlikely that the Baptist cause in Atlantic Canada would have become as significant as it eventually became.

Following Alline's death in 1784, many of his loosely connected New Light churches slipped into an extreme form of antinominism. By 1796 many New Light preachers sought a certain level of respectability. Motivated in part by certain millennial expectations, "the rage for dipping," as the populist religious movement was initially referred to by its critics, provided an opportunity for New Light leaders to usher hundreds of newly baptized individuals into properly constituted Calvinist churches. These churches embraced church discipline, the regular celebration of the ordinances, and by 1809, restricted (or close) communion. The marriage of Allinite religious experience and immersionist baptism created an almost irresistible baptismal spirituality which became the most effective tool of the Calvinist Baptists in evangelistic efforts. The evi-

association supports Toronto Baptist Seminary and Bible College, and its organ is *The Gospel Witness*. In addition to the above bodies, various Baptist missions from the USA have sent missionaries to Canada, attempting to establish churches among English-speaking and French-speaking Canadians.

Despite the differences and disputes that have created the numerous variations on the Baptist theme, the Baptist faith remains an experiential religion—a religion of the heart which embraces differing ethnical, cultural, and doctrinal tenets. With the growth of the French and Chinese-speaking Canadian Baptist communities, the continued missionary enterprise, and a renewed interest in religion within society, it is perhaps as I. E. Bill wrote more than a hundred years ago, "there is a future for Baptists."

George Rawlyk with Lorraine Coops and Dan Goodwin

BIBLIOGRAPHY: In recent years, there has been a remarkable number of volumes on Baptists in Canada. The history by Harry A. Renfree, *Heritage and Horizon: The Baptist Story in Canada* (Mississauga, Ont.: Canadian Baptist Federation, 1988), is a helpful survey and, although criticized for not incorporating the most recent research, is nevertheless a credible work which includes most Baptist bodies. Jarold K. Zeman has edited two volumes, *Baptists in Canada: Search for Identity Amidst Diversity* (Burlington, Ont.: G. R. Welch Company, 1980), and *Costly Vision: The Baptist Pilgrimage in Canada* (Burlington, Ont.: Welch Publishing Company, 1988), which provide excellent articles on a number of historical topics. The volume by Zeman, *Open Doors: Canadian Baptists 1950–1990* (Hantsport, N.S.: Lancelot Press, 1992), includes articles and popular addresses by the author. Zeman's article, "Baptists in Canada and Cooperative Christianity," *Foundations*, 15, no. 3 (July/Sep. 1972): 211–40, is an insightful article on Canadian Baptist relationships. A valuable contribution to understanding the revival movement in the Maritimes is the volume by George A. Rawlyk, *Ravished by the Spirit: Religious Revivals, Baptists, and Henry Alline* (Kingston and Montreal: McGill-Queen's University Press, 1984). A history on separatist evangelical/fundamentalist Baptists in Canada is the work by L. K. Tarr, *This Dominion His Dominion* (Willowdale, Ont.: FEBC, 1968). A helpful booklet on Southern Baptist beginnings in Canada is by Roland P. Hood, *Southern Baptist Work in Canada* (Portland, OR: Baptist General Convention of Oregon-Washington, 1968). For Ukrainian Baptists, see Peter Kindrat, *Ukraïn'kyĭ Baptysts'kiĭ Rukh u Kanadi* (Winnipeg and Toronto: "Doroha Prawdy," 1972). A valuable bibliography on Canadian Baptists is *Baptists in Canada 1760–1990: A Bibliography of Selected Printed Resources in English* (Hantsport, N.S.: Lancelot Press, 1989), prepared by Philip G. A. Griffin-Allwood, George A. Rawlyk, and Jarold K. Zeman.

BAPTIST AND BAPTIST-RELATED MISSIONS

BM-M (1950), EBM (1953), SBC (1953), CBHMS (1962), BBFI (1971), BrB (1978), BWM (1982), IFM, RBMS

*T*he United States of America (USA) is the center of world Baptist strength. With more than 28 million members, it includes about 75 percent of all Baptists. In the USA, only the Roman Catholic Church outnumbers Baptists, which leaves Baptists as the largest Protestant body. A recent poll found that almost one American in five claims to be a Baptist. More than half of the Baptists in the country belong to the Southern Baptist Convention, which is the single largest Protestant denomination in the country. Growth has been spectacular. In 1790 Baptists numbered a bit more than 67,000; in 1848 about 840,000, in 1918 about 7 million, and today more than four times as many. They are divided into more than fifty bodies, but 92 percent of them are found in five of them—Southern Baptist Convention (SBC); National Baptist Convention, USA, Inc. (NBC); National Baptist Convention of America, Inc. (NBCA); American Baptist Churches in the USA (ABC); and Baptist Bible Fellowship International (BBFI).

Baptist beginnings in the British colonies of the New World were inauspicious, and Baptists remained an insignificant group for about a century. They were a body which had to struggle from the ground up, beginning with small, scattered churches, and in some areas faced ecclesiastical restrictions, if not outright persecution. They were not part of any establishment, as were the Puritan Congregationalists in New England or the Anglicans in the South, and could not count on the thousands or even millions of immigrants which would come to help fill the ranks of such groups as the Presbyterians, Roman Catholics, and Lutherans.

Roger Williams (c. 1603–1683), the founder of Rhode Island as a haven of religious liberty, also established the first Baptist church in Providence. In 1638, after being baptized by sprinkling by Ezekiel Holliman, Williams then baptized Holliman and ten others. A second church under John Clarke was formed in Newport around 1644. It was probably Mark Lucar, who had been immersed in England in 1642 and then became a member of the Newport Church, who introduced believer's baptism by immersion in America. Williams soon left the church he founded to become a Seeker, awaiting God to reestablish the true church in His own way and time. Rhode Island Baptists were soon divided into three groups—General Six Principle Baptists who believed in Christ's general atonement, Regular Baptists, who as Calvinists believed in limited atonement, and Seventh Day Baptists.

Before the end of the seventeenth century Regular Baptists were present in both Pennsylvania and South Carolina, while General Baptists appeared in Virginia, but all Baptist groups were very weak until the Great Awakening in the middle of the eighteenth century. This revival, which was followed by the Second Great Awakening after the Revolutionary War, brought rapid growth to the Regular Baptists, who now became very evangelistic. In New England the revival gave birth to the Separate Baptists, who with their fiery evangelism grew rapidly in both New England and the

South. While the General and Seventh Day Baptists remained small bodies, most Regular and Separate Baptists joined as one body, continuing as Regular Baptists in the North or as United Baptists in the South. With their rapid increase, they became the mainstream of Baptist life and one of the leading religious bodies in the nation.

Although Baptist churches were congregational in church government, they nevertheless founded associations for mutual support and fellowship. Associations corresponded with each other and in some areas established general committees of correspondence. In the 1820s Baptists began to form state conventions. In 1814 the need for cooperation in foreign missions produced the first national Baptist organization: the General Missionary Convention of the Baptist Denomination in the United States for Foreign Missions (or the Triennial Convention). Baptists later formed other national societies and even national conventions to coordinate the work of the various societies or convention boards. Some Baptists, such as Primitive Baptists, reacted against the growth of denominational bodies outside the local church and associations by rejecting them entirely. In the twentieth century, fundamentalist Baptists have also reacted against too much centralization by forming associations of churches or fellowships of pastors which, in turn, are separate from the mission agencies and educational agencies which they support.

Seemingly, the many Baptist divisions present a maze of groups and subgroups, but they are much alike in theology and worship. Most Baptists in the United States are conservative evangelicals, ranging from moderate to strictly fundamental. Aside from doctrinal preaching in the small Calvinist groups, most sermons are warmly evangelical and biblical. If one were to exclude the dynamic worship patterns of the African-American community and the simplicity and older practices of the Primitivists, the worship patterns of most Baptist churches are similar. The average Baptist church follows an ordered service, but most reject a formal liturgy and include congregational singing, extemporaneous prayer, a sermon with an appeal for a personal response, and a folksy atmosphere of fellowship before and after the service. With the impact of the charismatic movement, many services are becoming less formal with praise hymns and choruses led by a worship team and accompanied by musical instruments, the projection of words for singing on screens or walls, and an informal delivery of the sermon.

Despite the similarities which unite most Baptists, at least four developments have divided them. A classification of Baptists in the USA should include the following factors:

1) *Theology.* Baptists started as two distinct theological groups—General Baptists (Arminian) and Regular Baptists (Calvinists). The theology of most Baptists is rooted in the Calvinist tradition which, in most Baptist bodies, has been greatly modified but retains the doctrine of eternal security. Some small groups remain strictly Calvinist, and others hold to a doctrine of free will. A further theological modification appears when some groups have made premillennialism a test of fellowship.

2) *Means.* Baptists have divided over means, that is, the use of methods to reach the unconverted. Small groups, such as Primitive Baptists, taking refuge in hyper-Calvinism, rejected all means.

3) *Culture and Ethnicity.* Baptists with either northern or southern cultural roots have often exhibited differences in worship, social mores, and ecclesiology. In addition, groups that worship in languages other than English or racial groups, such as African-Americans, have formed their own bodies.

4) *Denominational Relationships.* Most White Baptist groups as conservative evan-

gelicals reject the ecumenical movement but cooperate with other evangelicals who are like them in biblical belief and practice. On the left of them, however, are Baptists in the American Baptist Churches/USA, who are committed to the ecumenical movement and exhibit greater toleration for differences in belief than other Baptist bodies. On the right of the conservative evangelicals are separatist fundamentalists—those who are militantly opposed to theological liberalism and who separate from fellow evangelicals who may have relations with non-evangelicals. A fourth group includes bodies that refuse the baptism of other Baptists and do not fellowship with anyone outside of their own ecclesiological tradition, such as Landmark Missionary Baptists and Primitive Baptists.

The following is an outline of the different Baptist bodies that will be addressed in this work:

BAPTIST BODIES IN THE U.S.A.

I. Regular Baptists (Northern-Oriented)

  A. Ecumenical Mainline—American Baptist Churches in the U.S.A.

  B. Conservative Evangelical

   1. Baptist General Conference

   2. Conservative Baptist Association of America

   3. North American Baptist Conference

   4. Seventh Day Baptist General Conference

  C. Separatist Fundamentalist

   1. Fundamental Baptist Fellowship of America

   2. General Association of Regular Baptist Churches

   3. Independent Baptist Fellowship of North America

   4. New Testament Association of Independent Baptist Churches and related associations

II. Regular Baptists–Ethnic

  A. Ethnic Bodies in General

  B. Hispanic Baptists

III. Regular Baptists (Southern-Oriented)

  A. Conservative Evangelical—Southern Baptist Convention

  B. Landmark Missionary Baptist

   1. American Baptist Association

   2. Baptist Missionary Association

   3. Independent Landmark Missionary Baptist Associations/Churches

C. Separatist Fundamentalist
  1. Baptist Bible Fellowship International (BBFI)
  2. Independent Baptist Fellowship International (IBFI)
  3. Liberty Baptist Fellowship
  4. Southwide Baptist Fellowship
  5. World Baptist Fellowship

IV. Regular Baptists–National Baptists (African-American)
  1. National Baptist Convention of America, Inc.
  2. National Baptist Convention, U.S.A., Inc.
  3. National Missionary Baptist Convention of America
  4. National Primitive Baptist Convention, Inc.
  5. Progressive National Baptist Convention, Inc.

V. Regular Baptists (Southern-Oriented)—Primitivists
  A. Central Baptist Association
  B. General Association of Baptists (Duck River and Kindred Associations)
  C. Old Missionary Baptists
  D. Regular Baptists
    1. Old Regular Baptists
    2. Regular Baptists
    3. Enterprise Baptists
  E. Primitive Baptists
    1. Absoluters
    2. Old Liners
    3. Progressives
  F. Two-Seed-in-the-Spirit Predestinarian Baptists
  G. United Baptists

VI. Free Will/General Baptists
  A. Free Will Baptists
    1. National Association of Free Will Baptists
    2. Original Free Will Baptists
    3. Independent Free Will Baptist Associations
    4. United American Free Will Baptist Church
  B. General Association of General Baptists
  C. General Six Principle Baptists
  D. Separate Baptists in Christ

VII. Calvinistic (Reformed) Baptists

A. Reformed/Sovereign Grace Baptists

1. Reformed Baptists

2. Sovereign Grace Baptists

B. Strict Baptists

STATISTICS: The primary sources for the statistics of Baptist bodies in the U.S.A. which follow come from *Churches and Church Membership in the United States 1990* (Atlanta: Glenmary Research Center, 1992), yearbooks and directories of the various Baptist groups, and from correspondence by the editor.

REGULAR BAPTISTS (NORTHERN-ORIENTED)

	Members	Churches
I. Regular Baptists (Northern-Oriented)		
A. Ecumenical Mainline—		
1. American Baptist Churches in the U.S.A. (1907)	1,504,573	5,801
B. Conservative Evangelical		
2. Baptist General Conference (1879)	132,994	786
3. Conservative Baptist Association of America (1948)	200,000	1,197
4. North American Baptist Conference (1865)	42,689	267
5. Seventh Day Baptist General Conference (1801)	4,885	78
C. Separatist Fundamentalist		
6. Fundamental Baptist Fellowship of America (1920)	n/a	(402)*
7. General Association of Regular Baptist Churches (1932)	157,522	1,541
8. Independent Baptist Fellowship of North America (1990)	n/a	(106)*
9. New Testament Association of Independent Baptist Churches and related associations (1965)	66,500	467
	2,109,163	10,645

*The memberships of both the Fundamental Baptist Fellowship (FBF) and Independent Baptist Fellowship of North American (IBFNA) are composed of pastors and other individuals, not churches. The above figures for churches of these two groups represent pastors of churches who are members. Many of the churches related to the FBF would be included in associations which are aligned with the New Testament Association, if not also in one of the southern-oriented separatist fundamentalist fellowships. More than 40 percent of the pastors of the IBFNA are pastors of churches which continue in the General Association of Regular Baptists.

ECUMENICAL MAINLINE—AMERICAN BAPTIST CHURCHES IN THE U.S.A.

A merican Baptist Churches in the U.S.A. (ABC/USA) is both the oldest continuing body of Baptist Christians in North America and the first fellowship of Christian churches organized as essentially a creature of the New World. Almost all the other Christian bodies in the colonies were organized under the authority of British or European churches or emigrated as congregations to the North American continent. In contrast, American Baptists were largely an American development. Also significant for America and the world was the role of American Baptists in the founding of Rhode Island, the world's first state that practiced religious liberty.

The first two Baptist churches were formed by Roger Williams in 1638 in Providence and John Clarke in Newport around 1644. The Great Awakening, a revival in the 1740s, brought scores of New Light Congregational churches into the Baptist fold. It also began to change the basic theological orientation of most Baptist congregations to an emphasis on the human response of faith to God's grace in Jesus Christ. American Baptists have continued to influence and be influenced by the major trends in theology on the North American continent. William Newton Clarke and Augustus H. Strong tried to keep orthodox Christianity in touch with changes in modern thought. Walter Rauschenbusch, Leighton Williams, and the members of the Brotherhood of the Kingdom contributed greatly to the making and spread of the Social Gospel in American Christianity. Helen Barrett Montgomery brought a woman's perspective to Bible study and produced her own New Testament translation. Shailer Mathews and Harry Emerson Fosdick helped counter the fundamentalist movement, while E. J. Carnell, Carl F. H. Henry, and Bernard Ramm have been key thinkers in the development of a renewed evangelical theology. Martin Luther King, Jr., made a strong statement for peace, justice, and nonviolence, and Jitsuo Morikawa developed a cosmic doctrine of salvation. Phyllis Trible is an important contributor to the feminist critique and reworking of biblical interpretation.

The critical defining movement for American Baptist life, both theologically and organizationally, was the rising support for missions overseas and in the United States. Adoniram and Ann Judson and Luther Rice, missionaries under the American Board of Commissioners, were immersed as believers in India and thus began the American Baptist foreign mission enterprise. The Judsons went to Burma to start their work, while Rice returned to the United States to raise their support and to help lead in the formation in 1814 of the General Missionary Convention of the Baptist Denomination in the United States for Foreign Missions (also known as the Triennial Convention). This body, which also for a time sent out home missionaries, was the first national Baptist denominational body and, as the American Baptist Foreign Mission Society, became a constituent part of the Northern Baptist Convention in 1907. American Baptists not only provided mission support for Burma but also for China, Thailand, India, Japan, Philippines, Africa, and Europe. Under the American Baptist Home Mission Society (ABHMS), missionaries were supported in the Caribbean, Mexico, and Central America. More recent mission ties have been established with national conventions in Barbados, Bolivia, Brazil, Chile, Costa Rica, and Dominican Republic. The Board of International Ministries of ABC/USA is today responsible for all international work, including the Latin American and Caribbean fields, which were transferred to it in 1973.

American Baptists have always maintained a comprehensive approach to Christian witness abroad, including evangelization and church planting; education at primary, secondary, university and theological seminary levels; medical work in hospitals and clinics; and community development. In addition, in societies where women have had little or no status, they have emphasized educating women for leadership and conducting work with children, which had been a central focus of the Woman's American Baptist Foreign Mission Society.

Home missions were originally directed at two groups of people "in the West" (which in 1815 meant as far as the Mississippi River)—Native Americans and new settlers. When the Triennial Convention withdrew support from all home missionaries except Isaac McCoy, who had an Indian station in Indiana, John Mason Peck encouraged the formation of the American Baptist Home Mission Society (ABHMS) in 1832. The mission to Native Americans has remained a constant part of American efforts. Church planting has also been a continuing activity. Missionaries supported by the ABHMS organized both Sunday Schools and congregations, often in cooperation with the American Baptist Publication Society, which had its own system of colporteurs and later of chapel cars. In addition, many churches have received low-interest loans. Increased immigration to the USA from Europe called for mission efforts among the new arrivals. In most cases these groups formed their own conventions or associations, but many of their member churches continue as part of the American Baptist denomination. With a new flood of immigrants, especially from Latin America and Asia, American Baptists have once again picked up an emphasis on bilingual witness. Hispanic churches are becoming an increasingly significant proportion of the whole denomination.

Industrialization produced great cities with its own set of problems. Bilingual churches and new suburban congregations were part of the home missions strategy, but city societies and urban constituencies helped as well. In cooperation with the ABHMS and the Woman's ABHMS, they sponsored Christian centers, educational centers, and Christian Friendliness workers. During World War II, American Baptists provided a ministry to Japanese-Americans who had been forcibly detained in relocation centers after being evacuated from the West Coast and also developed trailer ministries to communities of defense workers. In cooperation with the regions, ABHMS fashioned a mission strategy for rural areas through town and country work. Home ministries today are under the Board of National Ministries, but this board now works less through its own missionaries and more through local congregations and community initiatives at the local level as well as with volunteers.

Social ministries have become a growing part of the home mission strategy. A Washington office is maintained to monitor governmental relations at the federal level. Grants and technical assistance support direct human services, particularly refugee resettlement, feeding, and shelter. Attention is also given to peace, ecology, racial justice, housing and urban strategy, and social and ethical responsibility in investments. Membership in the American Baptist Homes and Hospitals Association includes 76 retirement homes and communities, 27 hospitals and nursing homes, and 21 children's homes and special services. A national office accredits and supports chaplains and pastoral counselors.

American Baptists have had a continuing concern for education. Their first school for ministers was the academy organized in 1756 at Hopewell, New Jersey, by Isaac Eaton. With the encouragement of the Philadelphia Baptist Association, the school which became Brown University was organized in 1764 in Warren, Rhode Island, and then moved to Providence. Since that time Baptists connected with ABC/USA have established some ninety colleges and universities; sixteen continue to be American Baptist-related. The ABHMS assisted in establishing sixteen schools for freed men and women after the Civil War and aided two others. Seven colleges and theological seminaries remain as strong African-American educational institutions, four of which retain their relationship with ABC/USA. Bacone College, a fully accredited junior college for Native Americans, also grew out of home mission initiatives. Nine theological seminaries in the continental USA and Puerto Rico are still American Baptist-related.

The Baptist General Tract Society (later known as the American Baptist Publication Society) was organized by American Baptists in 1824. Until the end of the nineteenth century it was the principal source of Baptist educational materials for all Baptists in the United States. Today Educational Ministries offers a range of curriculum choices to meet the needs of an increasingly diverse constituency. Judson Press continues to be the publishing arm of American Baptists; it has gained recognition for practical books on church life and ministry and African-American works. American Baptists still publish the oldest continuing Protestant periodical in the USA, known today as *American Baptists in Mission*. It is supplemented by American Baptist News service and thirty-four regional publications. Other periodicals are *American Baptist Quarterly*, *Baptist Leader* for church school teachers, and *The Secret Place*, a quarterly devotional booklet. In 1943 American Baptists acquired a one thousand–acre estate in Green Lake, Wisconsin, and converted it into the American Baptist Assembly. Two strong lay organizations are American Baptist Women's Ministries and American Baptist Men.

American Baptists have been inclusive from their beginning but have become more intentional about their openness in recent decades. Recent statistics indicate that 43.1 percent of the present resident membership in ABC/USA belongs to racial and national groups other than White or European. With the emergence of the civil rights movement in the 1950s, an increasing number of African-American congregations applied for dual membership in American Baptist churches; a great many formerly White congregations, especially in the cities, became multiracial; and ABC/USA initiated an associated relationship with the Progressive National Baptist Convention (PNBC). Hispanic churches are an integral part of American Baptist churches and in recent years have been the leading group in new churches. There is also a growing influx of new Asian immigrants, some of whom are Baptists, and others who are being reached with evangelism in their own language.

One other area where American Baptists have been growing is in their acceptance of women as equal, not subordinate partners, in every area of life and work. American Baptists were among the first Baptist bodies to ordain women, the earliest being Lura Maines of Michigan in 1877. Although 747 of the 8,851 ordained American Baptists (8.4 percent) in 1992 were women, only 5 percent of all pastors were female. American Baptists have also included women as denominational staff and elected leaders. Helen Barrett Montgomery was the first woman president of the Northern Baptist Convention in 1921–1922, followed by Anna Canada Swain in 1944–1945.

Laywomen are now elected as ABC/USA president in rotation with laymen and ordained persons.

The membership of American Baptist congregations includes a wide span of socio-economic status but is heavily tipped toward the middle of the American class spectrum. In most communities American Baptist congregations are lower on the totem pole than the rest of the American mainline denominations. American Baptist churches, however, have had millionaires and celebrities—John D. Rockefeller, Jr., who gave generously to denominational causes; William C. Coleman, a manufacturer in Wichita, Kansas; and James L. Kraft, founder of the dairy and cheese empire bearing his name and a benefactor of the American Baptist Assembly. But the denomination has only small numbers of the very poor and the very rich.

In the early years, churches formed local associations and later state conventions. In more recent years, some state conventions have joined together into regions; some of the city societies have become regions (while others have been merged into a wider body); and all these intermediate organizations—at one time known as "regions, states, and cities"—have been designated as "regions," forming the third story of the American Baptist structure.

The first truly national body of American Baptists was the Triennial Convention (later called the American Baptist Foreign Mission Society). It was followed by the American Baptist Publication Society, the American Baptist Home Mission Society, the American and Foreign Bible Society, and the American Baptist Historical Society. American Baptists continued to operate on the society principle until the Northern Baptist Convention was organized in 1907 to coordinate the work of the denomination. It had taken almost three centuries from the organization of the first Baptist congregation in the New World before American Baptists added the fourth story to their denominational structure.

The name of the national organization was changed to "American Baptist Convention" in 1950 and then to "American Baptist Churches in the U.S.A." in 1972. Two major changes have been made in denominational structure in recent years. In 1972 the annual meetings of delegates from the churches were changed to biennial meetings. A two hundred–member General Board, with three-fourths elected on a representative basis from election districts and one-fourth elected at large by the biennial delegates, was given authority to make major policy decisions. Members of the General Board also serve on the national program boards for Educational Ministries, National Ministries, and International Ministries. Subsequently, election district representatives now also represent their region, and each region is entitled to send a limited number of delegates to the biennial meetings. The national Executive Council, composed of the general secretary and the executive directors of the program boards, meets regularly to coordinate the work of the national agencies, while the General Executive Council, composed of the regional executive ministers and a limited number of national executives, acts as staff backup to the General Board.

The Ministers and Missionaries Benefit Board, founded in 1911, administers both a retirement pension plan and a health plan; it also strives to improve pastoral compensation and provide salary support. The Commission on the Ministry coordinates efforts to recruit and guide persons into ministry, to support them in seminary, and to address problems faced by clergy. The Ministers Council was organized in 1936 to serve as a fellowship and advocacy organization.

Because of the theologically inclusive policies of the Northern Baptist Convention, a group of fundamentalists left in 1932 to form the General Association of Regular Baptists. Another defection occurred in the 1940s when Conservative Baptists established their own agencies. American Baptists have steadfastly refused efforts to adopt a denomination-wide confession of faith, preferring to abide by a statement first adopted in 1922 and then reaffirmed in 1946 by the controversy-wracked convention at Grand Rapids, Michigan: The New Testament is "a trustworthy, authoritative and all-sufficient rule of our faith and practice."

In most churches the sermon remains the centerpiece of the service except when the Lord's Supper is observed—which is customarily on the first Sunday of the month. Because there is no American Baptist book of worship—nor even a common hymnal— the form of worship varies greatly among congregations. The conventional service continues to include prayers, hymns, Scripture, sermon, and offering, with the choir or soloists singing an anthem or two. In churches influenced by the charismatic movement, the service opens with praise songs, followed by testimony and prayer that is not strictly limited to a given time period, and then the sermon and offering. In churches accustomed to a more formal and liturgical service, there may be use of the common lectionary of Scripture readings and set prayers. Still in some churches, worship is more of a free-form experience depending on the leader and kinds of participants available to bring music, drama, or even dance.

Communion is open to all Christian believers. While a majority of churches still restrict full membership to immersed believers, a growing number have open membership: Those who have been believing members of other Christian churches are received by letter or Christian experience, while those who come to faith for the first time through that congregation are baptized by immersion. Many American Baptist churches are members of more than one denomination, belonging also to another Baptist group or other Protestant body. Some congregations are union or federated churches.

In the early years of the nineteenth century, American Baptists participated in the formation of several interdenominational societies. They helped to organize both the Federal Council of Churches (1907) and the National Council of the Churches of Christ in the U.S.A. (1950) and became charter members of the World Council of Churches in 1948. A minority of American Baptist congregations exercise the right to be listed in the denominational directory as "not approving affiliation with or providing financial support" to the National Council of Churches. In keeping with its position as a denomination that spans almost the full theological spectrum of American Protestantism, American Baptist Churches also maintains an observer with the National Association of Evangelicals. Many of the outstanding leaders of ecumenical work in the United States have been American Baptists, including R. H. Edwin Espy, Edwin T. Dahlberg, and Stanley I. Stuber. American Baptist Churches also belongs to the Baptist World Alliance and the Baptist Joint Committee on Public Affairs.

American Baptists have served in government at all levels and continue to make a witness on public issues. The General Board of ABC/USA adopts statements of policy and resolutions that are communicated to those in government. Many regional bodies, associations, and congregations keep in regular correspondence with legislative representatives and others in government at all levels. Among the issues currently of concern to American Baptists are: health care, environment, human sexuality, women's issues, refugees, U.S. foreign policy, national budget priorities, and pastoral ethics of clergy.

George D. Younger

BIBLIOGRAPHY: Volumes which include an extended treatment of American Baptists are Robert G. Torbet, *A History of the Baptists*, 3d ed. (Valley Forge, Pa.: Judson Press, 1973), and William H. Brackney, *The Baptists* (Westport, Conn.: Greenwood Press, 1988). A helpful survey of American Baptists is the article by Edward C. Starr, "American Baptist Convention," *Baptist Advance* (Nashville: Broadman Press, 1964), 29–130. A valuable study of American Baptist polity is Paul M. Harrison, *Authority and Power in the Free Church Tradition: A Social Case Study of the American Baptist Convention* (Princeton: Princeton University Press, 1959).

CONSERVATIVE EVANGELICAL

*T*he constituencies of three of the four bodies in this category were identified at one time with the Northern Baptist Convention (now the American Baptist Churches/USA). Unlike the American Baptist Churches/USA, their national bodies have adopted confessions of faith, and they are not members of the Federal and World Councils. The North American Baptist Conference and Baptist General Conference were foreign language bodies with their own organizations, which eventually separated completely from the mother body. The Baptist General Conference, partly in opposition to a theological inclusivism in the American Baptist Foreign Mission Society, formed its own mission program, and has also joined the National Association of Evangelicals.

As a protest movement, the Conservative Baptists took a separatist position in respect to theological liberalism. But unlike separatist fundamentalists with whom they have much in common, Conservative Baptists cooperate with other evangelicals regardless of other ties and hold membership in the National Association of Evangelicals.

The Seventh Day Baptists, having a wider range of belief in their denomination than the other three, at one time might have been classified as a mainline ecumenical body but, with their withdrawal in the 1970s from both the Federal and World Council of Churches, this body better fits the conservative evangelical category. With the exception of the Conservative Baptists, these bodies are members of the Baptist World Alliance and the Baptist Joint Committee on Public Affairs.

Baptist General Conference

It was on August 8, 1852, that three newly arrived Swedish immigrants were baptized by Gustaf Palmquist in the Mississippi River at Rock Island, Illinois. On August 13 these three baptized believers with Palmquist organized a Swedish Baptist church. This marked the beginning of the Baptist General Conference (BGC). From this inauspicious beginning, the conference fellowship has grown to more than eight hundred churches in forty-three states, divided into fifteen districts and a membership of about 135,000. Its largest districts are Minnesota and Southwest (Arizona and Southern California) with around 25,000 members each.

The history of the BGC can be divided into three periods. The first is the Swedish period, 1852 to 1945. The early churches were divided between baptized believers from Sweden and the Swedish immigrants and their children who became a part of the evangelistic outreach of the churches. The Baptists in Sweden, many of whom suffered persecution, were part of a pietistic, separatist movement, which was given the name of *läsere* ("readers") because of their reading of the Bible. This period was marked by rapid church growth in the first half and slow growth in the second half. During the early to mid-1900s the flow of emigration practically dried up. In 1902 there were 324 churches, but in 1945 the number of churches had decreased to 293, although membership had nearly doubled to 40,224. Churches in cities with large Scandinavian populations, like Chicago, St. Paul, and Minneapolis, grew substantially.

John Alexis Edgren, a pastor in Chicago, founded two institutions in 1871 that helped define the role of the BGC. The first was a paper, *Zions Wacht* (The Watch of Zion), the outgrowth of which today is the denominational monthly, *The Standard*. Second, Edgren formed a theological seminary, even though there was only one student. Through the years this school moved to different locations, but finally in 1914 the seminary and an academy joined in St. Paul, Minnesota. Today the BGC operates Bethel College and Seminary as fully accredited schools. The liberal arts college currently has two thousand students, and the seminary, which includes an extension campus in San Diego, California, has 550 students.

The second period, 1945 to 1980, was marked by independence, global missions, post-war church growth, and evangelical cooperation. Because of dissatisfaction with the inclusive theological policy of the American Baptist Foreign Mission Society, through which it had sent most of its missionaries, and a desire for an independent mission program, the BGC established in 1944 its own Board of Foreign Missions. Today the conference supports personnel in fourteen nations, including 154 career missionaries and 51 short-term workers.

With the forming of the foreign mission board, the BGC broke its dependence upon the American Baptist Convention. During the 1950s, new churches were coming into the fellowship, nearly one a week. Church growth was especially significant in California, the Northwest, Rocky Mountain area, Minnesota, and Illinois. In 1980 the BGC listed 779 churches, including 68 churches in Canada, with a membership of 133,698. Optimism and denominational pride and loyalty were high. Active cooperation was increased with the Baptist World Alliance, the Baptist Joint Committee on Public Affairs, and the National Association of Evangelicals.

Even though the Swedish language was now a thing of the past, most of the leadership was made up of people who could trace their lineage to Sweden. The overtones of Swedish piety remained, and the linkage with the Baptists in Sweden was strengthened.

The third period, 1980 to the 1990s, has witnessed a dramatic change in denominational and pastoral leadership, a strong emphasis on church growth, and a rapid increase of multicultural ministries. During the 1980s 215 churches were added, however in 1985 seventy-two churches withdrew to form the Baptist General Conference of Canada. In 1980 there were sixty non-Anglo congregations, and in 1992 the number had grown to 139. During the 1991–1992 church year, of the sixty new churches added to the BGC, forty-two were non-Anglo churches.

In the 1980s a generational change in leadership began to take place in the BGC. Several of the newer leaders as well as pastors and laypersons in the local churches have, at best, a tenuous relationship, much less an understanding of the denominational heritage. From some perspectives it appears as if the BGC is cutting off from its past. It is beginning a different kind of journey, seeking to define a credible image in the evangelical global community.

Virgil A. Olson

BIBLIOGRAPHY: A well-written standard history of the first one hundred years of the Baptist General Conference is Adolf Olson, *A Centenary History as Related to the Baptist General Conference* (Chicago: Baptist Conference Press, 1952; reprint, New York: Arno Press, 1980). For further developments in the conference, see David Guston and Martin Erikison, *Fifteen Eventful Years* (Chicago: Harvest, 1961), and the volumes by Donald Anderson, ed., *The 1960s in the Ministry of the Baptist General Conference* (Evanston, Ill.: Harvest, 1971); *The 1970s in the Ministry of the Baptist General Conference* (Arlington Heights, Ill.: BGC, 1981); and *The 1980s in the Ministry of the Baptist General Conference* (Arlington Heights, Ill.: BGC, 1991). An excellent set of articles on Swedish Baptists and their relations with the American Baptists is in *American Baptist Quarterly*, 6 (Sep. 1987).

Conservative Baptist Association of America

The first institution among Conservative Baptists was the formation on December 15, 1943, in Chicago of the Conservative Baptist Foreign Mission Society (CBFMS). Other agencies followed—the Conservative Baptist Association of America (CBA of A, 1947), and the Conservative Baptist Home Mission Society (CBHMS, 1948). Conservative Baptists today have about twenty-five state or regional associations which coordinate the ministries of the churches in camping programs, missionary conferences, and ministerial placement. They are also affiliated with seven schools, including three seminaries, which enroll more than one thousand students, and three collegiate level schools, each operating independently with its own governing board.

Conservative Baptist links with broader evangelicalism are clearly revealed in the history, theology, and structures of the movement. Conservative Baptists have tried to avoid traditional denominational structures and control by forming independent agencies, which also helps to explain why they insist on referring to their organizational work as a movement.

Conservative Baptists played a significant role in the resurgence of evangelicalism, commencing during and after the Second World War. This included the ministry of Billy Graham and the emergence of the National Association of Evangelicals, Youth for Christ, World Vision, various evangelical schools, and other agencies.

The specific creation of CBFMS can be traced to a desire among a number of Northern Baptists to have an explicitly orthodox missionary society for their churches. As early as 1920 conservative pastors, led by an informal group called the Fundamentalist Fellowship, tried to establish doctrinal standards for missionary service, but several votes at the annual conventions (1922–1925) proved futile. After a lull in the 1930s—when many conservative churches were turning to nondenominational ministries—conservative pastors tried again in 1943 to create theological tests. But when their attempts showed no results, several hundred conservative churches joined in the call for the CBFMS. Pastor Richard Beal of the First Baptist Church of Tuscon, Arizona, and Pastor Albert Johnson at Hinson Memorial Baptist Church in Portland, Oregon, assumed the leadership of this action. Since that day CBFMS (today known as Conservative Baptist International or CBI) has sent more than one thousand missionaries to twenty countries.

The Conservative Baptist Association of America was organized at Atlantic City, New Jersey, in 1947. This resulted from the Northern Baptist Convention meeting at Grand Rapids, Michigan, in 1946 when the older convention would not tolerate a competing missionary agency within its structures. In the following years, hundreds of Northern Baptist churches left their national convention to join the Conservatives. In

Minnesota and Arizona, Conservatives even captured the state conventions. They were in a position to do the same in Oregon, but only by the exclusion of a number of conservative churches through political maneuver was the Oregon Convention saved for the Northern Convention.

By participating in the widening witness of evangelicals in America, Conservative Baptist agencies grew rapidly during the first fifteen years of their independent ministry. But from 1957 to 1964 Conservative Baptists went through a period of controversy—a minority favored a more militant fundamentalist position on separation. About two hundred churches finally withdrew, primarily in the Midwest and Rocky Mountain area.

In the late 1960s and 1970s Conservative Baptists made several attempts to unify their movement. The three national agencies moved their headquarters to adjacent properties in Wheaton, Illinois, and began cooperating in the publication of a common magazine. But several attempts to bring the three agencies into a more unified structure failed. In 1981 a Study Commission proposed two changes that were adopted: The first called for each school and agency to adopt a constitutional statement declaring affiliation with the Conservative Baptist Association of America. The second unified the procedures and requirements for churches affiliating with the national association.

Bruce L. Shelley

BIBLIOGRAPHY: Bruce L. Shelley, *A History of Conservative Baptists* (Wheaton, Ill.: CB Press, 1971). Hans W. Finzel, ed., *Partners Together: 50 Years of Global Impact, The CBFMS Story* (Wheaton, Ill.: CBFMS, 1993). For a conservative perspective on the struggle within the Northern Baptist Convention over mission policy which helped to produce the Conservative Baptists, see Chester E. Tulga, *The Foreign Missions Controversy in the Northern Baptist Convention* (Chicago: Conservative Baptist Fellowship, 1950).

North American Baptist Conference

The North American Baptist Conference (NABC) is a union of nearly sixty-five thousand Baptists in about four hundred churches in the USA and Canada. Local associations are currently supporting at least twenty-five church planting projects. Thirty percent of the constituency is in Canada.

The NABC originated with congregations organized since 1840 among German immigrants who were won to Christ as well as Baptist polity through the sponsorship of American and Canadian Baptists. German pietists, like Konrad Anton Fleischmann and August Rauschenbusch, embraced Baptist convictions after immigrating to the USA. Few of the Germans who immigrated before 1880 were already Baptists because the movement in Continental Europe itself had begun in Hamburg, Germany, only in 1834. The American Baptist Home Mission Society and the American Baptist Publication Society supported colporteurs as well as evangelists and church planters to work among the immigrants.

A first conference of pastors and church workers was held in 1851; it included representatives from one Canadian and four US churches and heard reports from three others. As the churches grew, regional conferences were organized with subsidiary associations to provide fellowship among the churches and coordinate the mission to the immigrants. In the 1880s and 1890s, Baptists were among the thousands of

German-Russians who moved to western Canada and the central United States. During the 1920s, additional German-Russians were able to leave the Soviet Union. These Baptist newcomers tended to be farmers rather than artisans and tradespeople, who had arrived in the earlier immigration.

German Baptists assimilated to American and Canadian ways rapidly. Patriotism and prejudice accelerated the switch to the English language in public services during World War I. A number of congregations ended their association with the German Conference and merged into the life of the adjacent English-speaking Baptist associations. In 1944 the conference dropped its ethnic identification altogether, adopting its present title. Nonetheless, another wave of German Baptist immigration occurred when thousands of Germans fled the Soviet Union and Soviet regimes being imposed in eastern Europe in the wake of the Second World War. Once again, the rather acculturated NABC churches in major urban centers received an infusion of German-speaking members; this changed the constituency of existing churches and produced new congregations.

Since the end of the First World War, German Baptists have financed their own work. While their young people were serving in many overseas mission fields under other mission agencies, NABs had a denominational foreign board responsible for Cameroon and a home mission board dedicated to church planting. They had their own network of associations and regional conferences, tied together in a triennial general convention. The NABC had its own printing press in Cleveland, Ohio, and headquarters in a Chicago suburb.

During the years 1920 to 1950 when modernist-fundamentalist controversies split the American Baptists and two regional unions of Canadian Baptists, the ethnic churches found it convenient to foster the institutions and ministries which bound them ethnically rather than to become partisans in political battles where their few numbers would have been ineffective. Since the 1930s they have become participants in the post-war expansion of evangelicalism throughout North America. Fundamentalism has influenced them through independent schools and publications whose biblicism suited their preference for a moderate conservatism.

The best-known thinker and writer to arise from among NABs was Walter Rauschenbusch, the son of the first theological instructor in the German Department of Rochester Theological Seminary. After nine years as pastor of a New York City German Baptist church where he forged his convictions on the Social Gospel, he joined his father as a tutor in the German Department (1897–1902), then took a chair at the Rochester Seminary until his death in 1918. German Baptists are more delighted with his evangelical passion than with his social agenda, so his ideas still enjoy a better reception in the larger Christian community than among the NABs; on the other hand, his Social Gospel colleagues were uncomfortable with his evangelicalism and pietism.

The present North American Baptist Seminary began as the German Department of the Rochester Seminary. August Rauschenbusch—Lutheran, pietist, theologian—was the first professor; for more than thirty years (joined in time by former students) he led in the theological education of ministers for the German Baptist churches. Progressively the German churches took over responsibility for the German Department, which gained its own building and incorporation although still part of Rochester Seminary. In the 1940s the school took its present name and moved in 1947 from Rochester to Sioux Falls, South Dakota.

As a result of short-term winter Bible schools hosted by various churches, German Baptist churches on Canada's prairies organized a residential school, the Christian

Training Institute, in Edmonton, Alberta, on the eve of World War II. In the 1960s it became the American Baptist College. Out of the college's undergraduate program of ministerial training, a second seminary for NABs was organized in 1980—Edmonton Baptist Seminary.

Initially under the missionary society of Baptists in Germany, German-American Baptists worked in what today is the Republic of Cameroon. In the 1930s the conference sent missionaries to the Cameroon under its own auspices and, particularly since World War II, this has been the premier foreign mission of the NABs. The Cameroon Baptist Convention, independently administered since 1954, actually exceeds its mother body in churches and has about the same number of members. After 1951 NABs expanded their cross-cultural ministries into Japan, Brazil, and the Philippines; this has occurred in cooperation with already existing structures formed by the Baptist General Conference or Southern Baptist Convention missionaries.

The NABC has struggled to plant churches among Hispanics in Colorado and Texas; the latter has become the springboard to a mission in Mexico since 1985. Population changes in a few metropolitan areas have resulted in congregations becoming predominantly Hispanic, Portuguese, or Black. Congregations in large urban centers of the USA and Canada have ministered with varying success to refugees from southeast Asia. NABs have also sought to establish congregations in the growing suburbs of Canadian and American cities.

The NABC continues the traditional practice of a triennial convention, increasingly planned more for fellowship than for business, although officers and members of boards are elected then. A General Council is effectively the governing body. It is comprised of lay and ministerial representatives from twenty-one regional associations. The professional staff is monitored by an executive committee formed out of the General Council.

Although other denominations also, as a consequence of migration and settlement patterns, have linked churches in Canada and the USA, the NABC is currently the only surviving cross-border union. Politics, economics, and other forces may finally end this unity, but for the foreseeable future the NABC will continue to operate as an international body.

David T. Priestley

BIBLIOGRAPHY: The standard history of the North American Baptist Conference is Frank H. Woyke, *Heritage and Ministry of the North American Baptist Conference* (Oakbrook Terrace, Ill.: NABC, 1979).

Seventh Day Baptists

Seventh Day Baptists are a covenant people based on a concept of regenerate membership, believer's baptism, congregational polity, and scriptural basis for belief and practice. Seventh Day Baptists have presented the Sabbath as a sign of obedience in a covenant relationship with God and not as a condition for salvation. They have not condemned those who do not accept the Sabbath but have been disappointed at the apparent inconsistency of those who claim to accept the Bible as their source of faith and practice, yet have followed ecclesiastical and popular traditions instead.

Seventh Day Baptists date their origin with the mid-seventeenth century separatist movement in England. With the renewed emphasis on the Scriptures for Free Church doctrine and practice, men such as William Saller, Peter Chamberlain, Francis Bampfield, and Edward and Joseph Stennett concluded that the keeping of the seventh day Sabbath was an inescapable requirement of biblical Christianity. Some maintained membership within the Baptist fellowship and simply added the private Sabbath observance to their other shared convictions. As the power of the state was used to enforce conformity to a common day of worship, separation became necessary. The first separate church of record was the Mill Yard church founded about 1650 in London.

One of those who maintained Sabbath convictions while a member of the Baptist Church in Tewksbury was Stephen Mumford, who came to Newport, Rhode Island, with his wife in 1664. Through his influence, several members of the First Baptist Church of Newport joined in fellowship with him while remaining members in the parent body. When two couples gave up their Sabbath convictions, the others found difficulty in sharing communion with them in the Newport Church, and a separation took place in December 1671, giving rise to the first Seventh Day Baptist church in America. Yet after the separation, close fellowship with other Baptist brothers remained, and twenty years later when the Newport Baptist Church was without pastoral leadership they voted to place themselves under the care of the Seventh Day Baptist pastor William Hiscox.

A similar separation occurred in 1705 at Piscataway, New Jersey, when a deacon of the Baptist church, Edmund Dunham, became convinced of the biblical basis of Sabbath observance. Dunham and sixteen others withdrew to form their own church.

A third group of churches came out of the Keithian split from Quakerism in the Philadelphia area about 1700. A pietistic movement among German immigrants was influenced by this third group. This led to the formation of a sister conference known as German Seventh Day Baptists which founded the cloisters in Ephrata, Pennsylvania, about 1728. From these three beginnings, Seventh Day Baptists followed the westward migration, arriving on the Pacific Coast by 1900.

Seventh Day Baptists have been characterized by their participation in missionary activity, educational endeavors, ecumenicity, and civic responsibility. The missionary spirit led to the formation of a General Conference in 1802. In preserving the autonomy of the local church, the Conference has relied upon societies for implementing a range of missions, publications, and education. Beginning in 1821 the denomination has had almost continuous publication, with the current house organ, *The Sabbath Recorder*, unbroken since 1844.

Several early missionary societies encouraged pastors to make extended journeys in the home field. The current Missionary Society was formed in 1843, and four years later missionaries began an effective mission in China, embracing both medical and educational phases until the Communist takeover in 1950. Most of the foreign missions of the twentieth century have been of the "Macedonian call" in response to Sabbath-keeping groups who have cried out, "Come over and help us." This led to missions in such areas as Jamaica and Guyana in the Caribbean region; Malawi and Ghana in Africa; India, Burma, and the Philippines in Asia; Australia and New Zealand in Oceania; and scattered responses in other areas. In 1965 a World Federation of Seventh Day Baptist Conferences was formed which by 1993 embraced seventeen conferences.

Seventh Day Baptist insistence on an enlightened conscience for beliefs and practice led to the formation of an Educational Society and the establishment of schools or academies as they migrated into the frontiers. These schools were never limited to members of the denomination but served the areas where public education had not yet become readily available. Three of those schools later became colleges at Alfred, New York; Milton, Wisconsin; and Salem, West Virginia. The desire for an educated clergy led to the establishment of a seminary at Alfred University in 1871. These schools were among the pioneers in women's education at the college and seminary level. What the academies and colleges did for higher education was duplicated for both children and adults in the local church through the Sabbath schools and materials prepared for them.

The sense of ecumenicity present in the earliest churches was continued as Seventh Day Baptists were charter members of such organizations as the National and World Council of Churches. The denomination withdrew from these ties in the 1970s when the direction of those bodies appeared to violate the autonomy of the local church and other principles of Baptist thought and practice. This withdrawal has strengthened their relationship with other Baptists in such organizations as the Baptist World Alliance, the North American Baptist Fellowship, the Baptist Joint Committee on Public Affairs, and related kindred groups involving women and societal interests.

Throughout their history, Seventh Day Baptists have had a strong sense of civic responsibility. Several leaders in the first churches in England held responsible positions in the government. In America both Richard and Samuel Ward were governors of Rhode Island in the eighteenth century, the latter also serving in the Continental Congress in 1775–1776. Others have served in government at various levels, including Congress where Senator Jennings Randolph of West Virginia represented his state for forty years in either the House or the Senate beginning in 1933. Many have served in the armed services, including chaplains in the Revolutionary War and more recently in World War II. The General Conference has taken strong stands on social issues such as temperance and sexual immorality and has urged its members to implement those principles and practices which would make for a more Christian society.

Because of its emphasis on freedom of thought and conscience, Seventh Day Baptists have represented a wide diversity of theological thought. Their common bond of the Sabbath enabled them to avoid a split during the fundamentalist-modernist controversy of the 1920s. For most of its history, the denomination has been rural oriented but has found in more recent years its greatest growth in developing urban ministries.

The Seventh Day Baptist General Conference is organized as a conference of churches; voting on most matters brought before the annual session is done by delegates from member churches. A General Council is empowered to act for the conference between sessions and prepare budget and program emphases. The council is composed of six elected members at large and six *ex officio* members representing the Missionary Society, the Board of Christian Education, the Tract and Communication Council, the Council on Ministry, the Women's Society, and the Memorial Fund Trustees. The General Council's offices are in Janesville, Wisconsin. The Missionary Society and Board of Christian Education have offices in Westerly, Rhode Island, and Alfred, New York, respectively. Eight geographically located associations help strengthen more local fellowship, youth activities, and witness.

Current reported membership in the General Conference, USA and Canada, is about five thousand in eigthy-eight churches. The World Federation of Seventh Day Baptist Conferences in 1991 reported membership of around fifty thousand in eighteen countries.

Don A. Sanford

BIBLIOGRAPHY: The standard history on Seventh Day Baptists is Don A. Sanford, *A Choosing People: The Story of Seventh Day Baptists* (Nashville: Broadman Press, 1992), which was published for the Seventh Day Baptist Historical Society. Another volume by Sanford is *Conscience Taken Captive: A Short History of Seventh Day Baptists* (Janesville, Wis.: Seventh Day Baptist Historical Society, 1992).

SEPARATIST FUNDAMENTALIST

*T*he four groups included in this classification have historical roots in the Northern Baptist Convention. In their opposition to theological liberalism, they take a militant position, regarding the separation from any organization which tolerates liberalism as "redemptive." They practice second-degree separation, refusing fellowship with other conservative evangelicals who, in turn, may have liberal or ecumenical relations. These bodies stress biblical inerrancy and the supernatural character of the Bible. They are premillennialists and, by and large, accept a dispensational interpretation of Scripture. The General Association of Regular Baptist Churches (GARBC) was the first Baptist group to separate from the Northern Baptist Convention; unlike the later Conservative Baptists, they forbade any dual affiliation with the old convention. Because of the feeling of some of its members that the GARBC is beginning to lose something of its historic position, a new fellowship has arisen from GARBC ranks, the Independent Baptist Fellowship of North America (IBFI).

The other two bodies come from Conservative Baptist ranks. In fact, the Fundamental Baptist Fellowship, composed of individuals, not churches, was itself the progenitor of the Conservative Baptist movement. Since the middle of the 1960s, it has followed its own independent course when Conservative Baptists have refused to take a more militant separatist position. Other militants formed a national association in 1965, the New Testament Association of Independent Baptist Churches. Churches or their pastors cooperate with either one of these two organizations or with both of them. Eventually, the militants took over the state associations of the Conservative Baptists in Minnesota, Illinois, and Michigan or formed their own associations. The state or regional associations, however, are entirely independent of the national bodies.

Fundamental Baptist Fellowship of America

The Fundamental Baptist Fellowship began in June 1920 with the convening of a Conference on Our Baptist Faith in the Delaware Avenue Baptist Church of Buffalo, New York, immediately before the annual session of the Northern Baptist Convention. In its early days the fellowship carried various names but came to be known as the Fundamentalist Fellowship of the Northern Baptist Convention. For many years it continued meeting before the sessions of the Northern Convention, serving as a special interest group to attempt to hold the convention to conservative theological norms. Although many of its members were premillennialists, at this time the Fellowship did not make premillennialism a test of affiliation nor did it favor separation.

Under new leadership in the 1940s, the Fellowship became more militant and led in the formation of the Conservative Baptist Association and two Conservative Baptist mission societies. In 1946 the Fellowship changed its name to the Conservative Baptist

Fellowship and cooperated with the other Conservative Baptist bodies with each, however, independent of the other.

In the early 1950s the Fellowship began to follow a strict separatist position and criticized individuals in the Conservative Baptist movement for their adherence to "neo-evangelicalism" and "ecumenical evangelism" (that is, cooperating in crusades led by Billy Graham). In 1955 the Fellowship ceased to cooperate with the other Conservative Baptist bodies and added to its doctrinal statement the premillennial return of Christ and the pretribulation rapture of the church. Because of growing disenchantment with the Conservative Baptist movement, it sponsored in 1961 the formation of the World Conservative Baptist Mission (now Baptist World Mission), and in 1965 it changed its name to Fundamental Baptist Fellowship of America. In 1965 some of its members formed the New Testament Association of Independent Baptist Churches of America, but others refused to support the new organization and simply continued supporting the Fellowship. After a period of strained relations between the Fellowship and the New Testament Association, the two groups effected a reconciliation but no merger in 1974.

For many years the Fellowship published the *Information Bulletin*, but beginning in 1991 it began *Frontline*, an attractively printed journal published in Schaumburg, Illinois. Besides annual meetings of the Fellowship, some members also participate in meetings of regional Fellowships, such as the Southeast Fundamental Baptist Fellowship and the Mid-America Baptist Fellowship. The 1993–1995 *Directory* of the Fundamentalist Fellowship recorded more than six hundred members in forty-four states, who, in turn, are related to 402 churches of which 134 of them have a relationship with other fundamentalist bodies. The fellowship is no longer confined to northern and western states but is a national body with surprising strength in the South, including in its membership both the chancellor and president of Bob Jones University. Institutions in sympathy with the Fellowship include Maranatha Baptist Bible College of Watertown, Wisconsin, Denver Baptist Bible College, and San Francisco Baptist Seminary.

BIBLIOGRAPHY: G. Archer Weninger, "A Brief History of the Conservative Baptist Fellowship," *North Star Baptist*, April 1965, 10–15, 18–19, and also printed as a brochure. Also see Richard V. Clearwaters, *The Great Conservative Baptist Compromise* (Minneapolis: Central Seminary Press, n.d.).

General Association of Regular Baptist Churches

The General Association of Regular Baptist Churches (GARBC) is a loose fellowship of more than 1,500 theologically conservative, independent congregations located mainly in the northern and western states and Florida. A few churches are in Canada. The churches have a membership of more than 150,000, mostly White working class and White middle class, but there are a few Hispanic congregations. The overwhelming majority of pastors regard themselves as "fundamentalists."

The GARBC arose out of the fundamentalist-modernist controversy which rocked the Northern Baptist Convention (NBC) in the 1920s and was reflected in the creation of the moderate Fundamentalist Fellowship and the separatist Baptist Bible Union (BBU). Unhappy with the NBC's refusal to adopt a confessional statement that would exclude theological liberals and the inclusive policy of the American Baptist Foreign

Mission Society, the BBU vowed to wage war on "modernism on all fronts," especially in missions and education, but its impact proved to be minimal.

By 1928 BBU leaders in Michigan, Ohio, and New York were insisting that separation was the only answer, and in 1930 it chose a committee to draw up plans for a new association. On May 15, 1932, thirty-four delegates from twenty-two congregations assembled at the Belden Avenue Baptist Church in Chicago for the BBU's last meeting and launched the new group. They decided to restrict its membership to churches rather than individuals, since individualism had been the main weakness of the BBU, and authorized the drafting of a constitution and confession of faith.

They called themselves the General Association of Regular Baptist Churches to emphasize that it was to be a national organization of independent churches and adopted the name used by Ohio fundamentalists who had earlier formed a union of "Regular Baptist Churches." This term had first appeared in the Great Awakening of the 1740s; the conservatives felt it would underscore that the Northern Baptists were "irregular" in their beliefs.

The new body inaugurated a publication, the *Baptist Bulletin*, in 1933 and accepted a constitution and confession in 1934 (ratified 1935). To avoid duplicating the mission structure of the NBC, it initiated in 1934 the practice of approving autonomous, independent faith missions, which would be reevaluated annually on the basis of their commitment to orthodox biblical Christianity and financial integrity. The first two were Baptist Mid-Missions (founded in 1920), now the largest GARBC-approved agency, and the Association of Baptists for World Evangelism (founded 1927). Evangelical Baptist Missions, which worked in Africa, was approved in 1938 and Continental Baptist Missions, a home missionary agency, in 1943. As of 1994 three smaller bodies are also on the approved list, as well as five "service ministries" that provide family assistance, foster care, and senior citizens' housing. Seven colleges and theological seminaries comprise the roster of educational institutions. The approved agencies, which must carry the word *Baptist* in their corporate names, have no organic connection with the GARBC. This program was, in effect, a return to the independent society concept of nineteenth-century Northern Baptists.

At the urging of Robert T. Ketcham, the GARBC's leading light, the executive structure was replaced in 1938 with a Council of Fourteen elected for two-year terms at the annual meeting. In 1972 it was expanded to a Council of Eighteen. In 1944 the GARBC rented an office in Chicago and created the post of "National Representative" to handle the growing administrative business of the denomination. State and regional associations were also formed, thirteen of which have appointed "State Representatives."

The GARBC became an increasingly complex body with the passage of time. During the Second World War it formed a Chaplaincy Commission and in 1950 established the Baptist Builders Club to aid young churches in securing construction funds. In that same year Regular Baptist Press was founded as a nonprofit corporation to produce Sunday School literature. During the 1970s the GARBC even experimented with a national radio program. As its enterprises multiplied, the Association moved to the Chicago suburbs, first Des Plaines in 1965 and then Schaumburg in 1976.

The hallmark of the GARBC is its emphasis on separation. This includes not cooperating in any religious venture with individuals who have ties with theological liberals or ecumenical bodies like the National and World Council of Churches (customarily referred to in GARBC polemics as "modernists" and "apostates"). The association's leaders backed Carl McIntire's creation of the American Council of Christian Churches in 1942 and the International Council of Christian Churches in 1948, but GARBC polity provided that only individual congregations could actually hold membership in them. It rejected any role in the National Association of Evangelicals and criticized the Conservative Baptist Association for not requiring its churches to make a complete break with the Northern Convention. The GARBC thoroughly condemned the cooperative evangelism of Billy Graham and Neo-Evangelicalism for their alleged compromises.

The group's policy of separating from evangelicals who maintain relationships with liberals is often called "second-degree separation," but some in the GARBC are uncomfortable with that label. Those who carry separation to extremes have caused problems for moderate GARBC Baptists who wish to cooperate with other fundamentalists.

Other distinctives include an emphasis on biblical inerrancy, the premillennial return of Christ, the pretribulational rapture of the church, and a categorical rejection of any evolutionary explanation of the creation of life. A moderately Calvinist group, the GARBC affirms the eternal security of the believer but does not take a Reformed stance on limited atonement. It also opposes the exercise of charismatic gifts such as tongues. Because of its accent on foreign missions and education, the GARBC is one of the most missionary-minded fundamentalist denominations, and the number of its young people who have taken up careers in higher education is impressive.

As a socially conservative body as well, the GARBC does not allow the ordination of women and stresses the leadership of men in the church and home. According to a survey of 1988, the denomination is unanimously "pro-life" on the abortion question, and only 1 percent of the pastors admit to being Democratic in their political party orientation. This conservatism has contributed to an erosion in the separatist emphasis, as many GARBC Baptists will cooperate with other Christians in promoting conservative political and social causes. Only time will tell whether this type of cooperation will lead to other collaborations in evangelism and church life.

Richard V. Pierard

BIBLIOGRAPHY: A recent history of the GARBC, written by its current National Representative, Paul N. Tassell, is *Quest for Faithfulness: The Account of a Unique Fellowship of Churches* (Schaumburg, Ill.: Regular Baptist Press, 1991). For a biography of the foremost leader of the GARBC in its early years, see J. Murray Murdoch, *Portrait of Obedience: The Biography of Robert T. Ketcham* (Schaumburg, Ill.: Regular Baptist Press, 1979). On the early history of the mission interests of the GARBC, see William J. Hopewell, *The Missionary Emphasis of the General Association of Regular Baptist Churches* (Chicago: Regular Baptist Press, 1963).

Independent Baptist Fellowship of North America

The Independent Baptist Fellowship of North America was formed in Oshkosh, Wisconsin, in October 1990 by individuals in the General Association of Regular Baptist Churches (GARBC) who felt the association was drifting from its original strict separationist position. In 1993 the Fellowship ratified its constitution in Providence, Rhode Island. It is composed of individuals, not churches, although local churches may become financial supporters. Its 1993–1994 *Directory* lists 250 members, besides spouses who may also belong. About half of the members have had or still have associations with the GARBC, while the others have been simply independent. Members represent 106 churches of which forty-six are listed with the GARBC. The Fellowship's greatest strength is in Pennsylvania and includes a few members from Canada. The Fellowship publishes a quarterly entitled *The Review*.

BIBLIOGRAPHY: L. Duane Brown, et al., *What Happened to the GARBC at Niagara Falls?* (Sellersville, Pa.: Bethel Baptist Press, n.d.).

New Testament Association of Independent Baptist Churches

In May 1965 messengers from more than one hundred churches, dissatisfied with Conservative Baptists for their lack of strict separation and the penetration of New Evangelicalism in their ranks, met at Beth Eden Baptist Church in Denver to consider establishing the New Testament Association. A provisional constitution and confession of faith were adopted. In the following year the association was formally organized at the Eagledale Baptist Church in Indianapolis. From 27 churches, the association today has 104 congregations, 23 of which are also members of other fellowships. It publishes a small paper, *Testimonies*. Its greatest strength is in Minnesota, where about one-third of its churches are located. Most of its Minnesota churches are also members of the Minnesota Baptist Association (formerly known as the Minnesota Baptist Convention), which at one time was in fellowship with the Northern Baptist Convention and then with the Conservative Baptists but is now independent.

A leading figure in the association has been Richard V. Clearwaters, who served forty-two years as pastor of Fourth Baptist Church of Minneapolis and was founder in 1956 of Central Baptist Theological Seminary in the same city. Under his leadership, Pillsbury Academy of Owatonna, Minnesota, became Pillsbury Baptist Bible College after a court battle in which the Minnesota Supreme Court ruled that the Minnesota association had the authority to appoint the school's trustees.

Besides the Minnesota Baptist Association, other state or regional associations either broke away from the Conservative Baptists or formed new associations or fellowships. Among these are the Wisconsin Fellowship of Baptist Churches, Association of Independent Baptist Churches of Illinois, Dakota Baptist Association, Inter-Mountain Baptist Fellowship (Montana and Wyoming), Mountain States Baptist Fellowship (Colorado), Association of Fundamental Baptist Churches of Northern California, and the Independent Fundamental Baptist Association (Michigan). Although ideologically in alignment with the New Testament Association, most of the churches in these associations remain independent of the New Testament Association.

BIBLIOGRAPHY: Richard V. Clearwaters, "The New Testament Association of Independent Baptist Churches of America," *Central Testimony*, July/August 1966, 1–4. Also see Clearwaters' autobiography, *On the Upward Road* (Minneapolis: Author, c. 1991).

REGULAR BAPTISTS—ETHNIC

	Members	Churches
II. Ethnic Baptists		
1. Association of Evangelicals for Italian Missions (1899)	n/a	n/a
2. Czechoslovak Baptist Convention (1912)	1,500	7
3. Hungarian Baptist Union (1908)*	n/a	11
4. Polish Baptist Association (1913)**	140	6
5. Portuguese Baptist Convention of New England (1903)	n/a	n/a
6. Romanian Baptist Association (1913)	n/a	n/a
7. Russian-Ukrainian Evangelical Baptist Union (1919)	800	21
8. Ukrainian Evangelical Baptist Convention (1946)	3,500	20
9. Union of Latvian Baptists (1950)	<u>385</u>	<u>8</u>
	6,325***	73***

*The Hungarian Baptist Union has 11 churches in the USA and 6 in Canada with a total membership of not more than 500.

**The Polish Baptist Association has one church in Canada with about sixty members.

***This list of ethnic Baptist bodies includes only autonomous bodies and not ethnic groups which are integrated into other Baptist bodies. Because of difficulty in gaining their statistics, their totals are incomplete. Since many of their churches are dually aligned, the statistics of these churches are included with other bodies. Consequently, the statistics of these bodies are not included as a separate item in the grand totals. All of the above bodies, except the Polish Baptist Association and Ukrainian Evangelical Baptist Convention, are in cooperation with the American Baptist Churches. The Polish Association is related to Southern Baptists, while five churches of the Ukrainian Convention are dually aligned with Southern Baptists and one church with the General Association of Regular Baptists.

ETHNIC BODIES IN GENERAL

Baptists in the USA who are outside the Anglo-Saxon majority have had a long and notable history. These Baptists have included the Native Americans, African-Americans who came as slaves, and immigrants from Europe, Canada, Asia, Latin America, and the Caribbean.

The earliest non-English immigrant group among Baptists in America was the Welsh. John Miles, a founder of Baptist churches in Wales, established a congregation in 1663 at Swansea, Massachusetts, with members he brought with him. Immigrants from Wales helped to establish seven early churches in the Philadelphia area between

1699 and 1745 as well as the Welsh Tract Church near Newark, Delaware (1701), and the Welsh Neck Church in the area of the Peedee River in South Carolina (1738). Welsh Baptists founded five of their own associations by the mid-nineteenth century and seven journals (six of them in Welsh), but they never established an independent denominational body. The American Baptist Home Mission Society (ABHMS), formed in 1832, began its first ethnic ministry among them in 1836.

In 1674 the Seventh Day Baptist Church in Newport, Rhode Island, baptized a Native American, the first known Indian to become a member of a Baptist church. Without mission assistance, nine Indian churches appeared in New England and New York, the first at Gay Head, Maine, about 1694 and the last in the 1830s, but did not form an all-Indian association. In the nineteenth century, there was a great upsurge of Baptist support for Indian missions. One notable effort was through the Triennial Convention, which began its Indian work in 1817 with the appointment of Isaac McCoy. The convention often worked with Baptist associations and mission societies. Later the American Indian Missionary Association, formed in 1842, entered the field.

In the nineteenth century, Baptists undertook some mission activity among Mexicans in American territory. The first missionary was Hiram W. Read, who in 1849 was the first Protestant missionary to New Mexico and an appointee of the American Baptist Mission Society. Some Mexican converts were gained. In the 1880s Mexican Baptist work in Texas also began to take root.

In 1854 J. L. Shuck, former missionary to China and under appointment of the Domestic Mission Board of the Southern Baptist Convention, opened the first Chinese mission in the USA at Sacramento, California. Because of financial constraint Southern Baptists gave up their work among the Chinese in California in 1884. The ABHMS opened work among Chinese on the West Coast in San Francisco in 1870 and in New York City in 1892. In the 1890s American (Northern) Baptists in Seattle began work among the Japanese.

Before the Civil War, African-Americans began to form congregations in the North and, in spite of slavery, even some in the South. In 1840 African-Americans in the North formed the first Black Baptist national convention; after the Civil War African-Americans, North and South, formed national organizations.

Beginning in the middle of the nineteenth century, the ABHMS and the American Baptist Publication Society, later joined by the Woman's American Baptist Home Mission Society, helped establish numerous churches composed of European immigrants. In turn, these churches formed their own conferences or associations, such as the German General Conference (1865), Swedish General Conference (1879), Italian Association (1899), Polish Association in U.S.A. and Canada (1903), Portuguese Convention of New England (1903), Hungarian Union (1908), Danish Conference (1910), Norwegian Conference (1910), Czechoslovak Convention (1912), Romanian Association (1913), Russian-Ukrainian Union (1919), and Union of Latvian Baptists (1950). With the tide of immigration shifting from northern Europeans to peoples from southern and eastern Europe in the late nineteenth and early twentieth century, many Baptists felt a double duty toward reaching them—not only to win them to Christ but also to help save the nation from the impact of alien values which they brought with them.

The greatest response was from the Germans and Swedes. They, however, not only assimilated rapidly but maintained their own conference structures and became entirely independent of the Northern Baptist Convention. After shedding their ethnic identity, they have attempted to reach fellow Americans and even other ethnics. On the other hand, the Danish and Norwegian Conferences dissolved in the 1950s and were absorbed by the American (formerly Northern) Baptist Convention. The remaining European Baptist bodies mentioned above have continued to maintain their ethnic identification. They also maintain an associate or dual relationship with the American Baptist Churches in the USA, except for the Polish Baptists, who turned to Southern Baptists for assistance. The Czechoslovak Convention, Latvian Baptist Union, and the Russian Ukrainian Union are also members of the Baptist World Alliance. Besides these bodies, one should add the Ukrainian Evangelical Baptist Convention (1946), some of whose churches maintain dual affiliations. In addition, Mexican Americans in California formed state conventions which related to American Baptists, while their compatriots in Texas and New Mexico did likewise but instead related to Southern Baptists.

In spite of moderate success among peoples with a Protestant background, such as Germans and Scandinavians, gains among adherents of the Roman Catholic faith from southern and eastern Europe and French Canada, were meager. With American assimilation and restrictions on immigration, the work among ethnics after World War I hit a plateau. In fact, with the demands for funds in new American communities after World World II, the American Baptist Convention began to curtail its bilingual work. Southern Baptists provided some support for ethnic work before the Second World War, primarily among Indians, Hispanics, and the French in Louisiana, but their efforts were limited.

Since World War II, however, with a great immigrant tide entering the country from Latin America and Asia, Baptist work among ethnics has grown by leaps and bounds, particularly among Hispanics and Asians, but also on a smaller scale among many other groups. Many Baptist groups in the USA now have significant multilingual ministries. At the beginning of the 1990s, the Southern Baptist Convention reported more than seventy-five ethnic fellowships/associations which included 236,827 Hispanics in 3,412 churches and missions, 133,891 Asiatic and Pacific Islanders in 2,008 congregations, and 36,970 Indians in 631 congregations. In 1956 the first Korean Baptist church was formed in the USA in Washington, D.C.; today Korean Baptists, with their own national fellowship, are one of the fastest growing ethnic bodies in the nation. American Baptist Churches/USA also has significant Hispanic, Indian, and Asian constituencies. One-third of the 135 churches in the Conservative Baptist Association of Southern California are ethnic.

Today ethnics do not form independent national bodies but generally are members of conventions, associations, or fellowships which are members of some larger predominantly Anglo-American body. Even the Mexican Convention of Texas, organized in 1910, became a department of the Texas Baptist Convention in 1964. Until recently most Baptists in the USA were either Anglo-American or African-American but, with the changing ethnic composition of the American population, the Baptist population in the USA is becoming increasingly diverse.

BIBLIOGRAPHY: For collective accounts of ethnic bodies, see *Chronicle*, 2, no. 3 (July 1939), which includes a number of articles on European ethnic groups; H. Leon McBeth, *The Baptist Heritage* (Nashville: Broadman Press, 1987), 724–49; "Ethnic Southern Baptists," in *Baptist History and Heritage*, 18 no. 3 (July 1983); and Joshua Grijalva, *Ethnic Baptist History* (San Antonio: Author, 1992). G. Pitt Beers, *Ministry to Turbulent America* (Philadelphia: Judson Press, 1957), 58–77, provides an overview of ethnic work of American Baptists to the 1950s. Insightful material on Northern Baptist attitudes toward immigrants and their evangelization is in Lawrence B. Davis, *Immigrants, Baptists, and the Immigrant Mind in America* (Urbana, Chicago, and London: University of Illinois Press, 1973), and

Paul William Walaskay, "The Entertainment of Angels: American Baptists and Americanization, 1890–1925," *Foundations*, 19, no. 4 (Oct./Dec. 1976): 346–60. Articles on individual groups may be found in Howard Clarkson Whitcomb, "Gay Head, Oldest Indian Baptist Church in America," *Chronicle*, 16, no. 2 (Apr. 1953): 104–12; Edward George Hartman, "Welsh Baptists in America," *Chronicle*, 19, no. 2 (Apr. 1956): 90–96; Frederick Hale, "Baptists and the Norwegian-American Immigrant Milieu," *Foundations*, 24, no. 2 (Apr./June 1981): 122–36; Salvatore Mondello, "Baptist Churches and Italian-Americans," *Foundations*, 16, no. 3 (July/Sep. 1973): 222–38; Paul M. Nagano, "Baptist Missionary Work Among the Japanese of California," *Chronicle*, 13 (July 1950): 126–34; and Salvatore Mondello, "The Integration of Japanese Baptists in American Society," *Foundations*, 20, no. 3 (July/Sep. 1977): 254–63.

For African-American Baptists, see the section, "National Baptist (African-American)."

HISPANIC BAPTISTS

*H*ispanics are becoming the largest minority in the United States. They include not only fifteen million Mexicans and Mexican Americans but also Cubans, Puerto Ricans, Central Americans, and South Americans. Although most are bilingual, a number speak only Spanish, and some American Hispanics speak only English. The never-ending cycle includes the exocultural, bicultural, and acculturative Hispanics.

Since the early days of colonization in Texas, Baptists have shown an interest in the evangelization of Hispanics. The First Baptist Church of San Antonio, Texas, organized the first mission in 1861, but it lasted only six months. Because of the work of John and Thomas Westrup, which began in 1880 in Laredo, a Mexican Baptist church was later formed. In 1888 a Mexican church was organized in San Antonio.

Upon the request of the Home Mission Board of the Southern Baptist Convention, C. D. Daniel became the first superintendent of Mexican missions in Texas in 1906. In 1907 he held the first of annual Bible institutes in San Antonio. In 1926 Paul C. Bell organized the first permanent Bible institute, which later ceased in 1941. The Mexican Baptist Bible Institute, formed in 1947 in San Antonio, is today known as the Hispanic Baptist Theological Seminary, an affiliate of Southwestern Baptist Theological Seminary. In 1910 Mexican Baptists in Texas organized their own convention.

Hispanic work was begun elsewhere. Through the American Baptist Home Mission Society, Hiram W. Read and Blas Chavez began Hispanic work in Santa Fe, New Mexico, in 1849. American Baptists also supported Hispanic work in California. In Key West, Florida, in 1884, W. F. Wood and a young Cuban convert, Adella Fales, began mission work.

After World War II, Hispanic congregations have spread like wildfire across the nation with work in practically every state. The Home Mission Board of the Southern Baptists has been particularly active through the leadership of men such as Lloyd Corder, Gerald Palmer, and Oscar Romo. A number of other Baptist bodies also have active Hispanic work. With present rates of growth, Hispanic Baptists are becoming a significant segment of the Baptist denomination in the USA.

Joshua Grijalva

BIBLIOGRAPHY: Joshua Grijalva, *A History of Mexican Baptists in Texas 1881–1981* (Dallas: Baptist General Convention of Texas/Mexican Baptist Convention of Texas, 1982).

REGULAR BAPTISTS (SOUTHERN-ORIENTED)

	Members	Churches
III. Regular Baptists (Southern-Oriented)		
A. Conservative Evangelical		
1. Southern Baptist Convention (1845)	15,400,487	38,458
B. Landmark Missionary Baptist		
2. American Baptist Association (1924)	250,000	1,705
3. Baptist Missionary Association (1950)	228,227	1,364
4. Independent Landmark Missionary Baptist Associations/Churches (Direct Mission)	n/a	n/a
C. Separatist Fundamentalist	1,935,000*	4,661*
5. Baptist Bible Fellowship International (BBFI) (1950)	(1,405,900)	(3,395)
6. Independent Baptist Fellowship International (IBFI) (1984)	n/a	(540)
7. Liberty Baptist Fellowship (LBF)	n/a	(100)
8. Southwide Baptist Fellowship (SBF) (1956)	n/a	(912)
9. World Baptist Fellowship (WBF) (1932)	n/a	(945)
10. First Baptist Church, Hammond Indiana	(75,000)	(1)
	17,359,614	46,187

*Separatist fundamentalist Baptist fellowships publish directories of cooperating churches or pastors but maintain no statistics of their members, which then must be estimated. Churches frequently appear in more than one directory. Figures in parenthesis are included in the estimated total for separatist fundamentalist bodies.

It is difficult to gain exact figures on membership for separatist fundamentalist fellowships. Some help may be gained from the directories of these bodies which list churches or pastors in fellowship. But there is a problem here in that many separatist fundamental Baptist churches fellowship with two or more fellowships. A study of the six directories of the BBFI, IBFI, SBF, WBF, Fundamental Baptist Fellowship (FBF), and New Testament Association (NTA) reveals 6,298 churches, of which 1,278 congregations were listed in one or more other fundamentalist Baptist directory. For BBFI, IBFI, SBF, and WBF, the southern-oriented fundamentalist fellowships, there were 5,792 churches listed with 1,132 of them listed with one or more of the other three. Liberty Baptist Fellowship, which is primarily a fellowship of pastors who have graduated from Liberty University, has no published directory, but its congregations would also be related to another fellowship. Using as a basis the average membership of a church of the BBFI as reported in the *Yearbook of American and Canadian Churches*, 1991, p. 259, and adding the membership of 75,000 of the First Baptist Church of Hammond, Indiana, a total of 1,935,000 is probably a reasonable figure for southern-oriented separatist fundamentalists since, in spite of many small churches, they have some very large congregations.

CONSERVATIVE EVANGELICAL—SOUTHERN BAPTIST CONVENTION

*B*aptists were in the South long before the founding of the Southern Baptist Convention in 1845. They first made their appearance in the South at the end of the seventeenth century and then throughout the eighteenth century. Those Baptists of Calvinistic persuasion who appeared first in New England and then in the Middle Colonies gradually spread into the South and were known as Regular Baptists. Others, holding Arminian views and known as General Baptists, established churches in the South about the same time.

William Screven, a shipbuilder and Baptist preacher from Kittery, Maine, who resettled in 1696 at Charleston, South Carolina, was influential in organizing the first Baptist church in the South. Baptists from other colonies and from England settled in Virginia and North Carolina. Then, as a result of the Great Awakening (c. 1725–1750), a new group of Baptists appeared. They were called Separate Baptists because they had separated from the Congregational churches in New England. Many of them migrated in the 1750s to the Southern colonies where they became numerous.

During the latter half of the eighteenth century, Baptists in the South grew by leaps and bounds. In 1751 the Charleston Association (Regular Baptist) was formed, and in 1758 the Sandy Creek Association (Separate Baptist) was organized. They were the second and third oldest associations in the country, after the Philadelphia Association (1707).

Between 1770 and 1801 many Regular Baptists and Separate Baptists discovered they had much in common, and the churches which did unite often called themselves United Baptists and became the mainstream of the Southern Baptist denomination. Some churches in both groups resisted union, and they continued to maintain their respective identities as Regular and Separate Baptists. After 1845 most United Baptists became known as Southern Baptists but, in some instances, churches retained the designation of United Baptist and kept themselves distinct from the Southern Baptist Convention. All three groups, the Regular, Separate, and United Baptists, have maintained an existence to the present and are found largely in Appalachia.

In the formation in 1814 of the first national organization of Baptists—the Triennial Convention (more properly known as the General Missionary Convention of the Baptist Denomination in the United States of America for Foreign Missions)—Baptists in the South participated wholeheartedly. Richard Furman, pastor of the First Baptist Church, Charleston, South Carolina, was elected president. In 1820 another Baptist pastor from the South, Robert B. Semple of Virginia, was elected president, and he served until his death in 1831. William B. Johnson of South Carolina, present at the formation of the convention in 1814, became president in 1841 and then in 1845 became the first president of the Southern Baptist Convention. In the second meeting of the Triennial Convention in 1817, the constitution was amended to include additional activities, such as home missions and education. In 1832, the American Baptist Home Mission Society (ABHMS) was organized, while the older Triennial Convention focused on foreign missions.

It was not long before conflicting views on the slavery issue were injected into the deliberations of both bodies, and the question was raised whether slaveholding disqualified a person from being appointed as a missionary. By 1841 such questions were being debated with considerable heat and bitterness. Just before the meeting of the Triennial Convention in 1841, however, some leaders who feared an imminent split drafted a Compromise Article. The document was critical of abolitionist Baptists who would add "new tests" as a basis for fellowship and cooperation. Seventy-four northern and southern leaders signed the statement. Thus, unity was temporarily preserved, and the breakup was delayed by three years.

Three issues contributed to the separation of the Baptists in the South from those in the North. The primary factor was slavery and abolitionism. Although some Southerners had opposed slavery earlier in the century, by the 1820s slavery was entrenched in the Southern states, and by the 1830s a vigorous abolitionist crusade was determined to end it. For Baptists in the South, the crisis occurred in 1844 when the ABHMS refused to appoint a slaveholder as a home missionary. Soon after, the Board of the Triennial Convention also declared that it could not in good conscience appoint a slaveholder as a foreign missionary. As a result, the Virginia Baptist Foreign Mission Society invited Baptists to meet in Augusta, Georgia, in May 1845 to discuss what actions might be taken to promote foreign missions and other interests of the denomination.

Besides slavery, two other issues played a part in the eventual organization of the Southern Baptist Convention. Baptists in the South charged that their region was not receiving a fair and proportionate number of missionaries appointed by the ABHMS. Apparently the ABHMS, located in New England, had difficulty finding qualified appointees willing to serve in the South in view of the slavery issue and a climate sometimes viewed as unhealthy. This complaint led to the formation of a Southern Baptist Home Mission Society in 1839; discontent with the ABHMS continued.

The other issue centered on differing preferences in the organization of denominational ministries. Baptists in the North tended to prefer the society method. A society was composed of interested individuals who paid annual dues to support the single ministry promoted by the organization. Thus, the society was based not on church participation but on the voluntary support of individuals. The other type of organization, largely preferred by Baptists in the South, followed the configuration of an association composed of churches and sought to promote a variety of ministries simultaneously. When the Southern Baptist Convention (SBC) was formed in 1845, it was organized to engage in both foreign missions and home missions at the outset with other activities to be added later. This pattern was called the associational or convention form of denominational organization.

As a result of the influence of these three issues, the SBC came into existence on May 8–12, 1845, when nearly three hundred messengers gathered in the First Baptist Church of Augusta, Georgia. Under the influence of William B. Johnson, the structure that emerged was designed "for eliciting, combining and directing the energies of the whole denomination in one sacred effort." Boards for foreign and domestic missions were authorized and soon began to function. When it was formed, this new body represented Baptists in 11 states, with 213 associations, 4,395 churches, and a membership of 365,000 persons.

The Foreign Mission Board, located in Richmond, Virginia, was led for the next twenty-five years by James B. Taylor, pastor of the Second Baptist Church of that city. The Board quickly established work in China and in 1850 opened work in Nigeria. The Domestic Mission Board, situated in Marion, Alabama, did not fare as well; it faced the problems of finance and leadership.

With the secession of Southern states from the Union and the formation in 1861 of the Confederate States of America, Southern Baptists encountered a variety of new challenges. Not long after the outbreak of hostilities, the work of home missions was largely suspended, and only limited foreign mission work continued. Arrangements were made for some funds to be conveyed to foreign missionaries from Baptists in the border states of Maryland, Kentucky, and Missouri. During the war years, men became soldiers, and many lost their lives. Property was neglected and families were broken up.

In the period which followed, known as Reconstruction (1865–1877), the SBC sought to cope with devastated assets, meager funds, widespread poverty, and a radically altered society which included the presence of Federal troops and a mass of Black freedmen. In the years following the war, there was discussion of reunion with Baptists in the North. Southern Baptists at their convention in 1879 finally decided that, while they acknowledged a common heritage and offered good wishes to their "Baptist brethren of the Northern states," they concluded, however, that "we can accomplish more for the cause of Christ when left to ourselves."

The Landmark movement, under the dynamic leadership of James R. Graves, editor of *The Tennessee Baptist*, had a widespread impact on Southern Baptists, particularly after the Civil War and in territory west of the Appalachian Mountains. The term *Landmark* is taken from a booklet entitled *An Old Landmark Reset* (1854), first written as a series of articles by James M. Pendleton, who rejected pulpit affiliation with pedobaptists. Landmarkers emphasized the primacy of the local church, starting with the historical succession and unique validity of Baptist churches. They claimed that an unbroken chain of Baptist congregations could be traced from New Testament times through dissenting groups which had separated from the Roman Catholic Church. Because only Baptist churches could be regarded as true churches, other Christian bodies were viewed as defective and their ministers, authority, and ordinances as invalid. So, friendly pulpit exchange was repudiated, and the immersion of believers by such groups was called "alien" and not acceptable.

Landmarkism ultimately advocated the practice of restricted (or close) communion, which limited participants in the Lord's Supper to the membership of the local church in which it was being observed. In 1859 Graves urged that missionary work be undertaken directly by churches rather than through the board system, This gave rise in the 1880s to the Gospel Mission movement. In all of these matters Graves insisted that he was restoring earlier traditions of Baptists and thereby "resetting the old landmarks." In 1880 Graves set forth his views in, *Old Landmarkism: What Is It?* In it he claimed that fifteen of the sixteen Baptist weekly papers in the South agreed with him and that there were some in the North as well.

The chief spokesman for Gospel Missions was T. P. Crawford, longtime missionary to China. He advocated that missionaries should conform to the social customs of the people to whom they ministered and that native work itself should be self-supporting and without subsidies. Churches should send out and support directly the missionaries. These views, however, gained only limited acceptance and were largely rejected by 1900.

The Southern Baptist Theological Seminary was founded in Greenville, South Carolina, in 1859. James P. Boyce led the initial faculty of four. An Abstract of Principles was drawn up in an effort to summarize the major views of Southern Baptists, and each professor subscribed to the document. In the seminary's first session twenty-six students enrolled from six states. During the Civil War classes were suspended, but the seminary reopened after hostilities ceased. Largely because of poor economic conditions in South Carolina, the seminary moved in 1877 to Louisville, Kentucky.

As early as 1851 the SBC established a Bible Board in Nashville, Tennessee, to direct Bible distribution, but it dissolved in 1863 during the Civil War. In the same year a Board of Sunday Schools at Greenville was formed, and in 1866 it began publishing a monthly paper, *Kind Words for the Sunday School Children,* a paper which survived until 1929. In 1873 the Home Mission Board assumed responsibility for Sunday School work. In 1891 in Nashville, the Sunday School Board was created to publish Sunday School materials and promote Sunday School work. Its first secretary was James M. Frost.

The Home Mission Board (named changed in 1874) continued to lack adequate leadership and funds and faced competition from the ABHMS. By the early 1880s some Southern states considered a connection with the northern society. In 1882 the Home Mission Board moved to Atlanta, Georgia. Under the leadership of Isaac T. Tichenor as secretary, who served from 1881 to 1899, the Board began a new era of aggressive action and a progressive program. Tichenor's vision included founding schools, hospitals, and orphanages as well as organizing new churches and ministering to the freedmen. In 1899 the board supported jointly with the state boards 671 missionaries. The Foreign Mission Board also expanded its work before the turn of the century by sending missionaries to Italy (1870), Mexico (1880), Brazil (1881), and Japan (1889).

Although Baptist women in the South were not admitted as messengers to the SBC until 1918, their activities were evident as early as the 1860s. In 1868 Southern Baptist women gathered in Baltimore at the time of the convention's meeting to hear reports on the work of R. H. Graves, a medical missionary to China. Then in 1888 when the SBC met in Richmond, the women gathered at a nearby Methodist church and organized the Woman's Missionary Union (WMU), auxiliary to the Southern Baptist Convention. The primary interest of the WMU was in missions, and its offices, first located in Baltimore, moved in 1921 to Birmingham, Alabama.

The first half of the twentieth century for the SBC was marked by new initiatives and significant progress in growth, geographical expansion, the founding of new institutions and agencies, increase in the work of missions both overseas and at home, and the development of a remarkably successful plan of financial support. In 1900 Southern Baptists reported a membership of 1,657,996 in 19,558 churches. By 1950 the number had grown to 7 million members in 27,788 churches. In 1900 there were fifteen state conventions in affiliation, but in 1950 there were twenty-four conventions stretching to the Pacific Ocean and including California, Alaska, and even Hawaii. The Great Depression and widespread drought of the 1930s and the move to take jobs in defense plants during World War II helped to disperse Southern Baptists into other regions.

The Annuity Board was established in 1918 to provide economic security for retired ministers and their families. Three new seminaries were formed: Southwestern (1908), New Orleans (1917), and Golden Gate (1944). The convention approved several commissions: Brotherhood (1908), Christian Life (1913), American Baptist Theological Seminary (1924), Education (1928), Radio and Television (1942), Historical (1951), and Stewardship (1960). In 1939 a Public Affairs Committee was formed to work in conjunction with other Baptist bodies to keep Baptists apprised of legislation and issues affecting religious liberty and the separation of church and state. In 1947 the

Southern Baptist Foundation was created to serve the SBC and its agencies and institutions by providing management of endowments and other funds as well as by offering advisory services on financial matters.

To replace the nineteenth-century system of funding agencies by a series of separate and emotional appeals to the churches for financial support, the SBC in 1925 adopted the Cooperative Program. This unified giving plan enabled congregations to contribute to the total work of the SBC. Each church sends a percentage of its offering receipts to the office of the state convention where a portion is kept for state Baptist ministries. The remaining percentage is then forwarded to SBC offices where there is an approved formula for a distribution of funds to foreign and home missions, theological education, the commissions, and other SBC programs.

In 1927 the SBC enlarged the scope of duties of its small Executive Committee (formed 1917) to include acting on behalf of the SBC between its annual sessions. The SBC elected a full-time administrator to give guidance to it. Although it does not control or direct the activities of the convention's agencies, the Executive Committee recommends the annual operating budget, reviews the financial statements of all agencies, and performs all tasks given to it by the SBC.

Between 1900 and 1950 the Foreign Mission Board entered twenty-five new countries. Missionaries established not only churches but also schools, hospitals, and publishing houses, and introduced other ministries. The Home Mission Board gave priority to founding churches and missions. Special attention was focused on the spiritual needs of the cities, Appalachia, African-Americans, and the western region of the USA. It also started language missions and work with the deaf. The Home Mission Board entered Panama in 1906 and expanded its work in Cuba. During the Second World War, it greatly expanded its ministry to servicemen and women through its chaplaincy program.

Notable achievements have continued since 1950. In 1993 the SBC reached 15,400,000 members in 38,741 churches and 1,218 associations, located in all 50 states. Baptisms numbered about 350,000. Total church giving for the year amounted to more than $5 billion and church property had an estimated value of more than $25 billion. The thirty-six cooperating state conventions provided a wide range of educational, benevolent, and mission programs. A Baptist paper served each state body with an overall circulation of almost one and a half million subscribers. Even though the membership of Southern Baptist churches is about 94 percent White (non-Hispanic), there has, however, been a notable rise in the number of racial/ethnic congregations in the SBC, whose members exceed 500,000.

In the fall of 1994 the Foreign Mission Board reported almost 4,100 missionaries in 129 countries. The Home Mission Board has more than 4,900 missionaries serving in all fifty states, the Caribbean, American Samoa, and Canada. Southern Baptists added two new seminaries in the 1950s—Southeastern (1951) and Midwestern (1957). Educational efforts also included fifty-three colleges and universities which draw support from the state conventions rather than directly from the SBC. In addition, there are four Bible schools and eight academies.

In recent decades the SBC has not been free from conflict. In the 1960s controversy arose over the publication of *The Message of Genesis*, a volume in which Ralph H. Elliott, professor at Midwestern Seminary, offered views which were at odds with many other Southern Baptists. Although Elliott was dismissed from the faculty, there was still a strong feeling that the SBC needed to take a stand on such doctrinal issues.

methods and policies of their respective state conventions. Dissident Landmark Baptists formed the East Texas Baptist Convention in 1900 (soon changed to Baptist Missionary Association of Texas), the State Association of Missionary Baptist Churches of Arkansas in 1902, and the Baptist General Assembly of Oklahoma in 1903.

In early 1905 messengers from a number of Arkansas churches met at Texarkana and formed a tentative general association and sent a memorial to the SBC demanding that each church have an equal voice in the convention, the removal of the money basis for church representation, and the elimination of the authority of boards to appoint and remove missionaries. With the rejection of their demands, the schism was complete. In November 1905 a permanent organization, the General Association of Baptists was formed (later called the Missionary Baptist General Association). The association never gained the full support of all Landmarkers outside the SBC and in the meantime the Baptist Missionary Association of Texas continued to support its own foreign mission program. In an effort to unify their forces nationally, Landmark Baptists formed in 1924 the American Baptist Association in Texarkana, which included churches of the Baptist Missionary Association.

One of the foremost leaders in the General Association and the American Baptist Association (ABA) was Ben M. Bogard (1868–1951), pastor of the Antioch Missionary Baptist Church of Little Rock, Arkansas, from 1920 to 1947, and a leading preacher, polemicist, and publicist of the movement. In 1934 he helped to establish the Missionary Baptist Seminary at the Antioch Church, and with others he began publishing Sunday School literature, which continues as an enterprise of the ABA.

Two factions began to develop in the association, one headed by Bogard and the other by W. J. Burgess, D. N. Jackson, and M. E. Childers. Differences came to a head in 1950 at the meeting of the ABA in Lakeland, Florida, over the issue of accepting messengers who did not belong to the church they represented. The Bogard faction, which supported the practice, prevailed; the other faction then formed the Baptist Missionary Association. The division touched almost everywhere, dividing state and local associations and even churches. The ABA lost about half its members and such major state associations as Texas, Misssissippi, and Missouri.

Today the ABA claims 250,000 members. About 40 percent of its membership is in Arkansas, where it even leads Southern Baptists in some counties, but it has churches in most other states. Its general headquarters and publishing center are in Texarkana, Texas. Besides the Missionary Baptist Seminary, three other major seminaries as well as numerous other schools and institutes are associated with the movement. In 1992 the churches of the ABA provided support for forty-two interstate missionaries, seventeen foreign missionaries, and numerous foreign nationals.

BIBLIOGRAPHY: Conrad N. Glover and Austin T. Powers, *The American Baptist Association, 1924–1974* (Texarkana, Tex.: Bogard Press, 1979). L. D. Foreman and Alta Payne, *The Life and Works of Benjamin Marcus Bogard*, 2 vols. (Little Rock: Authors, 1965–1966).

Baptist Missionary Association

The Baptist Missionary Association of America (BMA) was founded as the North American Baptist Association in May 1950 in Little Rock, Arkansas, by individuals who separated from the American Baptist Association. In 1969 it took its present name.

Its primary membership is in Texas (43 percent) with important constituencies in Arkansas and Mississippi, but it has churches in other parts of the United States. Its policies and programs are much like the American Baptist Association, except that its schools are controlled by an association and not by a single church. Its headquarters is in Little Rock, Arkansas, and it maintains a publishing house at Texarkana, Texas, a radio ministry, and a theological seminary at Jacksonville, Texas. BMA supports home missionaries as well as foreign missionaries (both American and national) in sixteen countries.

BIBLIOGRAPHY: John W. Duggar, *The Baptist Missionary Association of America (1950–1986)* (Texarkana, Tex.: Baptist Publishing House, 1988).

Independent Landmark Baptist Associations/Churches (Direct–Mission)

There are independent Landmark Missionary Baptist associations and churches which are independent of either the American Baptist Association or the Baptist Missionary Association, which follow the principles of Gospel Missionism, promoted by T. P. Crawford. These congregations practice direct missions, that is, they send mission support directly to the missionary, who is not supervised by any home board. Such churches may be found not only in the South but also on the Pacific Coast. For instance, in the 1890s Gospel Missionism began to take root among some Baptists in Oregon, and today twenty-three small churches in this state follow these tenets. Unfortunately, there is no national survey of these congregations, and their numbers and location remain largely unknown.

SEPARATIST FUNDAMENTALIST

*T*here are at least five separate fundamentalist fellowships with Southern antecedents, whose members are known as "Independent Baptists." Their main strength is in the South and the Midwest, but their churches are in every state of the union. With more than 4,500 congregations and a membership that is approaching 2 million, they are one of the most dynamic segments of the Baptist denomination in the USA. Their growth has come through aggressive church planting and evangelism, effectively utilizing the Sunday School, home visitation, bus ministries, and the mass media, including television, radio, and printed publications. They have also established many educational institutions, primarily Bible colleges with a strong emphasis on Bible instruction and practical Christian training, and Christian day schools.

Although this movement includes many small congregations, it also numbers some of the largest Baptist churches and Sunday Schools in the nation. Unlike Landmark Baptists, whose churches are often confined to small towns and rural areas, Independent Baptist churches are often located in urban centers. Leadership in Independent churches is centered on the pastor. Church buildings are built to be functional for a preaching and teaching ministry.

As a rule, Independent Baptists are premillennial dispensationalists and are strongly opposed to theological liberalism and the ecumenical movement. Although they advocate ecclesiastical separation from liberalism, they are not so fussy concerning second-degree separation as northern-oriented Fundamentalists, such as members of the Fundamental Baptist Fellowship, the New Testament Association, or Bob Jones University. They tend to stress a more traditional personal morality than many other Baptists. With heightened concern over the deterioration of morals in the country, they strongly oppose the philosophies and programs of political and social liberals in regard to sexual morality and the secularization of American life. Unlike many fundamentalists of an earlier age, many of them today have entered the political arena with a program which seeks to maintain traditional morality. The most notable exponent of this effort has been Jerry Falwell of Thomas Road Baptist Church, Lynchburg, Virginia, who founded in 1979 and headed for a number of years *The Moral Majority*, a coalition of the Religious Right.

In common with Landmark Baptists, Independent Baptists hold to the primacy of the local church and reject conventionism. Unlike Landmark Baptists, however, churches form no associations but cooperate through the participation of their pastors in state or national fellowships. Except for the Southwide Baptist Fellowship, which is composed of individuals and not churches, each national fellowship has a missions office through which churches may contribute support for missionaries, who, however, must raise their own support by deputation. They are much less concerned than Landmark Baptists with alien immersion and close communion and find their basis of cooperation, not on ecclesiology, but on common fundamentalist beliefs and methodology.

The Independent Baptist movement has revolved around charismatic leaders, who not only developed their own large congregations but through their leadership helped to bring into existence independent fellowships. In this process schools have played an important role. Each national fellowship is not only the extension of the personality of a Baptist leader but also of a school which he helped to found. Such premier schools which, with their alumni, help to bring a certain cohesion to their respective fellowships are Arlington Baptist College (1939) for World Baptist Fellowship, Tennessee Temple Schools (1946) for Southwide Baptist Fellowship, Baptist Bible College (1950) for Baptist Bible Fellowship International, Liberty University (1971) for Liberty Baptist Fellowship, and Norris Bible Baptist Institute (1984) for Independent Baptist Fellowship International.

Since the fellowships are loosely organized and with many churches associating with more than one fellowship and supporting a number of different mission agencies, further fragmentation is always possible if some leader wishes to develop his own movement or establish his own school. Fierce rivalries have at times produced warring factions with charges and countercharges.

Although they reject interdenominationalism, Independent Baptists will fellowship with other fundamentalist Baptists, such as in the Fundamental Baptist Congress of North America. Although the gulf is wide between Independent and Southern Baptists, there has been some fraternization of Independent Baptists, such as Jerry Falwell with conservative Southern Baptist leaders. Falwell, president of Liberty University in Lynchburg, Virginia, represents a neo-fundamentalist movement which seeks greater cooperation with conservative evangelicals and is willing to engage in constructive criticism of the fundamentalist movement itself. In addition, the mother church of the

Independent Baptist movement, First Baptist Church of Fort Worth, Texas, has voted to affiliate with the Southern Baptist Convention.

The spiritual father of the Independent movement is J. Frank Norris (1877–1952), the dynamic but controversial pastor of First Baptist Church of Fort Worth from 1909 until his death. In 1917 he began his own paper, *The Fundamentalist*. Because of his noncooperation and belligerent attacks on Southern Baptist leaders and institutions, the local association excluded his church from fellowship in 1922. Two years later the Texas General Baptist Convention permanently excluded him from its fellowship. He developed a large congregation, and through his preaching and publication ministry his influence spread over a wide area. In 1935 he also became pastor of the Temple Baptist Church of Detroit, Michigan, which he soon led out of the Northern Baptist Convention. In 1932 he established his own missionary fellowship, which he completely dominated, and formed in 1939 the Fundamental Baptist Bible Institute, today Arlington Baptist College.

A small rivulet which contributed to the Independent Baptist movement was the Orthodox Baptists from Oklahoma, which today is absorbed into the larger Independent Baptist movement. W. Lee Rector founded the First Orthodox Baptist Church of Ardmore, Oklahoma, in 1931, which severed ties in 1935 with Southern Baptists for alleged liberalism. In 1944 the church established the Orthodox Bible Institute. When the Trinity Temple Baptist Church in Dallas opened Orthodox Baptist College in 1964 (today Independent Baptist College), the Orthodox Bible Institute closed its doors to support the new venture. The Ardmore Church sponsored annual fellowship meetings, but an organization with defined membership never emerged.

BIBLIOGRAPHY: For a survey of fundamentalism in the South by a fundamentalist author, see George W. Dollar, *A History of Fundamentalism in America* (Greenville, S.C.: Bob Jones University Press, 1973), 122–34, 216–20, 226, 242–44, 246. For an appraisal of fundamentalism from a neo-fundamentalist perspective, see Ed Dobson, Ed Hindson, and Jerry Falwell, *The Fundamentalist Phenomenon* (Garden City, N.J.: Doubleday, 1981, 1st ed.; Grand Rapids: Baker Book House, 1986, 2d ed.). For an assessment by a Southern Baptist historian, see Bill J. Leonard, "Independent Baptists: From Sectarian Minority to 'Moral Majority,'" *Church History*, 56, no. 4 (Dec. 1987): 504–17. For a critical appraisal of J. Frank Norris, see "J. Frank Norris: Violent Fundamentalist," in C. Allyn Russell, *Voices of American Fundamentalism: Seven Biographical Studies* (Philadelphia: Westminster Press, 1976), 20–46. For a current survey of independent fundamentalist Baptists, both North and South, see Mike Randall, *A Profile of Independent Baptist Pastors & Churches* (Springfield, Mo.: Baptist Bible College, 1993). It, however, inflates the number of fundamentalist churches, since many of them are members of more than one fellowship. For an account of Jerry Falwell and other fundamentalists as political activists, see "Jerry Falwell's Crusade," and "Jerry Falwell Spreads the Word," *Time*, Sep. 2, 1985, 48–61.

Baptist Bible Fellowship International

The most dynamic fellowship of Independent Baptists is Baptist Bible Fellowship International (BBFI), formed in 1950 by members in the World Baptist Fellowship who separated from Norris' autocratic control. One of the major leaders was G. Beauchamp Vick (1901–1975), who had served as Norris' copastor of Temple Baptist Church in Detroit and president of Norris' school. In 1950 Vick became president of the newly established Baptist Bible College of Springfield, Missouri, which became the center of the new fellowship. With a new school, a paper *(Baptist Bible Tribune)*, and a mission office, the BBFI embarked on an aggressive program.

In 1972 the Fellowship reported churches in every state except two, and today is present in all fifty with an estimated membership of more than 1,400,000. Its *Directory* for 1993–1994 lists around 3,400 churches of which 434 are also members of the World Baptist Fellowship in addition to a number of other congregations with other dual affiliations. *Christian Life* magazine reported in 1971 that BBFI had twenty-three of the nation's one hundred largest Sunday Schools. Like the Southern Baptist Convention, the fellowship has found many fruitful fields among transplanted Southerners. Its greatest strength has been in the urban centers of the Trans-Mississippi South, the Upper South, Florida, Kansas, the Great Lakes region, and California. The BBFI has also had a strong foreign mission program. In August 1993 it reported 787 missionaries and eighty-seven fields.

BIBLIOGRAPHY: For works written by members of the BBFI on the beginnings and development of the movement, see Billy Vick Bartlett, *A History of Baptist Separatism* (Springfield, Mo.: Author, 1972), and Mike Randall, *G. B. Vick* (Springfield, Mo.: Author, 1987). For a statistical analysis of the movement, see "The 1990 Census of Independent Churches: Baptist Bible Fellowship," *Church Growth Today*, 5, no. 2 (1990): 1–3.

Independent Baptist Fellowship International

In 1984 Raymond W. Barber (b. 1932)—pastor of Worth Baptist Church of Fort Worth, Texas, former president of the World Baptist Fellowship, and professor at Arlington Baptist College—after having engaged in serious controversy with the college, led in establishing the Independent Baptist Fellowship International (IBFI). At the same time, he led the IBFI to found Norris Bible Baptist Institute, which meets at the Worth Baptist Church, to open a mission office, and to begin publication of *The Searchlight*. The IBFI has a total of 540 churches, 392 of which also cooperate with other fundamentalist fellowships. One of its largest congregations is the Worth Baptist Church, with a membership of two thousand. In 1992 IBFI was supporting fourteen missionaries, besides spouses, in five countries.

BIBLIOGRAPHY: For an account of the separation of the Independent Baptist Fellowship International from the World Baptist Fellowship from the perspective of adherents of the latter body, see Mr. and Mrs. Earl K. Oldham, *USS-WBF: Sail On* ([Grand Prairie, Tex.]): Authors, c. 1992), 338–346.

Liberty Baptist Fellowship

Liberty Baptist Fellowship is an outgrowth of the activity of Jerry Falwell (b. 1933), pastor of the Thomas Road Baptist Church (1956) of Lynchburg, Virginia, and his school, Liberty University. Most of the pastors of the churches in affiliation are alumni of Liberty University. According to the *Yearbook of American & Canadian Churches*, 1994, the fellowship claimed one hundred churches. The Thomas Road Church has 21,000 members and is also a member of the Baptist Bible Fellowship. Because of the unavailability of a directory for the fellowship, it is impossible to note the geographical distribution of the churches nor how many of them are related to some other fellowship.

Another related agency is Liberty Baptist Mission, founded in 1978. It currently reports twenty missionaries serving in seven countries.

BIBLIOGRAPHY: For a history of the Thomas Road Baptist Church, see Jerry Falwell and Elmer Towns, *Church Aflame* (Nashville: Impact Books, 1971). For other material, see the bibliography which introduces this section.

Southwide Baptist Fellowship

One of the strong fundamentalist leaders in the southeastern states has been Lee Roberson (b. 1909), who began serving the Highland Park Baptist Church of Chattanooga, Tennessee, in 1942. During his forty-year ministry, Highland Park became one of the largest Baptist congregations in the country. In 1971 the congregation reported 31,000 members, including members in forty-three chapels. In 1983 it claimed more than 57,000 members with around sixty chapels. Roberson also established Tennessee Temple Schools, which began in 1946 with Tennessee Temple Bible School but by 1951 included three other institutions—a seminary, college, and an elementary school. The schools were housed in buildings which clustered about the church. Because of criticism in 1955 from the Executive Committee of the Hamilton County Baptist Association for only token cooperation with the Southern Baptist program, Roberson and his church withdrew from Southern Baptists.

As early as 1948 Roberson was one of the leaders in founding a Tennessee Premillennial Fellowship in Chattanooga. In August 1955 a preparatory meeting for a fundamentalist fellowship was held in Aiken, South Carolina, where Roberson was guest speaker. This was followed in November by a preorganizational meeting at the Highland Park Church. In March 1956, 147 pastors and laymen formed the Southern Baptist Fellowship, today the Southwide Baptist Fellowship. It adopted a statement of faith with a premillennial article and elected Roberson president. At its first meeting at the same church in November, 423 individuals had become members. In 1960 Roberson led in founding Baptist International Missions, Inc., which today has more than five hundred missionaries serving in about sixty countries.

In its 1993–1994 *Directory*, Southwide Fellowship lists 1,847 individual members. These members, in turn, are related to 912 churches of which more than one-third are also aligned with other fellowships. Although it has members throughout much of the USA, its membership is concentrated in the southeastern states.

BIBLIOGRAPHY: See Southwide Baptist Fellowship, *Directory*, 1993–1994, which includes not only members but also a listing of the meetings of the Fellowship. Also see Kenneth Hubbard, (Th.D. dissertation, Southwestern Baptist Theological Seminary, 1968), 143, 203, 252–54, for the beginnings of the Fellowship and Roberson's relations with Southern Baptists. For a description of the Highland Park Church in the 1980s, see "Highland Park Baptist Church," in John N. Vaughn, *The World's Twenty Largest Churches* (Grand Rapids: Baker Book House, 1984), 109–16.

World Baptist Fellowship

At the third semi-annual Premillennial Bible School in November 1932 at the First Baptist Church of Fort Worth, Texas, J. Frank Norris, pastor of the church, led the assembled gathering to approve the formation of a Premillennial Baptist Missionary Fellowship and to send money directly to three stations in China. In 1938 the organization received a charter as the World Fundamental Baptist Missionary Fellowship, but since 1950 has been called the World Baptist Fellowship (WBF). Because of Norris' dictatorial tactics, in 1950 a large number of pastors left to form the Baptist Bible Fellowship International.

Because of the division and the death of Norris two years later, the fellowship has lost the momentum of its earlier years. In 1984 it was further weakened by a second division with the formation of the Independent Baptist Fellowship International. At present more than half of its 945 churches also cooperate with other fellowships. About half of its churches are in Texas, Florida, and Ohio. In 1992 the WBF had 133 missionaries under appointment for twenty countries.

BIBLIOGRAPHY: Wilburn S. Taylor, "World Baptist Fellowship," *Quarterly Review*, Apr./June 1959, 35–39. Mr. and Mrs. Earl K. Oldham, *USS-WBF: Sail On* ([Grand Prairie, Tex.]: Authors, c. 1992).

First Baptist Church, Hammond, Indiana

Besides Independent Baptists who are associated with the above fellowships, other Independents are unrelated to any fellowship. One of these is Jack Hyles of the First Baptist Church in Hammond, Indiana. Because of the magnitude of his work and influence among Independent Baptists, he has practically developed a fellowship of his own.

In 1957 the Dallas Baptist Association refused to seat the Miller Road Baptist Church of Garland, Texas, of which Hyles was pastor. The association cited Hyles' failure to cooperate with the Southern Baptist program. In 1959 Hyles became pastor of the First Baptist Church of Hammond and soon led it out of the American Baptist Convention to become independent. Through efforts on soul-winning, an extensive bus ministry, and special promotions, the church has grown to become the largest Baptist church in the world. In 1982 it reported almost 75,000 members and an average Sunday School attendance of 18,500. A more recent report records 14,000 in Sunday School, which still makes it the largest Sunday School in the nation. Hyles also established Hyles-Anderson College at Crown Point, Indiana, and a system of Christian schools at Schererville. Hyles' ministry has extended far beyond his own church and schools through his numerous books and pamphlets, speaking engagements, and sponsorship of an annual Pastor's School, which in 1993 numbered twelve thousand in attendance.

BIBLIOGRAPHY: "First Baptist Church, Hammond, Indiana," in John N. Vaughn, *The World's Twenty Largest Churches* (Grand Rapids: Baker Book House, 1984), 101–08.

REGULAR BAPTISTS–NATIONAL BAPTIST (AFRICAN-AMERICAN)

	Members	Churches
IV. National Baptist (African-American)	7,600,000*	25,000*
1. National Baptist Convention of America, Inc. (1880)	(1,700,000)	(6,716)

2. National Baptist Convention, USA, Inc.
   (1915)   (6,000,000)   (18,513)

3. National Missionary Baptist Convention
   of America (1988)   (200,000)   (701)

4. National Primitive Baptist Convention,
   Inc. (1907)   n/a   (616)

5. Progressive National Baptist Convention, Inc.
   (1961)   n/a   (741)

*These figures are a general estimate of the total Black Baptist constituency. They do not properly add up because there is widespread dual alignment among National Baptists. Because of the lack of data, the figures for the National Missionary Baptist Convention are probably understated. Figures in parenthesis are included in the estimated total for National Baptist churches.

It is most difficult to obtain statistics for National Baptists since they do not keep a listing of members by church. Two approaches were used to gain their statistics. Through personal contact, the membership of individual churches was obtained through the efforts of the editor in Tennessee and Oregon and by others in Georgia and then extrapolated for the nation. For the methodology used, see *Churches and Church Membership in the United States 1990* (CCMUS), Appendix F, 451–53. This approach yielded almost 7,000,000 communicant members.

The editor attempted a second approach by attempting to obtain statistics of state bodies since the published figures for National Baptist bodies on the national level are inflated estimates and many churches relate to more than one such body. He gained figures of eighty-four of ninety-four state bodies, generally by telephone from officials of state National Baptist bodies or from the statistics in Wardell J. Payne, ed., *Directory of African–American Religious Bodies* (Washington, D.C.: Howard University Press, 1991).

The state bodies contacted were related to the National Baptist Convention, USA, Inc. (NBC, USA, Inc.), the National Baptist Convention of America, Inc. (NBCA), and the National Missionary Baptist Convention. He also included the General Association of Baptists in Kentucky, which is not related directly to either body. Although the figures he obtained for the National Missionary Baptist Convention are probably incomplete, a number of the churches and members this body would claim for itself are probably still in state bodies listed with the National Baptist Convention of America, the body from which it separated. Moreover, he did not obtain state memberships of the Progressive National Baptist Convention since the greater number of its churches are still aligned in state bodies which relate to the National Baptist Convention, USA, Inc. Because of their unavailability, he did not gain the memberships of the churches of the National Primitive Baptist Convention, whose congregations are generally very small.

In arriving at his figures for estimated membership for all Black Baptists, the editor took the figures he obtained, subtracted 425,000 for North Carolina because it was included in the figures of two National Baptist bodies, and then added from CMMUS figures for the missing state bodies and arrived at a total of a bit more than 7,600,000 members, which came remarkably close to the total obtained by CMMUS. For churches of NBCA, Inc., and NBC, USA, Inc., the editor took the figures he obtained and then added an estimated number of churches for missing state bodies by using as a standard the average membership of the churches in each of these conventions for which figures were available.

ne of the largest segments of the Baptist denomination is the National, or African-American, Baptists—more than 25 percent of all Baptists in the USA. They compose the largest Black religious body in the nation. Their membership includes a bit more than 25 percent of the American Black population and possibly almost 33 percent if one includes children and other nonmembers who relate in some way to their churches. Combined membership totals of Black Baptist bodies suggest an even higher percentage. Two recent studies, however, indicate that these statistics appear to be inflated and duplicate, if not triple, the memberships of many churches which belong to more than one convention.

The National Baptists with other African-Americans have followed their own distinctive path of struggle—from slavery to freedom and then a struggle for equal rights. Unlike the majority of Baptists, their initial Christian experience was not based on a European but on an African consciousness. This factor together with their own special social status helped to mold a religious expression uniquely their own.

The local Black Baptist church is more than a religious organization—it is a social community which brings personal and social identity and support. Until recent times, the church has been the only institution which Blacks could truly control as their own. For many Blacks it has been their primary social center, an institution providing opportunity for the development of leadership and group solidarity.

The Black pastor, who is both the ruler and shepherd of the congregation, proclaims not only the gospel of personal salvation but is also a spokesperson for social justice. The intermingling of the personal and the social as well as the religious and the secular is far more a feature of the Black religious community than the White.

Worship in the Black Baptist church is celebration and seeks to engage the worshiper personally and emotionally—body, soul, and spirit. Worship includes a great variety of music, ranging from anthems to spirituals to improvised and syncopated gospel hymns. Adult and youth choirs often march into the sanctuary and rhythmically sway while singing. Many pastors, beginning on a slow note and encouraged by "amens" or other antiphonal responses from the congregation, will heighten the pace and intensity of the delivery, using descriptive, if not imaginative and picturesque, language to lead the worshiper to an emotional commitment. Unlike services in predominantly White churches, precise time contraints are not generally present.

Before the Great Awakening in the mid-eighteenth century, comparatively few Blacks were in a position to accept the Christian faith. Many slaveholders were indifferent or opposed to slaves becoming Christian, and the Christianity of the time hardly fulfilled the slave's religious and emotional needs. The Awakening brought a personal and ecstatic experience, which produced in the recipient the consciouness of being born anew. Water baptism confirmed to the believer that he or she had passed from the old life to a new one with Christ.

Mechal Sobel in her study *Trabelen' On* has documented the establishment of at least ten Black churches formally organized before 1800, all located in the South. Before the end of the Civil War, at least 205 had been constituted with 75 in the free states of the North and 130 in the slave South. These congregations by no means included all Black Baptists, since many were not in any position, socially or legally, to organize their own congregations. Large numbers belonged to multiracial congregations controlled by Whites. Others met secretly and left no records.

The first Black to join a Baptist church, was a man simply referred to as "Jack, a colored man," who became a member of the Baptist church in Newport, Rhode Island, in 1652, at a time when the Baptist denomination in America was still in its infancy. It would be more than 120 years later before the first all-Black Baptist church, Silver

Bluff, would be organized. At a revival on Silver Bluff plantation in South Carolina, some time between 1773 and 1775, a certain Palmer (probably Wait Palmer, a Baptist who had baptized Shubal Stearns), baptized eight Black candidates. Among them was David George, who would later become a Baptist leader in Canada and Sierra Leone.

Another early leader was George Liele, who was converted in 1773 and given freedom by his pastor to preach. Among other places, he ministered in Silver Bluff and, in December 1777, formed a church at Yamacraw, near Savannah, Georgia. Shortly before leaving for Jamaica, Liele baptized Andrew Bryan, who became the foremost Baptist leader after the departure of George and Liele. In January 1788 Abraham Marshall, a Separat Baptist, led in the formation of the First African Baptist Church of Savannah and, at the same time, ordained Andrew Bryan to the ministry. In 1819 the Sunbury Association was organized in Georgia, most of whose churches were Black congregations, which in the 1840s, however, lost their control to a White minority.

In the free North, Black Baptist churches also began to appear, including African Church in Boston (1805); Abyssinian Church in New York City (1808); First African in Philadelphia (1809); First Colored Church of Trenton, New Jersey (1812); and the Wood River Church in Wood River, Illinois (1819). The first independent Black associations were constituted in the Great Lakes region—Providence (1834) and Union (1836) in Ohio, Wood River in Illinois (1839), followed by others. In 1840 at the Abyssinian Church in New York City, Blacks formed their first national body, the American Baptist Missionary Convention, initially composed only of two churches from New York City and one in Philadelphia. By 1865 it had grown to forty-eight churches. In 1853 thirteen churches in Illinois and Missouri formed the Western Colored Baptist Convention but, because of the Civil War, did not meet from 1859 to 1864. In the latter year it was reorganized as the Northwestern and Southern Baptist Convention with churches in the Great Lakes area and Lower Mississippi Valley.

With the freedom of the slaves in the South as a result of the Civil War, all Blacks were free to form their own churches and denominational bodies. With already a comparatively large constituency in the South before the war, Black Baptists, rapidly leaving White-controlled churches and forming their own congregations, grew by leaps and bounds. Besides the organization of new associations, state conventions also appeared—Kentucky (1865), North Carolina (1867), Arkansas (1867), Virginia (1868), Alabama (1868), Mississippi (1869), Georgia (1870), Louisiana (1872), Tennessee (1872), Florida (1874), Texas (1874), South Carolina (1876), and West Virginia (1878). On the national level, the American Convention and the Northwestern and Southern Convention united in 1866 as the Consolidated American Baptist Missionary Convention. Because of the strength of the district conventions, which were to serve as auxiliaries, and the state conventions, the strength of the Consolidated Convention ebbed—it ceased to function by the end of the 1870s. One of the district conventions, the New England Missionary Baptist Convention (1874), still exists today as the oldest regional National Baptist body in the nation, but in a much weakened form.

Black Baptists also began to take some interest in foreign missions. In 1879 the state conventions of Virginia and South Carolina sent missionaries respectively to Nigeria and Liberia. In 1880 William W. Colley, who had served with the FMB of the Southern Baptist Convention in Nigeria, called for the formation in Montgomery, Alabama, of a missionary convention. More than one hundred delegates organized the Baptist Foreign Mission Convention of the USA, considered by Black Baptists as the beginning of their cooperative work as National Baptists. In 1895 the National Baptist Convention, USA, was formed by consolidating the Baptist Foreign Mission Convention, the American National Baptist Convention (1886), and the National Baptist Educational Convention (1882).

Despite the achievement of forming one national convention, National Baptists have been unable to remain in one body. The National Baptist Convention, USA, suffered division in 1897 over its foreign mission program, in 1915 over control of the National Baptist Publishing Board, and in 1961 over strategy in the civil rights struggle and tenure for convention officials. The National Baptist Convention of America, which was formed in 1915 to support the independence of the Publishing Board, itself divided in 1988 over the same issue.

With a plethora of national bodies, state conventions, and associations, National Baptists possess a labyrinth of organization, which nevertheless creates numerous positions for leadership. The divisions on the national level have helped to multiply bodies on the state level, most of which relate to one or another of the national bodies. Only the state bodies of North Carolina, South Carolina, Georgia, and Kentucky have been able to maintain a state body which includes all National Baptists in the state. In addition, two or more state bodies may relate to the same national body. There are at least eighty-six state bodies which are affiliated with the two largest national bodies: National Baptist Convention, USA, Inc., and National Baptist Convention of America, Inc. There are, of course, additional bodies which relate to the other national conventions. To make it even more difficult, the state body in North Carolina relates to three national bodies at the same time, while the state body in Kentucky does not relate to any of them. It also becomes a further maze when many local churches belong to more than one state body, each relating to a different national body. Many National Baptist churches also maintain a dual affiliation with a predominantly White body such as the American Baptist Churches/USA and the Southern Baptist Convention.

Both American and Southern Baptists have had an interest in furthering work among Blacks. By the early twentieth century, the American Baptist Home Mission Society and Woman's American Baptist Home Society had established twenty-seven educational institutions for the freedmen in the South, which provided education on various levels from common school up to university and seminary. Four such schools are still related to American Baptists—Benedict College, Shaw University, Florida Memorial College, and Virginia Union University. The American Home Mission Society also sponsored ministerial institutes. As a result of the civil rights struggle of the 1960s, a number of National Baptists began to seek dual affiliation with the American Baptist Churches, and in 1971 the American Baptist Churches of the South was formed, a primarily Black organization.

For many years Southern Baptists cooperated with National Baptists in providing limited funds for missionaries or missionary-teachers and also institutes for ministerial training. In 1924 the American Baptist Theological Seminary (now American Baptist College) opened its doors, a joint enterprise of the National Baptist Convention, USA, and Southern Baptists. In the 1940s the Home Mission Board began to support a secretary for student work among Blacks on college campuses and in 1959 changed the name of its Department of Negro Work to Department of Work with National Baptists. Southern Baptists have not only attempted to develop numerous cooperative ministries with National Baptists but have also favored dual affiliation with National Baptist churches which have been attracted to Southern Baptist literature and programs. Southern Baptists are now also actively engaged in forming Black Southern Baptist churches.

One of the notable accomplishments of the Black churches in the 1950s and 1960s was their contribution to the civil rights struggle. Black Baptist pastors provided much of the leadership, with Martin Luther King, Jr., (1929–1968) being the most notable. Today Black Baptist pastors continue to play important social and prophetic roles on the national level and in their communities. The three largest National Baptist conventions are members of the Baptist World Alliance and the Baptist Joint Committee on Public Affairs. Because of a concern for social and political justice, the three bodies are also members of the National Council of the Churches of Christ in the USA and the World Council of Churches. The three conventions, however, have shown comparatively little interest in issues of "Faith and Order" in the ecumenical movement. The National Missionary Baptist Convention is also a member of the Baptist Joint Committee on Public Affairs.

Although National Baptists continue to play a very significant religious role in the Black community, they nevertheless face serious challenges. From recent statistics, they do not appear to have within their religious community the numbers which have been traditionally ascribed to them. They probably include not more than one-third of the Black population. Because of migration, their rural churches have been drained of membership, and the city, accompanied by the breakdown of traditional family structure, is often a very difficult field. National Baptists are also facing competition from rapidly growing Pentecostals, on the one hand, and militant and disciplined Black Muslims on the other. The churches have been fortunate to have a loyal female membership, which are in the strong majority, but unfortunately they are failing to reach a great portion of the men and youth in the inner city.

Black Baptists have done well in developing their local churches but have been weak in cooperative endeavors. Aside from the two publishing houses in Nashville, National Baptists have always had a relatively limited denominational structure—weak in home and foreign mission organizations and in the development of their own educational institutions. Each convention board acts rather autonomously, and the concept of a unified financial program is either limited or nonexistent. Because of rivalries and division, National Baptists have also hurt their cause, and a number of churches are now being pulled toward other Baptist conventions with stronger programs.

BIBLIOGRAPHY: There is a wealth of material on African-American Baptists. For bibliographic materials, see *Quarterly Review* 31, no. 3 (Apr./June 1971): 46–55, and Lester B. Scherer and Susan M. Eltscher, "Afro-American Baptists: A Guide to Materials in the American Baptist Historical Society," *American Baptist Quarterly*, 4, no. 3 (Sep. 1985): 282–99. For a very helpful introduction to the religious life of Blacks, see the issue, "The Black Experience and the Church," *Review and Expositor*, 70, no. 3 (summer 1973). The volume by Leroy Fitts, *A History of Black Baptists* (Nashville: Broadman Press, 1985), provides a good historical survey of African-American Baptists. The works by Mechal Sobel, *Trabelin' On: The Slave Journey to an Afro-Baptist Faith* (Westport, Conn., and London: Greenwood Press, 1979), and Walter F. Pitts, Jr., *Old Ship of Zion: The Afro-Baptist Ritual in the African Diaspora* (Oxford and New York: Oxford University Press, 1993), study the development of the faith and worship of Black Baptists in light of their African heritage. Sobel also provides extensive material on the organization of Baptist churches in the antebellum period. For excellent studies of Black Baptists in the nineteenth century, see James Melvin Washington, *Frustrated Fellowship: The Black Baptist Quest for Social Power* (Macon, Ga.: Mercer University Press, 1986), and William E. Montgomery, *Under Their Own Vine Tree: The African-American Church in the South, 1865–1900* (Baton Rouge and London: Louisiana State University Press, 1993). For information on Jack, the first Black

Baptist, see Edwin S. Gaustad, "The First Black Baptist," *Baptist History and Heritage*, 15, no. 1 (Jan. 1980): 55–56, 64. For material on the first Black Baptist churches in the USA and their pastors, see Edward Holmes, Jr., "George Liele: Negro Slavery's Prophet of Deliverance," in *Baptist Quarterly*, 20, no. 8 (Oct. 1964): 340–51, 361, in *Baptist History and Heritage*, 1, no. 1 (Aug. 1965): 27–36, and in *Foundations* 9, no. 4 (Oct./Dec. 1966): 333–45; G. W. Rusling, "A Note on Early Negro Baptist History, *Foundations* 11, no. 4 (Oct./Dec. 1968): 362–68; Grant Gordon, *From Slavery to Freedom: The Life of David George, Pioneer Black Baptist Minister* (Hantsport, N.S.: Lancelot Press, 1992); and James M. Simms, *The First Colored Baptist Church in North America* (Philadelphia: J. B. Lippincott Co., 1888; reprint, New York: Negro Universities Press, 1969). For the contribution of American (Northern) Baptists to Black Baptist education, see the two issues, "Pursuit of the Promise: American Baptists and Black Higher Education," *American Baptist Quarterly* 11, no. 4 (Dec. 1992), and 12, no. 1 (Mar. 1993). For books which include material on Black Baptists and foreign missions in Africa, see Walter L. Williams, *Black Americans and the Evangelization of Africa, 1877–1900* (Madison: University of Wisconsin Press, 1982), and Sandy D. Martin, *Black Baptists and African Missions: The Origins of a Movement, 1880–1915* (Macon, Ga.: Mercer University Press, 1989).

National Baptist Convention of America, Inc.

The National Baptist Convention of America was formed in 1915 by National Baptists who supported Richard H. Boyd in his effort to keep the Baptist Publishing Board of Nashville independent of outside control. This convention has always played a secondary role to the much larger National Baptist Convention, USA, Inc., from which it separated. It has about twenty-nine state bodies in single alignment. Including the North Carolina Convention which relates to two other conventions as well, it has a membership of about 1,700,000. Its strength is greater west of the Mississippi River than east of it and has particularly strong support in Texas. In ideology during the civil rights struggle, it stood between the more liberal Progressive Baptists and the more conservative National Baptist Convention, USA, Inc. Like other conventions, it has a large number of boards and auxiliaries with a Foreign Mission Board in Dallas. It is attempting to develop a cooperative program (CAP), but its agencies receive much of their income independently.

Ironically, the convention experienced division in 1988 because of the National Baptist Publishing Board. The convention became an incorporated body in 1986 and desired more control of the Publishing Board and its successful Sunday Church School and Training Union Congress. The convention formed its own congress, thus severing its relations with the Publishing Board. This action led a number of churches to form the rival National Missionary Baptist Convention.

BIBLIOGRAPHY: The work by Bobby L. Lovett, *A Black Man's Dream: The First 100 Years—Richard Henry Boyd and the National Publishing Board* ([Nashville]: Mega Corporation, 1993), provides a very helpful account of the National Baptist Publishing Board and its relationship to the various National Baptist bodies.

National Baptist Convention, USA, Inc.

The National Baptist Convention, USA, Inc., is the largest National Baptist body in the United States. It traces its history back to the Baptist Foreign Mission Convention (1880) and the consolidation in 1895 of the three Black Baptist bodies. It has 57 or more state conventions affiliated with it which, in turn, have about 6,000,000 members and more than 18,000 congregations. Its churches are well distributed among the Black population, both east and west. It is the only National Baptist body to build a central headquarters—the Baptist World Center in Nashville—a magnificent structure, which was dedicated in 1989. Thus far, however, the various boards of the convention, including the Foreign Mission Board in Philadelphia, have not moved to the center.

The convention has suffered three divisions over the years. The controversy over the foreign mission enterprise took away support from the convention's foreign mission program. This controversy led to the formation of the Lott Carey Foreign Baptist Mission Convention in 1897 by individuals who favored retaining ties with White Baptists and resented the shift of the headquarters of the Foreign Mission Board of the Convention from Richmond to Louisville. The controversy over the National Baptist Publishing Board led to the formation of a rival convention in 1915, the National Baptist Convention of America, and the loss of a significant number of churches. A third division occurred in 1961 during the presidency of J. H. Jackson. Because the convention refused to take a stronger stand on civil rights and to enforce limited tenure for officials of the convention, a number of pastors led in forming the Progressive National Baptist Convention. Jackson also strongly condemned Black theology as contrary to the Christian gospel.

Of the National Baptist bodies, the National Baptist Convention, USA, Inc., has the strongest foreign mission program with work in twelve countries. In 1925 it completed a large building in downtown Nashville to house the Sunday School Publishing Board, its very successful publishing enterprise.

BIBLIOGRAPHY: The work of J. H. Jackson, *A Story of Christian Activism: The History of the National Baptist Convention, U.S.A., Inc.* (Nashville: Townsend Press, 1980), provides a narrative history of the convention as well as a defense of the author's policies while president of this body.

National Missionary Baptist Convention of America

The National Missionary Baptist Convention of America is the newest National Baptist body. Individuals in the National Baptist Convention of America who supported the independence of the National Baptist Publishing Board as an autonomous body formed the new body at a "Restoration Meeting," on November 15, 1988, in Dallas. The new body is not incorporated (nor was the parent body until 1986). The National Missionary Baptist Convention has also established boards and auxiliaries. Some state conventions in California, Oklahoma, and Indiana, which had been with the parent body, have transferred over to it. New state bodies are also being formed.

BIBLIOGRAPHY: For a historical account of the National Missionary Baptist Convention, see National Missionary Baptist Convention of America, *Directory*, 1993, 10–29.

National Primitive Baptist Convention, Inc.

The National Primitive Baptist Convention includes churches which at one time identified with the Primitive Baptist movement. With the organization in 1907 of a convention with boards and auxiliaries and the acceptance of Sunday Schools, musical instruments, and revivals, together with a departure from their Calvinist tenets, this group has become much like other National Baptist conventions. Their retention of the rite of footwashing and use of the pastoral title "elder" remain as reminders of their early heritage. Their churches, which are generally very small, are concentrated in the South. There are also some "old line" Primitive Baptist churches outside the convention with their own associations, which continue the traditional Primitive Baptist patterns of worship.

BIBLIOGRAPHY: The section "National Primitive Baptist Convention of the United States of America" in Arthur C. Piepkorn, *Profiles in Belief* (New York: Harper & Row, 1978), 2:447–48, includes a short historical and theological description of this body.

Progressive National Baptist Convention, Inc.

In November 1961 thirty-three delegates from fourteen states formed the National Progressive Baptist Convention. Its supporters broke with the National Baptist Convention, USA, Inc., when the leadership of this convention refused to recognize limited tenure for convention officers and was unwilling to give Martin Luther King, Jr., and his defenders full support for their program and tactics in the civil rights struggle.

In 1991 its church membership roster listed 741 churches, with many of them in dual relationship with the National Baptist Convention, USA, Inc. Since 1970 the Progressive Convention has also been an "associated organization" of the American Baptist Churches/USA with a number of its churches also individually aligned with this body. Like other National Baptist bodies, it includes a number of boards and auxiliaries. Its foreign mission work is under the Baptist Global Mission Bureau, which supports work in thirteen countries or territories. Although the boards receive funds directly from churches and individuals, the Progressive Convention has also promoted the concept of a unified budget. It is the most politically active of the National Baptist bodies and supports the NAACP, Urban League, and Southern Christian Leadership Conference.

BIBLIOGRAPHY: Wardell J. Payne, *Directory of African-American Religious Bodies* (Washington, D.C.: Howard University Press, 1991), 48–49, 231–32.

REGULAR BAPTISTS (SOUTHERN-ORIENTED)—PRIMITIVISTS

	Members	Churches
V. Regular Baptists (Southern Oriented)—Primitivists		
1. Central Baptist Association	3,297	35
2. General Association of Baptists (Duck River and Kindred Associations)	10,672	102
3. Old Missionary Baptists	13,093	73
4. Regular Baptists		
a. Old Regular Baptists	15,218	326

b. Regular Baptists	3,938	41
c. Enterprise Baptists	4,766	70
5. Primitive Baptists		
a. Absoluters	6,495	380
b. Old Liners	48,980	1,426
c. Progressives	8,000	119
6. Two-Seed-in-the-Spirit Predestinarian Baptists	70	3
7. United Baptists	<u>54,248</u>	<u>436</u>
	168,777	3,011

*S*everal titles could be given to this classification of Baptists, such as Primitivists, Traditionalists, or Old-Time. Unlike other Baptists who adopted missionary, benevolent, and educational institutions, these Baptists generally have sought to preserve older patterns of belief and practice. The main strength of these Baptists who are wedded to a simple rural culture is in the Appalachian South. They have, however, some pockets of strength in other areas of the rural South and in southern Ohio, Indiana, and Illinois; through migration they may be found in other areas of the Middle West and the Pacific Coast. The winds of modern life have not been kind to their growth or even, in some cases, to their survival. What indigenous strength they may once have had in the Northeast, Upper Midwest, and West has disappeared, and their presence there today is primarily due to Southerners migrating to these areas.

Primitivists generally reject not only missionary and educational institutions but also continue to oppose a theologically trained ministry. Many of their churches practice footwashing. A large number of their congregations meet once a month. It should be noted, however, that such churches may have a conference, possibly also with preaching, on Saturday with an extended preaching session on the following Sunday. Primitivists generally reject Sunday Schools, although some have them. Many congregations sing without instrumental accompaniment. As in older Baptist practice, ministers are generally addressed as "elder."

Not all Primitivists are necessarily static in faith and practice; they may sometimes modify their positions, such as forming Sunday Schools and benevolent institutions. There is a strong theological divide between Primitivists who hold to a theology of hyper-Calvinism and others who are very moderate Calvinists.

Since Primitivists include numerous independent associations, often in isolated areas outside the mainstream of Baptist life, it is difficult at times to locate and classify them. When a number of associations correspond with each other or recognize each other as belonging to a certain foundation of faith and practice, one can then list them as a separate Baptist entity. On the other hand, there are small associations which are isolated from almost everyone else. It would be foolish to list them as separate Baptist denominational bodies since it would increase the list of Baptist bodies to an unreasonable length and distort the number of different Baptist groups in the country. There is also the need to study further some church bodies so as to place them in the right category. For this reason this study does not treat individually the Barren River Missionary Baptist Association, Interstate and Foreign Landmark Missionary Baptist

Association, Jasper Baptist Association, Pleasant Valley Baptist Association, New Hope Baptist Association, Truevine Baptist Association, and Wayne Trail Missionary Baptist Association—totaling 216 churches and 27,430 members, even though they are listed as separate bodies in *Churches and Church Membership in the United States 1990* (Atlanta: Glenmary Research Center, 1992). Their statistics, however, are included in the total for Baptists in the USA.

BIBLIOGRAPHY: The corresponding editor possesses a copy of a letter from Clifford A. Grammich of Clarendon Hills, Illinois, to Richard Houseal, a research assistant in the Membership Study of the Association of Statisticians of American Religious Bodies, August 31, 1991, which includes a helpful discussion of some of the very small Baptist groups. Although there has been academic study of Primitive, Duck River, and Old Regular Baptists, there unfortunately has been little study of other Primitivists.

Central Baptist Association

The Central Baptist Association is a single association which extends from Hamilton County, Indiana, to Newberry County, South Carolina, with a concentration of its churches in eastern Tennessee and southwestern Virginia. It numbers 3,297 in thirty-five congregations. The association separated from the Eastern District Primitive Baptist Association and has a tabernacle, children's home, and youth camp at Duffield, Virginia. It is recognized as a separate body in the *Handbook of Denominations in the United States* by Frank S. Mead and Samuel S. Hill and the *Churches and Church Membership in the United States 1990*.

General Association of Baptists (Duck River and Kindred Associations)

The General Association of Baptists, is usually designated as the Duck River and Kindred Associations of Baptists. The Duck River Association, formed in 1826 by separating from the strongly Calvinistic Elk River Association, has served as a nucleus of a group of associations which correspond with each other. It has no central headquarters, but in 1939 this body formed an associational body with the name it bears today. It is a comparatively small body of seven associations with its primary strength in lower Middle Tennessee and northern Alabama. It is the leading Baptist body in Moore County, Tennessee. For many years its membership has remained about the same with between ten and eleven thousand members in around one hundred churches. They are moderately Calvinistic in theology and observe footwashing as an ordinance. Churches generally have Sunday Schools but support no mission or benevolent institutions.

BIBLIOGRAPHY: Forrest Shelton Clark, "A History of the Duck River Baptists," *Quarterly Review*, 33, no. 2 (Jan./Feb./Mar. 1973): 42–52. Arthur C. Piepkorn, *Profiles in Belief* (New York: Harper & Row, 1978), 2:443–44.

Old Missionary Baptists

The *Churches and Church Membership in the United States 1990* study recognizes the Old Missionary Baptist associations as a separate group. This study was able to obtain statistics from three associations—Enon, Siloam, and Wiseman—although there are additional associations related to this group which correspond with one or more of these associations. The three associations number about thirteen thousand members in seventy-three churches, which are located primarily in middle Tennessee and western Kentucky. These Baptists refer to themselves as "old-time" or "old-fashioned" Missionary Baptists and, like many other Primitivists, practice footwashing as a rite.

Regular Baptists

Regular Baptists are part of the Baptist mainstream which joined Separate and Regular Baptists as United Baptists. They have, however, elected to designate themselves as "Regular," which suggests that they maintain the old-time standards of faith and practice from which others have deviated. As most other Baptists, Regular Baptists are moderately Calvinistic. Like Primitivists, however, they have rejected modern methods and most mission, educational, and benevolent institutions. Although enumerated in the past by the U.S. religious census as one body, scholars today note deviations among them and separate them into three groups—Old Regular Baptists, Regular Baptists, and Enterprise Baptists.

A. Old Regular Baptists

These Baptists have kept the older practices of Regular Baptists more faithfully than the other Regular Baptist groups. They expect their ministers to preach by inspiration and not from preparation, engage in lined-singing without musical instruments, observe footwashing, reject Sunday Schools and mission organizations, and refuse to share pulpits with ministers outside their own fellowship. They deny women any role in leadership and oppose their following modern fashion in hairstyle and dress.

Most of the Old Regular associations descend from the New Salem Association or its offshoots. New Salem was organized in eastern Kentucky in 1825 as a United Baptist association but in 1854 changed its name to Regular and then in 1892 began using the designation of Old Regular. *The Churches and Church Membership in the United States 1990* survey located 326 churches with more than fifteen thousand members in seventeen associations. More than half of their churches are in Kentucky with significant numbers in Virginia and West Virginia and some strength in the Great Lakes region.

B. Regular Baptists

Regular Baptists are much like Old Regular Baptists in doctrine but are more open to change in worship and lifestyle. They have allowed Sunday Schools and occasionally use hymnals and musical instruments. *The Churches and Church Membership* survey located 4 associations with almost 4,000 members in 41 churches, located primarily in North Carolina.

C. Enterprise Baptists

The Enterprise Baptist Association in the past has been listed with other Regular Baptists. Today it does not correspond with any Regular Baptist association but only with United Baptists. Some of their churches now refer to themselves as Enterprise Baptist rather than Regular Baptist. Their worship is more open than the Old Regular Baptists. *According to the Churches and Church Membership* survey, this association has 70 churches and more than 4,700 members located primarily in Kentucky and Ohio.

BIBLIOGRAPHY: An excellent study of the Old Regular Baptists is the work by Howard Dorgan, *The Old Regular Baptists of Central Appalachia* (Knoxville: University of Tennessee Press, 1989), which also includes a helpful discussion of the differences between Old Regular and Regular Baptists. A work by a Regular Baptist on the Old Regular Baptists is Rufus Perrigan, *History of Regular Baptist(s) and Their Ancestors and Accessors* (Haysi, Va.: Author, 1961). Also see Chester Raymond Young, "Old Regular Baptists," *Encyclopedia of Religion in the South*, 569–70.

Primitive Baptists

One of the strongest groups of Primitivists is the Primitive Baptists, also called Predestinarian or Old School Baptists. They attacked mission, Bible, and tract societies as well as Sunday Schools, seminaries, and colleges as unbiblical and feared them because they introduced too much organization, were too impersonal, and threatened both the independence of the local church and the status of the unlettered farmer-preacher. For many Primitive Baptists, the demand of these organizations for money was almost like a religious tax. The Primitive Baptists attempted also to retain the primitive patterns of church life, which generally meant untrained ministers who received no stated salaries, monthly preaching, simple church structures, vocal music only, and, for many, footwashing.

In theology, Primitive Baptists shifted from the evangelical Calvinism of most Baptists to a form of hyper-Calvinism, rejecting all modern revival methods, or "means," as well as all organized mission efforts for the conversion of sinners. Preaching was only to edify the Christian and in no way was it an instrument to bring the sinner to repentance and faith, which, in any case, were gifts from God. Primitive Baptists became hardened in their theology and tended to defend Calvinism more than proclaiming the gospel itself.

The first separation of Primitive Baptists from other Baptists occurred in 1827 when the Kehukee Association in North Carolina condemned mission and educational organizations. By 1840 the division was complete. From the beginning the Primitive Baptist movement included two different emphases concerning predestination. The Old Line Primitive Baptists taught "conditional time salvation," which held that the Christian was responsible for the way he exercised the salvation which, by election, God had granted him. Conversely, the Absolute Primitive Baptists believed that God, although not the author of sin, had predestined all things. These two groups are separate today. A third group, Progressive Primitive Baptists, accepted certain innovations and thereby produced another division.

Originally, Primitive Baptists had strength in both the North and South, but today they are predominantly a Southern body. In the U.S. religious census of 1936, White Primitive Baptists numbered about 69,000 in 1,726 churches. According to a statistical survey in 1970 and 1971 of the three Primitive Baptist groups, Elder A. B. Hall of Arab, Alabama, discovered 66,518 members in 1,969 churches. Notwithstanding the enumeration of the *Churches and Church Membership in the United States 1990* survey (which found 39,354 members in 1,159 churches and 164 associations), Hall's study, although now dated and omitting some associations, still remains the best enumeration of membership for Old Line and Absolute Primitive Baptists. Hall included not only associations but also independent churches and calculated each Primitive Baptist group separately. Although their churches are comparatively small, Primitive Baptists appear to be holding their own in spite of increased urbanization in the South.

A. Absoluters

Absolute Primitive Baptists not only believe in God's election in salvation but extend God's sovereign control over all areas of life. They are a small body, probably numbering between six and seven thousand, and are concentrated in Virginia and North Carolina.

B. Old Liners

The Old Liners are more moderate than the Absoluters in respect to predestination, recognizing that individuals are responsible for their daily conduct. They are the most widely dispersed group of Primitive Baptists. *The Primitive Baptist Directory*, 1992, which attempts to list the Old Line churches, records 1,411 congregations. Their strongest states are Georgia, Alabama, Tennessee, Virginia, and Texas and include churches not only throughout the South but also in the Middle West and on the Pacific Coast. One of the foremost converts to the Primitive Baptist cause of the present day is Elder Lasserre Bradley, Jr., a Baptist minister who was rebaptized in 1958. He and fifty-four others became constituent members of the Cincinnati Primitive Baptist Church. Bradley maintains a radio ministry through his Baptist Bible Hour, which he had already begun before becoming a Primitive Baptist.

C. Progressives

Beginning in the early twentieth century, a progressive movement in Georgia produced the Progressive Primitive Baptists, who have accepted musical instruments, Sunday Schools, Bible conferences, homes for the aged, and organizations for men, women, and youth. They even organized a Primitive Baptist Foundation and Birdwood College, which exists today as Thomas County Junior College, a state institution. Although members of this group have gone far in departing from Primitive Baptist practice, they are still strict Calvinists and practice footwashing. Although rejecting their innovations, other Primitive Baptists still recognize them as part of the Primitive Baptist movement. Their greatest strength remains in the state of Georgia.

BIBLIOGRAPHY: Two outstanding dissertations on Primitive Baptists are by Byron Cecil Lambert, *The Rise of the Anti–Mission Baptists: Sources and Leaders, 1800–1840* (Ph.D. dissertation, University of Chicago, 1957; New York: Arno Press, 1980), and Julietta Haynes, *A History of the Primitive Baptists* (Ph.D. dissertation, University of Texas, 1959). An excellent discussion of Primitive Baptists is the article by Arthur C. Piepkorn, "The Primitive Baptists of North America," *Concordia Theological Monthly*, 42, no. 5 (May 1971): 297–24, which was reprinted in *Baptist History and Heritage*, 7, no. 1 (Jan. 1972): 33–51. An old-fashioned standard Primitive Baptist history with statistical data is Sylvester Hassell, *History of the Church of God* (Middletown, N.Y.: Gilbert Beebe's Sons, 1886; reprinted by Turner Lassetter, Atlanta, 1948, 1955). Primitive Baptist libraries which hold associational minutes and other materials are in Carthage, Illinois; Elon College, North Carolina; and Atwood, Tennessee.

Two-Seed-in-the-Spirit Predestinarian Baptists

The progenitor of this body was Daniel Parker (1781–1844). Among his accomplishments, in 1833 he led a congregation from Illinois into Texas—the Pilgrim Predestinarian Regular Baptist Church, the first Baptist church in the territory. Earlier he had become a leading spokesman against organized missions, publishing in Indiana in 1820 *A Public Address*, strongly attacking the Triennial Convention. In 1826 he reinforced his anti-missionism by adopting the "two-seed" doctrine, a type of Manichaeism which he propounded in 1826 in three pamphlets published in Illinois.

This doctrine teaches that individuals are born with either the good seed, which God implanted in Adam and Eve, or the evil seed, which Satan, himself an eternal being, implanted at the fall. The seeds are "in the spirit" and not of the flesh. Since one's eternal fate is determined by the seed he or she has received, mission activity is useless. Followers of this doctrine also reject a future corporeal resurrection. Christ Himself came in a spiritual body and did not suffer death or a physical resurrection. God resurrects His children spiritually as they die to the flesh, and after death their spirits go to God. After death, the spirits of those possessing the evil seed will remain eternally in a spiritual hell.

Although most Primitive Baptists rejected two-seedism, the Two-Seed Baptists have at times been confused with Primitive Baptists since their practices were the same. In addition, their doctrinal statements generally included no explicit two-seed doctrine and almost without exception their associations never included "Two-Seed" in their names and might even correspond with associations who did not hold the doctrine. Primitive Baptists strongly fought the doctrine in Texas, although it gained some support there. One of their most successful areas was a stretch of territory from southern Kentucky through middle Tennessee into northern Alabama, which included three associations which accepted this teaching.

This body's membership has precipitously declined. The U.S. religious census in 1906 claimed there were fifty-five churches and 781 members. In 1961 there were only twelve congregations. In 1991 there was only one remaining association, Trinity River, which included two churches—Little Hope near Jacksboro, Texas (42 members) and Otter Creek in Putnam County, Indiana (20 members). The Concord church in the Highland District near McMinville, Tennessee, existed independently with eight members.

BIBLIOGRAPHY: "Two-Seed-in-the-Spirit Predestinarian Baptists," *Religious Bodies: 1936*, vol. 2, pt. 1 (Washington, D.C.: Bureau of the Census, 1941), 234–38. For an account of the Two-Seed church in Putnam County, Indiana, see Terry E. Miller, "Voices from the Past: The Singing and the Preaching at Otter Creek Church," *Journal of American Folklore*, 88 (July/Sep. 1975): 266–82; and "Otter Creek Church, Indiana; Lonely Bastion of Daniel Parker's 'Two-seedism'," *Foundations*, 18 (Oct./Dec. 1975): 358–76.

United Baptists

As most other Baptists, United Baptists are also part of the main Baptist stream which united Regular and Separate Baptists. While most Baptists have dropped the designation of United, this group, has retained the name. They maintain local associations but do not participate in any Baptist convention. Some churches of the Cumberland River Association in Kentucky have, however, cooperated with the

American Baptist Association, a Landmark Missionary Baptist body. There are differences among them as to the acceptance of progressive measures. Some are more open to programs of Christian education and a trained ministry than others. Many of their churches practice footwashing.

The *Churches and Church Membership in the United States 1990* survey was able to locate 436 churches in 24 associations with a membership of around 54,000. The strength of this body is in Appalachia in eastern Kentucky (the leading Baptist group in two counties), eastern Tennessee, and southwestern West Virginia as well as in the Ozarks of Arkansas and Missouri and in southern Ohio near the Ohio River.

BIBLIOGRAPHY: Arthur C. Piepkorn, *Profiles in Belief* (New York: Harper & Row, 1978), 2:442–43.

FREE WILL/GENERAL BAPTISTS

	Members	Churches
VI. Free Will/General Baptists		
1. Free Will Baptists		
a. National Association of Free Will Baptists (1935)	234,588	2,461
b. Original Free Will Baptists (1961)	33,066	236
c. Independent Free Will Baptist Associations	22,000	295
d. United American Free Will Baptist Church	50,000	250
2. General Association of General Baptists (1870)	73,308	816
3. General Six Principle Baptists (1670)	140	2
4. Separate Baptists in Christ	8,318	100
	421,420	4,160

*F*ree Will and General Baptists advocate Christ's general atonement, free will, and the possibility of falling from grace. The mainstream of Baptist life, which began with the Regular or Particular Baptists, taught Christ's particular, or limited, atonement and God's initiative in salvation. Over the years the Regular Baptist mainstream has come closer to the Free Will/General position in that most of these Baptists now accept Christ's general atonement, reject unconditional election, and place far more stress on man's response to God rather than God's effectual calling. The big theological divide between the two groups of Baptists, however, is over the eternal security of the believer; Regular Baptists advocate eternal security, whereas the Free Will/General Baptists reject it. Unlike Regular Baptists, numbers of whom continue to practice close communion, Free Will/General Baptists have historically practiced open communion. Many of their churches also observe footwashing.

Free Will/General Baptists often include elements of connectionalism not found among Regular Baptists. While Regular Baptists place full authority for ordination in the local church with presbyteries serving only as advisory bodies, the General Association of General Baptists, the Free Will Baptists, and Separate Baptists maintain presbyteries or standing committees on the associational level. These presbyteries assume responsibility in approving ministerial candidates for ordination. Such councils within the General Association of General Baptists and the Free Will Baptists also control a minister's standing. Although recognizing congregational polity, the Original Free Will Baptists and the United American Free Will Baptist Church go even further in their connectionalism by empowering their associations or conferences to make disciplinary decisions in case of conflict.

While Baptists with a Regular Baptist heritage have, as a whole, flourished, Free Will/General Baptists have often had difficulty surviving. Regular Baptists absorbed most of the old General Baptists in North Carolina in the eighteenth century and absorbed most of the Free Will Baptists in the North in the early twentieth century. In addition, Free Will Baptists in the South underwent defections to Alexander Campbell's movement in the nineteenth century and to Pentecostalism in the twentieth century. One major factor for this group's limited growth compared to other Baptists is the fact that its memberships have been largely concentrated in rural areas. This factor is now beginning to change with more of its churches developing in metropolitan areas. The great majority of the churches are comparatively small and located in the South or in border areas influenced by Southern culture.

FREE WILL BAPTISTS

A. National Association of Free Will Baptists

The Free Will Baptist denomination can claim at least four separate points of origin—the General Baptists of eastern North Carolina, the United Baptists of western North Carolina, Free Will Baptists of New England, and the Separate Baptists of Kentucky and Tennessee. The oldest source can be traced back to Paul Palmer and his General Baptist congregation in Chowan County, North Carolina, in 1727. The New England source began as a separate movement in 1780 under Benjamin Randall and spread westward.

Recently discovered records show that the General Baptists in England used the name "Free Willers" near the beginning of the seventeenth century. Later documents trace Palmer's General Baptist successors, especially Joseph and William Parker, to churches that continue as Free Will churches today. The first official Free Will Baptist statement of faith, published in 1812, used the two names interchangeably. Early opponents had called the General Baptist preachers "Free Willers" because they taught the "heresy" that Christ had died for all men. By 1828 the denomination had officially adopted the new name.

In the nineteenth century the denomination witnessed the development of a strict code of conduct and a conservative platform of theology. At the end of the century, the denomination had several characteristics: Arminian and conservative in theology, severe in lifestyle, revivalistic, mission-minded (though the group would have to wait until the next century for a formal cross-cultural mission program), somewhat anti-intellectual, fearful of alliances with other movements, and predominantly rural.

By the late nineteenth century Free Will Baptists began to think of new relationships. The North Carolina group formed a Triennial General Conference in 1896. The new conference included churches from across the South and from as far north as Ohio. Though it was disbanded in 1910, a second General Conference was in place by 1920. In the meantime the New England movement merged in 1911 with the Northern or American Baptists, leaving a small remnant, largely in the Middle West and Southwest. In 1917 these small churches in Nebraska, Texas, Missouri, Kansas, and Oklahoma joined to form the General Co-operative Association of Free Will Baptists. A gift of property in Tecumseh, Oklahoma, made it practical for the new movement to locate its headquarters and its new school in that city.

By 1930 the remnants of the four original groups could be found in these two large conferences or associations: the General Conference in the South and the Co-operative Association in the West. In 1935 these two bodies combined to form the National Association of Free Will Baptists. By bringing together most of the Free Will Baptists in America, the new association provided for an extended and effective national ministry in missions, education, and evangelism. In the context of congregational church government, whose autonomy is jealously guarded, the National Association has served well as an advisory body for both the state associations and local congregations.

The Free Will Baptist of the late twentieth century would not differ significantly from his or her nineteenth-century ancestor. The denomination still continues with an Arminian and conservative theology, congregational government, a relatively severe lifestyle, and a heart for evangelism. Some churches, but not all, practice footwashing. If anything has significantly changed, it is that the old rural character has given way to a more urban and suburban ministry and a new emphasis on education. The denomination has four-year colleges in Tennessee, California, Oklahoma, and North Carolina. It has also expanded its foreign mission program, and today Free Will missionaries serve in nine countries. For a time the National Association was a member of the National Association of Evangelicals but withdrew from this body, leaving it to the local churches to support it if desired. It is not a member of the Baptist World Alliance.

At present the National Association has about 2,500 churches with more than 230,000 members. Growth has come slowly, but the denomination continues to be strong and healthy. Its greatest strength is in North Carolina, Tennessee, Alabama, Arkansas, Missouri, and Oklahoma. In 1991 the association moved into a new headquarters building in Nashville, Tennessee.

William F. Davidson

BIBLIOGRAPHY: For a standard history, see William F. Davidson, *The Free Will Baptists in America, 1727–1984* (Nashville: Randall House Publications, 1985). For a history of the Free Will Baptist movement in the North founded by Benjamin Randall, see Norman Allen Baxter, *History of the Freewill Baptists* (Rochester: American Baptist Historical Society, 1957).

B. Original Free Will Baptists

The Original Free Will Baptists have roots in the ministry of Paul Palmer, who established General Baptist work in North Carolina in the 1720s, organizing in 1727 the first Baptist church in the state. In the nineteenth century the General Baptists of the area adopted the name, Free Will Baptist. In 1912 they organized the "North Carolina State Convention of the Original Free Will Baptist Church of Jesus Christ." The number of churches, members, and cooperating conferences (associations) grew. In 1935 the North Carolina Convention became a charter member of the National Association of Free Will Baptists at which time it dropped "Original" in its title.

In 1961 a division occurred between the North Carolina Convention and the National Association, which resulted in the former's withdrawal from the national body. The division was over polity with the majority of Free Will Baptists in North Carolina upholding the right of an annual conference to discipline a local church, but the differences ran far deeper. Educational philosophies differed—the North Carolina Convention supported a liberal arts school, Mt. Olive College, while the association maintained the FreeWill Baptist Bible College in Nashville. In addition, the North Carolina Convention wished to retain control of its own press and production of Sunday School literature.

In the division, the North Carolina Convention lost many churches but kept a majority of its membership. In 1947 the convention again added "Original" to its name. In 1991 it reported thirty-three thousand members in seven conferences/associations. For some years its membership has been static. All of its churches are in North Carolina except for three in South Carolina and one in Florida. Besides maintaining Mt. Olive College and Free Will Baptist Press, Original Free Will Baptists support retirement homes, a children's home, and an assembly. In its foreign missions program, which began in Mexico in 1962, it also provides support for fields in the Philippines, India, Nepal, and Bulgaria.

BIBLIOGRAPHY: Floyd B. Cherry, *An Introduction to Original Free Will Baptists* (Ayden, N.C.: Free Will Baptist Press Foundation, Inc., c. 1974).

C. Independent Free Will Baptist Associations

A number of Free Will Baptist associations maintain an independent existence outside the National Association. A recent survey of eleven of their associations, using the statistics from seven current associational minutes and supplemented by older statistics for the other four, reveals more than 21,000 members and 286 churches. There are additional associations for which membership figures are unavailable—Western in North Carolina; Stone of Central Indiana; three associations in Oklahoma; and possibly others in West Virginia.

Tennessee with 8,723 members and 104 churches has the largest number of independents. Included in the state is the Free Will Christian Baptist Church of Christ of east central Tennessee, which is divided into two Stone Associations, one western and the other eastern. Tennessee also includes churches in the Muscle Shoals Stateline and Tennessee River Associations, both of which also have churches in Alabama; Toe River Association, with churches also in North and South Carolina; and one church in the French Board Association, whose other churches are in North Carolina. North Carolina, which has the next largest number of independents with around 4,400 members and sixty-three churches, includes churches not only in associations already mentioned but also in the Jack's Creek and Mt. Mitchell Associations. The single largest independent body is the John-Thomas Yearly Meeting, which includes five conferences in four states—Virginia, Kentucky, Ohio, and Indiana—and reports a membership of 6,261 and 94 churches. Of this number Kentucky has 3,450 members in 41 churches and Virginia has 2,614 members in 48 churches.

BIBLIOGRAPHY: For information on the independent associations, see the two works by

Robert E. Picirilli, *History of Free Will Baptist State Associations* (Nashville: Randall House Publications, 1976), and *The History of Tennessee Free Will Baptists* ([Nashville]: Historical Commission of the Tennessee State Association of Free Will Baptists, 1985).

D. United American Free Will Baptist Church

The United American Free Will Baptist Church (or Denomination) is an African-American body with most of its churches in North Carolina. The first church was formed in 1867. Its first general conference was held in 1899, which was incorporated in 1901. In 1966 it established its permanent headquarters in Kinston, North Carolina, where recently it has built an attractive headquarters building. In 1902 it established Kinston College, which ceased to exist in 1931 because of financial reasons. It publishes *The Free Will Baptist Advocate*. This body holds district, quarterly, annual, and general conferences, and since 1903 has published a book of discipline. Besides observing baptism and the Lord's Supper, it also practices footwashing and anointing with oil for the sick.

BIBLIOGRAPHY: For some limited historic data, see the program, United American Free Will Denomination, "Centennial Convocation," 1967. For current information, see "United American Free Will Baptist Denomination, Inc.," in Wardell J. Payne, ed., *Directory of African-American Religious Bodies* (Washington, D.C.: Howard University Press, 1991), 54.

General Association of General Baptists

Benoni Stinson (1789–1869), a Baptist minister in Kentucky and later Indiana, rejected the Calvinism of many of his Baptist contemporaries and preached that "Jesus tasted death for every man" (Heb. 2:9b). After being unable to get his views adopted by his association, which was then in the process of formation, he was determined to leave his Calvinist brethren. In 1823 he became pastor of the newly organized Liberty Baptist Church at Howell, Indiana (now in metropolitan Evansville), a congregation which included in its articles the doctrine of Christ's general atonement. Stinson soon formed three other churches of like faith, which joined the Liberty Church in 1824 to form the Liberty Association of General Baptists.

The movement took root in the joining area of the Ohio, Tennessee, and Mississippi Rivers, spreading in Indiana, Kentucky, Tennessee, Illinois, and Missouri. Although its strength remains today in this area, churches are found in other areas of the Midwest and South and also on the Pacific Coast.

In 1870 delegates from three associations formed the General Association of General Baptists. In time the General Association created a number of boards, including a General Home Mission Board in 1871 and a Foreign Mission Board in 1903. In 1891 General Baptists opened Oakland City College, a liberal arts college which today includes a Graduate School of Theology. In 1886 *The General Baptist Messenger* was launched, which continues as the denomination's chief organ. In 1942 General Baptists began to print their own Sunday School literature. The work of the denomination today is centralized at Poplar Bluff, Missouri, which also includes the Stinson Press.

Today General Baptists have around 60 associations but no state bodies and more than 73,000 members in 816 churches. The association still has a rural base, but increasingly its members live in urban areas. Its foreign mission program provides support for four fields—the Marianas (its earliest), Philippines, Jamaica, and India—with entry planned for Honduras. The General Association is a member of the Baptist World Alliance, the only Arminian Baptist body in the USA to assume this relationship, and the National Association of Evangelicals.

Ollie Latch and Albert W. Wardin, Jr.

BIBLIOGRAPHY: Ollie Latch, *History of the General Baptists* (Poplar Bluff, Mo.: General Baptist Press, 1954). For a later account, see Latch's article, "The General Association of General Baptists," *The Baptist Program*, Feb. 1971, 15–17, 21.

General Six Principle Baptists

The oldest General Baptist group in the United States is the General Six Principle Baptists. They hold to the six principles as outlined in Hebrews 6:1–2, which they interpret as including the rite of confirmation, or the laying on of hands, after baptism for the reception of the gifts of the Holy Spirit. Many Baptists in England and the American colonies, both General and Regular, observed the laying on of hands, but this group made it a test of fellowship.

The Baptist church at Providence, Rhode Island, which had been founded in 1638, in time gained members who held to a general atonement and the laying on of hands. With their gaining control of the church, a division occurred about 1653, when Thomas Olney left with others to form a Calvinistic church. Olney's church died out, but the Six Principle congregation continued and in 1771 dropped its requirement of the laying on of hands for participation in the Lord's Supper. In 1656 members who left the Baptist church of Newport, Rhode Island, formed a second Six Principle church.

With the formation of other congregations, Six Principle Baptists were the leading Baptist body in New England until the Great Awakening in the middle of the eighteenth century. Six Principle Baptists also moved west into New York (first church in 1724) and Pennsylvania (first church in 1821). In 1670 Six Principle Baptists in Rhode Island began a yearly meeting, the first associational body of Baptists in America. In 1824 the Rhode Island body recognized the New York Yearly Conference, which by 1836 had added "Pennsylvania" to its title. With the demise in 1865 of the last New York church, this body has been known as the General Six Principle Baptist Association of Pennsylvania. In 1895 the Rhode Island body incorporated as the General Six Principle Baptist Conference of Rhode Island.

Since the nineteenth century, the Six Principle Baptists have precipitously declined. They were little affected by the First and Second Great Awakenings, failed to maintain themselves in urban centers and, except for a few feeble attempts, never engaged in cooperative missions or publication work. They were also handicapped by the lack of trained ministers who lived in the vicinity of their charges and were supported by their churches. Finally in 1954 the Rhode Island Six Principle Baptists lifted their ban on communion with other Christians.

In 1955 there were only three churches in Rhode Island with 254 members and two small churches in Pennsylvania. In 1984 the Maple Root Church in Coventry suspended its participation in the Rhode Island Conference, leaving only the Wood River Church in Richmond and the Stony Lane Church in North Kingston to hold the last meeting (the 314th) of the Rhode Island Conference. Since then, the Maple Root and Wood River churches have dropped Six Principle from their names and are simply independent Baptist congregations whose pastors fellowship with the Conservative

Baptists. The Stony Lane Church, which has around 120 members, is now the only Six Principle congregation left in the Rhode Island Conference. The Pine Grove Church near Nicholson, Pennsylvania, with around twenty members, is the only Six Principle congregation left in the Pennsylvania Conference. After almost three and a half centuries of existence, this body appears close to extinction.

BIBLIOGRAPHY: The history by Richard Knight, *History of the General or Six Principle Baptists, in Europe and America* (Providence, R.I.: Smith and Parmenter, 1827; reprint, New York: Arno Press, 1980), is an old-fashioned study which included churches who practiced laying on of hands even though not Six Principle. A study with valuable statistical material is the work by Nelson Robert Elliott, *A History of the General Six Principle Baptists in America* (Th.D. dissertation, Southwestern Baptist Theological Seminary, 1958). Two helpful articles are W. T. Whitley, "The Six-Principle Baptists in America," *Chronicle*, 3, no. 1 (Jan. 1940): 3–9, and James E. Taulman, "The Origins of the (General) Six Principle Baptists," *Quarterly Review*, 33, no. 1 (Oct./Dec. 1972): 37–42.

Separate Baptists in Christ

Most Regular Baptists and Separate Baptists in Kentucky merged in 1801 to become United Baptists. In 1803 Baptists of the state refused to recognize the churches in the South District Association, which had refused a corresponding letter from another association, as constituting the true South District Association. These churches nevertheless continued as a separate association and in 1806 took the name of Kentucky Association of Separate Baptists in Christ. Besides the Kentucky Association in the south central section of the state, other associations were formed, including the following five which survive to the present—Nolynn (1819) in central Kentucky, Ambraw (1844) in Illinois, Northern Indiana (1854) and Central Indiana (1870) in Indiana, and Mt. Olive (1892) in Tennessee. Separate Baptists later corresponded with the Christian Unity Association (organized in 1935), a small Arminian body in North Carolina and Virginia.

Separate Baptists have been largely a rural people, served by theologically untrained pastors whose main income has come from secular work. Their preaching style is from an earlier period. Pastors speak with rising emotion by inspiration, not from outline or manuscript. Footwashing is observed as an ordinance once or twice a year with the Lord's Supper. Separate Baptists support Sunday Schools and youth camps but no educational institutions.

In 1877 Separate Baptists formed their first General Association, but it dissolved to be reestablished in 1912. They later overcame their early opposition to institutional missions by forming associational home mission boards and in 1969 Separate Baptist Missions, Inc., which promoted both home and foreign missions. Presbytery boards in the associations exercise final authority in the ordination of ministers and deacons and pass on ministerial credentials. Unlike their Separate Baptist ancestors, who tolerated a latitude of belief, Separate Baptists have made their articles of faith practically a creed.

In 1969 Separate Baptists had 7,734 members in 87 churches in six associations. Since then, the Christian Unity Association, after it had experienced a split, joined the General Association as Separate Baptists in 1965. In 1991 the General Association adopted an article which rejected a literal millennium after Christ's second coming. Upon this decision, the Ambraw Association withdrew in 1991, which was followed in the next year by the North Indiana Association. At the present time the General

Association includes four of the historic associations, the Christian Unity Association, two churches in West Virginia, and a church in Florida for a total of 84 congregations with an estimated membership of about 7,000. If one adds figures of 19 churches and 1,318 members for the withdrawing associations, Separate Baptists have a bit more than 100 churches and around 8,300 members. Separate Baptists support Steve and Rhonda Palmer, missionaries who went in 1994 to serve in Côte d'Ivoire.

> BIBLIOGRAPHY: For an informative review of Separate Baptists, see James Owen Renault, "The Changing Patterns of Separate Baptist Religious Life, 1803–1977," *Baptist History and Heritage*, 14, no. 4 (Oct. 1979): 16–25, 36. For an older history, see Morgan Scott, *History of the Separate Baptist Church* (Indianapolis: Hollenbeck Press, c. 1900).

CALVINISTIC (REFORMED) BAPTISTS

	Members	Churches
VII. Calvinistic (Reformed) Baptists		
A. Reformed/Sovereign Grace Baptists		
1. Reformed Baptists	8,000	200
2. Sovereign Grace Baptists	8,000	200
B. Strict Baptists	n/a	3
	16,000	403

REFORMED/SOVEREIGN GRACE BAPTISTS

R eformed/Sovereign Grace Baptists seek to return to the Puritan heritage of the Regular Baptists of the seventeenth century, a classical period in Baptist development, and recover their theology and ecclesiology. They, by and large, endorse the First London (1646), Second London (1689), and Philadelphia (1742) Confessions of Faith. They oppose, on the one hand, the evangelistic techniques of modern evangelicalism as too superficial and, on the other hand, reject the hyper-Calvinism and anti-missionism of the Primitive Baptists as too sterile. With their adherence to Calvinist tenets, they tend to oppose premillennialism and also reject the tenets of Landmarkism. They approve revivals, if properly conducted, foreign missionaries, Sunday Schools, Bible and pastors' conferences, the publication of literature, and Christian schools. They advocate the independence of the local church and avoid most other denominational structures. Some churches practice a plurality of elders, while others have only one pastor. The movement also seeks to recover the observance of church discipline, a practice which most Baptist churches have lost.

With roots both in the North and the South, Reformed/Sovereign Grace Baptists began to appear in the middle of the 1950s. Some of the impetus of the movement came from the efforts of Rolfe Barnard, an independent Baptist evangelist, and the writings of Arthur W. Pink. Probably the first formal organizational expression of the movement occurred in 1954 when Henry Mahan, pastor of the Thirteenth Street

Baptist Church of Ashland, Kentucky, and an alumnus of Tennessee Temple College of Chattanooga, Tennessee, convened at his church the first meeting of the Sovereign Grace Bible Conference. Annual conferences in other parts of the country have followed, including conferences at the Grace Baptist Church of Carlisle, Pennsylvania, the Calvary Baptist Church of Pine Bluff, Arkansas, and the Greenwood Baptist Church of Pasadena, Texas. The movement has also been advanced by books and periodicals, including such Calvinistic English periodicals as *Banner of Truth* and *Reformation Today*, edited by a Strict Baptist pastor.

The Reformed/Sovereign Grace movement, however, has divided into two camps. One group generally takes the name of Reformed Baptist, while the other is more apt to use the designation of Sovereign Grace Baptist. A local church in either camp may carry Baptist, Reformed Baptist, or Sovereign Grace Baptist in its name or may not use the name Baptist at all. This movement has been growing rather spontaneously both in the USA and abroad and includes a Reformed Baptist movement in England. Churches, however, are generally very small. It is estimated that the two groups of Reformed Baptists are about equal in number of congregations and membership.

The renewed interest in Calvinism among Baptists in the last several decades is not, however, confined to Reformed or Sovereign Grace Baptists. Support for a return to Calvinistic tenets has also appeared among Southern Baptists and other Baptist groups.

BIBLIOGRAPHY: David Scott, "A Survey of Particular Baptists: Their Origins, Doctrine, Dissension and Revival," *Baptist Reformation Review*, 3, no. 1 (spring 1974): 9–26. John Thornbury, "Calvinistic Baptists in America," *Banner of Truth*, Nov. 1968, 32–36. "Sovereign Grace Baptists," *Yearbook of American & Canadian Churches*, 1991, 115.

A. Reformed Baptists

One center of Reformed Baptist strength is in Pennsylvania and surrounding areas. In 1967 the Grace Baptist Church of Carlisle, Pennsylvania, began holding an annual pastors' conference under the leadership of its pastor, Walter Chantry, a graduate of Westminster Theological Seminary. A few years later an annual Reformed Baptist Family Conference was begun, which met on Labor Day weekend. Ten churches, adopting the Philadelphia Confession, established a Reformed Baptist Association. It includes churches in Pennsylvania, Delaware, and New Jersey.

In 1985 in Anderson, Indiana, delegates from Reformed Baptist churches established Reformed Baptist Mission Services (RBMS), a service agency for missions. The doctrinal basis of RBMS is the London Confession of 1689 to which its contributing churches and missionaries must also subscribe. The mission coordinator of RBMS resides in Carlisle. In 1994 thirty-seven churches were members, located from Connecticut to California, and also including a church in Canada.

B. Sovereign Grace Baptists

Sovereign Grace Baptists are a result of differences with Reformed Baptists, which began about 1980, over certain doctrinal points. Sovereign Grace Baptists relate more closely to the First London Confession (1646) rather than the Second London Confession. They are more critical of Covenant theology and place greater stress on the New Covenant. They are also less puritanical. The strength of this movement is in the Midwest, South, and West. One of the leaders in this movement is Jon Zens, editor of *Searching Together*, published in St. Croix, Wisconsin—a periodical which Norbert Ward began in 1972 in Nashville, Tennessee, as the *Baptist Reformation Review*.

STRICT BAPTISTS

*M*ost Strict Baptists are in England, where they separated from the Baptist Union for its toleration of broad theological views and practices and departure from Calvinistic tenets. There are presently three congregations in the USA which are Strict Baptist. In ideology they are closely related to Reformed and Sovereign Grace Baptists.

The first Strict Baptist church was the Salem Church in Cleveland, Ohio, which was begun in 1907 by English immigrants. It stood in alignment with the Gospel Standard group of Strict Baptists in England. The congregations's first pastor was Robert Mills. The church's second pastor, Sidney Sumsion, died in an accident in 1956 while on a visit to England, and the church has ceased to exist. Before his death, Sumsion had organized in 1947 the Hope Strict Baptist Church in Grand Rapids, Michigan, from a small group which had left an independent Baptist church in 1944 because of its association with Baptists who believed in free will. In 1952 the Hope Church changed its name to Zion Strict Baptist Church and purchased a building. Its membership today is nineteen, but its congregation is about ninety.

The Hope Baptist Church of Sheboygan, Wisconsin, traces its roots to a group of immigrants from the Netherlands. After meeting in homes, they erected almost seventy years ago a chapel but had no pastor. The group came under Baptist influence by reading Strict Baptist sermons and by visits of Baptist ministers from Grand Rapids, who in later years were Strict Baptists. They finally called their first pastor in 1989. The third congregation is the Old Paths Strict Baptist Church of Choteau, Montana. When it was a Reformed congregation, it ordained in the 1970s a minister not approved by the Reformed denomination and was cut off. After questioning infant baptism, the congregation began to practice believer's baptism by immersion. Some members were excluded when the church limited baptism to this practice. For a time the congregation cooperated with the Reformed Baptists but, after disagreement with them, it joined the Strict Baptists and was placed by them on three-year probation.

BIBLIOGRAPHY: "'Ebenezer'—Stone of Help," mss., a history of the Zion Strict Baptist Church to about 1960. The editor gained other material from correspondence with J. K. Stehouwer of Grand Rapids, Michigan, and G. L. TenBroeke of Sheboygan, Wisconsin, Strict Baptist pastors.

Appendix I

DISTRIBUTION OF BAPTISTS IN THE UNITED STATES BY REGION AND STATE

A distribution of Baptists in the United States by region and state provides both a perspective on Baptist regional strengths and weaknesses as well as the relative strengths of each Baptist body. In this survey the regions generally follow the census regions of the United States except that Delaware is placed in the Middle Atlantic region, the East and West North Central regions are treated as one Midwest region, and the South Atlantic and East South Central regions are merged into one Southeast region.

The state statistics may not exactly equal the national total for a Baptist body since the two sets of figures may have been gained from different sources or for a different time period. The listing of the number of churches is rather complete, but unfortunately it is often difficult to get figures on church membership for some Baptist groups. The biggest gap in the following tabulation is the membership of the Independent Baptist bodies, although their churches are listed. Nevertheless, the following statistical data will provide a good picture, even though sometimes not always in sharpest focus, of Baptist strength in each region and state.

Many of the state statistics are from *Churches and Church Membership in the United States 1990*. The directories of the Original Free Will Baptists and Progressive Primitive Baptists provided data on both membership and number of churches. Statistics for National Baptist bodies were generally gained from the *Directory of African-American Religious Bodies* (Washington, D.C.: Howard University Press, 1991), or from the editor's efforts through correspondence and telephone. The editor also gained statistics by telephone and correspondence for Conservative Baptists, Independent Free Will Baptists, and Separate Baptists.

For Southern Baptists, the editor generally used 1993 statistics provided to him by this body. Directories of the Independent Baptists and the Old Line Primitive Baptists gave data on the number of Baptist churches for each state but unfortunately no membership statistics. The directory of the American Baptist Churches/USA for 1991 provided information on dual affiliations of its congregations but, except for the District of Columbia and vicinity and Missouri, little information was available on dual affiliations of Southern Baptist churches.

Because of the unavailability of current figures on membership for the American Baptist Association (ABA), the editor used *Churches and Church Membership 1980* for this body. For the General Association of Regular Baptist Churches (GARBC), he frequently used figures he had gathered in the mid-1970s. Fortunately current statistics on the number of churches of the ABA and the GARBC were available from their respective directories. The 1970 study of Absolute Primitive Baptists by A. B. Hall provided data on the number of churches and memberships in associations but not for independent churches by state. Reformed Baptist churches are included as listed in *Missionary Update*, the periodical of Reformed Baptist Mission Services, but no complete listing of Reformed Baptist churches is available. The editor made no effort to include Liberty Baptist Fellowship, Sovereign Grace Baptists, National Primitive Baptists, United American Free Will Baptist Church, or ethnic bodies because of the lack of sufficient data. A new fellowship, Independent Baptist Fellowship of North America, was also not included—many of whose members belong to the GARBC.

ABBREVIATIONS

ABA	American Baptist Association
ABC	American Baptist Churches in the U.S.A.
BBFI	Baptist Bible Fellowship International
BGC	Baptist General Conference
BMA	Baptist Missionary Association
CBA	Conservative Baptist Association
CEN	Central Baptist Association
DR	Duck River and Kindred Baptist Associations
ENT	Enterprise Baptist Association
FB	Fundamental Baptist state bodies related to the Fundamental Baptist Fellowship or the New Testament Baptist Association of Independent Baptist Churches
FBF	Fundamental Baptist Fellowship
FWB	Free Will Baptists, National Association of
FWB-IND	Independent Free Will Baptist associations
FWB-OR	Original Free Will Baptists
GARBC	General Association of Regular Baptist Churches
GEN	General Association of General Baptists
GSPB	General Six Principle Baptists
IBFI	Independent Baptist Fellowship International
IND	Independent Baptist Church—First Baptist Church, Hammond, Indiana
LMB-DR	Landmark Missionary Baptists—Direct Mission
NABC	North American Baptist Conference
NB	National Baptists
NBC	National Baptist Convention, USA, Inc.
NBCA	National Baptist Convention of America, Inc.
NB-IND	National Baptists—Independent churches
NMBC	National Missionary Baptist Convention
NTA	New Testament Association of Independent Baptist Churches
OMB	Old Missionary Baptists
ORB	Old Regular Baptists
PB-AB	Primitive Baptists—Absoluters
PB-OL	Primitive Baptists-Old–Liners
PB-PR	Primitive Baptists—Progressives
PNB	Progressive National Baptist Convention

RB	Regular Baptists
REF	Reformed Baptists
SBC	Southern Baptists
SBF	Southwide Baptist Fellowship
SDB	Seventh Day Baptist General Conference
SEP	Separate Baptists in Christ
ST	Strict Baptists
TSS	Two-Seed-in-the-Spirit Predestinarian Baptists
UB	United Baptists
WBF	World Baptist Fellowship

In the following charts, the first figure is for membership while the second figure is for number of churches. The regions and states are not listed alphabetically but arranged in geographic progression.

NEW ENGLAND REGION

Maine

ABC	26,094	165
CBA	4,914	39
BBFI	n/a	24
SBC	1,614	13
GARBC	n/a	8
FBF	n/a	6
BGC	163	2
FWB	87	1
BMA	24	1
	32,896	259

New Hampshire

ABC*	14,892	93
CBA	3,128	29
BBFI	n/a	20
SBC	2,513	10
FBF	n/a	5
GARBC	n/a	4
FWB	98	1
NBC*	400	2
BGC	26	2
ABA	n/a	1
	21,057	167
Dual affiliation	-400	-2
	20,657	165

*2 ABC churches dually affiliated with NBC.

Vermont

ABC	6,987	63
SBC	670	16
BBFI	n/a	9
CBA	144	3

FBF	<u>n/a</u>	<u>2</u>
	7,801	93

Massachusetts

ABC*	54,417	261
NBC/PNB*	15,600	48
BBFI**	n/a	56
SBC*	7,751	55
CBA*	6,029	48
BGC*	3,597	26
FBF**	n/a	9
GARBC	n/a	6
SBF**	n/a	3
REF	n/a	1
ABA	<u>n/a</u>	<u>1</u>
	87,394	514
Dual affiliation	<u>n/a</u>	<u>-19</u>
		495

*17 ABC churches dually affiliated—10 with NBC, 4 with PNB, 1 with BGC, 1 with CBA, and 1 with SBC.
**2 dual affiliations with BBFI, FBF, and SBF.

Rhode Island

ABC*	17,824	77
BBFI	n/a	15
NBC/PNB*	2,000	6
SBC	1,506	7
CBA	723	6
SDB	356	3
GSPB	120	1
BGC	94	2
FWB	34	1
GARBC	n/a	2
FBF	n/a	1
SBF	<u>n/a</u>	<u>1</u>
	22,657	122
Dual affiliation	<u>-2,000</u>	<u>-6</u>
	20,657	116

*4 ABC churches dually affiliated with PNB and 2 with NBC.

Connecticut

ABC*	39,470	127
NBC/PNB*	19,800	66
SBC	7,252	32
BBFI**	n/a	24
BGC	1,981	13
CBA	1,780	16
FBF**	n/a	16
GARBC	n/a	5
SBF**	n/a	3
SDB	73	2
NABC	30	1
REF	n/a	1
ABA	n/a	1
	70,386	307
Dual affiliation	n/a	-47
		260

*41 ABC churches dually affiliated—30 with NBC, 8 with PNB, and 3 with NBC and PNB.
**6 dual affiliations with BBFI, FBF, and SBF.

*B*aptists in America first appeared in New England and have played an important historic role in the region. New England Baptists have been an influential body and are located in every New England county except two in Vermont (Grand Isle and Lamoille), but they never attained enough strength to dominate any one section of the region. Although Baptists are the largest Protestant body in Maine and are about equal with the Episcopalians in Rhode Island, they are a small body compared to the Roman Catholic Church. From available figures, all Baptists number about 225,000.

The American Baptist Churches/USA is the dominant Baptist body in each New England state, but it continues to decline. At the end of World War II its membership numbered 225,000; in 1980, 176,500; and today around 160,000 in 786 churches, which include a number of congregations dually affiliated with National Baptists. Conservative Baptists (141 churches) and Baptist General Conference (45 churches) have been static in membership, while the southern-oriented groups, particularly the Southern Baptist Convention (111 churches) and Baptist Bible International (148 churches) are showing surprising growth in both churches and membership, although still comparatively small bodies.

MIDDLE ATLANTIC REGION

New York

NBC/PNB*	250,000	430
ABC*	186,307	584
GARBC	19,451	149
SBC*	12,400	178
CBA*	12,076	98
BBFI**	n/a	75
BGC	1,549	11
NABC	1,530	12
FBF**	n/a	9
WBF**	n/a	6
SBF**	n/a	4
BMA	161	4
REF	n/a	3
IBFI**	n/a	2
ABA	n/a	1
NTA	n/a	1
	483,474	1,567
Dual affiliation	n/a	-136
		1,431

*132 ABC churches dually affiliated—93 with NBC, 29 with PNB, 3 with NBC and PNB, 2 with CBA, 1 with SBC, 1 with PNB and SBC, and 1 with NBC and SBC.
** 4 dual affiliations with BBFI, FBF, IBFI, SBF, and WBF.

New Jersey

NBC/PNB*	69,000	234
ABC*	67,409	254
GARBC	6,507	33
SBC*	6,459	56
CBA	6,000	53
BBFI**	n/a	26
SBF**	n/a	10
SDB	474	4
NABC	252	4
FBF	n/a	4
BGC	159	1

FWB	78	2
BMA	50	2
ABA	n/a	2
REF	n/a	1
WBF**	n/a	1
	156,388	687
Dual affiliation	n/a	-74
		613

*67 ABC churches dually affiliated—65 with NBC or PNB or both, 1 with SBC and NBC, and 1 with SBC.
**6 dual affiliations with BBFI, SBF, and WBF.

Pennsylvania

NBC/PNB*	250,000	400
ABC*	92,157	437
SBC	24,450	146
GARBC	10,894	81
CBA	10,136	56
BBFI**	n/a	67
SBF**	n/a	36
WBF**	n/a	34
FBF**	n/a	17
BGC	2,592	16
IBFI**	n/a	14
NBCA*	1,930	13
NABC	1,462	10
PB-OL	n/a	5
ABA	n/a	5
FWB	346	4
REF	n/a	4
SDB	129	3
RB	95	2
GSPB	20	1
	394,211	1,351
Dual affiliation	n/a	-88
		1,263

*58 ABC churches dually affiliated—57 with NBC, PNB, or both, and 1 NBCA.
**30 dual affiliations with BBFI, FBF, IBFI, SBF, WBF.

Delaware

SBC	4,515	14
NBC/PNB*	3,928	19
ABC*	3,379	10
BBFI**	2,600	13
BGC	762	2
FWB	496	4
GARBC	257	5
SBF**	n/a	3
ABA	280	1
CBA	179	1
PB-OL	<u>n/a</u>	<u>2</u>
	16,396	74
Dual affiliation	<u>n/a</u>	<u>-5</u>
		69

*3 ABC churches dually affiliated with NBC or PNB or both.
**2 dual affiliations with BBFI and SBF.

*W*ith large Roman Catholic and Jewish populations, Baptists are a comparatively small minority in the Middle Atlantic states (3.5 percent of the population). Baptists and Methodists, however, are the two largest Protestant bodies in the area. There are Baptist churches in every county of the region except one—Forest County in Pennsylvania. The African-American National Baptists with more than half the Baptist population are by far the largest Baptist group. In the above enumeration, they are, however, undercounted since no statistics were available for two bodies of the National Baptist Convention of America—General Baptist State Convention of New York and the Garden State Missionary Baptist State Convention of New Jersey.

The American Baptist Churches/USA is the next largest body with around 350,000 members. A number of its churches are dually affiliated with the National Baptists. This region is this body's heartland, containing its headquarters and some of its leading educational institutions. It has about two-thirds of all White Baptists in the region, and its numbers have been holding steady in recent years. From available statistics, it appears that Southern Baptists, Independent Baptists, General Association of Regular Baptists, and Conservative Baptists all have constituencies from 25 to 50 thousand members. The General Association of Regular Baptists has its primary strength in western New York and western Pennsylvania, while Conservative strength is primarily in eastern New York and New Jersey.

MIDWEST REGION

Ohio

NBC/PNB*	232,000	672
SBC*	153,343	506
ABC*	101,688	337
BBFI**	n/a	216
GARBC	27,908	191
FWB	11,336	150
WBF**	n/a	126
SBF**	n/a	50
IBFI**	n/a	49
UB	3,772	49
BGC	2,811	17
NBCA	2,640	22
ENT	1,864	34
NABC*	1,755	7
CBA	1,672	11
ABA	1,047	9
PB-OL	n/a	35
ORB	785	22
FBF**	n/a	12
BMA	150	1
OMB	136	2
FWB-IND	107	3
REF	n/a	2
SEP	n/a	1
SDB	26	1
	543,040	2,525
Dual affiliaton	n/a	-158
		2,367

*47 ABC churches dually affiliated—45 with NBC/PBC, 1 with NABC, and 1 with SBC.
**111 dual affilations with BBFI, FBF, IBFI, SBF, and WBF.

Indiana

NBC/PNB*	130,000	193
ABC*	106,106	397
SBC*	98,800	322

IND	75,000	1
BBFI**	n/a	132
GARBC	21,522	126
NMBC	18,706	105
GEN	10,951	106
NBCA*	4,100	55
PB-OL	n/a	40
UB	2,435	20
FWB	1,869	27
SBF**	n/a	26
SEP	n/a	25
ABA	1,615	19
WBF**	n/a	15
IBFI**	n/a	10
FBF**	n/a	7
BGC	647	7
ORB	384	17
FWB-IND	n/a	6
PB-PR	229	5
BMA	264	3
CEN	226	3
CBA	134	2
REF	n/a	2
NABC	66	1
ENT	56	1
TSS	<u>20</u>	<u>1</u>
	473,130	1,674
Dual affiliation	<u>n/a</u>	<u>-39</u>
		1,635

*9 ABC churches dually affiliated—6 with NBC, 1 with PNB, 1 with NBCA, and 1 with SBC.
**30 dual affiliations with BBFI, FBF, IBFI, SBF, and WBF.

Illinois

SBC*	240,498	941
NBCA*	190,000	150
ABC*	77,140	296
NBC/PNB*	77,000	174

BBFI**	n/a	108
FB**	15,000	78
BGC*	13,252	79
GARBC	10,862	77
GEN	8,363	139
CBA	6,638	35
FWB	4,229	41
PB-OL	n/a	36
NABC	1,876	14
SBF**	n/a	12
BMA	1,746	12
ABA	1,245	14
SEP	525	10
WBF**	n/a	3
IBFI**	n/a	2
PB-PR	80	2
SDB	55	1
ORB	54	2
UB	29	1
REF	n/a	1
	648,592	2,228
Dual affiliation	n/a	-40
		2,188

*29 ABC churches dually affiliated—14 with NBC, 8 with PNB, 1 with NBCA, 5 with SBC, and 1 with BGC.
**11 dual affilations with BBFI, FB, IBFI, SBF, and WBF.

Michigan

NBC/PNB*	185,000	400
ABC*	53,812	176
SBC*	50,382	254
GARBC	34,902	220
BBFI**	n/a	115
NMBC	31,500	90
FB**	15,000	60
WBF**	n/a	55
BGC	7,528	53
IBFI**	n/a	28

NBCA	6,500	21
NABC	5,353	22
CBA	4,553	20
SBF**	n/a	17
FWB	3,998	33
GEN	3,410	44
BMA	1,663	15
ABA	1,225	13
ORB	412	11
PB-OL	n/a	8
SDB	217	2
OMB	121	1
UB	26	1
ST	19	1
REF	<u>n/a</u>	<u>1</u>
	405,621	1,661
Dual affiliation	<u>n/a</u>	<u>-66</u>
		1,595

*19 ABC churches dually affiliated—17 with NBC/PNB and 2 with SBC.
**47 affiliations with BBFI, FB, IBFI, SBF, and WBF.

Wisconsin

NBC*	40,000	78
ABC*	15,386	84
FB**	12,000	85
SBC	9,868	51
BGC	6,134	58
GARBC	3,370	39
BBFI**	n/a	28
NABC*	2,557	13
CBA	944	12
SDB	614	7
WBF**	n/a	4
ABA	n/a	2
ST	n/a	1
IBFI**	n/a	1
SBF	n/a	1
PB-OL	n/a	1

UB	9	1
	90,882	466
Dual affiliation	n/a	-13
		453

*6 ABC churches dually affiliated—4 with NBC and 2 with NABC.
**7 dual affiliations with BBFI, FB, IBFI, and WBF.

Minnesota

BGC	25,153	142
NBC/PNB*	20,000	28
ABC*	10,136	39
FB**	7,045	68
CBA	4,800	48
SBC	4,714	42
GARBC	2,097	27
NABC	1,456	10
BBFI**	n/a	10
IBFI**	n/a	2
SBF**	n/a	2
ABA	n/a	2
SDB	97	1
WBF	n/a	1
	75,498	422
Dual affiliation	n/a	-12
		410

*7 ABC churches dually affiliated with NBC/PNB.
**5 dual affiliations with BBFI, FB, IBFI, and SBF.

Iowa

ABC*	25,619	124
GARBC	11,439	110
SBC	11,461	64
NBC*	7,000	33
BBFI**	n/a	36
BGC*	4,768	34
CBA	2,811	17
NABC	2,205	14
WBF**	n/a	8

PB-OL	n/a	7
SBF	n/a	3
IBFI**	n/a	2
FBF	n/a	1
NTA	<u>n/a</u>	<u>1</u>
	65,303	454
Dual affiliation	<u>n/a</u>	<u>-5</u>
		449

*3 ABC churches dually affiliated—2 with NBC and 1 with BGC.
**2 dual affiliations with BBFI, IBFI, and WBF.

Missouri

SBC*	637,328	1,861
NBC/PNB*	37,000	772
BBFI**	n/a	175
FWB	15,686	174
GEN	15,224	220
NBCA	11,500	65
ABC*	9,369	21
BMA	8,562	95
PB-OL	n/a	50
UB	2,514	30
FWB-IND	1,775	28
ABA	1,578	19
SBF**	n/a	14
GARBC	1,559	13
IBFI**	n/a	11
WBF**	n/a	7
BGC	396	5
PB-PR	160	2
SDB	83	3
NABC	51	1
FBF	<u>n/a</u>	<u>1</u>
	742,785	3,567
Dual affiliation	<u>n/a</u>	<u>-26</u>
		3,541

*7 ABC churches dually affiliated—5 with SBC and 2 with NBC.
**19 dual affiliations with BBFI, IBFI, SBF, and WBF.

Kansas

SBC*	77,718	231
ABC*	58,385	249
BBFI**	n/a	142
NBC*	28,748	117
NBCA	8,776	28
WBF**	n/a	41
GARBC	2,974	32
IBFI**	n/a	15
ABA	2,220	12
NABC	1,436	14
BMA	1,339	11
FWB	501	9
SBF**	n/a	6
FBF**	n/a	2
SDB	133	2
PB-OL	n/a	2
BGC	<u>24</u>	<u>1</u>
	182,254	914
Dual affiliation	<u>n/a</u>	<u>-58</u>
		856

*8 ABC churches dually affiliated—5 with NBC and 3 with SBC.
**50 dual affiliations with BBFI, FBF, IBFI, SBF, and WBF.

Nebraska

ABC*	12,207	62
SBC	10,593	38
NBC*	8,000	37
BGC*	2,906	33
BBFI**	n/a	23
GARBC	1,219	15
WBF**	n/a	11
NABC	219	5
FBF**	n/a	4
IBFI	n/a	3
SDB	189	1
CBA	65	2

FWB	58	2
ABA	n/a	2
PB-OL	n/a	2
NTA**	n/a	1
REF	<u>n/a</u>	<u>1</u>
	35,456	242
Dual affiliation	<u>n/a</u>	<u>-10</u>
		232

*3 ABC churches dually affiliated—2 with NBC and 1 with BGC.
**7 dual affiliations with BBFI, FBF, NTA, and WBF.

South Dakota

ABC	6,623	34
SBC	5,791	48
NABC	3,402	23
BGC	2,871	19
FB	600	8
BBFI**	n/a	8
GARBC	250	5
WBF**	n/a	2
SBF**	n/a	1
IBFI**	n/a	1
SDB	30	1
FWB	<u>25</u>	<u>1</u>
	19,592	151
Dual affiliation	<u>n/a</u>	<u>-3</u>
		148

**3 dual affiliations with BBFI, IBFI, SBF, and WBF.

North Dakota

NABC	4,663	34
SBC	2,737	20
ABC	1,856	19
BBFI	n/a	7
CBA	464	2
BGC	357	6
IBFI	<u>n/a</u>	<u>1</u>
	10,077	89

*T*he Middle West with its metropolitan centers, numerous small towns, and extensive rural areas is a cross section of America and of Baptist life. Ecumenical mainline Baptists, evangelical conservative Baptists, northern-oriented Fundamental bodies, Southern Baptists, southern-oriented Independent Baptists, and African-American National Baptists are all well represented and are often intermixed. The Roman Catholic Church is the largest religious body, but Baptists, closely following the Lutherans, are third in strength. Baptists are particularly strong in areas that border the South, such as in Missouri and southern Illinois. They are weak, however, in the north and west of the area, including Wisconsin, Minnesota, North Dakota, South Dakota, and Nebraska. These are states with large Roman Catholic and Lutheran populations and few large metropolitan centers. A number of counties in these states have no Baptist churches of any kind.

Southern Baptists are the single largest Baptist body; they lead in Missouri and Kansas and are approaching the lead in South Dakota and Nebraska. In addition, they are the largest predominantly White Baptist body in Ohio and Illinois and will undoubtedly soon gain the same standing in Indiana and Michigan. National Baptists with more than one million members are well represented in the metropolitan areas of Ohio, Indiana, Illinois, Michigan, and Wisconsin. Southern-oriented Independent Baptists with more than 1,200 churches have some of their largest churches in the area and are well represented in Ohio, Indiana, Illinois, Michigan, Missouri, and Kansas.

At the beginning of the century, Northern Baptists (today the American Baptist Churches/USA) could claim most of the White Baptist churches of the region within its constituency. With more than 475,000 members, American Baptists still claim a significant membership in the middle section of the region—in Ohio, Indiana, Illinois, Iowa, and Kansas. They have, however, lost most of their churches in Missouri and southern Illinois to Southern Baptists. Because of the fundamentalist controversy and the desire for independence of Baptist bodies with Nordic European roots, they also have lost heavily in the northern tier of states—Michigan, Wisconsin, Minnesota, North Dakota, and South Dakota.

Northern-oriented fundamentalist bodies—such as the General Association of Regular Baptist Churches, Fundamental Baptist Fellowship, and the New Testament Association or related state bodies—show strength in Ohio, Indiana, Illinois, Michigan, Wisconsin, Minnesota, and Iowa and also maintain schools in the area. The Conservative Baptists in the region, however, are comparatively weak, having lost important constituencies to the FBF and NTA. The Baptist General Conference, with Swedish roots, is the leading Baptist body in Minnesota, where it maintains a college and seminary. The North American Baptist Conference, with German roots, leads in North Dakota and maintains a seminary in South Dakota. Four of the conservative evangelical/fundamentalist bodies have their headquarters in the Chicago area.

SOUTHEASTERN REGION

Maryland

NBC/PNB*	169,000	159
SBC*	109,217	325
ABC*	30,039	67

BBFI**	n/a	49
SBF**	n/a	20
NBCA	4,000	18
GARBC	1,912	14
ABA	701	11
FWB	402	3
FBF**	n/a	7
WBF**	n/a	4
IBFI**	n/a	3
PB-OL	n/a	7
RB	251	2
CBA	212	3
ORB	48	1
NABC	44	1
SDB	31	1
BGC	27	1
	315,884	696
Dual affiliation	n/a	-78
		618

*57 ABC churches dually affiliated—42 with SBC, 2 with SBC and PNB, 6 with PNB, and 7 with NBC.
**19 dual affiliations with BBFI, FBF, IBFI, SBF, and WBF.

District of Columbia

NBC/PNB*	43,000	95
ABC*	28,560	39
SBC*	10,612	32
SDB	80	1
CBA	30	1
BBF	n/a	1
	82,282	169
Dual affiliation	-10,000	-34
	72,282	135

*29 ABC churches dually affiliated—24 with SBC and 5 with SBC and NBC/PNB.

Virginia

SBC*	606,157	1,535
NBC/PNB*	253,000	1,148
NBCA*	75,000	350

BBFI**	n/a	155
ABC*	41,399	88
FWB	9,688	98
SBF**	n/a	72
PB-OL	n/a	102
FWB-IND	2,614	48
ORB	1,903	46
FBF**	n/a	36
PB-AB	1,557	59
CEN	621	14
WBF**	n/a	13
GARBC	n/a	9
IBFI**	n/a	8
ABA	376	3
RB	271	3
CBA	n/a	2
BMA	150	1
BGC	72	1
PB-PR	35	1
REF	n/a	1
	992,843	3,793
Dual affiliation	n/a	-94
		3,699

*47 ABC churches dually affiliated—39 with NBC/PNB, 3 with NBCA, 1 with NBCA and PNB, 3 with SBC, and 1 with SBC and NBC/PNB.
**45 dual affiliations with BBFI, FBF, IBFI, SBF, and WBF.

West Virgina

ABC*	107,359	533
SBC	38,319	144
NBC*	12,000	250
FWB	11,753	179
BBFI**	n/a	55
WBF**	n/a	55
SBF**	n/a	42
FBF**	n/a	20
GARBC	n/a	18
UB	2,426	19
PB-OL	n/a	37

ORB	1,750	34
ABA	429	6
IBFI**	n/a	4
SDB	334	3
SEP	n/a	2
OMB	<u>33</u>	<u>2</u>
	174,403	1,403
Dual affiliation	<u>n/a</u>	<u>-29</u>
		1,374

*1 ABC church dually affiliated with NBC.
**28 dual affiliations with BBFI, FWB, IBFI, SBF, and WBF.

Kentucky

SBC	774,082	2,297
NB*	160,000	649
UB	35,945	250
GEN	19,811	171
FWB	13,089	129
BBFI**	n/a	74
ORB	9,562	181
SEP	4,924	55
FWB-IND	3,450	41
SBF**	n/a	21
PB-OL	n/a	67
OMB	3,030	16
ENT	2,846	35
WBF**	n/a	11
ABC*	742	4
IBFI**	n/a	4
CEN	372	4
GARBC	n/a	2
PB-AB	63	5
BGC	46	1
BMA	33	1
FBF	n/a	1
CBA	n/a	1
REF	<u>n/a</u>	<u>1</u>
	1,027,995	4,021

Dual affiliation	n/a	<u>-22</u>
		3,999

*2 ABC churches dually affiliated with NB.
**20 dual affiliations with BBFI, IBFI, SBF, and WBF.

Tennessee

SBC	1,108,739	2,836
NBC/PNB*	139,393	470
NBCA*	25,369	134
FWB	25,247	219
BBFI**	n/a	90
SBF**	n/a	73
OMB	9,755	51
FWB-IND	8,723	104
DR	7,035	71
PB-OL	n/a	117
NMBC*	6,373	9
UB	5,847	42
ABC*	4,592	12
WBF**	n/a	16
FBF**	n/a	13
ABA	4,240	16
GEN	3,311	24
CEN	1,878	12
BMA	1,507	11
PB-PR	305	8
IBFI**	n/a	6
SEP	n/a	3
GARBC	n/a	2
PB-AB	59	4
SDB	40	2
ORB	19	1
TSS	<u>8</u>	<u>1</u>
	1,352,440	4,347
Dual affiliation	n/a	<u>-42</u>
		4,305

*11 ABC churches dually affiliated—9 with NBC/PNB, 1 with NBCA, and 1 with NMBC.
**31 dual affiliations with BBFI, FBF, IBFI, SBF, and WBF.

North Carolina

SBC*	1,200,711	3,554
NB*	425,000	1,700
FWB-OR	31,384	232
FWB	29,373	230
SBF**	n/a	147
BBFI**	n/a	146
FWB-IND	4,391	63
FBF**	n/a	46
ABC*	22,212	37
PB-AB	2,852	155
PB-OL	n/a	86
RB	3,321	34
ABA	71	3
IBFI**	n/a	2
CBA	60	1
GARBC	n/a	1
BMA	n/a	1
REF	n/a	1
ORB	<u>20</u>	<u>2</u>
	1,719,395	6,441
Dual affiliation	<u>n/a</u>	<u>-80</u>
		6,361

*31 ABC churches dually affiliated with NB and 5 with SBC.
**49 affiliations with BBFI, FBF, IBFI, and SBF.

South Carolina

SBC	726,752	1,799
NB*	400,000	1,700
FWB	14,122	117
BBFI**	n/a	48
SBF**	n/a	44
FBF**	n/a	24
ABC*	1,294	3
PB-OL	n/a	10
ABA	545	9
CBA	257	2
CEN	200	2

PB-AB	128	7
WBF**	n/a	3
IBFI**	n/a	3
FWB-OR	117	3
FWB-IND	95	2
SDB	77	2
REF	<u>n/a</u>	<u>1</u>
	1,143,587	3,779
Dual affiliation	<u>n/a</u>	<u>-30</u>
		3,749

*3 ABC churches dually affiliated with NB.
**27 dual affiliations with BBFI, FBF, IBFI, SBF, and WBF.

Georgia

SBC*	1,287,237	3,092
NB*	500,000	800
SBF**	n/a	96
BBFI**	n/a	80
FWB	9,534	118
ABC*	9,114	16
PB-OL	n/a	207
PB-PR	6,265	79
WBF**	n/a	33
ABA	1,400	22
FBF**	n/a	15
IBFI**	n/a	9
GARBC	n/a	4
BMA	153	1
DR	121	2
PB-AB	91	9
REF	n/a	1
SDB	<u>35</u>	<u>1</u>
	1,813,950	4,585
Dual affiliation	<u>n/a</u>	<u>-47</u>
		4,538

*11 ABC churches dually affiliated—10 with NB and 1 with SBC.
**36 affiliations with BBFI, FBF, IBFI, SBF, and WBF.

Florida

SBC	992,697	1,809
NBC/PNB*	500,000	728
NBCA*	70,000	203
BBFI**	n/a	128
WBF**	n/a	126
ABA	15,520	107
SBF**	n/a	72
IBFI**	n/a	44
ABC*	7,805	33
FWB	6,103	77
GARBC	n/a	48
PB-OL	n/a	74
BGC	1,819	20
BMA	1,129	11
CBA	861	13
PB-PR	366	12
FBF**	n/a	8
SDB	233	5
ORB	198	6
PB-AB	116	8
NTA	n/a	2
NABC	85	2
FWB-OR	n/a	1
REF	n/a	1
SEP	n/a	1
UB	<u>15</u>	<u>1</u>
	1,596,947	3,540
Dual affiliation	<u>n/a</u>	<u>-146</u>
		3,394

*11 ABC churches dually affiliated—7 with NBC/PNB and 4 with NBCA.
**135 dual affiliations with BBFI, FBF, IBFI, SBF, and WBF.

Alabama

SBC	1,069,758	3,079
NBC/PNB*	645,000	2,555
NBCA	21,852	133
FWB	19,170	168

PB-OL	n/a	150
BBFI**	n/a	72
SBF**	n/a	47
ABA	4,476	33
DR	3,516	29
ABC*	2,025	3
BMA	1,769	20
WBF**	n/a	9
FBF**	n/a	9
IBFI**	n/a	5
PB-AB	671	61
PB-PR	418	6
SDB	<u>53</u>	<u>2</u>
	1,768,708	6,381
Dual affiliation	<u>n/a</u>	<u>-13</u>
		6,368

*2 ABC churches dually affiliated with NBC.
*11 affiliations with BBFI, FBF, IBFI, SBF, and WBF.

Mississippi

SBC	693,293	1,994
NPC/PNB*	367,000	917
NBCA	36,059	346
BMA	30,726	185
PB-OL	n/a	86
FWB	4,919	59
BBFI**	n/a	35
ABA	4,072	35
SBF**	n/a	13
WBF**	n/a	2
IBFI**	n/a	2
FBF	n/a	2
ABC*	350	2
SDF	<u>31</u>	<u>1</u>
	1,136,450	3,679
Dual affiliation	<u>n/a</u>	<u>-7</u>
		3,672

*1 ABC church dually affiliated with NBC.
**6 dual affiliations with BBFI, IBFI, SBF, and WBF.

B aptists are the predominant body in the Southeastern region and are present in every county. Except in Maryland, where Roman Catholics are far in the lead, Baptists are the largest religious body in every state as well as the District of Columbia. Methodists, however, are the strongest Protestant body among the White population in Maryland and almost equaling Baptist strength in West Virginia. In Florida the Roman Catholic Church, with a large Cuban constituency, almost equals Baptists there.

The Southern Baptist Convention with around 8.5 million members in more than twenty-two thousand churches is by far the largest Baptist body, followed by National Baptists, ranging between 3 and 4 million adherents in possibly twelve thousand churches. Because of sympathy for the Union cause during the Civil War, the majority of Baptists in West Virginia are members of the American Baptist Churches/USA. This body also has congregations in the other states, but they are predominantly Black and dually aligned with some National Baptist body. Independent Baptist churches, including both the southern-oriented groups and the Fundamental Baptist Fellowship and numbering more than 2,400 congregations, are rather well distributed throughout the region except in Maryland, District of Columbia, and Mississippi.

There are some significant differences between the coastal area and the territory west of the Appalachian Mountains. The coastal region rejected Landmarkism, while the western area was greatly influenced by it. One of the strongest areas of support for the the Cooperative Baptist Fellowship, a moderate Southern Baptist group, is in Virginia and North Carolina. In addition, Maryland, District of Columbia, Virginia, and North Carolina include more Black churches dually affiliated with the American Baptists than elsewhere in the region.

This area contains at least three Baptist subregions. One is in eastern North Carolina, the historical heartland of Free Will Baptists, where they still exhibit considerable strength. Another subregion is in southern Florida, where many Northerners have settled and where northern-oriented Baptists have established some churches. A third subregion is southern Appalachia, including western Virginia, western North Carolina, eastern Kentucky, eastern Tennessee, and West Virginia. This is a mountainous area, comparatively isolated from the rest of the nation, which includes many small rural or small-town congregations. This is a territory where, not surprisingly, primitivism has been able to survive in some strength. Regular Baptists, Old Regular Baptists, Enterprise Baptists, Central Baptists, Primitive Baptists, and United Baptists all are present. Free Will Baptists are also widely distributed, either belonging to the National Association or independent associations.

TRANS-MISSISSIPPI SOUTH REGION

Louisiana

SBC*	598,223	1,361
NBC/PNB	200,000 (?)	500 (?)
NBCA	84,900	290
ABA	15,140	73

BBFI**	n/a	44
BMA	8,309	41
NMBC	3,018	66
WBF**	n/a	22
IBFI**	n/a	15
SBF**	n/a	7
ABC*	2,359	6
PB-OL	n/a	23
FWB	345	5
FBF**	n/a	2
NABC	67	1
PB-PR	58	1
GARC	n/a	1
REF	<u>n/a</u>	<u>1</u>
	912,419	2,459
Dual affiliation	<u>n/a</u>	<u>-27</u>
		2,432

*1 church dually affiliated with ABC and SBC.
**26 dual affiliations with BBFI, FBF, IBFI, SBF, and WBF.

Arkansas

SBC	507,182	1,313
NBC	90,027	944
ABA	88,528	521
BMA	61,979	365
FWB	20,167	201
BBFI**	n/a	53
NBCA	3,200	40
PB-OL	n/a	48
UB	1,210	20
SBF**	n/a	8
WBF**	n/a	5
IBFI**	n/a	5
GARBC	n/a	7
BGC	257	1
PB-AB	219	16
SDB	183	4

ABC	46	1
NTA	n/a	1
	772,998	3,553
Dual affiliation	n/a	-9
		3,544

**9 dual affiliations with BBFI, IBFI, SBF, and WBF.

Oklahoma

SBC	780,675	1,496
NBC/PNB*	60,000	300
FWB	20,129	241
BBFI**	n/a	108
ABA	12,821	99
NMBC	10,000	100
BMA	7,803	52
NBCA	4,500	45
IBFI**	n/a	21
ABC*	1,897	13
PB-OL	n/a	25
WBF**	n/a	17
SBF**	n/a	5
NABC	347	5
GARBC	n/a	1
REF	n/a	1
SDB	30	1
	898,202	2,530
Dual affiliation	n/a	-27
		2,503

*1 church dually affiliated with ABC and NBC.
**26 dual affiliations with BBFI, IBFI, SBF, and WBF.

Texas

SBC*	2,609,599	4,435
NBCA*	404,798	1,525
NBC/PNB*	225,000 (?)	750 (?)
BBFI**	n/a	450
BMA	98,509	498

ABA	45,361	288
WBF**	n/a	232
IBFI**	n/a	210
PB-OL	n/a	131
SBF**	n/a	38
ABC*	10,046	24
FWB	3,883	55
NABC	1,262	14
GARBC	n/a	9
BGC	218	4
PB-AB	200	15
SDB	190	6
PB-PR	172	3
REF	n/a	2
FBF	n/a	1
TSS	42	1
CBA	30	1
	3,399,310	8,692
Dual affiliation	n/a	-330
		8,362

*13 ABC churches dually affiliated—7 with NBCA, 4 with NBC/PNB, and 2 with SBC.
** 317 affiliations with BBFI, IBFI, SBF, and WBF.

*T*he Trans-Mississippi South is overwhelmingly a Baptist region except for the French Catholic population in Louisiana and Mexican Catholics in Texas. Baptists lead in three states of the region, trailing only in Louisiana. They are in every county except two in Texas—Kenedy and Loving. Baptists far exceed the United Methodists, the next strongest Protestant body.

With more than 4 million members and 8,400 churches, Southern Baptists are considerably the largest Baptist body. National Baptists with around a million members and probably more than 4,500 churches are next in strength. Two Landmark Missionary Baptist bodies, the American Baptist Association and Baptist Missionary Association, have their largest constituencies here. Landmarkism continues to have considerable strength in the region not only because of these two Landmark bodies but also because of its continuing influence among Southern Baptists as well as Independent Baptists. In this area Baptists as a whole probably exhibit a greater sectarian spirit in respect to other denominations and with one another than anywhere else.

This is also a territory of aggressive southern-oriented Baptist expansionism. From this area Southern Baptists, greatly aided by southern migration, spread to the Pacific.

The American Baptist Association, the Baptist Missionary Association, and the World Baptist Fellowship, which all have headquarters and schools in the region, are all expansionists and have become national bodies. The Baptist Bible Fellowship International, although its headquarters is just over the line in southern Missouri, has its largest constituency in Texas and has conducted an aggressive program across the nation.

Within this area is a Baptist subregion, which extends into southern Missouri and includes the Ozarks, all of Arkansas, a bit of eastern Oklahoma, and eastern Texas to Dallas and Ft. Worth. This is a territory where Southern Baptists frequently have only a plurality and not a majority of the Baptist churches. This subregion is the heartland of the American Baptist Association and the Baptist Missionary Association. In some counties in Arkansas, where these two bodies are the strongest, Southern Baptists may even be in the minority. In the Ozarks, an area similar to southern Appalachia, some United Baptists and a rather strong representation of Free Will Baptists may be found.

MOUNTAIN REGION

Montana

SBC	10,475	90
ABC	3,321	26
FB**	1,800	22
GARBC	1,061	14
BBFI**	n/a	12
ABA	500	6
BGC	366	5
NABC	343	2
CBA	232	7
WBF**	n/a	3
SBF**	n/a	2
FWB	43	2
IBFI**	n/a	1
ST	n/a	1
	18,141	193
Dual affiliation	n/a	-5
		188

**5 dual affiliations with BBFI, FB, IBFI, SBF, and WBF.

Idaho

SBC	13,331	54
ABC*	7,729	39

CBA	1,381	15
GARBC	1,348	15
BBFI**	n/a	15
BGC	691	1
FWB	335	4
FBF	n/a	3
NABC	316	2
NBC*	250	2
ABA	225	3
IBFI**	n/a	2
WBF**	n/a	1
UB	<u>5</u>	<u>1</u>
	25,611	157
Dual affiliation	<u>n/a</u>	<u>-3</u>
		154

*1 church dually affiliated with ABC and NBC.
**2 dually affiliated with BBFI, IBFI, and WBF.

Wyoming

SBC	15,182	67
ABC	5,393	21
BBFI**	n/a	14
CBA	1,628	11
NBC	1,300	9
BGC	729	6
FB**	700	9
WBF**	n/a	4
IBFI**	n/a	3
GARBC	184	3
ABA	100	2
NABC	71	1
FWB	<u>67</u>	<u>2</u>
	25,354	152
Dual affiliation	<u>n/a</u>	<u>-9</u>
		143

**9 dual affiliations with BBFI, FB, IBFI, and WBF.

Colorado

SBC	67,549	205
ABC*	22,620	84
NBC*	15,650	40
BBFI**	n/a	72
CBA	10,982	47
FBF**	n/a	41
BGC	4,825	24
GARBC	1,573	19
WBF**	n/a	18
NTA	n/a	15
ABA	850	7
SDB	342	2
NABC	315	4
IBFI**	n/a	6
FWB	191	6
PB-OL	n/a	4
SBF**	n/a	2
BMA	72	2
OMB	18	1
	124,987	599
Dual affiliation	n/a	-43
		556

*7 churches dually affiliated with ABC and NBC.
**36 dual affiliations with BBFI, FBF, IBFI, NTA, SBF, and WBF.

Utah

SBC	10,890	52
ABC*	1,971	10
NBC*	1,200	7
BBFI**	n/a	10
CBA	888	9
WBF**	n/a	6
IBFI**	n/a	3
ABA	n/a	3
FBF**	n/a	2
GARBC	n/a	2
	14,949	104

Dual affiliation	n/a	-6
		98

*1 church dually affiliated with ABC and NBC.
**5 dual affiliations with BBFI, FBF, IBFI, and WBF.

Nevada

SBC*	26,856	83
NBC/PNB*	10,150	18
ABC*	5,374	21
BBFI**	n/a	7
CBA	506	4
GARBC	266	5
IBFI**	n/a	2
BMA	81	1
	43,233	141
Dual affiliation	n/a	-7
		134

*5 ABC churches dually affiliated—4 with NBC/PNB and 1 with SBC.
**2 dually affiliated with BBFI and IBFI.

New Mexico

SBC	113,088	272
BBFI**	n/a	49
NBC*	1,650	22
ABC*	1,502	4
WBF**	n/a	13
NBCA	730	11
ABA	693	6
BMA	355	8
PB-OL	n/a	9
CBA	291	6
IBFI**	n/a	6
FWB	146	5
FBF**	n/a	3
NTA**	n/a	1
SBF**	n/a	1
GARBC	n/a	1
	118,455	417

Dual affiliation	n/a	-18
		399

*1 church dually affiliated with ABC and NBC.
**17 dual affiliations with BBFI, FBF, IBFI, NTA, SBF, and WBF.

Arizona

SBC*	130,539	282
CBA	20,000	108
BBFI**	n/a	45
ABC*	9,526	42
NMBC	6,000	44
NBC*	5,400	36
NBCA*	3,775	21
FWB	773	13
WBF**	n/a	9
IBFI**	n/a	7
BGC	715	8
ABA	600	7
FBF**	n/a	5
GARBC	430	13
PB-OL	n/a	5
BMA	96	5
REF	n/a	2
SBF**	n/a	1
UB	15	1
ORB	9	1
	177,878	655
Dual affiliation	n/a	-21
		634

*4 ABC churches dually affiliated—2 NBC, 1 NBA, and 1 SBC.
**17 dual affiliations with BBFI, FBF, IBFI, SBF, and WBF.

B efore the Second World War, the Mountain region was not particularly receptive to Baptists. Several things have limited Baptist growth: the scattered population, the large Mormon concentration in Utah and southern Idaho which overlapped into Wyoming and Nevada, and Roman Catholic Hispanic and Indian populations. Although Baptists still face the same limitations, they have nevertheless grown significantly in the last couple of decades through migration and an aggressive program of church planting by Southern Baptists and Independent Baptists.

Although Roman Catholics and Mormons are far in the lead, Baptists are the third largest religious group in the area and the largest Protestant body in Arizona, New Mexico, and Colorado. They are, however, still comparatively weak in Montana, Idaho, and Utah, where a number of counties do not have one Baptist church. The region is rather devoid of Baptist educational institutions except in Phoenix and Denver.

Southern Baptists with 380,000 members in more than 1,000 churches are the strongest Baptist body in each of the Mountain states. Unlike other Baptist bodies, Southern Baptists maintain a separate state convention or fellowship in each state (except for Idaho and Utah which are united in one convention). American Baptists with 57,000 members and about 150 churches maintain an important constituency in Colorado but are comparatively weak elsewhere, having lost the New Mexico Convention to the Southern Baptists and the Arizona Convention to the Conservative Baptists. National Baptists with possibly around 50,000 members and about 200 churches are found in metropolitan areas of the region. Conservative Baptists have important constituencies in Arizona and Colorado and support a college in Arizona and a seminary in Colorado but are weak elsewhere. The Baptist Bible Fellowship International has considerable stength in Colorado, Arizona, and New Mexico, while northern-oriented fundamentalists have small groups in Montana, Wyoming, and Colorado.

PACIFIC REGION

California

SBC*	404,508	1,146
ABC*	145,509	555
NMBC	125,000	250
NBC/PNB*	115,000	525
CBA	47,435	215
BBFI**	n/a	149
NBCA*	43,750	125
BGC	34,442	125
GARBC	17,768	109
ABA	14,241	98
FB**	10,000	100
NABC	7,846	25
FWB	5,529	70
BMA	1,233	18
WBF**	n/a	11
IBFI**	n/a	10
PB-OL	n/a	29
SBF**	n/a	6
SDB	198	6

REF	n/a	4
	972,459	3,576
Dual affiliation	n/a	-74
		3,502

*51 ABC churches dually affiliated—34 with NBC/PNB, 15 with NBCA, and 2 with SBC.
**23 dual affiliations with BBFI, FB, IBFI, SBF, and WBF.

Oregon

CBA	34,001	171
SBC*	26,641	118
ABC*/***	13,529	61
BBFI**	5,000	35
NBCA/NMBC*	3,819	17
NABC	1,626	10
BGC	1,493	11
GARBC	1,475	17
NBC	975	2
LMB-DR	880	22
ABA	800	16
NB-IND	350	2
FWB	213	2
BMA	159	4
FBF**	n/a	1
IBFI**	n/a	1
SBF**	n/a	1
WBF**	n/a	1
PB-OL	49	4
SDB	25	1
REF	n/a	1
PB-AB	2	1
	91,037	499
Dual affiliation	-2,442	-14
	88,595	485

*9 NBCA/NMBC dual affiliations—6 with ABC, 1 with SBC, and 1 with ABC and SBC.
**4 BBFI churches each have a dual affiliation with another independent fellowship—
FBF, IBFI, SBF, and WBF.
***1 church dually affiliated with ABC and NBC.

Washington

SBC	50,937	206
ABC*	28,837	137
CBA	10,476	69
BGC	9,079	41
GARBC	9,001	71
BBFI**	n/a	57
NBC*	8,100	36
NBCA/NMBC*	4,400	22
NMBC	966	33
NABC	2,054	15
IBFI**	n/a	15
WBF**	n/a	14
ABA	521	14
FWB	397	6
BMA	227	4
FBF**	n/a	3
SDB	79	3
REF	n/a	3
SBF	n/a	1
ORB	74	2
PB-OL	<u>35</u>	<u>2</u>
	125,183	754
Dual affiliation	<u>n/a</u>	<u>-56</u>
		698

*36 ABC churches dually affiliated—25 with NBC and 11 with NBCA.
**20 dual affiliations with BBFI, FBF, IBFI, and WBF.

Alaska

SBC	24,602	62
NBC*	2,000	20
ABC*	1,463	10
BBFI**	n/a	9
CBA	333	5
BGC	293	5
FBF**	n/a	5
GARBC	159	5
BMA	38	1

ABA	n/a	1
	28,888	123
Dual affiliation	n/a	-5
		118

*4 churches dually affiliated with ABC and NBC.
**1 church dually affiliated with BBFI and FBF.

Hawaii

SBC	16,126	64
ABC	697	4
ABA	n/a	7
BBFI	n/a	5
CBA	268	3
BGC	152	3
WBF**	n/a	3
FBF**	n/a	1
SBF**	n/a	1
FWB	50	1
	17,293	92
Dual affiliation	n/a	-2
		90

**2 dual affiliations with FBF, SBF, and WBF.

D espite strong competition from many diverse religious groups which have found a home in the area or the religious indifference of many Westerners, Baptists have found the Pacific area a fruitful area of growth. After the Roman Catholic Church, Baptists are the largest religious body in the region and are the leading Protestant body in California, Oregon, and Alaska. Baptist churches are in every county in Oregon and Hawaii, all but one in California (Alpine), and all but three in Washington (Ferry, Garfield, and Wahkiakum).

Southern Baptists with 500,000 members and more than 1,500 churches lead in all of the states except Oregon, where Conservative Baptists are the largest body. American Baptists with 190,000 members in 767 churches have comparatively strong constituencies in California and Washington, while the Baptist General Conference is well represented in California and Washington. Conservative Baptists with 92,000 members in over 450 churches have almost half of their national constituency in this region. National Baptists with more than one thousand churches are strongly represented in the metropolitan areas and possess a large constituency in California. The National Baptist statistics for California are undercounted, however, since the membership of the Golden West Missionary Bible Convention could not be obtained. Independent Baptists, particularly the Baptist Bible Fellowship, have also found California and Washington to be fruitful fields.

Appendix II

BAPTIST WORLD STATISTICS

CONTINENTAL BAPTIST MEMBERSHIP

Continents	Members	Churches
Africa	3,084,674	19,572
Asia and Oceania	2,963,770	22,676
Europe/Eurasia	918,826	11,081
Latin America and the Caribbean	1,983,410	12,726
Northern America (Canada and USA)	<u>28,387,511</u>	<u>91,185</u>
	37,334,191	157,240

COUNTRIES WITH MORE THAN 100,000 BAPTISTS

1. United States of America	28,156,504
2. India	1,383,883
3. Brazil	1,176,098
4. Zaire	765,585
5. Nigeria	629,586
6. Myanmar (Burma)	497,731
7. Korea	323,750
8. Philippines	314,207
9. Haiti	235,463
10. Canada	231,007
11. Mozambique	210,200

12. Malawi	190,105
13. Cameroon	182,486
14. Kenya	163,051
15. Ukraine	160,481
16. England	156,540
17. Central African Republic	152,900
18. Zimbabwe	124,028
19. Mexico	120,877
20. Tanzania	120,000
21. Indonesia	118,500
22. Angola	115,318
23. Germany	114,231
24. Romania	109,043

COUNTRIES FROM 50,000 TO 100,000 BAPTISTS

25. Russia	98,848
26. South Africa	78,796
27. Australia	64,662
28. Argentina	61,812
29. Rwanda	61,625
30. Liberia	59,522
31. Zambia	55,800
32. Bahamas	55,000
33. Jamaica	51,055